Principles of Macroeconomics

Belton M. Fleisher
Ohio State University

Edward J. Ray
Ohio State University

Thomas J. Kniesner
University of North Carolina
Chapel Hill

wcb
Wm. C. Brown Publishers
Dubuque, Iowa

Book Team

John D. Stout *Editor*
Kathy Law Laube *Developmental Editor*
Mary K. Sailer *Designer*
Vickie Putman Caughron *Production Editor*
Vicki Krug *Permissions Editor*
Linda M. Gorchels *Product Manager*

wcb group

Wm. C. Brown *Chairman of the Board*
Mark. C. Falb *President and Chief Executive Officer*

wcb

Wm. C. Brown Publishers, College Division

G. Franklin Lewis *Executive Vice-President, General Manager*
George Wm. Bergquist *Editor in Chief*
Beverly Kolz *Director of Production*
Chris C. Guzzardo *Vice-President, Director of Sales and Marketing*
Bob McLaughlin *National Sales Manager*
Marilyn A. Phelps *Manager of Design*
Colleen A. Yonda *Production Editorial Manager*
Faye M. Schilling *Photo Research Manager*

Cover credit © Pat Peticolas/Fundamental Photographs

Library of Congress Catalog Card Number: 86-72959

ISBN 0-697-01035-X

Printed in the United States of America
10 9 8 7 6 5 4 3 2 1

Contents

Expanded Contents

Part I
Introduction

Part II
Introduction to Macroeconomics

3 Employment, Unemployment, and the Aggregate Production of Goods and Services *65*

4 Aggregate Expenditure on Goods and Services *89*

Part III

Macroeconomic Policy

11 Monetary and Fiscal Policies in Action *233*

12 Summing Up: Macroeconomic Controversies *251*

Part IV
The International Economy

15 Monetary and Macroeconomic Aspects of International Trade *313*

16 Current Issues in International Trade *335*

Part V

Economic Growth and Comparative Systems

Preface

What? Still one more principles text?

Yes. The reason we believe that we can contribute something of value to the already crowded field of introductory economics textbooks is that none of the other existing books matches our needs in teaching Principles of Macroeconomics. Needless to say, we hope that others perceive some of the needs that we have tried to address. We desired a text that uses a building-block approach, which means that each theoretical tool is developed on the basis of what has gone before, without time- and space-wasting repetition and without theoretical gaps or inconsistencies. Our goal has been a book that illustrates in every chapter the applicability of economic analysis to important social problems and integrates our knowledge of the economic process with social choices made in a political context. We also wanted a text that would be more effective than any other now available in helping students to understand the role of the United States in the rapidly changing international economy and to appreciate the political-economic problems faced by the world's developing nations. Finally, we believe it is crucial that the beginning student grasp the fundamental interrelationships between the real economy and monetary economy (microeconomics and macroeconomics). This requires understanding the "microfoundations" of the determination of unemployment, interest rate, price level, and aggregate production. However, we wanted to avoid the burden of the complex IS-LM analysis that is usually relegated to an appendix in other texts (if it appears at all). Pedagogically, we wished to avoid a text cluttered with "boxed inserts" that, in our judgment, divert students' attention from basic, important issues in economics.

Principles of Macroeconomics has been written on the assumption that a few tools, well-learned, provide insights that are unavailable to those who have not studied modern economic analysis. It serves as a summary of basic principles for those who may never enroll in another course beyond the usual two-term introductory sequence and as a foundation for additional courses taken by economics majors and business students. We have strived to keep theoretical analysis simple, yet correct, so that nothing need be "unlearned" by students going on to intermediate or graduate level course work. Numerous applications of economic analysis to policy issues are linked to an analysis of the political process through which social policies are developed. A broad spectrum of policy applications is covered, including health economics, agriculture, technological progress, poverty, the problems of the world's developing nations, current international economic problems, and more. Students' understanding of policy formulation is enhanced by repeated analysis of "winners" and "losers" from alternative policies and how their political power influences actual policy decisions.

▸ Organization

Part I is comprised of a single chapter that introduces the fundamental economic principles of scarcity, the *What, How,* and *For Whom* questions, the production possibilities frontier, opportunity cost, and comparative advantage, with some attention-grabbing applications, including the economics of life and death choices and the 55-mph speed limit. The role of economic theory and the distinction between positive and normative analysis are discussed.

Part II is the first macroeconomics section. Chapter 2 defines macroeconomics and introduces GNP and the other principal aggregate economic variables, the price level, interest rate, and unemployment. The appendix to this chapter summarizes the important factors of supply and demand that instructors can cover macroeconomics without having to cover microeconomics first. In fact, each element of supply, demand, and the equilibrium concept is introduced and defined within the main body of chapter 3, as well, so those instructors who wish to use their course time to cover applied topics more intensively can skip the appendix to chapter 2 without loss of required information in the macro course.

Chapter 3 introduces the labor market, a crucial microfoundation of modern macroeconomics. Chapter 4 describes the aggregate expenditure on goods and services that leads to a particular level of GNP in the goods market. The student is continuously reminded that full macroeconomic equilibrium depends on conditions in the labor market, as well, and that equilibrium in the goods market may or may not correspond to "full employment." Chapters 5, 6, and 7 introduce the financial sector and describe the determination of the interest rate, using a loanable funds approach. We believe that we are unique in using the loanable funds approach to link the real and monetary sectors and that this pedagogical device allows the student to learn much more about the mutual interaction of exogenous expenditure components with the interest rate and monetary and fiscal policies than is possible with any other existing text.

In Part III, we tie the labor, goods, and credit markets together to develop a model of general macroeconomic equilibrium in chapter 8. We use the model to illustrate what happens in each market during recessions and inflationary periods. Chapter 9 emphasizes determination of the price level, using the quantity theory and aggregate demand and supply. Chapters 10, 11, and 12 introduce fiscal and monetary policies in theory and practice. Our approach is unique in that the student does not have to unlearn the partial equilibrium aspects of fiscal policy that hinder understanding of how government expenditure and taxation policies interact with interest rate determination. Chapter 12 summarizes major issues in macroeconomics by comparing Keynesian, monetarist, and supply-side policies.

Part IV introduces international economics. Chapters 13 and 14 cover "real" trade, using the concepts of supply and demand to analyze imports, exports, and tariff and nontariff trade barriers. Chapter 15 covers monetary and macroeconomic trade issues, including exchange rate determination and the balance of payments. Chapter 16 addresses various current issues in the international economy, including the impact of OPEC on the world's developed and developing nations.

Part V includes the capstone chapters on economic growth and comparative systems. Once again, the applications of economic tools and empirical issues are stressed. In chapter 17, particular attention is paid to the productivity slowdown in the United States and to the role of "industrial policy" in economic development. Chapter 18 compares the allocation mechanisms of free market and mixed economies with those of planned, socialist economies and emphasizes a comparison of various measures of social and economic welfare between the planned economies and those of the other industrialized nations. This chapter also contains an appendix that deals with the theory of public choice.

▸ Pedagogy

Principles of Macroeconomics offers a variety of pedagogical aids for students and teachers. Each chapter opens with a chapter outline, learning objectives, and a prologue/scenario as part of the introduction. The introduction provides a real-world lead-in to the material and relates chapter content to previous and subsequent chapters. A running glossary is presented at the top of each page. The key terms are also listed and page referenced at the end of the chapter. Numerous end-of-chapter questions aid student comprehension of the material.

Each major section of the text concludes with a feature called Policy Issue. These policy puzzles direct students to put themselves in the position of an economic policymaker and formulate decisions regarding the issues presented. An appendix at the back of the book instructs students on how to analyze and work through the policy puzzles.

The careful use of appendices aids students in understanding the use and relevance of economic tools and concepts. The "careers" appendix after chapter 1 shows students the relevance of the subject to their future careers; it contradicts the notion that economics is a dismal science. The supply/demand appendix following chapter 2 provides condensed coverage of basic supply and demand concepts. Instructors can use this appendix to teach macroeconomics without unnecessary detail. Several other chapter-end appendices present mathematical analyses of material contained in the related chapters, allowing a clearer focus on concepts and applications in the body of the chapters.

The text contains numerous direct and rhetorical questions designed to get the student to think more deeply about economic principles and applications discussed. Outlines of answers to these questions are provided in the instructor's manual.

There are numerous applications of such important contemporary topics as public choice analysis, the economics of information, the economics of the allocation of time, and rational expectations. These applications repeatedly stress the political, or "public choice" ramifications of policy formation. At the same time, the authors have carefully avoided taking sides politically, while emphasizing the political limits on economic policymakers.

There is a distinct pedagogical advantage to our use of loanable funds analysis in developing a macroeconomic model of both the real and monetary sectors. Most texts use the loanable funds model in microeconomic analysis of the interest rate, but then drop it in the macro portion of the text. Some texts use the loanable funds theory of interest in describing how monetary policy works but do not integrate this analysis with the goods market and fiscal policy. This gives the appearance of two different theories of the interest rate and macroeconomic policy, which can only leave students confused. Our use of the loanable funds analysis of interest rates, depending only on the tools of supply and demand and combined with the microfoundations of supply and demand for labor, determination of real wage rates, and unemployment, shows how microeconomics applies to an understanding of the complex interrelationships of the macroeconomy. The loanable funds approach illustrates directly how monetary and fiscal policies are *related* means of achieving macroeconomic stability. The impacts of monetary and fiscal policies on GNP, employment, the interest rate, real investment, and the price level are easily compared. The power of this approach has enabled us to include brief histories of the Great Depression and economic experience in the United States since the 1960s that are superior in depth and scope to any existing principles text. The loanable funds approach is equally well adapted to a Keynesian or monetarist orientation, and the text clearly and succinctly explains the distinctions between modern Keynesians, monetarists, and supply siders in terms of the macroeconomic tools developed.

Teaching and Learning Aids

For the Instructor

Instructor's Manual: Each chapter includes a chapter outline with teaching tips, suggested answers to all end-of-chapter questions, and a set of additional readings from recent magazines and newspapers.

Transparencies: Forty-seven colorful acetates of selected economic diagrams facilitate instruction and learning.

Test Bank: Approximately 1,000 questions that have been carefully designed using guidelines established by the Joint Council on Economic Education. The questions are also available on complimentary **wcb** TestPak computer diskettes for instructors adopting the book.

Transparency Masters: Twenty-eight transparency masters and the test bank are included in the Instructor's Manual.

QuizPak: A student self-testing program offered free to adopters of *Principles of Macroeconomics*. Your students can review course material by quizzing themselves on the microcomputer. All questions in QuizPak are different from those in the Test Bank!

Software: Computer software will be available to help your students learn the principles of macroeconomics. The computer programs are designed to reinforce key concepts in the book.

For the Student

Student Study Guide: Each chapter contains an overview that summarizes the basic concepts introduced in each text chapter, a vocabulary check that reviews the key terms and definitions in the text, and numerous self-testing items, including true-false and multiple-choice questions and answers. Each chapter also contains at least one exercise and its solution.

StudyPak: An interactive student study guide on the microcomputer available for students to purchase. Students will review study materials selected for a particular text chapter and receive instant feedback. Printed study materials supplement the program to provide maximum coverage of each text chapter.

Highlights

To highlight the significant features of our text, we have summarized some of them below:

1. Uses a building-block approach that stresses the applicability of supply and demand analysis throughout.
2. Extensive policy applications to the household, business, health care, and government sectors and to developing nations.
3. Simply presented and current data.
4. A tools-oriented approach to the economist's way of thinking.
5. A unique, loanable funds approach to macroeconomics that facilitates incorporation of real and monetary disturbances in the basic macro model.
6. Stresses the microfoundations of macroeconomics.
7. Three chapters devoted to macroeconomic policy, including a unique historical analysis of two major episodes that continue to influence our lives today and an up-to-date comparison of Keynesian, monetarist, and supply-side policy positions.
8. Macroanalysis that focuses on the three crucial policy variables, inflation, unemployment, and interest rates.
9. Up-to-date analysis of the international economy as it affects the United States and the world's less-developed and -industrialized nations.
10. Fresh applications to the important policy areas of income distribution, externalities, public choice, international trade, and international financial problems.
11. Application of basic economic principles to the problems of developing nations.
12. Emphasis on comparing ideal policies with those that are practicable as determined by the reality of politics and the relationships of government to society.
13. Emphasizes international economic issues (most complete treatment available).

Acknowledgments

We would like to express special thanks to our reviewers, who provided ideas and suggestions of great importance:

Bruce L. Benson, Florida State University; Peter R. Kressler, Glassboro State College; Jerome McElroy, St. Mary's College; Michael G. Ellis, New Mexico State University; Michael Cook, William Jewell College; Richard Hansen, University of Northern Iowa; Randall W. Bennett, Clarkson University; William Shingleton, Ball State University; John Fizel, Pennsylvania State University-Erie; Eleanor C. Snellings, Virginia Commonwealth University; Geoff Carliner, National Bureau of Economic Research; Nancy Jianakoplos, Michigan State University; Timothy J. Perri, Appalachian State University; Mark Berger, University of Kentucky; Abdol Soofi, University of Wisconsin–Platteville; Charles Zech, Villanova University; John Wakeman-Linn, Williams College; Phil Graves, University of Colorado; Jerry Russo, University of Wisconsin–Madison; C. G. Williams, University of South Carolina.

In addition, we express our gratitude to our colleagues Richard Anderson, Lars Sandberg, and Nat Simons at Ohio State and Karen Smith, Helen Tauchen, and Jonathan Veum at the University of North Carolina, who provided many valuable comments that helped improve the text. We would also like to acknowledge the help of Greg Davidson in writing Appendix A.

Kenneth Kopecky graciously released rights to material from an earlier work, and the present text owes much to his influence. We also appreciate the cooperation of David Terry Paul in making publication of this book possible. Sarah Mason provided outstanding typing services.

Principles of Macroeconomics

Part I

Introduction

Chapter 1

Scarcity, the Three Questions of Economics, and an Economic System

Outline

Objectives

After reading this chapter, the student should be able to:

Explain what scarcity means and why scarcity requires that an economic system answer the three fundamental economic questions.
Distinguish between normative and positive economic issues.
Discuss how the government's policy on medical care affects the answers to the three economic questions.
Explain why economic models are crucial to the study of economics.
Use the concept of the production possibilities frontier to illustrate scarcity, efficiency, opportunity cost, comparative advantage, and economic growth.
Show how specialization leads to economic efficiency.
Use the concepts of opportunity cost and economic efficiency to discuss the formulation of government policies such as the 55-mph speed limit.
Distinguish among various types of economic systems.

Scarcity means that human wants or desires far exceed the capacity of the world's limited resources to satisfy those wants or desires.

*Every economic system must answer the **three fundamental economic questions**: What? How? For whom?*

Opportunity cost is the amount of one good or service that must be given in order to produce a unit of another good or service.

The Three Fundamental Economic Questions

The most important issue in economics can be summarized in a single sentence. If you understand all of the implications of this one sentence, you understand the essence of economics. A full understanding simply requires successively deeper and deeper analysis of its implications. You'll see as we go along. So let's go. The basic principle of economics concerns **scarcity,** *which means that we cannot ever have all we want of every good and service. That is the sentence. While our desires for goods and services are unlimited, our resources—land, raw materials, labor, machinery, energy, and so on that we use to produce goods and services—are limited. Thus, we cannot have everything we want. Without this problem of scarcity, there would be no need for the subject of economics. All of economics really just rests on this idea.*

The first implication of what you have just learned is that scarcity *forces us to choose among alternatives. Because we cannot have everything, scarcity forces society to make choices. Every economic system—whether a free market or government-controlled type—must answer* ***three fundamental economic questions:*** *(1)* What *goods and services will be produced? (2)* How *will they be produced? (3)* For whom *will they be produced? If it were not for scarcity, the answers to these questions would be unimportant. Because scarcity does confront us, the answers are crucial to our material well-being and to our social and political decisions. Economics, therefore, is a penetrating and important subject. Let us now think about scarcity in more concrete terms.*

A Thought Quiz

You have had your first lesson in economics. A quick thought quiz will reveal how well you have learned that scarcity forces us to choose among alternatives—*all of the time.*

Consider the following examples in which scarcity forces us to make choices:

1. Last summer you had to choose whether (a) to attend summer school in order to be better prepared for fall courses or to graduate earlier, (b) to take a job to earn money to buy a car, or (c) to join some friends who wanted to visit the national parks of the West.
2. You want to visit a friend at a another college for the weekend. For $300 you could take a round-trip by plane that takes a total of three hours, or you could drive ten hours each way. Should you take the plane or drive your car?
3. You work and go to school. The more you work, the more money you earn and the lower your grades. How many hours a day should you work, and how many hours a day should you study?

These are all simple examples in which scarce time and income force you to make choices. All involve the important concept of **opportunity cost,** which means that when you choose one alternative, you must sacrifice the benefits of choosing something else. Opportunity cost is the most fundamental implication of scarcity. It means that scarcity *forces* us to pay for what we choose. A few items that we value may be considered "free" in the sense that there is no opportunity cost of consuming a bit more. Perhaps taking an additional breath of air is the best example of something without opportunity cost. There are very few others.

In our first example, if you decided to take a summer job, you sacrificed the enjoyment of travel or the benefits of what you would have learned in summer school. In the second example, the opportunity cost of driving to save a large part of the $300 airfare is the seventeen hours you do not get to spend visiting your friend. In the third example, if you choose to work while attending school, the opportunity cost is not only likely to be lower grades but also the future job opportunities you may not receive because your lower grades make it harder to succeed in the job market after graduation.

Opportunity costs confront us in every choice we make in our day-to-day lives. They also force us to make difficult and important decisions when choosing among alternative social policies. Consider this statement and the two possible responses that follow it: No sacrifice is ever too great to save a human life. (1) To knowingly cause or permit a death violates our most basic moral principles. A life is so precious that no cost should be spared if one can be saved. (2) Spending tremendous amounts of money to extend artificially the life of a terminally ill person who is in great pain or exhibits minimal life signs is not always justified. Medical resources used in such efforts can often be used more fruitfully for other patients. In choosing to keep the first patient alive at all cost, one ignores the implications of such a decision for other patients.

Most people do not like to think about this unpleasant subject. However, as adults, we or our political representatives must deal with difficult decisions. One of the most important reasons for studying economics is to help you develop clearer thinking about important social issues. You probably find it difficult to choose between the two statements in the preceding paragraph. Perhaps you are inclined to accept the first argument but find that the second also has some merit. What can you do? Although there is no surefire guide to the right answer, economic analysis will help. It forces us to see that the first statement fails to recognize that choice is *always* necessary, unpleasant though it may be. In a world with scarcity, opportunity cost forces us to choose among alternatives whether we want to or not. To adhere exclusively to the first statement will not make opportunity cost disappear, although we may try to ignore it. Unfortunately, ignoring opportunity cost will only mean that we disregard the impact of saving one person's life on the life or death of other individuals. While the second statement recognizes that life and death decisions necessarily involve difficult and critical choices, it provides little insight into how to formulate rules society might use to choose who shall live. Let us elaborate.

If you understand the meaning of scarcity, you will realize that the first statement offers *no guide* to decision making in a world of scarcity. Think about it. *All* choices can be framed in a life or death context. At every moment, each of us could help to prolong our own (or someone else's) life by driving more carefully, giving up smoking, eating more healthful foods, or simply donating more of our income to the poor who cannot afford adequate food or medical care. We often choose activities that are enjoyable but that may shorten our own lives. Examples are driving over ten miles per hour, crossing a busy street, eating too many fatty foods, drinking alcoholic beverages, and smoking tobacco. Of course, by choosing to take only actions that prolong our lives, we would give up the pleasures we derive from eating foods that are "bad" for us, driving fast, and puffing on cigarettes. Thus, we return to the three basic economic questions. *What* should be produced—only those goods that prolong life? *For whom*—whose life should be prolonged? *How* should lives be saved? Suppose that all of our resources were devoted to extending life as long as possible. We would ultimately be forced to decide who should live longer and who should not. After all, no one lives forever, but in many cases life can be extended by extraordinary effort and expense. This brings us back to *for whom* again.

Positive economics is the study of how economic variables are related to one another.

A normative view concerns the ethics of an issue or what is "right" or "just" versus "wrong" or "unjust."

Economic analysis helps us to choose among personal and social alternatives by focusing on *positive* issues, which involve what *is* as opposed to what *ought to be.* The most important statement of **positive economics,** to repeat and summarize the "first lesson" stated above is this: *Nothing is free. Economists* do not place price tags on what we desire (including the saving of lives)—*scarcity* does it.

Economics also cannot provide a unique answer to a question such as Who shall live? The answer will always depend in part on the **normative view,** or ethics, of those who must make such decisions. In our life and death example, normative issues involve such questions as, Is it acceptable for someone to choose behavior that may shorten his or her own life (such as smoking cigarettes or eating unhealthfully)? Is it acceptable that some families and individuals have great wealth while others have insufficient resources to purchase life-saving medical care? Notice that the word *should* is usually involved in normative questions: *Should* you take a job while attending school? *Should* you travel by car or by plane to visit your friend at another college?

Most economists emphasize the *economic way of thinking,* which carefully distinguishes between positive and normative issues. The positive part of economic analysis constantly reminds us that our choices deal with scarcity because we cannot make scarcity disappear. Before we can even answer such questions as *should* we tax the rich in order to transfer income to the poor, or *should* we use public funds to support life-prolonging health care for patients who need organ transplants in order to live, we require the answers to the *positive* questions involving the opportunity costs of taking these actions. The costs are not simply measured by the dollars involved but by the *benefits foregone* when dollars are spent one way instead of another. Only when the positive issues are resolved (when the "facts" are known) can we combine our knowledge with our normative beliefs to develop informed opinions on the best choices to make in our personal lives and for society at large.

▸ Understanding Economic Events with Economic Analysis

When you have completed your economics course, you will be better prepared to recognize an economic issue when you hear or read about one. In addition you will have a clearer understanding of how scarcity determines the choices each issue presents. News analyses in the media often discuss economic issues without recognizing them as such. Frequently, the discussions are confusing and unhelpful because they are not organized around the three basic economic questions: What? How? and For Whom? A very helpful guide in sorting through complex issues as reported in the mass media is this: Look for the *for whom* question (how will the gains and losses be distributed). Economic issues involving the most heated public debate *always* involve some group's fear, whether realistic or not, that they will lose out under one or more solutions to the issue in question. For example, if we limit imports of foreign autos, steel, or clothing, consumers of these goods will have to pay higher prices of domestically produced items, while domestic producers (business firms and their employees) of these goods will be able to charge higher prices and receive greater profits and wages. Changes in the way the economy answers *for whom* (for example, who should win, steelworkers or steel consumers) *always* alter the ways in which the *what* and *how* questions are answered (if steelworkers are protected, more domestic steel will be produced and less of other goods). If you remember this hint, it will help you understand the basic issues.

Once you have recognized the three economic questions in debate over an economic issue, you will need some elementary tools of economic analysis to make headway in deciding where you stand. We will describe these tools and show you how to use them in this and following chapters. Before doing so, however, let us discuss another example of how government policy can affect the answers to *what, how,* and *for whom* goods and services are produced.

An Example of Government Policy and Its Impact on the Answers to the Three Economic Questions: Medical Care

In most countries, the United States included, government has intervened in the provision of medical care. The reason for this is the belief held by many that citizens deserve access to health whatever their economic status. Without government provision of some medical services, it is believed that many people would go without adequate medical care. Government policy toward the health care industry is primarily aimed at changing the way the economy answers the *for whom* question. The goal is to create a world in which no one is denied access to medical care because he or she is too poor to pay for it. As a result, certain groups of families and individuals get medical care at little or no monetary cost to them. Examples are the two federal government programs *Medicare,* which pays part of most medical bills for people age sixty-five and older, and *Medicaid,* which helps finance health expenditures for the poor of all ages. The United States is by no means the only country to provide medical care at little or no charge to the elderly and the poor. Most other nations do so, and many do so to a greater extent than the United States.

The main characteristic of programs such as Medicare and Medicaid is that the participants pay less (or nothing) for medical care because many of the costs are paid from general tax revenues or special taxes on wages, such as Social Security taxes. The result is that an eligible beneficiary feels (rightly) that each additional visit to the doctor or hospital costs little or nothing. Of course, this is in keeping with the main goal of the program—to encourage the use of health care and medical services by certain groups (the *what* and *for whom* questions). Unfortunately, there are certain economic side effects to this. The most important is that participants in Medicare and Medicaid have little or no incentive (1) to seek out health care specialists who provide services of a given quality at the lowest cost or (2) to substitute less expensive health care modes for more costly ones when feasible.

Kidney dialysis (placing people whose kidneys do not function on an artificial kidney machine) is a good example of a case in which alternatives are available at very different prices. Under the program in effect in the early 1980s the federal government paid all costs of anyone suffering from complete kidney failure. Kidney patients faced the following choices: (1) hospital treatment at an average cost of $159 per treatment (usually three times a week), or $25,000 a year; (2) clinic treatment at an average cost of $138 per treatment; (3) home treatment, in which family members aid the patient, at an average cost of $97 per treatment, or 30 percent less than in a clinic; and (4) a new approach that does not require a machine but requires the patient to wear a bag of fluid[1]. Because the dollar costs of treatment are not paid by the patients themselves, they have little incentive to save money by using clinic or home care rather than the more expensive hospital mode. This is one reason why the federal government's expenditures for the program have grown very rapidly and now account for a significant share of federal health care expenditures. Clearly, the *what* question (how much kidney dialysis as opposed to other medical and nonmedical goods and services) and the *how* question (which type of care) are being answered much differently because of changes in the answer to the *for whom* question in the case of kidney patients. Serious social issues surround the question of why kidney patients should be singled out for special treatment (instead of, for example, premature babies or heart disease victims). Many physicians fear that rising costs will ultimately force them to make life-or-death decisions regarding kidney patients. An alternative approach would be to provide patients with a fixed payment per month, letting them choose the method of treatment on which to spend the money. Do you think that this would provide increased incentives to reduce costs and thus limit federal expenditures? Explain. Do you favor such a policy? Explain. As you can see, economic decisions resulting from scarcity are often difficult and frequently have critically important consequences. Let us now try to generalize the ways in which scarcity affects an economic system.

*An economic **model** is an abstract, simplified representation of how decision makers interact, how their decisions are affected by the economic environment, and the behavior that results from these decisions.*

Scarcity and an Economic System

Economists and other scientists generally find that the easiest way to grasp the essential features of a subject (such as how an economic system deals with scarcity) is to first construct a **model,** which is a simplified description of how the environment affects behavior. We want you to learn more about what a scientific model is and why a model is an indispensable tool for grasping the essential features of our complex world.

What Is an Economic Model?

When you see the word *model,* you probably think of a model airplane or, perhaps, a model automobile, such as a hobbyist might build in a workshop. These are in fact very good examples. If you were to travel to Wichita, Kansas, and visit a factory of one of the major manufacturers of smaller private airplanes located there, such as Piper or Lear, you would probably be shown a department in which engineers and artists are working on models of various airplane designs that may be built and marketed in the future.

Physically, these models take on several forms. One of them is a miniature version of an airplane that might be built. When you examine such a model, you can instantly see that it is not an exact replication of a real airplane capable of carrying freight or passengers from one place to another. Depending on the stage of development, models by their very nature lack many elements of realism. For example, a model airplane may be completely hollow inside, with no seats, instrument panels, or other equipment. Still, it may be very helpful in studying the patterns of airflows over the wings and fuselage. This crucial stage in aircraft design will probably be conducted in a wind tunnel, which itself is not an exact replication of the atmosphere in which the plane may someday fly. Despite a lack of realism, the simple airplane model just described will enable researchers to focus on a crucial feature of interest—airflow. Indeed it would be correct to say that *because* the model airplane is incomplete or "unrealistic," it permits aeronautical engineers to focus on one or a few important features that the complexity of the real world would hide.

Models in economics serve much the same purpose as in aircraft design. Economic systems are very complex, and limitations on our time, physical resources, and mental capacity prohibit us from understanding every detail and interrelationship. Economic models help us to overcome these limitations by *abstracting,* or taking out of the complex society in which we live, the *essential* features of the economy. Unessential details are ignored. Models thus permit us to develop basic principles, to use them to understand past events, and to predict whether alternative economic policies will "fly" or "crash." Economic models are almost never *physical* counterparts of the economic system. Because of the nature of the subject matter, economic models are typically constructed verbally, geometrically, or algebraically. Their purpose is to help us to see important features of the economy that the complexity of the real world would otherwise hide. In using words, geometry, and algebra, economists are not all that different from aircraft designers. At crucial stages of their work, aircraft designers also use mathematical equations to describe important relationships such as the forces of lift and drag, which determine airworthiness. They also use drawings to represent, or to model, important features of an aircraft geometrically. But how does all of this help us to understand society?

*An **efficient economy** derives as much benefit as possible from its available resources; in this sense it wastes no resources.*

*A **production possibilities frontier (PPF)** illustrates the alternative output levels for an economy that gets the most it can from its given set of resources and available technology. It shows the maximum production possible for each good or service, given the output of all other goods and services.*

An Introductory Example: Dealing with Scarcity in a Small Economy

In order to understand how an economic system deals with scarcity, it is first helpful to discuss how a model economy might deal with scarcity. The problems that the economy must solve are similar to those that each of us must deal with in our everyday lives, but on a larger scale. The thought quiz at the beginning of this chapter addresses questions regarding the best ways to spend your time and income. Each choice requires that you give up something you would like in order to obtain more of something else. Now suppose that you are the director of economic affairs for a small country. You are responsible for how your country answers the three fundamental economic questions. Your goal is to make your country an **efficient economy,** which means that its citizens achieve the highest level of well-being possible, given available resources and their productive capabilities.

Your economy, though small, faces the same problems that most other economic systems must deal with. One of the most important economic decisions you must make is related to a question we have already discussed—how much medical care to provide for your citizens. Medical care is desired because it helps people achieve longer and more enjoyable lives. However, scarcity forces you to give up some consumer goods such as clothing, TVs, cars, vacation trips, movies, and so on, if you produce additional medical services. Circumstances are such that the only way people can get consumer goods *and* medical services is to produce them with resources available within the country. (Our economic model is obviously unrealistic in that trade with other countries is assumed to be impossible. Later on, we will deal with trade among nations in a more complex economic model.) As director of this economic system, your job is to assign individuals to the tasks of producing goods in such a way that they obtain the largest possible output consistent with their limited resources and abilities.

The Production Possibilities Frontier (PPF)

Here is an overview of your problem. Since medical services and consumer goods are both scarce, you want your economy to achieve the largest possible production of consumer goods, given its production of medical services, and the largest possible production of medical services, given its output of consumer goods. In order to achieve your goal, you require information on the economy's capacity to produce medical services and consumer goods. The information you need is contained in your economy's **production possibilities frontier (PPF),** which defines the *maximum* quantities of the consumer goods and medical services that can be produced if no resources are wasted. The PPF is illustrated in figure 1.1. The vertical axis measures production of medical services, and the horizontal axis measures production of consumer goods.

Here are some important features of the small country's PPF. Because their resources are limited, citizens in turn face an upper limit on the amount of medical services they can produce, even if they produce no consumer goods. There is also a maximum amount of consumer goods they can produce, even if they do not produce any medical services. Maximum medical services output is shown as 230 units per month in figure 1.1, and the upper limit on consumer goods is 180 units per month. Of course, the economy is not limited to producing only medical services *or* consumer goods. People can have both. Suppose that

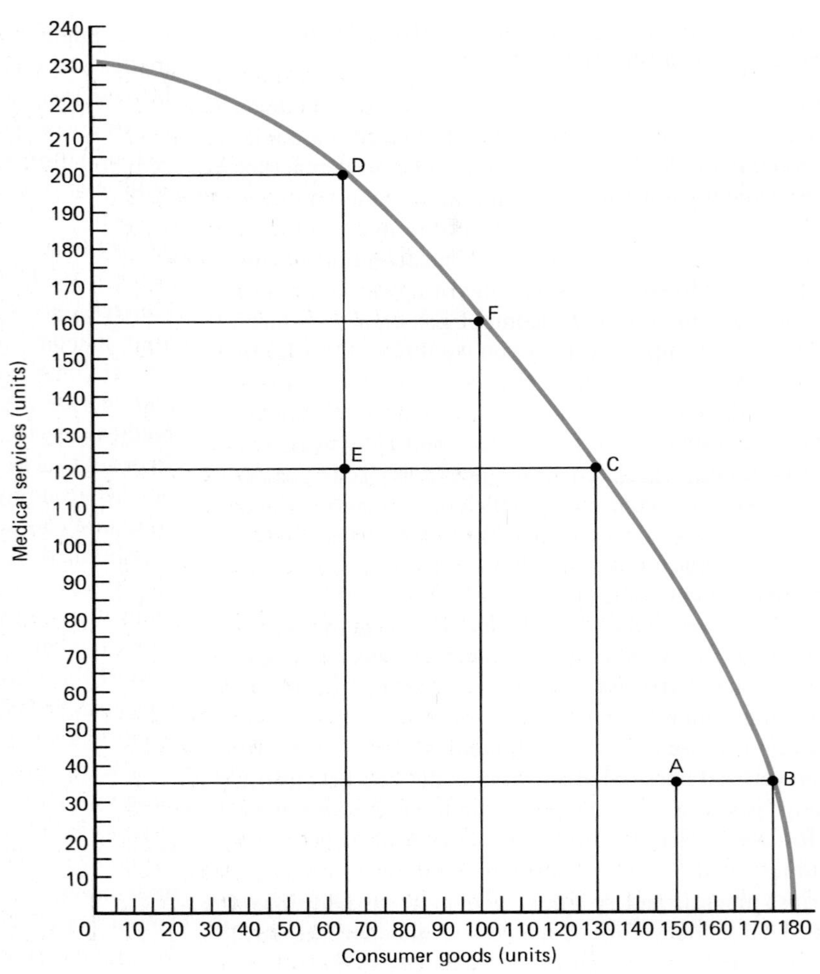

Figure 1.1 Production possibilities frontier for a small economy
The combination of health services and consumer goods along the curve represent the limits on production imposed by scarcity. Therefore, combinations of medical services and consumer goods *outside* the curve cannot be attained. Points A and E, inside the PPF, are inefficient because it is possible to reach points B and F, which represent increased production of at least one of the two goods/services and no less of the other.

the economy begins with maximum medical services output (230 units in figure 1.1). By giving up 30 units of medical services per month, the country can increase consumer goods production from zero to 65 units per month. This is indicated by point D on the PPF. There are many other possibilities. For instance, by sacrificing 40 *more* units of medical service production per month, *additional* consumer goods can be produced, but only 35 units more (point F on the PPF). Reducing medical services by still another 40 units allows a gain of only 30 more units of consumer goods (point C on the PPF). Reducing medical services output all the way to zero from point C, a 120-unit decline in medical services, would allow consumer goods output to expand to its maximum of 180 units per month.

Economic growth means that society is able to obtain more output and is illustrated by an outward shift of the PPF.

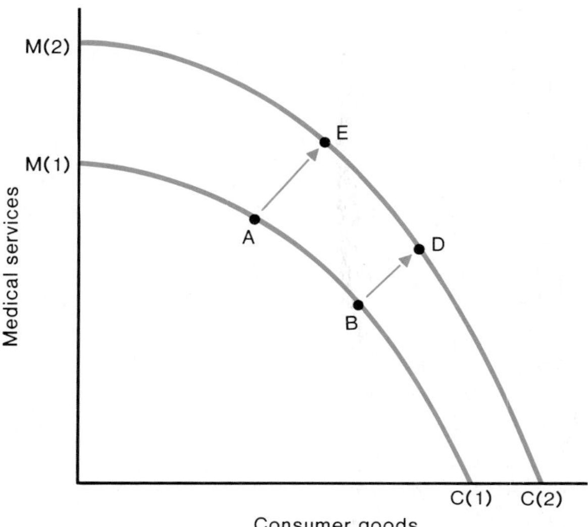

Figure 1.2 Economic growth means that society can produce more goods and services per person and involves an outward shift of the production possibilities frontier

Economic growth could also occur if an inefficient economy, producing at a point *inside* the PPF, became more efficient, moving *toward* or *to* its PPF. For example, a move from point E to point F in figure 1.1 would also be considered economic growth.

At any moment in time, the economy's PPF defines the limits on what can be produced and consumed. (It defines the possible answers to the *what* question.) How is it, then, that the level of consumption that characterizes a typical family or individual is higher now than it was ten, fifty, or one-hundred years ago? The answer is that the economy's PPF is not fixed in one position. Rather, it can shift outward over time. This is known as **economic growth.** An example of economic growth is shown in figure 1.2.

The PPF in figure 1.2 that goes from M(1) on the vertical axis to C(1) on the horizontal axis represents a lower level of potential consumption for the economy, and the PPF connecting M(2) and C(2) represents a higher level. This can easily be seen by noticing that for any point such as A or B on M(1)C(1), a larger output of *both* medical services and consumer goods is possible at points such as E and D on M(2)C(2).

The Production Possibilities Frontier, Opportunity Cost, and Economic Efficiency

If members of your society are to be as well off as possible, it is necessary to produce the maximum amount of consumer goods, given the amount of medical care produced, and vice versa. The production possibilities frontier defines the maximum amounts of medical care and/or consumer goods your economy is capable of producing and the trade-offs it faces. In short, economic efficiency requires that the economy reach its production possibilities frontier.

The PPF tells us something that is of general significance to all economic systems. *When an economy is operating efficiently, it is impossible to obtain more of one good or service without giving up something else.* If society wants more consumer goods, it must make do with fewer medical services. The value of the medical services society must forego in order to produce one more unit of consumer goods is the *opportunity cost* of consumer goods in terms of medical services. Conversely, if more medical services are desired, the opportunity cost is the value of the consumer goods that must be sacrificed. There is probably no economic concept more relevant to our everyday lives than opportunity costs of the choices we make.

In figure 1.1, the opportunity cost that must be paid for the first 65 units of consumer goods is 30 units of medical services. This is the *lowest* possible opportunity cost of obtaining these consumer goods. This follows from the definition of the PPF: The PPF represents the *maximum* quantity of consumer goods that can be obtained, given the amount of medical services produced. For the same reason, the lowest possible opportunity cost of an *additional* 65 units of consumer goods (going from point D on the PPF in figure 1.1 to point C) is an additional 80 units of medical services.

We have seen that the PPF reflects the lowest possible opportunity cost of obtaining any given amount of consumer goods, given its production of medical services. It is also true that if the economy is to reach its production possibilities frontier, opportunity costs must be as low as possible. If your economy is to be efficient, the opportunity cost of producing an additional consumer good (which is the quantity of medical services sacrificed) must be minimized, whatever the desired quantity of consumer good production happens to be. By the same reasoning, the opportunity cost of producing medical services (which is the quantity of consumer goods sacrificed) must also be as low as possible, whatever the amount of medical services desired. In order to reach your goal of achieving economic efficiency for your economy, then, you must minimize the opportuntity costs of producing whatever combination of consumer goods and medical services you or your society chooses.

To see why opportunity costs must be as low as possible if the economy is to reach its production possibilities frontier, suppose you have decided that you want to obtain 35 units of medical services and that you have done this by going to point A in figure 1.1, which is inside the PPF. At point A, you have your desired 35 units of medical services, but you only obtain 150 units of consumer goods. In other words, you have sacrificed 30 units (180–150) of consumer goods to reach point A. Since it is possible to obtain 35 units of medical services by sacrificing only 5 units (180–175) of consumer goods (point B, which is on the PPF), the economy cannot be efficient at point A. When the economy is at point A, more consumption goods are possible (175 units instead of 150 units) while still obtaining the desired 35 units of medical services. If your economy achieves its goal of 35 units of medical services by going to point A, the opportunity cost of medical services is not as low as it can be. When the opportunity cost of the desired level of medical services is made as low as possible, then the output of medical services and consumer goods will be described by a point on the production possibilities frontier of figure 1.1.

Even if you, as economic director, have no opinion concerning *where* on the PPF the economy should be (*what* is produced), you are not doing your job if you make a decision that leads to less production than is possible. That would be wasting resources. You are concerned, in other words, with *how* medical services and consumer goods are produced so that *opportunity costs are minimized*. If opportunity costs are not made as low as possible, resources are wasted. In general, wasted resources mean that your economy is not efficient. Later on in this chapter, we will examine in greater depth just how you might go about minimizing the opportunity costs of what your society produces. Of course, *where* your economy ends up *on* the PPF is also important. An efficient economy is one that not only produces goods and services somewhere along its PPF but also produces the combination of goods and services that is most desired. How desires for various goods and services determine *what* is produced is a topic we discuss throughout the next several chapters.

Notice that nowhere have we mentioned money in discussing opportunity costs. In everyday life, opportunity costs are often indicated to us through the money (dollar) prices we pay for the goods and services we buy. For example, the dollar cost of buying this book indicates the book's opportunity cost because it measures the value of the other things you could not buy when you spent your limited income on a book rather than other goods or services. Moreover, the opportunity cost of *using* this book includes the time you spend reading it. Right now you are probably acutely aware of the opportunity cost of reading this book. There are many other valuable uses of your time. Each decision you make to do one thing involves a decision not to something else. The best of the alternatives you choose not to pursue represents the opportunity cost you bear for each chosen course of action. Let us now return to the concept of the PPF and see what else it implies about society's opportunity costs by looking at figure 1.3.

The Shape of the Production Possibilities Frontier

Why do PPFs have the shape indicated in figures 1.1, 1.2, and 1.3? The PPFs we have drawn are not straight lines; rather, they get steeper as the production of consumer goods increases and flatter as the production of medical services increases. The curvature of the PPF means that citizens face *increasing* opportunity costs of producing more of either product.

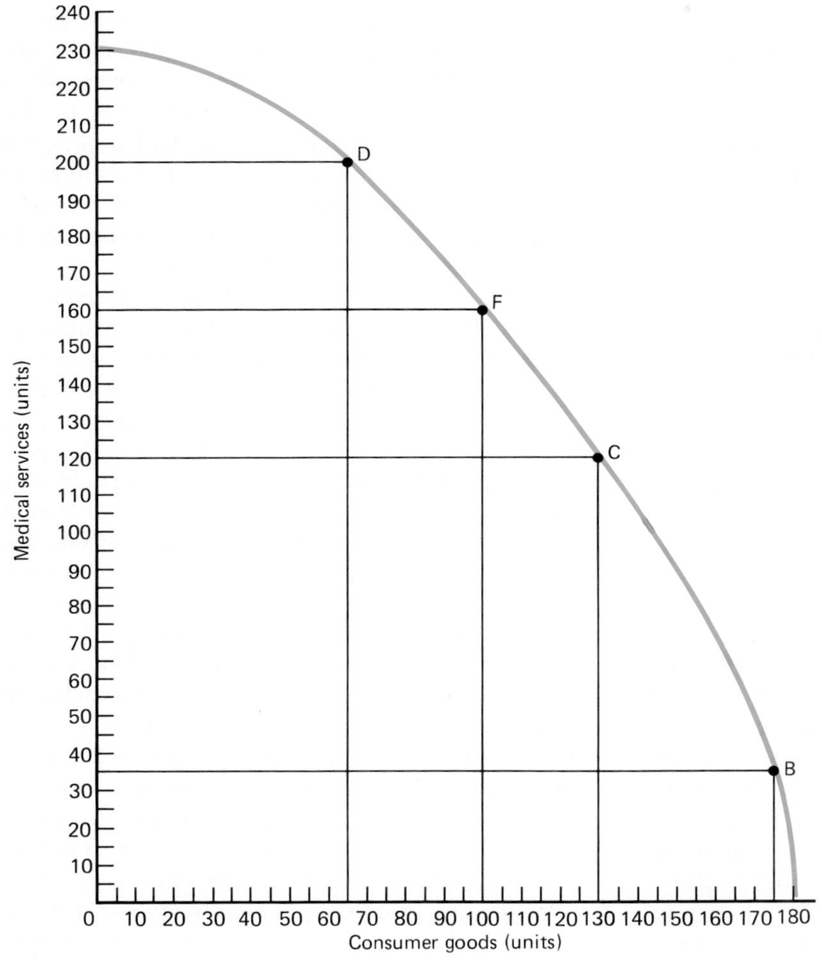

Figure 1.3 The production possibilities frontier and the law of increasing opportunity cost
The opportunity cost of the first 65 units of consumer goods is only 30 units of medical services. However, as more of the economy's resources are devoted to production of consumer goods, the opportunity cost of consumer goods increases. For example, increasing consumer goods production from 65 to 130 units (an additional 65 units) costs 80 units of medical services. Conversely, the opportunity cost of medical services rises as production increases. For example, the first 35 units of medical services require that society sacrifice only 5 units of consumer goods whereas increasing the production of medical services from 120 to 160 units requires giving up 30 units of consumer goods.

Moving *down* the PPF, the *additional* amount of medical services that must be foregone when *additional* consumer goods are produced increases as consumer goods output increases. Let us try to understand this more fully by looking at the numbers along the PPF in figure 1.3. The first 65 units of consumer goods cost only 30 units of medical services; however, increasing the production of consumer goods an additional 65 units, to 130, requires a sacrifice of 80 additional units of medical services. Going in the other direction, the first 35 units of medical services involve giving up only 5 units of consumer goods whereas increasing the production of medical services by 40 units from 160 to 200 requires a sacrifice of 35 units of consumer goods.

One reason why the opportunity cost of a good or service is likely to grow as more of it is produced is that we run out of resources that are best suited for it. If we go back to our example, the more medical services we produce, the more likely it is that we will have to use workers who are relatively better at producing consumer goods. The more specialized the economy becomes in producing either medical services or consumer goods, the more inappropriate the matching of workers to jobs is likely to become. The shape of the PPF in figures 1.1 through 1.3 corresponds to the increasing opportunity costs (difficulty) of having the economy produce more and more of either product. Do not fall into the trap of thinking that the economy is necessarily *less efficient* at the "ends" of the PPF than it is in the middle. Society may *desire* a great deal in terms of medical services and relatively little in the way of consumer goods or vice versa. These can both be efficient places to be on the PPF provided that the desired output is produced at the *lowest possible opportunity cost.*

Applications of the Production Possibilities Frontier and Opportunity Cost

Background

You should now understand why we argued earlier that we cannot ignore the cost of saving lives, even if ethically we abhor avoidable death. The PPF demonstrates graphically how scarcity forces us to make choices because scarcity imposes opportunity costs on us. Perhaps a good definition of heaven would be that it is the only place where scarcity does not exist, where opportunity costs are zero, and where nobody has to study economics. Here on earth, we cannot ignore for long the opportunity costs in choosing more of something we desire. The limitations on our capacity to produce ultimately make us reduce our consumption of another good or service, *whether we intend it or not.* Often government leaders would like to avoid this truth, but they must face up to it daily in choosing among higher military expenditures, taxes, welfare payments, public works, and deficits. Because facing up to opportunity costs is unpleasant, it is not surprising that in political campaigns the candidates often promise voters that they will adopt economic policies to improve economic well-being painlessly.

Here is an example. We are all aware of unemployment in the labor market. While not all unemployment represents economic waste, there are times that unemployment rises above levels that anyone could consider as "normal." When this happens, the economy is operating inside its PPF. The solutions to excessive unemployment, however, are not typically easy (cheap). Moreover, poorly designed policies to reduce unemployment can seriously harm the economy in the long run. Nevertheless, it is tempting for politicians to promise to reduce unemployment by increasing the size of the government sector and thus get from points such as A or E to points such as B or F in figure 1.1. Essentially, they are saying that we can have more output for society by having the government sector do more things. You will learn in your economics courses that such a seemingly costless gain in the output of our economy may be possible, but only under very special circumstances. Nevertheless, politicians are tempted to claim such achievements are attainable more often than is likely to be true. Moreover, we, as voters, often find it easy to believe them because we want to believe that solutions are cheap.

It is true that formulating economic policies is a difficult task and that the existing structure of government taxes, expenditures, and other controls may be less efficient than is possible. Voters, however, should always be skeptical of extravagant promises by politicians to improve the economy and provide benefits with no costs. It is far less painful for policymakers to suggest that their proposals will move us closer to our PPF than to emphasize the opportunity costs involved in moving along the PPF.

To summarize, if private individuals or government policymakers desire to increase the consumption of some good or service, they face two alternatives. Either they must forego consuming some other good or service, or they must find a way to move us closer to the PPF, assuming that current policies lead us to operate inside it. (You face this choice frequently in daily life. For example, if you find a way to use your study time more efficiently by finding a quiet place, without distractions, you will not have to give up a pizza break at ten o'clock the night before a midterm because you will have finished studying by then.) Unfortunately, discovering and adopting economic policies that will truly make our economy more efficient are themselves activities that usually involve opportunity costs. Failure to recognize these limitations is likely to lead to decisions that move *away* from an efficient use of our economy's resources. To make these points more concrete we will use the concept of opportunity cost to discuss the 55-mile-per-hour speed limit.

Reckoning with Opportunity Costs: The Case of the 55-mph Speed Limit

The principle of opportunity cost tells us that there are no free lunches, or that our choices always involve costs of some sort. For example, after oil prices rose sharply in 1973–74, Congress determined that the United States could reduce its gasoline consumption if motorists would reduce their driving speed. As a result, the federal government adopted legislation setting a 55-mph speed limit. Is the 55-mph speed limit good economic policy? Does it contribute to economic efficiency by pushing us closer to our economy's PPF?

Actually, *two* types of opportunity costs are involved in driving at high speeds. One relates to the individual driver and riders in his or her car. The cost of driving faster includes increased gasoline consumption per mile traveled and greater wear and tear on the car's tires and engine. There is also a greater risk of personal injury to the car's driver and passengers from driving faster. The second kind of cost is the increased risk of property damage and personal injury to drivers and passengers in *other* cars.

There is a crucial distinction between these two categories of opportunity costs. The first type involves only the driver of a car and its passengers. They are presumably able to take all of these costs into account in determining the best speed at which to drive. In return for bearing these costs, the driver and passengers reap the *benefit* of reduced travel time. Since time available for working, eating, and leisure activities is perhaps the most basic form of scarcity each of us confronts, the benefits of reduced travel time are substantial. The principal point to recognize with respect to these personal costs and benefits is that the best judge of whether the expected costs of driving faster exceed the benefits is probably those who bear them. This means that as far as saving gasoline or other resources is concerned, there would appear to be no obvious reason for government to interfere with private decisions. (One possible exception is that if injured individuals in the driver's car are eligible for Medicaid, others are paying part of their medical expenses. So, to some extent the driver and his or her passengers may not take all of the relevant costs of speeding into consideration, and they may drive too fast.)

The second type of cost is a different story, however. The driver of a car traveling at a high speed probably places less weight on the risk of injuring other drivers, their cars, and their passengers than do those who may be hurt by the speeder's behavior. Since some of the cost of driving fast is borne by others, a bias is created in favor of fast driving. Thus, there is a reasonably solid basis for speed limits. Is 55 miles per hour the correct speed limit for interstate highways, though? We cannot take the space to discuss all of the information needed to answer this question. We will take a brief look, however. The answer relies on the same basic framework and reasoning involved in our earlier discussion of whether any sacrifice is too great where human life is involved.

Because saving lives is costly, not *all* lives can be saved or prolonged. Choices must be made. Therefore, the question of *how* resources are allocated to prolong life is important. When speed limits are lowered more time is required to drive from one place to another. Over 25 percent more time per mile traveled is required by a driver who must travel at 55 miles per hour instead of 70 miles per hour. Since time is a scarce resource, it has value. Increased travel time is a resource that sales representatives, truckers, and others could use to carry out their business. A reduced speed limit extends the travel time to work for many commuters. Speed limits reduce the distances that can be traveled during a vacation period, thus diminishing the value of leisure and vacation time for many. Society's trade-off between saving lives and time available for activities other than driving is illustrated in figure 1.4.

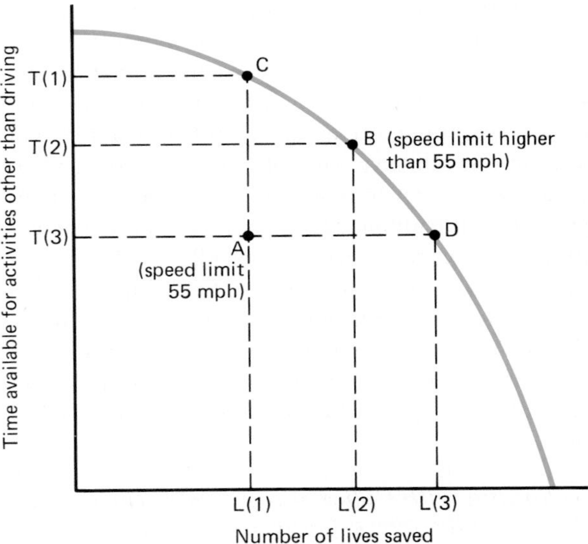

Figure 1.4 Society's trade-off between driving time and lives saved from automobile accidents
This PPF shows that society can choose between saving lives and using time for activities other than driving cars. By lowering the speed limit, we save more lives but we have less time available for other activities. However, there are other means of saving lives that have lower opportunity costs. Because time and lives are extremely valuable to most of us, this is an important social choice. Specifically, when the speed limit is 55 miles per hour, there are other things that can be done to save lives that make better use of our time and save more lives. An example would be to provide every family with a smoke detector. Then the speed limit could be raised while still saving more lives than we do now. This can be illustrated as moving from a point such as A to a point such as B, which is between points C and D on the PPF.

Economists have conducted studies of how people value their time. These studies are carried out not by interviewing individuals directly but rather by noting the modes of transportation people chose and how these choices depended on the costs in terms of dollars per mile traveled and time per mile traveled. The results of these studies imply that the average person is willing to spend an amount equal to about one-half his or her hourly wage to save one hour of travel time.[2]

Highway safety experts have calculated approximately how many lives are saved annually as a result of the 55-mph speed limit. Thus, it is possible to estimate the dollar cost per life saved. The finding is that it costs society about $2 million per life saved (in terms of average wages earned in 1986).

Is $2 million per life saved too much? Most of us would find it difficult to place a dollar value on our own or on our loved ones' lives, not to mention people we have never met. Still most people would agree that less costly life-saving methods should be chosen over more expensive ones. If the point of the 55-mph speed limit is to save lives, it is fair to ask if this is an efficient way to save lives. Why should we single out traffic deaths as the appropriate target for government policy? It has been estimated that placing smoke detectors in every home in the United States would save about as many lives per year as the 55-mph speed limit but at much lower cost, only $50,000 to $80,000 per life saved. Perhaps every home in the United States should be required to install smoke detectors. Do you agree?

Specialization occurs when people produce a good or service to trade or sell to others, not because they may wish to use the good or service they are producing.

The preceding discussion may be factually correct, but what would be a less expensive life-saving government policy with respect to automobiles? Here is one possible answer for you to think about. Instead of a 55-mph speed limit, let the federal government issue special license tags in different colors to permit driving up to various speeds on interstate highways. The higher the speed permitted, the higher the annual fee. Suppose that driving in the speed range of up to 70 miles per hour increases the risk of killing someone in another car by one death per year for every 30,000 licensed drivers. (This is based roughly on available statistics.) Suppose that in compensation for this risk, drivers were required to pay into an insurance fund that would compensate anyone injured or the families of anyone killed *plus* enough to save two lives by installation of smoke detectors. If the compensation paid were $1,500,000 per additional death caused by traveling over 55 mph and it cost $160,000 to install enough smoke detectors to save two lives, then anyone who wished to drive at speeds up to 70 mph would be required to pay approximately $55 annually for a license to do so ($55 × 30,000 = $1,650,000). The license revenue would be used to provide compensation to the families of people killed in car crashes and to purchase smoke detectors for the public. Would this essentially make drivers' licenses more of a license to kill than they are now? How would this proposal compare to current efforts to control speeding? Can you suggest what you think is a better alternative?

In the example of the 55-mph speed limit, we saw that there is more than one way to use our time and other resources in order to save lives. Some ways to save lives have lower opportunity costs than others, and in a world of scarcity it makes an important difference which methods are chosen. Before concluding our discussion of opportunity cost and the production possibilities frontier, we will take a closer look at how you, as director of a small economy, can help your economy become efficient by using your labor resources effectively.

Opportunity Cost, Comparative Advantage, and Specialization

Your task is to assign workers to produce either medical services or consumer goods so that production takes place along the production possibilities frontier. (To keep our example simple, we will assume that any worker has sufficient training to produce *some* medical services.) The production possibilities frontier describes the best "menu" from which society can then choose the most preferred combination of consumer goods and medical services.

As we have seen, reaching the production possibilities frontier requires minimizing opportunity costs. We shall see that opportunity costs can be minimized only when workers specialize in production. **Specialization** means that workers do not produce everything they consume; rather, they tend to concentrate their efforts on producing one or a few goods or services. *How* they specialize is of the utmost importance. Opportunity costs will be minimized and the country's maximum potential output, as defined by the PPF, will be obtained only if workers specialize in producing according to their *relative* skills.

A numerical example will show what we mean. Suppose that Larry and Laura are two new workers you must assign to producing either consumer goods or medical services. By carefully examining how Larry and Laura should be assigned, we can derive the basic principle that applies to the other workers as well. Specifically, suppose that Laura can produce at most *either* 50 units of medical services per year *or* 10 units of consumer goods. She can also produce some of both by giving up 50/10, or 5, units of medical services, for each (additional) unit of consumer goods she produces. Suppose that Larry, on the other hand, can produce at most only 40 units of medical services *or* 5 units of consumer goods and must sacrifice 40/5, or 8, units of medical services for each (additional) unit of consumer goods he provides.

Comparative advantage is determined by which producer has the lowest opportunity cost of producing a good or service. Since opportunity cost is measured in terms of the quantity of one good or service that must be sacrificed to produce one more unit of another good or service, everyone has a comparative advantage in producing something.

Table 1.1 Maximum production, opportunity cost, and comparative advantage

Laura's opportunity cost of producing consumer goods is lower than Larry's. The numbers also show that Larry's opportunity cost of producing medical services is lower than Laura's. It costs Larry only 5/40 = 1/8 unit of consumer goods to produce one more unit of medical services, while Laura's opportunity cost of an additional unit of medical services is 10/50 = 1/5 unit of consumer goods.

	Maximum production (units)		Opportunity cost of one more unit of consumer goods		Comparative advantage
	Larry	Laura	Larry	Laura	
Consumer goods	5	10	$\frac{40}{5} = 8$	$\frac{50}{10} = 5$	Laura in consumer goods and Larry in medical services
Medical services	40	50			

To complete our example, we will assume that every worker (besides Laura and Larry) in the economy has already been assigned to produce either consumer goods or medical services in the most efficient manner. We will also assume that society now desires 10 additional units of consumer goods. Given the information we have on Larry and Laura's production opportunity costs, it follows that Laura should produce the 10 additional units of consumer goods society desires. This is true even though by devoting her efforts only to medical services, Laura could produce 50 units, which is 10 more than Larry's capability. The reason is that the *opportunity cost* of producing each additional unit of consumer goods is 8 units of medical services for Larry but only 5 units of medical services for Laura. Because Laura has a lower opportunity cost of producing consumer goods than Larry does, we say that she has a **comparative advantage** in the production of consumer goods and should therefore specialize in producing consumer goods.

A moment's further thought will reveal that Larry has a comparative advantage in producing medical services. From the numbers given above, his opportunity cost of producing a unit of medical services is 5/40, or 1/8, unit of consumer goods. By contrast, Laura's opportunity cost of a unit of medical services is higher, 10/50, or 1/5, unit of consumer goods.

This simple example of opportunity cost, comparative advantage, and specialization is summarized in tables 1.1 and 1.2. It shows that if Larry were to help produce the 10 additional units of consumer goods, Laura would also have to produce 5 units. She would have to sacrifice 25 units of medical services, so society's total additional output would amount to 10 units of consumer goods and 25 of medical services. By contrast, if Laura were to specialize in consumer goods production, she could produce all of the additional 10 units by herself. Even though she would not produce any medical services, total (additional) production of medical services would be 40 units, all produced by Larry. This is a better outcome because it provides more medical services for society, given that society desires 10 additional units of consumer goods. The basic principle is that the economy can reach its production possibilities frontier only when workers produce those goods in which they have a *comparative* advantage, that is, a lower opportunity cost than other workers. In this way we see that the answers to the *what* and *how* questions are clearly intertwined.

*A **market economy** is one in which most goods and services are bought and sold in markets rather than each good and service being produced by each person or family that uses it.*

*A **market** may be an actual location, but in economics it is best thought of as an idealized concept that describes how buyers and sellers of a particular good or service come together.*

*A **barter economy** is one in which money plays an unimportant role and in which goods and services are traded directly.*

Table 1.2 Total production when 10 additional units of consumer goods are desired

If Laura specializes in the production of consumer goods, she will produce the additional 10 units society desires, leaving Larry free to devote all of his efforts to producing 40 units of medical services. This results in greater additional output of medical services than if Larry and Laura both produce consumer goods.

	If Larry produces only consumer goods			If Laura produces all the additional consumer goods desired		
	Larry's production	**Laura's production**	**Total**	**Larry's production**	**Laura's production**	**Total**
Consumer goods	5 units	5 units	10 units	0 units	10 units	10 units
Medical services	0 units	25 units	25 units	40 units	0 units	40 units

The Concept of a Market Economy and the Economy of the United States

This chapter has introduced the basic economic problem—scarcity. While people have desires for all types of goods and services, they cannot fully satisfy those desires because of limits to the resources they possess. In the following chapters, we will investigate how scarcity affects a **market economy,** which is a system in which producers and consumers interact to determine the output of goods and services. Market economies are dominant in the United States and most other nations. A **market** should be thought of as the arena in which buyers and sellers interact. Not all markets are formal, visible organizations in the sense that there is a particular geographical location where buyers and sellers come to do business such as in bazaars in the Middle East or at the New York Stock Exchange. These are markets, of course, but so is the labor market. The labor market is an example of a *conceptual* market, which cannot always be pinpointed in terms of a physical location. We have all heard of the labor market. In all likelihood you are either in it now, have been, or soon will be. But have you ever actually *seen* the labor market?

The point is that a market is a convenient analytical device economists use to organize their ideas. Sociologists do something similar when they refer to women's liberation or the civil rights movement. These are important social forces, but they are not things that you can actually touch. What we are saying is that exchanges do occur, even if they are not all in the same place, as in the case of the stock market. The way in which buyers and sellers of houses interact, for example, determines housing prices and how many houses are bought and sold. By developing the concept of a market more fully, we will see the forces that determine the prices and production of goods and services and their effect on the welfare of those individuals involved as buyers and sellers (the answers to the *what* and *for whom* questions).

An important aspect of most market economies is that purchases are made with money. To understand the importance of money we must imagine an economy *without* money, which is called a **barter economy.** In a barter economy, transactions involve trading one good or service for another. Successful trades require *mutual coincidence of want,* which means that if I wished to have my automobile fixed,

Free market economies *are those that operate with the least amount of government control over the prices and quantities of goods and services bought and sold; few such economies operate with absolutely no government influence, however.*

Controlled economies *are characterized by controlled markets, in which prices, and sometimes quantities bought and sold, are mandated by law or government decree. Some transactions may occur in uncontrolled markets.*

I would have to find a mechanic who wanted what I had to trade. If I baked rye bread for a living, the only way I could get a tune-up for my car would be to find a mechanic who just happened to want rye bread. This would be a very cumbersome way of getting something done and suggests why modern economies do not typically use the barter system. It is much simpler to sell the rye bread I produce for money and then use the money to purchase car repairs from any mechanic I might choose.

A market economy is an invaluable means of reducing scarcity because markets permit society to benefit from specialization. We have seen how specialization is crucial to achieving economic efficiency. When we specialize, almost none of us produce all of the goods and services we consume. Indeed, some of us work in jobs that involve goods or services we may never wish to purchase. For example, many famous designers of women's clothing are men; you do not have to like snow sports to work in a ski factory; many workers without pets help manufacture dog, cat, and canary food. If each of us tried to be self-sufficient, scarcity would be much more severe for us because we would not be able to direct our talents and abilities where they are most useful (the answer to the *how* question). We would all have to be Jacks or Jills of all trades. However, in the absence of markets, obtaining the goods and services we want in exchange for those we produce would take so much time and effort that the advantages of specialization would be largely lost. Before analyzing market economies in detail, we must further distinguish among various economic systems.

In this book, our focus is on those economic systems in which governments exert the least direct influence on the prices and quantities of goods bought and sold (the answer to the *what* question). In no nation are markets totally free of governmental controls. However, the economies of the United States, Canada, Japan, West Germany, and South Korea, among others, are characterized by the predominance of **free markets**—which means *relatively little* governmental intervention in the economy. **Controlled economies** lie at the opposite extreme. Examples are the systems of the Soviet Union, much of Eastern Europe, and the People's Republic of China, where relatively few transactions take place without the explicit approval of some government official. In this sense, government is much more involved in the answer to the *what* question in these countries.

Lying in between these two extremes are the **mixed economies** of such nations as France, Sweden, Great Britain, and Mexico, where government typically owns some major industries that are privately held in free market systems. The United States is sometimes also called a mixed economy because our government does control some industries (for example, mail delivery, some transportation, some utilities, and many schools). Other industries that are frequently owned by the government in mixed economies are basic steel production, petroleum, automobile manufacturing, airlines, and banks. There are various reasons why governments exert ownership over major industries in mixed economies. Some goals of government ownership are the achievement of high employment and high wages, independence from foreign suppliers, and the prestige associated with industrial "power." One of your tasks both as a citizen and as a student of economics will be to decide whether government ownership represents the best way of achieving these goals and, equally important, which economic goals you think it best for society to emphasize.

Mixed economies *contain many government-owned industries that are typically privately owned in free market systems.*

Summary and Conclusions

This chapter introduced the concept of scarcity and provided an overview of a simple economic system. You should now have a feel for the way an economic system answers the fundamental questions *what, how,* and *for whom.* The following points were emphasized in this chapter.

All economies face limits imposed by scarcity. When these limits are dealt with efficiently, opportunity costs measure the prices that must be paid when choosing among alternative goods and services.

Producing efficiently requires that individuals specialize according to their relative opportunity costs, or comparative advantage.

Opportunity cost and the production possibilities frontier (PPF) help us to understand the economic issues underlying much government policy, including determining the proper speed limit on interstate highways and labor productivity in the United States.

Few economies today are barter economies. In market economies, individuals typically exchange goods and services indirectly by using money. Market economies foster economic efficiency by encouraging specialization.

Market economies may be of the free market type, controlled economies, or mixed economies. The economy of the United States comes closer to a free market economy than most others. Nevertheless, it has many features of a mixed economy.

Key Terms

barter economy *21*
comparative advantage *20*
controlled economies *22*
economic growth *13*
efficient economy *11*
free market economies *22*
market *21*
market economy *21*
mixed economies *23*
model *10*
normative view *8*
opportunity cost *6*
positive economics *8*
production possibilities frontier (PPF) *11*
scarcity *6*
specialization *19*
three fundamental economic questions *6*

Questions for Discussion and Review

1. Define scarcity and positive economics.
2. Some restaurants advertise that after you pay for your meal you can have all the additional helpings you like free of charge. Have they found a way to eliminate scarcity? Is there any cost at all associated with "seconds" and "thirds" in these restaurants? Why do people patronize restaurants that do not price their meals this way?
3. Try to imagine a world in which scarcity did not exist. What would be the importance of answering the *what, how,* and *for whom* questions in such a world? What kind of economic system do you think would be best in this circumstance?

4. In one of the newspaper articles cited in this chapter, a kidney dialysis patient is quoted as saying, "I would not want to be forced into home dialysis just because it gave my doctor a greater profit. The question should be, is it good for the patient." Do you agree with the quotation? Can you imagine a situation in which someone would voluntarily agree to use home dialysis without receiving orders from a doctor or other authority to do so? Would such a situation be good for the patient? Would it be good for society?
5. Make a list of the types of models used in subjects other than economics. How do these models abstract from (ignore) details of the real world to focus on essentials?
6. Your Uncle Sid shows up at your college, takes you to lunch, and pays the bill. Is this really a free lunch? What costs, if any, do you pay for the lunch?
7. Are workers in the United States highly specialized? Do you believe that specialization has helped productivity growth?
8. In figure 1.1, what would happen to the PPF if a new discovery made producers of both medical services and consumer goods more productive?
9. In tables 1.1 and 1.2, how would Larry's and Laura's comparative advantage change if Larry were suddenly able to produce twice as much of both things, but Laura's capabilities did not change? Describe a change that would result in Larry's having a comparative advantage in the production of consumer goods. What would happen to Laura's comparative advantage?
10. In figure 1.2, suppose that workers producing medical services were provided with additional high-tech equipment to work with but that workers in the consumer goods area were not. What would be the effect on the PPF? What would happen to the opportunity cost of medical services? What would be the effect on the opportunity cost of consumer goods?
11. In congressional debates on pollution and environmental policy, one side frequently argues that our environment is too precious to be "sold" in return for higher industrial output. Others argue that the benefits of an improved environment must be weighed against the costs of reducing pollution. What are the costs and benefits they are arguing about? Which side do you support? Why?
12. Suppose that we did not have a market economy and that you had to produce everything you consumed. Make up a "time budget" showing how you would spend your time each week producing everything you need. How much time would you require? Be sure to allow time for eating and sleeping. How many of the goods and services that you now consume would you be able to have? How much time would be left over for leisure?
13. Suppose that you were in charge of organizing an all-volunteer army for the United States government. On the basis of what you have learned about the concept of opportunity cost, what issues would you consider in order to complete your task?

Appendix to Chapter 1

Economics and Your Career

▸ Why Take Economics?

Now that you are enrolled in your first or second course in economics, you are probably wondering just how this subject will help you in your future career. Some of you may, in fact, eventually become professional economists, although the probability of this is small. For most students, a course in the principles of economics is not the obvious doorway to a profession that preengineering or premed courses provide for many. Even so, economics can and should be a valuable part of your curriculum.

Economics courses are an important element in a program of liberal education. They offer an understanding of how the economy operates and provide a basis for informed opinions on many public issues. If you are majoring in one of the other social sciences or in business administration, a minor in economics will provide valuable information and training in understanding the social environment in which we live and work.

▸ Economics As a Major

There are various opportunities for economics majors. Although employment as a professional economist generally requires a graduate degree, an undergraduate major in economics that emphasizes the quantitative tools of economic theory and statistical applications (econometrics) provides excellent preparation for a career in government, banking, business, organized labor, trade associations, or teaching in the social sciences. Business firms and federal, state, and local government agencies look favorably on economics majors in their quest for bright, clear-thinking trainees capable of moving up the job ladder to positions of managerial responsibility.

An economics major also provides an excellent base for graduate work in law, business administration, public administration, and the health professions, as well as in economics. Admissions committees in these disciplines value economics majors because they know that economics provides sound training in logical thinking, assessment of alternatives, and quantitative skills.

▸ Careers in Economics

As we have suggested, taking a few courses or majoring in economics can provide the foundation for a variety of careers. A former advisee of one of the authors of this text who subsequently received a master's degree in public administration is now budget director of the state of Ohio. Two former students whose careers we have followed are professors at major law schools.

Graduate work in economics can lead to either a master's or a Ph.D. degree. Graduates with a master's degree find jobs as economic analysts with many business firms, in the banking industry, and as officials in city, state, and national governments and in international agencies such as the World Bank, International Monetary Fund, and so on. They also have access to teaching positions in high schools and many two-year colleges. Graduates with a Ph.D. frequently are employed by college and university faculties, but many have jobs with major financial institutions and research organizations. It is not uncommon for someone with a Ph.D. in economics to work (as an economist) at the level of vice president of one of the country's largest banks. During the past twenty years the heads of some of our major universities—including the University of California, Carnegie-Mellon University, Northwestern University, Princeton University, and the University of Colorado—have been economists. But so much for abstractions. We can also name names. The following list contains the names of over two dozen prominent people whose college undergraduate or graduate degrees were in economics. Who knows what heights you will attain if you choose economics as your major?

Prominent Economics Majors and Positions They Have Held

Brock Adams Representative from Washington and secretary of transportation

Robert O. Anderson CEO, Atlantic-Richfield Corporation

Roy Anderson CEO, Lockheed Corporation

Carlos Romero Barcelo Governor of Puerto Rico

Rose Elizabeth Bird Chief justice, California supreme court

W. Michael Blumenthal President, Bendix Corporation, and secretary of the treasury

Thomas A. Donovan President, Chicago Board of Trade

John Elway Quarterback, Denver Broncos

Michael Foot Prominent political leader, British Labor party

Mike Gravel Senator from Alaska

David Hartman Host, "Good Morning America"

Brian Holloway Defensive back, New England Patriots

Alfred Kahn Chairman, Interstate Commerce Commission

Juanita Kreps Secretary of commerce and vice president of Duke University

Drew Lewis Secretary of transportation

Hilla Limann President of Ghana

F. Ray Marshall Secretary of labor

Sandra Day O'Connor Associate justice of the Supreme Court

Merlin Olsen Professional football player and announcer

Charles Percy CEO, Bell and Howell Corporation, and senator from Illinois

Sylvia Porter Syndicated financial columnist

Ronald W. Reagan President of the United States

George P. Shultz President, Bechtel Corporation, secretary of state, secretary of the treasury, and secretary of labor

Cyrus P. Vance Secretary of state

Harold Wilson Prime Minister of Great Britain

Policy Issue: You Decide

Who Should Pay for Clean Air?

▸ The Action-Initiating Event

You are the chief economic adviser to the city council of a medium-sized industrial city. The city council is considering an ordinance requiring that the manufacturing firms in the city cut their air pollution by 50 percent during the next year. The head of the council has asked you to write a memo describing the key economic policy issue(s) that should be discussed by the council before it votes on the ordinance.

▸ The Issue

As you see it, the most important thing to consider here is *not* how the pollution will be curbed; you are reasonably sure that the firms will cooperate if the ordinance is passed and that they are technologically able to curb the pollution. The key issues in your mind involve trade-offs and opportunity costs. Clean air is good for the community, but it will not be free. Some group or groups must ultimately pay one way or another for that clean air. Moreover, the more one group of citizens pays, the less another group or groups will be burdened with the costs of cleaning up the air. Finally, you realize that each of the following groups have something to do with the problem of air pollution in your city: (1) owners of the polluting firms, (2) workers in the polluting firms, (3) the customers who buy the products of the polluting firms, (4) the taxpayers of your city, and (5) the members of the city government itself.

▸ Economic Policy Issues

Who should pay the cost of cleaning up the air in your city? The improvement in air quality that the city council is considering could cause some or all of the manufacturing firms in your city to close and move elsewhere. This would make each of the five groups identified above economically worse off. On the other hand, the people who live in the neighborhoods surrounding the manufacturing plants have been, in a sense, paying for the air pollution for a number of years by having to stay indoors more often, purchasing air conditioners and air purifiers for their homes, and suffering poorer health in the form of more frequent respiratory ailments. Should this continue? To make matters worse, you worry about your city being branded as antibusiness and unable to attract new businesses (and their jobs and tax revenues) to the city in the future—even ones that might not pollute at all, such as computer software companies.

▸ Recommendations

The head of the council wants you to identify in your memo the various groups of people that might be affected by an ordinance severely cutting air pollution. Included in your memo should be an explanation of some of the details of *how* each of the various groups involved might be harmed by the antipollution measures that might be adopted. At the end of the memo you are to outline an amendment to the ordinance being considered such that, should the ordinance pass, the costs of the required cutback in pollution would be *shared* by *all* of the affected groups.

Part II

Introduction to Macroeconomics

Chapter 2

Introduction to Macroeconomics

Outline

Objectives

After reading this chapter, the student should be able to:

Define macroeconomics and relate it to aggregate economics.
Define GNP and differentiate between nominal GNP and real GNP.
Explain the components of GNP, including consumption, investment, government spending, and net exports.
Describe the relationship between GNP and economic well-being.
Explain the circular flow of income.
Calculate and interpret price indexes.
Explain the relationship between GNP and the business cycle.
Define unemployment and explain its impact on economic issues.
Explain the types of interest rates and indicate how they are related to inflation.

Macroeconomics *analyzes the behavior of an entire economy.*

Aggregate economics *is a synonym for macroeconomics that reminds us that in order to be manageable, macroeconomic analysis must summarize the workings of an entire economy as the behavior of a few aggregate measures of economic performance including the inflation and unemployment rates.*

Gross national product (GNP) *measures the total value of all final goods and services the economy produces during a year.*

▸ An Introduction to the Study of Macroeconomics

On an early morning in February 1984 an Iowa farmer and his family stood and watched in numbed silence as federal agents auctioned off their farm equipment, house, and land to repay federal loans on which the farmer had defaulted. Some neighbors faced with the same grim prospects swore they would not participate in the sale and even talked abut using force to stop the auction. The farmer and his wife had worked the land for years, as had his father and grandfather before them. He had imagined that his children and their children would work the same land and share many of the same experiences that made the farm stand for everything he was and everything he ever hoped to be.

All of that was gone now. The farm, the equipment, the friends and neighbors, all the things that told this family who they were and what they should do, were gone. How could so much disappear so quickly?

Like many other farm families during the late 1970s, they borrowed substantial amounts of money to improve their land and buy new equipment. Interest rates were high, but prices were continuing to rise rapidly so the debts they acquired seemed easily manageable. Then the recession of 1981–1982 came; prices stopped rising rapidly. Farmland prices plunged, but interest rates remained high. The farmer could not meet his debt payments, and he could not get any new loans to keep the farm going. Why did land values decline by one-third to one-half of their 1980 value in only a few years? Why did crop prices stop rising at the double-digit rates experienced in 1979 and 1980? Why did interest rates stay so high that the farmer could not refinance his debt?

The next eleven chapters of this book will help explain the changes in prices, land values, and interest rates in the United States economy that ultimately spelled financial ruin for the farm family we have described, as well as for many others. These changes were beyond the farmer's control. Nevertheless, they had a profound effect on his life and the lives of many others. Millions of similar stories can be told about auto workers in Detroit, steelworkers in Pennsylvania, coal miners in West Virginia, and other workers in other places in America whose lives were dramatically affected by the changes that have occurred in the United States economy in the last few years. In more or less dramatic fashion, government actions regarding these changes will affect each of our lives. The purpose of the chapters that follow is to explain as clearly as we can how the aggregate economy works and how economic policies affect each of us.

Macroeconomics *deals with economywide problems such as inflation and unemployment. The Great Depression of the 1930s, the inflationary spiral of the 1970s, and the high unemployment of the early 1980s are examples of the important events that we will study in macroeconomics. In order to understand macroeconomics, it is necessary to simplify our view of the economic system quite a bit. One of the most important parts of this simplification is to add up—or aggregate—the inputs and outputs of thousands of firms and the expenditures of millions of households. The result of this adding up is a small*

Intermediate goods *are goods purchased by a firm to use in further production.*

Current prices *are the prices of goods and services actually in effect during the year in question.*

Nominal GNP *is the observed value of GNP during a given time period, say, a year, because goods and services are evaluated at current prices.*

Real GNP *is the value of the economy's total production adjusted to ignore changes in the prices of goods and services over time.*

number of aggregate variables *that summarize much of what goes on in our economic system. One of these aggregate variables, for example, is total consumption, which is the expenditures by all of the economy's households on most of the goods and services they use in their everyday lives.*

Because of this process of adding up crucial economic variables, perhaps a better name for macroeconomics would be ***aggregate economics,*** *because it deals with the summation of all markets into a few aggregate measures of the economy's performance. For the sake of simplicity, we will say that the aggregate economy can be represented by three very large markets: (1) the market for currently produced goods and services, (2) the market for financial instruments such as money and bonds, and (3) the labor market.*

Newspaper and magazine accounts of the macroeconomy's performance frequently mention inflation, unemployment, interest rates, and economic growth. We will clarify the meaning and measurement of these variables, which describe an economy's aggregate performance. We will examine what has happened to measures of macroeconomic performance both in recent years and over time and summarize important trends or relationships that our macroeconomic analysis must be able to explain.

This chapter, part of chapter 3, and chapters 5 and 6 present basic facts and institutional details needed to understand the macroeconomy. Part of chapter 3 and chapters 4, 7, 8, 9, and 10 present a basic theoretical analysis of the aggregate economy. Chapters 11 and 12 deal with macroeconomic policies and controversies that affect all of us.

▸ GNP: A Measure of a Society's Total Production

Background

Probably the most widely known measure of macroeconomic performance is the measure of aggregate production known as **gross national product (GNP),** which is the total market value of the *final* goods and services produced in the United States *during a given year.* (A closely related measure is gross domestic product, GDP. This measure is frequently used in international comparisons of aggregate economic performance. We will occasionally use it in later chapters dealing with the international economy and macroeconomic issues in countries other than the United States. When you see this term, you should think of it as equivalent to GNP.) The word *final* indicates that **intermediate goods,** which are goods purchased by a firm for further production, are not included in GNP. Purchases of goods produced in previous years are not part of GNP either because they were counted in an earlier year's GNP.

The federal government first calculates GNP in terms of **current prices,** which are the prices in effect during the year under consideration. This value of GNP is known as the **nominal GNP.** *Nominal* means that total production is calculated at prices currently prevailing in the economy. It is important to distinguish between the nominal value of GNP and the **real value of GNP,** which is the value of GNP calculated in such a way that it does not reflect changes in the prices of goods and services over time. We will soon see that the price level and the rate of inflation are what link the nominal and real values of GNP.

***Consumption** refers to households' expenditures on goods and services to be used primarily during the year in question.*

***Nondurable consumer goods** are goods used up by households in the year they are purchased.*

***Durable consumer goods** are pieces of equipment that provide services to households over a number of years.*

The Nominal Value of GNP

The nominal value of GNP is a measure of the economy's total production of goods and services in a particular time period. These data are taken from the *Economic Report of the President,*[1] which contains an extensive listing of the economic variables that describe the performance of the United States macroeconomy over time. If you are interested in such data, this publication is well worth buying. For selected values of macroeconomic data, the *Statistical Abstract of the United States* is a useful source of information.

Except for the depression era of the 1930s, nominal GNP has risen steadily, as shown in table 2.1. This table also contains data on personal consumption expenditures, investment by firms, exports (less imports) of goods and services, and the purchases of goods and services by the various government agencies in the United States. Together, these items represent the total value of all the goods and services produced in the United States economy and are, therefore, the basic components of GNP.

Table 2.1 shows that GNP consists of expenditures on several categories of goods and services, which are called consumption (C), investment (I), government (G), and net exports of goods and services to foreign countries (X). Because GNP is the sum of total expenditures for various items, we will use the symbol E to represent it. GNP can be expressed symbolically as

$$E \equiv C + I + G + X.$$

This identity will prove to be valuable when we build a model of how the macroeconomy works. For now let us store it in our memory banks and elaborate somewhat on each of the basic components of gross national product.

Consumption

Consumption (C) in table 2.1 includes those goods and services bought by households during the year being considered. Examples include clothing and food. Consumption expenditures include both **nondurable** and **durable consumer goods.** An ordinary nondurable consumer good, such as bread, is purchased and used up within a relatively short period of time. In contrast, a durable consumer good provides service over an extended period of time. For example, a car is usually expected to provide transportation for a number of years. Cars, refrigerators, and television sets are all examples of consumer durables. Strictly speaking, when we buy a car we really intend to use only a fraction of its total services during the year. Unless it is a real lemon, the car will give us use over its lifetime of, say, five years. Thus, the purchase price of the car, paid this year, exceeds the consumption value attached to the use of the car this year. To the extent that GNP lumps all consumption expenditures together, including the purchases of consumer *durable goods,* changes in GNP over time misrepresent changes in society's current consumption. (Purchases of new houses are *not* included in the consumer durable goods group; they are treated as investment expenditures. The reason for this is that there is a flow of benefits from a house to its users over a long period of years. These *annual* benefits, which are measured by rent in the case of people who do not own their own homes, are included in consumption. Thus GNP also includes the estimated rental value of owner-occupied homes.)

As an example, suppose a new discovery permits the manufacture of robots that can do all household chores. (This discovery also permits the robots to be produced with no reduction in the production of any other good.) These robots cost $25,000 each and last for twenty-five years, so their one-year consumption benefits are about $1,000. However, measured GNP will reflect the $25,000 purchase price. By including the total value of consumer durables purchased, GNP overstates the increase in consumption occurring in the year the robots are purchased. GNP calculations generally ignore the consumption value of consumer durables in the years *after* they are purchased, thus understating the consumption from consumer durables in these years. (As mentioned above, there is an exception. GNP includes the estimated rental value of the services received by people who own their homes.)

Investment occurs when businesses add to their collection of physical capital (plant and equipment) and inventories. It also includes the purchases of new dwellings, even if by individuals or families.

Table 2.1 Gross national product, expenditure components, 1929–85 (billions of current dollars)

Year	Gross national product (E)	Personal consumption expenditures (C)	Gross private domestic investment (I)	Government purchases of goods and services (G)	Net exports of goods and services (X)
1929	103.4	77.3	16.2	8.8	1.1
1933	55.8	45.8	1.4	8.2	0.4
1939	90.9	67.0	9.3	13.5	1.2
1940	100.0	71.0	13.1	14.2	1.8
1945	212.4	119.5	10.6	74.6	− 0.5
1950	286.5	192.0	53.8	38.5	2.2
1955	400.0	253.7	68.4	75.0	3.0
1960	506.5	324.9	75.9	100.3	5.5
1965	691.1	430.4	113.5	138.4	8.8
1970	992.7	621.7	144.2	220.1	6.7
1971	1077.6	672.2	166.4	234.9	4.1
1972	1185.9	737.1	195.0	253.1	0.7
1973	1326.4	812.0	229.8	270.4	14.2
1974	1434.2	888.1	228.7	304.1	13.4
1975	1549.2	976.4	206.1	339.9	26.8
1976	1718.0	1084.3	257.9	362.1	13.8
1977	1918.0	1204.4	324.1	393.8	−04.0
1978	2163.9	1346.5	386.6	431.9	−01.1
1979	2417.8	1507.2	423.0	474.4	13.2
1980	2633.1	1667.2	402.3	538.4	25.2
1981	2937.7	1843.2	471.5	596.9	26.1
1982	3073.0	1991.9	414.5	649.2	17.4
1983	3309.5	2158.6	471.3	690.2	−10.6
1984	3774.7	2423.0	674.0	736.8	−59.2
1985	3992.5	2581.9	670.4	814.6	−74.4

Source: From *Economic Report of the President,* 1986, Table B-1, pp. 252–253.

Definitions: E is the market value of (final) goods and services produced by the United States economy.

C is the market value of goods and services purchased by individuals and nonprofit institutions, the value of food, clothing, housing, and financial services received by them in kind and the rental value of owner-occupied housing. It does not include purchases of dwellings.

I is net acquisitions of fixed capital goods by private businesses and nonprofit institutions, net increases in inventories, and all private new dwellings.

G is net expenditures on goods and services by federal, state, and local governments.

X is sales to foreign countries less purchases from foreign countries.

Investment

Investment (I) consists of the economy's addition to capital during a year. Thus, the investment category of GNP basically represents purchases of *newly produced* goods that will be used as inputs into firms' production of other goods. We cannot emphasize too strongly that the economist's definition of *investment* does not match the everyday meaning of the word. In economics, investment does *not* include purchases of *existing* goods such as buildings constructed in earlier years or used machinery. It does *not* refer to items such as stocks and bonds issued by companies to finance their operations. (We shall discuss the role of these items, which are called financial assets, in chapters 5, 6, and 7.) Investment, in the language of economics, refers only to the part of *currently produced* GNP that consists of goods purchased by business firms and households for use over a period of years. Investment includes the construction of *new* buildings, production of *new* capital goods (machines), and purchases of machines, buildings, and equipment that replace old ones.

Government spending is the total dollar value of the purchases of goods and services by all government units—federal, state, and local.

Transfer payments are the opposite of taxes: payments from government to individuals or firms to raise their incomes.

The investment component of GNP includes firms' expenditures on building their inventories of goods. For example, suppose you buy a six-pack of your favorite soft drink from a supermarket. This is counted as consumption in GNP. However, in order to make sure that you can buy soft drinks whenever you want them, your favorite supermarket carries an inventory, or stock, of various brands on its shelves and in its warehouse. If the supermarket increases the value of soft drinks it has on hand from, say, \$100,000 to \$110,000, it must purchase \$10,000 worth of soft drinks from bottlers. This represents an increase in the sale of final goods and services (\$10,000 worth of soft drinks), but it is clearly not consumption, because the goods are being held for future use. Therefore, purchases of currently produced goods that go to increase inventories count as part of the investment component of GNP.

It is important to bear in mind that if one firm purchases an *existing* capital good (such as a used machine) from another firm, this is *not* investment in the GNP sense. The reason is that the seller of the used capital is *disinvesting* and the buyer is investing. When these activities are aggregated (added up) in the calculation of GNP, they cancel each other because they do not represent the *production* of investment goods during the year.

Given what you now know about the components of investment, does an increase in investment *necessarily* mean that society is better off? Why? (Investment is defined as the purchase of a *currently produced durable good.* It does *not* include the purchase of previously produced goods or financial assets such as stocks and bonds. Here is an instance where an economic definition differs from everyday usage.)

Government Spending

The next major part of GNP you need to be aware of is **government spending (G),** the expenditures for goods and services by government at all levels—federal, state, and local. The government spending portion of GNP runs the gamut from expenditures for FBI agents' salaries to the purchase of chemicals for your town's sewage-treatment plant. The government spending portion of GNP does *not* include a very important component of government *outlays. Transfers* to the private sector are direct payments that are not purchases of goods and services. They are called **transfer payments** because they *transfer* spending power from those individuals and households that pay taxes to other individuals or households (who may or may not pay taxes). Transfers are usually aimed at raising the incomes of certain groups that society chooses to aid. They support expenditures by their recipients, which are reflected in GNP when the expenditures are used to purchase currently produced goods and services.

Table 2.1 shows us that government spending has grown quite dramatically in the last forty years. If you compute the percentage of GNP accounted for by government spending in 1940 compared to 1980 or beyond, you will find an almost 50 percent increase in the relative size of the government sector. Government spending on currently produced goods and services was about 14 percent of GNP in 1940, and it grew to about 20 percent of GNP by 1980. As government spending has become an increasingly larger fraction of total GNP, other components of GNP must have fallen in relative importance. Has government spending increased across the board, or has it been concentrated at a particular level of government? Let us dig a little more deeply into these issues.

The relative importance of government spending in GNP has been matched almost point for point by a reduction in the share of personal consumption expenditures. The relative shares of net exports and gross private investment have changed little over the time that the government sector has grown. What appears to have happened is a substitution of *collective* consumption for *private* consumption by individuals. An even more interesting issue involves which level of government is responsible for the relative growth of the government sector. If you were to look at more detailed data from the *Economic Report of the President,*[2] you would see that most of the increase in government spending has come from state and local

Net exports represent the dollar value of a country's exports minus the dollar value of its imports.

governments. While politicians may blame the federal government for the increase in the size of government, purchases of goods and services at the federal level have not grown much more rapidly than GNP during the last forty years. For example, the federal government's purchases of goods and services amounted to about 6 percent of GNP in 1940 and to about 7.5 percent of GNP in 1980. In contrast, the expenditures by state and local governments accounted for approximately 8 percent of GNP in 1940 but had risen to about 13 percent by 1980. Evidently, citizens are demanding more public services from their state and local governments, to the extent their demands are reflected in their votes for tax and bond issues and for their legislative representatives.

Net Exports

When you buy an imported product, you are increasing the GNP of *another* country. The reason is that GNP includes **net exports (X),** the difference between goods and services exported and goods and services imported. When foreigners purchase goods and services from us, they contribute to *our* GNP. Note that in some years, X is negative in table 2.1. When a country has positive net exports, it has produced more goods and services for foreign customers than foreigners have produced for it. More goods and services flow out of the country than flow in. Often you read in the newspapers that a *trade deficit* is a bad thing. A trade deficit for the United States means that the value of goods and services foreigners sent us exceeded the value of goods and services we sent to them.

To make sure that you understand how the components of GNP make up the total, go through a couple of the rows of table 2.1 and actually calculate GNP. For example, in 1983, total gross national product of $3.309 trillion was the sum of personal consumption expenditure of $2.158 trillion + gross private domestic investment of $.471 trillion + government purchases of goods and services of $.69 trillion − net *imports* of $.01 trillion (why is there a minus sign here, and why have we relabeled net exports net imports?).

GNP and Economic Well-being

The news media often treat GNP as a measure of a society's economic well-being and an increase in GNP as an improvement in the welfare of a society. How valid is this? To understand the issue we must pay more attention to what is and is not included in aggregate production as measured by GNP. Remember that GNP is defined as the market value of the final goods and services produced during a given time period. Economic well-being, however, depends on many goods and services produced *outside* the market sector of the economy—mainly in households. Moreover, some production creates "bads," in the form of pollution, that detract from our welfare. In other words, not all production leads to consumption of items we value, and much of what we value economically is not measured in GNP statistics. In the next few sections we will discuss in greater detail some of the deviations of economic well-being from official measures of GNP.

The Role of Nonmarket Transactions

GNP measures the *market* value of goods and services produced. Market prices provide a convenient way to evaluate the production of diverse activities. Given the large number of different goods and services produced, it is an especially convenient way to calculate a grand total for production. As you might expect, some problems exist because of GNP's emphasis on market values. Problems occur whenever activities that clearly relate to society's well-being take place outside of any obvious market.

For the most part, GNP excludes nonmarket transactions. This does not create major difficulties for measuring changes in society's output and well-being as long as the *ratio* of market to nonmarket production remains reasonably constant. *Serious problems in the use of GNP to measure changes in society's economic welfare will occur, however, if there are changes in the relative proportion of market to nonmarket transactions.* There is no consensus on the actual size of nonmarket transactions relative to GNP in the United States. Estimates range from 3 percent to 60 percent of GNP.[3]

Labor Force Participation of Women To understand the role of nonmarket transactions more clearly, consider the changes in measured GNP that occur when married women enter the labor force in greater proportions, as they have been doing in the United States since the early 1900s. Prior to entering the labor force, the typical married woman spent at least part of her time in household activities such as shopping and cooking. Each of these activities contributed to the economic welfare of her family. Without this effort toward maintaining a clean, safe, and pleasant home environment, her family's well-being would have been substantially lower.

Suppose that we place a price tag of $100 per week on the value of the services that the homemaker rendered to her family. GNP places a zero value on these services that occur in the home, because they are outside the market system. It is important to realize that GNP basically ignores the services of individuals in home production of any sort. You do not have to be a full-time housewife or househusband. Every time you change the oil in your car or wash the windows of your house or apartment rather than pay someone else to do it, you have implicitly lowered the GNP of the United States.

Suppose that a homemaker decides to accept employment as, say, an installer with the telephone company. She now begins to receive a salary of $200 per week. In the process, her family probably uses part of her weekly income to purchase goods and services in the marketplace. Some will be substitutes for things the homemaker had previously been doing at home. In particular, the household may now buy more meals in restaurants and begin to use a laundry service. Suppose that these substitutes cost a total of $100 per week. The actual change in the welfare of our homemaker's family as a result of her new job (ignoring taxes) is really the *difference* between her current wage income and the value of the services she formerly produced as a homemaker. Her family is better off by $100 ($200 − $100) per week. GNP, on the other hand, calculates a welfare gain equal to the full $200 per week because it ignores the homemaker's contribution to her family's well-being.

As we said, GNP's emphasis on *market* value can overstate the change in society's well-being if people decide to do things differently. This issue is quite important whenever many people, as in this case, are simultaneously reducing the extent of their nonmarket activities and increasing their participation in market production. GNP is calculated as if market-employed women suddenly appeared as productive citizens on the economic scene. No allowance is made for previous contributions in their homes. When more women begin to participate in the labor force, then, the true increase in society's economic welfare is *less* than the amount measured by GNP. How would you suggest changing the way GNP is calculated so that it correctly evaluates the change in society's well-being as more and more married women enter the labor force?

Leisure Time

The treatment of leisure time is another example of how GNP misrepresents actual changes in economic welfare. Every year includes a fixed number of hours (approximately 8,760). Each individual divides these hours between work and other activities, including eating, sleeping, and recreation. The hours commonly referred to as *work* are purchased by firms in order to produce market goods and services. The hours not sold in labor markets are used by individuals in leisure activities and household production. We have just seen that household production is undervalued in GNP. GNP also attributes no value to the leisure time of its citizens.

This issue has a number of important economic implications. Let us briefly mention one. The average workweek in the United States was approximately fifty to sixty hours near the turn of the century and has fallen to under forty hours today. At the same time, GNP has risen fairly steadily. The increase in GNP does not account for this almost one-third reduction in the average workweek. How would you go about changing the way GNP is calculated so that it reflects the benefits of greater leisure time? What value would you place on an hour of leisure?

Illegal Transactions and Barter

Gross national product also ignores the value of goods and services exchanged in illegal markets. Whether this causes GNP to overstate or to understate the value of society's well-being depends on your point of view. Here is an example. The "underworld's" revenue from its gambling operations or its sales of cocaine is not included in GNP unless it is reported to the Internal Revenue Service. To the extent that society is worse off when more of these things occur, society's well-being is overstated by GNP.

Incomes and earnings in the United States are taxed under a progressive tax system, which means that tax rates increase with the level of income or earnings. One of the results of this has been that as earnings have risen over time, people have turned to forms of payment that avoid taxes. Recent news accounts note the exchange of services for services, or a return to a form of barter system. An example is a plumber who agrees to fix the toilet of an auto mechanic who in turn tunes up the plumber's car. While the goods that go into the repair of the toilet do get counted in GNP, the exchange of labor services does not. If these transactions are omitted from income tax returns (which is illegal), GNP does not measure them and it thereby undervalues production and society's economic well-being.

Intermediate Transactions

A firm usually does not make each and every component of its final product by itself. As we noted, a firm typically purchases goods from other firms in what are called intermediate transactions. These transactions are a key part of specialization. Specifically, a firm usually finds it advantageous not to make all the inputs that go into its final products. For example, a hospital usually finds it cost effective to buy medicines from drug companies rather than making them itself. What does this imply about the relationship between economic well-being, intermediate transactions, and the computed value of GNP? We will see that we are dealing with two issues here. The first is the fact that GNP *ignores* intermediate transactions. The second is whether that practice is desirable.

Suppose that we ignored the distinction between final and intermediate goods. In this case the economy's total production would be measured by the value of every single item that is bought and sold in a marketplace. Let us call this figure GNP'. Because GNP'counts *both* intermediate and final goods, GNP' can vary even though there is *no* net change in the economic well-being of society. This is best seen with a simple example.

Consider a person who purchases an $8,000 car and intends to use it on pleasure trips over the course of the year. The $8,000 spent represents the value of a final good produced, the automobile. Now suppose that the company that made the car had to purchase $3,000 worth of steel from a steel manufacturer and $500 worth of paint from a paint supplier. These two transactions are *intermediate* in the sense that the car company had to buy these two goods to make its finished product, the car. If we add together the car, steel, and paint purchases, the total value of all of these transactions equals $11,500. This sum is included in our *fictional* measure of society's output, GNP'.

Now suppose the car, steel, and paint companies merge into one large corporation. The inputs that the car company had previously been purchasing from the steel and paint companies will no longer appear as market transactions because the transfer of inputs now takes place *within* the new corporation. As a result of this change in corporate structure, the $3,500 worth of intermediate transactions disappears. In computing GNP', we are left with a total figure that is $8,000, the value of the car sold to the final buyer. Because GNP' falls by $3,500, it seems as though the formation of the large corporation reduces society's total welfare. In fact, economic welfare really remains unchanged because the car buyer still purchases exactly the same car at a price of $8,000. Because GNP includes only final goods and services and excludes all intermediate goods, we avoid such problems. In this way, we do not misinterpret data on changes in the total amount of output taking place when the industrial structure of the economy changes.

The ***circular flow of GNP (circular flow of income)*** *refers to the flow of money back and forth between the buyers and sellers of society's output and means that GNP can be calculated in either of two ways—as the flow of payments for the products of society or as the payments for the inputs used to make society's output.*

Proprietors' income *is the income earned by the self-employed from their business activities.*

GNP Is Also a Measure of a Society's Total Income

The Circular Flow of Income

Gross national product should be thought of as a set of exchanges between *producers* of goods and services and *purchasers* of goods and services. Remember that purchasers include households, business firms, and governments. Thus, the sum of those purchases (GNP) is a measure of total production by society. In the process of producing goods and services, however, producers purchase numerous inputs. They range from the services of workers to machinery and natural resources. Inputs used by producers also include the interest paid to people who lend them money and dividends paid to stockholders. The point of this is that we can also think of GNP as the sum of the expenditures on the inputs required to create it. This is illustrated in figure 2.1

To keep things simple, only exchanges between households and business firms are shown in figure 2.1. The inner circle of the figure shows us that business firms sell goods and services to households and receive payments for those goods and services in exchange. The outer circle reminds us that, at the same time, households are selling inputs to the firms, including the services of labor and money lent. In exchange, firms pay for these inputs through the wages and fringe benefits they pay workers and the dividends they pay out to stockholders. A simple principal of accounting is that all revenues must be accounted for. The total sales of goods and services by a firm must *exactly* balance the payments it makes in the course of producing that output. The two will balance if firms are careful in listing *all* payments, explicit and implicit. Some of the firm's expenditures are implicit because they are *opportunity costs,* which means that the owners of the firm must give up something, even if it is not a cash payment. For example, an implicit cost is depreciation. Firms may pay for machinery in one year and use it in a later year. If using the machinery makes it less productive in future years, then there is an implicit cost that is not explicitly accounted for by a cash payment during the year the cost is incurred.

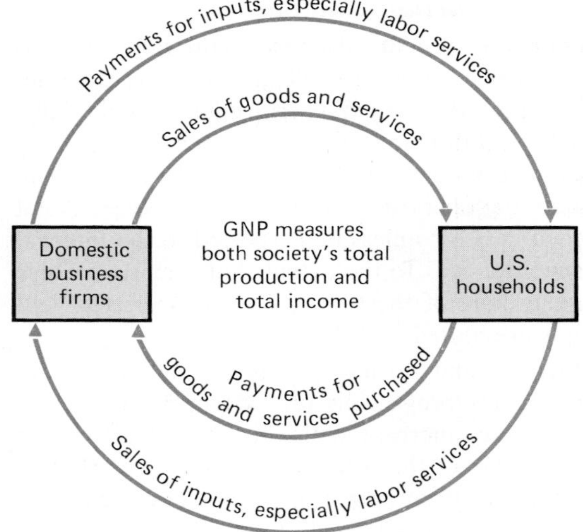

Figure 2.1 The circular flow of payments and purchases between households and firms
Households purchase goods and services from business firms. The total amount spent by households is the largest single component of GNP—Personal Consumption Expenditures. In the course of producing goods and services for sale, firms purchase the services of labor and other inputs, pay taxes to the government, and distribute profits to the people that own the firms. The sum of these also measures GNP, which can be thought of as society's total income. For this reason, GNP is sometimes loosely referred to as *national income.*

The flow of revenues back and forth between firms and households illustrated in figure 2.1 is known as the **circular flow of GNP** or **circular flow of income.** Because of this circular flow, GNP is sometimes casually referred to as national income, although as we shall see, the phrase "National Income" also refers to another, related measure of society's total production.

Data on GNP as a Source of Income

Figure 2.1 emphasizes that total expenditure on GNP is matched by income. In fact, GNP can be measured by adding up individuals and households' incomes as well as by expenditures on production. Business income, such as profit, is attributed to the people who own the business or shares in a corporation. Table 2.2 gives you an idea of the various ways in which GNP

Rental income is the income produced by renting out machinery or buildings for use in production or consumption.

Corporate profits represent the income people receive from dividends paid to them on the stocks they own and earnings retained by the corporation for reinvestment.

Indirect business taxes are those taxes paid by firms on the basis of the value of production taking place.

Table 2.2 Gross national product as sources of income, 1929–85 (billions of dollars)

Year	Gross national product (Y)	Compensation of employees	Proprietors' income	Rental income	Corporate profits	Interest	Depreciation	Indirect business taxes
1929	103.4	51.1	15.0	4.9	9.0	4.7	9.7	7.7
1933	55.8	29.5	5.9	2.2	−1.7	4.1	7.4	7.8
1939	90.9	48.1	11.8	2.6	5.3	3.6	8.8	9.9
1940	100.0	52.1	13.0	2.7	8.6	3.3	9.1	10.5
1945	212.4	123.1	31.8	4.6	19.0	2.2	12.2	20.0
1950	286.5	154.8	38.7	7.1	33.9	3.0	23.5	24.2
1955	400.0	224.9	42.9	11.3	45.5	5.9	34.8	33.4
1960	506.5	294.9	47.2	14.5	47.6	11.4	46.3	47.4
1965	691.1	396.5	56.9	18.0	80.0	21.0	56.0	65.4
1970	992.7	612.0	66.2	19.4	71.4	41.4	88.1	98.4
1971	1077.6	652.2	69.4	20.2	83.2	46.5	96.5	108.1
1972	1185.9	718.0	76.9	21.0	96.6	51.2	106.4	116.4
1973	1326.4	801.3	93.8	22.6	108.3	60.2	116.5	126.4
1974	1434.2	877.5	88.7	23.5	94.9	76.1	136.0	134.9
1975	1549.2	931.4	90.0	23.0	110.5	84.5	159.3	147.5
1976	1718.0	1036.3	94.1	23.5	138.1	87.2	175.0	159.6
1977	1918.3	1152.3	103.5	24.8	167.3	102.5	195.2	174.3
1978	2163.9	1301.1	118.5	26.2	192.1	121.7	222.5	187.5
1979	2417.8	1458.1	132.1	27.9	194.8	153.8	256.0	199.9
1980	2633.1	1598.6	116.3	31.5	181.6	187.7	293.2	224.4
1981	2937.7	1767.6	129.7	41.4	190.6	235.7	330.1	263.7
1982	3073.0	1865.7	109.0	49.9	164.8	261.1	359.2	258.3
1983	3309.5	1990.1	128.6	54.8	226.3	247.2	377.4	285.8
1984	3774.7	2221.3	233.7	10.8	273.3	300.2	418.9	310.6
1985	3992.5	2372.7	242.4	14.0	299.0	287.7	438.2	328.5

Source: From *Economic Report of the President,* 1986, Tables B–1, B–19, and B–21, pp. 276–279.

Notes: 1. Row totals will not exactly equal GNP because of measurement error (statistical discrepancy) and the subsidies less surplus of government enterprises.

2. The category labeled "Indirect business taxes" includes business transfer payments.

is measured as income of members of United States society. The income in table 2.2 is paid out to individuals and households and is used by them to purchase the goods and services produced. A few categories require some elaboration. **Proprietors' income** is the income of the self-employed. **Rental income** is what people receive when they let firms or households use the machinery or buildings they own, and **corporate profits** are divided between dividends corporations pay their stockholders and earnings retained for reinvestment in the corporation. As we noted, depreciation refers to the implicit costs of wearing out equipment in the course of production. The final category in table 2.2, **indirect business taxes,** represents excise and sales taxes paid by firms and is included in the costs of the goods produced. To make sure that you see how GNP calculated in table 2.2 compares to GNP calculated in table 2.1, go across the row for 1985. Prove to yourself that the sum of employee compensation of \$2.372 trillion + proprietors' income of \$.242 trillion + rental income of \$.014 trillion + corporate profits of \$.299 trillion + interest payments of \$.287 trillion + depreciation of \$.438 trillion + indirect business taxes of \$.328 trillion = GNP of \$3.992 trillion. (Note that there will always be a slight statistical discrepancy because these data come from different sources.)

*A **price index** is a number that indicates the ratio of the cost of purchasing or producing a given bundle of goods and services relative to some base year, multiplied by 100.*

*The **consumer price index (CPI)** for the United States is a number that represents the cost of purchasing a representative group of goods and services relative to some time in the past.*

*The **base year** is the date at which a cost of living index is set equal to 100 for the purpose of comparison with other years.*

Other Measures of Production and National Income

Background

Most of the time, GNP is the measure of society's production and income that is referred to in newspapers and other media discussions of the macroeconomy. For this reason, we will use GNP throughout most of our analysis of macroeconomics. However, sometimes more refined measures of income or production are needed to study how our economic well-being or total production has changed over time. For this reason, macroeconomists have developed additional measures of national production and income. So that you will know what these concepts measure, we have listed them, along with their definitions and recent magnitudes, in table 2.3. Notice that one of these measures, which is closely related to gross national product, is called National Income. As a rule, when the term *national income* is used it is a loose reference to GNP; however, in technical discussions, if this *particular* measure of society's production and income is meant, it is usually spelled with capital letters: as National Income rather than national income.

Table 2.3 Relation of GNP to other measures of aggregate production and income, 1985 (billions of dollars)

Gross national product	3573.5
Less: Capital consumption allowances (depreciation)	438.2
Equals: **Net national product**	3554.3
Less: Indirect business taxes	328.5
Business transfer payments	19.3
Statistical discrepancy	0.7
Plus: Net subsidies of government enterprises	9.9
Equals: **National Income**	3215.6
Less: Corporate profits	299.0
Net interest	287.7
Contributions for social insurance	354.9
Wage accruals less disbursements	−0.2
Plus: Government transfer payments to persons	465.2
Personal interest income	456.5
Personal dividend income	78.9
Business transfer payments	19.3
Equals: **Personal income**	3294.2
Less: Personal tax payments	493.1
Equals: Disposable personal income	2801.1

Source: From *Economic Report of the President*, 1986, Tables B–21, B–22, B–25.

Calculating Real GNP

Our discussions have centered on the nominal, or monetary, value of gross national product. We have seen that except for the years of the Great Depression, there has been a continual increase in nominal GNP. Inflation is one factor behind this trend. Remember that each year's GNP in table 2.1 is calculated at the prices in effect during the year in question. As a result, rising prices lead to larger nominal values of GNP even if the quantity of goods and services produced is unchanged. For example, an economy may produce ten units of a good in one year at a price of $1 apiece. Suppose that in the following year ten units are again produced but at a higher price, say, $2 apiece. The nominal value of GNP in the first year is $10; in the second year it is $20.

The increase in the monetary value of GNP from year to year sometimes creates a misleading impression of the growth in society's production and economic welfare. In the preceding example society's production has remained unchanged. In each year its citizens have ten units of output to satisfy their economic wants. Our economic welfare is basically dictated by our consumption of the goods and services themselves—not by their price tags. Of course we all like it when prices are lower, but the real source of our happiness lies in our ability to purchase the goods and services we want.

The Need for a Price Index

A crucial ingredient in determining real GNP is a **price index,** which indicates the cost of purchasing or producing a given set of goods and services at some time compared to the cost at another time. Probably the best-known price index constructed by the United States government is the **consumer price index (CPI).**

The consumer price index is constructed by calculating how much it costs to purchase a fixed bundle, or *market basket,* of goods and services at different times relative to a particular date. The choice of the date, or year, with which to compare the cost of goods and services at other times is arbitrary. The date that is chosen is called the **base year.** The value of a price index in the base year is always set at 100. For example, suppose the cost of a market basket of goods

The ***GNP deflator*** *is a special index number that expresses the average price of current GNP in terms of prices that prevailed in a base year.*

Table 2.4 How price indexes are calculated

Suppose that the economy consists of firms and households that produce and consume only two goods, steak and pizza. Between the base year, 1987, and the current year, 1988, the price of pizza rises from $1.00 to $1.50, while the price of steak doubles from $2.00 to $4.00. Because the price of steak has risen *relatively* more than the price of pizza, consumers decide to purchase fewer steaks and more pizzas. This can be seen in the 1988 quantities in the section showing how the GNP deflator is calculated.

The consumer price index depends on how much the quantities purchased in the base year cost in the base year and in the current year. The ratio of the cost in the current year (1988) divided by the cost in the base year, multiplied by 100, is the consumer price index.

The GNP deflator is calculated by using a somewhat different procedure. The base-year prices are used to calculate how much it would have cost to purchase the current year's actual purchases if prices had not changed. Then the amount that it actually costs to purchase the current year's quantities is divided by the amount that it would have cost had prices not changed. The resulting ratio, multiplied by 100, is the GNP deflator.

Consumer price index

	Base-year quantity of pizza	Price of pizza	Base-year quantity of steak	Price of steak	Cost of living	Consumer price index*
1987 (base year)	25	$1.00	35	$2.00	$ 95.00	100
1988	25	$1.50	35	$4.00	$177.50	187

GNP deflator

	Quantity of pizza	Base-year price of pizza	Quantity of steak	Base-year price of steak	Quantities valued in Base-year prices	Quantities valued in Current prices	GNP deflator**
1987 (base year)	25	$1.00	35	$2.00	$95	$ 95	100
1988	30	$1.00	33	$2.00	$96	$177	184

*Consumer price index ≡ (base-year quantities valued in current-year prices/base-year quantities valued in base-year prices) × 100.

**GNP deflator ≡ (Current quantities valued in current-year prices/current quantities valued in base-year prices) × 100.

was actually $150 in the base year. If, nine years later, the same quantities of these goods still cost $150, the price index would equal 100, because $150 is 100 percent of $150. However, if nine years later, the market basket of goods cost $225, the price index that year would be 150, because $225 is 1.5 (150 percent) times $150. The price index tells us that a representative bundle of goods cost 1.5 times as much in the second year as it did during the base year ($150 × 1.5 = $225). The upper part of table 2.4 contains an example of how the consumer price index is calculated in a simple economy where there are only two goods—steak and pizza.

Another commonly used price index is called the implicit GNP deflator, or **GNP deflator,** for short. The GNP deflator is based on the prices of *all* the goods and services included in GNP, not just the consumption goods component. In computing the GNP deflator, the value of goods and services purchased in the current year is measured by using the prices that prevailed during the base year. The result is called real GNP, or GNP measured in terms of base-year prices. If the nominal GNP for the current year is divided by the real value of the current year's GNP, the result is the GNP deflator. The GNP deflator is sometimes called the *implicit* deflator because it is the price index that is *implied* in calculating real GNP. An example of how you might calculate the GNP deflator is shown in the lower part of table 2.4. Notice in the table that the amount prices have risen as measured by the CPI (87 percent) is greater than the price increase measured by the GNP deflator (84 percent). This is generally the case because the GNP deflator takes into consideration the effect on purchases when the prices of some goods increase *relatively* more than other goods.

Table 2.5 Some important measures of the macroeconomy's performance, 1929–85

Year	Consumer price index (CPI)[a](base 1967)	Annual rate of inflation	Real GNP (base 1972) (billions of dollars)	Civilian unemployment rate[a]	Prime interest rate[a]	GNP deflator (base 1967)
1929	51.3	− 2.53%	$ 315.7	3.2%	5½–6%	43.0
1933	38.8	3.35	222.1	24.9	1½–4	33.4
1939	41.6	0.96	319.8	17.2	1.5	36.7
1940	42.0	5.0	344.1	14.6	1.5	37.3
1945	53.9	2.28	560.4	1.9	1.5	50.8
1950	72.1	0.98	534.8	5.3	2.07	68.2
1955	80.2	− 0.37	657.5	4.4	3.16	77.3
1960	88.7	1.60	732.2	5.5	4.82	87.8
1965	94.5	1.72	929.3	4.5	4.54	94.3
1970	116.3	5.92	1085.6	4.9	7.91	114.9
1971	121.3	4.30	1122.4	5.9	5.72	123.7
1972	125.3	3.30	1185.9	5.6	5.25	129.5
1973	133.1	6.23	1254.3	4.9	8.03	137.9
1974	147.7	10.97	1246.3	5.6	10.81	150.4
1975	161.2	9.14	1231.6	8.5	7.86	165.1
1976	170.5	5.77	1298.2	7.7	6.84	175.8
1977	181.5	6.45	1369.7	7.1	6.83	187.5
1978	195.4	7.66	1438.6	6.1	9.06	201.1
1979	217.4	11.26	1479.4	5.8	12.67	218.9
1980	246.8	13.52	1474.0	7.1	15.3	238.7
1981	272.4	10.37	1502.6	7.6	18.87	261.8
1982	289.1	6.13	1485.4	9.5	14.86	278.5
1983	298.4	3.22	1534.8	9.5	10.79	289.1
1984	311.1	4.0	1543.4	7.4	12.04	301.1
1985	322.2	3.8	1548.8	7.1	9.93	311.1

Source: From *Economic Report of the President,* 1986.

[a]The CPI, Unemployment Rate, and Prime Interest Rate are annual averages.

Definitions: The CPI is a measure of the average cost of a *market basket* of goods and services purchased by a typical family expressed in terms of 1967. The value of the CPI in 1967 is 100 in this table.

—The Rate of Inflation is the percentage change in the CPI between years.

—Real GNP is the value of GNP measured in terms of the prices that prevailed in 1972.

—The civilian unemployment rate is the number of people in the labor force who were actively seeking work or were on layoff expressed as a percentage of the total labor force.

—The prime interest rate is an interest rate banks stated they charged their most credit-worthy customers for loans.

—The GNP deflator measures the average cost of current GNP in terms of 1967 prices.

The CPI and GNP Deflator for the United States

Table 2.5 gives us some values of the consumer price index and GNP deflator since 1929. The CPI tells us that consumer goods are roughly three times more expensive today than they were in 1967. How much has the price level gone up, using the GNP deflator as a measure? How much more expensive are goods and services today than in 1940?

The numbers in table 2.5 do not tell us the particular items that have contributed most to the increase in the general price level in the last twenty years or so. If you were to get a copy of the *Economic Report of the President* and look at the individual categories of goods and services, you would find that three items have had especially large price increases since 1967. They are gasoline, home heating fuel, and houses. Each of these now costs nearly four times more than it did in 1967.

The ***rate of inflation*** *is the percentage change in the general price level and is typically measured by the percentage change in the CPI between two years.*

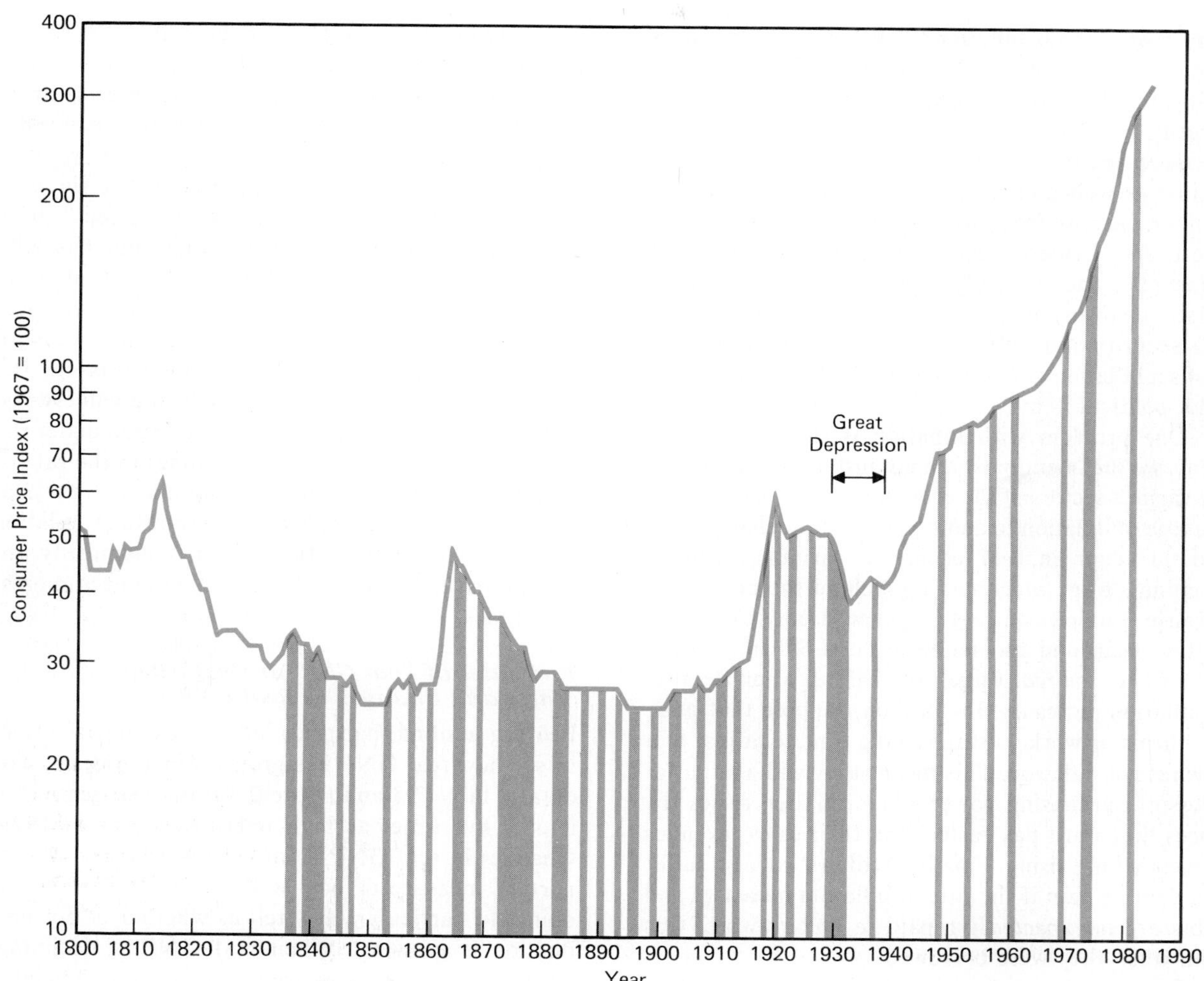

Figure 2.2 The consumer price index for the United States: 1800–1985 (1967 = 100)
The United States has experienced many periods of inflation and declining prices (deflation) in its history. However, the past fifty years' inflation is unprecedented. Recessions and depressions, as measured by the National Bureau of Economic Research, are indicated by the vertical shaded areas.

From *Historical Statistics of the United States,* Series E 135–166, pp. 210–211, 1970; *Economic Report of the President,* Table B-52, p. 221; *Journal of Economic Literature,* "Recent Works on Business Cycles in Historical Perspective: A Review of Theories and Evidence," Victor Zarnowitz, Vol. XXIII, (June, 1985), pp. 527–528; and *Economic Report of the President,* 1986, Table B-55, p. 315.

Price Indexes and Inflation

One interesting aspect of price indexes is that they can be used to tell us the **rate of inflation,** which is the percentage change in the general price level for one year. The second column of table 2.5 gives us the annual rate of inflation from year to year in the United States since 1929, based on the CPI. Figure 2.2 shows the CPI for the United States since the year 1800. One of the most interesting features of figure 2.2 is that there has been much more inflation in the last fifty years than during any comparable period in the history of the United States. (This inflationary tendency characterizes many other industrialized nations, too.)

***Indexing** is a means of adjusting nominal payments by referring to a price index so that their real value is unaffected by the rate of inflation.*

*A **recession** is a period of time when real GNP declines for two or more consecutive quarters.*

*A **depression** is a very severe recession, a period of time when a very severe decline in real GNP is occurring.*

Why Worry about Inflation? What difference does it make if the general price level is constant or grows at an annual rate of 5 percent, 15 percent, or even 500 percent, as it has in some foreign countries? If wages are increased to account for inflation, workers would do just as well under one rate of inflation as under another. Income from other sources such as rent, interest, and dividends can—and generally does—get adjusted by the forces of supply and demand to offset inflation. Government transfer payments such as Social Security and welfare are adjusted by legislation to offset inflation. So, why is double-digit inflation such a hot political item?

One problem with inflation is that the adjustments we just mentioned are not instantaneous. While the various sectors of the economy are adjusting from one rate of inflation to another, important changes can and do occur in *real* economic variables. Money (nominal) wage rates may lag behind the price level because a union contract is renewed only every two or three years and does not have a cost of living clause. In this case the *real* wage rate will fall when the rate of inflation increases. In addition, suppose that business firms or workers simply take time to adjust to a new rate of inflation. This means they will also suffer a loss of purchasing power when inflation raises the prices they must pay faster than their sales revenues or incomes are rising. Finally, creditors will also suffer and debtors gain if the rate of inflation increases and debts are *unexpectedly* repaid in dollars worth less than when they were borrowed.

In general, people whose *incomes* are fixed in nominal (money) terms are harmed by *unforeseen* accelerations in inflation. Those people whose *payments* are fixed in nominal terms benefit. These are not the only difficulties caused by inflation. Business decisions are difficult in an environment of unstable prices. Such decisions are much simpler when planning for the future can be based on accurate predictions of the wage and price levels.

The effects of unanticipated inflation can be lessened through a general scheme of **indexing,** which means tying all financial arrangements to the rate of inflation so that payments and receipts are adjusted proportionately. Prices and payments can be contractually or legislatively tied to the general rate of inflation. This would be similar to the way wage rates in many union contracts are currently tied to the consumer price index. If there were a "perfect" price index, or set of price indexes, indexing could basically eliminate any real effects of unanticipated inflation. However, we have already seen that our two most commonly used indexes do not give the same measure of the rate of inflation. Practically speaking, the chances are slim that "perfect" indexing will ever be possible. This means we can safely proceed under the assumption that unanticipated changes in the rate of inflation will continue to have significant real economic effects. As such, lowering the rate of inflation will continue to be politically and economically important in the United States and other noncommunist economies.

Estimates of Real GNP for the United States and Changes in Real GNP

Bearing in mind that price indexes are imperfect, let us see how real GNP has grown over the years. The data in table 2.5 and figure 2.3 show that real GNP is over five times as high today as it was in 1929. Changes in real GNP from year to year are an important measure of how well the macroeconomy is doing. In particular, they tell us whether or not production is growing. When real GNP is declining, economists say that we are in a **recession.** Officially, the beginning and ending of recessions are determined by a nonprofit private corporation, the National Bureau of Economic Research, in Cambridge, Massachusetts. This bureau defines a recession as two consecutive quarters of decline in real GNP (negative growth rate for real GNP), although there have been cases where one quarter was deemed sufficient (1980). Many economists, however, will speak of a recession when the growth rate of real GNP slows sharply, even though the rate of GNP growth is still positive. This is called a *growth recession.*

*The **business cycle** is the pattern of recession followed by recovery that characterizes the United States and other market economies.*

*The **interest rate** is the percentage of a dollar that a borrower must pay a lender per year for each $1 borrowed.*

*The **prime interest rate** is the standard or base rate of interest that banks charge borrowers for one-year loans.*

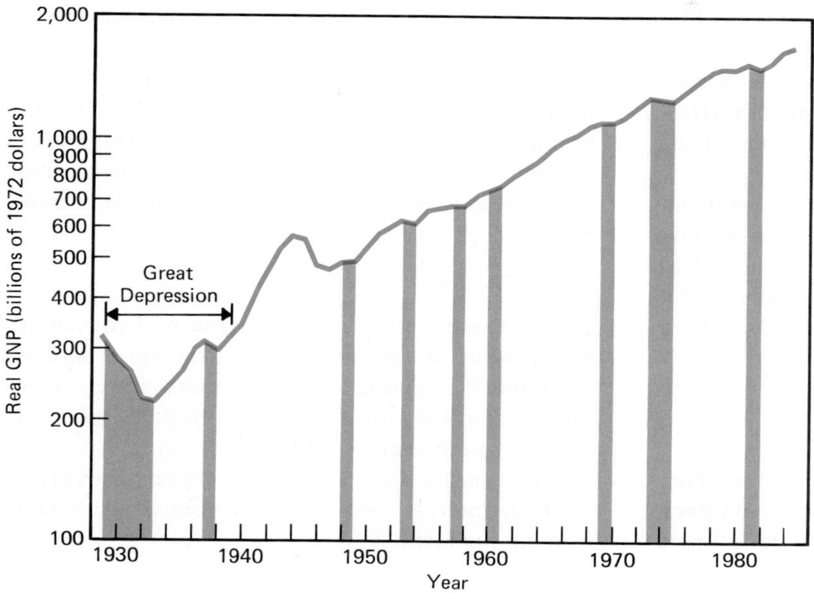

Figure 2.3 Real GNP in the United States, 1929–1984, in 1972 dollars
Real GNP has grown, with many ups and downs in between, so that it is several times higher today than it was in 1929. From *Economic Report of the President,* Table B-2, p. 164; *Economics Indicators,* p. 2; U.S. Department of Commerce (Bureau of Economics Analysis), *The National Income and Product Accounts of the United States,* 1929–1974, statistical tables; and *Economic Report of the President,* 1986, B-2, p. 254.

A very severe form of recession, that is, a very severe decline in real GNP, is called a **depression.** Major recessions and depressions of record are marked off in figure 2.3. Table 2.5 and figure 2.3 remind us of the substantial decline in real GNP that occurred during the Great Depression. Real GNP fell by 2.2 percent between 1932 and 1933. This is one of the largest reductions in output ever experienced in the United States. There was another recession severe enough to be labeled a depression in 1937–38, and we have had two relatively severe recessions in the postwar period. One was in the middle 1970s and the other in the early 1980s. Between 1974 and 1975 real GNP fell by 1.1 percent. Between 1981 and 1982 it fell by almost 2 percent, a quite severe recession by United States standards. It will be our goal in subsequent chapters to try to understand why real GNP sometimes rises and sometimes falls. The pattern of increases and decreases in real GNP is known as the **business cycle.**

Interest Rates

The easiest way to think of an **interest rate** is as the cost of credit. It is the number of cents per year that borrowers have to pay lenders for each dollar they borrow. Interest rates are a key economic variable in the macroeconomy because of their influence on investment decisions. The way in which government policy influences interest rates and thus investment, production, and unemployment is discussed in chapters 7 and 10–12.

Probably the best-known interest rate—the one you will often read about in the newspapers or hear about on television—is the **prime interest rate,** which is the standard or base rate of interest that is charged on loans of a predetermined risk level. Loans with greater than standard risk will be charged rates above the prime (prime plus); loans with lower than standard risk will be given discounts from the prime (prime minus). You should think of the prime rate of

*A **nominal interest rate** is sometimes referred to as the market rate of interest; it is the interest rate borrowers and banks agree to and is unadjusted for the rate of inflation.*

*The **real interest rate** is the nominal (market) interest rate minus the expected rate of inflation.*

interest as a reference point indicating the general level of interest rates on all types of loans. Changes in the prime rate tend to foreshadow similar changes in other key interest rates, such as the rate of interest charged on thirty-year home mortgage loans or four-year car loans.

Refer back to table 2.5 for data on the prime interest rate. Notice that when inflation rates are low, such as in the 1940s, the interest rate (as measured by the prime rate) is also low. However, when inflation is relatively high, such as in 1974 or from 1979 to 1981, interest rates follow suit.

Real versus Nominal Rates of Interest

In discussing macroeconomic concepts, we have been careful to distinguish between nominal and real values. For example, we discussed the difference between nominal GNP and real GNP. There is a similar distinction in the case of interest rates. The interest rate displayed in table 2.5 is a **nominal interest rate,** because it indicates the total price of credit borrowers pay lenders *unadjusted* for inflation. In considering the cost of credit and the return from lending, borrowers and lenders care about the real purchasing power of the interest payments. Lenders will account for the fact that the return on the credit is in reality lower when there is inflation. For example, suppose that you are considering lending $1,000 for one year at a 10 percent nominal rate of interest. This is what the borrower will pay you for the privilege of having $1,000 of credit for a year. Of course, it will make a big difference to you if the $100 interest you receive at the end of the year can purchase a lot or a little next year. Suppose the rate of inflation is zero. This means that your $100 interest payment could purchase the same amount of goods and services as $100 could now. However, if the rate of inflation is 10 percent, then your $100 interest payment is really worth only $90 in terms of its current purchasing power.

To account for the influence of inflation on the purchasing power of interest payments, economists have developed the concept of the **real interest rate,** which is the nominal interest rate adjusted for the rate of inflation that borrowers and lenders *expect* to prevail when they engage in credit transactions. Formally, we can write the expression for the real interest rate as

$$r \equiv i - \dot{P}.$$

In this expression, r represents the real rate of interest, which is equal to the nominal rate of interest (i) minus the expected rate of inflation $\dot{P}$. An example of a nominal rate of interest, i, would be the prime interest rate quoted in table 2.5.

We can view the relationship between the real and nominal interest rates slightly differently by rearranging the identity to read

$$i \equiv r + \dot{P}.$$

This shows us that the market rate of interest equals the real rate of interest plus the rate of inflation. Lenders expect a real return (r) plus an adjustment for the inflation rate to offset the fact that money repaid in the future has less purchasing power the higher the rate of inflation. It is important to note that for a short-term loan such as a three-month treasury security, the expected rate of inflation will generally equal the inflation experienced in recent years. For longer-term loans, the average inflation rate *expected* to be in effect during the loan period may differ among lenders and between borrowers and lenders much more than for short-term loans because predictions of inflation far into the future are very uncertain. To make sure that you understand the concept of the real interest rate, go back to table 2.5 and calculate the real prime rate of interest for the years 1975, 1976, 1980, and 1983. In which year was the real prime rate highest? In which year was the real prime rate lowest? When was the nominal prime rate highest and lowest? Are these the same years in which the real rate was highest and lowest? Was the real prime rate always positive (greater than zero)?

*The **Current Population Survey (CPS)** is a monthly survey of approximately 60,000 households in the United States for the purpose of gathering up-to-date data on personal characteristics and the labor force behavior of the U.S. population.*

Real versus Nominal Interest Rates in Recent Years

Think of an interest rate as the rental payment on the use of borrowed money, where this rental payment reflects not only the risk to the lender but also the real return that must be earned to make lenders willing to lend. The importance of this is that the nominal rate of interest seems to vary largely because of changes in the (expected) rate of inflation rather than because of changes in the real rate of interest.

These facts underlie the positive relationship between market interest rates and the rate of inflation. Consider the prime rate of interest. We can then use the actual inflation rate as a reasonable approximation of the expected inflation rate because the prime interest rate usually applies to relatively short-term loans. If you review the inflation rates and prime interest rates in table 2.5, you will see that the prime rate minus the inflation rate, which is the real prime rate, does not vary all that much. Of course, there is some variation with unexpected swings in the rate of inflation. For example, in 1974 the prime rate was 10.8 percent. The rate of inflation was unexpectedly high—nearly 11 percent. This means that in 1974 the real prime rate of interest was negative, −.16, approximately −0.2 percent. By the late 1970s, lenders had come to expect possible high inflation, so the real prime rate returned to a more typical long-run value. In 1980, when inflation was 13.5 percent, the nominal prime interest rate was 15.3 percent. These two figures yield a real prime rate of about 1.8 percent in 1979.

Unemployment

Unemployment in the United States for the period 1890–1984 is shown in figure 2.4. Unemployment has been a quite serious economic problem in the United States at various times in history. Obvious examples are the early 1920s, the Great Depression, and more recently, the early 1980s, especially 1982. Let us see where these figures come from, what they mean, and what unemployment data tell us about economic policy to reduce unemployment.

Definition and Measure of Unemployment

The total number of unemployed people is determined by how people respond to a set of questions in the **Current Population Survey, (CPS),** which is a monthly survey of about 60,000 households by the United States Census Bureau. The CPS is chosen to

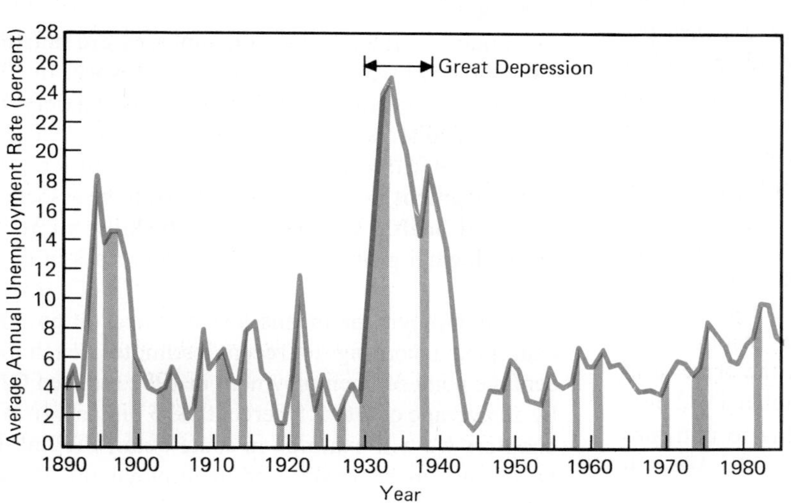

Figure 2.4 Unemployment rates for the United States, 1890–1985
Fluctuations in the unemployment rate coincide with the business cycle. Recessions and depressions are indicated by the vertical shaded areas. From *Historical Statistics of the United States, Economics Indicators.*

*The **unemployed** are people who did not work during the week before the CPS, but were available for work that week* and *(1) made specific efforts to find a job within the four weeks prior to the survey, (2) were waiting to be called back to jobs from which they had been laid off, or (3) were waiting to report to a new job within the next month.*

*The **unemployment rate** is the percentage of the labor force classified as unemployed.*

*The **labor force** is the sum of employed plus unemployed people in the population.*

provide reliable estimates of the characteristics of the nation as a whole, including the labor force status of individuals who are sixteen years of age or older. Someone is classified as **unemployed** if he or she has no job, wants one, and has tried to find one recently (generally within the previous four weeks). People waiting to start a new job or to be called back to an old one are also classified as unemployed by the CPS. The **unemployment rate** is the number of unemployed people expressed as a percentage of the labor force. The **labor force** is the total number of people employed or unemployed. In other words, the labor force consists of all people age sixteen and over who are either working, seeking work, or are on layoff from a job to which they expect to be recalled.

The definition of unemployment is an attempt to include only people who are actively willing and able to work and to exclude those who would prefer not to work or who are unable to work. In practice, this distinction is not as easy as it might seem. It has been claimed that in some cases the official definition includes too many people and in other cases too few.

Two categories of individuals are often cited as possible candidates for inclusion in the unemployed category. They are (1) people who are working part-time because they could not find full-time jobs and (2) people who have given up looking for work and have dropped out of the labor force because they believe that no jobs are available. On the other hand, it may be argued that the unemployment rate is an overstatement because it includes (1) part-time job seekers, (2) students attending school, (3) voluntary job quitters, and (4) workers on indefinite layoff who are not actively searching for new jobs.

Let us get some idea of the magnitude of a few of these categories. In December 1982 over twelve million people were unemployed.[4] At the same time, two million people said they were involuntarily working part-time schedules. Finally, the Bureau of Labor Statistics reported that in December 1982 over 1.8 million workers had given up trying to find jobs because they believed none were available. We will discuss unemployment in greater detail in chapter 3.

Why Is Unemployment Such an Important Economic Issue?

One obvious reason why we are concerned with unemployment is that much of the time spent looking for a job or waiting to be recalled might instead be used to increase our production of goods and services if only unemployment could be alleviated. As we shall show in chapter 3, however, not all unemployment is simply wasted time. Some unemployment is necessary if workers are to find the jobs that suit them best and in which they are most productive.

An equally important problem with unemployment is that in many instances it is a cause of poverty. Many of the unemployed live in families in which other members work extra hours to compensate for their unemployment. Moreover, many unemployed people receive unemployment insurance payments. However, unemployment is clearly linked to economic hardship for many families and individuals. Here are some facts. In 1981 families in which both the husband and wife worked had a median income of $31,600. Median family income was only $23,000 when either the husband or the wife was unemployed for one to twenty-six weeks. The median income of families in which either the husband or the wife was unemployed for more than half a year was less than $18,000.[5]

Financial losses of the unemployed are not their only costs associated with being out of work. In 1982 the media reported many stories of the anxiety and emotional distress felt by people who had lost their jobs or who feared that they might lose their jobs. The unemployment experience also seems to be associated with bad health, the decline of job skills, numerous psychological problems, and even increases in crime rates.[6]

Unemployment means lost national output. For example, according to recent estimates, each percentage point of unemployment in 1982 reduced GNP by an average of 2 to 2.5 percent ($75 billion). In later chapters we will examine in some detail the link between the business cycle and unemployment. We will also try to understand the reasons for the severe decline in output and severe increases in unemployment in the 1930s and early 1980s.

Summary and Conclusions

In this chapter we introduced the concept of the macroeconomy and explained the key measures of its performance. You have seen how inflation, recession, and increases in the real interest rate contributed to the personal tragedy of the farm family we described in the introduction. In the following chapters we will show how all of the unfortunate events that they experienced occurred. The following points were covered in this chapter.

Gross national product (GNP) measures the total market value of final goods and services produced in the United States during a year.

The nominal value of GNP refers to total production measured in current prices, and the real value of GNP adjusts for the fact that prices may be higher today than in the past.

Real GNP is an important measure of the economy's performance. Reductions in real GNP from year to year are what economists call a recession. A depression is a very severe decline in real GNP from year to year.

The ups and downs in real GNP experienced by economies are what economists call a business cycle.

An economy's economic growth is measured by examining the changes in real GNP over a long period of time, for example, ten to twenty years.

GNP is also a measure of society's income. This stems from the fact that total production has a cost, and when all input costs are tallied, they equal the total value of production.

The rate of interest is the cost of credit—it is the number of cents per dollar per year that borrowers pay to lenders for each dollar they borrow.

Nominal interest rates are related to the rate of inflation. When inflation is relatively high, so are nominal interest rates. When inflation is relatively low, so are nominal interest rates.

The unemployment rate is basically the percentage of the labor force that does not have jobs but wants them.

Unemployment is a major economic problem because it is associated with reduced incomes among the unemployed and lost real GNP.

Key Terms

aggregate economics *33*
base year *42*
business cycle *47*
circular flow of GNP (circular flow of income) *40*
consumer price index (CPI) *42*
consumption (C) *34*
corporate profits *41*
Current Population Survey (CPS) *49*
current prices *33*
depression *47*
durable consumer goods *34*
government spending (G) *36*
gross national product (GNP) *33*
GNP deflator *43*
indexing *46*
indirect business taxes *41*
interest rate *47*
intermediate goods *33*
investment (I) *35*
labor force *50*
macroeconomics *32*
net exports (X) *37*
nominal GNP *33*
nominal interest rate *48*
nondurable consumer goods *34*
price index *42*
prime interest rate *47*
proprietors' income *41*
rate of inflation *45*
real interest rate *48*
real value of GNP *33*
recession *46*
rental income *41*
transfer payments *36*
unemployed *50*
unemployment rate *50*

▸ Questions for Discussion and Review

1. You are given the following series for the consumer price index. The base year for this series is 1967 (that is, 1967 = 100). Suppose you need to calculate real wages in 1972 dollars. Show how you would adjust this series of index numbers to reflect a 1972 base.

Year	CPI
1968	110
1969	112
1970	118
1971	125
1972	129
1973	135

2. For a research project, you need a real investment series expressed in 1980 dollars. However, every reliable source of data has a base year of 1972 for this series of numbers. Describe how you could obtain the series that you need for your project.
3. Define macroeconomics. Give four examples of macroeconomic problems.
4. What is gross national product? What is the difference between nominal and real GNP?
5. How does GNP incorporate the value of consumer durables? Suppose that a person buys a $100,000 house. How does this affect the measured value of GNP? Be complete.
6. Evaluate this statement: it seems rather strange to call inventories a form of investment.
7. Discuss the following. When net exports are negative, this means that the value of goods and services foreigners send to us exceeds the value of goods and services we send to them. Thus, trade deficits are good.
8. Is the following true or false? Government spending has grown dramatically as a fraction of GNP since World War II. This has been the result of a large growth in the federal government. Support your answer with facts.
9. A new steel mill costing $10 million is built. It produces $1 million of steel this year. It creates pollution that costs people who live near the steel mill $100,000 to clean up. How much does all of this change GNP? Explain carefully. Does your answer overstate or understate the effect of the steel mill on society's economic well-being? Explain and draw a numerical conclusion.
10. Do you feel that the value of household production should be incorporated into GNP? Why? Suppose that the government decides it will indeed incorporate the value of home production into GNP. How would you recommend it make such a calculation?
11. The value of certain illegal transactions such as drug sales, prostitution, and gambling are not currently included in GNP. Discuss the pros and cons for including such transactions in GNP. How would you go about gathering the data to do such calculations?
12. Real GNP per capita is sometimes used as a simple measure of intercountry differences in well-being. Here is a topic for a short term paper. Go to your university library or the main library in your town and get some data for real GNP per capita in other countries. In your paper, discuss how real GNP in the United States stacks up against other western countries. Be sure your paper discusses the pitfalls of using real GNP per capita as a measure of the average person's well-being in a country. Focus on what real GNP per capita does or does not say about how well off a country's citizens are.
13. In 1944 nominal GNP was $210.6 billion. In 1947 it was $233.1 billion. The value of the GNP deflator is 37 for 1944 and 49.6 for 1947. Calculate real GNP in 1944 and in 1947. What was the dollar change in real GNP between the two years? Was there a relatively large

Demand is the relationship between the desire to buy various quantities of a good or service and its price.

Supply is the relationship between the desire to sell various quantities of a good or service and its price.

percentage change in real GNP between the two years? What do you think played a major role in the change in real GNP between 1944 and 1947? Support your answer with data presented in the chapter if you can.

14. Bob Dylan said, "Everybody's got to be someplace." Many people in the United States live in houses that they own. Others rent houses or apartments. For people who own their own homes, their house payments are constant for a relatively long period of time. They are zero when their houses are paid off. Find out how owner-occupied housing is accounted for in the consumer price index. Discuss recent changes in the consumer price index's treatment of owner-occupied housing.
15. If you were to look at data presented in the *Economic Report of the President,* you would find that historically the interest rate for thirty-year residential mortgage loans is noticeably higher than the prime rate of interest. What factors do you think contribute to making the interest rate on mortgages exceed the prime rate? Be complete. In 1979–81 this relationship changed. The prime rate was substantially higher than the interest rate charged for home mortgages. Speculate on some reasons for this twist in the structure of interest rates.
16. It is sometimes argued that the unemployment rate does not take account of people who are part-time workers but would like to be full-time workers and individuals who have given up looking for jobs. How would you go about changing the way unemployment is measured to include either or both of these groups? Do you think either of the two groups ought to be included in an official definition of unemployment? Justify your answer.

Appendix to Chapter 2

Introduction to Supply and Demand

If you have taken an economics course in the past, you undoubtedly are well-acquainted with the concepts of supply and demand and know how they interact with each other in markets for goods and services. However, if you are just beginning your study of economics, then learning about these simple but invaluable tools will make your study much more rewarding. Indeed, you cannot study economics without them.

Our analysis of a market economy has three elements: (1) **demand,** which refers to people's desire to purchase a good or service; (2) **supply,** the desire of firms to sell a good or service, and (3) the interaction of supply and demand, which determines prices and the quantities of goods bought and sold. Together, these three elements comprise a model or summary representation of the economic factors influencing the behavior of buyers and sellers. As a general rule, we will analyze how buyers and sellers behave in pursuit of their individual goals. As a second step, we will frequently show how government actions have intentionally or unintentionally altered the outcome that would prevail if supply and demand operated strictly on their own. We will then develop a framework that you can use to help decide for yourself the degree to which you believe that society's goals are better achieved when governmental policies affect the outcomes in a market economy. An understanding of demand and supply analysis can be useful when reading about economic issues in the newspaper or thinking about a government program being debated in Congress.

▸ The Demand Relationship

Basic Assumptions of Demand

Any scientific analysis has building blocks. To understand how economists analyze the demand for goods and services, we must first learn the basic assumptions or postulates upon which the theory of demand is built. There are two general

Ceteris paribus means that all but one factor influencing some form of economic behavior (such as demand) are assumed not to change.

categories of assumptions we must make. The first describes buyers' goals and how they try to reach those goals. The second concerns the constraints or limitations placed on a buyer.

The Goals of Buyers and How They Attempt to Achieve Them

1. We assume that individuals and firms plan for a particular amount of time into the future. At the end of that time, be it a week, a month, or a year, they again make purchase decisions. Practically speaking, this assumption means that we will measure the quantities of goods and services buyers use by the number of units they buy within a particular period of time. In other words, the theory of demand is based on the concept of the flow of goods or services purchased per time period, such as the amount of milk bought per week.
2. We assume that firms and individuals consider the future when making their decisions. Among other things, they will wait for prices to fall or buy now before prices go up. This is not to say that buyers are always correct in their expectations of future price changes. They will make mistakes. Still, their decisions are influenced by expectations of the future.
3. We assume that buyers know whether or not they would like a particular commodity. By this we simply mean that an individual buyer has tastes and preferences (likes and dislikes) and knows what they are. Economists really have very little to say about the details of preferences for particular goods and services. For example, you may like yogurt but not bean sprouts. Economists *do,* however, have some general ideas about the *structure* of tastes and preferences. This leads us to our next assumption.
4. We assume that people derive satisfaction from consuming a *variety* of goods and services and that *more than one combination* of goods and services can yield a particular amount of happiness. For example, you might enjoy drinking Cokes and eating pizza. In addition, you might get just as much enjoyment from eating a small pizza and drinking a large Coke as you would get from eating a large pizza and drinking a small Coke. Similarly, you might find it just as much fun to watch two basketball games and play one hour of tennis as to play three hours of tennis and watch only one basketball game.
5. Our final assumption concerning individuals' goals and feelings is that they prefer more to less pleasure from goods and services. This means that when given the choice of two activities that cost the same, say, going to a Woody Allen movie or seeing one of Shakespeare's plays, a person will pick the one that gives the greater enjoyment. The assumption that people wish to have happy and enjoyable lives means that they do their best not to be foolish or wasteful. In addition, they may take the feelings of others into account when making decisions. Clearly, individual economic decisions are influenced by feelings of love, caring, and empathy.

The set of assumptions introduced in this section relate to people's preferences and their attempts to lead satisfying lives. Apart from different tastes, why doesn't everyone have four Rolls Royces, a beach house at Malibu, and an apartment in midtown Manhattan? The answer lies in our next set of assumptions, which deal with the fact that the choices an individual has available are limited by a number of factors.

Limitations on Choices Buyers Can Make

1. We assume that no one has unlimited wealth. Your spending power is limited by your earnings from working and the amount of income you receive from stocks, bonds, and other investments, the government, and your family, or elsewhere. Because you cannot have everything, you must make choices. For example, if you choose to go to Florida for a couple of weeks in the spring, you might have to skip lunch for a month to save the money to pay for the trip.
2. We assume that buyers cannot control the prices they pay for goods and services. While you may look around for the store with the lowest-priced beer, once you find it, you must pay that price. We are merely assuming that no one has enough buying power to influence, to any great extent, the prices of goods and services. It is important to realize that in making this assumption we do not specify where those prices come from. They may be set by government decree, as in the case of a centrally planned economy such as that of the Soviet Union. They may also be set by market forces, as in most western nations.

*The **law of demand** states that there is a negative relationship between desired purchases and the price of a good or service,* cet. par.

*The **substitution effect** refers to the tendency for desired purchases of a good or service to rise when its price falls and to fall when its price rises relative to other prices,* cet. par.

*The **income effect** refers to the tendency of people to demand more of a good or service when their purchasing power rises and to demand less when their purchasing power falls.*

3. Finally, we assume that consuming a good or service takes time. In addition to the cost of the airline tickets, a Florida vacation takes time away from other activities. While we are doing one thing, there are limits on the extent to which we can be doing something else. For example, we might accomplish two things at the same time by watching the news during breakfast. However, while eating breakfast, we are not at work or polishing the car.

With these two sets of assumptions in mind, we will now say a few words about the way in which we will analyze the decisions people make concerning how much of a good or service to buy.

Method of Analysis

Throughout our analysis we will examine the forces influencing demand behavior *one at a time*. That is, we will first assume that all factors affecting demand are fixed or unchanging except for one. We will then proceed to look at the effect of changes in that one variable on the purchases desired by an individual or a set of individuals. This assumption is known as ***ceteris paribus,*** the Latin phrase for "other things equal." It means that when we analyze the impact of a change in a variable, such as a good's price, on the quantity of the good demanded, we will begin by assuming that *other* variables (such as buyers' incomes), do not change at the same time. *Ceteris paribus* is often abbreviated *cet. par.* Demand theory typically emphasizes the relationship between the price of a good or service and the quantity of that good or service buyers desire to purchase. So, in developing the theory of demand, we will first apply the *cet. par.* assumption to those forces affecting demand behavior *other than* the price of the good or service in question. If you review our list of building blocks of demand theory, you will see that these forces include the individual's time horizon for decision making, expectations of the future, tastes and preferences, income, prices of other goods and services, and the amount of time consumption must take.

It is extremely important to note that by imposing the *cet. par.* method of analysis, we are simply examining, *one at a time,* the factors that influence buyers' behavior. We can, and do, look at changes in factors other than price (also one at a time) to discover how they too affect the demand for a commodity. Just how and at what stage of our discussion we consider these other forces depends on the issues we wish to examine. Thus, as you will soon see, we develop the theory of demand by first determining how an individual buyer responds if the price of a particular good changes. We then proceed to analyze how changes in certain other variables—the amount of money available to spend, preferences, and so on—influence the amount of a good or service demanded. The importance of looking at forces *one by one* is that it enables us to get a much clearer picture of how governmental economic policy and private business practices affect consumption patterns.

The Law of Demand and the Demand Curve

The **law of demand** states that, *cet. par.,* (1) price reductions lead buyers to desire more of a good or service; and (2) price increases lead them to desire less of a good or service. This is the result of two effects that reinforce each other when a price changes. They are known as the substitution effect and the income effect of a price change. They are among the most important concepts economists have. The **substitution effect** states that when the price of a good or service falls, *cet. par.,* people have an economic incentive to use more of that particular good or service because it has become less expensive ***relative to*** all the other goods and services available. To be specific, suppose that rock concert tickets fall in price from $20 to $10, while movie tickets remain $5. Fans then have the incentive to attend more rock concerts while consuming fewer movies and other forms of entertainment. In effect, the reduced price of rock concerts compared to movies will make the concerts a better buy per dollar spent on them and therefore encourage buyers to purchase more concert tickets and less of other things. This desire to substitute rock concerts for other forms of entertainment is one of the reasons why rock fans attend more rock and roll concerts when ticket prices are reduced.

There is another effect of a price change yet to be considered. When the price of a good or service falls, real purchasing power rises, and people consume more because they feel wealthier. Economists call this the **income effect.** Not only can people purchase more of a good whose price has fallen, but they can also purchase more of everything else. To understand this more clearly, suppose that you have an income of $100 per week and you typically spend $21 of your weekly income on beer, which costs $3.00 a six-pack. Now suppose the distributor of your favorite brand lowers the price to $2.50 as part of a sales campaign. It is not hard to see that this is equivalent to an increase in your weekly income of $3.50 (7 six-packs × $0.50). With your fixed income of $100, you can now purchase exactly what you did before and still have $3.50 left over. That extra $3.50 can be used to buy a little more of all the things that you like

*A **demand curve** for a good or service is a geometric representation of the law of demand. It is sometimes called a demand schedule.*

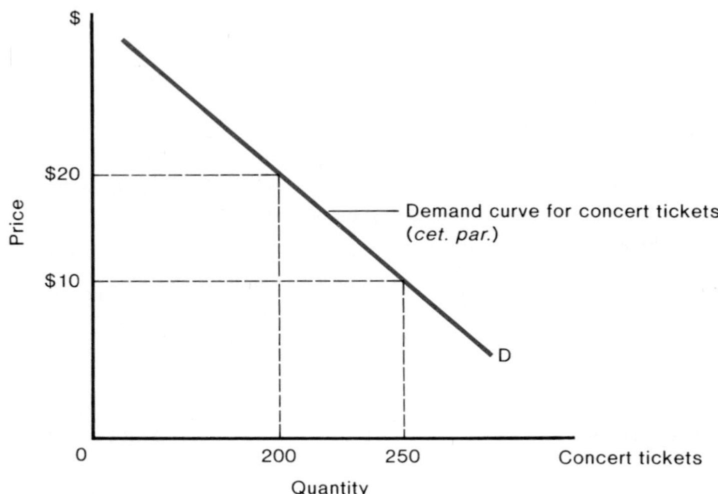

Figure 2.A Buyers' demand curve for a good or service
The substitution and income effects cause the quantity demanded to increase as price falls and to decline as price rises.

to consume. The overall increase in your consumption as a result of that freed up $3.50 in spending power is the income effect of the $0.50 fall in the price of beer.

As we said earlier, the income effect of a price change is reinforced by the substitution effect. Thus, when the price of something falls, there are two reasons to buy more of it. One reason is greater purchasing power (the income effect), and the other is a lower price relative to the prices of all other goods (substitution effect). Of course, the law of demand holds for a price increase as well. Just as a falling price, *cet. par.,* causes people to buy more, a rising price causes them to buy less.

It is important to recognize that the law of demand holds for *every* good or service whether a buyer "likes" it or not. To see why this is so, let's take an extreme example, in which you would not choose to consume any of a good, even if it were free. At the risk of being sued by the California Prune Advisory Board, suppose that prunes are such a good. Even if you would not eat a prune if it were free, we conjecture that if you were paid enough, you would be willing to eat at least one prune. Paying you to eat prunes is equivalent to having you pay a *negative* price for prunes. If our conjecture is true, there exists *some* price at which you would consume prunes even if it is not a *positive* price. You can probably think of other examples of some goods or services that you do not buy now because you do not like them very much. However, saying that you do not like something is generally equivalent to saying that its price is too high. If it became sufficiently cheaper, *cet. par.,* the law of demand predicts you will buy it.

Because the primary focus of social science in general and economics in particular is on group behavior, we are especially interested in the purchases by *all* of the buyers in a market. The relationship between the price of a good and the total amount purchased by all those who buy it is called demand, or, the **demand curve,** for a good. A demand curve for concert tickets is shown in figure 2.A. We measure the price of the particular good, concert tickets, on the vertical axis and the quantity buyers wish to purchase on the horizontal axis. Because individual buyers purchase less at high prices, the demand curve for all buyers is a downward-sloping line. The downward-sloping demand curve reminds us that the buyers of a good or service want more of it if price falls and less of it if price rises. For example, at a price of $20 the buyers in figure 2.A wish to purchase 200 tickets. At a lower price, say, $10, they increase their desired purchases to 250 tickets.

Shifts in Demand

Figure 2.B reminds us that the *quantity demanded* of a good or service corresponds to a *particular point* on a given demand curve, say, price $10 and quantity 100 on the demand curve in figure 2.B. Thus, when there is a change in the amount of a good or service people want to buy *because of a change in its price, other factors held constant,* we say that there has been a *change in the quantity demanded.* Of course, many other things in the economic environment can also change, and these lead to what economists call *a change in demand or a change in the demand curve.* When there

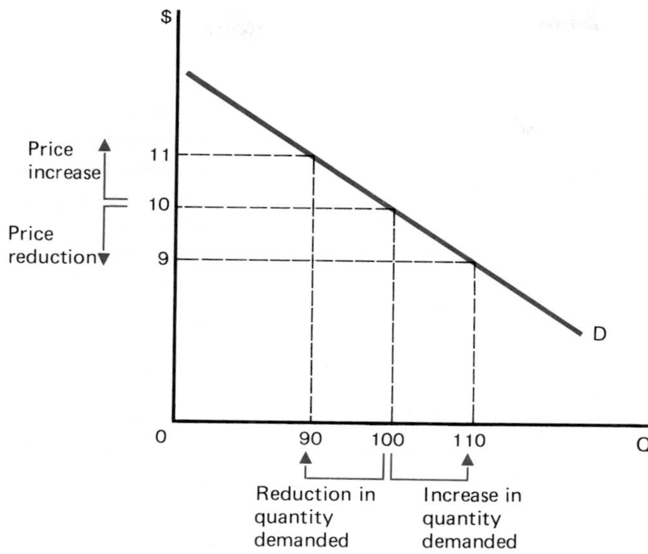

Figure 2.B Increases and decreases in the quantity demanded of a good or service
An increase in quantity demanded is a southeast movement along the demand curve due to a price reduction. A reduction in quantity demanded is a northwest movement along the demand curve due to a price increase.

is a shift in the demand curve, either to the right or left, we are dealing with a change in demand or a change in the demand curve. When the demand curve for a product shifts, it will also generally change the quantity demanded at any given price. It is very important in thinking about markets to be absolutely clear in your mind whether a change in quantity demanded results from a change in price, given the position of a good's demand curve, or whether it results from a shift in the position of the curve. Among the most important factors that shift demand curves are (1) increases or decreases in buyers' incomes, (2) changes in tastes and preferences, (3) changes in the prices of related goods, and (4) changes in expectations about future events.

For example, suppose consumers of a good or service receive salary increases. The increased income will lead them to purchase more of most of the things they currently buy. Moreover, as wealth increases even with prices unchanged, people often will substitute more expensive and/or higher quality products for less expensive and/or lower quality ones in consumption. An increase in demand is illustrated in figure 2.C by a rightward shift in the demand curve from D to D′. At any given price, more is desired along demand curve D′ than along demand curve D. As you might expect, a salary reduction would reduce demand. This would be denoted by a leftward shift in the demand curve from D to D″ in figure 2.C.

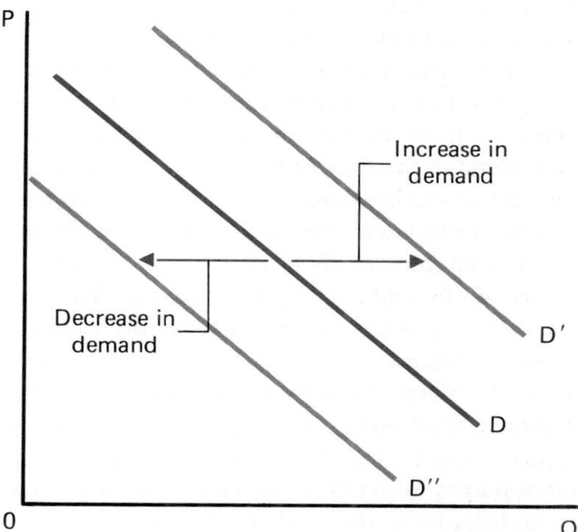

Figure 2.C Increases and decreases in the demand for a good or service
An increase in demand is a rightward shift in the demand curve. A decrease in demand is a leftward shift in the demand curve. Changes in demand occur if one of the factors held constant when the demand curve was initially drawn (for example, income) changes.

Another possible reason for demand to shift is a change in tastes or preferences of buyers. For example, if buyers' tastes for one good compared to another should change, the demand curve will be affected. If a certain good or service becomes *more* enjoyable, the demand curve will shift to the right. If it should become *less* desirable, the demand curve will shift to the left. Eventually, we will elaborate on some social forces that might cause tastes to change, and with them, demand schedules. For now, try to think of some on your own. For example, why might your feelings toward buying a navy blue suit change in the near future? (Hint: graduation.) How would these new feelings change some of your other demand curves?

It is often tempting to attribute a change in demand to a change in tastes. However, it is difficult to verify whether or not this is true because it is not easy to obtain accurate information about the public's feelings or goals. We must avoid the temptation to conclude that *whenever* purchases change, people's tastes have changed. We must have *reason* to suspect that tastes and preferences have changed *before* demand changes rather than inferring that tastes have changed because demand has changed.

Frequently, a change in the demand for one good reflects a change in the price of some closely related good or service. Suppose, for example, that the price of gasoline rises. Of course, the *quantity of gasoline demanded will decline*. However, people will also eventually desire fewer automobiles, and the *demand for cars* will fall. This, for example, happened in the late 1970s. Such a decline in the demand for cars does *not* reflect a change in people's tastes. When the price of gasoline rose rapidly in 1979 and 1980 people's demand for small fuel-efficient cars increased. That increase in demand for small cars did not simply reflect a change in people's tastes.

An increase in the price of one good may cause the demand for some related goods to increase, too. When two goods are typically used together (bread and butter, tape players and cassettes, automobiles and gasoline, or gin and vermouth), an increase in the price of one causes a decline in the demand for the other. However, if two goods can both be used for the same purpose, we say they can be *substituted* for each other, and an increase in the price of one will cause an *increase in demand* for the other. Some examples of substitutes are cotton and Dacron, Michelin and Firestone tires, gas ranges and electric ranges, or big luxury cars and small, more fuel-efficient cars.

Expectations play a crucial role in macroeconomics, and we will see that changes in expectations about the future can be a very important cause of changes in demand. For example, if I expect my favorite beer to cost 25 percent more next week, I will increase my demand for it this week (at the current price). Similarly, I will hold off buying a new car if I expect sizable rebates or price cuts to be offered next month. Of course, *how much* I change my demand depends on how anxious I am to have the good or service, how storable it is, and how certain I am about future price changes. For example, my freezer may be rather small, so I cannot increase my demand for ice cream by very much right now even if I expect a giant price increase tomorrow unless I also buy a new freezer. Whether or not I want to do that will also depend upon how certain I am about the increase in the price of ice cream and whether I think the price will remain high once it increases.

▸ The Supply Relationship

The preceding section introduced the principle of demand, which comprises the first half of the theory describing how prices are determined in a market economy. This section introduces the other half, the principle of supply. How markets work with both supply and demand is discussed in the next section. In the preceding section we explained the relationship between the quantity demanded of a product and price. In order to determine the price that buyers would have to pay to purchase various amounts of a product, we have to understand the principle of supply.

The *supply* of a good tells us how much is offered for sale at specified prices. In general, the supply of a good or service is the relationship between its price and the quantity offered for sale, *ceteris paribus*.

Basic Assumptions of Supply Theory

The building blocks, or assumptions, of supply theory parallel those underlying the demand relationship. They can be placed in two categories, one concerning suppliers' goals and the other concerning constraints on suppliers' behavior. The limitations suppliers—particularly business firms—face in achieving their goals will be analyzed in detail later. Therefore, we will only discuss suppliers' goals in detail here.

*A **firm** is the basic economic unit that makes production decisions in a market economy, just as the household is the basic unit that makes consumption decisions.*

***Economic profit** is the excess of a firm's revenue over* all *its costs of production.*

*The **law of supply** states that the quantity of a good or service firms desire to sell is greater the higher the price of the good or service,* cet. par.

Suppliers and Their Goals Any individual, household, or business firm is a potential supplier of a good or service. Most frequently, however, we will be concerned with business firms as producers and suppliers. A **firm** is simply a business entity whose management or owner hires inputs such as labor, machinery, and raw materials in order to provide a good or service. In a market economy this is normally done for profit. **Economic profit** is the difference between a firm's revenue and all its opportunity costs.

1. We assume that the firm's goal is to earn the largest possible profit. This is the *profit maximization assumption,* and it parallels the assumption that buyers seek to maximize the satisfaction they obtain from allocating their income among alternatives. Profit maximization requires that the firm accomplish three tasks successfully. These tasks lead us to three subsidiary assumptions that are necessary for profit maximization.
   a. The firm must decide *what* goods or services to produce. It cannot maximize its profit if it produces a good or service that cannot be sold at a high enough price to cover costs.
   b. The firm must decide *how* to produce each good at the lowest possible cost. That is, each firm must *minimize its costs* in light of the constraints imposed on it by available technology and its environment. Because a firm's profit is by definition the excess of its revenue over all of its costs, it should be obvious that it is impossible to *maximize* profit unless costs are *minimized.* Cost minimization does *not* mean that the firm is motivated to produce only cheap, low-quality output. Firms have a profit incentive to produce the level of quality that consumers are willing to pay for. Given that level of quality, however, profit maximization requires that costs be as low as possible.
   c. The firm must choose the *quantity* of production that assures it the greatest possible profit.
2. Firms, like consumers, are also assumed to calculate production in terms of *flows* of goods or services offered for sale *per time period.*
3. Firms also consider the *future* in their decisions. This has several important implications that will not be used immediately. It is a good idea to bear in mind, however, that consideration of the future implies that if firms expect prices of inputs or of their product to rise over time, they will have an incentive to speed up their purchases of inputs and slow down their sales of output. (What do you think this implies for the conservation of natural resources?) The assumption that firms consider the future also implies that actions that may increase current profits while damaging prospects for future sales, such as deceiving consumers about product quality, may not be consistent with overall profit maximization. What do you think this implies for consumer protection in a market economy?

The Law of Supply

Method of Analysis

Once again, as in the theory of demand, we will examine the forces that influence suppliers' decisions *one at a time.* Using the *ceteris paribus* assumption, we will first analyze the relationship between the price of a good or service and the amount offered for sale. After deriving this relationship—the supply curve itself—we will expand our understanding of supply by analyzing the effects of *other* forces on *shifts* in the supply curve.

The **law of supply** states that, *ceteris paribus,* price increases lead suppliers to supply more of a good or service, whereas price reductions lead them to supply less. To see why this should be so, we have to understand something about the way a supplier's *opportunity cost* of supplying its product varies as its output level changes. (You may wish to refresh your memory regarding the definition of opportunity cost in chapter 1.) Basically, we assume that the opportunity cost of producing more of a good eventually increases for a firm. This means that as a general rule, no individual supplier can produce all of a good or service that is demanded. However, suppliers are willing to increase their output if consumers are willing to pay a higher price. Moreover, as the price of a good or service increases, suppliers that had not found it profitable to supply the good or service

*A **change in supply** of a good or service or a shift in the supply curve is a movement of the supply curve that results when a variable other than price of the good or service changes.*

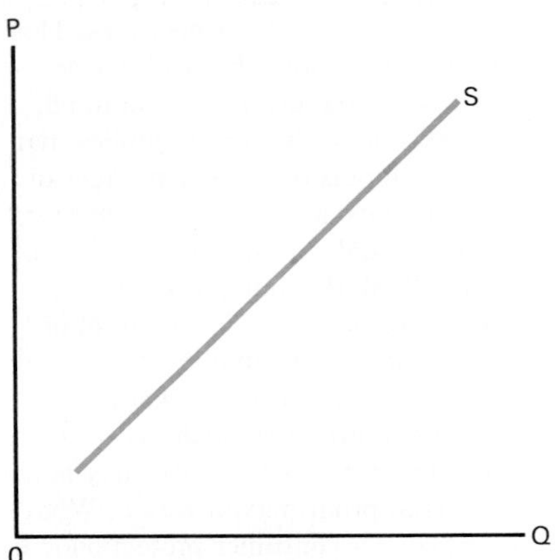

Figure 2.D The supply curve
The law of supply states that as a good's price increases, firms will produce more of it, and additional firms will offer it for sale.

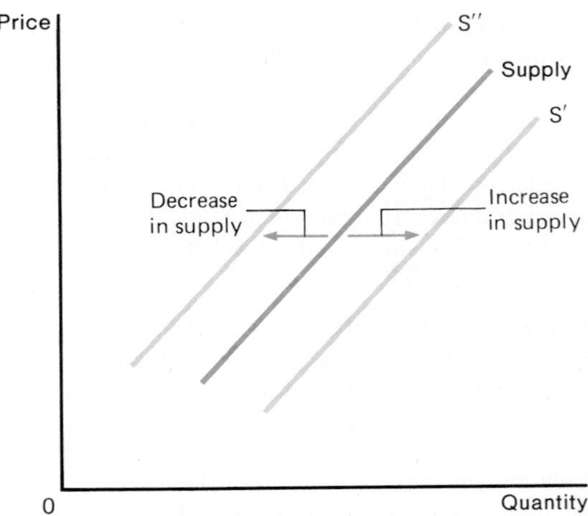

Figure 2.E Increases and decreases in the supply for a good or service
An increase in supply is a rightward shift in the supply curve. A decrease in supply is a leftward shift in the supply curve. Changes in supply occur if one of the factors held constant when the supply curve was initially drawn (for example, technology) changes.

previously may decide that it is worthwhile to do so in light of the increased revenue they can earn. For these two reasons, the quantity of a good or service supplied increases as its price rises. This relationship is illustrated in figure 2.D.

Factors that Shift Supply

The distinction between movements along a given supply curve and a change in the supply relationship follows the terminology we developed for the demand curve. When things other than price change, there results a **change in supply** or a **shift in the supply curve,** which means that suppliers wish to sell more or less than before at a given market price. Figure 2.D summarizes what has been said about the supply curve and reminds us of how a change in price affects the quantity supplied, *cet. par.*

Shifts in supply result from changes in anything that affects the quantity supplied except the good's price. Any change that affects the opportunity cost of producing a given quantity of output for sale will cause a change in supply. Some important factors that frequently result in supply shifts include the following: (1) changes in technology, (2) changes in input prices, and (3) changes in prices of other goods a firm might produce or in expected future prices of the good produced. A fourth factor that would shift an industry's supply curve would be a change in the number of firms in the industry. Changes in supply are illustrated in figure 2.E.

Changes in Technology Improvements in technology have been generally accepted as the single most important force responsible for the improved standard of living we enjoy compared to our great-great-great grandparents, say, 150 years ago. An improvement in technology means an increase in the amount of output firms can obtain for given quantities of inputs. When technology improves, fewer inputs are required, opportunity costs fall (given input prices), and the supply curve shifts downward and to the right as shown in figure 2.E. This represents an increase in supply (a rightward shift) because more is offered for sale at each price, or, equivalently, suppliers will accept a lower price in return for providing a given quantity.

A good example of this is pocket calculators. In the early 1960s students purchased slide rules for their math and science courses—pocket calculator technology as we know it today did not exist then. Slide rules cost about $25 and performed only a fraction of the operations that today's calculators can. Moreover, slide rules were much slower and far less accurate. Since the introduction of pocket calculators, technology has improved very rapidly. A pocket calculator that sells for $25 today would have cost $150 or more fifteen years ago. This immense price reduction (occurring over a period of time when inflation increased the prices of most other products) resulted from tremendous improvements in electronics technology.

Another striking example of the effects of changing technology on supply is in stereo equipment. Because of improvements that were almost inconceivable thirty years ago, a modest sum, say, $200, purchases audio equipment today that is by some measures ten times better than $200 worth of "hi-fi" equipment in the 1950s.

Improved technology in both the pocket calculator and stereo industries pushed supply curves to the right. This increase in supply made more product available at all prices and the same amount available at a lower price.

Changes in Input Prices In 1973 a war between Israel and its Arab neighbors resulted in an oil boycott that sharply reduced the quantity of petroleum available to most of the world. Subsequently, the Organization of Oil Producing and Exporting Countries (OPEC) found it had substantially strengthened its market power and was able to increase the prices it charged to nations that imported petroleum. The result was a quick and severe leftward shift in the supply of goods and services that use petroleum and its derivatives—fuels, plastics, important chemicals such as synthetic fabrics and rubber, and many others. The higher prices that consumers were required to pay for these products resulted in a lower standard of living for millions of people and in economic adjustments that continued into the early 1980s. What can we expect to happen to many supplies as a result of the oil price decreases that occurred in 1985 and 1986?

Changes in Expected Future Prices It may not be immediately obvious to you how *future* prices affect *current* supply. This relationship between the present and the future is extremely difficult to predict but important for the way the economy functions and for our economic welfare. When a good can be stored, the opportunity cost of *selling* it today may be greater than what must be given up to *produce* it today. For example, suppose you were a Texas rancher with oil wells on your property. If it costs you $15 to extract a barrel of oil for sale on today's market, you could sell it at a "profit" if today's price were, say, $20 per barrel. However, if you expect oil to sell for $30 per barrel a year from now, and if it costs, say, only $1 to store the oil for a year, your true opportunity cost of selling the oil today is $29, not $15. You would be losing, not profiting, by selling your oil at $20 today. In other words, an increase in the expected future price of oil or other storable commodity will result in a *leftward* shift in the supply of oil this year as producers place more in storage and offer less for current sale.

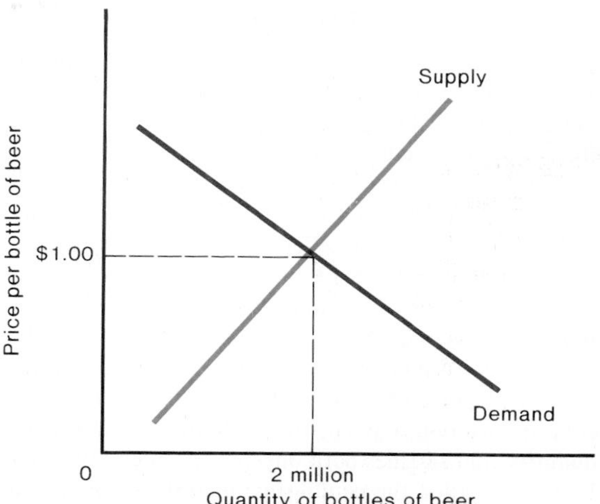

Figure 2.F Equilibrium price and quantity in a market for beer
The equilibrium price is $1 per bottle and the equilibrium quantity is two million bottles, where quantity supplied equals quantity demanded.

We have seen how the market price of a good or service affects the quantities demanded and supplied. But what determines the price? Both the supply and demand concepts are necessary if we are to understand how prices and quantities are determined. Supply and demand are the tools that provide immense insight into human behavior in the economy and the influence of government policies and business practices on production and consumption. They are linked together in the next section.

▸ How the Forces of Supply and Demand Determine Price and the Level of Production

We will begin by considering a market for beer, which is produced by many firms and consumed by many individuals. The first thing we will do is to put the beer demand curve and the beer supply curve together in one diagram. As depicted in figure 2.F, the demand curve is, of course, downward sloping and the supply curve upward sloping. When we see supply and demand together in the same picture, our eye is drawn to where they intersect. This is the most important price and quantity in figure 2.F. You will see why once we learn the concept of market equilibrium.

*The **equilibrium price** is the price at which the quantity of a good or service demanded equals the quantity supplied.*

*The **equilibrium quantity** is the quantity that results from the equilibrium price. It is both a quantity demanded and supplied.*

*An **excess demand,** or **shortage,** is the amount by which the quantity demanded exceeds the quantity supplied.*

The Concept of Equilibrium

In figure 2.F there is only *one* price at which the amount consumers want to buy exactly matches the amount producers want to sell. This price, $1 in figure 2.F, is called the **equilibrium price,** which occurs at the intersection of the supply and demand schedules. At *any other price,* one of the two parties is frustrated. Either buyers want to buy more than sellers want to sell or sellers want to sell more than buyers want to buy. Of course, buyers would be happier if the price were lower than $1 and they could still purchase as much as they wanted. Similarly, sellers would love to be able to sell two million or more bottles of beer at a price higher than $1 per bottle. Only at $1 per bottle, however, is there a transaction that satisfies both buyers and sellers. The quantity that satisfies both buyers and sellers, two million bottles, is called the **equilibrium quantity.** You should think of market equilibrium as a "point of rest" where no forces operate to make buyers or sellers change their agreement. In particular, price will remain at $1 and quantity at two million bottles until something causes a shift in either supply or demand.

We have just seen how to locate an equilibrium price and quantity in a diagram of a market. This is simple. What is crucially important, however, is to understand *why* the equilibrium price turns out to be the price that actually prevails in a market. Why is it, for example, that the price of a good or service does not get stuck below or above equilibrium? The answer is that unless equilibrium prevails, it is in the interest of both buyers and sellers to take actions that push the market price toward its equilibrium value.

For example, suppose the price of beer in figure 2.F were $0.75. Frustrated buyers would not be able to purchase all the beer they would like. An **excess demand, or shortage,** would exist. Sellers would notice lines forming in front of their stores early in the morning, before they opened. Some thirsty beer lovers might offer to pay a premium if only shopkeepers would sell them a six-pack or two. Profit-maximizing sellers, realizing that they could sell all they like at a higher price, would start raising their prices. (In other words, when there is a shortage, individual sellers *do* have some control over the prices they charge.) The upward trend in price would increase the quantity offered for sale

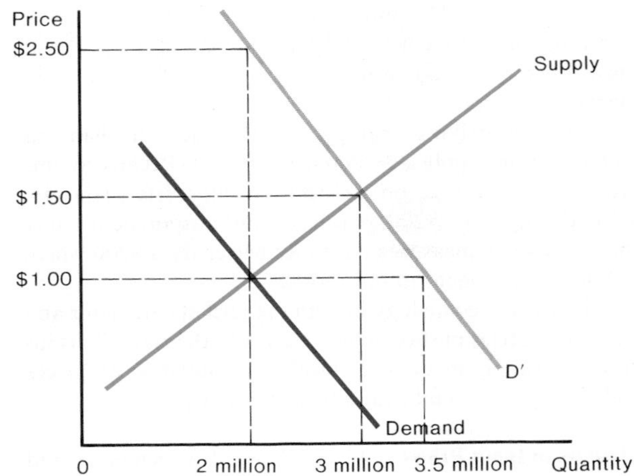

Figure 2.G The effect of a long-term increase in demand
A permanent increase in demand from D to D′ causes the equilibrium price to increase from $1 to $1.50 and the equilibrium quantity to increase from two million to three million.

and reduce the quantity demanded. This adjustment process would go on until the equilibrium price of $1 was reached.

You should be able to work through the adjustment process when the market price is greater than the equilibrium price. When this happens an **excess supply, or glut,** exists and sellers cannot find buyers for all the goods or services offered for sale.

The Effects of Shifts in Supply and Demand on Equilibrium Price and Quantity

Probably *the* major use of supply and demand theory is to predict how changes in demand or supply conditions affect prices and sales of a good or service. Consider the market for beer again as represented in figure 2.G. Initially, supply and demand are denoted by S and D. Now suppose that demand shifts to D′. Perhaps beer is found to have an anticholesterol agent in it that reduces the risk of heart disease. Equilibrium will not be restored until the price rises

*An **excess supply**, or **glut**, is the excess of the quantity supplied over the quantity demanded.*

Table 2.A **The qualitative effects of permanent supply and demand shifts on market equilibrium prices and quantities.**

	Supply increases	Supply decreases	Supply unchanged
Demand increases	Q↑ P↑, P↓, or P constant*	Q↑, Q↓, or Q constant* P↑	Q↑ P↑
Demand decreases	Q↑, Q↓, or Q constant* P↓	Q↓ P↑, P↓, or P constant*	Q↓ P↓
Demand unchanged	Q↑ P↓	Q↓ P↑	Q constant P constant

*Depends on whether demand or supply shifts more and on the relative steepness of demand and supply.

to $1.50 per bottle and quantity reaches three million bottles. At the old equilibrium price a shortage now exists. More beer is demanded than is supplied. This excess of demand over supply—3.5 million − 2 million bottles of beer—created when demand shifted to D′, leads to upward pressure on the price of beer. This in turn leads producers to expand their production.

Notice that the new equilibrium quantity, three million bottles, is more than the quantity originally demanded but less than buyers would buy had price *not* changed. The market in a sense serves as an auctioneer who matches buyers and sellers. When the auctioneer senses an increase in the amount buyers want to buy, the auction price is raised. The rising price mitigates the increased amount buyers want to buy.

We now have our first conclusion from the theory of supply and demand. *An increase in demand leads to higher prices and quantities bought and sold.* You should practice thinking things through in reverse order to make sure you understand the effect of a long-term *reduction* in demand. What would cause a reduction in demand? How do changes in supply and demand lead producers to cut back their output? When you think this through, you will come to the conclusion that *a reduction in demand leads to lower levels of production and sales as well as reduced prices.* This is our second major conclusion from supply and demand. In both cases, of course, we assume that "all else is unchanged."

Table 2.A summarizes how shifts in supply and demand affect equilibrium price and quantity. After you have studied table 2.A carefully, you will be ready to go on to see how these basic economic concepts are applied in later chapters.

▸ Key Terms

ceteris paribus *55*
change in supply, shift in the supply curve *60*
demand *53*
demand curve *56*
economic profit *59*
equilibrium price *62*
equilibrium quantity *62*
excess demand, or shortage *62*
excess supply, or glut *62*
firm *59*
income effect *55*
law of demand *55*
law of supply *59*
substitution effect *55*
supply *53*

Chapter 3

Employment, Unemployment, and the Aggregate Production of Goods and Services

Outline

Objectives

After reading this chapter, the student should be able to:

Explain how a firm's demand curve for labor is derived, and explain how the concepts of the production function, the marginal product of labor, and the value of the marginal product of labor are used.
Relate the aggregate demand for labor to the aggregate value of marginal product of labor.
Describe factors that affect an individual's labor supply decision.
Discuss the shape of the aggregate supply of labor curve and factors that will cause it to shift.
Explain how equilibrium is achieved in the labor market and how expectations affect the aggregate labor market.
Distinguish between frictional, structural, and cyclical unemployment, and discuss policies designed to reduce each.

▸ Introduction

Jo worked in the textile mill in her hometown for nearly ten years. By 1980, she was a supervisor earning more than $12,000 a year. She and her husband had a nice home, a boat, and new car, and she belonged to a strong union local. But by 1983, all that had changed. Jo lost her job in 1982 when the mill closed. Many people were looking for work. In the nation as a whole, the unemployment rate reached 10.8 percent, a rate that had only been exceeded during the depression of the 1930s.

When the economy picked up in 1983, the textile mill stayed closed and Jo got a job for about $7,000 a year as a night manager in an all-night convenience store. She didn't like that because her children were not getting enough supervision. By 1984, as the economy began to expand rapidly and unemployment dropped to 7.3 percent, Jo quit and took a job as a taxi driver. Unfortunately, the taxicab business went bankrupt, so she is unemployed again. However, she is presently looking into several jobs. She and her husband have had to sell their boat, the car is falling apart, and they have difficulty meeting their mortgage payments. Her old union local has dwindled to 50 percent of its former membership, and no new textile mills are on the horizon.

Jo can't figure out how or why things changed for the worse. She is the same woman who used to go to work every day and make more than $12,000 a year, isn't she? Why can't she make that kind of money some other way? Why, she wonders, couldn't she even keep a crummy job that paid less than she had been making before? In order to answer such questions, we have to understand how labor markets work and how they are affected by overall economic conditions.

In this chapter we set in place the first stone in our foundation of macroeconomic analysis. In particular, we examine the link between the input and output sides of the macroeconomy. Among other things, we focus on how firms' individual economic decisions lead them to produce a particular aggregate level of output for society (real GNP) and to hire a particular amount of labor. We also examine the forces that motivate households to provide the labor that firms use to produce society's goods and services. One of our primary goals will be to see how the interactions between buyers and sellers of labor (firms and individuals) influence wages, employment, and unemployment. If you have had a previous course in economics, much of the material in this chapter through page 77 will be familiar. Here we review the discussion of labor demand and supply to refresh your memory before we move on to a discussion of unemployment.

A worker who becomes unemployed suffers more than just an economic loss. During the severe recession of 1980–82, television and newspapers carried chilling accounts of the loss of self-esteem and of the pain and suffering experienced by the unemployed. Such feelings stem not only from lost income but also from uncertainty and anger. Unemployment is one of the most misunderstood economic concepts. Some, perhaps most, unemployment is a normal consequence of a large industrial economy such as ours. This means that government policy must be carefully constructed to take account of this. We will consider various government policies designed to reduce unemployment and, most important, begin to develop the macroeconomic model we will use to analyze recessions, inflation, and government policies to reverse them. The links we establish in this chapter between unemployment, employment, output, and prices play crucial roles in our discussions in chapters 8 through 12 of business cycles and macroeconomic policy.

The ***demand for labor*** *is the relationship that defines the quantity of labor a firm would like to hire.*

The ***supply of labor*** *is the relationship that defines the amount of labor offered to firms by individuals.*

The ***marginal product of labor (mpl)*** *measures the additional output a firm produces when it hires an additional unit of labor, all other inputs such as machinery held constant.*

▸ The Labor Market

A firm's desire to purchase labor is called its **demand for labor.** The amount a firm is willing to pay for some labor depends upon how much the firm receives for the good or service that labor helps to produce. Because of this dependence on the demand for a firm's product, the demand for labor (and other inputs) is called a *derived demand.* Although we concentrate on the demand for labor in this chapter, the ideas we develop can also be applied to the firm's demand for other inputs into its production process, such as machinery. We shall see that the amount of labor that a firm actually hires depends not only upon its demand but also on the willingness of individuals to offer their services, which is called the **supply of labor.**

The Demand for Labor

A simple example will help to see how a firm decides how much labor to employ. Suppose you decide to enter the calculator business. Since you are just beginning, your firm does just one thing. It assembles pocket calculators, using parts—integrated circuits, keyboards, displays, and cases—purchased from other companies. When you set up your firm, you purchase the equipment you and your workers will need to assemble any number of calculators up to 500 per day. Obviously, the output of your calculator-assembly firm is zero before you hire any workers. You do not assemble any calculators if you do not hire any assemblers. The number of calculators your company assembles increases with the number of workers you hire. If you hire one worker, your firm's total output would be thirty calculators assembled per day. This quantity of output is not only your total output, it is also the *additional output* you have produced by hiring your first worker. Should you hire a second worker? Your decision will depend upon how much additional output in terms of the number of calculators per day he or she can assemble. In general, the *extra* output produced whenever another worker is added is called the **marginal product of labor (mpl).**

Sometimes it is easier to use symbols for an expression like the marginal product of labor. When we are dealing with an economic concept that involves a *change* in one variable with respect to a *change* in another, we use the Greek letter delta (Δ) to indicate a change in a variable. Because mpl is defined as the *change* in output due to a change in the amount of labor used, we use the following expression:

$$\text{mpl} \equiv \Delta q / \Delta l.$$

In this expression for mpl, please note that we have used the symbol $\equiv$ (the identity symbol) rather than $=$ (the equality symbol). This is to remind you that mpl is *defined* to equal $\Delta q / \Delta l$ *in all places and at all times.* This is in contrast to an *equality* relationship in which two variables are equal to each other *only when certain conditions hold.* We will come back to the distinction between an equality and an identity later because it is very useful in understanding important economic relationships.

In calculating the marginal product of labor, you must be very careful to measure *only* the additional output produced by adding exactly one worker. For example, if at the same time you hired an additional worker, you also purchased more equipment for use in assembling computers, part of the additional output would be due to using more equipment, too. In other words, the marginal product of labor is the additional output gained by hiring an additional worker, *ceteris paribus,* or *holding constant* the amount of equipment your workers use. Remember, by imposing the *ceteris paribus* (*cet. par.*) method of analysis, we are simply examining, *one at a time,* the factors that influence a firm's behavior. We can, and do, look at changes in many factors (also one at a time) to discover how they too affect the demand for labor.

*A **price taker** is a buyer or seller that has no direct influence over the market price of a good or service.*

***Competitive firms** are price takers in the market for the good or service they produce and in the markets for the inputs that they use.*

Returning to our example, how much does output grow when you hire additional workers? When you hire the second employee, does the quantity of calculators assembled per day double? Hiring a second worker *could* actually *more* than double your calculator output, perhaps to something like seventy-five units per day. The reason is that with a second worker your employees can now be used more efficiently. Instead of one person's assembling all the parts to make one calculator, the two workers can specialize in performing a smaller set of tasks. This way, each worker becomes more efficient in assembling a part of a calculator than he or she would be when doing everything. Doing everything requires using a larger number of tools, starting and stopping to lay down and pick up different parts, and so on. At some point, however, the gains from additional worker specialization will taper off, and the marginal product of labor will start to diminish. You will reach the situation where additional workers increase the number of calculators assembled but *by progressively less and less.* By the time you hire a fifth worker, the *additional* number of calculators assembled drops to only four units per day. This decline in the marginal product of labor stems in part from the fact that you have only a certain amount of equipment for your workers to use. (Remember, this example of the marginal product of labor is *ceteris paribus.*)

While our example may be somewhat contrived for the purposes of demonstration, the basic principal is extremely important. *At a given level of other inputs, additional labor is productive, but the marginal product of labor eventually diminishes.* This basic principle is illustrated with numbers in table 3.1 and graphically in figure 3.1.

Put yourself in the position of the owner or manager of a firm trying to decide whether to add more workers. Perhaps business has been good and you are tempted to start a second shift, hoping that the extra sales will more than repay the cost and effort of hiring new workers and managing them. The marginal product of labor will play a crucial role in your decision. Whether or not adding the new workers will increase your profit will depend in a very important way on the marginal product of labor.

Table 3.1 The marginal product of labor in assembling pocket calculators

The marginal product of labor is the number of additional calculators assembled per day when an additional worker is hired. While marginal product is positive in this example, it becomes smaller and continues to decline after the second worker is employed.

Number of workers	Number of calculators assembled per day	Marginal product of labor ($\Delta q/\Delta l$) (in number of calculators)
0	0	
1	30	30
2	75	45
3	105	30
4	116	11
5	120	4
6	123	3

The Value of Labor's Marginal Product Is a Firm's Labor Demand Curve

In order to show that adding more workers may or may not increase profit, we need to know what happens to the price of your firm's product as output grows. We will assume that your firm is what economists call a **price taker,** which means that the price for which its output sells is influenced only by the combined output of all similar firms, *not* by the output of your firm alone. Your firm is simply too small to affect the market price of calculators. Because firms that are price takers must *compete* with each other for customers, they are often called **competitive firms.**

*The **value of the marginal product of labor (vmpl)** is the increase in a competitive firm's sales revenue resulting from the sale of the extra output produced when an additional worker is hired.*

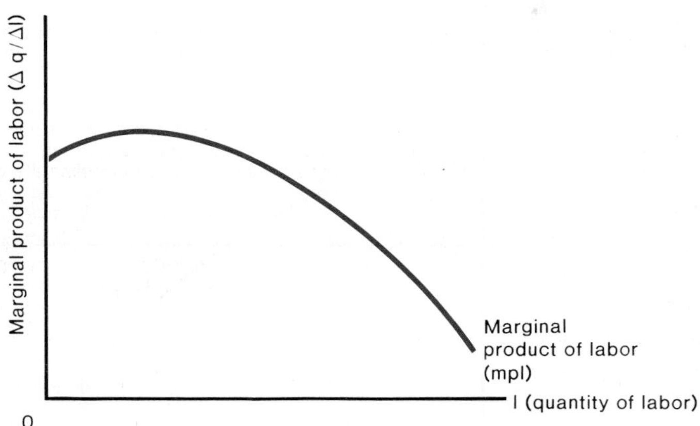

Figure 3.1 The marginal product of labor for a typical firm
The marginal product of labor (Δq/Δl) denotes the extra output (Δq) produced as a firm increases its labor input by one additional worker. The mpl for a typical firm is positive and diminishing—additional workers add to total output, but the increment shrinks as the firm's labor force grows, *cet. par.*

When a competitive firm hires an extra worker, it receives additional revenue, called the **value of the marginal product of labor (vmpl),** which is simply the marginal product of labor times the price of the firm's output. If we denote the market price for the firm's output as p, then the value of the marginal product of labor is

$$\text{vmpl} \equiv p \times \text{mpl} \equiv p \times \Delta q/\Delta l.$$

To be precise, we should recognize that a firm is concerned with the goods and services that can be purchased with the revenue it receives. Therefore, the firm's market price, p, used in the calculation of vmpl should be thought of as the *real price* at which it can sell its output. A simple way to calculate the real price faced by a firm is to divide the nominal (dollar) price at which it sells its product by a price index such as the Consumer Price Index (CPI) or GNP deflator. (You would set the price index equal to 1.0 in the base year rather than 100. Thus, if 1987 were the base year and your firm sold calculators at $5 each in 1987, the *real price* would equal $5. If calculators still sold for $5 in 1988 but the price index doubled, you would divide $5 by 2.0 to obtain a real price of only $2.50.)

Here and elsewhere in this chapter we will use the symbol p to denote the real price at which the firm sells its output and the symbol P to denote the CPI or GNP deflator.

Assuming that your calculator firm faces competition from many other calculator manufacturers, with a market price of $5 per calculator, the value of the first worker's marginal product in table 3.1 is $150 per day. At the price of $5.00 per calculator, the value to the firm of adding, say, a fourth worker is $55. Notice that the value of labor's marginal product is positive but eventually shrinks because of the diminishing marginal product of labor.

Because the value of marginal product is marginal product times price of output, vmpl has the same general shape as the the mpl curve in figure 3.1. The vmpl curve is illustrated in figure 3.2. The curve showing the value of labor's marginal product tells a story similar to that told by the mpl curve. Additional units of labor have positive value to the firm, but the firm benefits less and less from additional labor as the size of the firm's labor force grows.

*The **real wage (W/P)** is equal to the nominal (or paycheck) wage (W) divided by the aggregate price level (P); the real wage expresses a worker's pay in terms of its ability to purchase goods and services.*

*The **nominal, or paycheck, wage (W)** is the pay a worker receives measured in dollars per hour.*

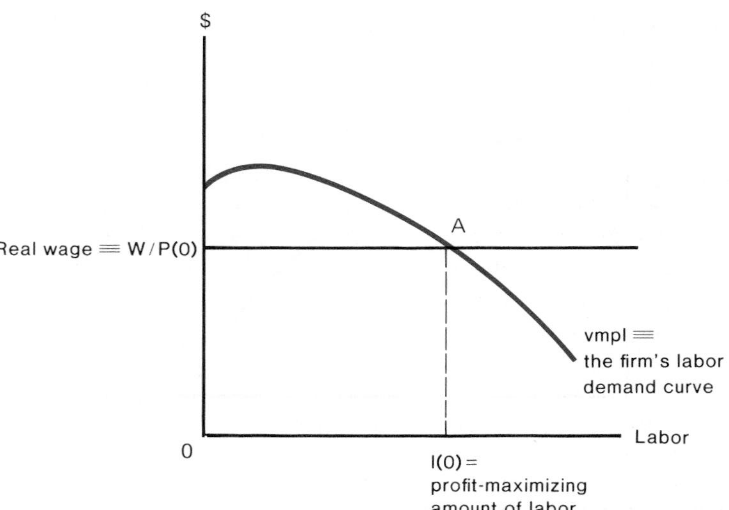

Figure 3.2 The value of labor's marginal product curve is also a firm's labor demand curve
The value of labor's marginal product (vmpl ≡ p × Δq/Δl) is the extra revenue a firm gets from selling the additional output generated by hiring one more worker. In order to earn the largest profit, a competitive firm chooses its labor input so that the last unit hired just pays for itself. This is where vmpl equals the (constant) real wage the firm must pay to attract workers.

In order to decide whether to hire additional workers, you also need to know what it will *cost*. We will assume that your firm is also a price taker in the labor market. This means that your hiring decisions have no direct effect on the **real wage (W/P)** you must offer, which is the **nominal, or paycheck, wage (W)** you pay, taking purchasing power into account. Workers, as well as firms, are concerned with how many goods and services they can buy with their earnings. Suppose, for example, you are a wage earner and your nominal wage increases by 10 percent between 1987 and 1988. How much better off are you? The answer depends on the price level next year versus today. If the price level (P) is the same in both 1987 and 1988, then you will be able to purchase 10 percent more next year with your salary. However, if the price level rises by 10 percent, you will be no better off. Should the price level rise by *more than* 10 percent, then your real wage will actually *fall*. Firms and workers will take inflation into account when deciding how much labor to buy or sell.

The horizontal line in figure 3.2 illustrates that the firm may hire as much labor as it wants at the going real wage, W/P (0). If you, as owner of the computer firm illustrated in table 3.1, are making a decision about whether to hire more workers, you will keep hiring as long as additional units of labor pay for themselves by adding more to revenue than to cost. You will stop hiring when you decide that one more unit of labor will add more to total cost than to revenue. This is the point where profit is greatest. In figure 3.2, if your work force is smaller than l(0), the value of additional workers exceeds their cost. Additional workers beyond l(0) worker cost more than they are worth because their wage rate exceeds the value of their marginal product. Thus, l(0) is the profit-maximizing amount of labor to hire in figure 3.2. This is marked by point A.

Suppose that your calculator firm shown in table 3.1 can hire all the workers it wants at $50 per day. If you can sell your calculators for $5 each, how many workers will you hire? If you answered four, you are correct. The fourth worker yields a value of marginal product equal to $55 but costs only $50 to hire. The fifth worker must also be paid $50 per day but yields a value of marginal product of only $5 x 4, or $20. If your answer was not four workers, we suggest you review the material in this section before you read on.

Symbolically, a firm earns the most profit by hiring workers up to the point that

$$vmpl = W/P(0).$$

A firm's labor demand curve [d(l)] is a graph illustrating the firm's desired labor force at various possible real wage rates.

Notice that we have used the *equality* sign (=) in this expression. This is because vmpl is *not the same thing as* W/P(0). They are *equal* to each other when, and only when, the firm hires just that quantity of labor that leads to the largest profit.

We have just seen how a firm chooses the size of its work force at the going real wage. If any of the conditions that determine the firm's choice change, then the choice of number of workers will change. For example, suppose your firm is so profitable that you decide to purchase additional equipment. With more machinery and tools, the marginal product of your workers will increase, and their value of marginal product will also rise. Given the wage rate, it will now be profitable to enlarge your labor force. Suppose, on the other hand, that increased foreign competition forces you to sell your calculators at $4.50 instead of $5 each. Because the demand for labor is a *derived demand,* this will reduce the value of marginal product of labor, and you will desire to reduce the number of workers hired. Using the numbers in table 3.1, calculate how much your employment and output will decline if the price of calculators falls from $5 to $4.50.

What happens to employment if the real wage rate changes? The answer to this question is given by a **firm's labor demand curve [d(l)].** We can think of this as a curve tracing out the firm's profit-maximizing labor force at the various real wage rates it might have to pay. Because the profit-maximizing competitive firm hires the amount of labor denoted by the vmpl curve at a given real wage, *the vmpl curve is also the firm's labor demand curve.*

To reinforce your understanding of the firm's labor demand curve, assume that you can hire all the labor you want at $50 per day and that calculators sell for $10 each. How many workers will you hire? How many will you hire at $35 per day? How many at $25 per day? Your answers should be four, five, and six workers, respectively. If these were not your answers, review the concept of the value of labor's marginal product and how the firm chooses its work force.

Events that Shift a Firm's Labor Demand Curve A firm's labor demand curve is downward sloping. This means that as labor becomes more expensive, the *quantity of labor demanded* by the firm declines. A firm adjusts to higher labor costs by becoming more capital intensive (using more machinery relative to labor) and cutting back on its level of production. Perhaps this seems paradoxical, though. If employment falls as real wage rates rise, then why hasn't employment in the United States diminished nearly to zero as real wage rates have grown over time? There is no doubt that even the lowest-paid workers today earn more per hour in terms of their purchasing power than workers did in 1900. Still, there are many more jobs in our economy today than there were at the turn of the century. The solution to this puzzle lies in remembering what we are holding constant (*ceteris paribus*) when we draw the labor demand curve in figure 3.2. In discussing the concept of the value of the marginal product of labor and the fact that it also serves as a firm's labor demand curve, we are *holding constant* the level of the firm's other inputs, such as machinery and energy. We are also holding constant the firm's technology. One key reason why workers are better off today than they were fifty or a hundred years ago is that technology has not in fact been constant. Increased use of machinery and energy sources and improved technology have led to an *increase in demand* (a rightward shift in the demand curve) for labor.

Suppose, for example, that you discover a new technology for assembling calculators, a technology that allows you to use labor more productively and lower your costs per calculator significantly. The change in technology means that the marginal product of labor shifts outward in figure 3.1 because there is more additional output per extra unit of labor. Similarly, the curve illustrating the firm's vmpl must be redrawn in figure 3.2 to reflect the fact that an additional worker will now be more valuable because of his or her greater marginal product. The result is to increase the value of labor's marginal product and the number of workers your firm will hire at any given wage.

*The **production function** quantifies the relationship between a firm's output and its inputs.*

*The **aggregate demand for labor** [D(L)] illustrates the total number of workers that society's firms wish to hire at various real wage rates.*

As a matter of historical record, the effects of improved technology have resulted in increased demand for labor. This has resulted in *both* higher wage rates and employment over time in the United States. For example, in the early part of this century, over a third of our labor force was required to produce food and other agricultural products for themselves and the rest of the nation. Vastly improved agricultural technology and investment in machinery now permit all of our food to be produced by less than 3 percent of today's labor force. Farmers and agricultural workers today have a far higher standard of living than they did seventy-five years ago. Workers no longer needed in agriculture have moved to jobs in other industries where they, too, earn much more than they would if they were still employed in menial jobs on the farm. Another way to see the effect of additional inputs and technology is to compare wages internationally. Those nations with the highest standards of living, such as the United States, the countries of Western Europe, and the industrialized nations of Asia, use a great deal of machinery, energy, and advanced technology. The poorest nations, those in Africa and parts of Asia and South America, use relatively small quantities of machinery and energy per worker and have not been able to adopt advanced technologies. They would like to do so to reduce the abject poverty of the majority of their populations.

A Firm's Demand for Labor, Its Production Function, and Its Total Output

We started off our discussion of a firm's demand for labor by focusing on the *marginal,* or *extra,* output obtained by hiring each additional worker. It will be very important as we develop our macromodel to relate employment to *total* output as well. This is a very simple step beyond our discussion of the marginal product of labor. At the heart of a firm's demand for labor is what economists call the **production function,** which is the technical relationship that shows how the firm's output is related to its input use. The term *production function* is derived from the mathematical definition of a *function.* A function is simply a relationship between one variable, such as the amount of output *produced,* and other variables that determine it. In the case of the production function, the amounts of labor and other inputs, such as machinery and raw materials, determine the amount of output a firm produces. A firm, such as an automobile maker, uses many inputs in its production process. Glass, steel, electricity, and the labor of various managerial and production workers are only a few of the inputs used in making a car.

We can simplify the production function by looking at the general relationship between a firm's output and its labor input alone, assuming that all of the other inputs used in production are unchanging. In the example of your calculator firm, the production function is illustrated by the first two columns of table 3.1—the relationship between employment and the production of calculators. A production function is illustrated in figure 3.3. The curve illustrates how a typical firm's output varies with the labor it uses, measured as the total number of workers (l). Notice that the marginal product of labor, mpl, is nothing more than the *slope* of the production function. Figure 3.3 illustrates the relationship between the firm's production function, its demand for labor, employment, and output. We will return to the production function later.

The Aggregate Demand for Labor

So far we have discussed the demand for labor of an individual firm. The focus of this chapter, however, is on the *aggregate* or *economywide* labor market. As a result, we are most interested in the **aggregate demand for labor [D(L)],** which is the *total* number of workers that all the economy's firms seek to hire.

Think of each firm in the economy adding one more worker. The benefit to society of one more worker's services in each firm is the real value of the additional GNP produced, which is the real aggregate value of marginal product of labor. Remember that when we calculate a variable such as real GNP, the price of each good or service is divided by the GNP deflator (P). When we use the GNP deflator, we must first divide it by 100. This is necessary because of the custom of setting price indexes equal to 100 in the

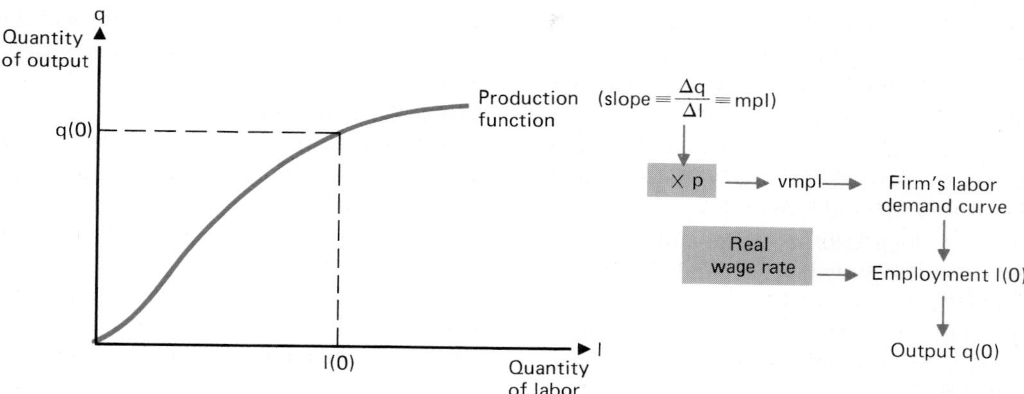

Figure 3.3 A firm's production function
A firm's production function illustrates how its output increases by using more labor, assuming that other inputs do not change. The slope of the production function is the marginal product of labor (mpl), which is the extra output produced by adding an additional unit of labor to the production process. The firm's output price, p, multiplied by mpl is the value of marginal product of labor, vmpl. The firm's vmpl curve is its labor demand curve. When a firm chooses a certain quantity of labor to hire, it also determines the output it will produce.

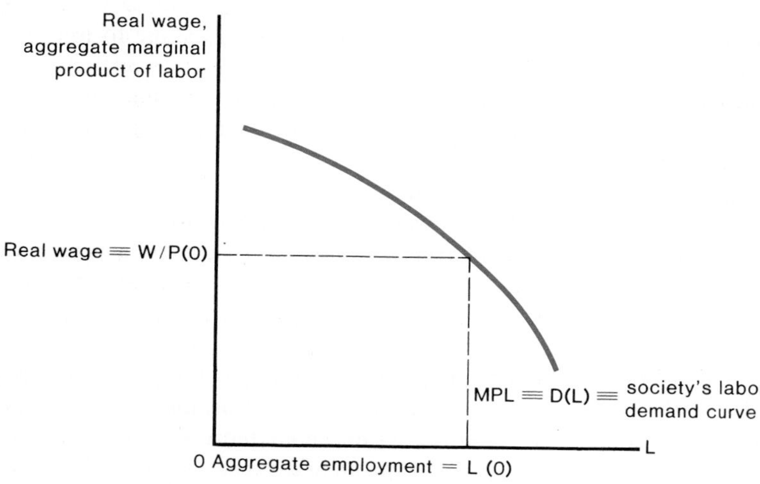

Figure 3.4 The aggregate demand for labor
The aggregate demand for labor, D(L), illustrates the total number of workers employers desire to hire at various real wage levels. The aggregate demand for labor reflects the marginal product of society's workers and is downward sloping because of diminishing marginal productivity of labor. At higher real wages firms hire fewer workers than at lower real wages, *cet. par.*

base year. For example, if nominal GNP equals $5 trillion and the GNP deflator equals 200, then real GNP is calculated as $5 trillion/2.00, or $2.5 trillion. If one more worker produces additional output that sells for $20,000 during a year, the real value of this additional GNP is $20,000/2.00 = $10,000.

The preceding paragraph shows that the aggregate demand curve for labor boils down to the aggregate marginal product of labor (valued in real dollars), MPL. This is illustrated in figure 3.4, where employment equals a total of L(0) workers when the real wage is W/P (0).

Nonmarket activities are the production of goods and services at home that are not sold for a price on a market.

The combined demand for labor of all the firms in the economy is depicted in figure 3.4, which illustrates the same idea as figure 3.2. The aggregate demand for labor is downward sloping, and it is a derived demand, just as a firm's labor demand is. As labor becomes more expensive in real terms, the economy produces less real GNP, and fewer workers are hired, *ceteris paribus*. As long as firms can sell all they produce, the economy's aggregate marginal product of labor curve (MPL) is also the aggregate demand for labor. A crucially important issue in macroeconomics, however, is that there are periods when firms cannot sell all of the goods and services produced when they hire the amount of labor indicated by the aggregate MPL curve in figure 3.4. When this occurs, the aggregate MPL curve is *not* the aggregate labor demand curve. Rather, firms will reduce the amount of labor they employ at any given real wage rate. Understanding the reasons for this problem is one of the basic tasks of macroeconomic analysis.

The demand for labor is only one side of the aggregate labor market, of course. It reflects workers' employment opportunities at various possible real wage rates. Labor market outcomes reflect not only the willingness of firms to hire workers but also the willingness of workers to offer their services to employers. In order to understand the key outcomes in the labor market—the real earning power workers receive, total employment, and the economy's level of unemployment—we also must consider the aggregate *supply* of labor.

The Supply of Labor

In examining the supply of labor we will proceed in a fashion similar to our discussion of the demand for labor. First, we will describe the decision an individual worker makes as to whether or not to supply labor. Next, we relate this to the aggregate supply of labor, or the total number of people who want jobs. In analyzing the supply of labor we will ignore population movements from other countries into the United States and focus only on changes in labor supply that stem from the number of U.S. citizens who seek employment. In the case of the United States, this is a fairly realistic assumption concerning aggregate labor supply.

Factors Underlying an Individual's Labor Supply Decision

Whether or not someone desires a job in the labor market depends upon a number of things. One consideration is whether that person wants to spend all available time in **nonmarket activities,** which include going to school, cooking, shoveling snow, taking care of children, painting the house, fixing the car, and watching television. Thus, someone's decision to supply labor (seek a job) depends upon whether that person desires (demands) 100 percent of his or her time for nonmarket activities. In other words, the amount of labor an individual *supplies* is the mirror image of his or her *demand* for time to use in nonmarket activities.

What determines individuals' demands for nonmarket activities? Three obvious candidates are income or spending power, tastes for market work versus spending time in other pursuits, and the opportunity cost of not working. The opportunity cost of engaging in nonmarket activities is, of course, a person's real wage rate, the amount that can be earned per hour of work in terms of its real purchasing power. The real wage is the opportunity cost of time spent in nonmarket activities because it is the purchasing power an individual gives up by working one hour less for pay and taking one hour more to cut the grass, for example. As you should expect, an individual is more likely to desire a job and seek employment in the labor market the higher the real wage, *cet. par.* At higher and higher real wages the cost of not working increases (the benefit of working grows), and at some point the individual hits an offer he or she cannot refuse.

Nonlabor income is the income someone receives that is independent of the amount worked.

The aggregate supply of labor [S(L)] illustrates the total number of people in society who want employment at the various real wage rates that might exist.

The real wage rate is not the only factor that determines an individual's supply of labor. Two other factors that economists feel are especially important are (1) tastes and preferences for home versus market work and (2) **nonlabor income,** which is the income someone receives outside of the job. People who really "like" nonmarket activities rather than a job will be less likely to work at any given real wage than other individuals. Similarly, high wage rates are less important to people with a great deal of nonlabor income. Thus, someone with a high income from stocks, bonds, real estate, or a trust fund will be less likely to want employment at any given wage rate. Of course, things work the other way too. People who do not like nonmarket activities all that much relative to working for pay will be more likely to want jobs at any given wage rate, and people with very low levels of nonlabor income will be more likely to want jobs at any given real wage.

It is important to recognize that the real wage and nonlabor income are two of the primary avenues through which government policy can influence whether or not a person wants a job. Numerous government programs—personal income tax, Social Security, food stamps, and welfare programs such as Aid to Families of Dependent Children—affect individuals' labor supply decisions by changing their real wages and nonlabor incomes.

The Aggregate Supply of Labor

The other side of the aggregate labor market is the **aggregate supply of labor [S(L)],** which illustrates the total number of people (L) who want jobs at various real wage rates. S(L) is upward sloping in figure 3.5 because higher real wages induce more people to enter the labor force by making nonmarket activities more expensive (market work more remunerative). Notice that the supply curve eventually approaches vertical. This is because at some point the total number of potential workers in society is "used up," and higher real wages cannot induce any more people to supply labor.

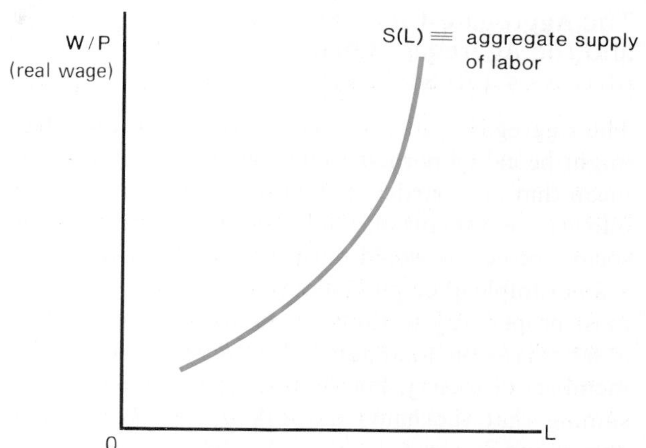

Figure 3.5 The aggregate supply of labor
The aggregate labor supply curve, S(L), illustrates the total number of workers seeking employment at various real wage rates, holding constant tastes for work and nonlabor income. The aggregate supply of labor is upward sloping because higher real wages draw more people into the labor force by making leisure more expensive. Changes in nonlabor income or tastes for work shift S(L).

It is important to recognize that the aggregate labor supply curve is drawn for a given set of tastes and preferences in the population concerning work and a given level of aggregate real nonlabor income. Should either of these change, the supply curve would have to be redrawn. For example, we know that increases in aggregate nonlabor income would shift the supply curve to the left in figure 3.5, and reductions in nonlabor income would shift it to the right. (Remember that demand and supply curves are drawn on the basis of the *ceteris paribus* assumption. If any of these other variables changes, the curve will shift to the right or to the left. When a labor demand or supply curve shifts to the right, the quantity demanded or supplied *at each wage rate* increases; a shift to the left means that the quantity demanded or supplied *at each wage rate* is less than it used to be.)

***Normal employment** (L^n) is the amount of employment denoted by the aggregate labor supply curve at a given real wage.*

*The **expected real wage** (W/P^e) is the nominal (paycheck) wage in terms of its purchasing power expected in the near future.*

***Equilibrium in the aggregate labor market** occurs when an employment–real wage combination is found that leaves no buyer or seller of labor unsatisfied.*

The Aggregate Labor Market and the Aggregate Quantity of Goods and Services Supplied

The aggregate labor supply curve illustrates what might be called **normal employment** (L^n). By this we mean that at a particular real wage the supply curve tells us the amount of employment that members of society prefer or would normally like to have. What is an example of employment that is *not* normal? The most proper way to think of the aggregate quantity of labor is as the total number of *hours* worked by the members of society. For simplicity, we have been assuming that the hours of work *per worker* do not change much over time. (This has been basically true for the United States since World War II. Thus, movements along the labor supply curve primarily reflect changes in employment.) There can, of course, be *temporary* situations where employees are required to work overtime, so that they are working more than is typical or normal. In this situation the aggregate quantity of labor employed would be to the *right* of the labor supply curve. Similarly, temporary layoffs or shortened workweeks would put total employment to the *left* of S(L) in figure 3.5. In this case employment would be below normal.

Expectations

Normal employment is based on the quantity of labor workers supply, given the real wage rate they *expect* to receive. A firm's employment and production decisions require planning into the future. At the beginning of each planning period, say, a year, a firm decides how much it expects to sell, at what price, and as a result, how much labor it desires to hire at the going real wage rate. Workers, on their side, must decide how much labor to offer employers on the basis of the real wage rates they expect to be paid. An element of uncertainty in carrying out these plans is a possible change in the price level, P, that determines the value of marginal product and the real wage rate.

Workers and firms must *predict* what the aggregate price level will be when making their decisions concerning how much labor to supply or demand. Any contract or informal agreement between a firm and its workers depends on what both sides expect prices to be *in the future*. This means that when planning how much labor to supply or demand during a year, workers and firms will base their decisions on the inflation they *expect*. Thus, the real wage rate we have been using in our discussion of the aggregate labor market is really the **expected real wage** (W/P^e), which is the nominal wage relative to the price level *expected* by firms and workers. If workers expect the prices of the goods and services they buy to rise in the near future, they will demand a higher nominal wage from their employers. On the other hand, if employers expect to be able to sell their output at a higher price, they will be willing to pay a higher nominal wage rate for a given number of workers. As we proceed, keep in mind that the aggregate labor supply and demand curves depend upon these expectations of firms and workers. We will see that expectations of inflation play an important role in the business cycle and the unemployment that goes with it.

Equilibrium in the Aggregate Labor Market

With this necessary background, we can now discuss **equilibrium in the aggregate labor market,** which occurs when a satisfactory transaction on the part of all buyers and sellers of labor can be found. This occurs at the intersection of the aggregate supply of labor [S(L)] and the aggregate demand for labor [D(L)] in figure 3.6. Notice that in figure 3.6 we have explicitly noted the important role of the *expected* price level in determining labor supply and demand. Only at the *expected* real wage rate $W/P^e(0)$ is the amount of employment firms desire exactly equal to the amount individuals seek. For now, we will assume that the price level has been constant for a while, so that firms' and workers' price expectations are both identical and correct. This means that the current price level is what firms and workers expected it to be and so is the real wage rate. Because workers are supplying the amount of labor they desire when there is labor market equilibrium, the employment level where supply equals demand in figure 3.6 is called equilibrium normal employment.

In the upper part of figure 3.6 we have drawn an aggregate production function for the economy, which relates the aggregate output of goods and services (real GNP) to aggregate employment. The aggregate production function in figure 3.6 illustrates how the economy's total output of goods and services varies with total employment in the economy. When there is equilibrium in the aggregate labor market, there is a normal employment level equal to $L^n(0)$. At the normal employment level, society produces real GNP equal to $Y(0)$ as shown in the upper part of figure 3.6. It is important to remember that along with equilibrium normal employment of labor comes a particular aggregate output of goods and services (real GNP). This is the aggregate quantity of goods and services supplied by the economy's firms. In the remainder of this chapter we examine how labor market equilibrium relates to observed unemployment. Events that disturb labor market equilibrium may move employment away from its normal level and are associated with fluctuations in unemployment and in the aggregate quantity of goods and services produced.

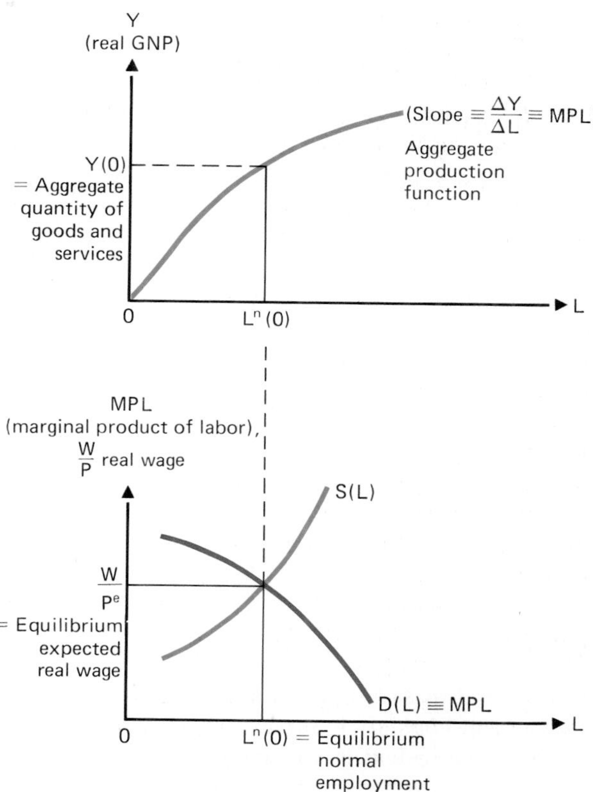

Figure 3.6 The aggregate labor market and the aggregate quantity of real GNP supplied
When there is aggregate labor market equilibrium, the amount of labor firms want to hire equals the number of people who want jobs. Labor market equilibrium is contingent on all the factors that underlie the aggregate labor supply and demand schedules plus the expected price level, P^e, used to calculate real wages. When the aggregate labor market is in equilibrium and the actual price level is equal to what firms and workers expected, employment is at its equilibrium normal level, $L^n(0)$. This level of employment leads to a particular aggregate level of goods and services supplied by firms.

Figure 3.7 Labor force attachment in the United States, 1985
From *Economic Report of the President,* 1986, Tables B-31, B-33, pp. 288, 291.

Unemployment

What Is Unemployment?

In chapter 2 we saw that the federal government uses the Current Population Survey to determine whether or not an individual is unemployed. Alternatives to being unemployed include being employed or out of the labor force. These possibilities are summarized in figure 3.7, which illustrates how the Current Population Survey categorizes people according to their labor force attachment. Keep in mind that the official definition of unemployment makes no reference to the wage rate that would lead someone to accept a job offer. A perfect definition of unemployment might take account of whether an unemployed worker is willing to work for a "reasonable" wage or whether an unemployed worker is looking for an "unrealistic" job in light of current opportunities.

Our objectives in this chapter include trying to understand how the flow of workers into and out of unemployment is related to economic well-being and how much unemployment is "normal" as opposed to "excessive." We will develop some subcategories of unemployment and classify different types of unemployment by their root economic causes. We will see that a portion of unemployment is due to relatively low aggregate demand for output and another portion is due to shifts in the regional or industrial structure of the economy. Still another portion stems from the fact that it takes time for new workers and other job seekers to find employment. By understanding the various components of total unemployment, we will get a much clearer understanding of government policies to reduce unemployment and its detrimental effects on economic welfare.

Varieties of Unemployment and Their Causes

Frictional Unemployment

Figure 3.7 suggests that unemployment would still exist even if there were no recessions or the economy never underwent any changes in its regional or industrial structure. Why? Every month some people

***Frictional unemployment** occurs because it takes time for newly unemployed workers to find jobs even though there are enough jobs to go around.*

leave school, others return to the labor force after having children, and still others come out of retirement. In each of these situations an individual must seek information concerning job opportunities. During the process of discovering what jobs are available, a person is classified as unemployed. Moreover, there will always be experienced workers who feel that they could get better jobs than their last or current jobs. In the process of looking around for better jobs they may be unemployed.

Information is scarce concerning what jobs are available. As a result, some, perhaps many, labor force participants must *necessarily* be unemployed as a way of obtaining good or better jobs. The twenty-one-year-old who spends the summer after graduating from college looking for her first job or the forty-five-year-old assembly line worker who tells his boss to "take this job and shove it; I ain't working here no more" are two examples of what economists call **frictional unemployment.** Employers also play a direct role in creating frictional unemployment. Firms continually seek to improve the quality of their labor forces by testing out new employees and then laying off or firing those they find unacceptable.

Labor market "frictions" occur because both workers and firms have less than perfect knowledge of job opportunities and available employees. The pool of unemployed workers is regularly replenished because it takes time for jobs and workers to find each other. Frictional unemployment is a *normal* situation in a modern industrial society. Workers and firms simply cannot find each other instantaneously. This is not to say, of course, that our economy generates what could be called an acceptable, or ideal, amount of frictional unemployment. Similarly, this is not to say that economic policy cannot or should not reduce the typical period that a frictionally unemployed worker searches for a job.

Policies to Reduce Frictional Unemployment The primary way government policy in the United States attempts to reduce frictional unemployment is by funding the Employment Service. The Employment Service is your state employment agency, which is a joint federal-state venture with 20,000 to 30,000 employees who run branch offices. These branch offices are where you can go to check the jobs listed by employers who tell the service they have vacancies. The goal behind the Employment Service is to make it easier for workers and employers to find one another. The Employment Service is designed to make information more readily available, and in this way help an unemployed worker find a job more quickly. The intended result is a reduction in the unemployment rate.

There are also a number of government programs that *indirectly* affect frictional unemployment by providing income support to the unemployed or by encouraging workers to enter or leave the labor force. For example, the goal of the unemployment insurance system is to provide needed financial support to workers who are unemployed. Unemployment compensation is sometimes made available to workers who have quit their previous jobs. This financial support enables workers to be more careful and take longer in finding their next jobs. The result is an increase in frictional unemployment. The unemployment compensation payments are paid for by a system of taxes on employers. In many states taxes are structured so as to increase the use of layoffs by firms during off seasons. In this way the unemployment insurance system contributes to frictional unemployment.[1] It is important to recognize the trade-off inherent in the unemployment compensation system in particular and programs to help people with low incomes in general when discussing economic policy. The trade-off is that the valuable economic support provided to the unemployed also increases the unemployment rate somewhat.

Structural unemployment arises from the job losses people suffer when firms move out of a region, the skill requirements of the work force change, or when there is a minimum wage rate.

Frictional unemployment is beyond the scope of government policy to a certain extent. The age and the sex mix of the population both have much to do with the number of people who are entering or reentering the labor force. The number of people who are entering the labor force for the first time is strongly related to the number of students graduating or leaving school, and this is largely the result of how many people are sixteen to twenty-two years of age or so. The same situation describes the relative number of women who have decided to return to work after rearing their children. For example, in 1950 only about 30 percent of women twenty years old and over were in the labor force; today the figure is about 50 percent. Many economists feel that demographic factors are the primary reason that frictional unemployment varies over time.

Structural Unemployment

Structural unemployment occurs when major changes in the industrial, occupational, or regional structure of the economy cause a substantial decline in the job opportunities in a particular labor market or among a particular group of workers. Examples include the unemployment caused when many steel mills closed in Youngstown, Ohio, when the federal government deemphasized the space program, and when automatic elevators replaced elevator operators. In short, structural unemployment results from a mismatch of workers' skills and the available jobs either because the jobs and workers are in different parts of the country or workers' skills are not "right" for today's job market.

Since changes in the industrial and occupational structures of the economy occur quite often, why don't workers and firms make adjustments to prevent structural unemployment? First of all, structural unemployment does not *always* happen when firms move out of an area or when there is a technological innovation such as robotics. Most economists note how well firms and workers adjust, even to rather major changes in the economy. Still, workers and firms may adjust too slowly to changing economic conditions to prevent structural unemployment. Reacting to a changing economic environment is costly. Workers may have to relocate or retrain, or firms may have to install new equipment or alter their old plants to take account of changes in their available work forces. Neither firms nor workers will necessarily take such steps unless the changes in their economic environment seem to be reasonably permanent, or at least permanent enough to justify the substantial expenses involved. Neither workers nor firms have perfect information. If you are a worker, for example, it takes time to decide whether or not job opportunities have declined permanently or whether job opportunities will eventually return. Similarly, the decision to move to another part of the country will not be made in haste. In addition to the economic costs of moving, there are psychological costs of adjustment to a new environment and changed surroundings.[2]

The interdependence of the aggregate supply and demand for labor can also produce structural unemployment. When the labor force adjusts to changing demand conditions—perhaps by moving out of an economically declining community—this often further reduces the demand for labor. For example, when people move out of an area, they stop buying goods and services there. The demand for labor in food stores, auto repair shops, and hospitals, to name a few places, is reduced. Moreover, firms may keep wages high rather than lowering them and spreading available employment around because they (1) fear social disapproval, (2) confront unions with contracts that prohibit wage reductions, or (3) are subject to state or federal minimum wage rates that prohibit offering more employment opportunities at lower wages.

Cyclical unemployment results when workers are laid off because the aggregate demand for output declines and firms cut back on production.

Policies to Reduce Structural Unemployment Examples of the structurally unemployed include many teenagers as well as adults experiencing long-term unemployment in industries such as meat packing, automobiles, steel, rubber, and textiles. Policies to reduce structural unemployment must consider the special problem faced by these workers. A problem in the teenage labor market is the relative lack of *career-ladder* employment opportunities. There is much economic support available to young people who go on to get postsecondary educations in publicly subsidized colleges and universities and scholarships. Similar financial support has not typically been given to young people in the United States who choose to enter the labor force after high school. Moreover, employers may not offer much on-the-job training to teenagers for various reasons, including minimum wage legislation. Minimum wage laws discourage employers from hiring unskilled workers at very low wages while compensating them further in other ways—including providing training. To the extent that this is prevented by minimum wage laws in the United States, such laws contribute to our extremely high teenage unemployment rate.

Reducing the instability of employment and the high unemployment of youths requires more career-oriented employment and training opportunities. A variety of programs in the United States are designed to accomplish this. The two most important are probably the Job Training and Partnership Act of 1982 (JTPA) and the Targeted Jobs Tax Credit (TJTC). The JTPA is a major federal initiative designed to reduce structural unemployment among youths and adults. It is different from previous federal employment training programs because of its greater involvement with private industry and vocational training institutions. Under JTPA, federal funds are targeted to individuals identified in the law as being substantially in need, including economically disadvantaged youths.[3]

The JTPA also attempts to alleviate long-term unemployment experienced by adults. It creates state-administered programs of employment and training assistance for (1) workers who have become unemployed as a result of plant closures, (2) laid-off workers who are unlikely to return to their previous industry or occupation, and (3) individuals experiencing long-term unemployment in occupations with limited employment opportunities.[4] The JTPA helps states to establish a wide variety of employment and training activities, including job search assistance, job training, employment counseling, and relocation assistance. It is too soon to judge whether the JTPA has had its hoped-for effect on structural unemployment.

Cyclical Unemployment

Much of the concern with unemployment in general stems from the Great Depression of the 1930s or the severe recession of 1981–82. It would be fair to say that most economists and policymakers still associate unemployment with the economy's periodic reduction in the rate of growth of aggregate demand for output and the derived demand for labor. Such fluctuations in business activity (the business cycle) result in a parallel movement in the overall unemployment rate, called **cyclical unemployment.**

Our understanding of cyclical unemployment is improved if we know the process by which people become unemployed. The data underlying figure 3.7 permit us to classify the unemployed into one of five groups: (1) people who are laid off but can expect to return to their previous jobs, (2) people who have lost jobs to which they cannot expect to return, (3) people who have quit their jobs, (4) people who are returning to the labor force after a period of neither working nor looking for work (reentrants), and (5) people who have never worked at full-time jobs before but are now seeking employment (new entrants).

***Full employment** occurs when there is no cyclical unemployment.*

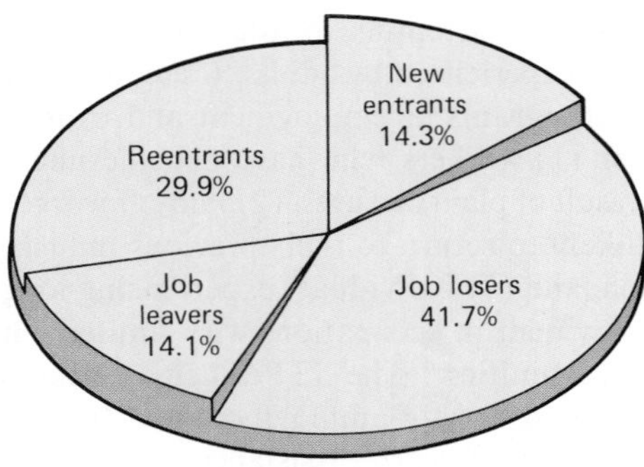

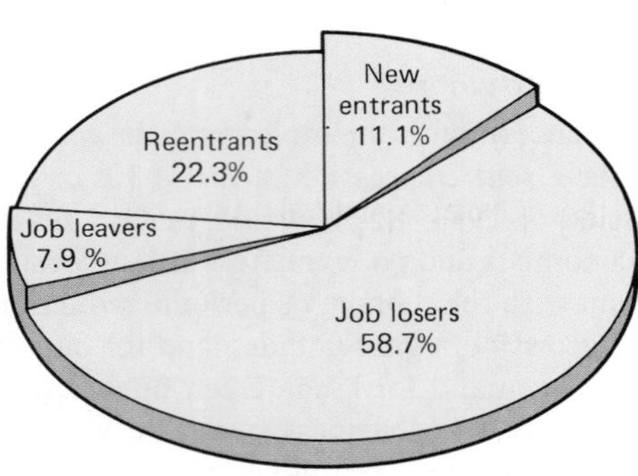

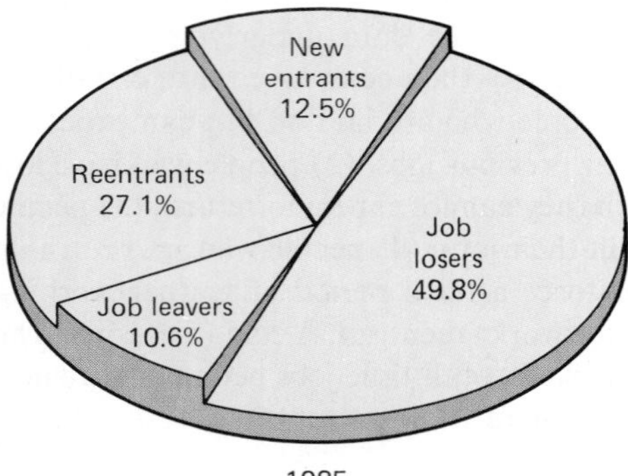

Figure 3.8 The distribution of unemployment by reason
Note: data relate to people sixteen years old and over.
From *Economic Report of the President,* 1986, Table B-33, p. 291.

Figure 3.8 shows us that the distribution of the unemployed among these categories is quite sensitive to the business cycle. We see this by comparing 1982, when the economy was in a recession, to 1978, when there was approximately **full employment,** and by definition, no cyclical unemployment. Remember that while full employment means that there was basically no cyclical unemployment, there was still frictional and structural unemployment. The unemployment rate was 6.1 percent in 1978. In contrast, 1982 was a year of relatively severe recession by U.S. standards. The unemployment rate hit 10.8 percent (twelve million people) during December of 1982. This was higher than at any other date since the Great Depression.

Figure 3.8 helps us to see that the relative number of people who have lost their jobs, either temporarily or permanently, rises noticeably during a recession. During 1978–82, this fraction rose from 42 percent to approximately 59 percent of the total unemployed. The total number of job losers more than doubled. Figure 3.8 also suggests a significant decline in employment opportunities for the unemployed during the 1981–82 recession. The share of unemployment traceable to workers voluntarily leaving their jobs declined from 14 percent in 1978 to 8 percent in 1982. Finally, the relative number of labor force entrants and reentrants declined from over 44 percent in 1978 to 33 percent of the total unemployed during the 1981–82 recession.

Why Are Workers Laid Off During Recessions? It is not immediately obvious why cyclical unemployment occurs. Why don't firms smooth out production so that it remains fairly constant over the business cycle? Or why don't workers accept lower wages during recessions to maintain employment opportunities?

Suppose that firms could predict future fluctuations in economic activity and that goods and services could be stored for future sale at low cost. If this were true, a *temporary* reduction in aggregate demand for goods and services due to the business cycle would not necessarily result in a decline in the demand for labor. Firms would find it profitable to continue production

*The **normal unemployment rate** (u^n) is the unemployment rate when the labor market is in equilibrium; it is the percentage of the labor force that is frictionally or structurally unemployed.*

at a constant level. Realistically, of course, these conditions do not hold. Firms do not know how long a given recession will last or probably even how it will affect their particular product line. Services and many goods (perishables) cannot be stored at low cost. The result is that the demand for labor will shift in the same direction as the demand for output over the business cycle. This means that during recessions, firms will want to reduce either the real wage rate or the amount of labor they hire.

Figure 3.9 will help us understand the interrelationship between the demand for output, the demand for labor, real wage rates, layoffs, and cyclical unemployment. The labor market is initially in equilibrium at point A where the aggregate labor supply curve intersects the aggregate labor demand curve. At point A employment is at its normal level, and the expected real wage is at its equilibrium value. There is no cyclical unemployment when the labor market is in equilibrium. However, there *is* still normal unemployment, so that the unemployment rate is u^n, which is known as the **normal unemployment rate.**

Suppose that a downturn in economic activity reduces the demand for labor. Remember that the labor demand curve, D(L), represents the aggregate marginal product of labor. How can the demand curve shift if the aggregate production function and the marginal product of labor have not changed? The answer is that the demand for labor is a *derived* demand. If firms cannot sell all the output they produce when they hire labor up to the point where the expected real wage equals the aggregate marginal product of labor, then the aggregate demand curve for labor will shift leftward.

If the expected real wage were to fall when aggregate labor demand declines, equilibrium could be reestablished at point B in figure 3.9, and *no* cyclical unemployment would be created. While *employment* would be reduced, no new *unemployment* would result. How can this be? The answer is that the reduced demand for labor and the employment opportunities that go with it reduce the real return on an hour of work enough so that workers leave the labor force. At the (lower) real wage rate, W/P^e (1), labor market work is no longer as attractive relative to the alternatives available outside the labor market. The exit

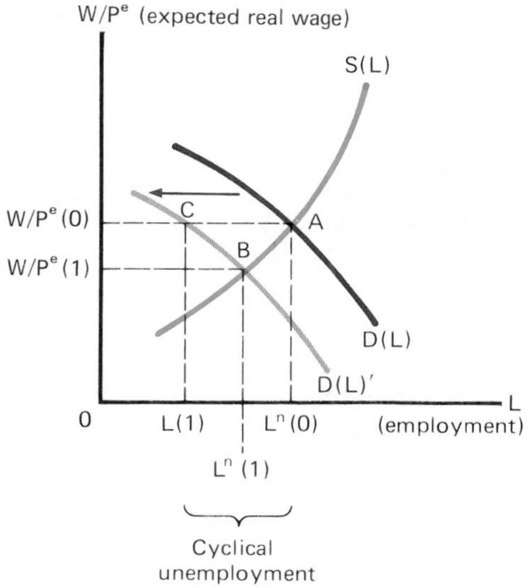

Figure 3.9 Recession, the demand for labor, and cyclical unemployment
Point A illustrates initial equilibrium in the aggregate labor market. There is no cyclical unemployment at point A because there are enough jobs to go around. Of course, there is still normal unemployment at A because new workers and labor force reentrants do not immediately find work and workers do not immediately retrain or migrate when the occupational or regional structure of labor markets changes.

During a recession the demand for labor is reduced to, say, D(L)′. If the real wage is flexible, it will fall and equilibrium is reestablished at point B, where there is reduced employment but not cyclical unemployment (everyone who wants a job can eventually get one). If wages are rigid at, say, $W/P^e(0)$, then cyclical unemployment results. More people want jobs, $L^n(0)$, than there are jobs available, L(1).

of some individuals from the labor force results in *less employment* but *no cyclical unemployment.*

Cyclical unemployment is generated when real wages do not fall to their new equilibrium level. Why might this happen? Specifically, why don't firms and workers agree to reduce real wage rates rather than keeping them rigid? One possibility is that unions and their collective bargaining agreements prevent real wage reductions and require layoffs as the adjustment firms must make to a recession. As long as less than half the labor force of a firm is laid off, a majority vote by workers might tend to prefer *some layoffs* to reduced wages for *everyone.*

Real wages *do* get reduced in the United States, even under collective bargaining, during severe recessions. Newspapers and magazines carried numerous stories of "give backs" by industrial unions, such as the United Steelworkers, during the early 1980s.[5] More important, layoffs, as opposed to wage reductions, also occur in industries and occupations that are not covered by union collective bargaining agreements. The negative relationship between cyclical unemployment and aggregate economic activity is not just a creature of the past forty years, the time in history when unions have been most plentiful in the United States. And about 80 percent of workers are currently *not* covered by collective bargaining agreements. Thus, while unionism may seem an obvious reason for wage rigidity, forces more fundamental to labor markets must be responsible for cyclical unemployment.

Two reasons are frequently offered for employers' unwillingness to lower their real wages during a recession. The first relates to employers' credibility and their ability to attract new employees in the long term. Economists have recently come to view the employment relationship as a contract (sometimes written, other times unwritten) specifying the terms of employment over a relatively long time. Although lowering the real wage to take advantage of depressed labor market conditions might be profitable for the firm in the short term, long-term profitability of a firm could be severely harmed if its workers had expected stable or increasing real wages as part of their bargain with an employer. For example, workers often expect their employers to provide not only employment and training opportunities but also some degree of protection, or insurance, against a fluctuating real income. In return, employees agree to accept a stream of wage payments that is lower than it would be if real wages were allowed to fluctuate over the business cycle. In this sense workers often "purchase" what could be called income insurance. Keep in mind that such income insurance is not free; it is paid for in terms of a lower average rate of pay. Therefore, employees seldom choose complete freedom from the risk of a fluctuating income. Thus, during times of extremely low demand for output (severe recessions), the employment relationship still permits firms to lay off some workers.

This leads us to another question. Why don't these implicit income-insurance contracts permit wage reductions when the demand for labor falls below a critical level? After all, when a worker is laid off his or her income is dramatically reduced. Wouldn't employment at a reduced wage be better than no employment? Not necessarily. When a worker is laid off, income is not reduced to zero because unemployment compensation and other forms of transfer (welfare) payments take effect. Moreover, many workers prefer to stay home and do domestic chores or care for their children rather than accept a drastically reduced wage. Therefore, if the real wage were cut by enough to make firms willing to keep employment at its normal level, L^n in figure 3.9, when aggregate demand was reduced to $D(L)'$, some workers would simply leave the labor force. Notice how the quantity of labor that workers supply is reduced from point A to point B when the aggregate demand for labor is reduced and real wages are allowed to fall. Thus, firms may lay off workers during a recession because they know their employees would not want to work at the wage the firms would be willing to pay them.

There is a second possible reason for layoffs as opposed to wage cuts when the demand for labor declines. Workers may want to be sure that firms are not trying to "fool" them into accepting lower pay for no good reason. A firm will always be better off if workers agree to accept lower pay. However, when employment is reduced so is production, and the firm loses some of its profits. Thus, by refusing to accept lower wage rates and forcing the firm to lay off workers instead, workers are keeping the firm "honest." Employers will only lay off workers when they really have to, because they share in lost income along with their employees.

Before concluding this section on layoffs, we should note that the opposite often occurs during short periods of unusually high labor demand. Written or unwritten agreements between employees and employers often call for the employees to work overtime when asked to do so. Sometimes an overtime premium is paid for this additional work, and at other times it is not. The main point is that if employers treat employees fairly during periods of reduced demand for output, employees are expected to refrain from "holding up" their employers—demanding sharply higher wage rates—when a firm experiences a temporarily high demand for its output.

In addition, employees are often glad to have temporary extra work, because it allows them to compensate for the days when they are laid off.

Normal versus Cyclical Unemployment and Government Policy We noted that *normal unemployment* is that portion of total unemployment that results from the fact that it takes time (1) for workers who have just quit, or entered, or reentered the labor force to find jobs and (2) for workers to relocate in another firm, industry, or occupation because the structure of the labor market has changed. As such, the normal unemployment rate characterizes the economy in the *absence* of macroeconomic "shocks." Thus, cyclical unemployment, which is the result of the business cycle, is *not* part of the economy's normal unemployment. Currently, economists suspect that the normal rate of unemployment is in the range of 6 to 7 percent.[6]

Cyclical unemployment is the result of relatively rigid real wages in the face of a decline in the demand for labor during a recession. This means that government policies that make real wages less rigid or "smooth out" the aggregate demand for output will reduce cyclical unemployment. Unemployment compensation helps to make real wages more rigid because workers know that they have income available outside of their jobs. This brings us back to one of the trade-offs that policymakers face when attempting to reduce cyclical unemployment. Unemployment compensation provides valuable assistance to the needy. However, it also may contribute to increased unemployment. As yet, no policymaker has developed a socially popular way to fine-tune our unemployment compensation program in a way that increases wage flexibility and thus reduces cyclical unemployment.

Summary and Conclusions

This chapter sets in place the first stone in our foundation of macroeconomic analysis. We can now understand the experience of the unemployed textile worker that introduced this chapter in terms of structural and cyclical unemployment. By analyzing the supply and demand for labor we see how the interaction between firms and individuals in the aggregate labor market leads to a particular (1) real wage, (2) level of employment, (3) aggregate production of goods and services, and (4) unemployment rate. These links play crucial roles in our later discussions of the commodity and loan contract markets in chapters 4 and 7 and our analysis of recession and inflationary episodes in chapters 8 through 12. The key points in this chapter include the following.

- Diminishing marginal productivity of labor means that firms will only hire more labor if the real wage rate falls, *cet. par.* As a result, the aggregate demand for labor is downward sloping.
- Higher real wages induce more individuals to seek employment by making the opportunity cost of nonmarket activities more expensive. As a result, the aggregate supply of labor is upward sloping.
- Equilibrium in the aggregate labor market occurs where supply equals demand. At equilibrium, the expected real wage equals the actual real wage and employment is at a level acceptable to all firms and households.
- The equilibrium level of employment implies a particular aggregate quantity of goods and services supplied by the economy's firms.
- Economists classify unemployment according to whether it is caused by frictional, structural, or cyclical factors. The purpose of this classification is to emphasize the need for different types of economic policy to reduce unemployment.
- Frictional unemployment and structural unemployment are part of what economists call normal unemployment. This is not to say that they are "good" for society but rather that they are an unavoidable part of a modern industrial economy in a democratic country.

Cyclical unemployment results when the demand for labor declines but real wages do not. Economists are just beginning to understand why real wages may not adjust sufficiently to prevent substantial cyclical unemployment. One possibility is that workers prefer a job "package" that contains relatively rigid real wage rates and fluctuations in employment to one that permits real wage rates to vary but stabilizes employment.

When there is no cyclical unemployment, the economy is said to be at full employment. Full employment takes account of the fact that there will still be unemployment even if there are enough jobs to go around.

▸ Key Terms

aggregate demand for labor [D(L)] *72*
aggregate supply of labor [S(L)] *75*
competitive firms *68*
cyclical unemployment *81*
demand for labor *67*
equilibrium in the aggregate labor market *76*
expected real wage (W/P^e) *76*
firm's labor demand curve [d(l)] *71*
frictional unemployment *79*
full employment *82*
marginal product of labor (mpl) *67*
nominal, or paycheck, wage (W) *70*
nonlabor income *75*
nonmarket activities *74*
normal employment (L^n) *76*
normal unemployment rate *83*
production function *72*
price taker *68*
real wage (W/P) *70*
structural unemployment *80*
supply of labor *67*
value of the marginal product of labor (vmpl) *69*

▸ Questions for Discussion and Review

1. What is the marginal product of labor? What are the two key properties of marginal product of labor? What is the difference between the marginal product of labor and the value of labor's marginal product?
2. Explain why the value of labor's marginal product is also the competitive firm's labor demand curve. Support your answer graphically.
3. Pete's Pizzeria of Piscataway makes (what else?) pizzas. Pete has a fixed capital input (ovens, etc.) and purchases only one additional input, the labor of pizza makers. There are many similar pizza shops in Piscataway so that Pete sells pizzas and purchases labor under competitive conditions. You have the following information about Pete's operation.

l	**q**	**mpl**	**vmpl**
0	0		
1	15	15	75
2		22	
3	67		150
4	90		
5	108		
6		15	
7	135		
8			
9	150	6	
10	153	3	15

where l ≡ number of pizza makers
q ≡ number of pizzas made per day
mpl ≡ marginal product of labor
vmpl ≡ value of the marginal product of labor

a. How many pizzas are made when six pizza makers are employed? Explain.
b. What is the marginal product (mpl) of the seventh pizza maker? Explain.

c. What is the price of a pizza in Piscataway? Explain.
d. What is the value of marginal product of the eighth pizza maker? Explain.
e. Suppose that the competitive daily wage for pizza makers is $90? How many pizza makers will Pete hire so as to maximize his profit? Explain.

4. Listed below are an economy's aggregate labor demand and supply schedules.

Aggregate labor demand schedule		**Aggregate labor supply schedule**	
Daily real wage (dollars)	*Employment (000's)*	*Daily real wage (dollars)*	*Employment (000's)*
60	0	0	0
55	500	5	500
50	1,000	10	1,000
45	1,500	15	1,500
40	2,000	20	2,000
35	2,500	25	2,500
30	3,000	30	3,000
25	3,500	35	3,500
20	4,000	40	4,000
15	4,500	45	4,500
10	5,000	50	5,000
5	5,500	55	5,500

What is the equilibrium real wage? What is equilibrium employment? Explain how you arrived at your answer.

5. Describe the set of government policies that would be required to make frictional unemployment disappear. Why do you think that the United States government has not totally eliminated frictional unemployment?

6. Why is structural unemployment a part of normal unemployment? Explain why there would be much less structural unemployment if adjustments to economic change were *free*.

7. Economists say that frictional and structural unemployment are part of normal unemployment. Explain. Is cyclical unemployment also part of normal unemployment? Explain. Does it make sense to classify some unemployment as normal? Discuss.

8. Explain why cyclical unemployment results if the demand for labor declines but real wages do not. Support your answer graphically. Describe some economic policies that would make real wages more "flexible." Why do you think the government has not adopted all of your suggestions?

9. Some economists feel that the rigid real wages leading to cyclical unemployment are the result of worker preference. Put differently, economists suspect that workers might prefer relatively constant real wages and the threat of unemployment to a job "package" that would have stable employment but more variable rates of pay. This amounts to assuming that workers themselves are responsible for cyclical unemployment. Evaluate and discuss. Why do *you* think cyclical unemployment exists?

10. Suppose that the teenage labor market is in equilibrium at the legislated minimum wage rate. If a recession occurs in the economy, what is the likely effect on this market?

Chapter 4

Aggregate Expenditure on Goods and Services

Outline

Objectives

After reading this chapter, the student should be able to:

Identify the four components of aggregate expenditure.
Identify the three uses of society's total income.
Distinguish between endogenous and exogenous consumption and the factors that influence each.
Explain the significance of the consumption function's various components, such as its slope and the vertical intercept.
Discuss the factors underlying the level of investment.
Explain the relationship between planned aggregate expenditure, the 45° line, and GNP.
Describe algebraically and graphically the relationship between planned investment, planned saving, and the government deficit at equilibrium GNP.
Use the multiplier to determine the change in equilibrium GNP that results from a given change in planned expenditures.

Introduction

A well-known economist who served as an economic adviser to policymakers in developing countries related the following experience in one emerging African nation during the 1960s. When he first arrived in the country, he visited the Ministry of Planning and asked to see any available data that might give him a picture of recent and current economic conditions there. He was stunned by the wealth of data available both in terms of the number of years covered and the amount of detail on various sectors of the economy. Experience had taught him that such data were hard, if not impossible, to find in most developing countries.

The solution to the mystery became apparent when he discovered that for the previous ten years the country's measured total production was always equal to 1 percent of that in the United States. Further investigation revealed that bureaucrats in the planning office in the capital city had no idea what was actually going on in the economy. Under pressure from their superiors to produce numbers, they simply took United States data and created what they thought were "good" numbers for their country.

Clearly, numbers are not very useful for appraising how an economy is developing over time if they are pure inventions. How can intelligent government policies be developed if the government itself is ignorant about conditions in the economy?

Even if one wanted to conscientiously collect data for a particular economy and had a well-trained staff to perform the task, there still would be a number of questions to answer before the job could begin: What kind of data should be collected? How should data on household, business, and government activities be grouped? Are some measures more useful than others? How can data be added up to provide useful information about the economy? Once the data are collected, how can they be used to help understand the way past economic conditions affect those of today and to forecast the economic scene in the near future? What macroeconomic theory enables one to make sense of various measures of aggregate economic activity? These are some of the questions we will look into in this chapter.

▸ Aggregate Expenditure on Goods and Services: Background

In this chapter we set in place the second stone in the foundation of macroeconomic analysis. In particular, we describe aggregate expenditure on goods and services and how this leads to a particular level of gross national product. Keep in mind that this chapter really deals with only *one* aspect of the macroeconomy, aggregate *expenditure* on goods and services. In chapters 8 and 9 we put things together into a complete representation of the aggregate economy.

The Components of Aggregate Expenditure: A Brief Review

We will begin by briefly reviewing the components of society's aggregate expenditure on goods and services. In chapter 2 we saw that one way to categorize these components is according to which group is doing the spending. We saw that aggregate expenditure is composed of personal consumption expenditures by individuals (C), investments by firms (I), purchases of goods and services by the various government agencies in the United States (G), and net exports of goods and services to foreign consumers (X). Added up they equal the total aggregate expenditure for goods and services (E). This relationship can be described simply as

$$E = C + I + G + X.$$

You should assume in our discussions of aggregate expenditure and gross national product that we are concerned with *real* values. This means that aggregate expenditure on GNP in any year will be expressed in terms of the prices that prevailed during the base year for calculating real gross national product.

GNP Also Measures Society's Total Income

A Brief Review

In chapter 2 we saw that real GNP is *always* equal to the real value of the income people receive from the sale of their labor and other productive resources to firms. This is illustrated in the circular flow diagram of figure 2.1. All those goods and services produced in an economy do not just appear out of thin air. To create them, firms use resources such as labor, land, energy, and physical capital. Whenever producers decide how many final goods and services to make, they must also decide what inputs to purchase. When firms purchase productive resources, this generates income to the owners of those resources—the individuals in society. We have been using the symbol Y to represent the total income paid out to the owners of society's productive resources. At this point we suggest you review table 2.2 for data on how the production of GNP in the United States creates different categories of payments or income for the owners of society's various productive resources.

The Uses of Society's Total Income

The income people receive is used in three general ways: to purchase consumer goods and services (C), to save (S), and to pay taxes to the government (T). At this point, one difference between macroeconomics and microeconomics becomes clear. If we were concerned with microeconomics, for instance, we would be discussing the various types of taxes individuals pay, including sales taxes, property taxes, and taxes on earnings and nonlabor income. We would also be discussing the particular components of consumption, such as food versus housing. We are now interested in the macroeconomy, however, so we concern ourselves only with aggregate or total consumption, saving, and taxes paid to the government.

Saving *is the difference between total income and the amount spent on the consumption of goods and services or paid to the government in taxes.*

Full-employment GNP *requires that there is equilibrium in the aggregate market for goods and services and full employment in the aggregate labor market at the same time.*

The ***consumption function*** *is a schedule, or equation, indicating society's total intended consumption expenditures at various levels of aggregate income.*

The portion of people's income that is not paid in taxes or used to purchase consumption goods and services is **saving.** Saving may entail adding to a bank account, buying a stock or bond portfolio, or contributing to a pension fund. In our discussion saving does not refer to any particular form of adding to one's wealth.

Figure 4.1 contains a simple numerical example that illustrates the relationship between income, consumption, saving, and taxes. Suppose that the aggregate real income received by households is $200 billion and that they are required to pay taxes of $20 billion. If the households decide to spend $130 billion on consumption of goods and services, then we know that saving, the remainder, must equal $50 billion. If households had instead spent more on consumption of goods and services, they would, of course, have saved less. This relationship between income, taxes, consumption, and saving can be illustrated by using the following equation:

$$Y = C + S + T.$$

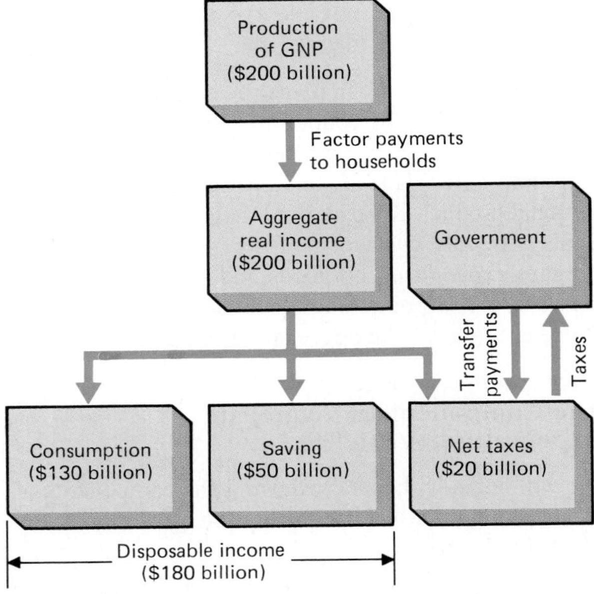

Figure 4.1 The relationship between GNP, total income, disposable income, consumption, and saving
Production of GNP equals $200 billion, which generates factor payments to households of $200 billion (wages, profit, interest, rent, etc.). Households also receive transfer payments from the government and pay taxes to the government. *Net* taxes equal the taxes households pay to the government less the transfer payments they receive from the government. The income households receive from factor payments less *net* taxes equals their *disposable income.* Net taxes equals $20 billion, and households allocate their disposable income of $180 billion to consumption ($130 billion) and saving ($50 billion).

The relationship between total income, net taxes, consumption, and saving can also be illustrated using the equation

$$\begin{array}{cccc} Y = & C + & S + & T \\ 200 = & 130 & 50 & 20. \end{array}$$

An Analysis of Aggregate Expenditure on Goods and Services

In developing our analysis of aggregate expenditure on goods and services, we draw upon our understanding of its components—consumption, investment, government spending, and net exports. One of the major points to bear in mind as we analyze aggregate expenditure is that our macroeconomic model is concerned with *planned* or *intended* behavior. By this we mean that we wish to understand the various forces that lead households to *choose* one level of consumption over another and investors to *choose* a certain quantity of spending on investment goods. Thus, we need to detail the forces underlying consumption and investment *plans,* along with what drives government spending and net exports to their particular levels. We will see that only when all expenditure plans are actually realized will the aggregate market for goods and services be in equilibrium. Whether full employment in the labor market will prevail when the goods and services market is in equilibrium—leading to **full-employment GNP**—is another question. It is answered in chapter 8. In this chapter, we are concerned *only* with the circumstances that lead to equilibrium in the aggregate market for goods and services.

***Endogenous consumption** is that part of planned consumption that depends on GNP.*

***Exogenous consumption** is that part of planned consumption that depends on factors other than GNP.*

***Disposable income (YD)** is the total income consumers have to spend after their taxes (T) are paid, so that $YD \equiv Y - T$.*

The Consumption Function

The cornerstone of the aggregate expenditure relationship is the **consumption function,** which illustrates the relationship between planned consumption and society's total income (GNP). It is called the consumption function because it is a relationship between the variable *consumption* and another set of variables that determine how much households desire to consume in any given year.

Economists who analyze macroeconomic issues have found it very useful to distinguish between two categories of factors that affect household consumption behavior. One category includes only one variable—the income that households receive. The other category includes all of the factors *other* than household income that affect consumption, such as basic subsistence needs, expectations about the future, the desire to save income now so that more may be consumed later, and so on. We have seen that GNP, which determines the income of households, depends itself on the level of planned consumption expenditure. For this reason, that part of consumption that depends on household income is called **endogenous consumption.** The word *endogenous* is used because it refers to that part of consumption that originates *in* the circular flow between GNP and income. That part of consumption that depends on factors other than income and GNP is determined *outside* the circular flow and is therefore called **exogenous consumption.** To summarize, we divide planned consumption into two parts: endogenous consumption and exogenous consumption. Using the symbol $\overset{*}{C}$ to denote total planned consumption, we say that

$$\overset{*}{C} \equiv \text{(planned) endogenous consumption} + \text{(planned) exogenous consumption.}$$

The income *available* for consumption, which is the amount households have left over after paying their taxes, is called **disposable income (YD),** as indicated in figure 4.1. (We shall ignore the fact that in the official national income statistics as shown in chapter 2, *depreciation* of plant and equipment must also be subtracted from GNP to derive disposable income.) If you take another look at table 2.3 on page 42, you will see that disposable income (or disposable personal income as it is officially named) includes *government transfer payments,* which include Social Security, Aid to Families with Dependent Children, and similar payments that add to the spending power of individuals and families over and above what they earn. You should think of government transfer payments as taxes in reverse, or negative taxes. In figure 4.1, we have simply subtracted government transfer payments from the taxes the public pays the government to obtain *net taxes* of \$20 billion. For example, if taxes paid were \$35 billion and transfers paid by the government to households were \$15 billion, then net taxes paid by households to the government would be \$20 billion. Since taxes paid to the government typically exceed transfer payments from the government, net taxes are usually positive. What households have left to save or consume after net taxes are subtracted from their incomes is disposable income.

A good way to remember how GNP, net taxes, disposable income, and consumption are related is this. A change in GNP (national income) will change disposable income and endogenous consumption but not exogenous consumption. Variables *other* than a change in GNP will change exogenous consumption but not endogenous consumption. A change in taxes that does *not* itself result from a change in GNP will cause exogenous consumption to change. If tax policy does not change, then exogenous consumption will change only when forces other than GNP or taxes change.

The Consumption Function Expressed Quantitatively

We will now put some meat on the bare bones of the exogenous and endogenous consumption concepts. Table 4.1 contains a numerical example of the relationship between GNP, taxes, disposable income

Table 4.1 A numerical example of the consumption function

GNP (Y)	Net Taxes (T)	Disposable income (YD) ≡ (Y − T)	Exogenous consumption (a constant)	Endogenous consumption (depends on Y)	Total consumption (C)		Saving (S) ≡ (YD − C)	
(billions of dollars)						$\Delta C/\Delta Y$ (MPC)		$\Delta S/\Delta Y$ (MPS)
25	20	5	10	15	25		−20	
						0.6		0.4
60	20	40	10	36	46		−6	
						0.6		0.4
75	20	55	10	45	55		0	
						0.6		0.4
80	20	60	10	48	58		2	
						0.6		0.4
100	20	80	10	60	70		10	
						0.6		0.4
120	20	100	10	72	82		18	
						0.6		0.4
125	20	105	10	75	85		20	
						0.6		0.4
150	20	130	10	90	100		30	
						0.6		0.4
200	20	180	10	120	130		50	
						0.6		0.4
300	20	280	10	180	190		90	

Exogenous consumption is $10 billion annually. Endogenous consumption equals GNP × 0.6. Total consumption is exogenous consumption plus endogenous consumption, and saving is disposable income (YD) less total consumption. When GNP falls below $75 billion, total consumption exceeds disposable income, and households *dissave,* or draw down their savings to maintain their standard of living. As GNP rises above $75 billion, saving becomes positive. Notice that whenever GNP rises or falls, disposable income changes by the same amount because we have assumed taxes are fixed.

Both endogenous and total consumption change by exactly 60 percent of the amount that GNP and YD change, and saving changes by exactly 40 percent of any change in GNP and YD. The *change* in consumption per dollar *change* in GNP can be expressed symbolically as $\Delta C/\Delta Y$ and is called the ***marginal propensity to consume (MPC).*** Similarly, the *change* in saving per dollar *change* in GNP is expressed symbolically as $\Delta S/\Delta Y$ and is called the ***marginal propensity to save (MPS).*** For example, when GNP goes from $150 billion to $200 billion, YD also increases by $50 billion, and consumption increases by $50 billion × 0.6, or $30 billion, going from $100 billion to $130 billion. Saving goes up by $50 billion × 0.4, or $20 billion, from $30 billion to $50 billion.

Factors that influence exogenous consumption
basic consumption needs
expectations about the future
tastes and preferences
accumulated savings
access to borrowed funds
net taxes that don't depend on GNP

Factor that influences endogenous consumption
GNP

***Dissaving** occurs when people consume more than their disposable income.*

(YD), exogenous consumption, endogenous consumption, total consumption, and saving. In this example, we assume that net taxes are fixed at $20 billion annually and that exogenous consumption is fixed at $10 billion per year. Endogenous consumption, as defined, depends on the level of total income, or GNP. To be precise, endogenous consumption equals 60 percent of GNP, so when GNP and disposable income change, total consumption changes by exactly 60 percent as much. Notice that when GNP equals $200 billion, total consumption equals $130 billion, as in figure 4.1. What figure 4.1 does not show is that total consumption consists of $120 billion endogenous consumption and $10 billion exogenous consumption.

The general nature of the consumption function will be easier to understand if we use some simple algebra. In our algebraic representation of the consumption function, we will use the symbol A to represent exogenous consumption. In table 4.1, A equals $10 billion. Where does A come from; why and how is it determined? The list at the bottom of table 4.1 indicates that exogenous consumption depends on basic consumption needs, expectations about the future, tastes and preferences, accumulated savings, access to borrowed funds, and, *very important,* taxes and transfer payments that do not change with the level of GNP. If a household's disposable income were temporarily to fall to zero, it would not eliminate consumption entirely, for to do so would make it impossible to survive. The consumption that would persist even if disposable income were zero is part of exogenous consumption. The funds to purchase consumption goods might come from savings accounts, borrowed funds, or private charity. When people spend more than their disposable income, we say they are **dissaving.**

To elaborate somewhat, when consumers anticipate inflation, they will spend now to "beat" the price increases. This was the case in the late 1970s and early 1980s. Later, in 1982–83, consumption became "sluggish" because inflation expectations slacked off as a result of the relatively low inflation rates and falling prices.[1] Suppose your job prospects are especially bright and you expect to be promoted soon. You are likely to increase the amount you consume out of your current income. This is equivalent to an exogenous increase in your consumption function. Tastes can also affect exogenous consumption by influencing the amount of expenditure an individual or household views as "necessary" for basic subsistence. Comparing two individuals whose incomes temporarily fall to zero, one of them might be more willing to draw down savings or to borrow from friends or relatives to maintain a given standard of living than the other one. The first individual would have a higher level of exogenous consumption (value of A) than the second.

Endogenous consumption depends on GNP and variables, such as disposable income, that change when GNP changes. In the simple example in table 4.1, taxes do not change with people's incomes. Therefore, disposable income changes only when GNP changes. (We will treat taxes more realistically later on, after we establish the basic nature of the consumption function and how it relates to the aggregate goods market.) Notice that whenever GNP and disposable income change, we have assumed that endogenous consumption changes by a constant 60 percent as much. To formulate the consumption function in terms of an equation, we will use the symbol b to indicate the amount by which endogenous consumption changes whenever GNP or disposable income change by a given amount. As we show in table

*The **marginal propensity to consume (MPC)** is the additional aggregate consumption spending that occurs out of each additional dollar of disposable income; MPC is a fraction (b) between 0 and 1.*

*The **45° line** exactly divides the right angle created by the two axes of the consumption function graph. Along this line, whatever expenditure components are measured along the vertical axis exactly equal GNP, which is measured along the horizontal axis.*

4.1, this fraction, b, is known as the **marginal propensity to consume (MPC).** It tells us the *change* in consumption when consumers receive an *additional* dollar of disposable income. (Remember that with net taxes fixed, disposable income changes by exactly the same amount that GNP changes.) We will use the symbol Δ to denote a *change* in consumption and a *change* in income. Thus, b, the marginal propensity to consume, can be denoted as $\Delta \overset{*}{C}/\Delta Y$. The asterisk (*) indicates that we are referring to *planned* consumption. In table 4.1, the marginal propensity to consume equals 0.6.

We can summarize everything we have said about consumption and the consumption function with the following simple expression for the consumption function:

$$\overset{*}{C} = A + bY,$$

where b ≡ MPC = 0.6 in our example and A = $10 billion. To see how this formula for the consumption function works, simply plug in some of the numbers from table 4.1. When GNP is only $25 billion, endogenous consumption equals 0.6 x $25 billion, or $15 billion, so total consumption equals $10 billion plus $15 billion, or $25 billion, as shown in the total consumption column of table 4.1. Verify for yourself that when GNP equals $100 billion, total consumption equals $70 billion, according both to the equation above and table 4.1.

The Consumption Function Expressed Graphically

Figure 4.2 illustrates the consumption function graphically. The horizontal axis is gross national product (households' total income), which is measured in billions of real dollars. The vertical axis is planned consumption and net taxes, also measured in billions of real dollars. One way to think of the consumption function is as a computer program. This program first takes aggregate income before net taxes (real GNP), then calculates the net taxes consumers must pay, and thus also calculates their disposable income (YD). The program then considers consumers' tastes and preferences and determines an amount they desire to spend on goods and services. It is the first

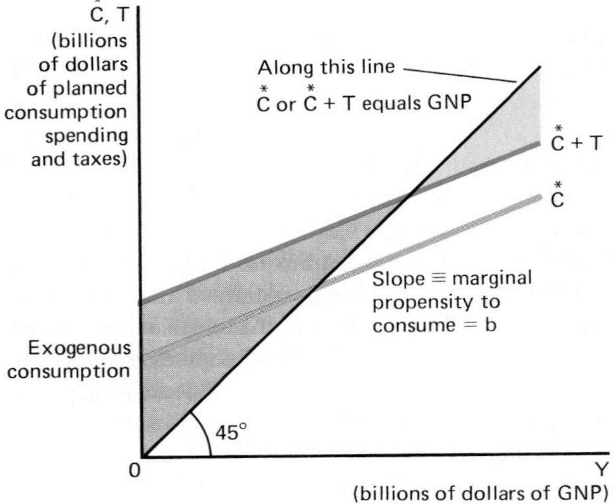

Figure 4.2 The consumption function
The consumption function illustrates how real income (GNP) influences society's consumption spending. The slope of the consumption function is the marginal propensity to consume (b). The point where the consumption function crosses the vertical axis measures the quantity of exogenous consumption.
The upper line, marked $\overset{*}{C} + T$, represents planned consumption plus taxes. Where the $\overset{*}{C} + T$ line crosses the 45° line, planned consumption plus taxes equals GNP. In other words, at this point, planned saving is zero. To the right of this point, planned saving is positive, and to the left, planned saving is negative (there is planned dissaving).

and last statements in this computer program that we see in the line marked $\overset{*}{C}$ in figure 4.2. The upper line in the figure measures planned consumption plus net taxes that people are required to pay out of the income they receive. It is labeled $\overset{*}{C} + T$. We will discuss this line later.

There is a special line in figure 4.2 that is the same distance from the horizontal axis as from the vertical axis. Because it runs through the middle of the right (90°) angle created by the horizontal axis and the vertical axis, this line is known as the **45° line.** At all points along the 45° line, the variables measured along the vertical axis are *exactly* equal to real GNP. How does the consumption function ($\overset{*}{C}$) relate to the two axis and the 45° line?

Figure 4.2 illustrates that the consumption function has two components. The first component, the marginal propensity to consume, is represented in the diagram by the slope of the line labeled $\overset{*}{C}$. We have already seen that the marginal propensity to consume is the fraction b, the change in planned consumption for every dollar change in disposable income. The fact that the $\overset{*}{C}$ line is flatter than the 45° line reminds us that consumers do not plan to spend all of each additional dollar of disposable income on consumption goods. Some of it they plan to save. In other words, while b is greater than 0, it is less than 1. The second component of the consumption function is exogenous consumption. In figure 4.2, exogenous consumption is measured as the amount consumed when GNP equals zero. (In table 4.1, consumption would equal $10 billion, even if GNP dropped to zero.) It is measured by the height of the consumption function where it crosses the vertical axis, because at this point, GNP equals zero.

Given that exogenous consumption is positive, while the slope of the consumption function is less than the slope of the 45° line, the consumption function *must* cross the 45° line at some point. At this point, planned consumption (measured along the vertical axis) is exactly equal to GNP (measured along the horizontal axis of figure 21.2). In table 4.1 this point occurs at GNP equal to $25 billion.

Now we can explain why the line labeled $\overset{*}{C} + T$ is also shown in figure 4.2. From what we have said already, it should be clear that where the $\overset{*}{C} + T$ line crosses the 45° line, planned consumption *plus net taxes* equals GNP. It will help to say the same thing algebraically, as follows: the point at which the $\overset{*}{C} + T$ line crosses the 45° line can be expressed as

$$Y = \overset{*}{C} + T.$$

However, we have already seen that saving is defined as the portion of households' disposable incomes that is not consumed. In other words, planned saving is GNP minus net taxes minus planned consumption, or

$$\overset{*}{S} \equiv Y - T - \overset{*}{C}.$$

Therefore, when planned consumption plus net taxes equals GNP, planned saving must be zero. In table 4.1, this occurs at GNP equal to $75 billion. You can see this algebraically if you substitute the first equation in this paragraph for Y in the second expression. In figure 4.2, the shaded area to the right of the intersection of the $\overset{*}{C} + T$ line indicates that planned saving is positive and grows larger as GNP increases. The shaded area to the left of this point indicates planned dissaving (negative saving).

Figure 4.2 is a basic representation of aggregate consumption that *models* the observed behavior of United States consumers. Figure 4.3, by comparison, plots out *actual data* on aggregate consumption and disposable (after net tax) income for 1929 to 1985. Notice the similarity with figure 4.1. In 1933, when aggregate disposable income was quite low, people were dissaving. More recently people have been saving about 9 percent of their aggregate disposable income. For example, in 1981 real aggregate disposable income was $1.04 trillion and real aggregate consumption expenditure was about $948 billion. On a *per capita* basis, real disposable income in 1981 was about $4,538 (measured in 1972 prices) and real consumption expenditure was about $4,123 (also measured in 1972 prices).[2] If you were to calculate the marginal propensity to consume in recent years from the slope of the consumption function in figure 4.2, you would see that consumers actually spent about 80 to 90 percent of an additional dollar of income after net taxes.

Investment

In chapter 2 we saw that investment includes spending by firms for their buildings, equipment, and inventories. As we discuss the role played by investment in aggregate expenditure, it is important to keep a number of things in mind. First, investment has both planned and unplanned components. Firms "draw down" on their inventories when their sales exceed what they had anticipated. They build up their inventories unexpectedly when sales fall short. Second, purchases of plant and equipment may be the result of either capacity expansion or the need to replace equipment because of wear and tear from past usage. The most important point, however, is that current investment is largely *independent* of firms' *current* sales. Let us explain this more fully and identify the economic variables that have the greatest impact on aggregate investment.

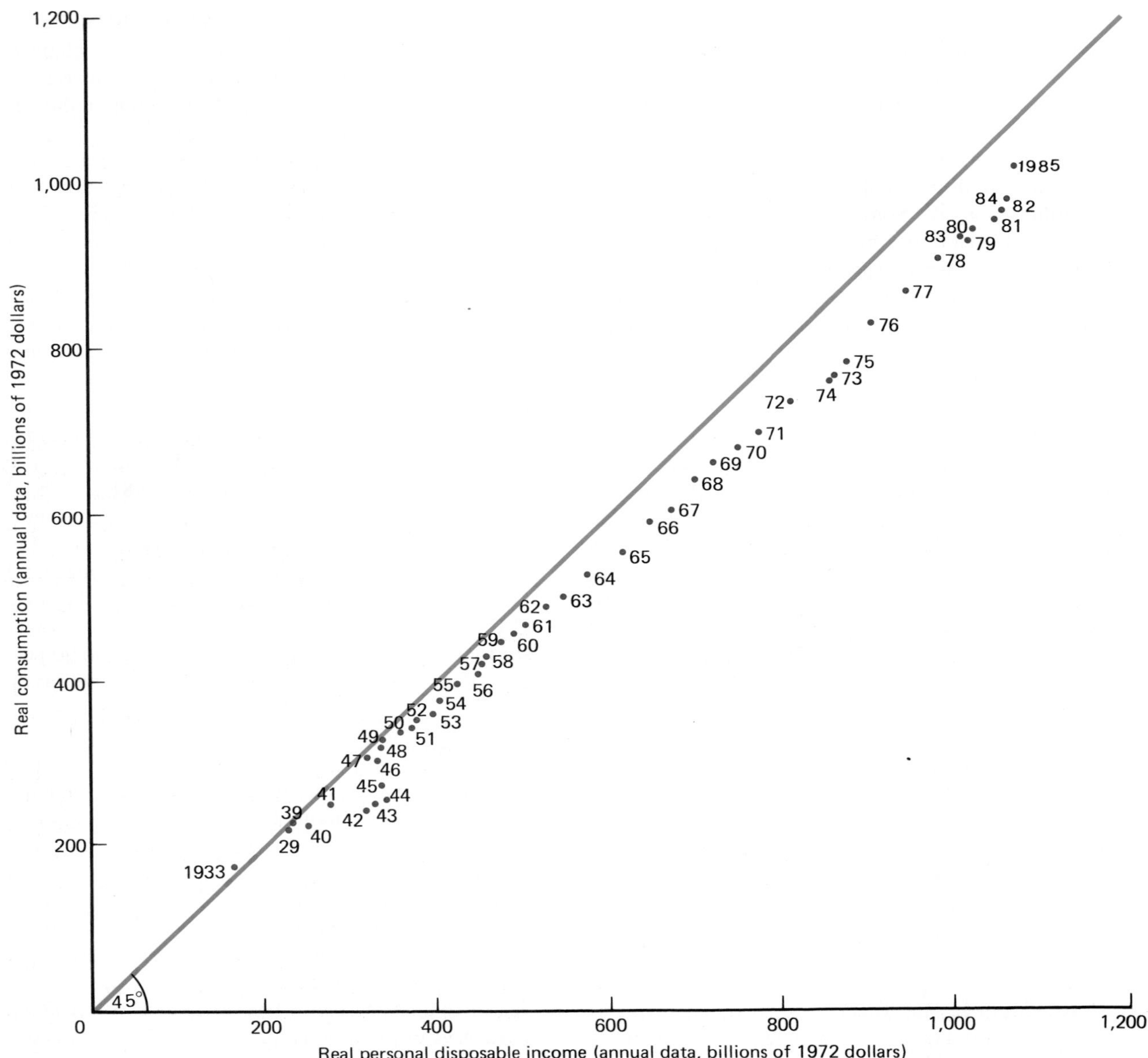

Figure 4.3 Aggregate consumption and disposable income in the United States, 1929–1985
From *Economic Report of the President,* 1983, Table B-24 and 1986, Table B-26, p. 283.

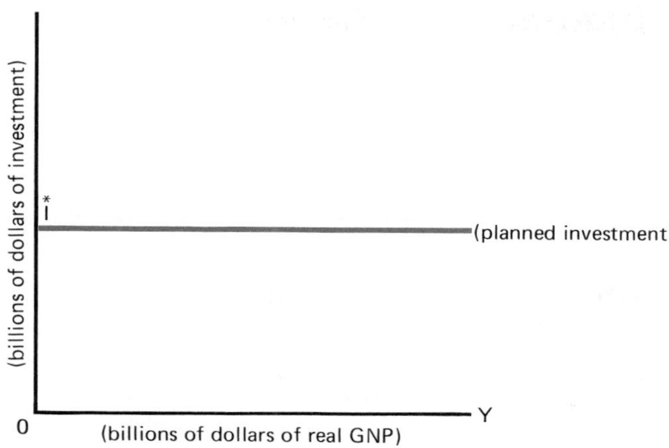

Figure 4.4 Planned investment
Investment largely depends upon (1) the interest rate at which firms borrow to finance growth of their productive capacity, (2) expectations of future output growth, and (3) past levels of production. Thus, intended investment tends to be unaffected by short-term changes in production (real GNP). $\overset{*}{I}$ represents the level of investment that firms plan to make during the current period.

The interest rate is very important in determining firms' investment decisions. High interest rates make it expensive to borrow funds for investment. Sometimes, however, the investor does not have to borrow funds. In this case, the investor uses his or her own funds to purchase investment goods. However, these funds could have been lent to others at the prevailing interest rate. This means that an opportunity cost is incurred—the interest that could have been earned on the money that financed the investment. Thus, it really does not matter whether a firm has to borrow from a lending institution such as a bank or borrow implicitly from itself. In either case, there is an interest cost of investing, and that cost rises with the interest rate. This means that the "backend" of investment—the future payoff—becomes less profitable. Thus, investment will be lower the higher the cost of credit (the interest rate). Conversely, lower interest rates encourage greater investment.

The profitability of investment is also related to the rules for taxing the return on an investment. Examples are depreciation allowances and tax rates on capital gains. The goal of the Economic Recovery Tax Act of 1981 (ERTA) is to make investment more profitable in general and especially more profitable in specific areas such as research and development. The hope is that by encouraging investment, ERTA will promote increased production (economic growth).[3]

Another factor to consider is that investment takes time and pays off in the future. As a result, today's investment is heavily influenced by a firm's anticipations of what sales are likely to be over a period of years. Thus, many economists would say that expected *future* growth in production, not current production, plays the major role in determining new investment.

Finally, we know that a part of current investment is the replacement of worn-out buildings and machinery. In fact, one-half to three-fourths of total investment in recent years falls into the category of replacement or depreciation. Thus, a good deal of current investment depends upon how rapidly machines and other equipment become obsolete and how they were used *in the past*. This means that *past* production, but not necessarily current production, also plays an important role in determining current *investment*.

One of the main implications of this section is that it is appropriate to treat planned investment as independent of *current* production (real GNP). Intended investment can be shown as the horizontal line labeled $\overset{*}{I}$ in figure 4.4. The fact that the line representing intended investment is horizontal means that aggregate investment does not change if current output (real GNP) changes.

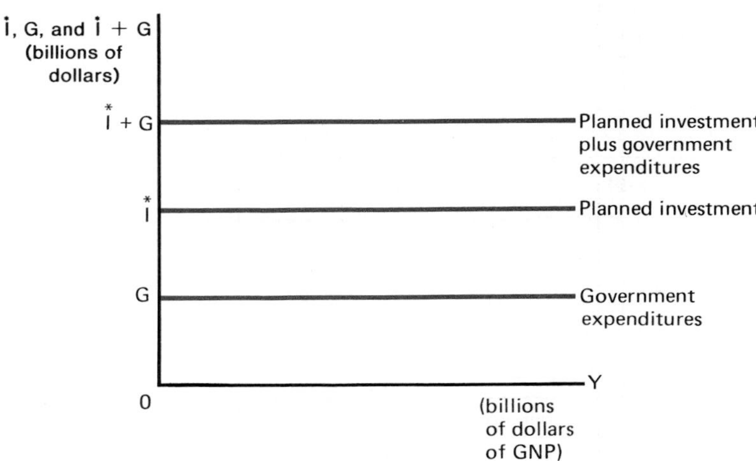

Figure 4.5 Planned aggregate investment and government spending Planned aggregate investment and government expenditures are each largely independent of current real GNP. Thus, they can be represented by the horizontal lines $\overset{*}{I}$ and G, respectively. We can designate their sum by the horizontal line that hits the vertical axis at the height $\overset{*}{I}$ + G.

To summarize, planned investment depends on such factors as taxation policy, the rate of interest, past production, and expected future production. Investment should be viewed as *exogenous* with respect to current real GNP, just as part of consumption expenditure is. This does *not* mean investment never changes. If, for example, the interest rate were to fall, then intended investment would change from $\overset{*}{I}$ in figure 4.4 to some higher level, say, $\overset{*}{I}'$. If the government reduced taxes on business profits, or if investors expected future sales to grow sharply, then planned investment would also be likely to increase.

Government Spending and Net Exports

We will only briefly discuss the two remaining components of aggregate expenditure, government spending on goods and services and net exports. These topics are treated at greater length in other chapters.

In completing our model of aggregate expenditure on goods and services, we will assume for now that the trade sector of the aggregate economy is "in balance" so that imports equal exports, or net exports (X) equal zero. Government spending on goods and services, like investment, will be treated as exogenous, or independent, of real GNP. (By government spending we refer only to spending on goods and services. Government also spends on transfer payments, but this form of government expenditure is already accounted for by our calculation of net taxes.) We will assume that government spending is for the most part determined by past budget decisions that are updated relatively slowly.

Government spending is shown by the horizontal line in figure 4.5. This figure also shows us that it is easy to illustrate the sum of planned investment plus government spending. The line labeled $\overset{*}{I}$ + G indicates aggregate investment plus government spending. The technique of adding components of aggregate demand will soon prove useful. It is important to reemphasize that while planned investment, government spending, and their sum are exogenous (not dependent on the current level of GNP) in figure 4.5, this does not mean that they never change. For example, governments can and do change the level of their expenditures on public works, such as highway construction and new buildings.

Planned aggregate expenditure ($\overset{*}{E}$) is the sum of aggregate planned consumption by households ($\overset{*}{C}$), investment planned by firms ($\overset{*}{I}$), and government spending (G)—as well as net exports (X), assumed to equal 0 in this chapter.

***Equilibrium real GNP** occurs when the aggregate real quantity of goods and services produced exactly equals planned aggregate expenditure.*

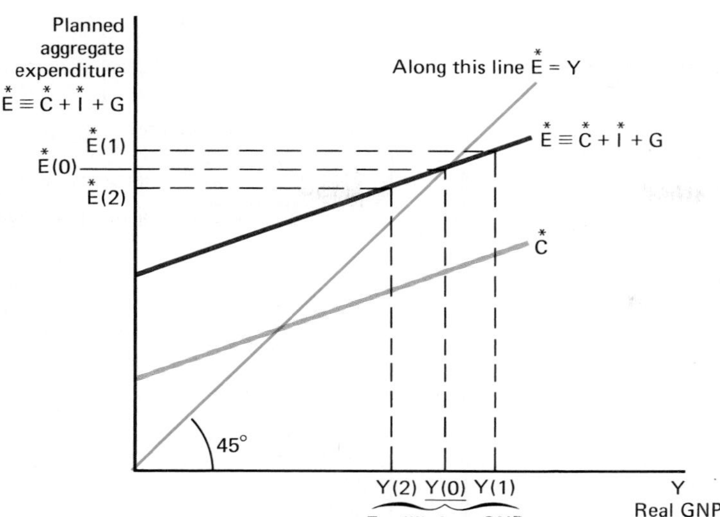

Figure 4.6 Equilibrium real gross national product
$\overset{*}{E}$ represents planned aggregate expenditure, $\overset{*}{C} + \overset{*}{I} + G$. The point at which $\overset{*}{E}$ crosses the 45° line shows where planned aggregate expenditure equals GNP. Since producers are able to sell all they produce at this level of GNP and consumers, investors, and the government can purchase all the goods and services they desire, Y(0) represents equilibrium GNP, which is equal to $\overset{*}{E}(0)$, planned aggregate expenditure on GNP.

If GNP produced equals Y(1), then planned aggregate expenditure, $\overset{*}{E}(1)$, will be less than Y(1), and firms will have to reduce their production. If GNP produced equals Y(2), then planned aggregate expenditure, $\overset{*}{E}(2)$, will be more than Y(2), and firms will increase their production.

Aggregate Expenditure, Aggregate Production, and Equilibrium GNP

Planned aggregate expenditure ($\overset{*}{E}$) is simply the sum of planned expenditures by firms, households, and the government. It is defined as planned consumption plus planned investment plus government spending, or

$$\overset{*}{E} \equiv \overset{*}{C} + \overset{*}{I} + G.$$

At this point you may be asking yourself why there is no asterisk (*) over G. Remember that firms' or consumers' planned behavior may not be realized, so that firms, for example, may end up investing more or less than intended. However, we are assuming that the government always spends what it planned to spend, so that actual and desired spending typically coincide. Thus, there is no need to put an asterisk over G.

Planned aggregate expenditure, $\overset{*}{E}$, can be depicted in a graph that starts out with the basic consumption function illustrated in figure 4.2 and then adding to it planned investment and government expenditure, as illustrated in figure 4.5. Since figure 4.5 shows that planned investment plus government expenditure does not vary with GNP, the shape of the aggregate expenditure line, $\overset{*}{E}$, in figure 4.6 is exactly the same as the consumption function. However, the $\overset{*}{E}$ line lies above $\overset{*}{C}$ by the amount of $\overset{*}{I} + G$. Remember that the 45° line plots out all the points where whatever is measured along the vertical axis equals what is measured along the horizontal axis. Therefore, at the point where the planned aggregate expenditure line, $\overset{*}{E}$, crosses the 45° line, $\overset{*}{E} = \text{GNP}$. This means that at the level of GNP at which planned aggregate expenditure crosses the 45° line, firms sell exactly the quantity of goods and services (GNP) that they have produced, and all consumers, investors, and the government are able to carry out their expenditure plans. In short, Y(0) is called **equilibrium real GNP** because firms sell all they had planned to sell and buyers' plans also are exactly realized. $\overset{*}{E}(0)$, which is equal to Y(0), represents equilibrium planned expenditure.

The common sense of this is that if firms decide to produce one dollar more than Y(0), the additional income generated will lead to *less* than an additional dollar of planned expenditure. This is because planned consumption rises by less than $1 for each $1 increase in disposable income. Planned saving also increases, but there is no direct effect of the increased planned saving on planned investment or government spending. Therefore, planned expenditure rises only as much as planned consumption increases. If firms decide to produce one dollar less than Y(0), the reduction in income received by households will induce them to reduce their planned consumption spending by *less* than one dollar. Planned saving also falls, but planned investment and government spending do not respond directly to reduced planned saving.

Of all production levels firms might choose, only one, which we have called Y(0), exactly matches the total quantity of goods and services that households, firms, and the government want to buy. If the decisions of firms lead them to produce at Y(0), then the quantity they produce will just match aggregate expenditure. This is illustrated numerically in figure 4.7, which is nothing more than a review of the circular flow of GNP we first illustrated in chapter 2. Figure 4.7 shows how the situation depicted in figure 4.1 would turn out to be one of equilibrium in the aggregate market for goods and services. The level of planned consumption generated by aggregate real income of $200 billion equals $130 billion. Government expenditure on goods and services exactly equals net taxes ($20 billion). Therefore, if planned investment happens to equal $50 billion, then planned expenditure will be $200 billion, exactly the amount of GNP produced.

Returning to figure 4.6, suppose that firms choose to produce a level of real GNP, call it Y(1), that is greater than planned aggregate expenditure. This leads to a situation where firms cannot sell all they have produced and therefore cut back on their production. Real GNP falls, and some workers will lose their jobs.

The story is reversed if firms' decisions lead them to produce at a real GNP level that is less than planned aggregate expenditure, call it Y(2). In this case, society demands more goods and services than firms have produced. Production and/or prices will increase as buyers bid for the items they desire and firms try to meet sales that exceed their projections.

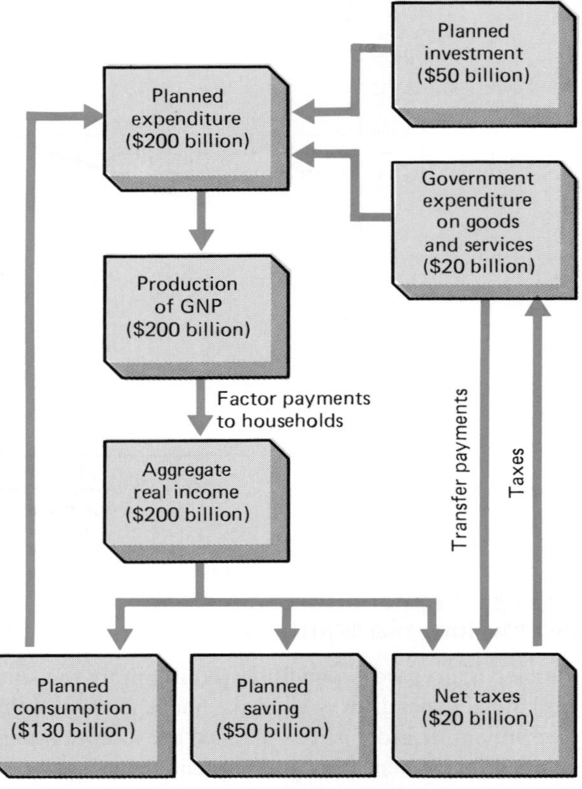

Figure 4.7 A numerical example of equilibrium GNP
With net expenditures, taxes equal to government GNP = $200 billion will be an equilibrium level of GNP if planned investment happens to equal $50 billion. Only then will planned aggregate expenditure, $\hat{E}$, exactly equal $200, the amount of GNP produced.

In summary, given planned investment, government expenditure, net taxes, and the consumption function, there is only *one* level of real GNP that is an equilibrium. At equilibrium real GNP, firms sell what they had planned and buyers purchase exactly what they had planned. The aggregate market for goods and services is at a point of rest, so to speak. Equilibrium means that GNP will not change unless there is a change in one of the exogenous factors underlying planned aggregate expenditure. Should any of these factors change, planned investment for instance, so will equilibrium GNP. In chapter 8 we dis-

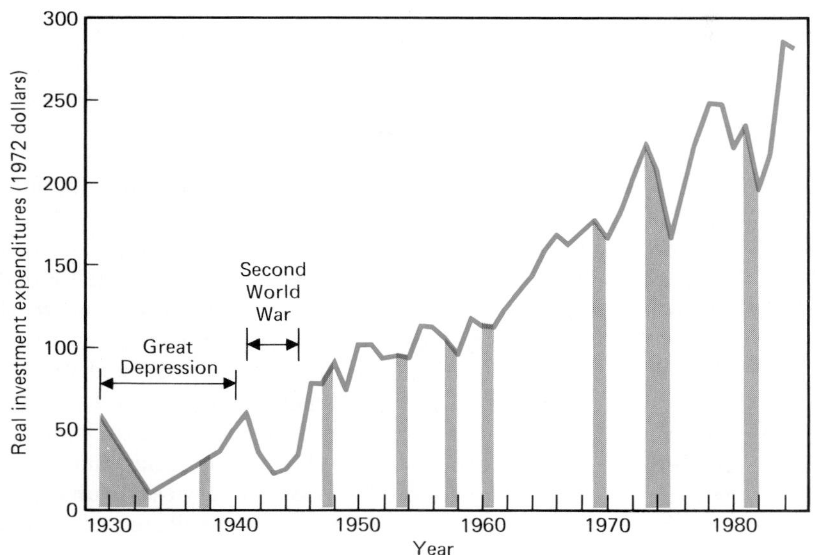

Figure 4.8 Swings in investment and business cycles in the United States, 1929–1985
From *Economic Report of the President,* 1986, Table B-16, p. 271.

cuss changes in investment and how they affect the macroeconomy, and in chapter 11 we look carefully at the role of investment spending during the Great Depression. For now let us give you some startling facts. Between 1929 and 1933 real aggregate investment (in 1972 dollars) fell from \$55.8 billion to \$8.4 billion, a decline of 85 percent. Not until 1941 did real investment again reach its 1929 levels. This severe reduction in investment between 1929 and 1933 contributed to the decline in aggregate expenditure that led to the period of substantial idle productive capacity and unemployment known as the Great Depression. The large swings in investment and their association with business cycles in the United States is illustrated in figure 4.8

Another Look at Equilibrium GNP: Saving, Investment, and the Government Deficit

In developing a full view of macroeconomic equilibrium, it will be very helpful to look at equilibrium in the aggregate market for goods and services from another perspective. In this view, the cornerstone of our analysis remains the relationship between the production of GNP and aggregate income. To review briefly, remember that there are three ways for this income to be used: planned consumption, planned saving, and net tax payments. Remember, too, that planned aggregate expenditure has three components: consumption, investment, and government spending. Finally, remember that in equilibrium, planned production equals planned expenditure on GNP. This means that in equilibrium, planned spending on goods and services in the aggregate ($\overset{*}{E}$) is equal to the income people receive from producing these goods and services, which we have labeled Y(0).

As we have seen, planned aggregate expenditure is defined as planned consumption plus planned investment plus government expenditure, or

$$\overset{*}{E} \equiv \overset{*}{C} + \overset{*}{I} + G.$$

Similarly, income can be broken down into its three components of planned consumption, planned saving, and net taxes paid so that

$$Y \equiv \overset{*}{C} + \overset{*}{S} + T.$$

(We do not use the asterisk (*) over the Y, because we assume that producers always carry out their production plans exactly.) When there is equilibrium GNP, production equals planned aggregate expenditure, or

$$\overset{*}{E} = Y(0).$$

This is the same as saying that planned consumption plus planned investment plus government expenditure equals planned consumption plus planned saving plus net taxes, or

$$\overset{*}{C} + \overset{*}{I} + G = \overset{*}{C} + \overset{*}{S} + T.$$

Note that we have used the equality sign (=) in the preceding two expressions. This is because planned production and planned expenditure are *not* the same variable. They are *equal* to each other *only* when the aggregate market for goods and services is in equilibrium.

We can gain further insight into equilibrium GNP by noting that planned consumption ($\overset{*}{C}$) appears on both sides of the equation. Thus, we can subtract it from both sides. If we also subtract net taxes (T) from both sides, we see that in equilibrium, planned saving must equal planned investment plus the difference between government spending and net taxes, or

$$\overset{*}{I} + (G - T) = \overset{*}{S}.$$

If government spending (G) exceeds net taxes (T), then G − T is positive, and we say there is a *government deficit*. If the opposite holds true, then there is a *government surplus. We conclude that equilibrium GNP can be described as the level of GNP where investment plus the government deficit equals society's intended saving.*

Now, to clinch your understanding of this important relationship between planned investment, the government deficit, and planned saving, go back and review figure 4.7. There we have assumed that the government's budget is balanced, so that G − T = 0. Consequently, equilibrium in the aggregate market for goods and services requires that planned investment equal planned saving. In figure 4.7, planned investment and planned saving are both $50 billion, and equilibrium prevails.

Another way to think about the relationship between planned saving, planned investment, the government deficit, and equilibrium GNP is this. When people save or pay taxes, they are withdrawing funds from the flow of GNP-income-consumption-GNP that is illustrated in figure 4.7. Sometimes, saving and taxes are therefore called "leakages" from the flow of income and expenditure described in our model of the goods and services market. On the other hand, the government and investors "inject" funds back into income-expenditure flow. Therefore, equilibrium in the aggregate market for goods and services requires that "injections" into the flow of expenditure and income equal "leakages" out of the flow. In this terminology, net taxes constitute a leakage, too, whereas government expenditure is an injection. Another comparison that may help you understand equilibrium GNP is to think of it as similar to the level of water in a lake. If the water level does not rise or fall, we can say that the lake is in equilibrium. But what does this require? An equilibrium lake level results when the amount of water flowing in (injections) is exactly equal to the amount that flows (leaks) out or evaporates.

It should be clear that if the level of government spending or planned investment were to change, the situation depicted in figure 4.7 would no longer be one of equilibrium. That is, if either government expenditure or planned investment were to increase, the equilibrium level of GNP would no longer be $200 billion because planned expenditure would exceed that amount. Similarly, if either planned investment or government spending were to fall, firms would be unable to sell all their output if they produced GNP worth $200 billion. In both these situations, the equilibrium level of GNP would change. In the next section we will see exactly how equilibrium GNP relates to the level of planned investment and government expenditure. This relationship is called the *multiplier,* for reasons that you will soon understand.

*The **marginal propensity to save (MPS)** is the extra aggregate saving that occurs out of each additional dollar of disposable income; MPS ≡ 1 − MPC = 1 − b and is therefore a fraction between 0 and 1.*

*The **multiplier** (also called the **exogenous expenditure multiplier**) is the ratio 1/(1 − b), where b is the marginal propensity to consume, which shows how changes in exogenous expenditure (planned investment, government spending, or exogenous consumption) are related to changes in equilibrium GNP.*

The Multiplier To begin, we will work through a simple numerical example showing just how much equilibrium GNP would change if planned investment or government spending were to change in figure 4.7. For instance, suppose planned investment increases *permanently* by $10 billion per year, to $60 billion. This will upset the equilibrium flow of income, consumption, investment, government spending, and taxes. Planned investment plus the government deficit will now exceed planned saving by exactly $10 billion, and there will be excess planned expenditure. GNP will begin to rise. Increased GNP leads to increased disposable income and, hence, an increase in planned consumption expenditure. When more consumption goods are produced, a further increase in GNP and disposable income results, leading to a further, somewhat smaller increase in planned consumption expenditure. This chain of increased consumption expenditure, increased income, and further increased planned consumption continues until the goods market is once again in equilibrium. (Can you explain why each subsequent increase in planned consumption is smaller than the last?) Equilibrium will be restored only when planned saving is once again equal to planned investment plus the government deficit. An increase in GNP can eventually restore equilibrium because planned saving rises as GNP increases. The aggregate market for goods and services will return to equilibrium when planned saving has risen by exactly $10 billion, which was the initial increase in planned investment.

We can calculate exactly the amount GNP must increase before planned saving increases by $10 billion by referring back to table 4.1 on page 94. In table 4.1, we see that for every dollar increase in GNP, planned saving increases by $0.40. This relationship between changes in planned saving and changes in GNP is called the **marginal propensity to save (MPS)**. Because an increase in disposable income must be either saved or consumed, the marginal propensity to save is nothing more than one minus the marginal propensity to consume (the fraction b). Symbolically,

$$MPS \equiv 1 - MPC = 1 - b.$$

Using our knowledge that the marginal propensity to consume in the numerical example in table 4.1 is 0.6, we see that the marginal propensity to save is 0.4. Thus, planned saving will rise by $10 billion when GNP increases by $25 billion ($25 billion x 0.4 = $10 billion). Only at this new equilibrium level of GNP will leakages from the circular income-expenditure flow once again equal injections.

Notice that the increase in GNP needed to restore equilibrium in the aggregate market for goods and services is much larger than the initial increase in planned investment. It is, in fact, 2.5 times as large. The change in GNP divided by the initial change in planned investment equals 2.5. This ratio is **the multiplier** we mentioned at the end of the preceding section. A little simple arithmetic will show you that *the multiplier equals the reciprocal of the marginal propensity to save, or 1/MPS*. Symbolically, in terms of our example,

$$\text{the multiplier} \equiv \Delta Y(0)/\Delta I = 1/MPS = 2.5.$$

The multiplier relationship is also useful for analyzing the influence of government policy on planned expenditure. For example, if government expenditure in figure 4.7 rose by $10 billion, *cet. par.* equilibrium GNP would increase to $225 billion. This effect of an increase in government expenditure on equilibrium GNP is exactly the same as the effect of a $10 billion increase in planned investment in the preceding example. Can you explain why? What do you think would happen if the increase in GNP required to restore equilibrium were greater than the economy's productive capacity? Can you explain what would happen to equilibrium GNP if planned investment or government expenditure were to *decline* by $10 billion?

Interestingly, a reduction in net taxes will also raise planned expenditure, but by a somewhat smaller amount than an equal increase in government expenditure. For example, suppose that in figure 4.7, net taxes fall by $10 billion with government expenditure unchanged. This means that the government deficit (G − T) rises by $10 billion, and planned investment plus the deficit will now exceed planned saving by $10

*The **saving function** is a schedule, or equation, indicating how much society plans to save at various possible levels of real income.*

billion. The aggregate goods and services market will no longer be in equilibrium, and equilibrium will be restored only when planned saving increases by $10 billion.

The difference between the multiplier effect of a $10 billion increase in government expenditure and a $10 billion decrease in taxes lies in their initial impact on total expenditure and saving. Whereas the increase in government expenditure has no *direct* impact on saving and increases total expenditure on GNP by $10 billion, the reduction in taxes has two *direct* impacts. One is to increase exogenous consumption by $10 billion multiplied by the MPC (0.6), and the other is directly to increase planned saving by $10 billion multiplied by the MPS (0.4).

Now, we know that planned saving must increase by $10 billion before equilibrium GNP is restored. Since the direct impact of a tax reduction is to increase planned saving by $4 billion, GNP need increase only by enough to get planned saving the rest of the way to $10 billion. How much does GNP have to increase to raise planned saving an additional $6 billion? The marginal propensity to save tells all. If GNP increases by $15 billion, planned saving will increase by $15 billion x 0.4, or $6 billion. Prove to yourself that this is correct. Notice that $15 billion equals $25 billion (the increase in equilibrium GNP when either government expenditure or planned investment increases by $10 billion) multiplied by 0.6—the marginal propensity to consume! In other words, the multiplier effect of a *reduction* in taxes is

$$-(\Delta Y(0)/\Delta T) = b/MPS.$$

(Remember that ΔT is a *negative* quantity when taxes are *reduced*.) Since the marginal propensity to consume, b, is less than 1, this tax multiplier is smaller than the multiplier effect of an increase in government expenditure or planned investment. What will happen to equilibrium GNP if government transfer payments increase by $10 billion?

A Final Look at Equilibrium GNP We can now take a brief, final look at equilibrium GNP that will graphically illustrate what equilibrium looks like in terms of planned saving, planned investment, and the government deficit. To begin, we need to show more formally how planned saving is related to GNP. The relationship between planned saving and GNP is called the **saving function,** and it is a kind of mirror image of the consumption function.

To derive the saving function, review table 4.1 on page 94 once again. Notice, for example, that when GNP rises from $100 billion to $120 billion, planned saving rises from $10 billion to $18 billion, or by $8 billion. If GNP were to fall from $100 billion to $25 billion, planned saving would fall from $10 billion to −$20 billion. In other words, at this very low level of GNP, there would be *dissaving*. Notice that the change in planned saving divided by the change in GNP is always $\Delta S/\Delta Y \equiv MPS = 0.4$. This logic shows us that if GNP were to fall to zero from $25 billion, planned saving would drop even further, by $25 billion x 0.4, or $10 billion, to −$30 billion. In other words, there would be dissaving of $30 billion. (Of course, GNP never actually falls to zero. The saving function tells us, mathematically, what planned saving would be under these imaginary circumstances.) We have already seen that if GNP were to fall to zero, planned consumption would remain positive. We called this *exogenous consumption* and denoted it by the symbol A. Similarly, when GNP equals zero, the quantity of planned saving is called *exogenous saving*. In the example in table 4.1, exogenous saving is negative. This follows from the fact that exogenous consumption is positive and consumption equals disposable income less saving. The saving function tells us that planned saving equals exogenous saving plus endogenous saving, just as the consumption function tells us that planned consumption equals exogenous consumption plus endogenous consumption. Symbolically, we can write the saving function as

$$\overset{*}{S} = -A' + (1 - b)Y,$$

where $-A'$ stands for exogenous saving (which is negative) and $(1 - b)Y$ is endogenous saving, or the marginal propensity to save multiplied by GNP. In terms of the table 4.1 example, $-A' = -\$30$ billion and $1 - b = 0.4$.

We will now illustrate equilibrium GNP with a diagram that contains the saving function. The horizontal line in figure 4.9 depicts planned investment plus the government deficit, and the upward-sloping line labeled $\overset{*}{S}$ is the saving function. The point at which the saving function intersects the horizontal line that represents planned investment plus the government deficit marks equilibrium GNP.

What happens when planned saving exceeds planned investment plus the deficit? This is equivalent to an excess of production over planned aggregate expenditure. To see this, we need simply restate the relationship between planned expenditure and production when production is greater than planned expenditure:

$$Y > \overset{*}{E},$$

or,

$$\overset{*}{C} + \overset{*}{S} + T > \overset{*}{C} + \overset{*}{I} + G.$$

When production rises above planned expenditure, we see that planned consumption plus planned saving plus net taxes will exceed the sum of planned consumption, planned investment, and government spending. This boils down to planned saving exceeding planned investment plus the government deficit, or

$$\overset{*}{S} > \overset{*}{I} + (G - T).$$

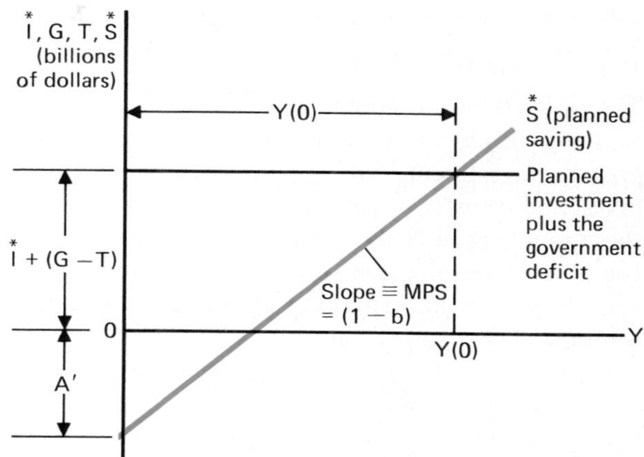

Figure 4.9 Aggregate expenditure in terms of planned saving, planned investment, and the government deficit Equilibrium GNP, Y(0), occurs at the point where the saving function (the planned saving line) crosses the line representing planned investment plus the government deficit.

If planned saving exceeds planned investment plus the government deficit, then production exceeds Y(0), and GNP and employment will fall. If planned saving is less than planned investment plus the government deficit, then production is less than Y(0), and production, employment, and/or the price level will increase.

Using the same analysis, we can see that when planned saving is *less* than planned investment plus the government deficit, we have planned expenditure *greater* than aggregate production, and business firms will be able to sell more than they have produced.

To summarize, when planned saving exceeds planned investment plus the government deficit, then production exceeds Y(0), and GNP and employment will tend to fall because firms will not be able to sell all they have produced. When planned saving is less than planned investment plus the deficit, production will be less than firms can sell, and production, employment, and/or the price level will increase.

The National Income Accounts: Measured Saving, Measured Investment, the Government Deficit, and Measured GNP

The national income accounts published by the United States government contain separate entries for aggregate investment, saving, government spending, taxes, and transfer payments. Can we compare all of these numbers published in the national income accounts to determine the state of equilibrium or disequilibrium in the aggregate market for goods and services? The answer is no.

The reason that the national income accounts do not provide direct information on the state of equilibrium or disequilibrium in the aggregate market for goods and services arises from the way the accounts are constructed. In the GNP accounts, measured saving is *always* equal to measured investment plus the government deficit (and net exports, which we have temporarily ignored in this chapter). In other words, the national income or GNP accounts do not identify the *planned* behavior of business firms and households in our economy. They simply measure the purchases and sales that have actually taken place. A numerical example may be useful.

Consider a fictitious country with national income accounts constructed in the same way as in the United States. This fictitious country has planned aggregate expenditure equal to $125 billion, but aggregate production is only $110 billion. Thus there is excess aggregate expenditure of $15 billion. Let us suppose that this occurs because $\overset{*}{S}$ = $25 billion while $\overset{*}{I}$ = $30 billion and G − T = $10 billion. Despite this excess, we will assume that everyone is successful in carrying out planned purchases because firms carry inventories of goods that were produced in previous years. The national income accounts in our fictitious country will show that *measured* investment equals $15 billion, even though *planned* investment equals $30 billion. The reason is that investment is defined to include both the production of new investment goods *and* the change in the firms' inventories. In our example, producers' inventories will fall by $15 billion because firms sell $125 billion worth of goods and services but produce output worth only $110 billion.

A reduction in inventories is treated as negative investment in the national income accounts. Although *we* know that this inventory reduction is contrary to the intentions of the producers in the economy, the accounts do not make any distinction between planned and actual behavior. The national income accounts in our example will report $30 billion worth of goods sold as investment goods and $15 billion worth of goods subtracted from inventories. In terms of the national income accounts, *measured* investment is $30 billion − $15 billion = $15 billion. This is how measured investment plus the government deficit equals $25 billion, which is also *measured saving.*

Similar situations will occur when planned aggregate expenditure is less than GNP. The difference is that in the case of excess aggregate production, additions to inventories, while unplanned, will be treated as a positive act of investment in the national income accounts. Measured saving will again be precisely equal to measured investment plus the government deficit. To summarize the point of this section, *GNP figures on investment, saving, government deficit (and net exports) tell us nothing about the state of disequilibrium in the aggregate market for goods and services.* These items *always* balance in the national income accounts.

Can you work through an example, using the same level of planned expenditure and production, but assuming that households and firms are *unable* to purchase goods and services in excess of actual production? What would the GNP accounts look like? Whose *measured* behavior (consumption, investment, etc.) would represent actual plans and whose would represent disequilibrium—a deviation of actual from intended expenditures or production?

Summary and Conclusions

This chapter develops the concept of equilibrium in the aggregate market for goods and services. It is not an analysis of the entire macroeconomy; rather, it deals with only *one* of its aggregate markets. Nevertheless, you should now have a clearer picture of the frustration faced by the visiting economic expert in the introduction to this chapter. In order to analyze how the aggregate goods and services market works, accurate data on gross national product and its components are absolutely essential. The following points were discussed.

Consumption is a key component of aggregate expenditure. Consumption is generally less than total income because consumers pay taxes and save.

Equilibrium in the aggregate market for goods and services occurs when planned aggregate expenditure by consumers, firms, and the government coincides with the aggregate quantity of goods and services produced.

When discussing government policy in later chapters it will be convenient to have an alternative way of describing equilibrium aggregate expenditure for goods and services. This is that equilibrium planned aggregate expenditure is the level of aggregate income at which planned saving equals planned investment plus the government deficit.

The equilibrium level of GNP can be expressed as the product of the multiplier and an expression containing the exogenous components of planned expenditure.

When society produces fewer goods and services than consumers, firms, and the government seek to buy, this leads to increases in production, employment, and/or the price level as buyers seek to purchase more goods and services and firms try to meet their demands.

When firms produce more goods and services than society seeks to purchase, this leads to reduced production and employment as firms cut back on their production.

The national income accounts of the United States contain information on actual expenditures and production. They do not contain information that directly tells us what planned expenditure or production was in a year.

Key Terms

consumption function *93*

disposable income (YD) *93*

dissaving *95*

endogenous consumption *93*

equilibrium real GNP *101*

exogenous consumption *93*

45° line *96*

full-employment GNP *92*

marginal propensity to consume (MPC) *96*

marginal propensity to save (MPS) *105*

the multiplier, exogenous expenditure multiplier *105*

planned aggregate expenditure ($\overset{*}{E}$) *101*

saving *92*

saving function *106*

Questions for Discussion and Review

1. What are the components of expenditure?
2. What determines the amount of investment firms make? Is it reasonable to treat investment as independent of *current* output (real GNP)? Through what avenues does government policy influence investment? Is the following statement consistent with our treatment of investment as exogenous:
   Investment depends, in part, on last year's GNP. Explain.
3. Explain the concept of equilibrium real GNP. Describe equilibrium real GNP in a diagram.

4. Suppose that there is a country with
   $\overset{*}{C} = 10 + 0.9(Y - T)$
   $T = 10$
   $\overset{*}{I} = 25$
   $G = 10$
   where the numbers represent billions of dollars. Show that the equilibrium aggregate expenditure on goods and services is $360 billion.
5. Take the data in question 4 and use it to derive a saving function. On the basis of this expression, what is the value for the marginal propensity to save?
6. A hypothetical country's macroeconomy is described by the following information
   $\overset{*}{S} = -10 + 0.1(Y - T)$
   $\overset{*}{I} = 25$
   $T = 10$
   $G = 10$
   Solve for its equilibrium GNP. Show that the aggregate market for goods and services in this economy is *identical* to that in question 4.
7. During the Great Depression saving was thought to be "bad" because it held down aggregate expenditure. Newspaper articles often say that saving is "good" for the macroeconomy. Can it be true that saving is both good *and* bad for the macroeconomy? Discuss.
8. True or false? The macroeconomy is always in equilibrium because the national income accounts show that saving *always* equals investment. Explain your answer carefully.
9. Using the hypothetical model in question 4, solve for the exogenous spending multiplier. What is the tax multiplier equal to in this model?
10. Using the same model as in question 4, let taxes depend on income ($T = tY$ where t is a constant). Now solve for the exogenous spending multiplier. How does this compare with the exogenous spending multiplier in your answer to question 9?

Appendix to Chapter 4

A Deeper Look at the Multiplier and Graphical Analysis

We can develop a deeper understanding of the multiplier by using the equilibrium relationship between planned saving and planned investment plus the government deficit. This will provide additional insight into how changes in planned investment, government spending, or net taxes affect GNP, employment, and unemployment.

First, we will derive the saving function somewhat more rigorously than we did in chapter 4. Recall that saving is defined as what remains after net taxes are paid and planned consumption expenditure is carried out, or

$$\overset{*}{S} \equiv Y - T - \overset{*}{C}.$$

We also need to remember that planned consumption consists of exogenous consumption plus endogenous consumption as described by the consumption function

$$\overset{*}{C} = A + bY.$$

If we substitute the consumption function in the definition of saving above, we can derive the saving function as follows. By substituting the consumption function for $\overset{*}{C}$ in the preceding definition of saving, we obtain

$$\overset{*}{S} = Y - T - A - bY.$$

When we combine the two terms that have Y in them, we obtain the saving function,

$$\overset{*}{S} = -A - T + (1 - b)Y,$$

which says that planned saving depends on GNP, (Y), exogenous consumption multiplied by -1, and net taxes. Remember, in our simple model of the aggregate goods market, taxes are exogenous; that is, taxes do not change with the level of GNP. Because both A (exogenous consumption) and T are independent of the level of GNP, it will simplify things if we combine them into a new term, A′, where

$$A' = A + T,$$

so that the saving function can be written as

$$\overset{*}{S} = -A' + (1 - b)Y,$$

which is the saving function specified in chapter 4.

The next step in our in-depth analysis of the multiplier is to substitute the saving function in the equation for equilibrium GNP, which tells us that in equilibrium, planned saving must equal planned investment plus the government deficit:

$$\underbrace{\bar{I} + (G - T)}_{\text{planned investment plus govt. deficit}} = \underbrace{-A' + (1 - b)Y.}_{\text{planned saving}}$$

We can now show how rewriting the equation for equilibrium GNP leads the way to a deeper understanding of how planned investment and government spending affect equilibrium GNP. We need only solve the above equation for Y. First, we move the one term with Y in it, $(1 - b)Y$, to the left-hand side of the equation, then we place all of the other terms on the right-hand side and multiply both sides of the equation by -1. Then, we divide through by $1 - b$. This gives us the following equation describing equilibrium gross national product:

$$Y = [A' + \bar{I} + (G - T)]/(1 - b).$$

Now, recall that $A' = A + T$. Therefore, the expression above can be further simplified to

$$Y = [A + \bar{I} + G]/(1 - b) = Y(0), \text{ or}$$

$$\text{equilibrium GNP} = \frac{\text{exogenous consumption} + \text{planned investment} + \text{government spending}}{\text{marginal propensity to save}}.$$

To further simplify the above expression for equilibrium GNP, we can use the expression Y (0) to denote equilibrium GNP and EX to stand for all of the *exogenous* variables, G, $\bar{I}$, and A. Then we can rewrite it simply as

$$Y(0) = EX/(1 - b).$$

This equation says that equilibrium GNP depends on two major variables. The first major variable, which we have named EX, includes all of the components of exogenous expenditures on GNP—exogenous consumption, planned investment, and government spending. The second major variable is the marginal propensity to save. More precisely, equilibrium GNP equals EX multiplied by the ratio $1/(1 - b)$, which as we have already seen, is the multiplier.

To make sure that you understand the multiplier equation, we will show how it applies to the numerical example in table 4.1 and figure 4.7. We have claimed that the level of GNP in figure 4.7 is an equilibrium value, because planned saving equals planned investment plus the government deficit. If this is true, then we should be able to show that the level of GNP, \$200 billion, equals EX times the multiplier. From table 4.1 and figure 4.7, we see that exogenous consumption equals \$10 billion and planned investment plus government spending equals \$70 billion, yielding a total value for EX equal to \$80 billion. The MPC equals 0.6, the MPS—(1 − MPC)—equals 0.4, so the multiplier, 1/0.4, equals 2.5. EX × the multiplier is \$80 billion × 2.5 = \$200 billion, which is the level of GNP shown in figure 4.7. Thus, figure 4.7 does represent equilibrium in the aggregate market for goods and services.

There is nothing mysterious about the conclusion that equilibrium GNP depends on exogenous expenditure and the multiplier. It is just an *alternative* way of describing the situation in which society's planned expenditure on goods and services exactly matches aggregate production.

Figure 4.9 also shows how equilibrium GNP relates to exogenous expenditure and the multiplier. To see this, take the following steps. (1) First note that the point at which the saving function cuts the vertical axis lies below the zero line by the amount $A' = A + T$. This is the quantity that appears (with a minus sign in front of it) as the first term of the saving function on p. 107. (2) Now add this quantity to planned investment plus the government deficit. The result is the quantity EX in the multiplier equation. That is, the distance from the point that the saving function intersects the vertical axis up to the horizontal line representing planned investment plus the government deficit equals EX. You may wish to mark the distance EX on your copy of figure 4.9. (3) Next note that the slope of the saving function, which is the MPS, $(1 - b)$, can be expressed as the ratio of the two quantities EX and Y(0). Therefore, the multiplier, $1/(1 - b)$ equals Y(0)/EX. (4) Finally, you can see that the multiplier equation on p. 105 is equivalent to

$$Y(0) = EX \times Y(0)/EX.$$

To show how the multiplier works from a somewhat different perspective, figure 4.A presents a numerical example. The data in this example are somewhat different from those in table 4.1 and figure 4.7. Figure 4.A shows how a *change* in exogenous expenditure, such as an increase in planned investment, affects production *over time* as the economy gradually approaches the new equilibrium level of GNP. When the new equilibrium is finally attained, the change in GNP compared to the original equilibrium GNP equals the change in exogenous expenditure multiplied by the multiplier.

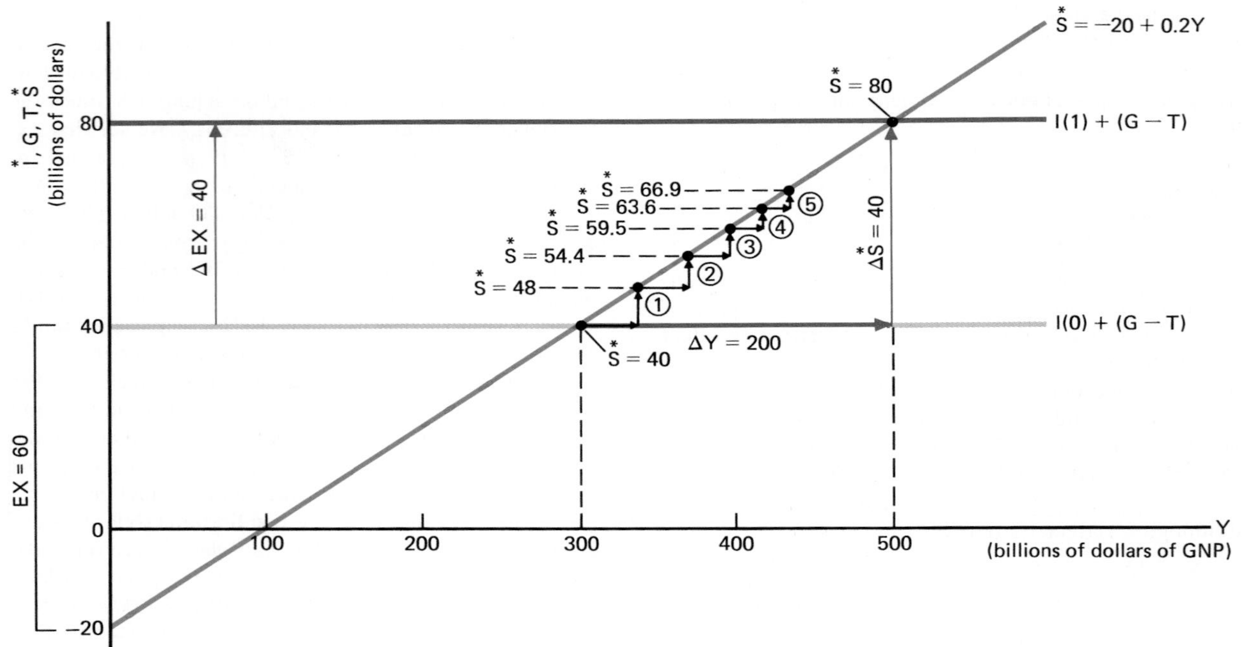

	ΔEX	ΔY	$\Delta \overset{*}{C}$	$\Delta \overset{*}{S}$	$\Delta \overset{*}{E} = \Delta EX + \Delta C$
Start	40	0	0	0	40
1st round	40	40	32	8	72
2nd round	40	72	57.6	14.4	97.6
3rd round	40	97.6	78.1	19.5	118.1
4th round	40	118.1	94.5	23.6	134.5
5th round	40	134.5	107.6	26.9	147.6
6th round	40	147.6	118.1	29.5	158.1
7th round	40	158.1	126.5	31.6	166.5
8th round	40	166.5	133.2	33.3	173.2
9th round	40	173.6	138.6	34.6	178.6
•	•	•	•	•	•
•	•	•	•	•	•
•	•	•	•	•	•
Final round (new equilibrium)	40	200.0	160.0	40.0	200.0

(all changes measured in comparison to their initial equilibrium values)

Figure 4.A The multiplier

In this example, the saving function tells us that planned saving equals −$20 billion plus 0.2 times GNP, or

$$\overset{*}{S} = -20 + 0.2 \text{ GNP}.$$

Planned investment plus the government deficit equals $40 billion. Therefore, the quantity EX equals $40 billion plus $20 billion, or $60 billion. Using the multiplier formula tells us that equilibrium GNP, Y(0), must be $60 × 1/0.2 = $60 × 5 = $300 billion.

Now suppose that a $40 billion increase in planned investment raises the value of EX from $40 billion to $80 billion. The multiplier formula tells us that the resulting *change* in equilibrium GNP will be

$$\Delta Y = \Delta EX \times 5 = \$40 \times 5 = \$200.$$

The new equilibrium GNP will be $500 billion.

It is helpful in understanding how the economy reaches the new level of GNP to think of the changes in planned expenditure as occurring in "rounds" or steps as follows. To start, as shown in the diagram, planned investment expenditure increases by $40 billion, resulting in an increase in planned aggregate expenditure, $\overset{*}{E}$, of the same amount. This increase in exogenous expenditure means that firms could have sold $40 billion more output than they have produced. Thus, in the first round, they increase their production, Y, by $40 billion. Because income has risen by $40 billion, planned saving and consumption now increase. Since the MPS is 0.2, we know that the MPC is 0.8. Therefore, in the first round, there is an increase in planned consumption equal to 0.8 × $40 billion, or $32 billion. There is increased planned saving of 0.2 × $40 billion, or $8 billion. While planned saving has risen to $48 billion, this is still less than the new amount of planned investment plus the government deficit ($80 billion).

Now you should be able to see how consumption expenditure and saving increase in the second and subsequent rounds. Firms had not expected to be able to sell $32 billion additional output, so they have unfilled orders for their output at the end of the first round. Responding to this excess of desired expenditure over production, firms increase production by $32 billion, which leads to $32 billion increased income and, in the second round, a *further* increase of 0.8 × $32 billion = $25.6 billion *more* planned consumption and $6.4 billion *additional* planned saving. Planned saving has now risen by a total of $14.4 billion, to $54.4 billion.

The amount that planned saving increases during each round is shown graphically up through the 5th round. As you can see, at each step, planned consumption and planned saving increase by smaller and smaller amounts as GNP, planned consumption, and planned saving approach their new equilibrium values. By the ninth round, planned saving has risen $34.6 billion over its original value, to $74.6 billion. This is 86.5 percent of the amount that planned saving must rise to reach its new equilibrium value of $80 billion. In equilibrium, planned saving will have increased by exactly the amount that planned investment has risen. Once again, planned aggregate expenditure will equal aggregate production.

Chapter 5

Money and the Banking System

Outline

Objectives

After reading this chapter, the student should be able to:

List and discuss the three functions of money.
Compare a commodity standard with a paper standard of money.
Describe how the banking system creates money through the process of multiple deposit expansion.
Give three official government definitions of money.
Explain why credit cards are not money.

*The **financial sector** consists of the economy's money and credit markets.*

***Credit markets** are markets in which loans of various time lengths are arranged between borrowers and lenders.*

*A **bank** is a financial institution that accepts deposits and makes loans.*

*A **depository institution** accepts deposits from the general public and from other banks.*

Introduction

There are two common sayings about how banks work. The first is that "a bank will only lend you money if you don't need it." Whether or not that saying strikes you as having an element of truth, it does make one wonder what role banks play in the economy when they lend money and why people borrow money. Could a bank really lend money if nobody needed it, and why would anyone borrow money if he or she did not need it? Why do we need money in a modern economy, and what role does the banking system play in meeting that need?

The second saying, which is sometimes attributed to the famous economist John Maynard Keynes, is that "if you owe a bank a dollar, the bank owns you; but if you owe a bank a million dollars, you own the bank." We cannot really judge the truthfulness of this observation unless we have some understanding of how banks work. What is it that a bank has to sell? How does a bank produce the services it offers, and do profit-maximizing banks work like other profit-seeking businesses?

Complementing the macroeconomy's real sector *is its **financial sector**, which includes the money and credit markets. **Credit markets** are where corporate bonds, stocks, United States Treasury bills, and other forms of debt are bought and sold. In this chapter we focus on money—what it is, its function in the economy, how it is produced, and its relationship to the real (nonfinancial) sector of the economy. The banking system plays a crucial role in the interactions between money, finance, and the markets for goods and services. Therefore, a fundamental task of this chapter is to spell out the place of banks in the macroeconomy. While almost everyone has a good idea of what a bank is, a definition is in order. Briefly, we shall refer to a **bank** as any institution that accepts deposits and makes loans. As savings and loan associations and credit unions fit this definition, we shall refer to them as banks, too. Because banks accept deposits, they are also called **depository institutions**.*

__Money__ consists mainly of checking account balances owned by business firms and individuals (not those owned by banks and the government) plus paper money and coins (currency) outside banks' vaults.

A __medium of exchange__ is something that is widely accepted by people in return for the sale of commodities or services or as payment for a loan.

A __unit of account__ is the way in which an economy's prices are expressed (such as in dollars or yen).

The Role of Money

The best way to understand the nature of money is to learn what functions it performs. We analyze these functions of money in the next few sections. Later we will outline the specific definitions of money in the United States economy, but for now, it is sufficient to know that in the United States and in most modern economies, **money** primarily consists of checking accounts, paper currency ("folding money"), and coins owned by the general public.

Money as a Medium of Exchange

If we were forced to choose the most important role of money, it would probably be its function as a **medium of exchange,** which is anything that members of society are commonly willing to accept in return for goods and services or in payment of debts. Money, by this definition, may include gold, silver, personal checks, or paper currency printed by a government agency. Various commodities other than gold and silver have also been used as money. For example, at various times and places, cattle, tobacco, stones, and seashells have all been used as money. Some of these commodities are used as money in primitive economies even today.

The Advantage of a Monetary Economy Over a Barter Economy

We saw in chapter 1 that modern, market economies are also monetary economies. It is inconceivable that the tremendous advantages of specialization could be obtained in a barter economy because in barter situations every transaction requires a mutual coincidence of wants. Without money, we would all have to produce much of what we consume, and our standard of living would be much closer to bare subsistence.

The essential difference between an item used in a barter exchange and a monetary transaction is whether it is valued for its intrinsic characteristics or simply because it can readily be exchanged in further transactions at a known value. Thus, if I trade my cow for your goat in today's economy, this does not mean that cattle are money. However, if you were to accept my cow simply because you and others find cows to be a convenient and efficient means of executing transactions, not because you want to own my cow as such, then cows would be a medium of exchange—money, in short.

With the money from the goods you buy, sellers pay their employees and suppliers, who in turn buy whatever *they* want. Only one party in each transaction must consider the quantity and quality of the particular goods or services bought. The other party is perfectly willing to accept money. With money, markets work smoothly and efficiently. Without it, in a barter economy, much time and material resources are required before anyone can exchange one commodity for another.

Money as a Unit of Account

When a society has adopted a currency as a medium of exchange, it is natural to use it also as the country's **unit of account,** the measure in which prices are denominated. Thus, in the United States, the dollar is not only the official currency, but prices are also stated in terms of dollars and cents. Curiosities and anachronisms occur, however. For example, prices in United States stock markets are denominated in *eighths* of a dollar, even though there is no combination of coins worth exactly 12 1/2 cents. This practice probably has historical roots in early Spanish coins called "pieces of eight" that could be cut into eight "bits" to make

***Hyperinflation** is an extremely rapid and continuous increase in the price level.*

*A **store of value** is any means of keeping wealth over time.*

*A **monetary standard** defines the basis of an economy's money.*

transactions. Thus, the colloquial expression "two bits" for a quarter dollar is an informal unit of account in the United States. In the United Kingdom, before the pound was decimalized it consisted of twenty shillings, each containing twelve pence. Nevertheless, fashionable stores, high-class lawyers, and doctors to the rich quoted prices in *guineas*. In modern times, there has been no such thing as a guinea coin or note, and if you bought a coat for 100 guineas, you would write a check for 105 pounds because a guinea equaled twenty-one shillings.

An official currency may cease being used as a medium of exchange and a unit of account when legal price controls destroy its usefulness. For example, in occupied Germany at the end of World War II, price ceilings were so low and rigid that currency became useless in making transactions. For small purchases, cigarettes were much more useful. They were quite scarce and easily carried about, so it was easy to substitute cigarettes for currency and to measure prices in cigarettes rather than deutsch marks. Larger transactions were consummated with cognac. Milton Friedman, the Nobel Prize-winning economist and a historian of money, refers to cognac as "by all odds the most liquid currency of which we have record."[1]

Another example of a change in a monetary system, also from Germany, dates back to the almost unimaginable inflation following World War I. Between August 1922 and November 1923, the German price level increased by over *10,000,000,000 percent*. The German currency of the time became useless as a medium of exchange because its value was declining so rapidly. As a result, the United States dollar became the measure of prices until stability was restored.[2] Such extremely inflationary periods are called **hyperinflations.** The impact of hyperinflation on the German economy was very severe because transactions became difficult and the benefits of specialization in production were diminished. The resulting economic devastation was so great that it inspired Germany during World War II to try to sabotage the British economy by introducing counterfeit five-pound notes designed to cause hyperinflation in Great Britain. One description of the impact of hyperinflation in Germany in the 1920s can be loosely quoted as follows: "We used to go shopping with our money in our pockets and our groceries in our wheelbarrow. Now, we go shopping with our money in our wheelbarrow and return home with our groceries in our pockets."

Money as a Store of Value

The principal purpose for adopting some kind of money as a medium of exchange is to achieve substantially lower costs of everyday transactions. There are two reasons why money achieves this goal. One, as we have seen, is that barter is generally very time-consuming. The second reason is that at the time at which a commodity is demanded, a purchaser may not have a good or service available for sale. Money allows purchases and income to be separated. When you place money in a drawer or put it in a checking account today so that you can spend it in the future, say, on a vacation or for your education, money serves as a **store of value.**

Of course, many commodities in addition to money serve as stores of value. Any asset that does not rot or wear out quickly can be a store of value and a means of transmitting purchasing power from one date to another. At different times in history, depending on economic conditions—particularly the expected rate of inflation and interest rates—money has been a relatively good or poor store of value. Some of the most important macroeconomic relationships we will discuss in later chapters relate to this issue. For example, the rapid rise in the prices of houses and of farmland in the United States in the late 1970s was to a considerable extent due to a switch from money to "real" assets as a store of value. This was a period of high inflation and low interest rates (restricted by law). Consequently, money depreciated in spending power as prices of goods rose, and lending money to others was unrewarding because of legal ceilings on interest rates. During the early 1980s, interest rates were deregulated and rose rapidly, while inflation was reduced greatly. Consequently, farmland and house prices declined dramatically.

*Under a **commodity standard of money**, the quantity of money is determined by the amount of a specific commodity, such as gold.*

*Under a **paper standard**, the quantity of money is determined by a monetary authority and is unrelated to any commodity.*

***Fiat money** is money because the government has declared it to be so.*

Monetary Standards and the Value of Money

Whatever custom or law that determines a society's money is called its **monetary standard.** The standard that is adopted is of fundamental importance in determining how the financial sector of the economy relates to the nonfinancial (real) sector. When stones, cattle, tobacco, gold, silver, or some other commodity is used as money, we say that society has adopted a **commodity standard of money.**

It should be apparent why commodity monetary standards were adopted early in the economic history of the world. No central authority is needed to maintain a monetary system in which a commodity serves as the medium of exchange, unit of account, and store of wealth. Money under a commodity standard is produced as an ordinary economic activity. Any commodity will do as long as it serves as a satisfactory medium of exchange. Because of this, it should also be fairly obvious why such exotic standards as stones, tobacco, and cattle have never achieved wide popularity as monetary standards. Can you imagine using a cow to buy a candy bar from a vending machine? How many boulders would you have to carry to your bursar's office to pay your tuition? Could tobacco or some other readily reproducible commodity serve as money for long without strict limitations on the amount farmers could plant and harvest? Could such restrictions be efficiently enforced without martial law?

Gold and silver have had nearly universal appeal as monetary standards because of the ease of making them into coins, their high value per unit of weight, and the relative difficulty of producing more. This means that a precious metal fulfills the functions of money very efficiently compared to most other commodities. Why do you suppose that diamonds have not been a popular monetary standard?

Even though no modern society today uses money based on a commodity standard, nearly all modern monetary systems have evolved from systems based on commodities. This is reflected in the names of various currency units. For example, the *pound* and the *peso* both refer to a given weight of gold or silver. The term *dollar* dates back to Spanish and American coins made from silver. Modern economies have adopted monetary systems based on a **paper standard,** which means that the money society uses has no intrinsic value and that the government determines how much money is in circulation. Today's monetary systems use **fiat money,** from the Latin word *fiat* meaning "let it be." This means that money is whatever a government says it is.

What determines paper money's value, then? We have already seen that a government edict is not sufficient to give money value. The examples from Germany show that if one monetary standard ceases to be a useful medium of exchange, society will adopt another, regardless of what government officials say. Money's value, like any other commodity's, is based on its scarcity relative to society's desire for it, that is, on supply and demand. We have seen that without money, everyone's standard of living would be much lower than is attainable given available resources. Thus, the higher standard of living attainable in a monetary economy gives rise to the demand for money. Government's role in determining the value of fiat money is to make sure that people have *faith* that the money they accept today will be accepted later by others. This faith in the value of a particular currency is essential to maintain the demand for it.

With a commodity standard, such as gold, faith in the value of money is based on the well-known difficulty of creating more of it. To maintain faith in a paper standard, it must be clear that the government will not supply (produce) an unlimited amount. As with any other commodity, money's value will plummet toward zero if it ceases to become scarce. Because a dollar bill's value as a piece of paper (its commodity value) is far less than its exchange value as money, it is tempting for a government to print a lot of it to purchase goods and services or to buy political support. This is the principal danger with a paper standard. (Commodity standards are not immune from a practice called *debasing the currency,* which occurs when the government adds "base" materials, such as lead, to precious metals, such as gold, in its coinage as a means of increasing the amount it

***Reserves** consist of assets banks retain to pay their depositors when they wish to withdraw from their accounts. In today's banking system, reserves include a bank's cash on hand and demand deposits it holds in other banks. The most important component of commercial banks' reserves are deposits they hold with the central bank—the Fed in the United States.*

*The **central bank** is a nation's monetary authority and is responsible for determining the quantity of money under a paper monetary standard.*

can spend.) As we will see in later chapters, the temptation for government to sacrifice the long-term benefits of maintaining the public's faith in the value of money for short-term political gains is a fundamental cause of macroeconomic difficulties—particularly inflation. In the remainder of this chapter we will see how the government and the banking system interact to determine the quantity of money under a paper standard.

▸ The Banking System and Money

The banking system is of fundamental importance in the production of paper money. Modern banks have arisen from two historical roots. One is early business firms (depository institutions) that accepted deposits of commodity money—particularly gold and silver—for safekeeping. The other root is wealthy families and firms that lent money to merchants and landowners who borrowed to finance their ventures or their consumption needs. Early depository institutions also soon developed into lending institutions. After all, depositors seldom withdrew their accounts all at once. In the meantime the firm holding the gold or silver could profit by lending part of the assets it held to eager borrowers willing to pay interest. It only needed to keep a *fraction* of its deposits as **reserves,** which are assets retained to pay customers who wish to withdraw their deposits. We shall soon see that an important feature of banks today is that they could not pay cash if all—or even a large number—of their depositors wanted to withdraw their deposits at the same time.

The banking systems of modern economies consist of two parts. The first part includes all of the banks that are the institutions most of us deal with in our everyday activities of depositing funds, borrowing money, and so on. The second part consists of the **central bank,** which is responsible for regulating the commercial banks and controlling the quantity of money in the economy. The central bank is usually a branch of government or a semigovernmental institution. In the United States, the central bank is called the **Federal Reserve System,** or the **Fed** for short. We will study the role of the Fed in detail in chapter 6. In this chapter, we will deal mainly with the role of the banks other than Fed in the financial sector of the economy. When we use the term *bank,* we mean one of these banks unless we specifically refer to the Fed.

The crucial role of banks today is their ability to create money by adding to their depositors' checking accounts. Of course, banks do not credit our accounts because they enjoy playing Santa Claus. They do so only when we give them something of value in return. Either we must deposit funds, or we must give the bank a promise to repay at a future date the amounts it credits to our checking accounts, along with an additional payment of interest for the service it has provided. We will call this promise to repay a loan a **loan contract,** which is merely another expression for an IOU. The interest payments banks receive on the loan contracts they accept represent their principal source of revenue.

A loan contract is only one example of a **financial instrument,** which is a financial obligation between two parties. In general, financial instruments represent liabilities of governments, firms, or individuals to other governments, firms, or individuals. Another example of a financial instrument is a checking or savings account. When we deposit funds in a bank, a claim is created on the bank's assets, but this is not a loan contract in the sense usually meant by a loan. If we purchase stock in a new business firm, we buy still another type of financial instrument.

*The **Federal Reserve System**, or Fed for short, is the central bank of the United States.*

*A **loan contract** is an agreement created when one party borrows from another. The financial instrument specifies a repayment schedule along with interest owed to the lender.*

*A **financial instrument** is an asset for one party and a liability for another party.*

***Demand deposits** include any bank account from which the owner may demand immediate payment to the owner or to a third party by means of a check, telephone call, or telegram.*

The Balance Sheet of a Bank

In order to see how banks create money, we need to examine a simplified version of the balance sheet of a typical bank. Remember that banks are institutions that make loans and accept deposits. In particular, we shall be concerned with a particular type of deposit called a demand deposit. **Demand deposits** are accounts that the owners may redeem *anytime* without financial penalty. Checking accounts are the most widely used form of demand deposits, but accounts that can be transferred by telegram or electronic systems also qualify. In recent years, savings and loan companies, savings banks, and other financial firms such as credit unions have received the legal right to establish demand deposit accounts. They are all banks by our definition and are therefore part of the banking system.

A simplified balance sheet for a bank is shown in table 5.1. Those of you who have taken an accounting course will know that a bank's balance sheet is similar to that of any business or individual in that it is based on the **basic accounting identity:**

$$\text{Net worth} \equiv \text{assets} - \text{liabilities.}$$

Simply put, what you are worth is defined as what you own less what you owe. This applies to banks, too.

We are primarily interested in the *composition* of a bank's assets and liabilities, which differs from other types of firms. In particular, a substantial component of banks' assets consists of loan contracts, and a substantial fraction of their liabilities consists of deposits. Over three-fourths of United States banks' assets consists of various kinds of loan contracts, and approximately the same fraction of their liabilities consists of checking accounts and other deposits.[3] Table 5.1, following accounting convention, lists all assets on the left-hand side of the balance sheet. Liabilities and net worth are listed on the right-hand side. The accounting identity assures that when we add up the items on the right side they always *exactly equal* the sum of all the items on the left.

Table 5.1 A simplified balance sheet for a bank

Assets	Liabilities and net worth[a]
Loan contracts	Demand deposits
Reserves (checking account balances of the bank at the central bank, vault cash)	Time deposits[b] (some savings accounts, certificates of deposit, and similar accounts)
Physical assets (buildings and equipment)	IOU's payable to others (accrued payroll, taxes, borrowed funds)
	Net worth (stockholders' or owners' equity)

[a]Net worth is defined as assets minus liabilities.

[b]Time deposits cannot be withdrawn before a specified date without incurring a penalty.

We can now use the bank's balance sheet to become more precise in defining and measuring the quantity of money in our economy. Since money consists primarily of checking accounts plus currency and coins outside of banks' vaults, it follows that the demand deposit liabilities of each bank make up an important component of the quantity of money.

There is no reason in principle why *any* liability of a bank could not be used as money. As a matter of fact, it was not until 1913 that the right to issue paper currency was granted solely to agencies of the federal government. Before that time, authorized banks not only issued checking account liabilities but also their own notes, which circulated just as dollar and larger-denomination bills (Federal Reserve notes) do today.[4]

The ***basic accounting identity*** *describes the structure of all balance sheets; it says that net worth is defined as the difference between assets and liabilities.*

Table 5.2 First FRK Bank balance sheet

Assets		Liabilities and net worth	
First day of business			
Office furniture	$25	Liabilities (none)	
Cash (reserves)	25		
		Net worth $50	
Second day of business			
Loan contract	$10	Liabilities	
Office furniture	25	Demand deposit	$10
Cash (reserves)	25		
		Net worth $50	

How Banks Create Money

To illustrate how a bank's liabilities form part of the nation's money stock, let us suppose that your authors were to use the royalties they receive from sales of this text to establish a bank. (In reality, it is necessary to obtain permission of state and sometimes federal regulatory agencies to open a bank.) Their goal is, of course, to earn profits. The balance sheet of the First FRK Bank on the first day of business is shown in table 5.2. Your authors have used their first royalty payment of $50 in cash to purchase $25 worth of office furniture and have retained $25 in cash for use as reserves. Just after lunch on the second business day, the bank's first and only customer asks to borrow $10. After checking the borrower's references and credit history, FRK agrees to accept the customer's loan contract (the customer's promissory note or IOU) for $10. The loan is completed by creating a checking account for the borrower and crediting it with $10. As a result of the bank's activities on its second business day, its assets and liabilities have both increased by $10.

Remember that the principal component of the money supply consists of demand deposits. By lending $10 to its first customer and creating a checking account (demand deposit) for the same amount, *the First FRK Bank has created a $10 increase in the economy's money supply*. Moreover, this transaction will lead to a chain of events that increases the money supply even more. To see how this happens, we will make the simplifying assumption that the entire banking system consists of two banks: the First FRK Bank and the Other Bank. Table 5.3 shows the balance sheets of the First FRK Bank and the Other Bank immediately following FRK's transaction creating the new $10 checking account outlined in the preceding paragraph. Since the Other Bank is a long-established bank, we will only show *changes* in its balance sheet in table 5.3, starting from the point at which FRK's first customer spends the borrowed money.

When FRK's customer spends the borrowed $10, the customer writes a check for $10. The payee deposits the check in an account with the Other Bank. In step 2 of table 5.3, we see that this results in changes for both FRK's balance sheet and that of the Other Bank. Upon receiving the deposit, the Other Bank presents the check to FRK for payment. FRK pays the Other Bank from its cash reserves, which fall to $15; at the same time, FRK charges (debits) its customer's checking account for $10, so that FRK's demand deposit liabilities fall back to zero. (In the banking system that now exists in the United States, FRK would have deposited most of its initial $25 in reserves with the Fed. The Other Bank would have sent the FRK customer's check to the Fed for collection, and the Fed would have paid the Other Bank by subtracting $10 from FRK's reserve account.) The Other Bank's assets have increased by $10 in cash. This cash is considered reserves by the Other Bank. We see that the money supply is still $10 higher than before the entire process started but that the new checking account balance of $10 is now located in the

Table 5.3 Multiple deposit expansion and the money supply

Step	Assets		Liabilities and net worth	
Step 1—FRK lends $10 to its first customer	**Balance sheet of First FRK Bank**			
	Office furniture	$25	Liabilities	
	Cash (reserves)	$25	Demand deposit	$10
	Loan contract	$10		
			Net worth	$50
Step 2—FRK's customer spends the borrowed money	**Balance sheet of First FRK Bank**			
	Office furniture	$25	Liabilities	
	Cash (reserves)	$15	Demand deposit	$ 0
	Loan contract	$10		
			Net worth	$50
	Change in balance sheet of Other Bank			
	Cash (reserves)	$10	Liabilities	
			Demand deposits	$10
			Net worth	$ 0
Step 3—Other Bank uses its new reserves to lend $8 to a customer	**Change in balance sheet of Other Bank**			
	Cash (reserves)	$10	Liabilities	
	Loan contracts	$ 8	Demand deposits	$18
			Net worth	$ 0
Step 4—Other Bank's customer spends the borrowed money	**Balance sheet of First FRK Bank**			
	Office furniture	$25	Liabilities	
	Cash (reserves)	$23	Demand deposit	$ 8
	Loan contract	10		
			Net worth	$50
	Change in balance sheet of Other Bank			
	Cash	$ 2	Liabilities	
	Loan contracts	$ 8	Demand deposits	$10
			Net worth	$ 0

Multiple deposit expansion means that when the banking system's reserves increase, the quantity of checking account liabilities can be increased by a larger amount.

The money multiplier is the ratio of the change in the quantity of money that results from a change in banks' reserves.

Other Bank rather than in the First FRK Bank, where it originated. At the same time, $10 in reserves has been transferred from FRK to the Other Bank.

The *increase* in the Other Bank's cash (reserves) of $10 now places it in a position where it can purchase a loan contract. It would like to do so because the interest it will collect will increase its profits. However, the Other Bank is unlikely to lend $10 to one of its customers. The reason is that the Other Bank fully expects the new checking account balance to be spent and that when this happens, the check may find its way to FRK. Moreover, the Other Bank is likely to want to be sure that it always has enough cash on hand to meet the demands of its customers for currency when they request it. Therefore the Other Bank lends only $8 as a result of the $10 increase in its reserves. This loan occurs in step 3 of table 5.3.

Compared to its situation before step 2, the Other Bank now has both assets and liabilities that are $18 greater. These changes consist of (1) an increase in cash assets of $10, (2) an increase in loan contracts of $8, and (3) an increase in demand deposits of $18. For the *banking system as a whole*, checking account liabilities have risen by $18 compared to the beginning of our example. The essential point of step 3 is that the initial increase in the money supply of $10 created by the First FRK Bank has led to an *additional* increase of $8 created by the Other Bank! Nor is this the end of the story.

In step 4 of table 5.3, we see that the Other Bank's customer has spent the borrowed money and the check has indeed been deposited in the First FRK Bank. FRK has collected its check from the Other Bank, so that its cash reserves are now $23, while its demand deposit liabilities are only $8. Therefore, FRK can buy new loan contracts, paying for them with new checking accounts or increases in existing checking accounts. This means that the money supply will continue to rise.

The process we have described in steps 1 through 4 of table 5.3 is called **multiple deposit expansion,** which means that an increase in banks' reserves will lead to an increase in banks' deposits and in the money supply that is a multiple (greater than 1) of the initial increase in reserves. The ratio of the additional quantity of money that results to an increase in reserves is called the **money multiplier.** We will have more to say about multiple deposit expansion and the money multiplier in chapter 6. Obviously, multiple deposit expansion must come to an end, or the money supply would grow without limit. Two factors limit multiple deposit expansion. The basic limit in the United States economy is that banks are required by regulations to maintain a certain ratio of reserves to their deposit liabilities; this means that, given their reserves, they cannot continue to buy loan contracts forever. In chapter 6, we will examine the way in which these reserve requirements operate. However, even in the absence of specific reserve requirements, it is unlikely that the banking system would generate an unlimited amount of money on its own. The reason for this is implicit in our description of the multiple deposit expansion process in steps 1 through 4 of table 5.3. It is that individual banks will always wish to retain their ability to honor their customers' (depositors') demands for cash withdrawals and the demands for payment that are created when a depositor writes a check that is deposited in another bank. The amount of reserves each bank desires will depend on the amount of deposits it has. Thus, even if they were not required to do so, banks would maintain their reserve balances at a certain fraction of their outstanding deposit liabilities. This means that, given their reserves, banks will limit the amount of loans they issue and the new money balances they create. To do otherwise would result in the risk that they would be unable to meet obligations to their customers (depositors) and to other banks. The need to retain the confidence of

Cash drain is the flow of money into the public's holding of currency when there is an increase in the total money stock.

the public forces banks to limit the deposits they create, even though buying loan contracts is their principal source of income.

Cash Drain and Multiple Deposit Expansion

Our analysis of multiple deposit expansion has dealt only with one form of money—checking accounts. We have already noted, however, that another principal component of the money stock is currency held by the public. The desire of the public to hold currency affects the relationship between the addition of new reserves to the banking system and the amount of new money that is eventually created. The reason is that cash held by the public cannot be used at the same time by banks as reserves. Because the public's demand for cash, in addition to checking account money, reduces the size of the money multiplier, the relationship between the amount of money held by the public and its demand for cash results in what is called a **cash drain.**

A numerical example will help you see how cash drain reduces the money multiplier. Suppose that the public desires to hold 30 percent of its money in the form of cash. Thus, at step 2 of table 5.3, instead of $10 being deposited in the Other Bank, only $7 is deposited. The remainder, $3, is held as cash. The new reserves of the Other Bank are only 70 percent as large as they would be if there were no cash drain. Thus, it will make new loans of only $5.60 (80 percent of $7) instead of $8. The money supply has grown by $15.60 instead of $18 (the original FRK loan of $10 plus the Other Bank's new loan of $5.60). At the beginning of step 4 in table 5.3, the First FRK Bank receives a new deposit of only $3.92 (70 percent of $5.60) instead of $8. Thus, in step 4 of table 5.3, the First FRK Bank has reserves of only $18.92 instead of $23. Instead of excess reserves of $21.40, it has only $18.14. (Excess reserves equal total reserves less 20 percent of demand deposits in this example.) If FRK uses all of its excess reserves to buy new loan contracts, it can purchase only about $18 worth instead of over $21 worth. It is obvious that at each succeeding step, the amount of loans and new money created will be smaller than if there were no cash drain and that the money multiplier is reduced.*

*The money multiplier with cash drain is more complex than the simple money multiplier defined in the text. Let the public's desired currency holdings be determined as follows:

$$C = k(C + D),$$

where C represents currency holdings, D represents checking account money, and k is the fraction of its total money balances the public desires to hold as cash. We have already seen that checking account deposits are related to banks' reserves by the relationship

$$D = R/r,$$

where r represents the required reserve ratio and R represents bank reserves. We assume that banks will always increase their loans if they have excess reserves. By substituting the second expression for D into the first expression and combining terms, we derive the relationship

$$C = (R/r) \times k/(1 - k).$$

The next step is to define the ratio of the total money supply to the sum of currency plus bank reserves. (This sum is called the *monetary base,* which is discussed in the text on page 139.) This ratio is

$$(C + D)/(C + R).$$

When two preceding expressions for C and D are substituted into this ratio and the result is simplified, we derive the equation

$$(C + D)/(C + R) = 1/[k(1 - r) + r],$$

which is the money multiplier when there is a currency drain. When r and k are both fractions, this multiplier is clearly smaller than 1/r, the money multiplier when there is no currency drain. For example, if r = 0.1, the money multiplier without a currency drain is simply 1/0.1 = 10. However, if k = 0.3, the multiplier given by the formula we have developed here is only 1/(.3 × .9 + .1) = 2.7. The way to understand the formula is to think of the Fed as changing the monetary base when it engages in an open market operation, not simply bank reserves.

M1 includes all deposits (except those of the United States Treasury) in the banking system's consolidated balance sheet on which checks can be written plus currency and traveler's checks in the hands of the nonbank public.

Table 5.4 **Consolidated balance sheet (millions of dollars) of the banking system, December 1985**

The banking system[a]			
Assets		**Liabilities and net worth**	
1. Loan contracts		1. Deposits	
a. Non-United States government obligations[b]	1,614.6	a. Demand deposits	536.4
b. United States government obligations	249.9	b. Savings accounts	450.0
2. Cash	211.6	c. Certificates of deposit and other time deposits[c]	777.1
3. Other assets	189.4	2. Total liabilities	1,763.5
4. Total assets	2,265.5	3. Net worth	502.0

Source: From *Federal Reserve Bulletin*, March 1986. Column totals may not be exact due to rounding.

[a]Domestically chartered commercial banks.

[b]Includes obligations of states and subdivisions and commercial, industrial, and real estate loans.

[c]Certificates of deposit (CDs) are a special type of time deposit whereby the depositor agrees not to withdraw the funds during a specified time period, usually ninety days or more; a time deposit is a deposit that earns a fixed rate of interest over a specified time period with a substantial interest penalty for early withdrawal.

The Consolidated Balance Sheet of the Banking System

Table 5.3 presents a simplified picture of how individual banks interact to create new money balances through multiple deposit expansion. Now that we have seen how this process works, it will be easier to analyze the economy's financial sector if we view the banking system as a whole. Macroeconomics is aggregate economic analysis, and from now on, we will refer to the *aggregated*, or *consolidated*, balance sheet of the economy's banks in discussing the financial sector. In other words, we will treat the entire banking system as if it were one gigantic bank with a balance sheet of its own.

Consolidation involves *adding up* (aggregating) all of the individual banks' assets, liabilities, and net worths, but *not including* the assets of one bank that are liabilities of other banks in the system. For example, in table 5.3, we might have shown an intermediate step between steps 1 and 2, step 1a. At step 1a, FRK's customer would have spent the $10 it borrowed, and the check would have just been deposited in the Other Bank. If the Other Bank were to *immediately* credit its depositor's account for $10 but were to delay a day in presenting the check to FRK for payment, the Other Bank's assets would not show an increase in cash of $10. Rather, its assets would show an increase in uncollected checks of $10, and the $10 in cash would still be shown on the books of FRK. At the same time, FRK would also have a *liability* in the form of a $10 demand deposit that would be eliminated as soon as it paid the Other Bank. If we were to *consolidate* the FRK and Other Banks' balance sheets at step 1a, the Other Bank's $10 uncollected check and FRK's $10 demand deposit would be eliminated. The consolidated balance sheet would show only the cash (reserve) assets of the two banks and the $10 demand deposit that is recorded as a liability of the Other Bank in step 2.

The consolidated balance sheet of the banking system contains only assets that are *not* claims of one bank on another bank within the system. Similarly, the liabilities in the consolidated balance sheet of the banking system consist only of obligations payable to individuals, firms, and governments *outside* the

M2 includes M1 plus "small" certificates of deposit, savings accounts, money market mutual fund accounts, and certain other bank obligations that banks' depositors treat as readily available to carry out transactions.

M3 includes M2 plus "large" CD's and other deposits that are relatively liquid but are inconvenient to use in day-to-day transactions.

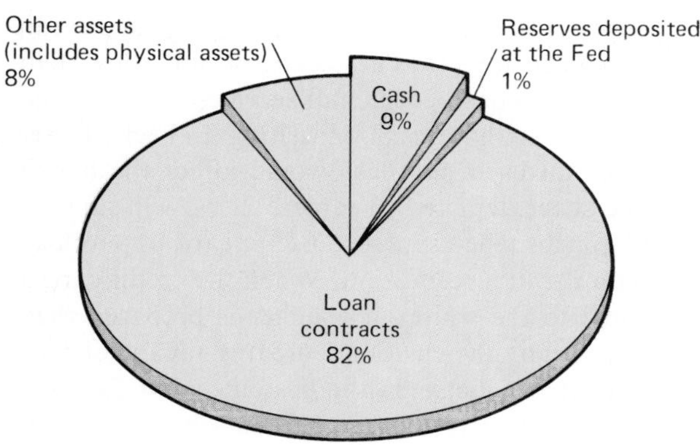

Figure 5.1 Assets of United States commercial banks
From *Federal Reserve Bulletin,* December 1985, Table 1-25.

banking system. Items inside the system cancel out. The consolidated balance sheet of the United States banking system is shown in table 5.4 and summarized in figure 5.1.

Figure 5.1 shows us that about 82 percent of the banking system's assets consist of *earning assets*—loan contracts on which the banks receive interest payments. In the banking system's assets, cash amounts to about 9 percent of the total and to only 12 percent of deposit liabilities. Obviously, if all depositors tried to withdraw the amounts credited to their checking accounts, savings accounts, and certificates of deposits all at once, there would not be nearly enough funds to pay them. Of course, individual depositors have no reason to cash in as long as they believe their deposits can either be converted to currency or used to carry out transactions as desired. A monetary system works as long as people believe it will work. In the next chapter, we will see how the banking system's ability to purchase loan contracts and create money balances is regulated in the United States.

The Definitions of Money in the United States Economy

We are now able to define money more precisely. We have seen that in most modern economies money consists of demand deposits plus paper currency and coin. In the United States there are three official government definitions of what constitutes our money supply, two of which are commonly used in media discussions of economic issues. The reason for multiple definitions is that savings accounts and other deposits are *substitutes* for checking accounts and currency in satisfying needs for the means to pay for transactions. Some economists prefer the government's narrowest definition of money, which excludes savings accounts and other deposits that are not available on demand. Others find the broader definitions more useful.

M1 includes all currency held by the general public, traveler's checks, and all bank deposits held by the general public on which checks can be written.

M2 includes M1 plus money market fund shares, savings accounts, and time deposits (certificates of deposit) up to $100,000, also called "small" time deposits, plus other highly liquid assets.

M3 which is a far less commonly used definition than M1 or M2, includes M2 plus "large" time deposits.[5]

Time deposits in excess of $100,000 are not included in M2 because they usually involve severe restrictions on when their owners can claim payment. Therefore, they are not very close substitutes for demand deposits and small savings and time deposits. Currency and deposits owned by the Fed, the banking system, or the federal government are *not* part of the money supply.

Federal Reserve notes are our paper currency.

Money consists mainly of items that are liabilities on the banking system's consolidated balance sheet. One important item, however, is not a liability of privately held banks. This is currency, which consists mainly of Federal Reserve notes. **Federal Reserve notes** are our paper money, generally in \$1, \$5, \$10, \$20, \$50, and \$100 bills. Legally, Federal Reserve notes are liabilities of the Fed and are issued by the twelve Federal Reserve Banks in quantities sufficient to satisfy the public's demand for this form of money. However, suppose you went to your local Federal Reserve Bank and demanded payment for, say, a \$20 bill. You might, if you persisted, receive the Fed's check for \$20, which you could deposit in a checking or savings account at your bank. Traveler's checks issued by nonbanks such as American Express are not liabilities of either the banking system or the Fed. Coins are minted by the U.S. Treasury and do not constitute a claim on any financial institution.

Are Credit Cards Money?

Many of us carry "plastic money" in the form of at least one major credit card. Even if we pay the full balance every month, credit cards such as VISA, MasterCard, American Express, and Diner's Club are great conveniences because we can make purchases without having to worry about having enough cash in our wallets. Are credit cards money? You now have enough information to answer this question.

Suppose the First FRK Bank were to issue credit cards to its customers. These cards would allow their holders to purchase goods and services from participating firms without cash or writing a check. To see how a credit card purchase would affect the bank's balance sheet depicted in table 5.2, we will analyze what happens when someone uses a card to purchase a \$25 dinner at a restaurant. When the credit card is presented to the waiter, a voucher is prepared that, when signed by the customer, creates a loan contract liability for \$25 between the customer and the First FRK Bank. The restaurant presents a copy of the voucher to the bank, and the bank makes the following entries in its books: (1) increase the bank's loan contract assets by \$25 to reflect the credit provided to the purchaser of the meal; (2) increase the bank's liabilities by \$25 (less a service charge retained by the bank) to reflect an addition to the restaurant's checking account with the bank. The second entry will be reflected as an increase in the checking account liabilities of the consolidated balance sheet of the banking system. Thus, M1, M2, and M3 will rise by the amount the restaurant receives. Clearly, credit cards are not money themselves, but when they are used to make purchases, money is created. When the First FRK Bank credits the restaurant's checking account for \$25 less the service charge, the money supply increases by the same amount. What happens to the money supply when the customer receives a statement for \$25 at the end of the month and pays the balance in full?

▸ Summary and Conclusions

In this chapter we learned what banks have to sell, how they earn their profits, and why a bank may not be willing to lend you money when you really need it. We outlined the structure of the banking system and its relationship to the supply of checking account money. The basic features of a paper monetary standard and a banking system in which reserves amount to only a fraction of banks' outstanding checking and savings account liabilities characterize all modern economies today. The following main points were emphasized.

Money serves as a medium of exchange, unit of account, and store of value.

Under a paper standard, money is a liability of the banking system.

The banking system creates money when it satisfies the public's desire to finance purchases of goods and services with borrowed funds.

▸ Key Terms

bank *116*
basic accounting identity *121*
cash drain *125*
central bank *120*
commodity standard of money *119*
credit markets *116*
demand deposits *121*
depository institutions *116*
Federal Reserve System (Fed) *120*
Federal Reserve notes *128*
fiat money *119*
financial instrument *120*
financial sector *116*
hyperinflations *118*
loan contract *120*
M1, M2, M3 *127*
medium of exchange *117*
monetary standard *119*
money *117*
money multiplier *124*
multiple deposit expansion *124*
paper standard *119*
reserves *120*
store of value *118*
unit of account *117*

▸ Questions for Discussion and Review

Are the statements in questions 1 through 5 true, false, or uncertain? Defend your answers.

1. The United States dollar is not "backed" by anything of intrinsic value.
2. Money is both an asset and a liability.
3. Writing a check and depositing it in your money market fund account increases M2.
4. Increasing the amount of money that you carry in your wallet will affect a banking system's ability to expand deposits.
5. If you close out your checking account and take the balance in dollar bills, your actions reduce the quantity of money.
6. Can an item fulfill money's role as a medium of exchange if it is not also a store of value? Cite historical examples to defend your answer.
7. If only one bank were chartered to do business in a country, how would this affect the deposit expansion process?
8. Do people ever have more money than they want? Explain.
9. Suppose a traveler takes $10,000 from a cookie jar and purchases traveler's checks. How does this affect M1, M2, and M3?
10. Suppose the Federal Reserve paid market rates of interest on bank reserves held at the Fed. How would this affect the size of the money supply?

Chapter 6

The Central Bank and Regulation of Money and the Banking System

Outline

Objectives

After reading this chapter, the student should be able to:

Describe the structure of the Federal Reserve System.
Explain how each of the three major instruments of monetary policy (open market operations, changing the reserve requirement, and changing the discount rate) are used by the Fed to expand or contract the money supply.
Explain how direct credit controls, interest rate restrictions, and moral suasion can affect the money supply.
Describe the role of the Federal Deposit Insurance Corporation.
Discuss recent attempts to deregulate banking.

*A nation's **monetary authority** is usually its central bank, which is responsible for determining the quantity of money under a paper monetary standard.*

Introduction

When the Johnson family moved to a quiet suburb in Ohio in 1980, they put their modest savings in a neighborhood savings and loan association. They think it was owned by a Cleveland-based bank that is federally insured. After a couple of years, ownership of the savings and loan association changed hands, but the Johnsons didn't give it much thought. In fact, it was purchased by a firm that insured through a state fund rather than with the Federal Deposit Insurance Corporation.

In February 1985 something called ESM Investment Securities Corporation in Florida went bankrupt, and by March 1985 all Ohio savings and loan associations that were insured by the Ohio state deposit insurance fund were closed to depositors by order of the governor. The Johnson family had $5,000 in one of those savings and loans, and both Dick and Mary Johnson's monthly paychecks had been automatically deposited just before it closed its doors.

Checks that they had written to pay the mortgage, utilities, and other monthly bills were all returned unpaid. The Johnsons borrowed money from their parents and friends to buy groceries. For three agonizing months, the Johnson family waited to learn if they would ever see their money again, if they would be evicted from their home, if their car would be repossessed, and how long they could keep borrowing from friends and relatives to survive. Finally, an out-of-town savings and loan association with federal deposit insurance took over the bank in which the Johnson family had its money, and life returned to normal.

During the course of that financial and emotional roller-coaster ride, Dick and Mary Johnson learned a lot more than they had ever thought they would care to know about how banks earn profits and how safe deposits are under federal and state insurance programs. How much do you know about the bank in which you keep your money? Can what happened to the Johnson family happen to you? How effectively are bank deposits protected by federal insurance programs that became effective in the mid-1930s? During the Great Depression (before federal deposit insurance became effective) there were 4,000 bank suspensions in 1933 alone, and over 8,000 banks were closed at least temporarily between 1930 and 1933, before President Roosevelt ordered all banks closed, just as the governor of Ohio did in 1985. In 1985, bank failures in the United States hit a post-Great Depression high of 120.[1] While this is a much smaller figure than that reached in 1933, many people began to wonder whether anything like Great Depression levels of bank failures could happen again. We will explore this question, among others, in this chapter, where we study the role of the Fed in regulating the banking system and the money supply.

*In chapter 5 we saw that the United States and most of the world's economies employ a paper standard of money. Under a paper standard, the quantity of reserves is not determined by the cost of producing a commodity such as gold or silver. Rather, the banking system's reserves, which limit the quantity of money that banks can supply, are determined by a nation's monetary authority. A nation's **monetary authority** is the government agency responsible for controlling the banking system's ability to create money. The monetary authority in most countries today is its central bank. Actually, a nation's central bank need not be an official government agency, but most of them are. For example, the Bank of England, Great Britain's central bank, was originally a privately owned firm. Nationalization of the Bank of England essentially formalized the functions it had customarily assumed over the years. Some other countries' central banks are the Australian National Bank, the Bank of Japan, and the German Federal Bank. In chapter 5 we noted that the central bank in the United States is the Federal Reserve System, frequently referred to as the Fed. In this chapter, we shall explore the role of the Fed in the financial sector of the United States economy.*

The ***Depository Institutions Deregulation and Monetary Control Act of 1980*** *extends control of the Fed to all depository institutions and provides for greater competition among banks and for eventual decontrol of most interest rates they charge and pay.*

The Fed's ***monetary policy*** *determines how much money circulates in the United States economy.*

Table 6.1 **Balance sheet of the Fed, March 1986 (millions of dollars)**

The Fed			
Assets		**Liabilities and net worth**	
1. Gold certificates[a]	$11,090	1. Federal Reserve Notes (paper money)	$177,189
2. Coins	570	2. Deposits	
3. Loan contracts		a. Banking system	30,782
a. Banking system obligations	818	b. United States Treasury	3,280
b. United States government		c. Foreign governments	274
obligations (government bonds)	176,620	d. Other	511
4. Other assets[b]	34,035	3. Other liabilities[c]	7,119
5. Total assets	223,133	4. Total liabilities	219,155
		5. Net worth	3,978

Source: From *Federal Reserve Bulletin,* June 1986. Column totals may not be exact due to rounding.

[a]Can be turned over to the United States Treasury in exchange for gold.

[b]Includes Special Drawing Rights (SDRs), which are an account the United States government has with the International Monetary Fund (IMF) as an official reserve to finance balance of payments deficits.

[c]Includes deferred availability cash items and accrued dividends.

Keeping Money Scarce: The Role of the Fed

The United States' central bank is not located in a single place, although its headquarters are in Washington, D.C. The Federal Reserve *System* includes twelve Federal Reserve District Banks. Each Federal Reserve District is named for the city that is the home of its principal Federal Reserve Branch Bank. These cities are Boston, New York, Philadelphia, Cleveland, Richmond, Atlanta, Chicago, St. Louis, Minneapolis, Kansas City, Dallas, and San Francisco. Overseeing the district banks is a board of governors, the members of which are appointed by the president of the United States. The members of the board serve fourteen-year terms, which are staggered so that every two years someone's term expires.

Also included in the Federal Reserve System are a large number of commercial banks, which are called *member banks.* (Commercial banks are institutions that accept deposits and make loans but are not savings and loan institutions, mutual banks, or credit unions.) The member banks own common stock of the Fed and must subscribe to certain rules and regulations that until recently were more stringent than those governing nonmember banks. Only about half of the commercial banks in the United States are member banks. They tend to be larger than nonmember banks and account for about three-quarters of all deposits of member and nonmember banks combined. Under the **Depository Institutions Deregulation and Monetary Control Act of 1980,** Congress has mandated that nonmember banks are subject to most of the same controls by the Fed as are member banks. At the same time, many services that the Fed used to perform only for member banks are now provided for all banks, savings and loan associations, and credit unions. These services include check clearing, wire transfer of funds, and access to borrowing from the Fed.

The Fed's activities that determine the supply of money constitute its **monetary policy.** In order to understand how the Fed carries out its monetary policy, we need to see how the Fed's balance sheet ties into that of the consolidated balance sheet of the banking system, which is shown in table 5.4. The Fed's balance sheet is shown in table 6.1.

*The Fed's **instruments of monetary policy** are the different types of actions it can take to control the money supply.*

*The **required reserve ratio** is the amount of reserves that banks must keep with the Fed or on hand, expressed as a fraction of the banks' deposit liabilities.*

*In a **fractional reserve system**, required reserves are less than the banks' deposit liabilities.*

The Balance Sheet of the Fed and the Banking System

The principal connection between the Fed's balance sheet and the consolidated balance sheet of the commercial banking system is through the reserve accounts the commercial banks keep with the Fed. These accounts are deposit liabilities of the Fed and assets of the commercial banks. The commercial banking system's reserves include its cash on hand and its reserve accounts with the Fed. In chapter 5, we noted that the First FRK Bank began business with a certain amount of reserves. In today's financial world, the First FRK Bank would have deposited most of its reserves with the Fed and kept only a small portion as cash on hand to meet its customers' daily demands for currency.

The FRK's reserve account with the Fed would be very similar to a checking account that any of us might hold with a commercial bank, such as FRK. The First FRK Bank would be able to draw upon its reserves to meet the demands of its customers to withdraw their funds or the demands of other banks to honor checks that FRK's customers have written and that have been deposited in accounts elsewhere. As we shall see, the Fed controls the money supply essentially by controlling the banking system's reserves and by requiring a certain ratio of reserves to the commercial banks' deposit liabilities.

One aspect of the Fed's balance sheet may surprise you. Nearly three-quarters of the Fed's assets consist of loan contracts that are obligations of the United States government—bonds and notes used to finance the federal deficit. Notice also that less than 6 percent of the Fed's assets consist of gold certificates, which are claims on the government's stock of gold. As we have said, and as you can see, gold has virtually nothing to do with the quantity of money in circulation in the United States. Table 6.1 shows us that our money is essentially backed by whatever the Fed has as an asset, very little of which is gold.

The Means of Monetary Control: The Instruments of Monetary Policy

We can now take a closer look at the **instruments of monetary policy,** which are the means used by the Fed to control the quantity of money. As we suggested, the most powerful means of limiting the money supply is to control the amount of reserves in the banking system or the quantity of reserves banks must hold for each dollar they have as checking account and savings account liabilities. In other words, the Fed has the power to control the size of the reserve accounts commercial banks hold with it. We will see how shortly. The Fed also has the power to rule that for every dollar in the deposit accounts of commercial banks' customers, the commercial banks must themselves keep a certain fraction of a dollar as cash in their vaults or in their reserve accounts with the Fed. For example, if a commercial bank's customers have deposits worth, say, $1 billion, the Fed can require the commercial bank to hold reserves of 10 percent of this amount, or $100 million.

The amount of reserves banks are required to hold relative to their checking account and savings account liabilities is determined by the **required reserve ratio.** The United States has a **fractional reserve system,** which means that this ratio is less than 100 percent. For every dollar commercial banks owe their customers in the form of checking or savings accounts, they are required to keep less than a dollar in reserves.

In order to satisfy their reserve requirements, individual banks must maintain minimum balances in their accounts with the Fed. The Fed can alter either the required reserve ratio or the amount of reserves available as a means of monetary control. If the Fed wants to reduce the quantity of money, or reduce its rate of growth, it need only reduce the quantity of reserves available to the banks, or its rate of growth. Alternately, the Fed can increase the required reserve ratio, which also reduces banks' ability to lend, given the quantity of reserves available.

*The **Federal Open Market Committee (FOMC)** is the part of the Fed that controls bank reserves.*

__Excess reserves__ are banks' deposits at the Fed and other reserves in excess of their required amount.

__Open market operations__ are the purchases and sales of government bonds by the Fed on the open market (the market for government bonds).

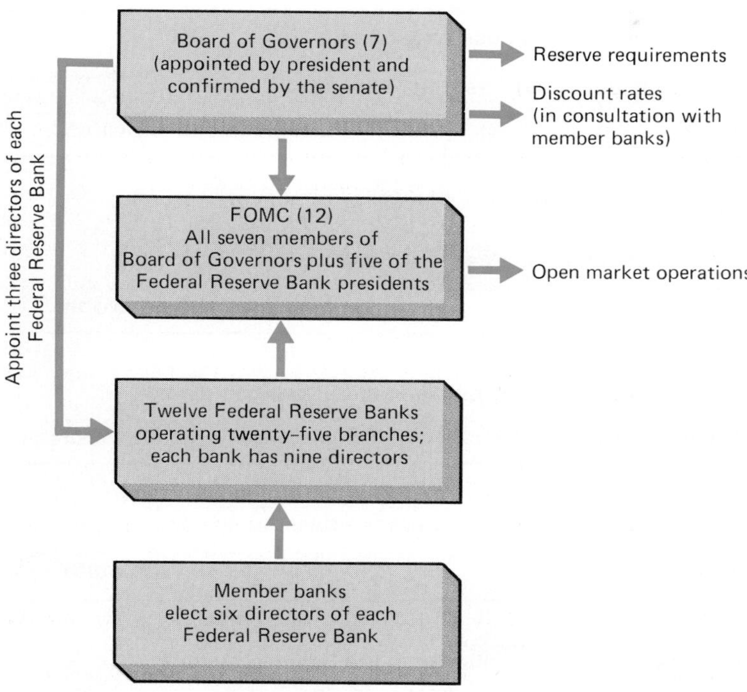

Figure 6.1 The Federal Reserve System

The question of whether the quantity of reserves available to the banking system is too large or too small is determined by a part of the Fed called the **Federal Open Market Committee (FOMC),** which consists of the entire Board of Governors, the president of the Federal Reserve Bank of New York, and four chairpersons of the other Federal Reserve Banks, who serve on a rotating basis. The FOMC is the agency most directly concerned with the short-run management of the money supply and meets approximately every six weeks to determine monetary policy. The relationship of the FOMC to the Board of Governors and the member banks is illustrated in Figure 6.1

For example, suppose the banking system's demand deposit liabilities total $1 billion and the required reserve ratio is 10 percent. As a result, banks' required reserves equal $100 million. If actual reserves held as deposits with the Fed equal $100 million, then the banking system has no **excess reserves,** which are reserves over and above the legally required amount. Let us suppose the FOMC decides it would be desirable to change the quantity of money in circulation. In order to achieve its goal, the Fed will most likely act to change the quantity of reserves available. Just how does it accomplish this task?

Open Market Operations and the Quantity of Money with No Currency Drain

The means that the FOMC is most likely to use to change the quantity of reserves is called an **open market operation,** in which employees of the Fed are directed to buy or sell United States government bonds

Table 6.2 Open market operations and multiple deposit expansion

Step	Balance sheet	Assets		Liabilities and net worth	
Step 1—the Fed buys a $10,000 bond from the FRK	Balance sheet of the First FRK Bank (FRK)	United States Govt. bonds	−$10,000	Demand deposits	+$10,000
		Reserve account at the Fed	+$10,000		
		Loan contracts	+$10,000		
Step 2—the customer of the FRK who received the new $10,000 loan contract spends the money	Balance sheet of the First FRK Bank	Reserve account at the Fed	−$10,000	Demand deposits	−$10,000
	Balance sheet of other banks in the banking system	Reserve account at the Fed	+$10,000	Demand deposits	+$10,000
Step 3—the banking system eliminates its $9,000 of excess reserves by issuing new loan contracts	Balance sheet of other banks in the banking system	Loan contracts	+$9,000	Demand deposits	+$9,000
Step 4—the borrowers of the money write checks, which are then deposited in the FRK	Balance sheet of other banks in the banking system	Reserve account at the Fed	−$9,000	Demand deposits	−$9,000
	Balance sheet of the First FRK Bank	Reserve account at the Fed	+$9,000	Demand deposits	+$9,000

on the open market, that is, the market for United States government bonds. Let us see how when the Fed purchases bonds on the open market this affects banks' reserves and the money supply when all of the additional money created is held by the public in the form of checking accounts. Suppose the First FRK Bank owns United States government bonds worth $100,000 and decides to sell a $10,000 bond to the Fed. The Fed pays by crediting FRK's account at the Fed for $10,000. The result is that FRK's balance sheet will show the changes indicated by step 1 in table 6.2 and figure 6.2—the assets side of the balance sheet shows *plus* $10,000 in reserves and *minus* $10,000 in United States government bonds. This is a very important change for the First FRK Bank, even though *total* assets are unchanged.

The easiest way to see how the Fed's open market operation affects the money supply is to assume that the First FRK Bank, like the banking system as a whole, had no excess reserves before the Fed took action. (Banks may actually hold excess reserves—reserves over and above their requirements—to

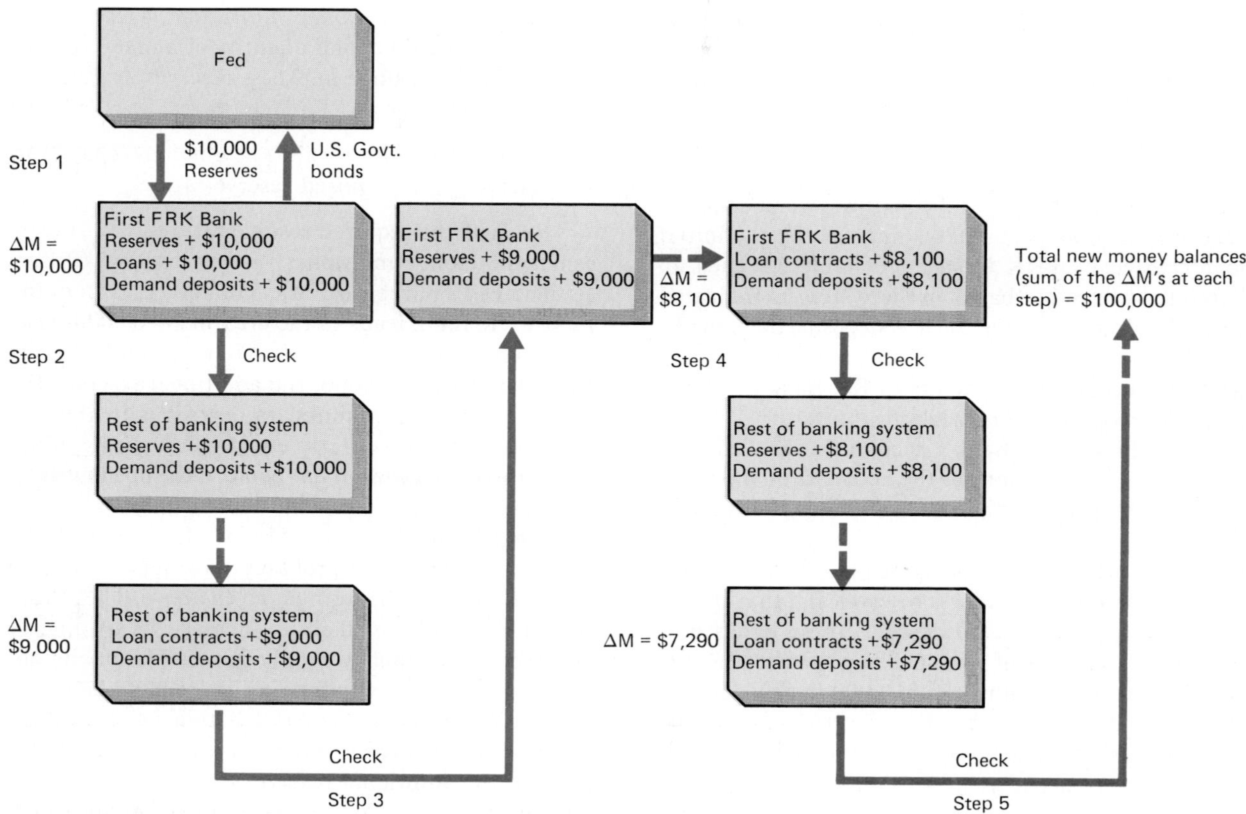

Figure 6.2 An open market operation and multiple deposit expansion
The arrows show how the initial purchase of government bonds worth $10,000 by the Fed leads to an increase in reserves, demand deposits, and new loans by the First FRK Bank. Subsequently, the $10,000 in new loans leads to increased reserves for the rest of the banking system and new loans of $9,000. Each new loan raises the money supply (ΔM). By the time the fourth step has been completed, the money supply has been increased by $10,000 + $9,000 + $8,100 + $7,290 = $34,390. When the process is complete, the money supply will have increased by $100,000.

accommodate unforeseen demands for cash by their customers. However, they must forego the interest revenue on the loan contracts they might have otherwise purchased.) With no excess reserves, the First FRK Bank is unable to increase the amount of credit supplied to its customers, because it is not allowed to add to its demand deposit liabilities. With the $10,000 in excess reserves it receives through sale of the bond, the bank is now in a position to buy more loan contracts and to create new demand deposits. Since the First FRK Bank would like to increase its profits whenever possible, it lends $10,000 to a customer. Thus, the almost immediate effect of the Fed's purchase of a $10,000 bond from the First FRK Bank is to indirectly increase the quantity of money by $10,000.

As we saw in chapter 5, our story is by no means over. A borrower who gave the First FRK Bank a $10,000 loan contract in return for an addition to its checking account did so to use the money for purchases. Let us review the process of multiple deposit expansion as we follow the $10,000 in new reserves and new money through the banking system. Suppose that the $10,000 in purchases financed by the initial loan created by FRK in step 1 of table 6.2 ends up deposited with other banks in the system as indicated by step 2. After receiving the new deposits, these banks present checks worth $10,000 for payment. The Fed helps them collect from the First FRK Bank by acting as a *clearinghouse* for checks, *subtracting* $10,000 from the First FRK Bank's account at the Fed, and adding the same amount to the accounts of the other banks at the Fed. In other words, FRK's reserves are reduced by $10,000, while the reserves of the other banks are increased by the same amount. Assuming they originally had no excess reserves and that the required reserve ratio is 10 percent, these banks now have excess reserves of $9,000. They need retain only $1,000 in reserve against the $10,000 in new demand deposits and are free to buy loan contracts and create new demand deposits totaling $9,000 (step 3 in table 6.2).

The story continues. The borrowers of the $9,000 also write checks totaling this amount, and the money is deposited in the First FRK Bank (step 4). The First FRK Bank needs to hold only $900 in reserves, and in the next set of transactions (which *you* should write in the balance sheet), it lends $8,100. So far, the money supply has increased by $27,100, which is equal to the $10,000 created in step 1, plus the $9,000 created in step 3, plus the new $8,100 just noted. If you were to carry out the succeeding chain of transactions, you would see that the initial open market operation of purchasing a $10,000 bond from the First FRK Bank will lead to a *total* increase in the money supply of $100,000. This is because *when there is no currency drain,* the *money multiplier,* which determines how much the total quantity of money changes as a result of a change in excess reserves, is given by the formula

money multiplier = total new money/change in reserves = 1/required reserve ratio.

Because the required reserve ratio is 0.1 (10 percent), the money multiplier in this case is 1/0.1 = 10. The Fed's purchase of the $10,000 bond from the First FRK Bank leads to the creation of $100,000 of new money for the economy. After demand deposits have grown by $100,000, the additional reserves the banking system is required to deposit with the Fed will total $10,000, exactly equal to the Fed's initial purchase of the government bond on the open market.

The Impact of Currency Drain In practice, the money multiplier will probably be smaller than the amount shown in the formula given above. The reason is that the public is likely to increase its holding of currency as the money supply grows. The public obtains currency by withdrawing it from its bank accounts. When the banks pay out this currency, they must draw down their cash reserves. In other words, some of the additional reserves created by the Fed's open market operation "leaks" into the public's currency holdings, limiting banks' ability to purchase new loan contracts and expand deposits. In practice, part of the initial $10,000 in new reserves created by the Fed in the preceding example ends up as currency held by the public instead of bank reserves. The *sum* of new bank reserves and additional currency held by the public will equal the initial $10,000 the Fed injected into the banking system. Suppose, as in our example of currency drain in chapter 5, the public desires to hold 30 percent of its total money balances in the form of cash. Then, when the monetary expansion induced by the Fed's open market operation is complete, the money supply will not have risen by $100,000. Instead, it will have grown by only $27,028.

*The **monetary base** is the raw material from which banks create deposit liabilities and is equal to the sum of banks' reserves, currency in their vaults, and currency in the hands of the public.*

Of this total, 30 percent, or $8,108 will be held as cash by the public. The difference between the public's increased cash holdings and the initial increase in reserves of $10,000, or $1,892, will remain as increased bank reserves. As a consequence, banks will have increased their loans by $18,920 (ten times their increase in reserves). The increase in checking account money plus the increase in the public's holding of cash equals the $27,028 increase in the money supply. (See footnote on page 125.)

However, the actual story is likely to be still more complex. The increased money supply may cause the public to wish to transfer funds from checking accounts to savings accounts. The immediate impact is to reduce M1 but leave M2 and M3 unchanged. (Why?) Since required reserve ratios are generally lower for banks' savings account liabilities than for their checking account liabilities, this action by the public leads to a money multiplier that is larger than it otherwise would be. The main point to remember is that excess reserves encourage banks to increase the quantity of money by a multiple greater than one. Currency drain tends to make this multiple closer to one than it would otherwise be, but transfers from checking accounts to savings accounts may make the multiple larger when M2 is used to measure the quantity of money.

There is another side of the "coin" of cash drain. Cash held by the public, if deposited with banks, becomes bank reserves. The sum of bank reserves and currency, either held by banks in their vaults or held by the general public, is known as the **monetary base** because it represents the basic raw material for creating money. The Fed, when it purchases bonds, either by increasing bank reserves or by paying in cash, increases the monetary base and lays the groundwork for an increase in the money supply. However, when the public desires to increase its cash holdings, it allocates part of the monetary base toward a form that cannot be used by banks to increase checking account money further.

It would be a good idea for you to work through the example illustrated in figure 6.2 and table 6.2 and show that if the Fed were to *sell* United States government bonds on the open market, the money supply would *fall* by a multiple of the initial decline in excess reserves. In a sense, money is destroyed. To see this, think about how banks meet their reserve requirements when the Fed sells United States government bonds on the open market. What happens to banks' outstanding loans and to demand deposits?

Other Instruments of Monetary Policy

Buying and selling government bonds on the open market is the Fed's most frequently used instrument of monetary policy. We also noted that the Fed sometimes changes, albeit rarely, required reserve ratios. There are still other instruments of monetary policy that the Fed uses either in conjunction with its open market operations or sometimes as substitutes for them. We will consider these other tools of monetary policy briefly in the next sections.

The Required Reserve Ratio In the example of an expansionary open market operation illustrated in table 6.2 and figure 6.2, the Fed purchased government bonds to expand the money supply. The required reserve ratio was 10 percent. Suppose now that the Fed decides to reverse its policy and wishes to reduce the money supply. We have already seen that the most likely course of action will be a contractionary open market policy, which involves *selling* government bonds to the public or to the banking system directly. However, another possibility is for the Fed to *increase* the required reserve ratio. Suppose the banking system is "loaned up," in that it has no excess reserves, that the money supply is $1 billion in checking accounts, and that reserves equal $100 million (10 percent of outstanding checking accounts), exactly what the Fed requires.

*The **discount rate** is the interest rate banks must pay when they borrow from the Fed. The term **discount** refers to the payment of the interest charge in advance so that the actual loan is the net of the total interest payment.*

__Direct credit controls__ allow the Fed to tell banks how much they can lend and to whom.

If the Fed wants to reduce the money supply by $100 million, it can sell $10 million worth of government securities, or it can achieve the same result by raising the required reserve ratio to 11.1 percent. With $1 billion in checking accounts, increasing the required reserve ratio to 11.1 percent will increase required reserves from $100 million to $111.1 million. Banks will be deficient in meeting this requirement by $11.1 million and will have to start a process of reducing their outstanding loans. As loans come up for renewal, the banks will simply refuse to renew them. When the loans are paid off, the banks' demand deposits will decline and so will their required reserves. Finally, when $100 million in loans has been paid off, demand deposits will have fallen by $100 million, and required reserves will be .111 × $900 million, or $100 million. Since $100 million equals the actual reserves of the banking system, there will be no more pressure to reduce outstanding loans, and the decline in the money supply will come to an end.

The Discount Rate In the discussion of open market operations and the reserve requirement, we asked you to work through the transactions involved in a *contraction* of the money supply. A contraction results from a sale of government bonds by the Fed on the open market. We have also seen that a contraction can be the result of an increase in the required reserve ratio. Still another possible cause of declining reserves is an increase in the public's desire to hold money in the form of currency rather than checking accounts. If banks have no excess reserves, then their reserves will fall below the legally required minimum. What happens then?

When banks' reserves fall below the required level, banks will reduce the value of loan contracts they hold. As loans are repaid, the banking system's checking account liabilities will fall, and banks will eventually be able to meet their reserve requirements. But this takes time. What is a bank to do while its reserve balances are legally too low? (A bank can actually lose its charter if deficient reserves are a persistent problem.) One possibility is for a bank to *borrow* reserves from the Fed, using its loan contract assets (earning assests) as security. Of course, the Fed charges banks for these loans. The interest rate the Fed charges banks when they borrow reserves is called the **discount rate.** By raising the discount rate, the Fed increases banks' costs for allowing their checking account liabilities to remain above the legally permissible level. This discourages them from allowing their borrowers to repay their loans slowly and from making new loans. By lowering the discount rate, the Fed can encourage banks to borrow reserves to meet their obligations and even to expand the amount of money in the economy.

Financial analysts often place considerable importance on announcements by the Fed that it is changing the discount rate. This is because the Fed sometimes changes the discount rate as a means of announcing to the general public its intentions regarding the money supply. This can be a quicker way to inform the public of the Fed's intentions than waiting for the news of changes in open market operations and their effects on the money supply to filter down through detailed statistical summaries in the news media.

Direct Credit Controls, Interest Rate Regulations, and Moral Suasion Banking is a regulated industry, and the Fed is one of its principal regulatory agencies. (Other regulators include various state banking agencies, the Comptroller of the Currency, and the Federal Deposit Insurance Corporation.) From time to time, Congress has authorized the Fed to impose **direct credit controls** on the banking system, which involve restricting the banks' right to supply credit to

***Moral suasion** is one of the Fed's methods of encouraging banks to lend more or less than they would like or to favor certain classes of customers.*

*A **bank run** occurs when a large proportion of a bank's depositors want to withdraw their funds all at once.*

*The **Federal Deposit Insurance Corporation (FDIC)** insures "small" bank deposits (those not exceeding $100,000) against losses if a bank fails.*

certain classes of borrowers. For instance, credit may be limited to large businesses that want to purchase trucks as opposed to small businesses or consumers who want to purchase cars. Direct credit controls are difficult to justify in a market economy. They almost always lead to various distortions in what is produced and consumed. Direct credit controls could conceivably be used to restrict the overall ability of the banking system to expand the money supply, but the direct control of credit is a much less effective tool than open market operations.

The Fed also has an instrument of monetary control known as **moral suasion,** which has been called the Fed's "open mouth" policy, as opposed to its open market policy, because it involves persuading banks to behave in a way that pleases the Fed. An implied threat may be that if banks fail to please the Fed, it may restrict their access to the "discount window" (bankers' jargon for the process of borrowing reserves). The channels through which moral suasion can affect the quantity of money are similar to those through which direct credit controls operate.

Deposit Insurance and Bank Bailouts The most troublesome feature of a fractional reserve monetary system is its susceptibility to **bank runs,** which occur when depositors lose faith in a bank's ability to meet its deposit obligations. As we have seen, reserves are never sufficient to convert all deposits into cash under a fractional reserve banking system. One of the major factors that caused the Great Depression was a one-third decline in the quantity of money between 1930 and 1933. This drop was partly caused by bank runs, which led to bank failures.

A review of the multiple deposit expansion process will show you how a decline in the public's confidence in the banking system leads to a fall in the quantity of money. Suppose depositors begin to cash in their deposits. Banks lose reserves as a result and must call in their loans—demanding repayment as soon as they legally can. This reduces the quantity of money. If bank reserves fall to zero, banks will be unable to meet their depositors' demands. Panic may then set in, spreading throughout the banking system. Under the worst circumstances, everyone wants to cash in, banks fail, and depositors may lose part or all of the wealth represented by their deposits.

The Fed has always had the power to provide reserves to avoid a financial panic, but it failed to exercise that power during the Great Depression. (We will say more about this in chapter 11.) The **Federal Deposit Insurance Corporation (FDIC)** was created by an act of Congress in 1933 for the purpose of insuring "small" deposits in participating banks. As of 1984, the definition of a small deposit was one not in excess of $100,000. The Federal Savings and Loan Insurance Corporation (FSLIC) performs a similar service for savings and loan institutions.

Since the mid-1930s, the FDIC and FSLIC have guaranteed that most depositors need not fear banks' inability to honor their deposit liabilities. If a bank is about to fail, the FDIC (or FSLIC) first tries to find a financially solvent bank to take over the failing bank's assets and liabilities so that no depositors, large or small, need suffer a loss. If a bank does fail, the FDIC steps in and operates it until a purchaser is found. The bank's stockholders will probably lose their equity, but most deposits are guaranteed. Therefore, depositors have little incentive to start a run on the bank. Since the FDIC was established, bank runs have been uncommon in the United States. However, in the early 1980s, several major banks found themselves in serious difficulty. Some large regional banks and savings and loan institutions became insolvent, and depositors began to withdraw their balances in bank runs that most financial analysts had thought disappeared with the 1930s. The run on banks in Ohio in the spring of 1985, referred to in the introduction, stemmed from the fact that the savings and loan institutions involved were members of a private, state-based insurance program. Their deposits were not guaranteed by official federal and state agencies.

Perhaps the most startling of the bank difficulties of this period was the de facto bankruptcy of one of the nation's largest banks, Continental Illinois National Bank of Chicago. Continental was heavily involved in loans to the United States petroleum industry. When oil prices began to decline in the early 1980s, many of these borrowers defaulted, and Continental saw its net worth plummet toward zero. A bank run ensued, and many observers feared that panic would spread to the rest of the banking system if Continental were not protected from actually declaring bankruptcy. The FDIC could not find any bank willing to take over Continental's assets and liabilities without substantial guarantees against financial loss. In other words, potential merger partners viewed Continental's net worth as negative. The FDIC faced the difficult choice of intervention to save the bank from bankruptcy, protecting its large depositors and possibly its stockholders, or letting events take their natural course toward actual bankruptcy.

Economists and financial analysts engaged in intense debate over the wisdom of intervention to bail out Continental. Proponents of intervention felt it was essential to protect the banking system from possible massive runs and collapse. Opponents believed a bank failure was necessary to signal large uninsured depositors and stockholders that they should be more careful by not placing deposits in, and buying the stock of, banks with careless management. While the bank was "saved," along with the accounts of both small and large depositors, stockholders lost practically all of their equity in Continental because the value of their stock was reduced to nearly zero. Nevertheless, those who opposed intervention felt that large depositors were not punished enough for failing to exercise discretion in placing funds with a potentially very risky bank.[2]

Until 1980, the FDIC also enforced interest rate ceilings set by the Fed on checking accounts (no interest allowed) and savings accounts. However, the Depository Institutions Deregulation and Monetary Control Act of 1980 established the Depository Institution Deregulation Committee to phase out most interest ceilings by 1986. As a result, most individuals now receive interest payments on their checking accounts and rates determined by the market on other accounts.

Deregulation of the Banking System: Increased Competition and Increased Risk In recent years, many aspects of banking have been increasingly deregulated under the Depository Institutions Deregulation and Monetary Control Act of 1980. The rationale for banking deregulation is that by fostering increased competition among financial institutions of all types, borrowers will benefit from greater access to funds and depositors will receive higher interest rates. We have already mentioned several provisions of the act as it affects required reserves and services available to banks. To a certain extent, the act is misnamed because some of its provisions actually *increase* banking regulation by subjecting nonmember banks, savings and loan associations, and other depository institutions to the same controls that the Fed exercises over member banks.

One provision of the act grants permission for all depository institutions to offer NOW (negotiable order of withdrawal) accounts throughout the United States.

These are essentially interest-bearing checking accounts. Providing them has eliminated the most significant difference distinguishing commercial banks (those that have always offered conventional checking accounts and a full range of loan services to individuals and businesses), savings banks, savings and loan associations, and credit unions. The act has set up machinery to phase out most interest rate ceilings on bank deposits and restricted the power of states to place ceilings on the interest rates banks are allowed to charge their customers (usury laws).

Under provisions of the act, banks are now freer to compete for deposits by paying higher interest rates. They are permitted to venture into riskier markets, seeking loan contracts yielding higher returns. As we saw in the discussion of the Continental Illinois bailout, deregulation has created serious questions regarding the degree to which the Fed and the FDIC should bail out banks and protect large depositors from the risk of making bad loans.[3]

Before deregulation, people seeking high returns on their funds were frequently forced to bypass the banking system and lend directly to borrowers. These lenders had a strong incentive to assess the risk of default because they would bear the full cost of a borrower's failure to pay interest or repay principal. Suppose now that a major United States bank has attracted large deposits by offering high interest based on relatively risky loans to foreign governments and businesses. (See chapter 16 for a discussion of the international debt problem and its effect on United States banks.) Depositors seeking these interest rates are likely to worry much less about the riskiness of these loans if they believe banks will be bailed out should default appear imminent.

Unfortunately, such bailouts are not costless. If the Fed or the FDIC uses moral suasion to force a solvent bank to lend money to other banks or to borrowers in difficulty in order to avoid their default, these funds are not available for less risky loans. As a result, some potential borrowers must do without. An alternative would be to pay off small depositors if a bank should fail, letting the bank's large depositors and its stockholders bear the penalty of making a business error in search of higher returns. This is an issue that will occupy much space in the economic news during the next several years.

▸ Preview: The Linkage between Money, Credit, and National Income

As the Johnson family in the introduction to this chapter learned very unfortunately, when the Fed or members of the banking system do anything to disrupt the normal relationship between the supply of money and the rest of the economy, the consequences can be quite serious. In the following chapters on the macroeconomy, we will explore the crucial linkages between the monetary system and the goods-producing sector. The principal connection is through credit markets. Banks are among the most important purchasers of loan contracts from households and business firms. The money balances created through this channel are used to purchase consumer durable goods and finance business investments. Thus, they are a crucial link in the relationship between aggregate expenditure on goods and services and aggregate production. Some important aggregate measures of the money stock, the monetary base, and bank-financed credit are contained in table 6.3 and illustrated in figure 6.3.

Table 6.3 Money stock, monetary base, and bank loans and investments, 1959–85 (billions of dollars)

Year	M1[a] (annual average)	M2[b] (annual average)	Monetary base[c] (figures for December of each year)	Bank loans and purchases of United States Treasury and other securities (figures for December of each year)
1959	$140.9	$ 297.7	$ 44.3	$ 188.7
1960	141.9	312.3	44.5	197.4
1961	146.5	335.5	45.7	212.8
1962	149.2	362.8	47.1	231.2
1963	154.7	393.4	49.4	250.2
1964	161.9	425.1	51.9	272.3
1965	169.5	459.5	54.7	300.1
1966	173.7	481.3	56.8	316.1
1967	185.1	526.6	60.5	352.0
1968	199.4	569.4	64.8	390.2
1969	205.8	591.3	67.9	401.7
1970	216.5	628.8	72.0	435.5
1971	230.6	713.6	77.1	485.7
1972	251.9	806.4	84.2	572.6
1973	265.8	863.2	90.3	647.8
1974	277.4	911.2	98.3	713.6
1975	291.0	1,026.9	104.5	745.2
1976	310.4	1,171.2	112.0	804.2
1977	335.5	1,297.7	121.4	891.5
1978	363.2	1,403.9	132.2	1,013.5
1979	389.0	1,518.9	142.5	1,135.9
1980	414.5	1,656.2	155.0	1,239.6
1981	440.9	1,822.7	162.7	1,316.3
1982	478.5	1,999.1	175.1	1,412.4
1983	528.0	2,188.8	185.5	1,553.0
1984	558.5	2,371.7	199.0	1,716.8
1985	624.7	2,563.6	216.9	1,895.5

Source: From *Economic Report of the President, 1986,* Tables B-64, B-66, B-67, pp. 327, 330, 333.

[a]M1 includes all demand deposits in the banking system (except those of the United States Treasury) upon which checks can be written or that can be transferred by telephone or electronic means, plus currency and travelers' checks in the hands of the nonbank public.

[b]M2 includes M1 plus "small" (under $100,000) certificates of deposit, savings accounts, money market mutual funds, and certain other bank obligations that depositors treat as readily available to carry out transactions.

[c]Monetary base is the sum of the bank's reserves, currency in their vaults, and currency in the hands of the public.

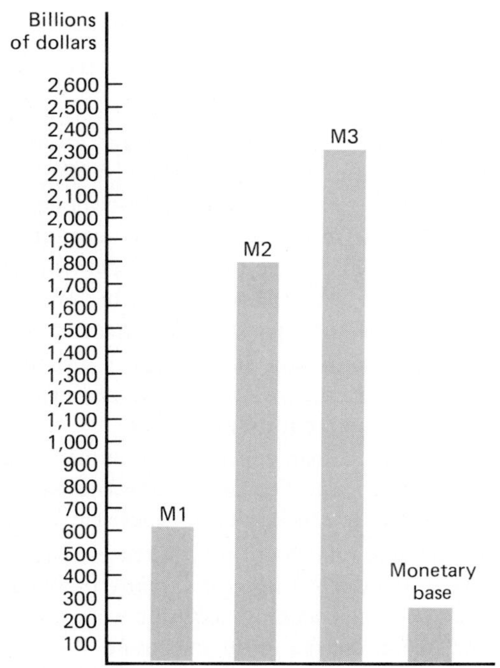

Figure 6.3 Important monetary aggregates for the United States, June, 1985
From *Federal Reserve Bulletin,* December 1985, Tables 1-20, 1-21.

▸ Summary and Conclusions

In this chapter we showed how the Fed, the central bank of the United States, regulates the quantity of money in our economy. We also described the role of the Federal Deposit Insurance Corporation. Although the institutional details describe the economy of the United States, the basic features of a paper monetary standard and fractional reserve banking characterize all modern market economies today. A complete listing of how the Fed can affect the money supply is given in table 6.4.

Table 6.4 How the Fed controls the money supply

Action by the Fed	Effect on the money supply
Buy government bonds from banks or the public	Increases total bank reserves, which causes deposit expansion and an increase in the money supply
Sell government bonds to banks or the public	Reduces total bank reserves, which causes deposit contraction and a decrease in the money supply
Lower the reserve requirement (the required reserve ratio)	Decreases banks' *required* reserves, which causes deposit expansion and an increase in the money supply
Raise the reserve requirement (the required reserve ratio)	Increases banks' *required* reserves, which causes deposit contraction and a decrease in the money supply
Lower the discount rate	Encourages banks to borrow reserves from the Fed, which causes deposit expansion and an increase in the money supply
Raise the discount rate	Discourages banks from borrowing reserves from the Fed, which causes deposit contraction and a decrease in the money supply
Direct credit controls	Prevents certain types of lending by banks, which restricts the money supply
Moral suasion	Restricts (encourages) lending by banks, which restricts (increases) the money supply
Interest rate restrictions	Lowers the attractiveness of certain deposit liabilities, which discourages deposit expansion and restricts the money supply
Deposit insurance (by the FDIC)	Encourages people to use bank deposits instead of cash, which tends to increase the money supply

Key Terms

bank runs *141*
Depository Institutions Deregulation and Monetary Control Act of 1980 *133*
direct credit controls *140*
discount rate *140*
excess reserves *135*
Federal Deposit Insurance Corporation (FDIC) *141*
Federal Open Market Committee (FOMC) *135*
fractional reserve system *134*
instruments of monetary policy *134*
monetary authority *132*
monetary base *139*
monetary policy *133*
moral suasion *141*
open market operation *135*
required reserve ratio *134*

Questions for Discussion and Review

Are the statements in questions 1 through 3 true, false, or uncertain? Defend your answers.

1. The Fed, through an open market operation, buys a bond from John Smith for $10,000. Smith decides to keep $1,000 as mad money and deposit the rest in his checking account. With a required reserve ratio of 10 percent, the banking system can create $90,000 in new money through multiple deposit expansion.
2. To ensure that the poor have access to credit, the Fed should impose interest rate ceilings on lenders below current market rates.
3. If a bank buys a loan contract, the money stock increases, but if the Fed buys a government bond, the money stock does not increase.
4. After the deregulation of interest rates that banks pay on deposit accounts, many banking services such as checking accounts were no longer free of charge to the customer. Why?
5. Some institutions, such as Merrill Lynch and Sears, offer financial services similar to those of banks but are not subject to the same regulations as banks. Why?
6. The stated intention of Federal deposit insurance is to insure depositors against the loss of their funds should the depository institution fail. What incentives do managers of financial institutions have as a result of this insurance?

7. Show how the following transactions initially affect the banking system's assets, liabilities, and the quantity of money as measured by M1 and M2. Use balance sheets such as those in tables 5.1, 5.2, 5.4, and 6.2 to illustrate your answers.
   a. A business firm pays off a $100,000 bank loan by writing a check.
   b. The Fed buys $1 million worth of government bonds from the United States Treasury.
   c. The United States Treasury sells a $1,000 bond to a private citizen and uses the proceeds to buy office equipment. The citizen pays for the bond by withdrawing $1,000 from a savings account.
   d. The Treasury pays off $1 million of the national debt by redeeming (buying back) bonds from the public. It pays for these bonds by writing checks on its account with the Fed. The public deposits the $1 million in savings accounts.
   e. Suppose that in the transaction in part d, the Treasury pays by collecting $1 million in taxes from the public. The taxes are paid by drawing down checking accounts.
   f. One bank borrows $1 million in reserves from another bank (*not* from the Fed).

   Why does the question specify the *initial* effects of the transactions on the quantity of money? Is there a further impact? If so, how large is it? Show how each of the transactions affects the monetary base and the amount of loan contracts held by banks.
8. Suppose that there was no central bank, that open market operations were never carried out, and that there were no reserve requirements. Would the money supply grow without limit under a paper standard? What might comprise the monetary base? What could cause the monetary base to change? How could currency be issued? Would it help you to answer this question if there were paper currency issued by the government's treasury? Hint: How would banks' profit motive lead them to act?
9. Suppose the federal government decided to pay off the entire government debt. This would mean that the Fed's open market operations as we now know them would no longer be feasible. What means might the Fed adopt to control the quantity of money?
10. Assume there are no excess reserves. Use the balance sheets of the Fed and the banking system to show the way an open market sale of government bonds reduces the monetary base and the quantity of money.

Chapter 7

Money, Credit, and the Rate of Interest

Outline

Objectives

After reading this chapter, the student should be able to:

Discuss the roles of the lender and the borrower in a loan contract.
Explain why firms' demand for loanable funds is downward sloping.
Explain how the government's demand for loanable funds is related to its budget deficit.
Describe the aggregate demand for loanable funds and what factors cause it to shift.
Explain what factors affect households' decisions to save and how households allocate their financial assets between money and loan contracts.
Describe why banks add to the supply of loanable funds and the role the real interest rate plays in this decision.
List factors that shift the supply of loanable funds.
Use households' and banks' supplies of loanable funds to derive the aggregate supply of loanable funds.
Explain how equilibrium in the loan contract market determines the real interest rate.
Discuss factors that affect the structure of interest rates.

▸ Introduction

In 1979, real GNP in the United States grew 2.8 percent. In 1980, it declined by 0.8 percent. In 1978, unemployment was 5.8 percent of the labor force and grew to 7.0 percent in 1979. Although these figures were both high by historical standards, the CPI increased 11.3 percent in 1978 and 13.5 percent in 1979. These data were typical of the "stagflation" that plagued the United States economy in the 1970s. Such conditions boded ill for the reelection of the Carter administration in November 1980.

Throughout 1978–79 economists forecast a recession that did not materialize. The political calculation had been that a recession in 1978 and/or 1979 would precede an economic expansion in 1980. In the early stages of an economic expansion, real GNP grows at a faster rate, inflation falls, and so does unemployment. Such conditions obviously would be favorable to a president seeking reelection.

In October 1979 the Fed announced a major change in its monetary policy. Instead of trying to achieve an ideal interest rate, it claimed it would focus primarily on achieving a desirable rate of growth of the quantity of money as measured by M1 and M2. This change was well-received by many economists. However, the promised change in policy goals was not achieved. Over the next twelve months, the money supply in the United States grew first at the slowest rate in twenty-five years and then at the fastest rate in many years. The economy experienced the shortest recession and then the shortest recovery in recorded business cycle history. The Fed was accused of trying to manipulate the economy to reelect a president. Whether this accusation was true or not, the timing of Fed policy was such that the economy sank into a minirecession in mid-1980.

In this chapter, we will take a closer look at the connection between the financial sector of the economy and the goods sector. We will explore how government policies can affect interest rates and inflation. We will begin to explore how monetary policy may be used to affect macroeconomic conditions.

Things to Come

In chapter 4 we noted that it is impossible to understand how the macroeconomy works by analyzing the goods and services sector alone. Full understanding requires incorporating the connections between the market for goods and services and the financial sector of the economy.

In this chapter we develop a simple, yet realistic, model of the supply and demand for financial assets such as bank deposits, corporate bonds, and United States Treasury securities. This clarifies a number of important economic issues. Among them are the economic variables that influence the behavior of buyers and sellers of financial assets, including the price level. We will also concern ourselves with the concept of equilibrium in financial markets and how it results in a particular interest rate or set of interest rates. In this chapter we reiterate the importance of the difference between the nominal and the real rate of interest. An important objective of this chapter is to link the financial and nonfinancial sectors of the economy. In particular, we show how the analysis we develop helps us to understand how government policy affects interest rates and thus affects investment and aggregate expenditure for goods and services.

Table 7.1 Some credit market instruments held by households, 1960–1983

	Billions of dollars 1960	1970	1981	1983	Percent of total 1960	1970	1981	1983
Total credit market instruments[a]	**$150**	**$262**	**$646**	**$868.1**	**100%**	**100%**	**100%**	**100%**
United States government securities	$ 73.8	$ 93.9	$313.4	$425.0	49	36	49	49
State and local government obligations	30.8	48.4	89.1	160.0	21	18	13	18
Corporate and foreign bonds	10.0	53.1	76.5	58.6	7	20	12	7
Mortgages	33.4	60.5	130.2	184.3	23	23	20	21

Source: From *Statistical Abstract of the United States: 1982–83* (103d edition), U.S. Bureau of the Census, 1982, Table 814 and 1985, Table 810, p. 488.
[a]These are loans made by households in various forms to institutions and people.

Financial Instruments

There are many financial markets in a modern economy such as that of the United States. If you turn to the business section of your city's newspaper, you will see numerous ads for financial instruments, which as we saw in chapter 5, are the various ways you can hold your financial wealth. One possibility is to hold it as money. Another possibility is to hold your wealth in a loan contract. In exchange for lending money to some borrower, you will receive interest payments plus a promise that your money will be repaid by the end of the loan period. The best way to think of a loan contract is as a bond, such as one issued by a large corporation (General Motors or Sears) or the federal government. At first glance, the term *loan contract* seems a very cumbersome name for a bond. The reason we will use it is that it is a more general expression, which also includes other forms of loans, such as a mortgage to finance a construction project or funds that a bank may lend an individual to start a small business.

Table 7.1 presents data on the total dollar value of credit market instruments held by United States households in recent years. (Banks and other institutions hold financial instruments, too. Their behavior in the loan contract market will be discussed later.) Between 1960 and 1983, households increased the nominal dollar value of the credit market instruments they held by almost 600 percent. During the same period, consumer prices rose by about 300 percent. Based on these data, what happened to the real holdings of credit market instruments by households? Table 7.1 also tells us that the dollar value of corporate and foreign bonds holdings by households in 1983 was almost *six times* what it was in 1960. Of course, corporate bonds are not the only credit market instruments owned by households. In fact, the largest single category in 1983 was United States government securities. Keep in mind that the data in table 7.1 ignore the assets held as reserves by private pension funds. In 1983, United States pension funds' reserves totaled almost $1 trillion. These are a form of loan contract held by individuals in a group sense and include the types of loans listed in table 7.1. Loan contracts held as pension fund reserves were nine times larger in 1983 than in 1960.

*The **loan contract, financial,** or **credit market** is where borrowers and lenders of money arrange the terms of loans.*

***Loanable funds** consist of money borrowed and lent in the credit market.*

The Decision to Hold Money versus Loan Contracts

It is important to point out that money and loan contracts are linked in the individual's decision to hold financial wealth. In particular, if we know someone's spending behavior in the market for currently produced goods and services and his or her behavior in the loan contract market, then we *automatically* know his or her behavior in the money market.

To better understand this, a simple example is helpful. Suppose that a person with an after-tax income of $1,000 this month decides to buy $750 worth of consumption goods and $150 worth of bonds. This means that $100 is left over ($1,000 − $900) to be kept as an addition to this person's money balances. This behavior concerning how much money to be held (the additional $100) can be immediately inferred once we know the behavior of the individual in the goods and services market (purchases of $750) and the loan contract market ($150 lent out). The point is that although we will focus on the loan contract market in this chapter, we are also implicitly examining people's decisions concerning how much money they wish to hold.

▸ The Loan Contract Market

Background

In a modern economy such as that of the United States, some individuals would like to purchase goods and services now but lack the necessary dollars to pay the sellers of those goods and services. Of course, at the same time there are other individuals with a completely different problem. They would prefer *not* to use all of their dollars currently available to purchase goods and services. These are not necessarily people who are rich or who don't know what to do with their money. Instead, they are individuals who would like to purchase more goods in the future compared to today. The market for **loan contracts** is also called the **financial or credit market,** which brings these individuals together. The loan contract market is the "place" where the two types of people "meet" to transfer their money. Money is transferred from those who have more than they want for current uses to those who want more than they now have. A loan contract arranges such a reallocation of spending power.

It is important that we define loan contract precisely. A loan contract is basically a piece of paper that obligates someone to repay money borrowed from someone else. Two parties are obviously involved in any loan contract transaction—the borrower of current dollars and the lender of current dollars. Those of you who go on to law school will study the detailed legal language of a loan contract. When all the details are stripped away, though, a loan contract is simply an exchange of today's dollars for a promise of future dollars.

A Closer Look at the Details of a Loan Contract

To understand the commitments involved in a loan contract, we can examine what is involved from the viewpoints of the two parties involved. In our analysis, the *demander* in the loan contract market is the *borrower*. The demander (or borrower) wishes to receive a certain number of dollars from the lender; these dollars are known as **loanable funds.** In exchange, the demander (or borrower) of loanable funds gives the lender an IOU. This IOU is the loan contract in which the borrower promises to pay back the money borrowed plus interest. The loan contract specifies very clearly the future dates when these payments are to be made. The *demander* of loanable funds, then, *supplies* a loan contract and, as a result, gains *current dollars*. At the same time, the loan contract obligates the demander to return *future dollars* to the lender. The demander of loanable funds is willing to go into debt today because of the potential benefits he or she expects from putting borrowed dollars to good use.

The dollar commitments made by the *supplier* of loanable funds, the *lender,* are mirror images of the dollar commitments made by the demander of loanable funds. The supplier of loanable funds parts with current dollars and in return acquires ownership of the demander's IOU. Because the IOU represents a claim over a specified sequence of payments of future dollars, the supplier of loanable funds has basically traded current money for the money the demander is obliged to pay back in the future.

At the outset it is important to correct any impression that the lender is a loser in the deal. Remember that interest is paid on a loan contract. The rate of interest, and typically not altruistic feelings, is what motivates the lender to willingly part with current dollars. Also keep in mind that it is the *real* interest rate that concerns borrowers and lenders, not the observed or nominal interest rate. If this distinction is unclear, review the definitions of these terms in chapter 2, pages 48–49. Later we will discuss the precise role played by the rate of interest in the decisions of borrowers and lenders in the loan contract market.

The Model of the Loan Contract Market to Be Developed

Two points should be made concerning how our model of the loan contract market relates to the financial markets currently in existence in the United States economy. First, the financial markets in a large modern economy develop according to the principle of specialization. This means that many different types of IOUs are traded. Each IOU pays its own specified rate of interest. Thus, at any time many different interest rates are in effect in the economy. To keep things manageable, our model of the loan contract market will ignore this complexity and simply use the concept of a loan contract or IOU as a generic term. The rate of interest paid on this representative loan contract will be the economy's average interest rate. The second point is that our model is not concerned with the total volume of outstanding loan contracts that have been bought and sold in the *past*. Our model is concerned only with how *new* issues of loan contracts are created in the economy and how this process relates to the determination of aggregate economic activity.

The Demand for Loanable Funds

Firms

Business firms demand loanable funds by selling corporate bonds, by selling their stock, and by borrowing from banks. Firms also borrow loanable funds in another way. Sometimes firms retain earnings, which are profits that go undistributed to stockholders. Because households own the firms in society, retained earnings or business saving is simply another component of firms' demand for loanable funds. The basic reason firms demand loanable funds is to finance investments. Consider, for example, the case of a builder who wants to start an investment project such as the construction of a new building. The contractor is faced with a dilemma. On the one hand, he or she has to buy materials such as bricks, concrete, electrical wiring, and so on from producers who make and sell these products. Construction workers will only be willing to supply their labor services if they receive the current market wage. These and the other expenditures require dollars *now*. However, the builder will not realize any profits from renting space in the building to be constructed until it is completed, which means that profits will be realized in the future. Our builder might try to pay for the goods and services currently supplied by promising future dollars. The fact that this is not the way things actually happen suggests that construction workers and materials suppliers tend not to be interested in producing investment goods unless they are paid in *current* dollars.

We will simply assume that to satisfy the need for current dollars, our builder can enter the loan contract market and exchange an IOU for current dollars. What is the value of the loan contract the builder will demand? It is exactly the same as the value of the current goods and services he or she wishes to buy for the investment project.

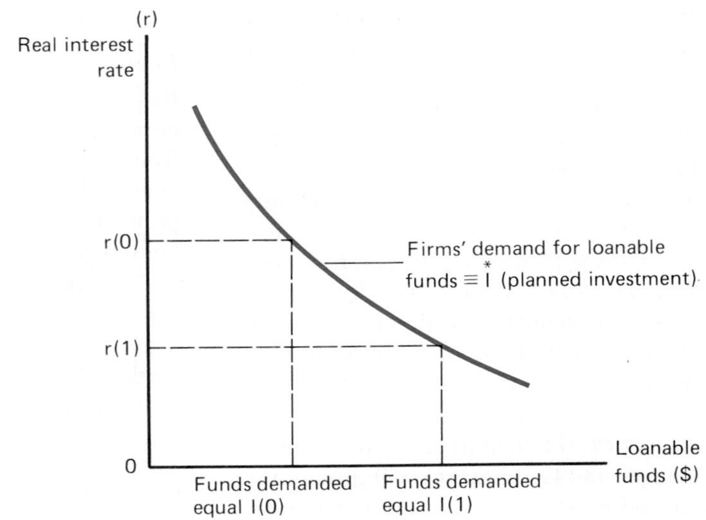

Figure 7.1 Firms' demand for loanable funds
Lower interest rates make additional investments profitable because the interest rate is the cost of the credit necessary to finance investment. As a result, the quantity of funds firms wish to borrow increases as the interest rate falls. Thus, the amount of money firms wish to borrow at any particular interest rate is equal to the amount they plan to invest ($\overset{*}{I}$).

Firms' Demand for Loanable Funds We assume that a firm's decision to demand loanable funds will reflect its decision to purchase investment goods and that firms borrow for no other reason. This means that firms' demand for loanable funds schedule in figure 7.1 has a negative slope. As the interest rate falls, the amount of funds firms wish to borrow rises. The inverse relationship between the real interest rate (r) and firms' demand for funds stems from the effect of the interest rate on the profitability of investments they might make. There are always more investment projects that will be profitable when the interest rate declines.

The interest rate provides investors with a way of calculating the economic value of potential investment projects, each of which generates a stream of payoffs at various dates in the future. Because a higher interest rate reduces the profitability of investment projects, firms' demand for funds to finance these investments is downward sloping. An investment decision involves present costs and future returns to firms from the services of the additional capital. The rate of interest is what allows a proper economic comparison of these present costs and future returns. As such, it plays a key role in the investment decision.

The total dollars needed to complete *all* the projects deemed profitable at the prevailing interest rate is also the total dollar value of investment goods demanded. When the interest rate is r(0) in figure 7.1, this quantity equals $\overset{*}{I}(0)$. To finance this investment, investors will try to borrow an equivalent amount of money in the loanable funds market. Although additional investment projects are available, investors will reject them because the cost involved exceeds the value of their returns.

Suppose the interest rate is lower, say, r(1) in figure 7.1. This makes each investment project more profitable. Some projects that were unprofitable at interest rate r(0) become winning ventures at the lower interest rate, r(1). To finance the purchase of this larger quantity of investment goods, investors increase the amount of funds they wish to borrow. Thus, the dollar value of the loans firms desire at interest rate r(1) is $\overset{*}{I}(1)$, which is greater than $\overset{*}{I}(0)$. Remember that we are concerned with the *real value* of loanable funds demanded. This means that we are evaluating the funds that firms wish to borrow at prices that prevailed during some base period (year).

The Government

We know that the federal government purchases goods and services from producers in the economy and provides income support to certain poor, sick, and elderly members of society. One way it pays for these is with revenue collected through taxes. When government expenditure exceeds the tax revenue it collects, we say that the government runs a *deficit*. Only once since 1960 has the federal government in the United States not been in a deficit situation where its total tax revenue (T) fell short of its total expenditure (G). Prior to 1960, budget *surpluses,* the situation where tax revenue exceeds government expenditures, were not uncommon.[1] Let us represent the budget deficit by (G − T), the real value of the difference between the government's expenditure and its tax revenue. The size of the government deficit is a source of great controversy in debates over macroeconomic policy. We will have much more to say about the government deficit in the following chapters—particularly chapters 10–12. For now, we will explore how the government finances a deficit.

Monetizing the Budget Deficit There are two basic ways the federal government can deal with a budget deficit. First, the United States Treasury can borrow directly from the Fed. This is equivalent to the federal government's simply printing the money necessary to finance the deficit. When firms demand cash before turning over their goods to a government buyer, the government could simply produce the exact number of dollar bills required to pay for the goods.

Many Latin American governments use their ability to borrow from their central banks or to print money as a "magical" source of financing for their budget deficits. In chapter 11 we analyze the link between inflation and the rapid expansion of the money supply. For now, we turn our attention to another, more commonly used method of financing budget deficits in modern Western economies.

Financing the Budget Deficit in the Loan Contract Market Suppose that the Treasury does not borrow directly from the Fed when faced with a budget deficit. This means that the government behaves like a private investor in the loan contract market. When government expenditures exceed tax revenues, then, the government enters the loanable funds market as a borrower, seeking enough dollars to finance its budget deficits from the private sector of the economy. In exchange for the loans it receives, the government issues new loan contracts (government bonds) and promises to pay back its debt with future dollars plus interest.

Households and the commercial banking system are perfectly willing to part with their dollars in exchange for the loan contracts the government provides for one basic reason. The federal government can *never* go bankrupt. As a last resort it can always raise taxes or print new money to pay its debt. This means that government IOUs have the lowest risk of all loan contracts and therefore usually pay a lower rate of interest than the bonds of private borrowers. Remember, though, that in our simple model of the aggregate loan contract market we are dealing with a single (average) interest rate.

The ***aggregate demand for loanable funds (DLF)*** *is a schedule illustrating the total amount of loanable funds borrowers seek to borrow at various real interest rates.*

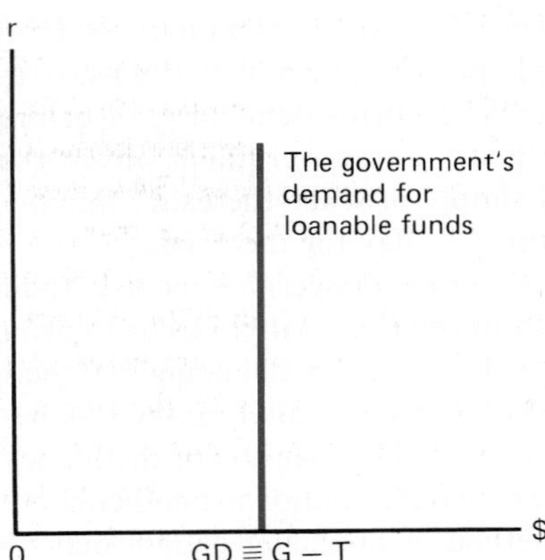

Figure 7.2 The government's demand for loanable funds
The government demands loanable funds equal to its budget deficit and pays whatever interest rate is necessary.

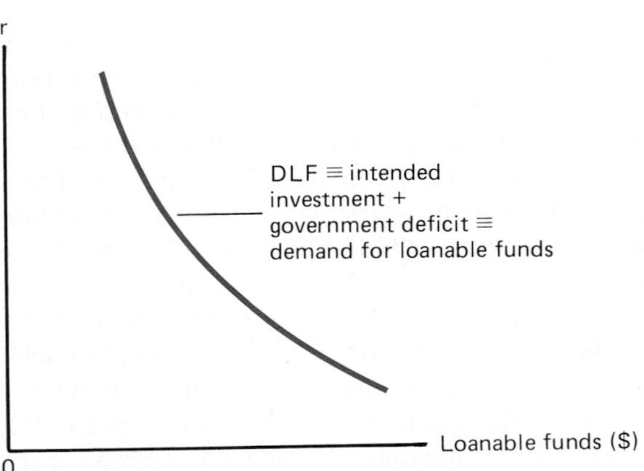

Figure 7.3 The aggregate demand curve for loanable funds
The aggregate demand for loanable funds (DLF) comes from two sources: private investors and the government.

The Government's Demand for Loanable Funds Figure 7.2 illustrates the real value of the loanable funds demanded by the government. We have drawn the government's demand curve as a vertical line. This implies that the government will finance its entire deficit, G − T, in the loan contract market regardless of the interest rate it must pay. The government's need for dollars to finance any deficit is so immediate that it accepts the prevailing rate of interest in the loan contract market.

Exactly how does this happen in practice? Currently, all government securities are auctioned off to the highest bidders. The difference between the face value of the security and the price paid by the lender is the implicit interest rate on the loan contract. For example, suppose that the government wants to borrow $100,000 for one year. It might auction off a security that is a promise to pay the lender $100,000 one year from today. If the winning bidder offers $90,000 for this security, then the implicit rate of interest paid by the government is about 11 percent. The interest rate is higher the lower the amount paid for the promise that the government will pay the lender a fixed $100,000 one year from now.

The Aggregate Demand Curve for Loanable Funds and the Rate of Interest

The **aggregate demand for loanable funds (DLF)** has the two components just discussed: the demand for funds stemming from investment by firms in the private sector of the economy and the government's demand due to any budget deficit. These two sources of demand for loanable funds produce the aggregate demand curve for loanable funds shown in figure 7.3. The real rate of interest is measured on the vertical axis and the total real dollars of loanable funds on the horizontal axis. To obtain the points for the aggregate demand for loanable funds, we have simply added the amount the government wishes to borrow (its budget deficit) to the amount demanded by private investors at the various rates of interest. By considering the various possible real rates of interest, we can plot the aggregate demand for loanable funds schedule, DLF in figure 7.3, from the information in figures 7.1 and 7.2. The demand for loanable funds schedule takes the shape of the demand for loanable funds by investors. In our model, private investors are the only borrowers who are sensitive to changes in the real rate of interest. Thus, the market demand for loanable funds is simply the investors' demand for loanable funds moved to the right or left by an amount equal to the government deficit or surplus.

The aggregate demand for loanable funds shows us how borrowers *as a group* respond to changes in the rate of interest. It is important to realize that the DLF schedule is drawn holding constant the other factors that influence the demand for credit. Should anything that determines investment or the government deficit change (other than the real interest rate), this will disturb the aggregate demand for loanable funds. What are some examples?

Think about factors that would change the individual components of the demand for loanable funds. First, anything that reduces the government deficit, such as a reduction in government expenditures or an increase in taxes, shifts the demand for loanable funds schedule to the left. The opposite holds if the political process generates a larger government deficit through increased government expenditures, reduced taxes, or both. Finally, anything that affects the profitability of investment will also shift the demand for loanable funds schedule. Suppose, for example, firms suddenly hit upon a new technology that makes all investments more profitable. This means that at any given interest rate, firms will desire to invest more and therefore demand more loanable funds.

The Supply of Loanable Funds

Households as Suppliers of Loanable Funds

The Household's Financial Wealth At the beginning of a given period of time—say, a month—a household will possess a certain level of financial wealth. One way households hold their wealth is in money, which is largely checkable deposits at banks plus currency issued by the government. A second way households hold their wealth is in loan contracts—bonds issued by private firms, foreign countries, or the United States government.

The Household's Saving Decision Households own productive resources that they ultimately sell to producers of goods and services in exchange for income. All households then face two basic decisions. One is that they must decide how many currently produced goods and services to consume. How many chicken dinners, light bulbs, and vacation trips will they buy?

We know from the discussion in chapter 4 that once a household has made its consumption purchases and paid its taxes, the remainder is its saving. This brings us to a second basic economic decision households make. How will they allocate saving between the two financial assets we are discussing, money and loan contracts? Money is useful to have on hand because it facilitates purchases. However, it pays relatively little or no interest. Holding your wealth in bonds will earn relatively high interest, but then you cannot use it to buy that new car. There are costs and benefits to holding money versus lending it out. The decisions of how much to consume and how to allocate saving are the basic economic choices faced by households on a day-to-day basis. Many complex factors are involved in a household's financial decisions, but two generalizations are reasonable.

1. Day-to-day fluctuations in the rate of interest seem to play no role in how much households save versus consume. Economists disagree over the long-term impact of a permanent change in the return people expect to receive on the amount they save. However, they tend to agree that over short periods of time, other factors are much more important determinants of saving behavior. If the interest rate is not what determines the total amount of saving, then what is? We already have an answer to this question from chapter 4. The saving function discussed there showed us that *total aggregate saving is largely based on aggregate disposable income.* But if the real interest rate does not affect aggregate saving, what role does it play in households' financial decisions?

2. The rate of interest is crucial in determining the *distribution* of households' wealth *between* money and loan contracts. Households will place more and more of their wealth into interest-bearing financial instruments—loan contracts—as the real rate of interest rises. Higher interest rates induce households to increase the amount of money they lend (loan contracts they buy) and also induce them to reduce the amount of money they desire to hold.

For example, suppose we have a household with financial wealth at the beginning of this month that includes $100 in the form of a checking account deposit and $300 worth of loan contracts. These loan contracts may, for example, be held as shares in a mutual fund that purchases corporate and government bonds. Suppose further that the household intends to sell $200 of labor services to an employer this month. The household intends to spend $100 of its earnings on consumption goods, including food and recreation. Its tax bill is $50. These data mean that our hypothetical household is saving $50 ($200 − $150), the portion of its income not consumed or paid out in taxes. This $50 in saving will allow the household to consume more in the future.

The household's next choice concerns the form in which it will hold its $50 saving. The answer depends on the real rate of interest at the time the decision is made, because the interest rate is the opportunity cost of holding financial wealth in currency or in a checking account. Remember, the alternative is to lend the money out and receive an interest payment in return. While a household values dollars in its checking account to facilitate purchases of goods and services, unfortunately it must give up something for that privilege. To hold dollars, the household has to give up the interest it could have earned had it held its savings in loan contracts as opposed to cash or a checking account. The higher the interest rate, the higher is the cost attached to holding money in cash or in a checking account and the greater is the incentive to turn these dollars into interest-bearing loan contracts. (We are discussing the very basic case where the household owns a checking account that pays no interest. In reality, many checking accounts, such as NOW accounts and money market accounts do pay interest. However, the interest that can be earned on loan contracts is higher. The opportunity cost of holding money in a NOW-type checking account is the *difference* between the interest rate paid in the loan contract market and that paid on the NOW account.)

The Rate of Interest and the Household's Supply of Loanable Funds Let us dig a little deeper into the relationships between the interest rate and the quantity of funds that households supply to the loan contract market. Suppose that within the context of the example we have been developing the interest rate is very low. This means that the opportunity cost of holding money (currency and checking accounts) is also low. The result is that the household in our example decides to save its $50 by placing $10 in its checking account and $40 in a mutual fund that purchases corporate bonds. Thus, the household exactly uses up the $50 it planned to save. Keep in mind that at the low rate of interest we are discussing, the household's supply of loanable funds is less than its current total saving. The low rate of interest makes adding to its checking account a relatively attractive option. By putting some of its saving in a checking account, the household is thereby lending less money ($40) than the maximum it could if it had placed all its saving in a loan contract ($50).

If the real rate of interest rises, a checking account becomes a more expensive asset to hold because total interest rises with the interest rate. Eventually, the interest rate can increase to the point where the household considers the *initial* $100 in its checking account as just the right amount.This means that it will not add any of its intended saving to its checking account. At that particular interest rate, the household's planned saving ($50) will precisely equal the amount it supplies to the loanable funds market ($50).

As the interest rate rises further, the household will reevaluate the benefits it receives from its initial $100 checking account balance. Higher and higher rates of interest mean that the costs of holding a checking account rise relative to the benefits. The financially astute household will therefore decide to keep less than the initial $100 in its checking account. As the interest rate continues to rise, the household will move more and more of its financial wealth out of its checking account and into the loan contract market. At relatively high interest rates, then, households may purchase *more* loan contracts than their saving alone can finance. The balance comes from reducing their holdings of cash and checking account balances.

Households' Supply Curve of Loanable Funds Figure 7.4 illustrates households' supply of loanable funds. The vertical axis indicates the real rate of interest, r, and the horizontal axis measures the real value of the money households supply to the loanable funds market. (Remember that the real value of funds supplied to the bond market is the amount of money households lend expressed in terms of the base period's prices for currently produced goods and services.)

Based on our discussion, the households' supply curve of loanable funds in figure 7.4 is drawn with a positive slope. Before proceeding, it is important to point out that households do not *only* supply loanable funds (save). Many households borrow to finance purchases of houses, cars, farms, mobile homes, and so on (dissave). However, households are *net* savers.

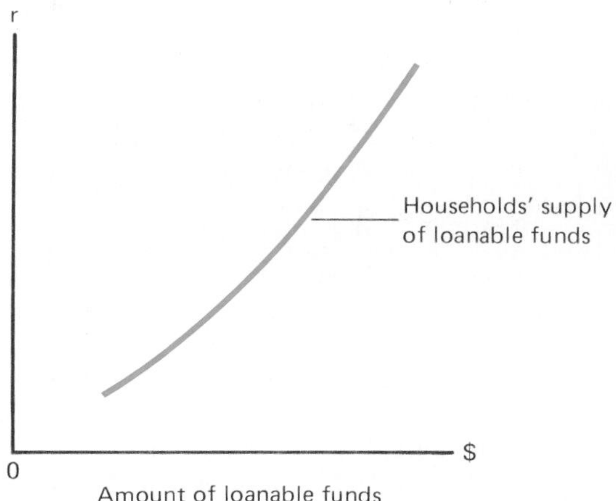

Figure 7.4 Households' supply of loanable funds
Households offer more funds to the loanable funds (credit) market as the real interest rate rises. At higher and higher interest rates the opportunity cost of holding money rises and loan contracts become a financially more attractive way to hold wealth.

For example, in 1983 the average United States family had an average net worth (assets − liabilities) of $66,050.[2] Thus, the supply of loanable funds by households in figure 7.4 should be thought of as the amount households offer to lend *in excess of* any funds they borrow.

Banks As Suppliers of Funds

The banking system is a second major supplier of loanable funds in the economy. Because we studied the banking system and money creation in detail in chapters 5 and 6, we need only review briefly the money creation process and how it is a source of loanable funds. The key point to remember is that as long as banks have sufficient reserves, they can supply (write) loans without first receiving dollars from other sources. Banks can do this by creating new checkable deposits.

Table 7.2 A bank's loan operation

The bank supplies loanable funds by purchasing a loan contract and creating a new checking account balance

Assets	Liabilities
+$100,000 loan contract	+$100,000 checking account

Consider a simple example. A potential borrower comes into a bank wishing to finance a construction project. He or she enters into negotiations with the loan officer, and the loan officer views the investment project as a profitable one for the bank. As a result, the bank agrees to supply loanable funds (buy the borrower's loan contract). To fulfill its part of the transaction, the bank gives our investor the loan in the form of a new checking account. The borrower now has dollars that can be used to buy the goods and services necessary to complete the construction project.

Table 7.2 reminds us how the banking system conducts a loan operation. When a borrower buys a $100,000 loan contract, the bank takes the $100,000 loan contract and adds it to its assets. At the same time, the bank increases its liabilities by crediting the borrower with a *new* $100,000 checking account (or increasing the balance in the borrower's existing account). *The crucial issue illustrated in table 7.2 is that the commercial bank did not depend on household saving to make this transaction.* The loan occurred entirely within the banking system through the creation of new money in the form of a checking account balance.

Another way to state what we have just learned about the banking system's supply of loanable funds is that the checking account balances created by the loan activities of banks add to the value of society's money supply (M). To see this more clearly let us use the symbol P to represent the current price level *relative* to the base period price level. P might, for example, be the consumer price index or the GNP deflator. Finally, let us use the symbol Δ to signify a change, so that we have

$$\text{banks' supply of loanable funds} \equiv \Delta M/P.$$

Banks' supply of loanable funds is an addition to the real stock of money in the economy.

The Rate of Interest and Banks' Supply of Loanable Funds Banks' reserve position is probably the main factor determining the amount of loanable funds banks supply to the economy. However, higher interest rates may induce the banking system to expand the amount of loanable funds it offers. The reason for this is that banks suffer an opportunity cost whenever they hold reserves in excess of the amount required by the Fed.

Remember that without excess reserves banks would find it difficult to satisfy both the desires of the public (for example, a sudden, unexpected withdrawal from checking accounts) *and* the Fed's reserve requirements. If a bank were to have no excess reserves when it cashed a customer's check, it would be placed in the position of holding less than its required reserves. This is a result of fractional reserve banking. To return its reserves to the required level, a bank would have to do something fairly costly, such as borrow from the Fed, call in a loan contract early, or sell off an earning asset. The point is that excess reserves are a valuable source of flexibility for a bank.

The opportunity cost of holding excess reserves is the interest income banks *could have* earned had they supplied loanable funds to the full extent permitted by the reserve requirements of the Fed. As the real rate of interest rises, this opportunity cost also increases. In an attempt to obtain profits, the banking system has an incentive to reduce its excess reserves and to supply more loanable funds to the public whenever the interest rate rises.

Banks' Supply of Loanable Funds Schedule Figure 7.5 depicts the supply of loanable funds by the banking system. The real rate of interest is measured on the vertical axis, and the real quantity of loanable funds supplied by banks is measured on the horizontal axis. The upward slope indicates that higher rates of interest induce banks to offer greater amounts of loanable funds to their customers.

Two events can shift banks' real supply of loanable funds: (1) a change in the price level and (2) a change in banks' excess reserves. The first event is worth discussing in order to explain how the rate of inflation and the real rate of interest are related. The second event gives us the avenue through which monetary policy affects credit markets, saving, investment, and economic activity in general.

Banks supply loanable funds by creating *new* checking account money. A change in the price level of goods and services (P) alters the quantity of goods and services that can be purchased with a given amount of money. In terms of the expression $\Delta M/P$, an increase or decrease in P will change the denominator. Since banks' supply of loanable funds is the real value of the *change* in the money stock resulting from their loan activities, a change in the price level changes the real value of this additional money supplied. A higher price level shifts the banks' supply of loanable funds to the left because a given amount of money created has a lower real value at a higher price level. Similarly, a reduction in the price level shifts the banks' real supply of loanable funds to the right.

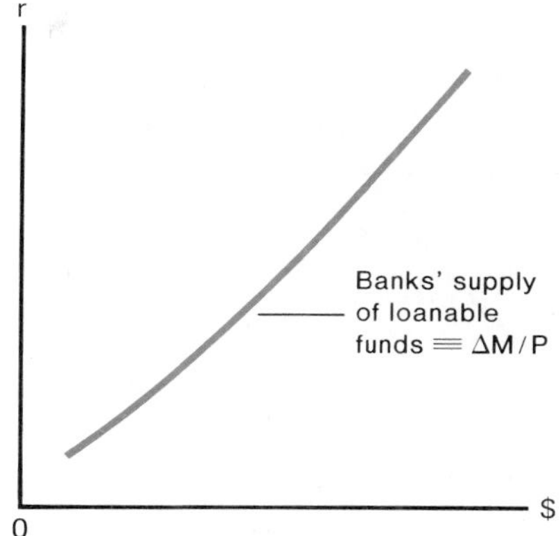

Figure 7.5 Banks' supply of loanable funds
The banking system supplies more loanable funds at higher real interest rates. At higher interest rates the opportunity cost of holding excess reserves rises. This leads banks to reduce their excess reserves and supply more loanable funds.

In this case, a given amount of new checking account money has a greater purchasing power and a greater real value.

It is also important to remember that the supply curve of loanable funds by banks depicted in figure 7.5 illustrates their willingness to turn a *given* amount of excess reserves into loans at various interest rates; that is, the curve is valid for a particular level of excess reserves. Should monetary policy change those excess reserves, banks' supply of loanable funds would shift. More excess reserves means that banks will offer greater amounts of loanable funds to borrowers at any given interest rate and the supply curve will shift to the right. Monetary policy that reduces banks' excess reserves will result in a leftward shift in the supply schedule in figure 7.5. At any given interest rate, banks will supply less loanable funds should monetary policy reduce their excess reserves.

*The **aggregate supply of loanable funds (SLF)** is a schedule illustrating the total amount of loanable funds lenders offer at various real interest rates.*

*The **equilibrium interest rate** is the real interest rate that equates the aggregate supply and demand for loanable funds; at the equilibrium interest rate borrowers want to borrow exactly the amount of funds that lenders want to lend.*

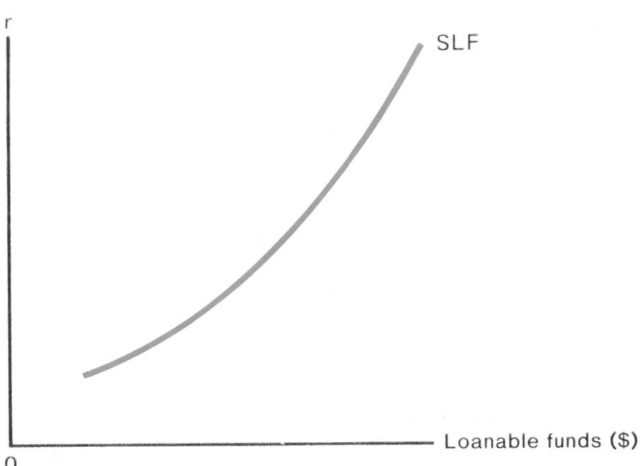

Figure 7.6 The aggregate supply curve of loanable funds
SLF is the sum of households' net supply and banks' supply of funds to the loan contract market. It is positively sloped because both banks and households are willing to lend more at higher real interest rates.

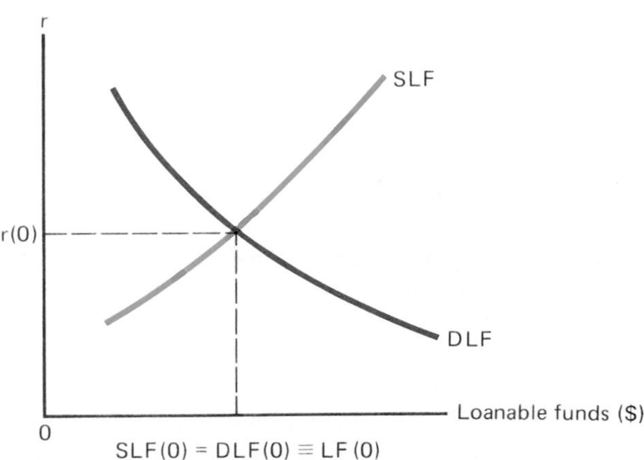

Figure 7.7 Equilibrium in the aggregate loan contract market
The equilibrium interest rate, r(0), is the price of credit where the amount of money borrowers wish to borrow exactly matches the amount lenders offer to lend. Anything that disturbs the demand curve (the demand for investment projects, for example) or the supply curve (banks' excess reserves or households' saving, for example) will lead to a new equilibrium real rate of interest.

The Aggregate Supply of Loanable Funds

The total supply of loanable funds to the credit market stems from the supply of funds by households and the banking system and is known as the **aggregate supply of loanable funds (SLF).** It represents the *real value* of the total dollars supplied to the loan contract (credit) market by banks and households.

Figure 7.6 illustrates the market supply curve for new loan contracts with respect to the real rate of interest. To derive points on SLF, we first choose a particular value of the real rate of interest. We then look at the total funds offered by households at the rate of interest in figure 7.4 and at the total loanable funds offered by banks at the rate of interest in figure 7.5. The sum of these two numbers is plotted in figure 7.6 against the real rate of interest we chose. Repeating this exercise for various interest rates traces out the SLF in figure 7.6. Because both banks' and households' supply of loanable funds schedules are upward sloping with respect to the interest rate, so is the aggregate supply of loanable funds.

Equilibrium in the Loan Contract Market

The Determination of the Real Interest Rate

The loan contract market performs two extremely important functions for the aggregate economy. First, it is where scarce funds available for lending are allocated among different borrowers. Second, the interaction of borrowers and lenders in the loan contract market leads to the current real interest rate.

Figure 7.7 contains both the aggregate supply and demand schedules for loanable funds. The intersection of these two curves shows us that at interest rate r(0), the real value of new loan contracts demanded in the economy equals the amount supplied. The **equilibrium interest rate** is r(0) because no other rate of interest can satisfy both the desired plans of borrowers and lenders in the aggregate loan contract market.

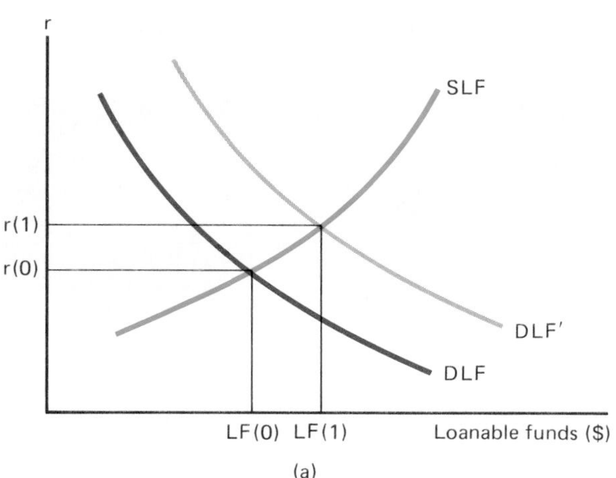

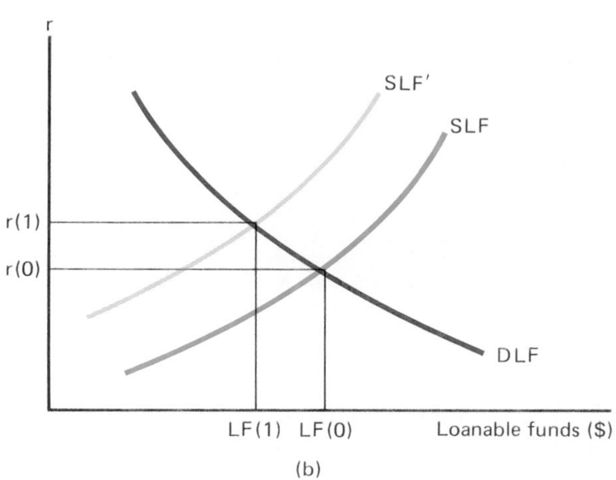

Figure 7.8 Shifts in the demand and supply of loanable funds
In part (a) an increase in planned investment or in the government deficit has shifted the demand for loanable funds to the right. The result is an increase in the rate of interest and an increase in the quantity of money borrowed.

In part (b) an increase in the desire of households to add to their cash balances or a decline in the willingness of banks to make new loans has shifted the supply of loanable funds to the left. The result is an increase in the rate of interest and a reduction in the quantity of money lent.

When the interest rate is above equilibrium, the quantity of loanable funds offered by lenders exceeds the quantity of funds borrowers wish to borrow. In a sense, borrowers are in the driver's seat. Money for investment projects is more than readily available. However, some lenders will not be able to find borrowers with whom they can satisfactorily negotiate loan contracts. As lenders begin to realize the extent of the market's disequilibrium, downward pressure will be exerted on the real interest rate. This pressure ceases when the loan contract market finally reaches its equilibrium interest rate, r(0).

The opposite effects are felt in the aggregate loanable funds market when the interest rate is below equilibrium. In this case, *suppliers* of loanable funds are in the driver's seat. Borrowers are unable to find all the funds they want, but lenders have no trouble getting loan contracts that meet their approval. Eventually, some potential borrowers will fear that they might get caught short in their total borrowing and start to compete with one another by bidding up the interest rate. The excess demand for loanable funds at the lower interest rate will generate upward pressure on the market rate of interest until the aggregate loanable funds market settles into an equilibrium at real interest rate r(0).

When either the demand or supply of loanable funds shifts, the equilibrium interest rate will also change. Shifts in the demand and supply of loanable funds are illustrated in figure 7.8. In part (a), an increase in planned investment or in the government deficit has shifted the demand for loanable funds to the right. The result is an increase in the rate of interest and an increase in the quantity of loanable funds borrowed and lent. In part (b) of figure 7.8, an increase in the desire of households to add to their cash balances or a reduction in the willingness of banks to lend money has shifted the supply of loanable funds to the left. The result is, again, an increase in the rate of interest but a *reduction* in the quantity of loanable funds borrowed and lent.

The ***structure of interest rates*** *refers to the variation in interest rates across loans by the type of borrower and the term of the loan (loan period).*

Table 7.3 Selected nominal interest rates, 1960–1986

	1960	1965	1970	1975	1978	1980	1982	1983	1986
United States Treasury securities									
1-year Treasury bill	3.41	4.06	6.48	6.28	7.74	10.89	11.07	8.80	6.65
3-year maturity	3.98	4.22	7.29	7.49	8.29	11.55	12.92	10.45	7.27
10-year maturity	4.12	4.28	7.35	7.99	8.41	11.46	13.00	11.10	7.71
High-grade (Aaa) corporate bonds	4.41	4.49	8.04	8.83	8.73	11.94	13.79	12.04	9.09

Source: From *Statistical Abstract of the United States: 1982–83* (103d edition), U.S. Bureau of the Census, 1982; *Economic Indicators,* January 1983, and *Statistical Abstract of the United States,* 1985, Table 850, p. 515.

The equilibrium interest rate r(0) satisfies all suppliers and demanders in the loanable funds market. Table 7.3 illustrates selected nominal interest rates in the United States for 1960 through 1986. In chapter 2 we saw that nominal interest rates and the rate of inflation tend to move together. For example, the interest rates for 1960 in table 7.3 are in the range of 3 to 4 percent. In 1960, the rate of inflation was 1.6 percent. In 1970, when the rates of interest were 6 to 8 percent, the rate of inflation was 5.9 percent. A generally positive relationship between interest and inflation rates continued in the 1980s. In 1980, the inflation rate was 14.5 percent and the interest rates were 11 to 12 percent. After inflation fears subsided considerably, interest rates fell to an average of about 7.5 percent in 1986.

It is important to reemphasize the distinction between the nominal, or so-called market, interest rate and the real rate of interest. The interest rates in table 7.3 are the total price of credit borrowers pay lenders *unadjusted* for inflation. When borrowers and lenders consider the cost of credit and return from lending, they care about the real purchasing power of the interest payments. Both will take account of the fact that at a given nominal interest rate, the real interest rate is lower the greater the rate of inflation expected to prevail. Thus, at higher rates of inflation borrowers insist on higher nominal interest rates to offset the reduced purchasing power of the dollars they will receive in the future when goods and services cost more.

The Structure of Interest Rates

A number of factors underlie the **structure of interest rates,** which is the variation in interest rates depending upon the type of borrower and the duration of the loan contract as listed in table 7.3. Notice that for the three different types of United States Treasury securities listed, generally the longer the term of the loan, the higher the rate of interest. Second, corporate bonds have a rate of interest that is higher than that on United States Treasury securities. Thus, we see that interest rates in a given year vary by the term of the loan contract (number of years) and who the borrower is.

A key factor underlying the rate of interest a borrower must pay is the risk to the lender that the loan will not be repaid. We have already discussed the unlikelihood of the United States government's going bankrupt. This means that United States Treasury securities have lower default risk than corporate bonds because a given corporation is more likey to go bankrupt and not pay its loan obligations. This is one of the reasons why the United States Treasury securities listed in table 7.3 generally bear lower interest rates than high-quality (Aaa) corporate bonds.

Another aspect of risk is that the farther into the future you consider, the more dramatically the economy may change. Who is to know, for example, whether there will be extremely high inflation or taxes on interest earnings five to ten years from now? As a lender, I will require a higher compensation to tie up my money for ten years than if I will be repaid at the end of this year. Because many things can happen in my personal life in ten years—for example, death or a new baby, just to name two—I must receive relatively high compensation to be willing to tie up my funds in a ten-year bond. The riskier the loan (from the perspective of the lender), the higher the rate of interest on the loan. This is what underlies the fact that long-term United States securities pay higher interest rates than one-year Treasury bills and that United States Treasury securities generally pay lower rates of interest than corporate bonds.

Summary and Conclusions

It is impossible to understand how the macroeconomy works without taking careful account of the financial sector. In this chapter we have seen how the Fed's decisions on whether to use its powerful policy tools to control the money supply or the interest rate can have a crucial influence on the course of the macroeconomy and the fortunes of politicians in office during periods of prosperity or recession. We discussed the economic factors that underlie the supply and demand of loanable funds and developed the concept of equilibrium in the aggregate loanable funds market. The following points were emphasized.

Knowledge of the individual's behavior in the market for goods and services and the market for loan contracts implies the amount of money he or she will choose to hold.

The loan contract market brings together two different groups—those who would like to divert expenditure into the future and those who would like to move their expenditure from the future into the present.

The aggregate demand for loanable funds is downward sloping. At higher real interest rates borrowers wish to borrow less money, and at lower interest rates they wish to borrow more.

The aggregate supply of loanable funds is the sum of the net supply of funds by households and the banking system. The aggregate supply of loanable funds is positively sloped with respect to the real interest rate.

The loan contract market performs two important functions for the aggregate economy: (1) it is where scarce funds available for loans are allocated among various borrowers, and (2) the interactions of borrowers and lenders in the aggregate loan contract market determine the real interest rate.

From the standpoint of the aggregate economy, the real interest rate is what matters to borrowers and lenders.

The longer the term of a loan, typically the higher the rate of interest on the loan, *cet. par.*

The greater the risk of default on a loan, typically the higher the rate of interest on the loan, *cet. par.*

Key Terms

aggregate demand for loanable funds (DLF) *156*

aggregate supply of loanable funds (SLF) *162*

equilibrium interest rate *162*

loanable funds *152*

loan contract, financial, or credit market *152*

structure of interest rates *164*

Questions for Discussion and Review

1. Lenders are rich people and borrowers are poor people. Discuss and evaluate this statement. In the course of answering be sure to discuss the motives underlying the respective behavior of borrowers and lenders.
2. What are the basic properties of a loan contract; that is, what are the respective economic motivations of the borrower and the lender?
3. The lenders in a loan contract are the winners because they get back more money than they lent. Evaluate this statement.
4. The lenders in a loan contract are the losers because they are repaid with money that will buy less because of inflation. Evaluate this statement.
5. What are the sources of the market demand for loanable funds? Which of them is sensitive to the rate of interest? Why are some of the demanders of loanable funds not influenced by the rate of interest?
6. Make a list of events that would shift the demand for loanable funds. Next to your list indicate the direction in which each event would shift the aggregate demand for loanable funds. Next to that indicate a government policy, if any, that would produce the event you have listed.
7. Who are the two major suppliers of loanable funds? Why is each of them willing to supply more loanable funds the higher the real rate of interest?
8. Explain and graphically describe the equilibrium point in the loan contract market. Now suppose that a (usury) law is introduced placing a ceiling on the rate of interest that is below the equilibrium value r(0). How do you take account of the usury law in your diagram? If the law is effectively enforced, what will the market rate of interest and the amount of loanable funds borrowed and lent be? Who are the winners from the usury law? Who are the losers?
9. The rate of inflation is 10 percent per year. You open a newspaper and see that long-term government bonds in the United States pay an annual rate of interest of 15 percent. Is this a high or a low rate of interest? Explain carefully. Would your answer be any different if the rate of inflation were 14 percent? Explain.
10. A recent newscast reported that high interest rates are bad because borrowers cannot afford them. Another newscast reported that low interest rates are bad because lenders cannot make any money. Is any particular rate of interest good for society? Discuss carefully.
11. In the early 1980s there was a great deal of concern over large government deficits. It was felt that these deficits raised the interest rate and, in the process, crowded out private investment. Analyze this conclusion within the context of the model of the loanable funds market developed in this chapter. Support your answer graphically.
12. Considering the supply and demand framework of the loanable funds market, what is the relationship between real interest rates and bond prices?

Policy Issue: You Decide

Deregulation of the Banking Industry

▸ The Action-Initiating Event

The House Subcommittee on Money and Banking has begun hearings with a view toward stopping and perhaps reversing the deregulation of financial institutions begun in 1980. The committee is being lobbied heavily by representatives of savings and loan institutions and commercial banks. The political judgment is that the committee is evenly split on the issue. There will be an attempt to draft legislation within the committee for House consideration after the next recess. Apparently, the committee is considering raising reserve requirements on all types of deposits, eliminating branch banking, and imposing ceilings on all lending and deposit interest rates.

▸ The Issue

The economics of the situation seem fairly straightforward. Deregulation of the banking industry has cut into local savings and loan bank monopolies and those of commercial banks in general at a time when savings and loans are still trying to recover from losses caused by long-term mortgages with rates of interest well below the current interest rates they must pay to retain existing deposits and acquire new ones. In addition, many commercial banks of all sizes are facing default on a significant portion of their loans to developing nations. Moreover, the substantial number of bank failures throughout the 1980s has made the public afraid for the safety of their deposits. Consequently, the President needs to take a strong position on this issue going into the upcoming national elections.

▸ Economic Policy Issues

I have been asked by the President to solicit your opinion on a number of substantive issues. First, to what extent would protection of local bank monopolies against competition from new banks entering their local markets help avoid bank failures? How would protecting them against competition affect interest rates? What would be the effect of reregulation of banks on consumer debt, the housing market, and business investment plans? Can you propose alternative schemes to assist banks that would address their problems more directly, with fewer potential adverse affects on the economy? Should the administration take a promarket approach and let weak institutions fail? If so, is there any danger of a 1930s-style financial collapse?

▸ Recommendations

In brief, I would like you to consider a wide range of policy options, from doing nothing to returning to the pre-1980 regulatory conditions in which banks had local monopolies (i.e., were protected against competition from other banks entering their local markets by state regulations) and in which both deposit and lending interest rates were limited by law. First, I need your assessment of the economic pros and cons of alternative policy options and your estimate of what would be best for the country. Second, I need your judgments regarding who the potential winners and losers would be for the alternatives you consider. The office of the President will then try to make a political judgment about the feasibility of supporting the various options you outline, considering the upcoming elections. We want to maintain a posture of leadership by getting out front on this issue. But we do not want to set the administration up as an easy target for the opposition in the next campaign.

Part III

Macroeconomic Policy

Chapter 8

How the Macroeconomy Works

Outline

Objectives

After reading this chapter, the student should be able to:

List the three markets that must be in equilibrium and the conditions that exist in each when full macroeconomic equilibrium exists.

Use the market for loanable funds and the goods and services market to diagram full macroeconomic equilibrium.

Show how a decrease in planned investment can lead to a short-run equilibrium with the economy in a recessionary episode.

Show how flexible prices can return a recessionary short-run equilibrium to full macroeconomic equilibrium.

Show how an increase in planned investment can lead to an inflationary episode and discuss what brings the economy back to full macroeconomic equilibrium.

Full macroeconomic equilibrium *occurs when equilibrium exists in the labor, goods, and credit markets simultaneously.*

Short-run macroeconomic equilibrium *occurs when there is equilibrium in the aggregate market for goods and services but not in all other aggregate markets.*

Introduction

In August 1971, President Nixon announced a number of major economic policy changes. At that time, both the rate of inflation and the unemployment rate in the United States were rising toward 6 percent per year. Nixon had lost a close race for the presidency against John F. Kennedy in 1960 partly because of a recession for which the Republicans received some blame. In 1968, Nixon won the presidency with less than 50 percent of the popular vote and fewer actual votes than he had received in his losing campaign of 1960. Pointing toward the presidential campaign of 1972, the president seemed determined to make sure that overall economic conditions did not reduce his chance for reelection.

With the Viet Nam War grinding on, the prospects of a serious recession seemed slight, but the inflation rate appeared to be rising rapidly. Despite his conservative reputation on economic issues, President Nixon imposed wage and price controls on the United States economy for the first time since the Korean War of the early 1950s.

How clever it might seem to stop inflation by simply making it against the law. In fact, however, inflationary pressures continued to build up in the economy, and wage and price controls disrupted markets everywhere. By 1974, the economy was heading into a recession, with an overall unemployment rate of 5.5 percent and consumer prices rising at an annual rate of 11 percent. By 1975, the inflation rate was still 9.1 percent, and the unemployment rate had risen sharply to 8.3 percent. For the first time, people were talking about "stagflation."

It would be naive to believe that the combination of high rates of inflation and unemployment and the low rate of economic growth in the mid-1970s could be blamed solely on the Nixon wage/price controls of August 1971. However, it will be clear after studying this chapter why it is nonsensical to believe that performance of the macroeconomy can be dictated by law and why it is reasonable to believe that President Nixon's policies contributed to the country's economic problems in the mid-1970s.

The stones that we have set in place in our foundation of macroeconomic analysis are the different aggregate markets—the market for labor, the market for goods and services, and the market for credit. The result is a model of the macroeconomy. ***Full macroeconomic equilibrium*** *requires that there be no excess supply or demand in any sector of the macroeconomy. As long as even one market is in disequilibrium, adjustments will eventually occur that affect all sectors of the economy. After we show what the macroeconomy looks like when full equilibrium prevails, we will then "shock" the economy with changes in one of the individual sectors and observe whether, and how, full macroequilibrium is reestablished. In this chapter, we show how adjustments in the rate of interest and the price level can help restore macroeconomic equilibrium when the economy enters a recession or a period of inflation. Briefly, during a recession, reductions in the rate of interest and the price level help return the economy to full employment. During periods of inflation, increased interest rates and rising prices help bring the inflationary process to an end. In chapter 9 we will explore in greater depth the forces that determine the price level and money wages.*

Before returning to full equilibrium the macroeconomy may exhibit ***short-run macroeconomic equilibrium****, which means that planned expenditure equals production in the aggregate market for goods and services but that disequilibrium exists in other markets. During a phase in which the economy is in short-run macroequilibrium, we shall see that it is possible for employment and GNP to fall below (or rise above) the levels that prevail in full equilibrium. When "low-level" short-run equilibrium occurs, the* *economy is in* recession, *and cyclical unemployment is positive. When the economy is in short-run macroequilibrium at a level above full macroequilibrium, the unemployment rate is less than its normal value, and an* inflationary episode *is inevitable.*

Since the end of World War II, the United States has experienced six severe recessions and four mild recessions. During the severe recessions, GNP declined by an average of 3.3 percent, while the unemployment rate increased by an average of 3.8 percentage points. In the mild recessions, GNP declined on average by 1.7 percent and unemployment increased by an average of 2.3 percentage points. Each contraction of economic activity was followed by an expansion, in which GNP growth was greater than average and the unemployment rate declined.[1] *In chapter 11, we review in detail the inflationary episode that started in the mid-1960s, some effects of which continue to the present time.*

We will focus particularly on the role of interest rate and price level adjustments in pushing the economy toward macroequilibrium. Once you understand how the macroeconomy behaves when it is "disturbed," it will be relatively easy to understand how various government policies influence unemployment and inflation. This subject will be investigated in chapter 10.

A model of the economy with only three markets may seem simplistic given the vast number of markets in the actual economy. Even with only three markets, you will see that keeping track of everything at the same time *can get a little tough. In a macroeconomic setting, events happen simultaneously in all markets. A change in demand in the goods market will affect the credit market and the labor market. What happens in the credit and labor markets will feed back into the goods sector. Because of this cause-and-effect cycle, we must keep careful account of supply and demand conditions in* all *markets* simultaneously. *This task is made much easier by simplifying our macroeconomic model to contain only three aggregate markets.*

Full Macroeconomic Equilibrium: Satisfying Three Markets Simultaneously

First, we will review equilibrium in each of the separate aggregate markets we have studied in chapters 2 through 7. These are the markets for labor, goods and services, and credit. During this review, remember that only when equilibrium prevails in *each* market *at the same time* can we say that the entire macroeconomy is in equilibrium.

1. The aggregate labor market is in equilibrium when the quantity of labor demanded equals the quantity of labor that the population wishes to supply. Moreover, when full macroeconomic equilibrium prevails, there is full employment in the labor market (cyclical unemployment equals zero), and the total unemployment rate is at its so-called normal level. The real wage rate will equal the marginal product of labor. The real wage is equal to the real wage workers expect to be paid because no one is surprised by an unexpected change in the price level.

   Equilibrium in the aggregate labor market determines not only the real wage rate, the level of employment, and the level of unemployment but also the aggregate quantity of goods and services produced. Figure 8.1 shows how the aggregate supply of labor and aggregate demand for labor interact to determine the equilibrium real wage rate and equilibrium employment, L(0). Employment determines aggregate production, GNP, through the aggregate production function. We have seen that this is called *full-employment GNP.* (You may wish to review pages 76–77 to remind yourself of how employment determines GNP through the aggregate production function.) In 1986, employment averaged more than 108 million and GNP was close to $4 trillion.
2. The aggregate market for currently produced goods and services is in equilibrium when *planned expenditure equals production.* In chapter 4, we learned that the aggregate

Figure 8.1 The aggregate labor market and the quantity of real GNP supplied
Equilibrium employment and the real wage rate are determined by the aggregate supply and demand for labor.

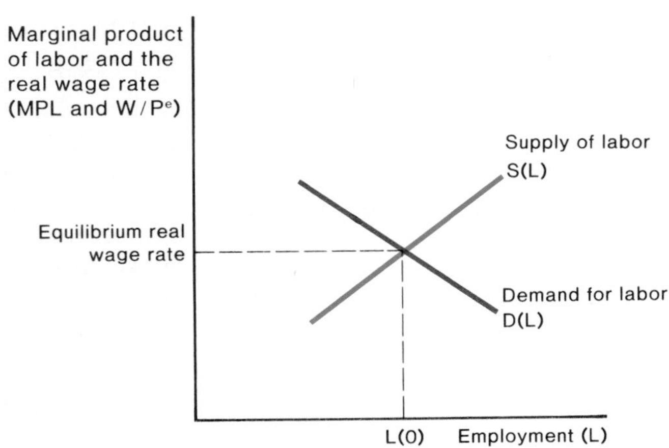

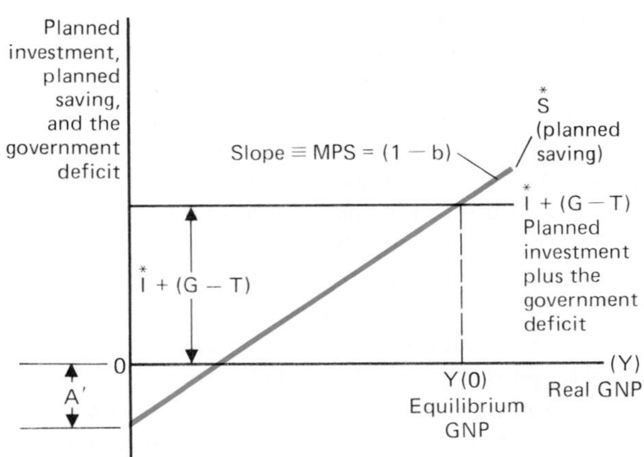

Figure 8.2 The aggregate market for goods and services The aggregate market for goods and services is in equilibrium when planned saving equals planned investment plus the government deficit. The market for goods and services and the labor market must *both* reach equilibrium at the *same* value of gross national product.

market for goods and services is in equilibrium when planned investment plus the government deficit equals planned aggregate saving or when

$$\overset{*}{I} + (G - T) = \overset{*}{S}.$$

In figure 8.2, we see that planned investment plus the government deficit does not rise as GNP rises. Planned saving, however, does increase with GNP. Therefore, there is one, and only one, value of GNP at which the previous equation holds. At this level of GNP, Y(0), planned saving equals planned investment plus the government deficit, and aggregate planned expenditure on goods and services exactly equals the quantity firms have produced. In full macroeconomic equilibrium (and *only* then), the level of GNP will equal the amount produced when the labor force is fully employed. That is, in full macroeconomic equilibrium cyclical unemployment will not exist.

3. The aggregate credit market is in equilibrium when the quantity of loanable funds demanded by borrowers equals the quantity supplied. Remember that the aggregate supply of loanable funds includes the new money balances (measured in real dollars) provided by banks' desired purchases of new loan contracts. The demand for loanable funds is created by planned investment expenditures and borrowing by the government to finance its own deficit. Figure 8.3 summarizes equilibrium in the credit market. Equilibrium in the market for loan contracts requires that the real interest rate be at exactly the level that makes the quantity of loanable funds demanded equal to the quantity supplied.

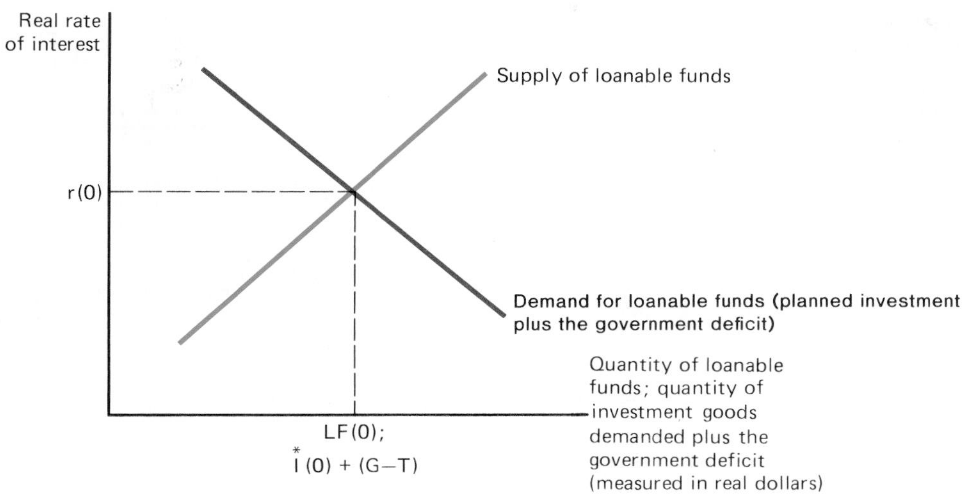

Figure 8.3 The aggregate market for loanable funds
The demand for funds comes from the demand by borrowers to purchase investment goods (I) and from the government to finance its deficit (G − T). At the equilibrium real interest rate, the quantity of funds demanded exactly equals the quantity supplied. Full macroeconomic equilibrium requires that $\overset{*}{I} + (G - T)$ in this diagram equal planned investment plus the government deficit in figure 8.2. In other words, equilibrium in the credit market and equilibrium in the market for goods and services must both occur at the same time, and the value of GNP, Y(0), must be the same in both figures 8.1 and 8.2.

Remember that the quantity of loanable funds demanded is, by assumption, equal to investment plus the government deficit. Therefore, the rate of interest is a crucial variable linking the credit market to the market for goods and services. In full macroeconomic equilibrium, the rate of interest must be at precisely the level that assures that planned investment plus the government deficit equals planned saving at the *full-employment level of GNP.* This assures that the goods and services market equilibrium as depicted in figure 8.2 is the same as implied by figure 8.1.

In full macroeconomic equilibrium, inflation is zero. The price level is stable and is not expected to change. Therefore, the real and nominal rates of interest are equal because the real rate of interest is the nominal rate minus the inflation rate.

▸ A Closer Look at Full Macroeconomic Equilibrium

To understand how the macroeconomy works and the means government policymakers may use to prevent recessions or inflations, it is helpful to combine as many macroeconomic variables as possible into one diagram. Figure 8.4 depicts full macroeconomic equilibrium with GNP = $200 billion. Part (a) of this figure is a flowchart representation of macroequilibrium, showing how the aggregate labor, goods, and credit markets are interrelated. For convenience, we depict a situation in which government expenditure is equal to taxes so that the government deficit is zero. However, the representation of macroequilibrium would be just as valid if, for example, the government deficit were positive or negative (a surplus). To make sure you understand part (a) of figure 8.4, redraw it on a piece of paper with a government deficit of $10

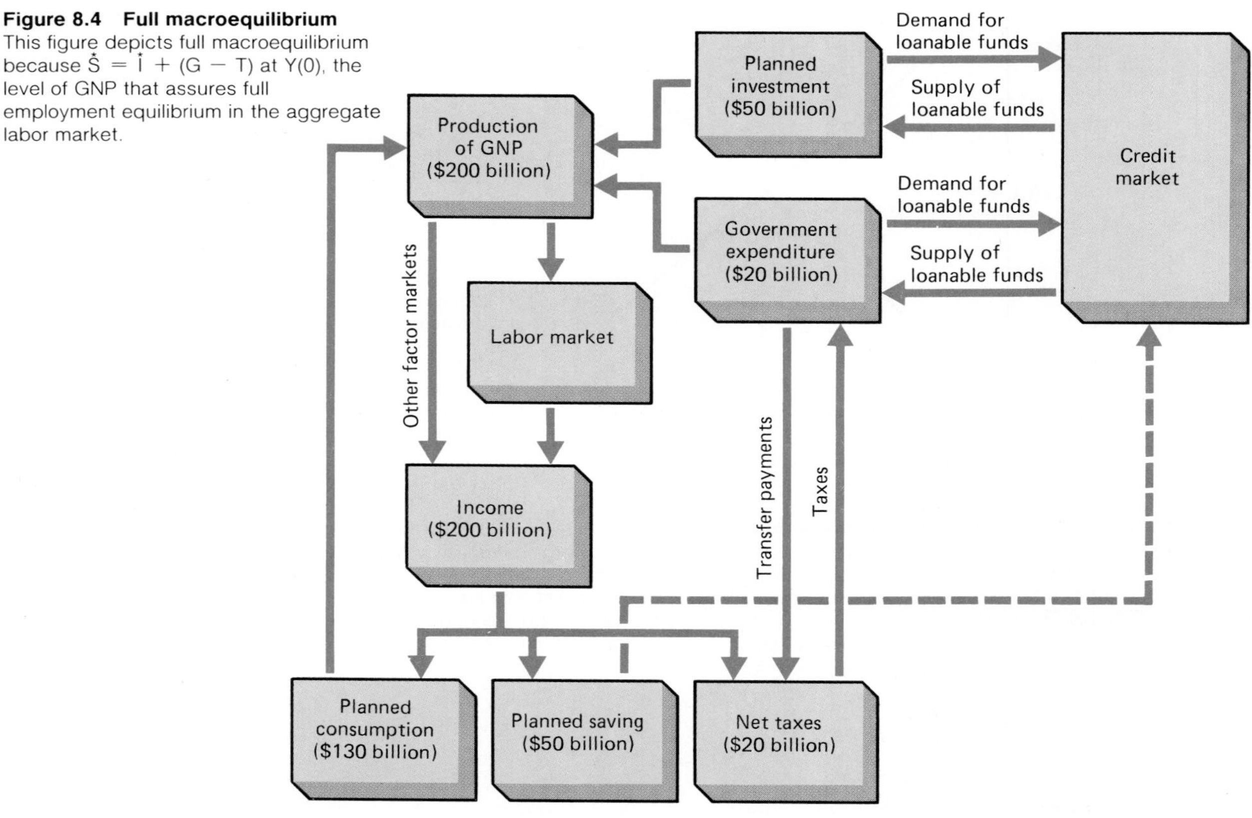

Figure 8.4 Full macroequilibrium
This figure depicts full macroequilibrium because $\dot{S} = \dot{I} + (G - T)$ at Y(0), the level of GNP that assures full employment equilibrium in the aggregate labor market.

billion. (Will you lower taxes or raise expenditure?) Now adjust planned investment so as to maintain macroeconomic equilibrium. (Do you have to raise planned investment or lower it? Could you also adjust planned consumption and saving to maintain macroeconomic equilibrium?)

Figure 8.4, part (b) describes macroeconomic equilibrium geometrically in terms of supply and demand in the aggregate credit market and on the market for goods and services. We can combine these two markets in one diagram because the real value of loanable funds, the real value of investment expenditure and the government deficit, and the real value of saving all have the same unit of measurement (real dollars). This means that they can all be measured along the horizontal axis.

Remember, figure 8.2 shows that equilibrium in the goods market occurs at the level of GNP where planned saving equals planned investment plus the

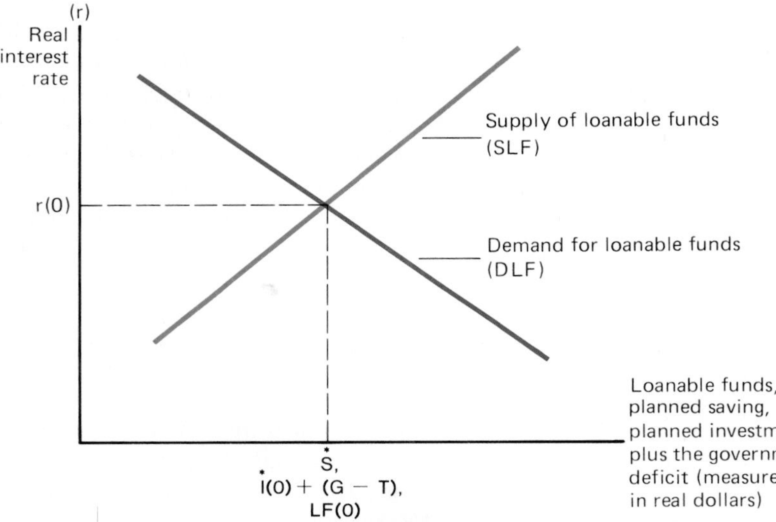

These symbols show that the quantity of loanable funds demanded and supplied, investment plus the government deficit, and planned saving, are all equal to each other.

(b)

government deficit. Along the horizontal axis of part (b) of figure 8.4, we have marked the level of planned saving that occurs when GNP is at its *full-employment level.* The DLF curve marks off the quantities of loanable funds demanded to finance new investment projects at various interest rates plus the amount the government needs to borrow to finance its deficit. The DLF curve crosses the SLF curve (which represents the quantity of loanable funds supplied at various interest rates) at just the point that assures planned investment plus the government deficit equals planned saving. Thus, in part (b) of figure 8.4, we depict a situation in which planned saving equals planned investment plus the government deficit, assuring equilibrium in both the loan contract market and the market for goods and services *at the full-employment level of GNP.* We know the labor market is at full employment because the level of planned saving marked by $\overset{*}{S}$ has been specified to be the amount of saving that households desire when the labor market is in full-employment equilibrium. This corresponds to the level of employment shown in figure 8.1. Therefore, figure 8.4 describes full macroeconomic equilibrium.

We can now use figure 8.4 to show what happens when the economy heads toward a recession or an inflationary episode. Will the economy ever return to full macroequilibrium after it begins to move away, or will it get "stuck" in a short-run equilibrium at less than full employment or with permanent inflation? The answer to this question is crucial in understanding how the macroeconomy works and how government policies can help or hurt macroeconomic performance.

Recessions and Inflationary Episodes

We will now analyze how the macroeconomy responds to exogenous changes in some of the variables that affect the full equilibrium levels of employment, GNP, the real interest rate, and the price level. Economists who specialize in studying macroeconomic adjustments generally agree that the major events affecting macroequilibrium involve changes in investors' optimism about the profitability of investment projects and changes in government expenditure, taxation, and monetary policy. In the remainder of this chapter and in chapter 9, we will explore the impact of changes in planned investment and planned saving during a recession and during an inflationary episode. Changes in government expenditure, taxation, and monetary policy will be treated in depth in chapters 10–12.

Our analysis of recessions and inflationary episodes is based on figure 8.4. Starting from an initial position of full macroeconomic equilibrium, we will assume a change in the economic behavior of some group. In response to this shock, a new intersection of supply and demand for loanable funds will produce a new equilibrium real interest rate. Once we know the value of this new rate of interest, we can compare planned saving with planned investment plus the government deficit, which monitors the state of disequilibrium in the goods market. The goods market will then adjust to achieve a state of *short-run* equilibrium in which planned expenditure equals production but GNP is less than its full-employment level. We will then note which conditions of *full* macroeconomic equilibrium are *not* satisfied. Thus, we will be able to predict whether, and how, the cycle of adjustment will continue until the economy regains full macroequilibrium.

Recession: The Effect of a Decline in Planned Investment

Recall that *today's* planned investment depends on investors' expectations about the *future* stream of profits, or returns, from new investment projects. Suppose investors observe that a major decline in the birthrate twenty years ago will result in fewer young adults marrying, forming households, buying new cars, and so on. This forecasted change in expenditures on consumer durable goods leads to a more pessimistic view of the returns on investing in new plants and equipment to produce lumber products, automobiles, household appliances, and other goods. This decline in investment leads to further reductions in planned investment in the industries producing capital goods in the economy. In other words, since the *future* no longer appears as profitable as it once did, investors will respond *today* by reducing their current rate of planned expenditure. The economy's probable initial reactions to this change are outlined on the following pages.

A Leftward Shift in the Demand for Loanable Funds

The assumed change in investors' expectations can be represented graphically on the basis of figure 8.4 part (b). In figure 8.5, part (a), the lines DLF and SLF represent macroeconomic conditions *prior* to the change in investment expectations. Full macroeconomic equilibrium prevails with real interest rate r(0). To remind you what is going on in the goods and labor markets, we have reproduced figures 8.2 and 3.9 in figure 8.5, parts (b) and (c), respectively. In part (b) you can see that the full-employment level of GNP is Y(0), where planned saving equals planned investment plus the government deficit. In the labor market, part (c) of figure 8.5, full employment occurs at expected real wage $W/P^e(0)$, with employment equal to $L^n(0)$.

In part (a) of figure 8.5, we can depict the effects of reduced investor optimism about the future by noting that a reduction in planned investment shifts the demand curve for loanable funds leftward to DLF′. Given the change in investor expectations, DLF′ tells us how many dollars are now demanded when borrowers are confronted with various interest rates. Planned investment at *each* rate of interest is now *less* than it was. Thus, at interest rate r(0) investors intend to spend less than previously. This decline in the demand for loanable funds due to a reduction in planned investment is indicated by the arrow pointing leftward in the loanable funds market diagram.

A Decline in the Interest Rate

With the new demand for loanable funds, the interest rate r(0) no longer equates the demand and supply for loanable funds. At interest rate r(0), the loanable of loanable funds (households and banks) will then compete for the reduced number of loan contracts offered to them by bidding down the interest rate until the loanable funds market is again in equilibrium, at interest rate r(1) in figure 8.5, part (a). This decline in the interest rate, which closes the gap between the quantity of loanable funds demanded and supplied, is indicated by the downward-pointing arrow.

Viewed from the supply side of the credit market, the lower rate of interest induces households to devote *more* of their saving to acquiring additional money balances (and hence less to the purchase of loan contracts) because the opportunity cost attached to holding money has gone down. The lower interest rate also induces banks to purchase smaller amounts of loan contracts. Viewed from the demand side of the loanable funds market, the decline in the rate of interest to r(1) *partially* offsets the effects of the reduction in the demand for loanable funds. In part (a) of figure 8.5, the lower interest rate r(1) has induced investors to move down along their *new* loanable funds demand curve. Thus, they wind up purchasing *more* investment goods than they would have purchased at the old interest rate r(0) given their current pessimism about the future. However, they still do not want to purchase as many investment goods as they did before they became pessimistic and when full macroeconomic equilibrium prevailed. Along DLF′, planned investment plus the government deficit now equals $\overset{**}{I}(1) + (G - T)$, which is also the quantity of loanable funds demanded. (The two asterisks, **, over the symbol I indicate that the planned investment schedule has shifted to a different position compared to the initial planned investment schedule, which is marked with one asterisk, *.)

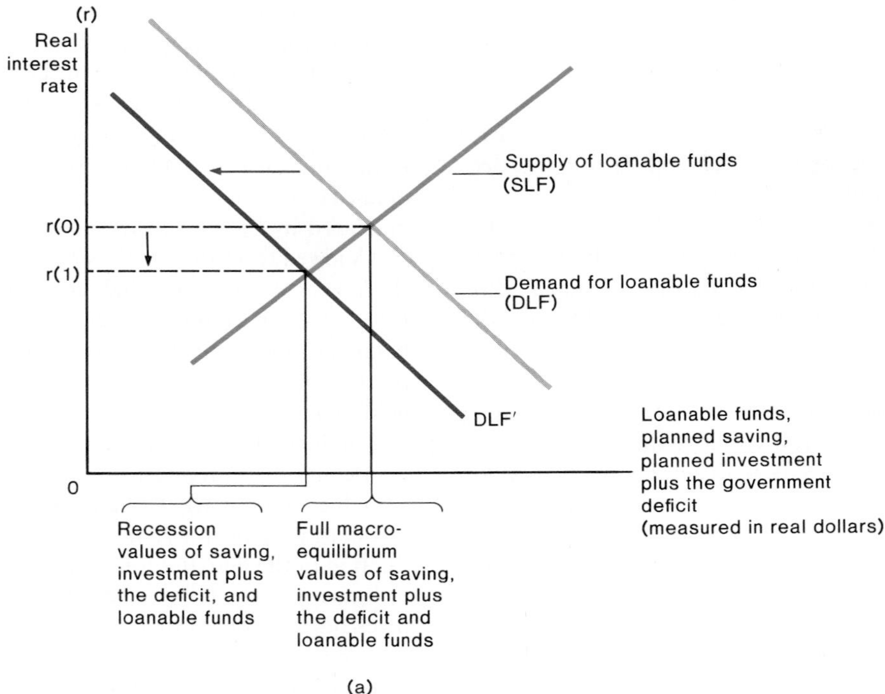

Figure 8.5 A decrease in planned investment leading to short-run macroeconomic equilibrium in a recession
In part (a) planned investment and the demand for loanable funds have declined. This leads to a decline in real GNP and in the real rate of interest. As GNP falls, planned saving falls as well.

In part (b) equilibrium in the market for goods and services has changed. GNP is now lower than its full macroequilibrium value because planned investment has declined.

In part (c) we note that during a recession the demand for labor is reduced to D(L)′. If the real wage rate is "stuck" at $W/P^e(0)$, then cyclical unemployment results. More people want jobs, $L^n(0)$, than there are jobs available, L(1).

You might wonder how the decline in the interest rate in part (a) of figure 8.5 increases the quantity of planned investment, since we started by assuming that investor expectations had declined to a point where investors want to invest less (and hence demand less loanable funds). The answer lies in the process by which the interest rate determines the quantity of investment goods demanded. Although investors may believe that future returns on investment projects have declined, they may nonetheless *revise* their decision concerning any particular investment project *if in the meantime* the interest rate has also declined. Why? Because lower rates of interest reduce the cost of paying for investment projects. Thus, when the interest rate falls, investors' initially pessimistic view is offset *somewhat* by the prospect of lower investment costs. This reasoning underlies the movement *along* the new demand for loanable funds from r(0) to interest rate r(1). While investors may view the future as less rosy, it can still be reasonable to invest if the interest rate also falls. The result is that the decline in the interest rate has offset somewhat, but not fully, the decline in investment due to pessimistic expectations about the future.

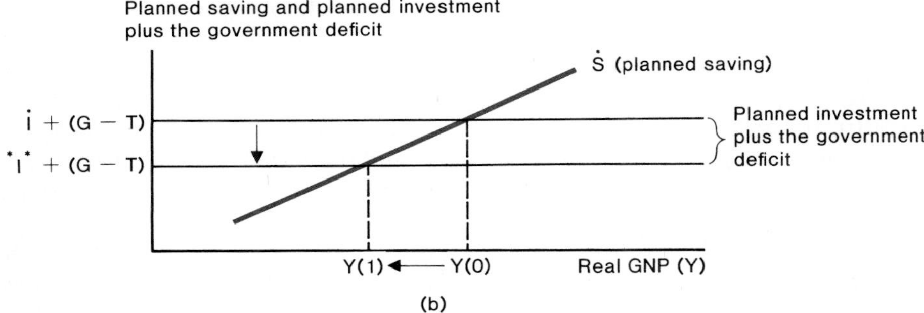

(b)

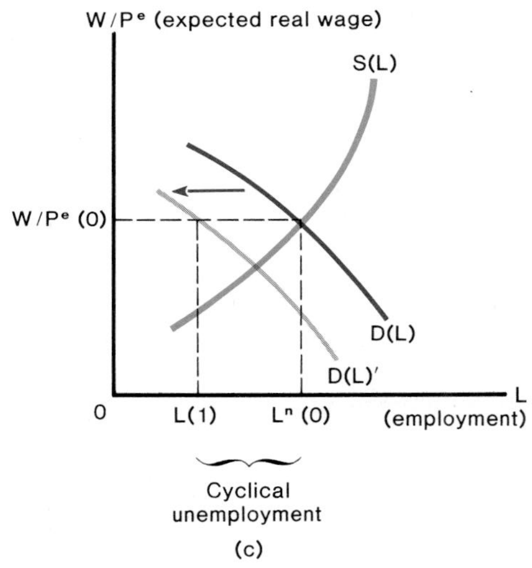

(c)

A major event in recent times that reduced investor optimism was the increase in world oil prices that occurred in two stages during the middle and late 1970s. We will analyze the impact of the oil-price "shock" on the United States and world economies in greater detail in chapters 11 and 16. However, we can note here that following both major increases in world oil prices, unemployment rose and GNP growth slowed. In addition, there was a decline in real interest rates in the United States following both episodes. *One* reason for this decline was probably the reduced demand for loanable funds during the recessions that followed the oil-price shocks.

Reaction in the Goods and Labor Markets

The interest rate performs the extremely important function of *cushioning* the shocks produced by sudden changes in macroeconomic variables such as aggregate investment. The loanable funds market returns to equilibrium at interest rate r(1). In the macroeconomic setting, however, we must also consider what is taking place in the goods and labor markets. Despite the cushioning effect of the decline in the rate of interest from r(0) to r(1), the goods and labor markets are no longer in full-employment equilibrium. The reduced level of planned investment plus the government deficit, $\ddot{I}(1) + (G - T)$, is *less* than planned saving when GNP is at its full-employment level. At the full-employment level of production, the goods market is now in a state of *excess production*. Since the goods market is in disequilibrium at a level of GNP equal to Y(0), full macroeconomic equilibrium no longer exists. Business firms cannot sell all they would like if they hire enough workers to preserve full employment in the labor market.

A Decline in Saving: Short-Run Macroeconomic Equilibrium in a Recession

A glance at part (b) of figure 8.5 shows us that the aggregate market for goods and services will not remain in a state of excess production. As aggregate production, employment, and income decline, so does planned saving. As you can see in the figure, as planned investment, an *exogenous* component of planned expenditure, declines, the resulting fall in GNP leads to a lower level of planned saving. The goods market reaches a new short-run equilibrium in which production equals planned expenditure, with GNP reduced to Y(1). At this lower level of GNP, planned saving once again equals planned investment plus the government deficit. The economy is now in a recession, with higher than normal unemployment. Notice that if the interest rate had not fallen to r(1), the line representing planned investment plus the government deficit in part (b) of figure 8.5 would be even lower than $\overset{**}{I} + (G - T)$ and GNP would have fallen still farther. Moreover, as we shall shortly see, the equilibrium that occurs at GNP equal to Y(1) will probably not persist because further macroeconomic changes are likely to cause the interest rate to fall even lower than r(1).

Figure 8.5, part (c) shows that in the labor market, the decline in firms' ability to sell their output has caused the aggregate labor demand curve to shift leftward from D(L) to D(L)′. In other words, declining production in the goods market leads to smaller desired employment in the labor market. We saw in chapter 3 that in the short run, the real wage rate remains "stuck" at $W/P^e(0)$, so employment falls to L(1), and cyclical unemployment equal to $L^n(0) - L(1)$ results.

The *multiplier* concept tells us exactly how much GNP will fall to reach its lower, short-run equilibrium level provided planned investment remains at its lower level, $\overset{**}{I}$. Since the multiplier relates all of the exogenous components of planned expenditure to the equilibrium level of GNP, the *change* in equilibrium GNP is equal to the *change* in exogenous planned expenditure (the change in planned investment in this case) times the multiplier. It may help you to remember how the multiplier works if we recall the numerical example of chapter 4. In that example, the MPC is 0.6, the MPS is 0.4, and the multiplier, 1/MPS, equals 2.5. Therefore, if planned investment $\overset{**}{I}$ (1) is now \$10 billion less than the *initial* level of planned investment $\overset{*}{I}$ (0), the new short-run macroeconomic equilibrium level of GNP Y(1) will be \$25 billion less than Y(0). Algebraically,

$$\begin{aligned}\Delta Y \equiv Y(0) - Y(1) &= \Delta I \times 1/MPS,\\ \$25 &= \$10 \times 1/0.4 \text{ (in billions)},\end{aligned}$$

where as usual, the symbol Δ indicates the *change* in a variable. (Can you show that the decline in planned saving is *exactly* equal to the decline in planned investment? Hint: The decline in planned saving equals the MPS multiplied by the decline in GNP.)

Adjustment toward Full Macroeconomic Equilibrium with Flexible Prices

In chapter 10, we shall discuss the different types of government policies that can be used to combat a recession. The rationale behind these policies can be better understood, however, if we first discuss how a market economy *might* regain a new position of full-employment macroeconomic equilibrium when it is in a recession.

In figure 8.5, we have seen that firms have cut back on their production so that short-run equilibrium exists in the goods and credit markets at interest rate r(1) and a level of GNP equal to Y(1). Both firms and workers, however, will become increasingly distressed as sales and job opportunities remain below their full-employment levels. Unemployment compensation does not last forever. Firms' profits decline.

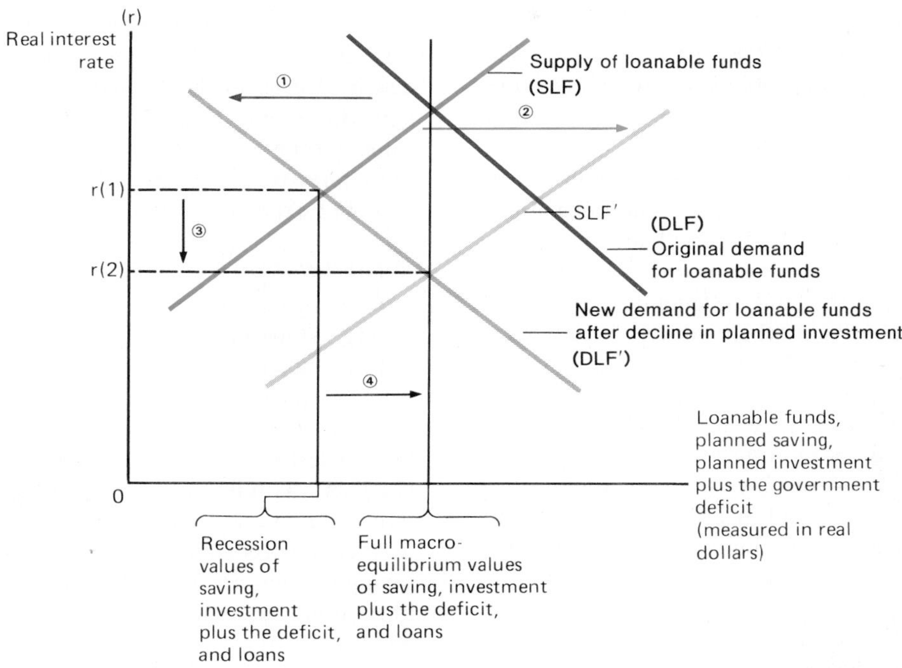

Figure 8.6 A decline in the price level leading to an increase in the real value of the supply of loanable funds When the economy is in recession, prices and wages will eventually decline. As prices fall, a given nominal (money) value of loans will purchase more investment goods. Therefore, the supply curve of loans, measured in *real* dollars, shifts rightward as prices fall. This leads to a movement down along DLF′ and an *increase* in planned investment, which eventually rises back to the level of planned investment before the recession began. It is the decline in the interest rate, not optimistic expectations, that returns the economy to full employment.

As their discomfort increases, business firms will become more aggressively competitive with their rivals and begin to cut prices on a wider and wider range of their products in an attempt to recapture lost customers. Firms will also place increasing pressure on their employees to accept wage cuts, or "givebacks," to help firms survive and to reduce employees' risk of further layoffs.

Declining Prices and the Supply Curve of Loanable Funds The way in which declining prices may eventually lead back to full macroeconomic equilibrium is through their effect on the *real value* of the supply of loanable funds originating in the banking system. In our discussion of the credit market, we showed that the *real value* of the banking system's supply of loanable funds is $\Delta M/P$, the change in the *real* money supply. If the denominator, P, of $\Delta M/P$ falls, the value of the fraction must rise. Thus, a decline in the prices of goods and services leads to an increase in the *real value* of the banking system's supply of loanable funds.

Since the aggregate supply of loanable funds is the sum of the households' supply and the banks' supply ($\Delta M/P$), the aggregate supply of loanable funds shifts to the right when the price level declines. This rightward shift in the supply curve of loanable funds is depicted in figure 8.6. At each and every rate of interest, the *real value* of new loans will be larger when the price level declines.

As the supply of loanable funds shifts rightward from the position occupied by SLF in figure 8.6, downward pressure is placed on the rate of interest in the loanable funds market. Downward adjustment of prices in the aggregate market for goods and services will persist as long as firms are unable to sell all the output they would like to sell under conditions of full employment. Eventually workers will adjust their expectations of future prices downward. This is a very important part of the macroeconomic adjustment process. Remember that when workers accept jobs, they do so in the *expectation* that every hour will yield a certain level of *real* earnings. If they expect the price level that prevails when they spend their earnings to be lower than it has been in the recent past, then they will be willing to accept lower *nominal* wage rates. Thus, the downward trend in prices and wages will continue as long as the economy is not in full macroequilibrium.

A Further Decline in the Interest Rate with Wage-Price Flexibility and Self-Correction in the Goods and Labor Markets As long as there is wage-price flexibility, there will be self-correction in the goods and labor markets. As suppliers of loanable funds compete with one another for loan contracts, the rate of interest will continue to decline. This reduction in the rate of interest will affect expenditures on investment goods. A lower interest rate lowers the cost of investment projects, thereby inducing increased investment. As investment rises, so does real GNP. This increase in production shifts the aggregate demand for labor to the right and raises employment. As incomes increase, planned consumption and saving also grow. *This downward trend in prices and wages and the upward spiral of investment, income, consumption, and saving continues until full macroeconomic equilibrium is restored.*

In figure 8.6 we show that at full macroeconomic equilibrium, planned investment plus the government deficit returns to the level that had prevailed originally. Investors' views of the future are still more pessimistic than they used to be. However, a decline in the interest rate has encouraged them to restore investment expenditure to its original level.

Recapitulation

Let us retrace the events that have occurred, following the arrows in figures 8.5 and 8.6. (1) The initial macroeconomic shock was a decline in business firms' planned investments at the interest rate r(0), shown by a *leftward shift* in the DLF curve indicated by the leftward-pointing arrows in each diagram. (2) This was followed by a *decline* in the rate of interest to r(1) and excess production in the aggregate market for goods and services. A decline in planned saving brought about short-run macroeconomic equilibrium in a recession at a lower level of real income Y(1) in figure 8.5, with higher than normal unemployment. A *decline* in prices and wages led to a *rightward* shift in the supply of loanable funds to SLF′ in figure 8.6, indicated by the arrow labeled 2, and a further *decline* in the interest rate to r(2) in figure 8.6, indicated by the arrow labeled 3. Even though the DLF curve had shifted to the left, the rightward shift in the SLF curve caused a movement *down* along the new DLF curve associated with the decline in the interest rate from r(1) to r(2) in figure 8.6. The decline in the interest rate caused an increase in planned investment, indicated by the arrow labeled 4, which led to higher GNP. Increased production of GNP led to a greater demand for labor and higher employment, income, and planned saving. Finally, full macroeconomic equilibrium was restored. This new full-employment equilibrium is depicted in figure 8.6 by the intersection of DLF′ and SLF′ at interest rate r(2).

Planned investment plus the government deficit once again equals planned saving at the full-employment level of GNP. Buyers and sellers in all markets are now simultaneously satisfied, and the economy is in a position of full macroequilibrium. The crucial variables that allowed the economy to reattain full-employment equilibrium are *the price and wage levels* and the *rate of interest*.

It is important to note that although both the price level and the *money* wage rate have fallen, the *real* wage rate in the new, full-employment equilibrium is *exactly the same* as before the recession. This is because the aggregate demand for labor, derived from aggregate production in the goods market, has been restored to its full-employment level. Full equilibrium requires the same real wage and employment level as before the recession began. In full-employment equilibrium, both employers and employees have learned to accept a new, lower price level and *money* wage level as permanent. Therefore, the expected *change* in the price level is again zero.

An Inflationary Episode Resulting from an Increase in Planned Investment

Now that we have examined the adjustments that occur in the macroeconomy as it cycles from full equilibrium through a recession and back to full equilibrium, we can summarize a movement through an inflationary episode quite easily. To begin, we assume that an event takes place that causes investors to become more optimistic about the future. Suppose, for example, that the discovery of a new electronic principle revolutionizes all forms of manufacturing and communications. All firms now desire to invest in new equipment to take advantage of the new processes made profitable by this discovery. The result is that planned investment at *every* rate of interest is greater than before.

Using figure 8.5 as a guide, construct a diagram with the DLF and SLF curves showing the economy at full-employment macroequilibrium. Then construct a DLF′ curve, showing a *rightward* shift in the demand for loanable funds corresponding to investors' more optimistic view of the future. If you have drawn your diagram correctly, there will be an *excess demand* for loanable funds at the original equilibrium rate of interest, r(0), after DLF increases to DLF′. However, the credit market will quickly move to a new (higher) equilibrium interest rate, r(1), as investors compete among themselves for available dollars to borrow.

The *rise* in the interest rate has two immediate effects. (1) Suppliers of loanable funds now find it desirable to economize on their cash balances and reserves, and they increase the quantity of loan contracts they are willing to purchase. (2) Some potential borrowers drop out of the market in the face of the higher interest rate. Despite the higher returns they anticipate on investment projects, the increased interest rate raises their costs and turns some attractive projects into losers. Nevertheless, at the new short-run equilibrium rate of interest, r(1), the quantity of loanable funds supplied and demanded will be higher than the original full equilibrium quantity.

Even though the credit market is now in equilibrium, there is a problem in the aggregate market for currently produced goods and services. In particular, planned expenditure now exceeds production. Business firms are pleased that their sales are growing and ask their employees to work extra hours; they also hire additional help as they attempt to expand production. As production and incomes increase, so does planned saving. As saving grows, the goods market approaches a short-run equilibrium with higher than normal production. In the labor market, employment is greater than normal, and the unemployment rate falls below its normal level.

In the labor market, employment rises in part because workers agree to put in longer hours temporarily when their employers ask them to do so. Of course, overtime work often requires that employers agree to pay extra money per hour. New employees may be hired, too, but they are unlikely to be as productive as a firm's experienced workers. Thus, labor costs per unit of output begin to rise. Employers, facing excess demand for their products, will begin to charge higher prices. Despite the fact that the price level is beginning to rise, workers do not yet expect inflation to continue. Moreover, past experience has shown that it is wise to accept additional work during periods of high demand to build up savings for a rainy day. Therefore, the population is willing to supply more labor for a while without demanding major wage increases. Thus, *short-run* macroeconomic equilibrium can be achieved at a level *above* full employment, with higher output sustained by above-normal employment and overtime hours.

It won't be long, however, before bottlenecks begin to appear in various markets in the economy. Certain raw materials will become more costly to obtain. Some industries have limited flexibility to expand output to meet higher than expected demand. The resulting potential shortages will lead to price hikes that purchasers view as increased costs of supplies. Thus, the initial increase in aggregate expenditure on goods and services will be followed by increased production costs for many firms. These cost increases, along with increased labor costs, will lead to further price increases, and gradually the economy will enter an inflationary phase, with rising prices becoming the rule.

As the price level increases, workers begin to notice that their real wages are not as high as they thought they were going to be. As inflation becomes the norm, employers find that they are unable to retain their workers unless they grant major wage increases. Members of unions with cost of living allowances begin to receive automatic wage hikes. New collective bargaining agreements now call for larger wage increases than in the past. The economy is now in the middle of an inflationary episode.

The inflationary, upward spiral of prices is likely to move the economy relatively quickly back to full macroequilibrium compared to the relatively slow speed of adjustment during a recession. When prices are rising, workers will be relatively quick to demand compensatory wage increases that lead to further price increases. While contracts with labor unions set floors on wage rates, they do not establish ceilings. Since businesses are enjoying increased prosperity, they may not be as cautious about raising their prices as they are about lowering them during a recession.

As the price level increases, there is an important impact in the loanable funds market. As the price level (P) rises, $\Delta M/P$ declines. An increase in the price of goods and services shifts the banking system's supply of loanable funds, $\Delta M/P$, to the left. Draw the leftward shift of the aggregate supply of loanable funds in your diagram. Prices will continue to rise, and SLF will continue shifting to the left as long as production remains above its full-equilibrium level. Thus, the process continues until SLF′ crosses DLF′ at r(2), the interest rate that is high enough to restore equality between planned aggregate expenditure and the aggregate production of goods and services. When this occurs, both planned investment and planned saving have fallen back to the levels observed in the initial full macroeconomic equilibrium. A higher interest rate has offset increased investor optimism. Planned investment plus the government deficit once again equals planned saving at GNP equal to Y(0), the full macroeconomic equilibrium value of GNP.

Once full macroequilibrium has been regained, inflation ceases. At the new, higher price level, a typical firm no longer experiences either increasing costs or excess demand. Borrowers can satisfy their demands for loanable funds at the new, higher interest rate. In the labor market, the quantity of labor demanded will have declined back to its normal, full-employment level and the unemployment rate will have risen back to its normal value. The real wage rate will also have returned to its preinflation value, with both the nominal wage rate (W) and the price level (P) higher than before. Neither firms nor workers have any reason to anticipate further inflation. Although the price level, the nominal wage level, and the interest rate are higher at the new full macroequilibrium than before the initial increase in planned investment, they are *no longer increasing.*

Let us briefly retrace the events that have occurred, following the arrows that you have drawn in your diagram. If you did not draw in arrows indicating shifts in the curves, you should do so as we go along. (1) The initial macroeconomic shock was an increase in business firms' planned investments at the interest rate r(0), shown by a *rightward shift* in the DLF curve. (2) This was followed by an *increase* in the rate of interest and excess planned expenditure in the aggregate market for goods and services. An increase in planned saving brought about short-run macroeconomic equilibrium in an inflationary episode, with less than normal unemployment. An *increase* in prices and wages led to a *leftward* shift in the supply of loanable funds, leading to a further *increase* in the interest rate and a movement *upward* along the new DLF curve. The increase in the interest rate caused a decline in planned investment, which led to lower GNP, income, employment, and planned saving. Finally, full macroeconomic equilibrium was restored. Once again, the crucial factors that allowed the economy to reattain full-employment equilibrium were *the price and wage level adjustments* and the *rate of interest.*

▸ Summary and Conclusions

In this chapter, we saw how the macroeconomic adjustment process generates powerful forces that even President Nixon could not overrule with laws governing legal maximum wages and prices in the 1970s. We have used a macroeconomic model to trace the impact of changes in planned investment, the money supply, the quantity of capital, and the cost of labor on GNP, unemployment, the price level, and the rate of interest. The following points were emphasized.

In the *short run,* a decline in planned investment (or any other component of exogenous expenditure) will cause a decline in the equilibrium level of GNP and in employment. This leads to short-run equilibrium in a recession.

In the *long run,* a decline in the price level and a further decline in the rate of interest are capable of restoring full-employment macroeconomic equilibrium. Once the economy reaches a new full macroequilibrium, however, unemployment and real income end up unchanged from their initial equilibrium values.

In the *short run,* an increase in planned investment (or any other component of exogenous expenditure) will cause an increase in the equilibrium level of GNP and in employment. This leads to an inflationary episode.

An *increase* in planned investment has a positive initial impact on the price level, the rate of interest, and real GNP, and it has a negative effect on the unemployment rate in the short run. Once the economy reaches a new full macroequilibrium, however, unemployment and real income are unchanged from their initial equilibrium values. The nominal wage rate, the price level, and the interest rate have all increased.

Key Terms

full macroeconomic equilibrium *172*

short-run macroeconomic equilibrium *172*

Questions for Discussion and Review

Are the statements in questions 1 to 4 true, false, or uncertain? Defend your answers.

1. In short-run recessionary macroequilibrium, all macroeconomic variables are unchanging, by definition.
2. In comparing one position of full macroeconomic equilibrium to another, the price level generally is unchanged.
3. The interest rate is the principal variable promoting short-run macroequilibrium when planned investment changes.
4. An important difference between short-run and full macroeconomic equilibrium is the behavior of the price level.
5. Assume that the marginal propensity to consume is 0.8, taxes are zero, exogenous consumption is $100, planned investment is $1,000, the government deficit is $50, and net exports are zero. (All these data refer to a one-year time period and are in billions of dollars.) Calculate aggregate expenditure for goods and services. Suppose that households' desire to save equals $1,200 when the economy is at the full-employment level of national income. What do you think will happen to the price level and the interest rate in the future? What conditions must be held constant to make your forecast? What change in net exports would bring about full macroequilibrium immediately?
6. Explain why a flexible price level is crucial to achievement of full macroeconomic equilibrium.
7. How would a decline in the marginal propensity to save affect full macroequilibrium? (You can use the data in question 5 to answer this question.) What would be the long-term impact on economic growth?
8. Suppose the government decided to repeal the income tax on corporation profits. Assuming that this tax is essentially a tax on the returns on investments, how would macroeconomic equilibrium be affected in the short run? How would full equilibrium be different compared to before the tax was repealed? What effect would this policy have on economic growth?

Chapter 9

Aggregate Demand, Aggregate Supply, and the Price Level

Outline

Objectives

After reading this chapter, the student should be able to:

State the quantity equation and what each variable represents.
Explain how the quantity equation leads to the quantity theory of nominal GNP.
Explain the linkage between the money supply and the price level.
Explain why the aggregate demand curve slopes downward and what factors are held constant when constructing it.
Explain why the short-run aggregate supply curve slopes upward and what factors are held constant when constructing it.
Describe factors that would cause the aggregate demand curve or the aggregate supply curve to shift.
Explain why the long-run aggregate supply curve is vertical.
Use aggregate demand and supply to describe a recession and an inflationary episode.
Use aggregate demand and supply to describe recession and inflation in a growth scenario.
Describe the relationship between unemployment and the rate of inflation in the short run and in the long run.
Distinguish between demand-induced inflation and cost-push inflation.

Introduction

At the beginning of chapter 8 we discussed the political concerns that contributed to President Nixon's decision to impose wage and price controls on the United States economy in August 1971. There is one key element in that decision that we did not explain. Why did an economically conservative president decide that conditions warranted such drastic and uncharacteristic actions by his administration? After all, while an inflation of nearly 6 percent per year along with an unemployment rate of 6 percent might seem disappointing, the experience of the late 1970s and early 1980s was not much better, and neither Democrats nor Republicans have pushed for similar controls.

The ability of Democrats to make political gains by calling for controls in 1971 and the administration's decision to proceed in that direction can be understood best by placing the issues in historical perspective. In the first two decades following World War II, economists and political leaders developed a general consensus on how the macroeconomy works. On the basis of the experience of the Great Depression of the 1930s, the economic research of John Maynard Keynes and others, and early postwar experience, it seemed clear at the time that during economic downturns prices either remained fairly constant or declined. On the other hand, when the economy was at or near full employment, inflation tended to be the major macroeconomic problem—not unemployment.

Therefore, the disturbing picture that emerged in 1971 was that both inflation and unemployment were high by recent historical standards and that both were rising. In a sense, it appeared that the conventional economic story did not correspond to the facts. No wonder unconventional policy initiatives seemed plausable and popular. This chapter explains why the strange events of the early 1970s occurred.

In chapter 8 we saw that full macroeconomic equilibrium involves full employment in the labor market, an interest rate that equates the quantity of loanable funds demanded and supplied, and planned expenditure equal to the production of GNP in the aggregate market for goods and services. We also saw that the price level is a key variable in restoring macroeconomic equilibrium during recessions and inflationary episodes. What we did not *learn, however, is what determines the actual price level that exists when macroeconomic equilibrium prevails. Why does a typical market basket of goods cost, say, $100 rather than $0.10 or $1 million? In this chapter, we will answer this question. We will develop two sets of tools that enable us to deal with the forces underlying changes in the average price of goods and services. These tools—the quantity theory of nominal GNP and aggregate demand and supply curves—provide another way of summarizing inflationary episodes and recessions. They also provide additional insights into the causes of macroeconomic disequilibrium, as well as suggestions for some possible cures.*

*The **quantity equation** expresses the quantity of money as proportional to nominal GNP.*

***Velocity (V)** tells us the constant of proportionality in the quantity equation: 1/V is the constant of proportionality between nominal GNP and the quantity of money required to sustain it.*

▸ The Equilibrium Price Level: The Quantity Theory

As we have seen, when the economy is in macroequilibrium, the price level is stable. However, we have not pinned down the reason that macroeconomic equilibrium occurs at the *particular* price level corresponding to equilibrium in the goods, labor, and credit markets. One simple view that is accepted by many economists explains the average price of goods and services in terms of the amount of money available to spend on them. This view states simply that if the number of dollar bills (or pound or lira or peso notes) increases but the quantity of goods and services produced stays the same, then there will be "too much money chasing too few goods" and prices will rise. Similarly, if the quantity of money in circulation falls, *ceteris paribus,* the price level will decline.

To understand the importance of the quantity of money in explaining the price level, remember that one of the variables held constant in deriving our model of macroeconomic equilibrium is the quantity of banks' reserves. Banks' reserves determine their willingness to lend funds to borrowers and thereby increase the money supply. In the explanation of the price level we have just described, the average price of goods and services is determined by the *total quantity* of money balances in the economy and by the *quantity of goods and services* on which those money balances can be spent. In an economy with a large amount of reserves, banks will furnish a great deal of money and the price level will be relatively high compared to an economy in which reserves and the amount of money in circulation is smaller but the quantity of goods and services is the same.

We will now state this theory of the price level more precisely. If you multiply the price level, P, by the real value of GNP, Y, the result is the *money or nominal value of GNP.* In the theory of the price level we have just described, the economy's quantity of money is related to nominal GNP by what is called the **quantity equation,** which is expressed

$$MV = PY.$$

In the quantity equation, M is the quantity of money, P is the price level, Y is real GNP, and PY is nominal GNP. The variable V is extremely important in the quantity equation and is called the **velocity of money.** The velocity of money is nothing more than a number relating the nominal value of GNP (PY) to the quantity of money. It is called velocity because it reflects the "speed" with which money circulates in the economy. For example, suppose PY equals $1 trillion and V equals 4. Then the quantity of money required to sustain this level of nominal GNP is $250 billion because each dollar "changes hands" an average of four times during the year.

The quantity equation is the basis of what is called the *quantity theory of nominal GNP,* or the quantity theory for short. Economists who accept the quantity theory tend to believe that V is constant or changes slowly and predictably. Economists who accept the quantity theory with few, if any, qualifications are called *monetarists.* Monetarists believe that at full employment, current changes in the money supply are the best predictor of changes in nominal GNP—PY in the quantity equation—six months into the future.

(Their views will be contrasted with alternative views of the macroeconomy in chapter 12.) According to the quantity theory, if the quantity of money is not equal to the amount needed to sustain the current level of nominal GNP, nominal GNP will change. The quantity equation makes it clear how much money is needed to sustain any given amount of nominal GNP. To find out how much money is needed, we simply solve the previous equation for the quantity of money M, obtaining

$$M = (PY)/V.$$

Using the preceding numerical example, if nominal GNP is $1 trillion and velocity is 4, then $250 billion is required to support aggregate expenditure. If the actual money supply is greater or less than the amount specified by this equation and if V is a constant, then the quantity theory says that either P or Y will be forced to adjust.

Why is it that the quantity theory is an explanation of the price level rather than the level of real GNP? The reason is that economists who accept the quantity theory believe that in the long run the production of real GNP is determined by "real" variables, which are the economy's available resources—its labor, capital equipment, technology, and so on. They also believe that upward or downward adjustment of the price level will lead the economy to the full-employment level of GNP. Full-employment GNP, they believe, is not determined by the quantity of money or the velocity of money. Therefore, when full-employment GNP is represented by the variable Y in the quantity equation, it is treated as a constant. That is, full-employment GNP is treated as *exogenous*—not determined by the quantity equation itself but by other variables. With V also a constant, it follows that the price level, P, is proportional to the quantity of money. This can be seen by rearranging the terms of the quantity equation, placing P alone on the left-hand side. We then have the following equation that describes how the quantity of money is related to the price level:

$$P = (V/Y)M.$$

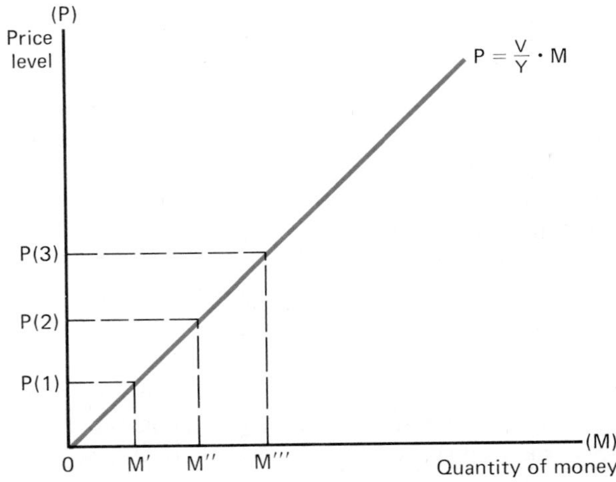

Figure 9.1 The relationship between the price level and the quantity of money according to the quantity theory
The straight-line relationship between the price level and the quantity of money indicates that the price level is directly proportional to the quantity of money, as indicated by the price-level equation we have just derived from the quantity equation. If velocity should increase, holding Y constant, the slope of the price line would increase, too. If real GNP should increase, the slope of the line would decrease.

This equation says that, given velocity and real GNP, the price level is proportional to the quantity of money. Notice that an increase in velocity (the "speed" at which money changes hands), given real GNP and the quantity of money, will increase the equilibrium price level. An increase in real GNP, given velocity and the quantity of money, will reduce the price level.

Figure 9.1 illustrates the relationship between the price level and the quantity of money as described by the quantity theory. In figure 9.1, velocity, V, and real GNP, Y, are assumed to be constant. Therefore, an increase in the quantity of money from an amount such as M′ to an amount such as M″ will cause the price level to increase from P(1) to P(2). The straight-line relationship between the price level and the quantity of money indicates that the price level is directly proportional to the quantity of money, as indicated by the price-level equation we have just derived from the quantity equation. If velocity should increase, holding

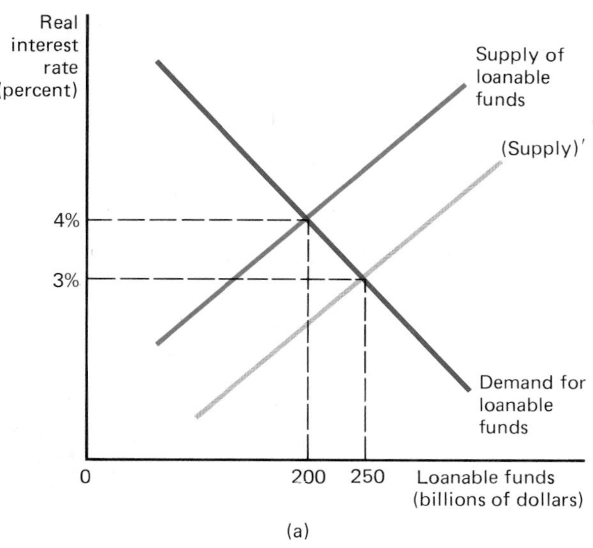

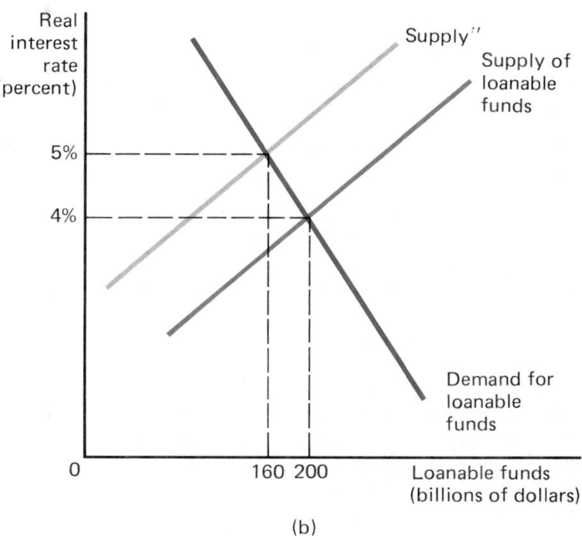

Figure 9.2 Money supply and the loanable funds market
In part (a) the increase in the money supply shifts the supply of loanable funds to the right. The real interest rate falls from 4 percent to 3 percent, and loans rise from $200 billion to $250 billion. At full employment the increased demand for goods and services of $50 billion pushes the price level up.

In part (b) the decrease in the money supply shifts the supply of loanable funds to the left. The real interest rate rises to 5 percent, and loans decrease by $40 billion. At full employment the decrease in demand for goods and services of $40 billion exerts downward pressure on the price level.

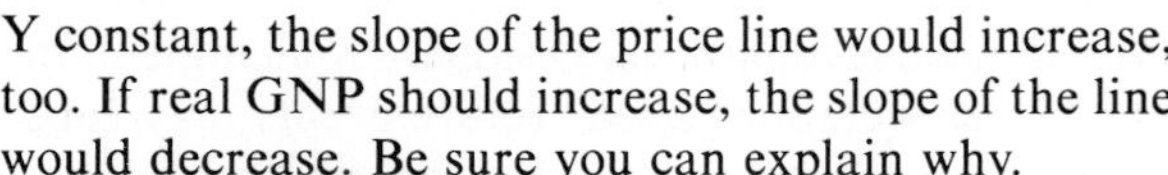

Y constant, the slope of the price line would increase, too. If real GNP should increase, the slope of the line would decrease. Be sure you can explain why.

Just how does an increase in M lead to an increase in P? What is the *linkage* between the quantity of money and the price level? The connection can be seen if we work through the effects of a change in the quantity of money on the loan contract and goods markets. Assume that the economy is currently at full-employment equilibrium and that something happens to increase the quantity of banks' reserves. Banks respond by increasing the aggregate supply of loanable funds. Since more loanable funds are available, the interest rate declines, investors borrow more, and the money supply (M) increases. With the economy at full employment, the rightward shift in the supply of loanable funds has led to higher levels of planned expenditure and production of GNP than are consistent with stable prices. An inflationary episode results. When the economy returns to macroequilibrium, real GNP will be unchanged but the price level will have gone up. The quantity equation tells us that the price level will have increased by the same proportion that M increased. Figure 9.2, part (a), illustrates the rightward shift in the loanable funds supply curve and the increase in the quantity of loanable funds borrowed in response to the reduced real interest rate.

The same logic tells us how a decrease in the quantity of money will shift the aggregate supply of loanable funds to the left. This will lead to an increase in the rate of interest, a reduction in planned investment, and a recession. However, there is no effect on the *full-employment* level of GNP. The recession will ultimately result in declining prices that lead the economy back to full employment. The quantity theory tells us that when full employment is restored, the price level will have fallen by the same proportion that M decreased. Part (b) of figure 9.2 illustrates the leftward shift in the loanable funds curve caused by a contraction of the money supply. As a result, the real interest rate increases and the quantity of funds borrowed declines. It is important to note that the reduction of the interest rate in part (a) and the increase in part (b) are both temporary. Be sure you can explain why the interest rate returns to 4 percent when full macroequilibrium is restored.

As illustrated, the increase in the money supply creates $50 billion of new planned expenditure that induced price increases at full employment. The decline in the money supply reduces the supply of loanable funds in part (b) and, therefore, the planned expenditure on goods and services by $40 billion. At full employment, the decline in planned expenditure on goods and services puts downward pressure on prices.

The Role of Velocity

The heart of the quantity theory is the assumption that velocity, V, is constant or changes only slowly and predictably over time. If you were to divide the nominal values of GNP reported in chapter 2 by the values of M2 reported in chapter 6 you would see that the ratio has varied in the narrow range of 1.55 to 1.67. This means that an average dollar of M2 changes hands 1½ to 1⅔ times per year. This measure of V has exhibited little long-run change and represents a relatively stable relationship between M2 and PY. Velocity as measured with M1 has varied over a considerably wider range. (Economists are not in general agreement regarding whether M1 or M2 is the better measure of the quantity of money to use when calculating velocity, but popular attention remains focused on M1. In recent years, deregulation of the banking system has resulted in interest's being paid on demand deposits and checking privileges allowed with savings accounts and money market funds. The usefulness of most components of M2 balances for transactions resulting from these changes suggests that M2 may be a good measure of the quantity of money when we want to calculate velocity in discussions of the quantity theory and the price level.) Remember, the quantity equation says that

$$V = PY/M.$$

An average dollar in our supply of M1 currently "changes hands" about six times per year.

The value of velocity does change gradually over time. It is determined in the long run by the technology of carrying out transactions, by the expected riskiness of holding assets in nonmonetary forms such as loan contracts, and by the rate of interest. An improvement in the technology of conducting our everyday business, such as the increased use of electronic funds transfer systems, would reduce our need to hold cash for transaction purposes. This would reduce the quantity of money balances required to sustain a given level of nominal GNP and increase velocity. An increase in the rate of interest would also increase velocity because the opportunity cost of holding wealth in the form of checking accounts or currency rather than loan contracts would be higher.

Economists who accept the quantity theory base their belief on the idea that velocity is relatively constant and predictable over long periods of time. However, they do recognize that temporary changes in the public's expectations about future events may cause rather sharp fluctuations in V for short time periods. For example, if households and firms should suddenly turn pessimistic about the likelihood of selling goods and services in the near future, they might seek safety in holding larger money balances. This would result in a reduction in the velocity of money until the public regained its confidence.

We will have more to say about economists who disagree with the quantity theory (most of whom are known as *Keynesians*) in chapter 12. Briefly, however, they believe that velocity, V, is very sensitive to changes in interest rates and to the public's perceptions of current and future economic events. In their view, a change in M is equally, or more, likely to result in a change in V (in the opposite direction) than

*The **aggregate demand and supply curves** describe the relationship between the price level and the quantities of real GNP demanded and supplied, respectively.*

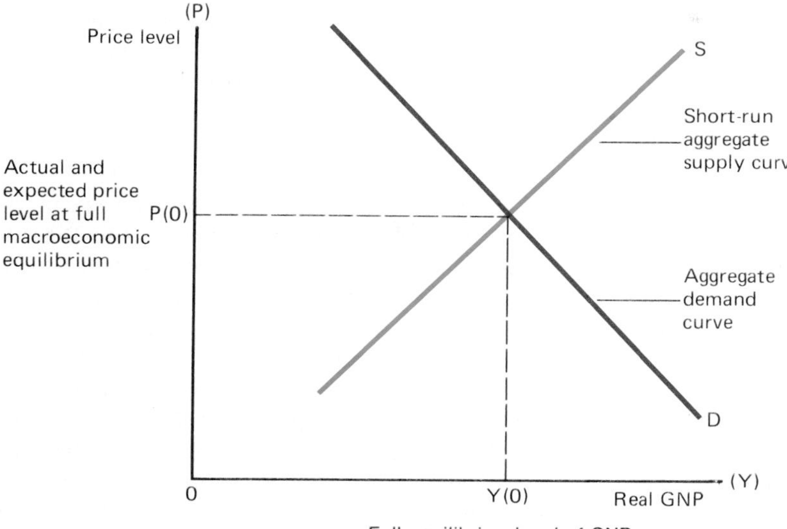

Figure 9.3 Aggregate demand and short-run aggregate supply
The aggregate demand and supply curves show how the quantities of GNP demanded and supplied change along with the price level. Several variables are assumed constant in deriving aggregate demand and supply, including the expected price level. A change in any of these variables results in a shift of either the aggregate demand curve or the aggregate supply curve.

a proportional change in the price level. For example, if an increase in the quantity of money simply leads the public to enlarge checking account balances, this will not result in increased planned investment, GNP, or the price level.

To summarize, the reason that the quantity theory provides an explanation of the price level in the long run is the belief that in the long run real GNP (Y) is determined by the economy's available resources and technology. Velocity (V), however, is believed to be determined mainly by the technology of executing transactions and to a lesser extent by the opportunity cost of holding money versus other assets. That is, the values of V and Y are *exogenously* determined by forces that the quantity of money does not affect. Therefore, the quantity equation tells us that when the monetary authority determines M, it also indirectly determines P, the only *endogenous* variable of the quantity equation in the long run.

Summarizing Changes in Aggregate Production and the Price Level: Aggregate Demand and Supply

A more elaborate framework for analyzing the price level involves developing the concepts of demand and supply curves in the aggregate market for goods and services. We have already seen how production of goods and services and the price level change during recessions and inflationary episodes. We have also seen how the quantity theory of nominal GNP offers an explanation of what determines the price level when macroeconomic equilibrium prevails. Many students find it easier to remember how all of the pieces of the macroeconomy fit together when they are summarized in terms of demand and supply curves for GNP. Such curves are depicted in figure 9.3. The curves relating the price level and the level of real GNP shown in the figure are called the **aggregate demand** and **supply curves** because they describe how the quan-

The ***short-run aggregate supply curve*** *shows what happens to the price level and real GNP during inflationary episodes and recessions.*

The ***long-run aggregate supply curve*** *is a vertical line relating the price level to the full macroeconomic equilibrium value of real GNP.*

quantities of GNP demanded and supplied are related to the price level during recessions and inflationary episodes.

After deriving the aggregate demand curve, we will derive the **short-run aggregate supply curve,** which describes the aggregate supply of GNP during recessions and inflationary episodes. We will then show how their intersection describes the equilibrium price level and the production of goods and services. Finally, we will derive the **long-run aggregate supply curve,** which shows how the price level and the quantity of GNP supplied are related when the economy is in full macroequilibrium.

All of the conditions that were assumed constant when we discussed the aggregate labor market, the aggregate market for goods and services, and the credit market are assumed constant as we derive the aggregate demand and supply curves. Among other things, we assumed that the economy has a given stock of physical capital and a fixed population and that the aggregate supply curve of labor is given. We shall see that a change in any of these variables results in a *shift* in aggregate supply. Another very important variable that is assumed constant when we derive the aggregate supply curve is the *expected price level.* We shall see that if the expected price level changes, the short-run aggregate supply curve shifts in the same direction (up or down).

Another set of conditions is assumed constant when we derive the aggregate demand curve for GNP. First, we assume that investors' desire to purchase investment goods is given. This means that the relationship between the quantity of investment goods demanded and the rate of interest does not change. If it does, the aggregate demand for GNP will shift. If, for example, investors become more optimistic about the future and wish to purchase more investment goods at any given interest rate, then the aggregate demand for GNP will shift. Second, we assume that the levels of government expenditure and taxation are given. A change in either of these variables will cause a shift in aggregate demand.

Finally, we have seen that an increase in the quantity of money (or any other change that increases banks' or other lenders' willingness to lend funds) will result in an increase in aggregate expenditure. This is equivalent to saying that an increase in the quantity of money causes a rightward shift in *aggregate demand* for GNP. The reason is that a rightward shift in the supply of loanable funds, *cet. par.,* will lead to a fall in the rate of interest. The lower interest rate increases the quantity of investment goods demanded, which increases the quantity of GNP demanded *at every price level.* Of course, a reduction in the quantity of money following a leftward shift in the supply of loanable funds will accompany a decline in the aggregate demand for GNP. Less GNP will be demanded *at every price level.* We will return to our earlier example of the relationship between changes in the money supply and changes in the price level after we illustrate aggregate demand and aggregate supply.

Aggregate Demand

The aggregate demand curve in figure 9.3 slopes downward and to the right. The reason is that planned expenditure on goods and services (real GNP) falls as the price level increases and grows larger as the price level declines. To see why, we need only review the macroeconomic adjustments that take place during recessions and inflationary episodes. As the price level declines, a given amount of dollars will purchase more goods. Thus, a decline in the price level shifts the aggregate supply of loanable funds (measured in *real* dollars) to the right, as described in figures 8.5 and 8.6 on pages 180–81 and 183. This causes a decline in the rate of interest. As the interest rate falls, planned investment expenditures increase. This raises the level of total expenditure on GNP. In other words, the quantity of real GNP *demanded* rises as the price level falls, and it declines when the price level rises.

Aggregate Supply

The aggregate supply curve in figure 9.3 slopes upward and to the right. Once again, a quick review of macroeconomic adjustments during recessions and inflationary episodes will show why. During a recession firms reduce production (and employment) to avoid accumulating unsold goods. As excess productive capacity persists, firms start to lower their prices in an attempt to regain lost sales. Thus, during recessions, we observe a decline in the price level and in the quantity of GNP supplied. During an inflationary episode, by contrast, the price level tends to increase as firms produce larger quantities of output for sale. Workers supply the additional labor needed to produce this output because in the short run they are glad to have the extra work and typical employer-employee relationships call for working overtime when asked to. Moreover, workers are usually surprised by the decline in the purchasing power of their wages at the beginning of an inflationary episode. At first they are not likely to perceive price increases. When they do notice the beginnings of inflation, they do not immediately view an increase in the price level as a permanent change. (Remember our assumption that the *expected* price level is constant.) Because workers expect prices to return to "normal" in the near future, they do not anticipate permanent decline in their *real* wage rates. Thus, in the *short run,* there is a positive relationship between the quantity of goods and services supplied and the price level.

Equilibrium of Aggregate Demand and Supply

Just as with other demand and supply curves we have dealt with, there is only one price level and quantity of GNP at which the aggregate demand and supply curves cross. If the price level is higher than P(0) in figure 9.3, the quantity of GNP demanded will be less than the quantity supplied. If the price level is less than P(0), there will be excess demand for GNP. Given all the conditions we assumed constant in deriving the aggregate demand and supply curves, there is one, and only one, equilibrium price level and quantity of real GNP. In figure 9.3, we have drawn the aggregate demand and supply curves when full macroeconomic equilibrium prevails. It is easy to use the aggregate demand and supply curves to summarize the changes that take place in the macroeconomy during a recession or an inflationary episode. By tracing the macroeconomic adjustments that occur during such episodes, we will also be able to derive the *long-run aggregate supply curve.*

Aggregate Demand and Supply during a Recession

Remember that the macroeconomic "shock" that starts the economy into a recession was assumed to be a decline in investors' optimism about the returns on future investment projects. This means that the planned investment component of the demand for

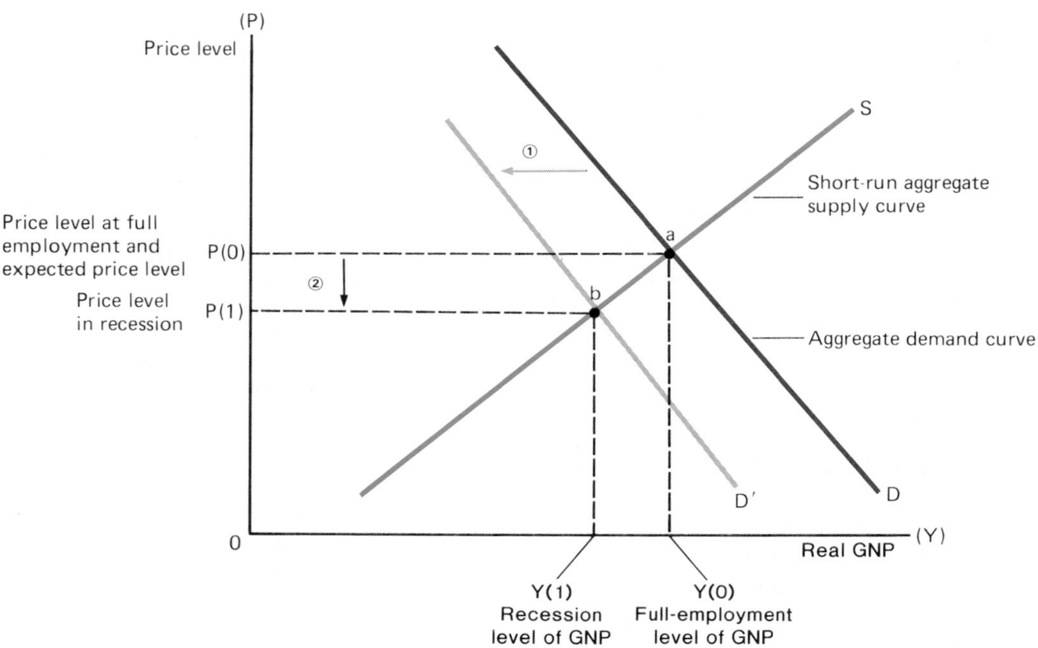

Figure 9.4 Aggregate demand and short-run aggregate supply in a recession
A recession begins with a leftward shift in the aggregate demand curve. The intersection of aggregate demand and aggregate supply moves from point a to point b. The economy moves into a recession as GNP falls from Y(0) to Y(1) and the price level falls from P(0) to P(1).

loans shifts to the left. At every rate of interest, fewer investment goods are demanded. This change causes a leftward shift in the aggregate demand curve, as shown by the arrow numbered 1 in figure 9.4 The prerecession aggregate demand curve intersected the short-run aggregate supply curve at point a, with an equilibrium price level of P(0) and GNP at its full-employment level Y(0). The new aggregate demand curve intersects the short-run aggregate supply curve at point b, with a lower price level, P(1). The arrow numbered 2 shows the decline in the price level from P(0) to P(1). GNP is also lower during the recession, at Y(1). During the initial stages of the recession, workers are unwilling to accept lower nominal (money) wage rates because they believe that the price level will soon return to its older, higher value of P(0).

Figure 9.5 shows the macroeconomic adjustments that take place as the declining price level gradually brings about an end to the recession and a return to full employment. Part (a) of figure 9.5 is a copy of figure 9.4. It shows the beginning of the recession with a leftward shift of the aggregate demand curve. Part (b) of figure 9.5 introduces a new change in the macroeconomy. As the recession persists and the price level continues to fall, workers begin to adjust their belief about the future course of the prices of the goods they buy. They no longer expect the price level to return to P(0). They realize that what is "normal" for the economy in the future is going to be different than in the past. Because their *expected* price level falls, workers are now willing to accept jobs at *lower* nominal wage rates. As nominal wage rates fall,

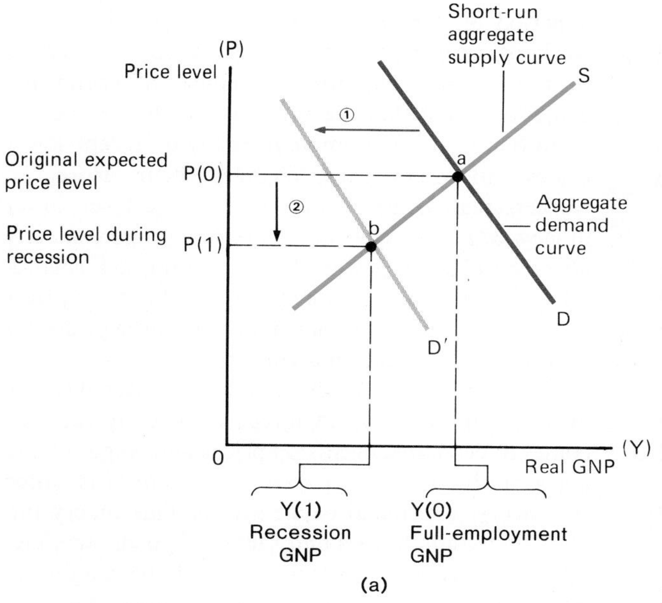

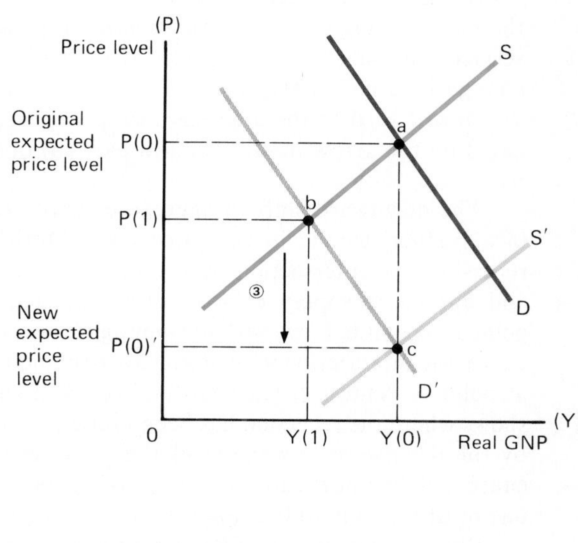

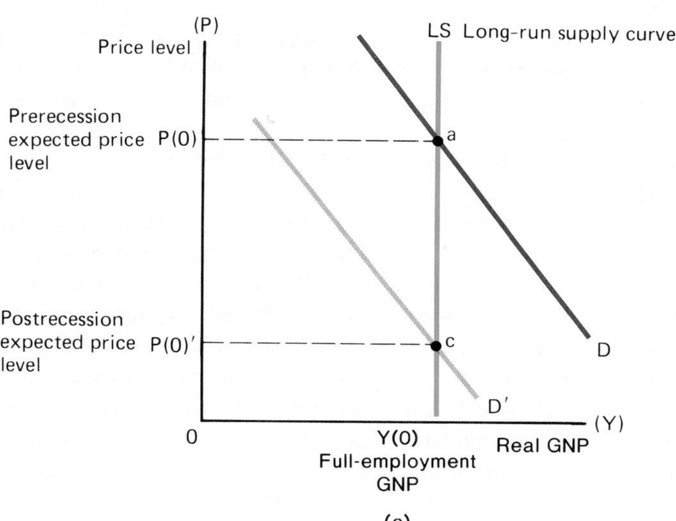

Figure 9.5 Aggregate demand and aggregate supply as the economy recovers from a recession with a lower price level
In part (a) the recession begins: (1) aggregate demand shifts to the left and (2) the price level and GNP decline.

In part (b), as the recession continues, (3) the aggregate supply curve shifts downward as the expected price level falls.

In part (c) the recession is over. The expected price level has fallen from P(0) to P(0)′. GNP has once again reached its full-employment level. Points a and c are on the *long-run aggregate supply curve.*

The ***theory of rational expectations*** *says that firms and households correctly incorporate available information in making decisions about their work effort, level of production, willingness to borrow and lend, and so forth; they are not fooled over and over by the effects of persistent or repeated economic events and government policy actions.*

firms experience a decline in their costs. They are therefore willing to offer *every quantity* of goods and services for sale at lower prices than before. This change in firms' supply conditions is depicted by a *downward shift* in the aggregate supply curve, indicated by the arrow numbered 3 in part (b) of figure 9.5.

The downward shift in aggregate supply results in a further decline in the price level. During the recession, the intersection of the aggregate demand and aggregate supply curves initially shifted from point a to point b. Now, with the new aggregate supply curve, the intersection with aggregate demand occurs at point c. Point c in parts (b) and (c) of the figure shows where the recession has been brought to an end by the downward movement of the price level. Because a dollar now can purchase more goods, GNP has returned to its full-employment level, Y(0).

Since both points a and c correspond to the equilibrium values of the price level and of GNP when the economy is in full macroequilibrium, they both lie on the *long-run* aggregate supply curve. To illustrate the long-run aggregate supply curve, we have connected points a and c in part (c) of figure 9.5. The long-run aggregate supply curve is a vertical line that shows, in the long run, that the equilibrium level of GNP has only one value—its full-employment level—and that the price level adjusts so as to push the macroeconomy back to equilibrium when it enters a recession.

Our development of the long-run aggregate supply curve is based on the assumption that firms and households learn from their experience and adjust their expectations of future economic events accordingly. During the initial stages of a recession, it is difficult to tell whether the economy has actually entered a period of depressed business activity. Therefore, workers and firms are reluctant to accept lower prices for their services and products. However, when it becomes apparent that the only way to sell more output or to obtain desired employment is to accept lower prices and wages, these changes occur. Moreover, workers realize that with a lower price level, lower money wage rates do not represent proportionately lower purchasing power of their earnings. Firms realize that with lower money wages and lower prices for nonlabor inputs, they can accept lower prices for their output without incurring losses.

The idea that businesses and households use available information to forecast correctly the outcomes of economic events on prices and wages and to act accordingly in their own best interests is called the **theory of rational expectations.** This theory implies that while buyers and sellers of goods, services, labor, and loanable funds may initially be caught unaware by a sudden change in their economic environment, they learn to anticipate accurately the results of macroeconomic shocks that persist or occur repeatedly. Those who do not learn to adjust accurately to such changes in their economic environment lose out.

The basic idea imbedded in the long-run aggregate supply curve is that real GNP is determined in the long run by the capacity of the economy to produce goods and services (the aggregate production function) and by the willingness of workers to supply labor at various real wage rates (aggregate labor supply), not by the price level. The theory of rational expectations states that firms and workers adjust their behavior to their perception of "real" variables and are not fooled for long by changes in the level of money wage rates and prices. Therefore, in the long run, the quantity of GNP produced does not depend on the price level. An important implication of the theory of rational expectations is that recessions and inflationary episodes take place quickly. The return to full macroequilibrium will not be a prolonged process when firms and households learn to anticipate price level adjustments and react quickly. This implication of the rational expectations concept is still controversial among economists.

Aggregate Demand and Supply during an Inflationary Episode

The adjustments of aggregate demand and supply to determine the price level and equilibrium GNP during an inflationary episode are summarized in figure 9.6. In part (a), a macroeconomic "shock," such as a sudden improvement in investment opportunities, shifts the aggregate demand curve to the right. The preinflation aggregate demand curve intersected the short-run aggregate supply curve at point a, with an equilibrium price level of P(0) and GNP at its full-employment level, Y(0). The new aggregate demand curve intersects the short-run aggregate supply curve at point b, with a higher price level, P(1). This rightward shift in aggregate demand is indicated by the arrow numbered 1 in part (a) of figure 9.6. The increase in the price level is indicated by the arrow numbered 2. GNP has also risen to a higher level, Y(1). During the initial stages of the inflationary episode, employees feel they must honor their employers' request to work more and are glad to have the extra income. They may earn an agreed upon wage premium for overtime work, but they do not demand wage increases to compensate for a rising price level. If they see prices increasing, workers initially expect that the price level will soon return to "normal," which they believe to be P(0).

The events that take place as the inflationary episode continues are shown in part (b) of figure 9.6. As the inflation persists, workers gradually come to expect a permanent increase in the price level. Therefore, they demand increases in their nominal wage rates even when they are not working overtime, and employers find they can no longer hire all the labor they want unless they are willing to pay more for it. This increase in labor costs means that firms must receive a higher price at every level of production. That is, the aggregate supply curve *shifts upward* as indicated by the arrow numbered 3 in part (b) of figure 9.6. The upward shift in aggregate supply leads to further inflation as prices continue to rise. Finally, the new aggregate supply curve intersects the aggregate demand curve at point c. Point c shows where the inflationary episode has been brought to an end. As the price level has risen, the supply of loanable funds has moved to the left because of the increase in the denominator of $\Delta M/P$. The resulting rise in the interest rate has choked off investment, GNP, and the demand for labor. In general, the increase in prices has caused the purchasing power of a dollar to decline, and real GNP has fallen back to its full-employment level, Y(0).

Just as in the scenario traced during a recession, points a and c lie on the economy's *long-run* aggregate supply curve. The long-run aggregate supply curve is depicted in part (c) of figure 9.6, which shows that the inflationary episode has not caused a long-run increase in the level of real GNP. In the long run, real GNP is determined by the economy's available resources and technology. If the demand for goods and services increases when the economy is at full employment, the price level will rise so that real GNP cannot long remain above the initial level attained before the inflationary episode began.

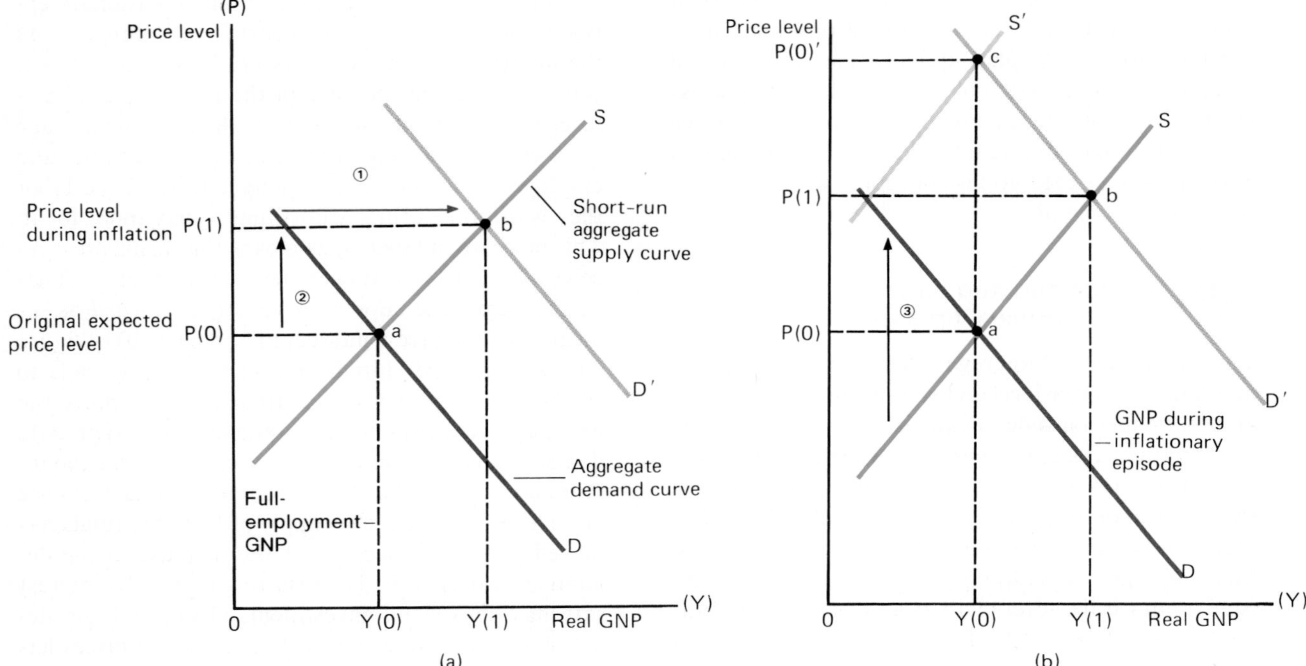

Figure 9.6 Aggregate demand and supply during an inflationary episode
In part (a) the inflation begins: (1) aggregate demand shifts to the right, and (2) the price level and GNP increase.
In part (b), as the inflation continues, (3) the aggregate supply curve shifts upward as the expected price level rises.
In part (c) the inflationary episode is over. The expected price level has risen from P(0) to P(0)′. GNP has once again reached its full-employment level. Points a and c are on the *long-run aggregate supply curve.*

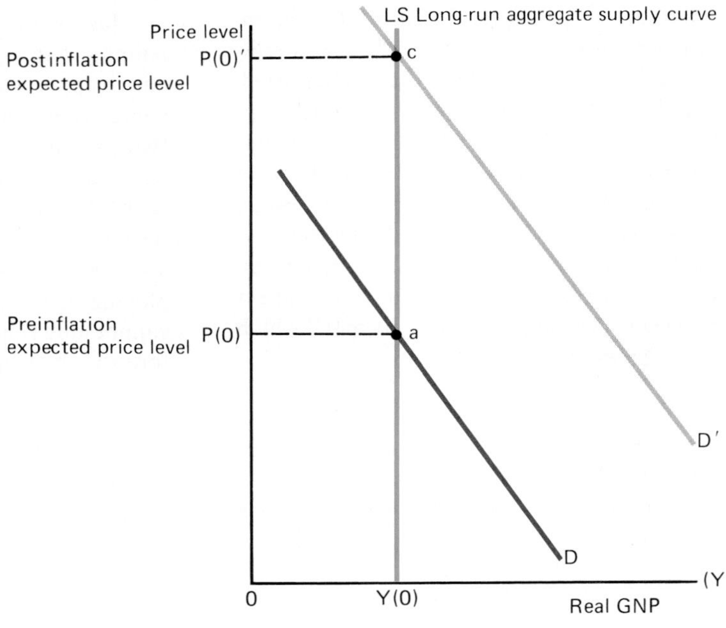

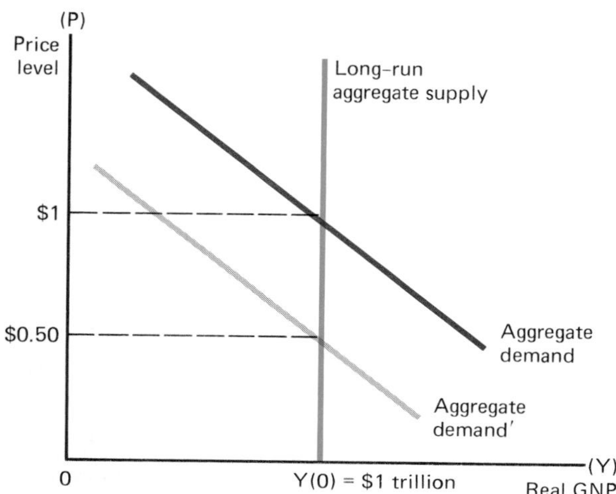

Figure 9.7 Money and prices
With full-employment real GNP equal to $1 trillion, a decrease in the money supply from $250 billion to $125 billion, assuming V = 4, will reduce the average commodity price from $1 to $0.50 and nominal GNP from $1 trillion to $500 billion. Real GNP measured in terms of the prices prevailing before the money supply contracted is unchanged.

Figures 9.5 and 9.6 can be used to follow up our earlier numerical example of the relationship between the quantity of money and the price level. Referring to figure 9.7, which summarizes the stories told in figures 9.5 and 9.6, suppose the economy is at full employment with nominal and real GNP equal to $1 trillion. Assume that one unit of a typical "good" costs $1, that the quantity of money is $250 billion, and that velocity equals 4. The quantity theory says that if something should happen to reduce the quantity of money in circulation from $250 billion to $125 billion, then the resulting decline in the price of a typical good will be $0.50. The economy will return to macroequilibrium with the price of a typical good only half as great as before but with real GNP unchanged. Nominal GNP will have declined from $1 trillion to $500 billion, however. What will happen to the price level and to real GNP if the quantity of money should *increase* from $250 billion to $500 billion?*

We have shown how the aggregate demand and supply curves summarize the relationship between the quantity of money, the level of real GNP, and the price level. Holding constant the economy's production function, the supply of labor, the demand for investment goods, the level of government spending, taxes, and the consumption function, the quantity of money will determine a unique price level described by the intersection of the aggregate demand curve and the long-run aggregate supply curve. In the short run, the aggregate supply curve slopes upward from left to right, meaning that an increase in aggregate demand will temporarily result in an increase in the price level, GNP, and employment. A reduction in aggregate demand has the opposite effects. However, depending on how quickly firms and workers anticipate the impact of raised or lowered prices, GNP and employment will return to their original levels as indicated by the vertical, long-run aggregate supply curve.

We have also shown how changes in "real" variables, such as an increase or decrease in planned investment or in government spending, will cause the aggregate demand curve to shift to the right or left (with a given quantity of money). Again, a rightward shift in aggregate demand leads to increasing prices and in the short run increasing GNP and employment. In the long run, however, GNP is determined by the (vertical) long-run aggregate supply curve, and only the price level is determined by the position of the aggregate demand curve. A leftward shift in aggregate demand causes a short-run reduction in GNP and employment, but in the long run only the price level declines, with GNP and employment determined by long-run aggregate supply conditions.

*The aggregate demand curves in figures 9.3 through 9.7 have been drawn as straight lines for convenience. Actually, if the quantity equation holds, the aggregate demand curve must get flatter at lower price levels and steeper at higher price levels. This is true because as long as real GNP and the quantity of money are greater than zero, then the aggregate demand curve cannot intersect either the vertical (price) or horizontal (real GNP) axis.

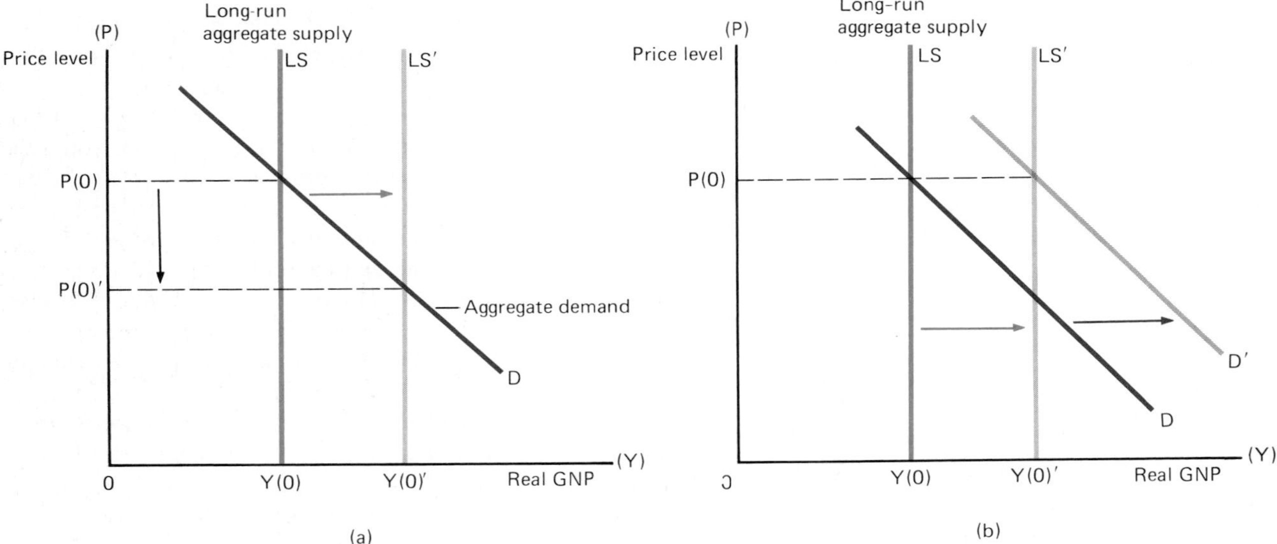

Figure 9.8 The equilibrium price level and GNP in a growth scenario
In part (a) economic growth is reflected in a rightward shift of the aggregate supply curve. Unless aggregate demand also shifts to the right, the equilibrium price level will fall.

As shown in part (b), if the Fed promotes a sufficient increase in the money supply, aggregate demand will shift to the right so as to maintain a stable price level.

Macroequilibrium, Recession, and Inflation in a Growth Scenario

We have seen that in the long run, the equilibrium values of GNP and the price level depend on society's available resources, technology, and the quantity of money. When we discussed the relationship between the quantity of money and the price level, we assumed that resources and technology are unchanging. Now let us see what happens when we recognize that our capacity to produce real GNP may change over time. Specifically, if the stock of physical capital increases, labor becomes more productive. This is reflected in an upward shift in the aggregate production function, an increase in the marginal product of labor, and a rightward shift in the demand for labor. (Review figure 3.6 and see how these changes affect employment, GNP, and the real wage rate.) Since the full-employment level of GNP increases, the long-run aggregate supply curve will shift to the right.

It is important to recognize that as long as real investment expenditure is positive, the amount of physical capital is *constantly growing.* So the economy's full equilibrium value of GNP will also grow constantly. In figures 9.5, 9.6, and 9.7, we depicted the economy's long-run aggregate supply curve. The scenario for the economy we are describing now shows that in full macroequilibrium, economic growth occurs. This means that the long-run aggregate supply curve is constantly shifting to the right. This increase in long-run aggregate supply adds a new wrinkle to the problem of maintaining macroeconomic equilibrium, as figure 9.8 shows.

In part (a) of figure 9.8, we show the long-run aggregate supply curve shifting to the right, reflecting growth of the economy's capacity to produce GNP. With a *given* aggregate demand curve, this economic growth will result in a *decline* in the equilibrium price level from P(0) to P(0)′. Why does the equilibrium price *decline* when the economy is

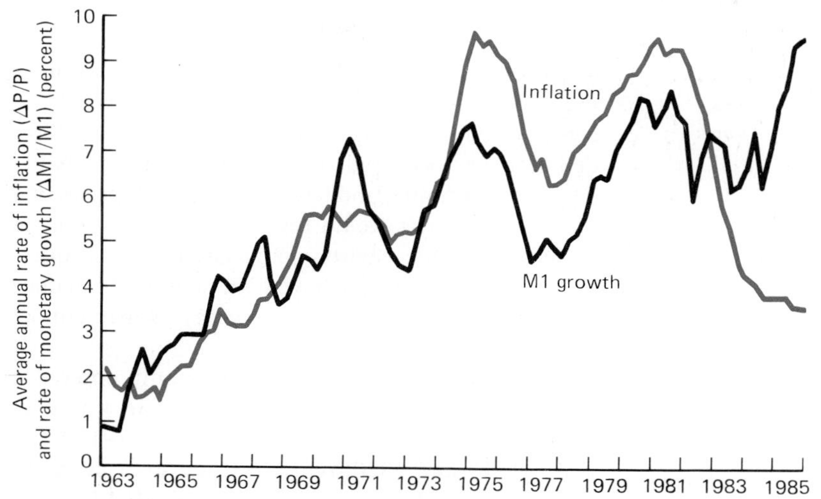

Figure 9.9 The percentage growth of money supply (M1) and the percentage rate of inflation, 1963–1985
This chart compares the average annual rate of increase in M1 with the average annual rate of inflation. It shows that the money supply has grown more rapidly than the capacity to produce GNP. This has led to persistent inflation that has usually been greatest when the money supply has grown most rapidly.
From *Economic Report of the President,* 1986, p. 28.

growing in real terms? The quantity equation tells all. If the quantity of money, M, is constant but real GNP, Y, is growing and velocity, V, does not change, the price level must fall. Otherwise, the quantity of money available will not be able to sustain a level of nominal GNP, PY, corresponding to the new, higher level of real output. If you examine figure 9.11 on page 207, you will note that the years 1814–1857 and 1864–1900 were periods of rather prolonged *deflation.* A probable major cause of these periods of declining prices was a relatively slow growth in the money supply accompanying a rapidly growing capacity to produce goods and services. The United States was on the gold standard then, and there was no Fed. When monetary growth was slow relative to the growth of real GNP, the price level was pushed downward and recessions were relatively frequent and severe.

Figure 9.8, part (b), shows that if the Fed causes the money supply to grow as rapidly as the economy's capacity to produce goods and services, the aggregate demand curve will shift to the right by just the amount needed to keep the equilibrium price level from falling.

The quantity theory provides an explanation of one of the important causes of inflationary episodes and recessions in our economy. If the Fed allows the money supply to grow more rapidly than the economy's capacity to produce goods and services grows, inflation is the inevitable long-run result. If monetary growth is too slow, the price level will eventually fall but the economy will be afflicted with persistent tendencies toward recession. A major reason for the recessions is that slow monetary growth leads in the short run to high real interest rates and reduced planned investment. During the last twenty-five years, the money supply has grown at a considerably greater rate than the economy's capacity has increased, and this has led to persistent inflation. That is why we have come to view a constantly rising price level as more or less normal. After the experience of the Great Depression and the lesson learned about the disastrous consequences of too little growth in the money supply (see chapter 11), it is perhaps understandable that the Fed has preferred to maintain too much rather than too little monetary growth.

Figure 9.9 shows the annual inflation rate from 1963 through 1985 and the annual rate of growth of M1 two years earlier in the United States. It is clear from this chart that inflation was closely associated with the rate of growth of the money supply, at least through 1982. In chapter 11, we will take a closer look at the causes of the inflation the United States

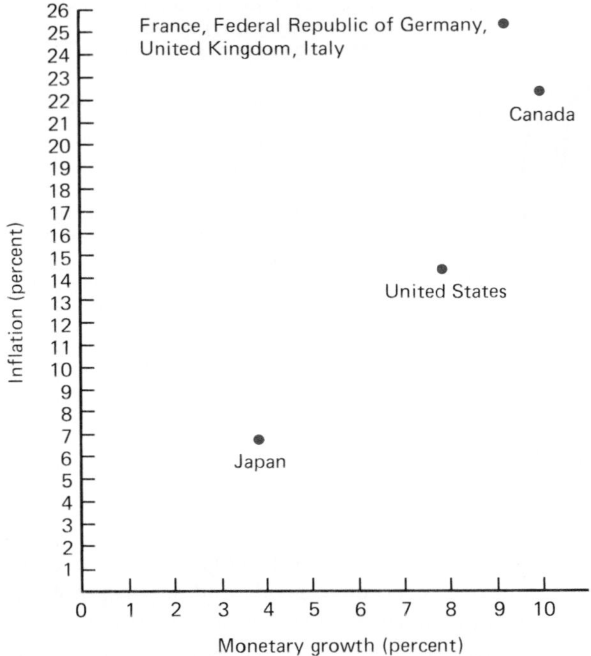

Figure 9.10 An international comparison of inflation and monetary growth, 1981–1985
The rate of inflation in several major industrial nations is positively related to the rate of monetary growth.
From International Monetary Fund, *World Economic Outlook*, 1985, Table 13, p. 218, and *Economic Report of the President*, 1986, Table B-108, p. 376.

economy has experienced over the past two and a half decades. We will also offer some speculation regarding the divergence between M1 growth and inflation that occurred after 1982.

The positive relationship between monetary growth and inflation is not confined to the United States. Figure 9.10 shows how increases in the money supply (M1) and inflation (as measured by the CPI) compare for some major industrial nations over the period 1981–85. It is clear that relatively high rates of monetary growth were positively related to high rates of inflation internationally, as well as within the United States.

A Brief Historical Note

Our economy has not always experienced inflation as the norm. Figure 9.11 illustrates that earlier in this century and on several occasions during the 1800s, deflation has occurred. Economists would probably disagree on whether and how rapidly falling prices and money wage rates would restore full employment in today's economic environment. There is little question, however, that they have done so more than once in the past. A particularly noteworthy adjustment occurred shortly after World War I.

In 1920, the United States economy entered a sharp recession. The unemployment rate was over three times as high in 1920 as it was in 1919.[1] Between 1919 and 1920, real GNP fell by 5 percent.[2] The price level fell sharply, however, so that by 1922 the consumer price index was one-sixth lower than in 1920. Wholesale prices dropped by over one-third. Recovery was rapid, so that by 1923 unemployment had fallen to a low level and real GNP stood above its 1919 level.

The Rate of Inflation and Unemployment during Recessions and Inflationary Episodes

Now that we have seen why our economy has typically experienced rising prices, even during recessions, over the period of the past twenty-five to thirty years, it would be a good idea to briefly review the macroeconomic events that occur during recessions and inflationary episodes. All of the events that we described as part of the macroeconomic adjustment process still represent a valid scenario provided that we make one minor adjustment. Instead of observing a *decline* in the price level during a recession, in recent years we have typically observed a *smaller* rate of inflation. When planned aggregate expenditure has exceeded aggregate production of goods and services, the price level has increased *more rapidly* than when full macroeconomic equilibrium prevails.

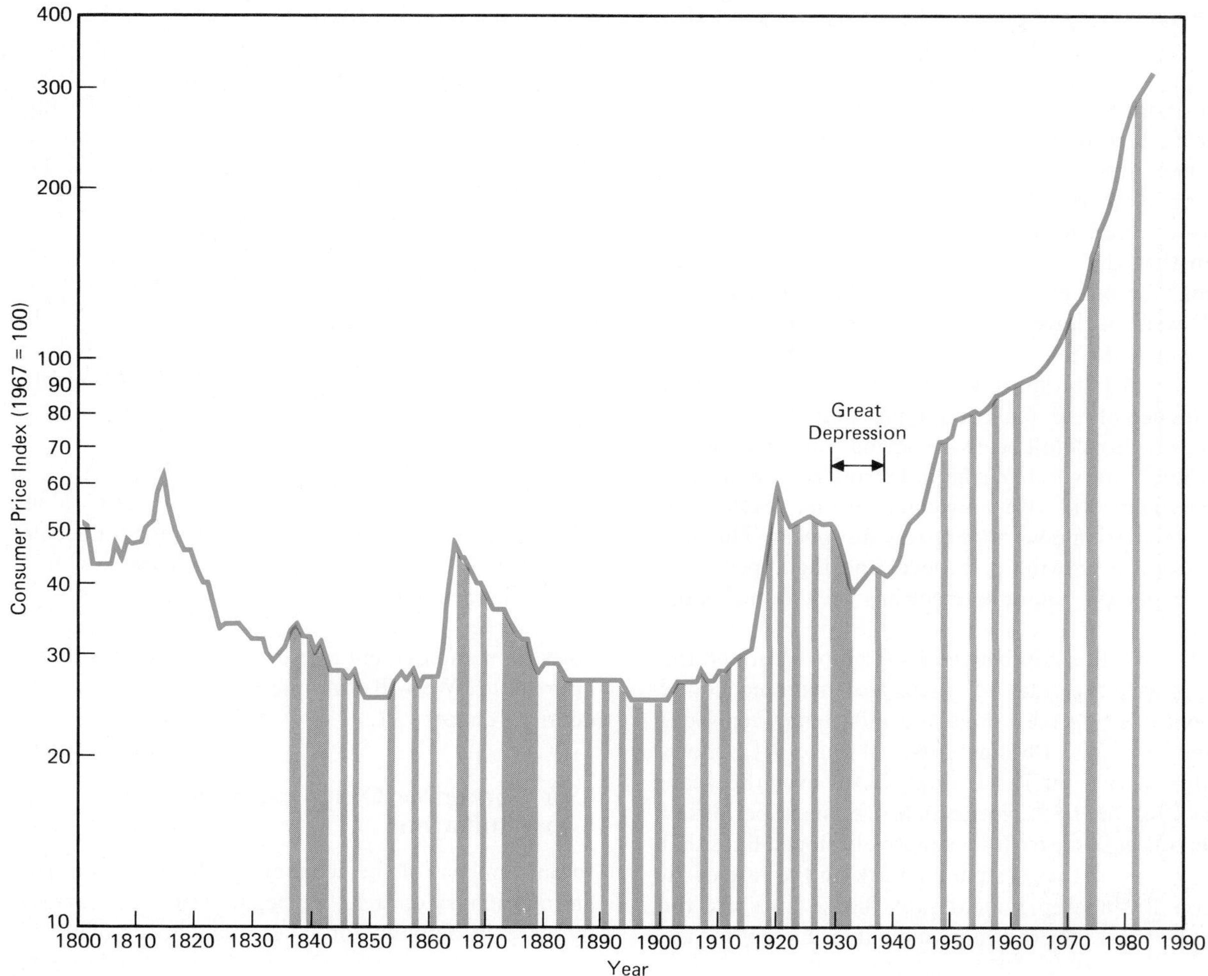

Figure 9.11 Inflation and deflation in the United States from colonial times to the present

This chart shows that deflations and inflationary episodes have alternated throughout the history of the United States. The period since World War II, however, has been characterized by rising prices.

From U.S. Bureau of the Census, *Economic Report of the President,* 1986, Table B-55, p. 315, and *Historical Statistics of the United States,* pp. 210, 211.

***Stagflation** is the coexistence of inflation and above-normal unemployment.*

*The **Phillips curve** is a statistical relationship between the unemployment rate and the rate of inflation that is observed in the short run during inflationary episodes and recessions.*

***Demand-induced inflation** is caused by forces that shift the aggregate demand curve to the right.*

Economists and policymakers have frequently focused attention on the parallel adjustments of the rate of inflation and the unemployment rate during recessions and inflationary episodes. We have seen that a basic feature of recessions is an increase in unemployment above its normal, "full-employment," level. During inflationary episodes, unemployment temporarily declines to abnormally low values. Does this mean that the inflation we have come to accept as normal for our economy has somehow been associated with a lower normal unemployment rate? Nothing could be further from the truth. When a certain rate of inflation has come to be *expected,* then our model of the macroeconomy predicts that unemployment will fall below its normal value only when inflation is *unexpectedly* high. During recessions, unemployment will rise above its normal level, even though inflation does not entirely disappear. The persistence of a growing price level and the appearance of recessionary unemployment has been named **stagflation.**

The relationship between unemployment and the rate of inflation that characterizes macroeconomic behavior during recessions and inflationary episodes is known as the **Phillips curve.**[3] Figure 9.12 shows Phillips curves for the United States over the years from 1965 to 1985. Notice that over short periods of time, it is possible to draw negatively sloped lines that more or less match the points marking the rate of inflation and unemployment rate. These lines are the Phillips curves for the years indicated. Except for the "outliers" of 1974, 1975, and 1982, all of the points plotted in figure 9.12 fall fairly close to one of the five Phillips curves.

The horizontal lines in figure 9.12 show how the average rate of inflation increased over the years from 1960 to 1981 and then decreased after 1981. As the inflation rate increased and then decreased, it is reasonable to assume that the public's expectation of future inflation changed in the same direction. Our macroeconomic model tells us that an upward trend of expected inflation will result in an upward shift of the Phillips curve and a downward trend will result in downward shift of the Phillips curve. That is exactly what appears to have taken place. The Phillips curve for each successive time period through 1980–83 lies higher and higher in figure 9.12. The most recent Phillips curve (1983–85) has shifted down, showing that by the mid-1980s the public had come to expect lower inflation. In other words, as the rate of inflation rose over time, the average unemployment rate showed no long-run tendency to decline. Moreover, the unemployment rate fell back toward 7 percent as soon as the public realized that lower rates of inflation were likely to persist after 1982.

Notice that the average unemployment rate tended to rise over the period from 1965 to 1982, along with the rate of inflation. Our macromodel does not predict that the normal rate of unemployment will increase along with the rate of inflation. Evidently, some other forces in the economy were pushing up the normal unemployment rate over the period covered in figure 9.12. We will examine these forces in greater detail in chapter 11.

Can Workers or Other Suppliers Cause Inflation?

In our analysis of the economy's adjustments during an inflationary episode, we began with an *exogenous* increase in demand for investment goods. This exogenous increase in demand was the fundamental cause of the inflationary episode. We have also seen that too rapid an increase in the quantity of money is also inflationary. In chapter 11 we will find that still another cause of inflation can be an increase in government spending if it is not accompanied by an increase in taxes. All of these instances are examples of **demand-induced inflation,** which means that the initial macroeconomic shock shifts the aggregate demand curve to the right. Yet, when you read

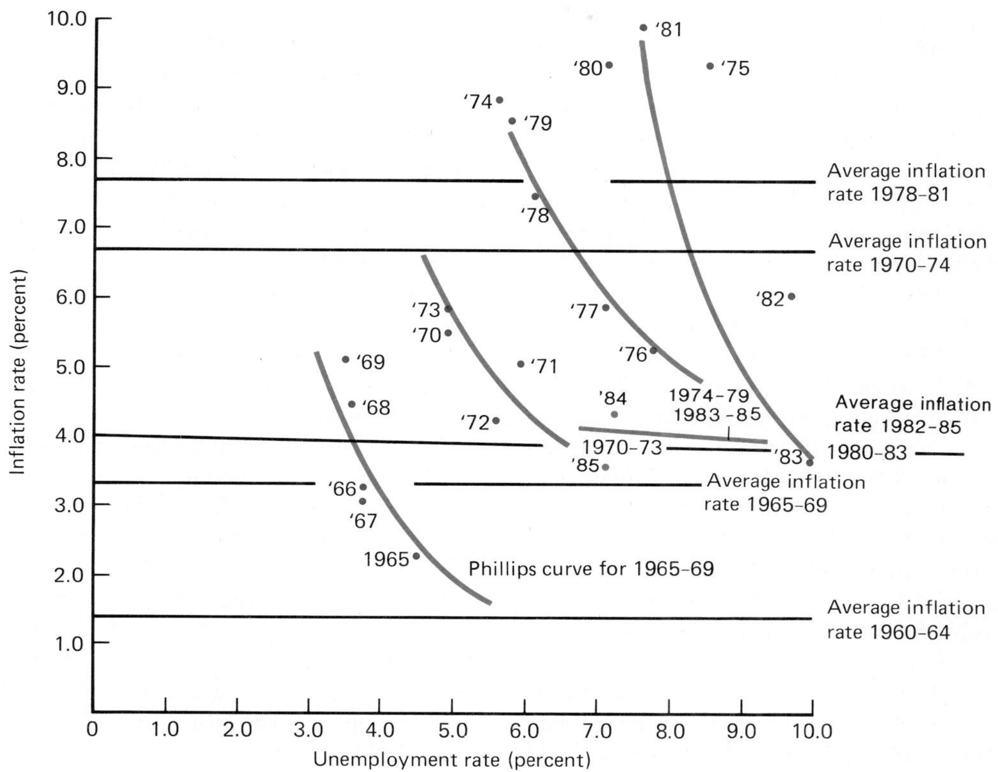

Figure 9.12 Phillips curves for the United States, 1965–1985
Over short periods of time, unemployment tends to be lower when the rate of inflation is greater than expected. This relationship is called the Phillips curve. This graph shows how the average inflation rate rose over the years after 1964. As expectations of inflation rose, the Phillips curves for the United States economy shifted upward, and as expectations of inflation declined, the Phillips curve shifted downward. Thus, a higher rate of inflation did not cause the unemployment rate to fall in the long run.
From *Economic Report of the President,* 1983, Federal Reserve Bank of St. Louis; *National Economic Trends,* October, 1983, *Economic Report of the President,* 1986, Table B-59, p. 320, Table B-35, p. 293.

newspaper accounts of inflation or watch the business news on television, you will often see or hear that inflation is "caused" by an increase in a specific price, such as the price of petroleum, construction, or wage rates. If you understand our discussion of inflation, you will view such "obvious" explanations with great skepticism.

In narrow sense, it is always true that inflation can be linked to a few prices in a price index. There are always some prices rising while some prices fall even during inflationary episodes. To "blame" inflation on those components of CPI or the GNP deflator is not only naive but it can also be dangerous if it leads to the wrong policies to combat rising prices.

Cost-push inflation is caused by increases in costs that shift the aggregate supply curve to the left.

If you recall our description of an inflationary episode, you will remember that prices begin to rise only *after* aggregate demand has increased. A likely scenario is that certain raw materials industries and some producers of manufactured goods develop shortages, which lead to price increases. Since these materials are inputs into further production, their price increases are *cost* increases in other industries. As these *costs* rise, the *prices* of goods these inputs are used to produce will increase. Therefore, to the casual observer, it will appear that *costs* are "pushing up" prices. As the CPI begins to rise, workers will demand increases in their wage rates to catch up with inflation. These wage increases will cause further cost increases for employers and will appear to push up prices even more. Hence we are often urged to believe that we are experiencing **cost-push inflation,** which results from a leftward shift in the aggregate supply curve, when the actual cause has been a rightward shift in aggregate demand.

It *is* possible for an exogenous increase in costs to cause inflation. Since the inflationary process is somewhat different than when an exogenous increase in aggregate demand results in a demand-induced inflation, the behavior of important macroeconomic variables will also be different. Consequently, the wrong macroeconomic policies may be chosen to cure what appears to ail the economy unless the causes of the symptoms are correcty diagnosed.

To understand the basic differences between cost-push and demand-induced inflation, we will use as an example an increase in the cost of labor. It is important to bear in mind, however, that an exogenous increase in the price of *any resource that accounts for a substantial fraction of production costs* will have a similar macroeconomic impact. For example, we could as easily discuss the cost-push effects of OPEC oil price increases in 1974 and again in 1979.

To see how a cost-push inflation might originate, refer to figure 8.1 on page 174. Suppose that a substantial majority of the labor force is unionized and that all the labor unions collaborate with one another to raise the real wage rates of their members. This would be represented in figure 8.1 by an *increase* in the real wage above its equilibrium value. Employment will fall as employers move back along their labor demand curves in response to the higher real wage they must pay. Since the aggregate labor supply curve has not shifted, however, *more* labor will be supplied just as the quantity of labor demanded declines. Thus, unemployment is likely to increase above its normal level.

When employment declines, so will real GNP. In other words, the economy's *aggregate supply curve* will shift to the left. This means that at every price level, the economy will now produce less GNP than before because labor costs have risen. An increase in costs shifts the aggregate supply curve to the left. To see what happens next, take a piece of paper and draw an aggregate demand and an aggregate supply curve. When you shift the aggregate supply curve to the left, what happens? The price level increases and GNP falls. This increase in the price level will be viewed as an inflationary episode by the public. At the same time, we have seen that the unemployment rate will have risen *above* its normal level. Thus, we have the seemingly paradoxical situation of a recession at the same time that the price level has increased. (When a certain amount of inflation is the norm, we observe an unexpected *increase* in the rate of inflation with unemployment rising above its normal level.) Notice that this relationship between inflation and unemployment is *exactly opposite* to that described by the Phillips curves in figure 9.12.

*An **accelerated inflation** is one in which the percentage rate of increase of prices increases from year to year.*

Unless labor unions demand and obtain a further increase in real wages, the inflation will stop at this point. The economy will remain at underemployment equilibrium with the price level higher than it was and GNP lower. However, the government will be under tremendous pressure to bring down the unemployment rate. In particular, political pressures on the Fed may lead it to *validate the cost-push inflation,* which means increasing the quantity of money more rapidly so that the aggregate demand curve shifts far enough to the right to return GNP (and unemployment) to its full-employment level.

Of course, if the Fed validates a cost-push inflation, the economy will end up with an even higher price level than before because the aggregate demand curve will shift to the right following a leftward shift in the aggregate supply curve. Unemployment will return to its normal level because the further increase in the price level, P, causes the *real wage rate,* W/P, to fall back to the level that brings about equilibrium in the labor market. This means, of course, that the initial increase in the real wage rate that began this inflationary episode will be wiped out by inflation. If workers try to regain their higher real wage rate and at the same time the Fed continues to validate the resulting cost-push inflation by increasing the quantity of money, a continuing inflation of wages and prices, called an **accelerated inflation** or an inflationary spiral, in which nominal wages and prices rise at faster and faster rates, will result. Take a moment to draw the aggregate demand and supply curves associated with cost-push inflation and for cost-push inflation with the Fed's support. It is important to note the higher equilibrium price level in the latter case and the fact that the price level does reach a new equilibrium in each case. Cost-push inflation can only persist for long periods of time if unions make repeated higher wage demands and/or the Fed continually pumps up the money supply more rapidly.

▸ Summary and Conclusions

In this chapter we explained how economic conditions can give rise to both rising inflation and unemployment rates and why price controls could not have cured the macroeconomic problems of the 1970s or early 1980s. We reviewed macroeconomic equilibrium and the adjustments made by the price level when disequilibrium prevails. The following points were emphasized.

The quantity theory of nominal GNP is a widely accepted explanation of the price level that prevails when the economy is in full-employment equilibrium.

Economists who accept the quantity theory tend to believe that velocity is relatively constant or changes slowly and predictably and that the full-employment level of GNP is determined by "real" variables. These economists are called monetarists.

A more elaborate view of the equilibrium price level and equilibrium GNP is given by the aggregate demand and aggregate supply curves.

Long-run aggregate supply is determined by the economy's available resources and its production function.

In a growth context, both the aggregate demand curve and the aggregate supply curve must shift rightward at the same rate to maintain a stable price level.

We have experienced inflation as the norm over the past twenty years because increases in the quantity of money have pushed the aggregate demand curve to the right faster than the aggregate supply curve has shifted.

In the long run, inflation does not cause GNP to be greater than its full-employment value or the unemployment rate to fall below the full-employment level.

It is possible for an exogenous increase in *costs* to cause inflation, but the behavior of major macroeconomic variables is different in cost-push inflation than in demand-pull inflation. In particular, cost-push inflation is associated with *above-normal* unemployment and a *lower* real GNP than the economy is capable of producing at full macroeconomic equilibrium.

▸ Key Terms

accelerated inflation *211*
aggregate demand and supply curves *195*
cost-push inflation *210*
demand-induced inflation *208*
long-run aggregate supply curve *196*
Phillips curve *208*
quantity equation *191*
short-run aggregate supply curve *196*
stagflation *208*
theory of rational expectations *200*
velocity of money *191*

▸ Questions for Discussion and Review

Are the statements in questions 1 through 5 true, false, or uncertain? Defend your answers.

1. An increase in the money supply will always lead to an increase in the price level assuming velocity is stable.
2. During periods of high inflation, the velocity of money will decline because rising prices will deter consumers from making purchases.
3. During periods of high inflation, people will want to hold more money so as to be able to afford the higher prices charged for goods and services.
4. Macroeconomic equilibrium can only occur at one particular level of prices in the long run.
5. In the long run, economic growth will cause the full-employment level of output to change.
6. Show by means of a graph what happens to aggregate demand and aggregate supply from a position of full-employment equilibrium in each of the following circumstances.
   a. The Fed sells government securities.
   b. Firms anticipate inflation in the near future.
   c. The UAW wins a large wage increase in contract negotiations, and the Fed increases the money supply to sustain it.
   d. The Fed raises the discount rate.
   e. The average number of years of schooling of the population increases.
7. What if any effect do innovations in banking such as credit cards, automated teller machines, and debit cards have on the price level?
8. Using the Phillips curve diagram, illustrate the following situations starting from the full-employment level of unemployment.
   a. The Fed buys government securities, short and long run.
   b. The expected price level rises.
   c. The price level rises unexpectedly.
9. Can the monetary authorities reduce inflation as easily as they can increase it through validation?
10. Considering the theory of rational expectations, what if anything could render government fiscal and monetary policies ineffective?

Chapter 10

Fiscal and Monetary Policies

Outline

Objectives

After reading this chapter, the student should be able to:

Describe how discretionary fiscal policy can be used to prevent a recession.
Describe how discretionary fiscal policy can be used to prevent an inflationary episode.
Discuss the problems with implementing discretionary fiscal policy.
Discuss the types of nondiscretionary fiscal policies that exist and how each is countercyclical.
Describe how discretionary monetary policy can be used to prevent a recession.
Describe how discretionary monetary policy can be used to prevent an inflationary episode.
Compare the short-run and long-run effects of fiscal and monetary policies.

▸ Introduction

During the period 1961–68 real GNP rose 5.7 percent per year from a value of $756.7 billion in 1972 to $1.058 trillion. The unemployment rate declined steadily from 6.7 percent to 3.6 percent, and consumer prices rose at a modest 1.7 percent annually. Economists announced the end of the business cycle and declared that with the prudent application of fiscal and monetary policy, the government could "fine-tune" the economy. Like a well-tuned automobile, the United States economy was expected to continue to move forward rapidly and smoothly. For many reasons, the overall performance of the United States economy over the next two decades bore no resemblance either to actual economic experience during the 1961–68 period or to the almost unanimous predictions of economists. In chapters 11 and 12 we will have a great deal to say about what happened after 1968 and why. In this chapter we will focus on how fiscal and monetary policies affect the macroeconomy. Among other things, the discussion will provide some insight into why we could not fine-tune the United States economy in 1968 and why we cannot fine-tune the United States economy today.

In chapters 8 and 9 we paid little attention to the role of government in our model of the macroeconomy. In this chapter we emphasize the gov-

Figure 10.1 A quick review of full macroequilibrium
Part (a) shows the economy in full macroequilibrium.
In part (b) the economy is in full macroequilibrium because $\hat{S} = \hat{I} + (G - T)$ at Y(0), the full employment level of GNP, and because DLF = SLF at interest rate r(0).
In part (c) the aggregate demand and long-run aggregate supply curves intersect at the equilibrium price level P(0) and equilibrium level of GNP, Y(0).

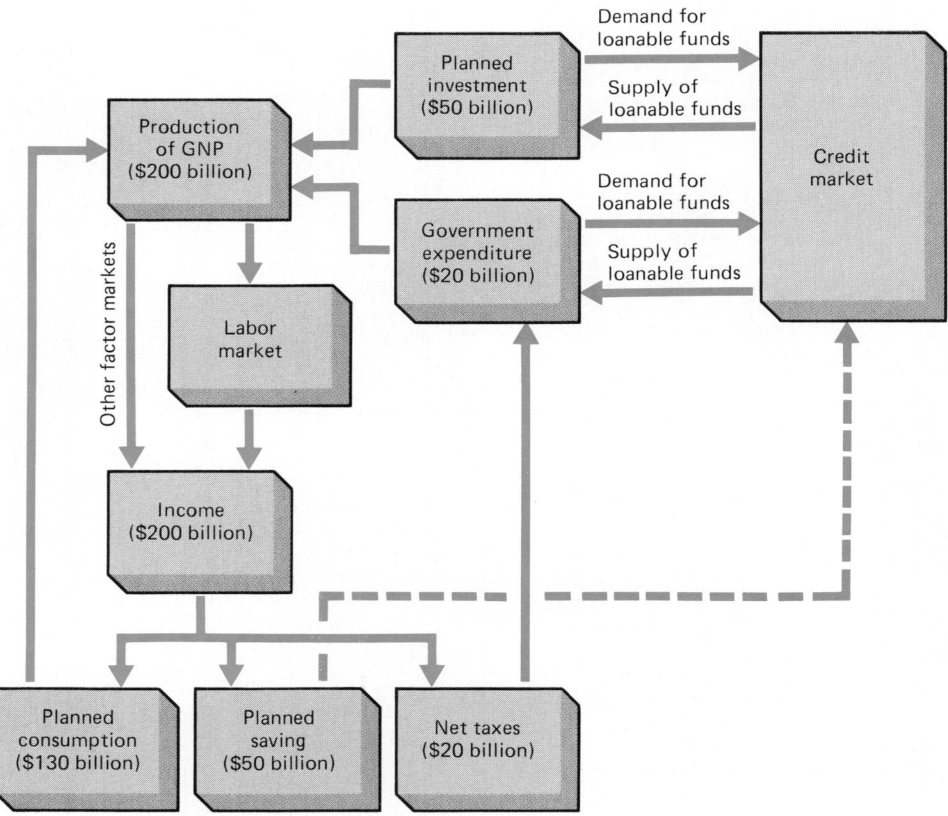

***Fiscal policy** is the adjustment of taxes or government spending.*

*ernment's role in the goods market and the credit market. We will see how government expenditure and taxation policies, which are both included in the category of **fiscal policy**, can affect adjustments to short-run equilibrium in a recession or in an inflationary episode. In theory, fiscal policy can prevent recessions and inflationary episodes. We will also investigate how monetary policy might be used to eliminate cyclical unemployment and inflation.*

Before describing how government might prevent recessions and inflationary episodes, we will illustrate full macroeconomic equilibrium once again. Figure 10.1 depicts a situation of full-employment macroeconomic equilibrium.

Part (a) of figure 10.1 recaps the numerical example of macroeconomic equilibrium presented in chapters 4 and 8. Gross national product is $200 billion, which is an equilibrium value because planned saving equals planned investment plus the government deficit. We have assumed that this is just the amount of GNP that satisfies the condition of no cyclical unemployment in the labor market. Parts (b) and (c) depict a more general view of macroeconomic equilibrium. The equilibrium interest rate, shown in part (b), is r(0), and the full-employment level of GNP, shown in part (c), is Y(0). The equilibrium price level, P(0), is indicated by the intersection of the aggregate demand and long-run aggregate supply curves in part (c) of figure 10.1.

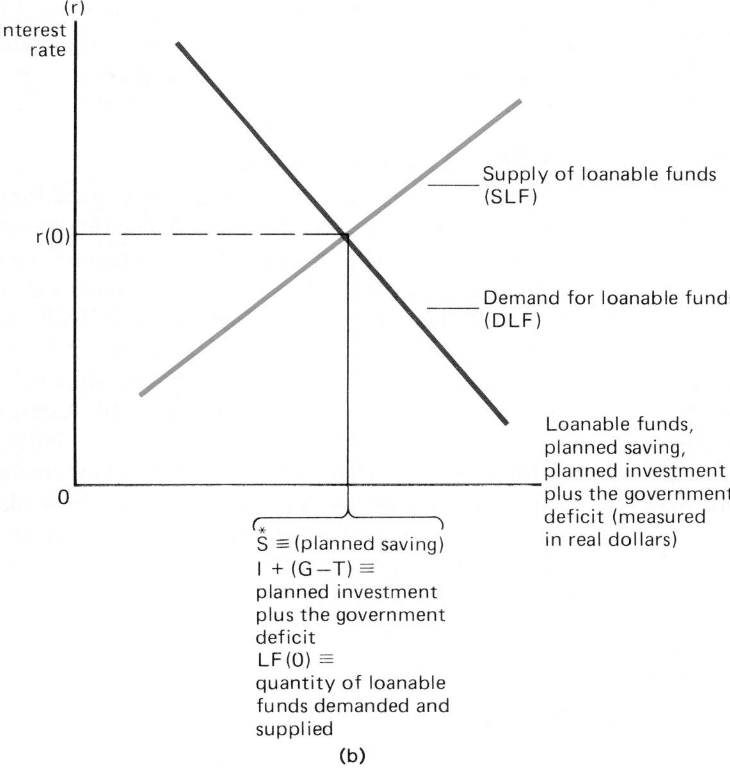

(b)

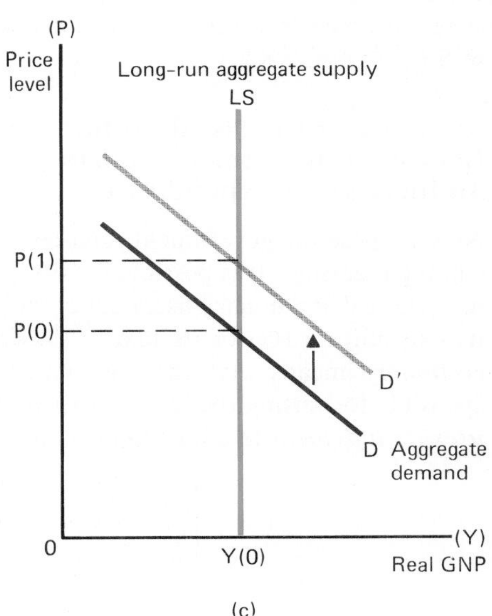

(c)

Discretionary Fiscal Policy in a Recession

The economy will remain in equilibrium as long as no disturbances upset the balance between supply and demand in the goods, loanable funds, or labor market. Suppose, however, that planned investment declines by $10 billion. In part (a) of figure 10.1, this would involve a decline of planned investment to $40 billion, with no immediate change in any other macroeconomic magnitude except GNP. This recessionary tendency is indicated by the arrows pointing to the left in figure 10.2.

As we have seen, a decline in planned expenditure will create excess production of goods and services and lead to a recession. We learned in chapters 4 and 8 that the impact of a decline in planned investment on the goods market is given by the multiplier equation. (See page 105.) To make the arithmetic simple, suppose that the MPC is 0.8 and the MPS is 0.2. Then, the multiplier, which is 1/MPS, equals 5, and a decline in planned investment of $10 billion will lead to a potential short-run decline in equilibrium GNP of $10 billion × 5 = $50 billion. (Actually, the decline in planned investment and equilibrium GNP will be somewhat less to the extent that the interest rate declines and keeps planned investment from falling quite so far. See figure 8.5.)

Response of the Fiscal Authority to a Decline in Investment Demand: An Increase in Expenditure

Now suppose the government foresees the economy's coming recession. It is possible for the government to undertake discretionary fiscal policy, adjusting either its expenditure (G) or its taxes (T). The word *discretionary* means that the government agency responsible for setting the level of expenditure or taxes *uses its judgment* to adjust G or T to counteract the economy's recessionary tendency. Suppose the government decides to increase *immediately* its expenditure by an amount *exactly equal* to the decline in planned investment—$10 billion. Such an immediate increase in government expenditure on goods and services will prevent the recession from actually occurring. Neither aggregate demand nor the demand for loanable funds will shift leftward, and full macroeconomic equilibrium will continue.

Reaction in the Goods Market

The government's discretionary increase in its spending is just the right amount to prevent planned aggregate production in the goods market from exceeding planned aggregate expenditure at full-employment GNP. Planned saving at full employment is exactly equal to planned investment plus the government deficit because an increase in government spending has exactly offset the decline in planned investment. This means that the economy is no longer heading toward recession because the aggregate market for goods and services is once again in equilibrium.

Reaction in the Credit Market

The effect of an increase in government expenditure will also be felt in the credit market. Since the size of the government's tax revenue, T, has remained unchanged, an increase in G of $10 billion means that the budget deficit (G − T) also grows by $10 billion. In terms of figure 10.2, the larger budget deficit keeps the demand for loanable funds, DLF, exactly where it was before planned investment declined. Consequently, the real interest rate remains at its initial equilibrium value, r(0). However, DLF is now made up of a *smaller private demand* for loanable funds and a *larger government demand.* Government expenditure has replaced some private investment expenditure in GNP.

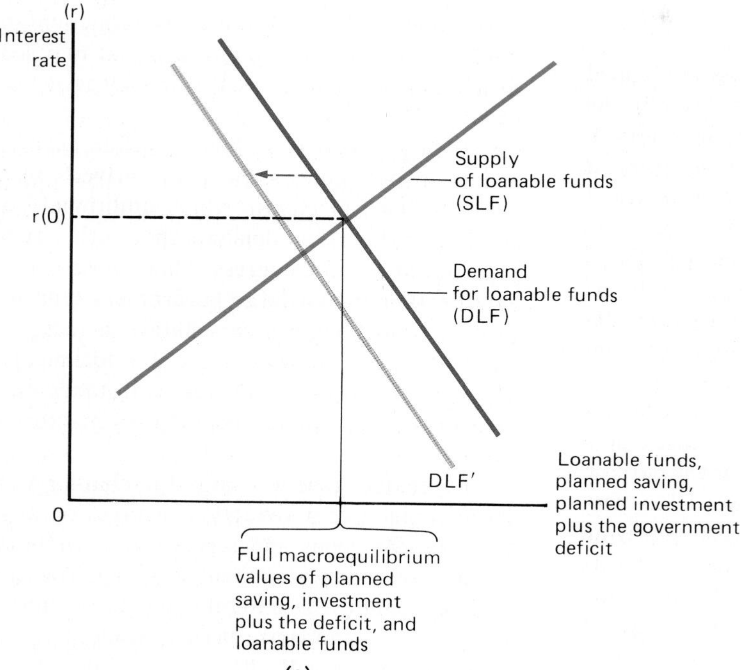

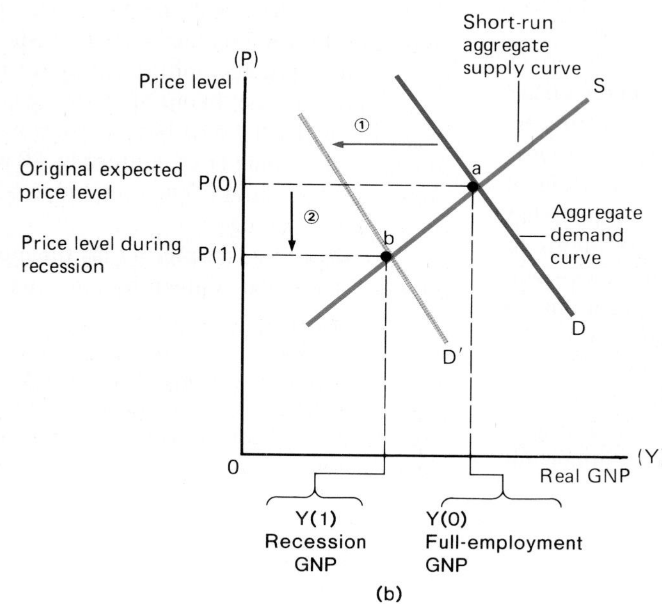

Figure 10.2 The government increases spending to combat a recession with fiscal policy
The arrows show that planned investment expenditure and aggregate demand have declined. If planned investment plus the government deficit [$\dot{I}$ + (G − T)] declines, then the economy will head toward a recession as indicated by the leftward-pointing arrow. However, if the government immediately increases G, then [$\dot{I}$ + (G − T)] and aggregate demand need not decline and the recession can be avoided.

In part (b) the recession begins: aggregate demand shifts to the left and the price level and GNP decline.

Why Fiscal Policy Works

Recall that we started out with a decline in planned investment, which of course led to a reduction in the amount of goods producers sold private investors in the economy. However, *assuming the government possesses perfect information about the economy,* it can enter the goods market and quickly increase its purchases of goods. The multiplier equation shows that fiscal policy works because it makes no difference to suppliers of goods and services whether exogenous expenditure, EX, is made up of government purchases or those of private investors. The private buyers of products such as steel and bricks who decide to reduce their purchases are replaced by government agents buying the same goods for the purpose of constructing schools, bridges, and so on. Any particular firm may be saddened by the loss of its private customers, but it will not change its prices or alter its production if, in the meantime, the government makes up the loss in sales by increasing its own purchases of goods and services.

Discretionary Fiscal Policy When Taxes Are Adjusted

If the government decides to reduce net taxes rather than increase its expenditures to carry out antirecessionary fiscal policy, it is relying on an increase in *private planned consumption* to offset the decline in planned investment. (It is important to recognize that an *increase in transfer expenditures*—payments to individuals or families to increase their incomes—will have an impact on the deficit and on consumption expenditures similar to a *reduction in taxes.*) In our macroeconomic analysis, reduced taxes and increased consumption work just as well to maintain full-employment equilibrium as does an increase in government expenditure. However, there are important differences in the effects of a tax reduction and of a government expenditure increase that may lead to a preference of one form of fiscal policy action over the other.

To begin, there is the obvious difference that a tax reduction puts consumers in the driver's seat so to speak. They can choose which additional goods to purchase rather than delegate that authority to their representatives in Congress. Thus, those who favor a small rather than a large government tend to advocate tax reductions over expenditure increases in fiscal policy debates. Second, there are technical differences in the impact of decreases in taxes versus increases in government spending on macroeconomic equilibrium.

Remember that we showed in chapter 4 that the *initial* impact of a reduction in taxes on aggregate spending for goods and services is *smaller* than an equal increase in government spending. You may wish to review pages 105–6 to refresh your memory before going on. To summarize briefly, when taxes are lowered, consumers will allocate only *part* of their increased disposable income to consumption. Specifically, they will increase their planned consumption by the increase in their disposable income (the decline in taxes) multiplied by the marginal propensity to consume. In our numerical example, if taxes were to decline by \$10 billion, consumers would increase their planned expenditure by 80 percent of this amount, or \$8 billion. The remainder, \$2 billion, goes to increased saving.

We showed in chapter 4 that the multiplier effect of a tax reduction is given by the equation

$$-(\Delta Y(0)/\Delta T) = b/(1 - b),$$

where b is the marginal propensity to consume and $1 - b$ is the marginal propensity to save. The multiplier effect of an increase in government expenditure, however, is $1/(1 - b)$. In our example, with an

Crowding out means that an increase in the government deficit raises the interest rate, leading to a reduction in planned investment expenditure.

MPC of 0.8, the multiplier effect of a tax reduction is only 80 percent as large as an equal increase in government expenditure. Therefore, the tax reduction required to maintain full employment is 1.25 (1/0.8) times as large as the required increase in government expenditure. If net taxes are reduced by $12.5 million, planned consumption will increase by 80 percent of this amount, or $10 million, which is precisely the decline in planned investment. Thus, full-employment equilibrium in the goods market will be maintained.

Our analysis of a reduction in taxes versus an increase in government spending has shown that discretionary fiscal policy reducing taxes requires a larger increase in the government deficit than a policy that raises expenditures—$2.5 billion more to be precise. Other things equal, this greater demand for loanable funds will result in an interest rate that is higher than otherwise. If an increase in the government deficit does raise the interest rate, it will lead to what is called **crowding out** of private investment because the quantity of investment goods demanded falls as the interest rate increases, *cet. par.* Does this mean that increasing government spending is a more desirable fiscal policy than reducing taxes? The answer to this question is not simple and leads to a great deal of economic and political debate. A fuller discussion of crowding out will follow, especially on pages 264–66.

Our macroeconomic model will help us sort out the issues. A tax reduction directly increases disposable income, which is GNP less taxes. Smaller taxes mean larger disposable income. Thus, when taxes fall, planned consumption and saving increase. In our example, planned saving will increase by the increased disposable income multiplied by the MPS of 0.2. If taxes are reduced $12.5 billion to prevent a recession, both disposable income and the deficit increase by $12.5 billion. Increased saving amounts to $12.5 billion × 0.2 = $2.5 billion. Thus, the public's *increase in planned saving* when there is a tax reduction (as opposed to an increase in government expenditure) is *exactly* equal to the *additional* government deficit of $2.5 billion, *cet. par.* It is likely that this increase in planned saving will offset the additional government deficit by increasing the supply of loanable funds. Thus, the larger deficit caused by a tax reduction of $12.5 billion need not raise the rate of interest more than an increase in government expenditure of $10 billion would.

Moreover, other conditions in the economy may be affected by a tax reduction. *Additional* effects of the tax reduction may make reducing taxes *more* rather than *less* effective than an expenditure increase in combating the recession. The tax reduction, particularly if corporate income tax rates are reduced, will lead to an increase in the *after-tax* profitability of investment projects and the *after-tax* returns on loan contracts. It is what you "take home" *after* taxes that determines your willingness to invest or to purchase a loan contract. Therefore, this increase in after-tax returns on investments will lead to an increase in planned investment expenditure. At every rate of interest, planned private investment will be larger with a reduction in taxes than with an increase in government spending because after-tax returns to lenders and investors (borrowers) will be higher. To summarize, the *direct* effect of an increase in government spending may initially make it seem more effective in combating a recession. However, the *indirect* effects of tax reductions on planned saving and the supply of loanable funds and investment expenditures create powerful arguments in favor of reducing taxes.

Figure 10.3 The government reduces spending to combat an inflationary episode with fiscal policy The arrows show that planned investment and aggregate demand have increased. If planned investment plus the government deficit $[\mathring{I} + (G - T)]$ increases, then the economy will head toward an inflationary episode. However, if the government immediately reduces G or raises T, the inflationary episode can be avoided.

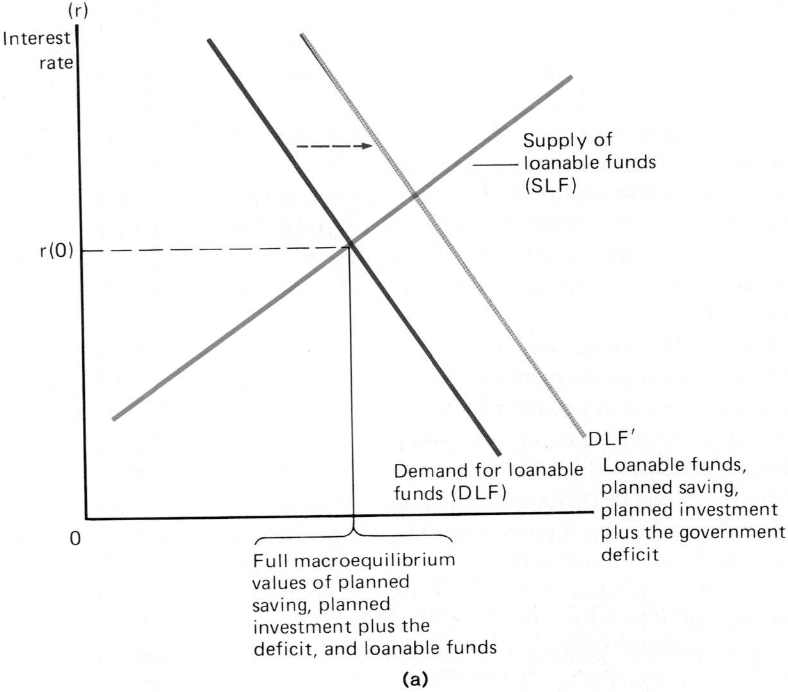

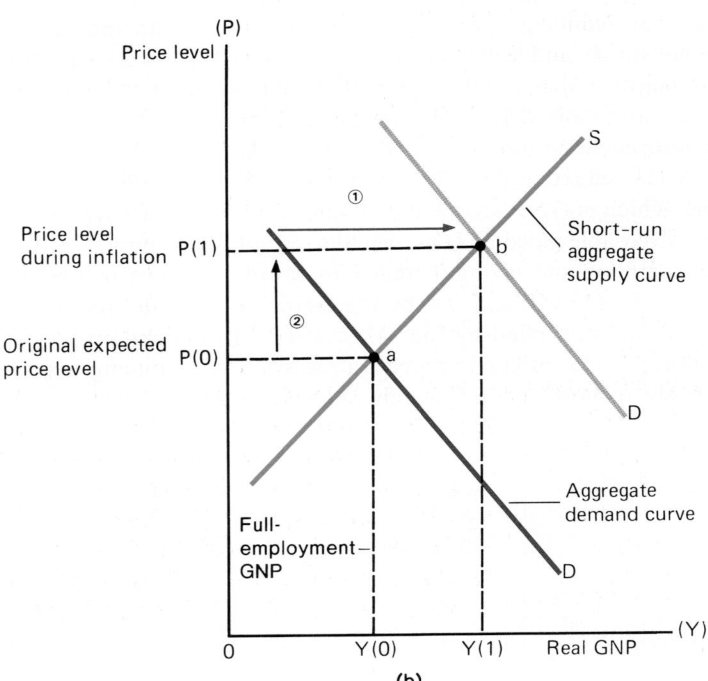

▸ Discretionary Fiscal Policy to Prevent an Inflationary Episode

Theoretically, changes in government expenditures and taxes can be used to prevent an inflationary episode as well as a recession. The fiscal policy required is, of course, opposite in direction to the policies that would counteract a recessionary tendency in the economy.

Figure 10.3 depicts the economy in full macroequilibrium. Should investment demand increase as indicated by the arrows pointing to the right in part (a) of figure 10.3, an inflationary episode is imminent. As the arrows in part (b) show, (1) a rightward shift in aggregate demand will lead to (2) an increase in the price level. A discretionary *reduction* in government spending equal to the increase in planned investment can prevent the inflationary episode from occurring. Government will have reduced its expenditure in order to accommodate investors' desires to use more of the economy's resources. Planned investment will rise, but government spending will decline by just the right amount to prevent an excess demand for goods and services.

The government can also carry out its antiinflationary fiscal policy by increasing taxes. Either a reduction in spending or an increase in taxes will prevent inflation. However, the effects of these two alternative fiscal policies have different impacts on important macroeconomic variables, as we saw when analyzing the impact of antirecessionary government actions. The direct impact of a tax increase is to reduce private consumption expenditure and planned saving. The resources for increased investment are taken from the production of consumers' goods and services. Moreover, taxes must be increased by a *greater* amount than government expenditures need be reduced to result in a decline in planned consumption equal to the increase in planned investment. The reason, of course, is that planned consumption will fall by *less* than the tax increase. To be sure that you fully understand why the increase in taxes must be greater than the reduction in government expenditure, work through the examples given for a reduction in taxes when planned investment falls. Now everything is reversed. Show *exactly* the *increase* in taxes when planned investment increases $10 billion that is required to maintain macroeconomic equilibrium.

As we have seen, there are additional effects of increasing taxes. The supply of loanable funds will fall because reduced disposable income will reduce saving. Moreover, an increase in tax *rates* reduces the after-tax return to holding loan contracts. On the demand for loanable funds side of the market, increased tax rates will reduce the after-tax returns on investment. This will reduce planned investment and shift the DLF curve to the left. The leftward shift will to some extent offset the initial increase in the demand for investment goods, causing planned investment to rise by less than it would if government expenditures were reduced instead of taxes increased. Table 10.1 summarizes the basic fiscal policy actions the government can take to fight inflationary episodes and recessions.

Table 10.1 Summary of fiscal policy to offset recessions or inflationary episodes

To combat	The government can adjust either Taxes	or Expenditure	Effect on deficit
Recessions (expansionary fiscal policy needed)	Reduce	Increase	Increase
Inflationary episodes (contractionary fiscal policy needed)	Increase	Reduce	Reduce

*A **lag** is the time that elapses between the occurrence of an event and a reaction to the event.*

*A **recognition lag** is the time that elapses between the occurrence of an event and the observation that the event has occurred.*

Lags, Politics, and Fiscal Policy

We have seen that as long as the government responds *quickly* and in the *appropriate direction,* changes in spending or taxes can offset any recessionary or inflationary tendencies that threaten the economy. Fiscal policy is *theoretically* sound; its basic problem is in *practice,* given the rapid pace of everyday changes in the economic life of a nation. Because of constitutional restraints and political realities, the government does not have the power to turn expenditures or taxes on or off at will. In the United States, congressional committees must meet and legislation must be passed before government agents can implement a policy calling for changing expenditures or taxes. Economists use the word **lag** to describe the delays inherent in fiscal policy. Whether these lags are sufficiently lengthy to destroy the effectiveness of fiscal policy is a matter that can be resolved only by careful empirical analysis of macroeconomic data. However, if lags are not too long, our analysis shows that discretionary fiscal policy can be a powerful stabilization tool.

An example from the severe recession of 1981–82 illustrates the difficulties in carrying out an increase in government spending to help cure a recession. In late 1982, Congress voted a substantial increase in federal funds allocated to state highway construction projects. One argument for the increased expenditure was that it would help reduce unemployment. In the state of Ohio, unemployment had risen to a higher level than in almost any other state. Therefore, the increased funds available for highway construction in 1983 should have been very welcome news. So they were, but paradoxically, expenditure on highway repair and construction actually *fell* during early 1983 compared to 1982.

This decline in highway expenditure was contrary to the intent of Congress and probably contributed to prolonged high unemployment in Ohio. One reason for the decline was, ironically, the existence of increased federal aid. To make sure that the state received full advantage from the available federal aid, Ohio postponed signing contracts for highway construction until it was sure the contracts would be eligible for federal support. This delay contributed to a *50 percent decline* in authorized highway expenditures through April 1983 compared to the first four months of 1982.[1]

Even if the legislative process did not introduce lags in implementing fiscal policy, there are further problems in acting *quickly* enough for fiscal policy to be effective. As we have seen, preventing a recession requires that increases in government spending or reductions in taxes take place *before* planned investment actually declines. Unfortunately, it takes several months before the data that the government needs to recognize a recession or inflationary episode are available. This is called a **recognition lag.** Only then, when it may already be too late, will Congress *begin* the lengthy legislative process that precedes a discretionary tax or expenditure change. There may be further lags in starting up new projects if expenditures are to be increased. Implementing a change in tax policy, once the decision is made to do so, need not take as long.

The lags of *recognition* and *implementation* of fiscal policy are serious enough when recession threatens. However, fiscal policy is even less likely to be timed accurately enough to prevent an inflationary episode. The reason for this is the political danger to legislators in raising taxes or reducing government expenditures. While the public and its congressional representatives may strongly favor antirecessionary fiscal policy *in principle,* few people really believe that it is a good idea to increase *their* taxes or reduce allocations to *their* favorite projects.

Political realities as well as recognition and implementation lags lead many economists to believe that *discretionary* fiscal policy is unlikely to work well as an antiinflationary or antirecession macroeconomic tool. Fortunately, however, there are elements of fiscal policy that do not require new legislation every time an inflation or a recession threatens macroeconomic stability.

Countercyclical fiscal policy is fiscal policy designed explicitly to moderate fluctuations in GNP and employment.

Automatic fiscal stabilizers are fiscal policies that do not require new legislation or executive decisions to become effective because they are built into existing laws.

Nondiscretionary Fiscal Policy

Various tax and expenditure programs serve as **countercyclical fiscal policy** (fiscal policy to offset recessions and inflationary episodes) that is relatively free of recognition and implementation lags.

Even without new legislation, changes in important aspects of the government's budget *automatically* come into play whenever the economy moves into a recessionary or inflationary phase. This is very important because market economies everywhere are characterized by business cycles that lead to alternating periods of excess expenditure and excess production in the goods market and to increases and decreases in unemployment in the labor market. The economy's **automatic fiscal stabilizers** are elements of fiscal policy that do not require new legislation each time they are used. They are valuable tools to reduce economic fluctuations, although they cannot be expected to prevent them. Automatic, or nondiscretionary, fiscal policy stems from the fact that our tax laws and certain government expenditures are programmed to increase or decrease *automatically* in the correct direction to offset recessions and inflations.

On the tax side, income and sales taxes automatically fall when incomes and the sales of goods and services decline. They rise as business conditions "heat up." Thus, such taxes *automatically* tend to slow down both the leftward shift of the aggregate demand curve during recessions and the rightward shift of aggregate demand during inflationary episodes. Beginning in 1984, the federal personal income tax brackets were adjusted for inflation. Through a process called *indexing,* increases in your income that are offset by inflation will not push you into a higher tax bracket under the changes implemented in 1984. The tax *rates* on individual incomes are not to increase just because of inflation. With indexing of tax brackets, income taxes will now rise less rapidly during inflationary episodes than they did in the past. Many economists favor indexing because it means that the tax rates we pay must be determined by legislation, not by inflation. However, indexing does reduce somewhat the effectiveness of the income tax as an automatic fiscal stabilizer during inflationary episodes.

Several categories of transfer expenditures increase when the economy heads into recessions and decline when incomes rise and unemployment falls. One program is unemployment insurance. During recessions, most laid-off workers become eligible for unemployment compensation. Thus, their lost wage income is partially replaced. Because their disposable income does not fall as much as their lost wage income, unemployed workers who receive unemployment compensation are able to maintain their consumption expenditures at a higher level than would be possible if they were completely on their own. The consumption expenditures supported by unemployment compensation payments help maintain the level of aggregate demand and thus reduce the severity of the recessions.

Other transfer expenditures that increase automatically during recessions and fall during movements toward inflationary episodes are all income maintenance programs, such as Aid to Families with Dependent Children (AFDC) and federal food stamps. When family incomes fall below legislatively determined levels, these programs provide additional income in the form of cash payments (AFDC) or stamps that can be traded in for food purchases. Under both programs, disposable income is maintained during recessions and reduced when earnings increase. Thus they act like unemployment compensation does: to offset declines in planned consumption during recessions and to reduce increases in planned consumption during inflationary episodes.

Recent Fiscal Policy Developments

While it is useful to distinguish between countercyclical fiscal policy and long-term fiscal policy, the experience with changes in tax policy in the United States in the 1980s illustrates that distinctions are sometimes difficult to make. Federal income tax cuts in the early 1980s represented historic changes that could have positively affected long-term growth in the economy. Yet, as discussed more fully in chapter 12, more zealous advocates of the income tax changes argued that tax cuts would quickly stimulate the economy in countercyclical fashion.

In 1985, the Reagan administration proposed a "flat tax" that would drastically simplify and restructure the incentive effects of the personal and corporate income tax laws. Again, such efforts, if successful, could have a substantial long-term growth impact on the economy. Yet the surprisingly sluggish performance of the United States economy in 1985 was attributed in part to uncertainty by consumers and businesses about when and if tax law changes would take place and what those changes would look like. The more uncertain consumers and producers are about the rules of the game with respect to taxes, the more tentative they will be with respect to spending, saving, and investment decisions.

In short, the experience of the first half of the 1980s made it clear that long-term fiscal policy requiring changes in tax rates takes a long time to implement. The transition period was lengthy and the implications of the changes were uncertain. Increased uncertainty about where United States tax policy was going in the long run had significant and adverse short-run effects on the United States economy in the mid-1980s.

▸ Discretionary Monetary Policy in a Recession

As with fiscal policy, monetary policy can be a very potent weapon in forestalling macroeconomic disequilibrium. In fact, under present institutional arrangements, monetary policy may be more flexible and, hence, a more effective discretionary tool than fiscal policy. This is because the day-to-day conduct of monetary policy does not require the prior approval of the executive or congressional branches of government. It is conducted by the Fed, which is theoretically independent of Congress in deciding how to conduct monetary policies that affect the macroeconomy. In the sections that follow, we first see how discretionary monetary policy can prevent a recession and then how it can forestall an inflationary episode. Before going on you may wish to review the discussion of monetary policy and the role of the Fed in chapters 6 and 7.

In figure 10.4, parts (a) and (b), we illustrate the start of the same recession described in figure 10.2. Planned investment has declined as indicated by the leftward-pointing arrow in part (b) of figure 10.4. If no further changes occur, the economy is headed toward a recessionary equilibrium. In the recession, the interest rate will fall as indicated in part (b) of figure 10.4. GNP will decline as indicated by the arrow pointing leftward in part (a) of figure 10.4, and the price level will begin to fall (arrow pointing downward). However, if the Fed—the monetary authority—possesses this information about the coming recession, it can prevent it by engaging in an expansionary open market operation. If the Fed increases the banking system's reserves by a sufficient amount, the supply curve of loanable funds (SLF) and the aggregate demand curve (D) will shift far enough to the right to maintain planned investment and GNP at the full-employment level as shown in part (c) of figure 10.4.

The economy's supply of loanable funds consists of households' net supply of loanable funds plus the banking system's supply. The banking system's supply of loanable funds equals the rate of growth of real money balances, $\Delta M/P$. Therefore, the Fed's expansionary monetary policy must cause an *increase* in the *growth* of the real money supply large enough to keep planned investment at its initial level. Such an expansionary monetary policy is illustrated in part (c) of figure 10.4, where the arrow points to the right.

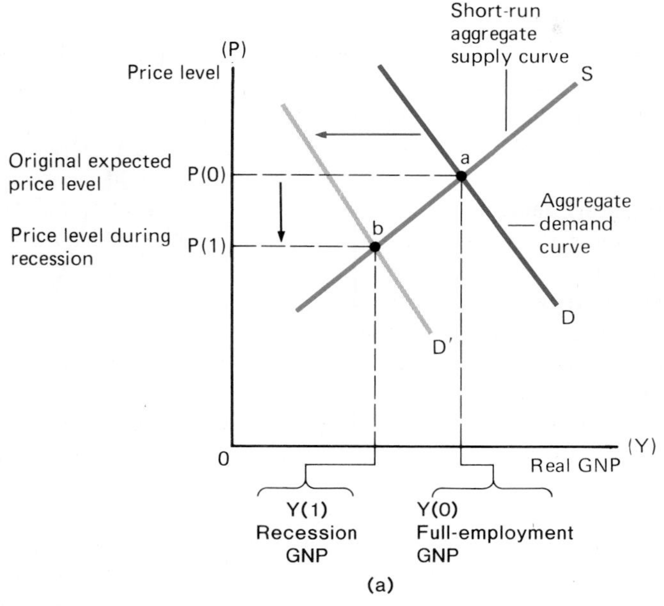

(a)

Figure 10.4 The Fed adopts an expansionary monetary policy to prevent a recession
The arrows in parts (a) and (b) show that planned investment expenditure has declined and the economy will enter a recession unless immediate action is taken to prevent the recession.

As shown in part (c), if the Fed immediately buys government bonds to increase the reserves of the banking system, the supply of loanable funds will shift to the right (see arrow). The interest rate will fall, so that planned investment does not decline, avoiding the recession.

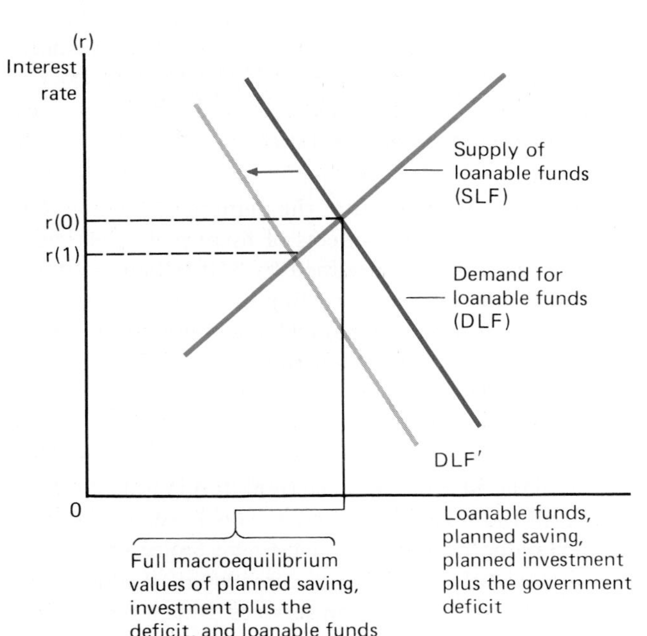

(b) The arrow shows that planned investment expenditures have declined and the economy will enter a recession unless immediate action is taken to prevent it.

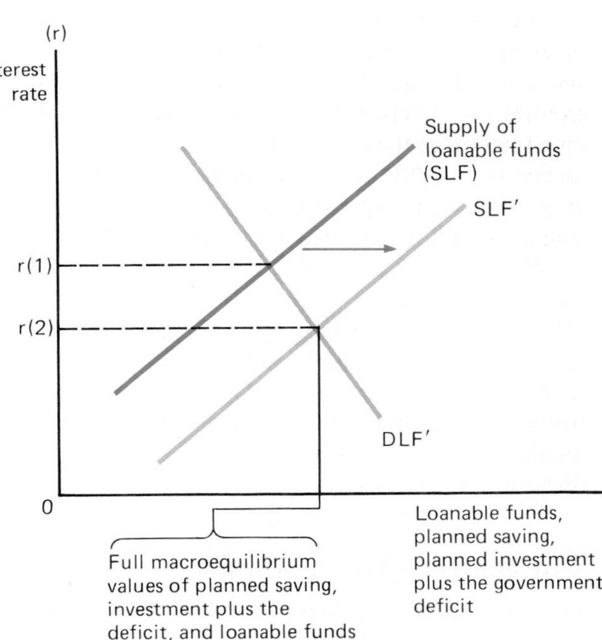

(c) If the Fed immediately buys government bonds to increase the reserves of the banking system, the supply of loanable funds will shift to the right as shown by the arrow. The interest rate will fall, so that planned investment does not decline, avoiding the recession.

The Initial Effect in the Loanable Funds Market

We will assume that the Fed has increased banking system reserves by the amount that leads to an increase in the rate of growth of the money supply *exactly* sufficient to offset the impending recession. This expansionary monetary policy shifts the supply curve of loanable funds rightward to SLF′. Given the new demand curve for loanable funds, DLF′, there is now an excess supply of loanable funds at interest rate r(1). To eliminate this excess supply, lenders compete with one another to buy loan contracts. This competition forces the rate of interest all the way down to r(2), where SLF′ intersects DLF′. At this interest rate, the loanable funds market is in equilibrium.

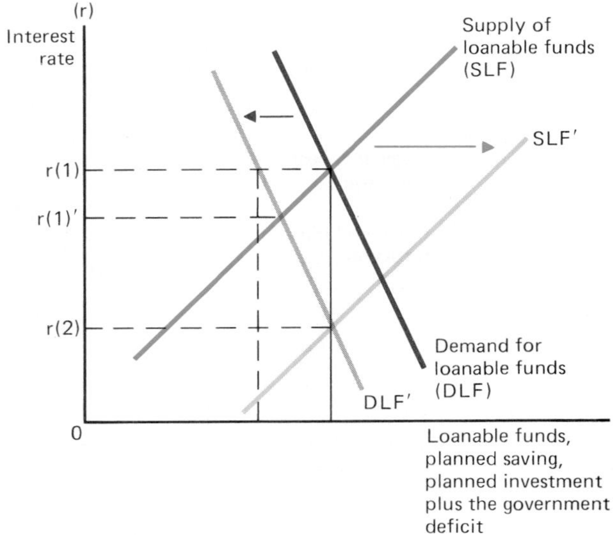

Figure 10.5 How monetary policy works to prevent a recession
Planned investment has declined, as indicated by the leftward-pointing arrow. However, the Fed can prevent a recession by an expansionary monetary policy that shifts the SLF sufficiently far to the right, as indicated by the rightward-pointing arrow, to force the interest rate down to r(2). This keeps planned investment and the quantity of loanable funds demanded and supplied at their full-employment levels.

The Effect in the Goods Market

The success of the Fed's intervention in the macroeconomy results because the interest rate falls to the lower value of r(2). As a result of this decline, planned investment remains at the level that prevailed when the economy was in its initial state of full macroequilibrium. Therefore, at interest rate r(2), planned investment plus the government deficit equals planned saving with GNP at its full-employment level. Aggregate demand intersects aggregate supply at the original equilibrium price level, P(0).

With production and sales synchronized, firms have no incentive to lay off workers. The Fed's policy of expanding the banking system's reserves has removed the fundamental cause of the threatening recession, excess production in the goods market. Since equilibrium exists simultaneously in the goods, credit, and labor markets, full macroeconomic equilibrium has been maintained.

Why Monetary Policy Works

The Fed was able to counteract the recessionary threat resulting from the decline in the demand for investment goods by exerting a powerful influence on the rate of interest. By acting quickly to increase the supply of loanable funds, the Fed forced the rate of interest down. In terms of the numerical example we used to illustrate the effects of fiscal policy, planned investment initially declined by $10 billion, as indicated by the leftward-pointing arrow in figure 10.5. Without any action by the Fed, the interest rate would have declined to r(1)′, but this would not have been sufficient to boost planned investment back to its original level. The rightward-pointing arrow shows that the Fed's expansionary open market operation has shifted the SLF curve to the right, forcing the interest rate all the way down to r(2). This lower rate of interest reduced the cost of investment projects and thus stimulated the investment component of aggregate expenditure for goods and services. Recall that investors had initially planned to reduce their purchases of goods because of their pessimistic expectations about the future. At a sufficiently *lower* rate of interest, even these pessimistic investors wished to purchase the same quantity of investment goods as they had been buying *prior* to the decline in planned investment. Notice that at the lower rate of interest, r(2), both planned investment *and* the quantity of loanable funds demanded and supplied are exactly the same as before the initial decline in planned investment.

The mechanism by which monetary policy transmits its effects throughout the economy bears a striking resemblance to the way flexible prices automatically adjust the economy following a decline in planned investment. Monetary policy and flexible prices both affect the real value of the new money balances created when the banking system buys loan contracts. Remember that the real value of these new money balances is represented symbolically by the expression $\Delta M/P$, where ΔM is the change in *nominal* money balances and P is the price level. In the case of flexible prices, excess aggregate supply in the goods market produces a decline in prices, which makes the *denominator* of $\Delta M/P$ smaller and hence raises the value of the $\Delta M/P$ ratio. Monetary policy, on the other hand, works directly on the *numerator* of $\Delta M/P$ by making ΔM larger. The net effect in both cases is a rightward shift in SLF, the aggregate supply of loanable funds, and a resulting decline in the interest rate. Therefore, by using monetary policy, the Fed can achieve the same result that flexible prices do, without the economy's having to experience the undesirable symptoms of a recession—high unemployment and low production.

One reason that monetary policy can be such an effective weapon against recession should be clear. If the Fed wants to initiate a particular policy action, it can do so without going through a lengthy process of legislation. This potentially speedy response is a virtue as long as the Fed accurately anticipates changes in the goods market and takes the appropriate policy action to offset them. Remember, in this chapter we assumed that the Fed always chooses the correct policy because it is fully informed about the events unfolding in the real and financial sectors of the economy. The real world, unfortunately, is such a complicated place that the Fed often has to resort to educated guesses about what is happening in the aggregate economy. Recognition lag affects monetary policy just as it does fiscal policy. For example, the Fed has to wait for three months or longer before it receives accurate data on the quantity of investment goods purchased in the goods market during any given period. In the meantime, it has to guess whether planned investment during that period has increased, decreased, or remained constant.

Discretionary Monetary Policy to Prevent Inflation

The Fed's ability to affect bank reserves can be used to prevent an inflationary episode as well as a recession. The monetary policy required is, of course, *restrictive,* or *contractionary,* just the opposite of the expansionary monetary policy needed to combat recession.

To make sure that you understand the theory of antiinflationary monetary policy, construct a diagram with the economy in macroequilibrium. Shift the demand curve for loanable funds to the right to indicate that investors' increased optimism about the future leads them to desire to invest *more* than previously. This will also result in a shift to the right of the aggregate demand curve, leading to the beginning of an inflationary episode. The Fed can prevent an inflationary episode from occurring, however, if it knows that planned investment is about to increase and takes immediate action to *reduce* bank reserves by just the amount needed to restore planned investment to its original level.

By *selling* government bonds in an open market operation, the Fed can accomplish its desired aim, and the supply of loanable funds will shift *leftward.* As a result of the ensuing *increase* in the rate of interest, investors see the cost of prospective investment projects increase. The Fed's restrictive monetary policy will offset the rightward shift in the demand for investment goods and prevent excess demand from occurring in the goods market. The Fed has achieved this goal by *reducing* the *numerator* of $\Delta M/P$.

Table 10.2 Comparison of monetary and fiscal policies

Policy needed to combat	The Fed should	Congress should	Impact of policy on DLF or SLF
Recession			
Expansionary monetary policy (open market operation)	Buy government bonds to increase bank reserves		Shifts SLF to the right
Expansionary fiscal policy		Increase expenditures or reduce taxes	Shifts DLF to the right
Inflationary episode			
Contractionary monetary policy (open market operation)	Sell government bonds to reduce bank reserves		Shifts SLF to the left
Contractionary fiscal policy		Reduce expenditures or increase taxes	Shifts DLF to the left

Table 10.2 summarizes and compares monetary and fiscal policies to offset recessions and inflationary episodes. The table also shows the impact of each type of policy on the supply of loanable funds (SLF) or the demand for loanable funds (DLF).

The Politics of Discretionary Antiinflation Monetary Policy

In our discussion of fiscal policy, we pointed out that in addition to the technical problems of recognizing when countercyclical fiscal policy is needed and of implementing the correct actions once their need is agreed upon, there is an additional problem when inflation threatens. It is simply that the cure for inflation always appears more painful than that for recession. Taking something away from borrowers or consumers is always going to be a less popular activity than giving something to them. We shall see in chapter 11 that this political reality has been an important factor contributing to the inflationary era in the United States that characterized the period from the late 1960s well into the 1980s.

The members of the Federal Open Market Committee (FOMC) do not stand for election as members of Congress must. Therefore, there is little question that they face less pressure when implementing antiinflationary policy than Congress does. However, the members of the Fed's Board of Governors are appointed by the President, and Congress has the power to pass laws that restrict the Fed's power to conduct monetary policy. Therefore, the Board of Governors and the FOMC cannot completely ignore public and congressional reaction to their monetary policies.

The principal problem faced by the Fed in its efforts to prevent inflationary episodes arises from the fact that an increase in investment demand is very unlikely to be spread uniformly over all industries. The expected returns on future investments may have increased much more in some areas (for example, computers or consumer electronics) than in others (for example, construction or automobile manufacturing). Therefore, when the Fed takes actions that raise the rate of interest, this will be seen as "choking off" investment in those areas of the economy where the investment demand schedule has *not* shifted to the right. Of course, this is simply a reflection of the need to reallocate resources from, say, the housing industry to the computer industry. The market is giving the correct signals to investors through the interest rate.

Unfortunately, the process of adjusting to the changed composition of investment goods demanded will not be painless for firms and workers who had been active in the sector of the economy not sharing in the growth of productivity or demand. The non-growing firms and their labor forces will experience reduced profits and increased unemployment as the needed adjustments occur. Their complaints to their elected representatives will lead to unpleasantness for the Fed as it tries to prevent inflation. This political pressure, then, represents an obstacle to the conduct of appropriate monetary policies to prevent inflation. Throughout the period 1980–83, the Fed committed itself to bringing inflation down from the double-digit levels of 1979 and 1980. The Reagan administration and many in Congress were highly critical of Fed Chairman Paul Volcker and blamed the Fed's restrictive monetary policy for the recession in 1981–82. By 1983 the economy began to expand rapidly and inflation appeared to be under control. Paul Volcker became popular in political circles for having arrested inflation. Although Volcker had originally been appointed by Democrat Jimmy Carter, the Republican incumbent reappointed him in 1983.

Comparing the Short-run and Long-run Effects of Fiscal and Monetary Policies

Fiscal and monetary policies are the tools the government uses in influencing the aggregate economy. Both can correct a disequilibrium that will lead into a recession or a period of rising prices. *Fiscal policy* operates *directly* on the *goods market* because the government-spending component of fiscal policy is itself part of aggregate expenditure for goods and the tax component affects households' consumption demand for goods. *Monetary policy,* on the other hand, does not affect the goods market directly. The initial impact of *monetary policy* is felt in the *credit market,* as *bank reserves* are affected. A change in the banks' supply of loanable funds in turn affects investment expenditure in the goods sector via changes in the interest rate.

Both fiscal and monetary policies can be used to offset business cycles. However, there are significant differences in the lags that occur before they are implemented and in their effects on various macroeconomic variables, such as government spending, taxes, saving, investment, consumption, and interest rates. Because of these differences, there is much political debate, and even some disagreement among economists, about the desirability of using one type of policy or the other. There is also disagreement regarding the form of fiscal policy—tax adjustments or expenditure changes—that should be used to promote aggregate economic health. We will survey the major features of these debates in chapter 12. Remember that *both* forms of policy can in theory restore or maintain full macroeconomic equilibrium. However, our concept of full equilibrium ignores the long-run impact of investment on the economy's capital stock and, hence, its capacity to produce goods and services. For example, fiscal policy to counteract a recession will in general result in a *lower level* of investment and a *higher level* of consumption or government spending than will monetary policy. Review figures 10.2 and 10.4 if you do not see why this is so. A great deal of political debate over the relative merits of alternative macroeconomic policies involves confusion over their immediate and long-run effects.

Is Discretionary Policy Useless?

In chapter 12 we will analyze a subtle issue hotly debated among economists called *monetarists* and *Keynesians,* but first we must introduce it here. The issue is twofold. First a number of empirical studies purport to show that because of the lags associated with implementing countercyclical monetary and fiscal policy, the timing for the use of each has been all wrong. In effect, the argument is that ill-timed countercyclical policies have actually made business cycles worse than they would have been without government discretionary actions. That evidence has led some economists (monetarists) to call for less use of discretionary monetary and fiscal policy until and unless we develop better methods for recognizing the need for policy action and for implementing policies in a timely fashion.

The second element of the debate is even more profound in its implications. Professor Robert Lucas of the University of Chicago and others view discretionary monetary and fiscal actions as attempts to smooth the growth process in a market economy by fooling consumers, savers, and investors into believing that the economy will not slow down or speed up despite evidence that such changes are taking place. As the public becomes more informed and sophisticated in its reading of economic variables indicating changes in the economy, they will become harder to fool with discretionary policies. This argument suggests that aggregate economic activity can only be smoothed by means of discretionary policy actions that surprise consumers, savers, and investors. The conclusion of these economists is that smoothing the rate of growth of the economy will only reduce long-run growth. If this view is correct, we would expect to observe that even well-timed fiscal and monetary policies would lose their effectiveness in modifying the short-run growth path of the macroeconomy.

These two positions—that recognition and implementation lags are at present insurmountable and that the public cannot continually be fooled by discretionary policies—present strong arguments against the use of discretionary monetary and/or fiscal policies. Keynesians, on the other hand, still favor the use of discretionary countercyclical monetary and fiscal policies.

▸ Summary and Conclusions

By now, you should be beginning to decide for yourself whether you believe that discretionary monetary and/or fiscal policies can help offset inflationary episodes or recessions. You will learn more about macroeconomic policies in practice in the next two chapters. Discretionary fiscal and monetary policies are, in *theory,* extraordinarily powerful weapons of macroeconomic control. By manipulating the dials of government expenditures, government taxation, and banks' reserves, government authorities can presumably ward off many of the destabilizing elements that affect the private sector of the economy. The following main points were emphasized.

Expansionary or restrictive fiscal and monetary policies can theoretically reduce the severity of business cycles.

Fiscal policy that operates through a change in taxes will have effects that differ from those of fiscal policy that operates through a change in government expenditures.

Monetary and fiscal policies have different impacts on major macroeconomic variables in both the short and the long run.

Both information lags and political considerations impede the effectiveness of discretionary countercyclical monetary and fiscal policies.

▸ Key Terms

automatic fiscal stabilizers *223*

countercyclical fiscal policy *223*

crowding out *219*

fiscal policy *215*

lag *222*

recognition lag *222*

▸ Questions for Discussion and Review

1. Are the following statements true, false, or uncertain? Defend your answers.
   a. Monetary and fiscal policies are equally effective in preventing inflationary episodes and recessions.
   b. One advantage of monetary over fiscal policy is that the Fed need not consider the political implications of its actions.
   c. One advantage of fiscal over monetary policy to combat inflationary episodes is that it promotes investment in physical capital to a greater extent.
2. Describe the differences between monetary and fiscal policies with regard to:
   a. the macroeconomic variables that are directly affected by the policies;
   b. the governmental authorities that are responsible for them.
3. Suppose you are in charge of discretionary fiscal policy and your computer model of the aggregate economy has just furnished you with the following information about the economy for the next twelve months:

Full-employment GNP	= $1,000
Consumption function	= $100 + .72(GNP−T)
Taxes (T)	= $100
Planned investment	= $100
Government spending	= $100

   Design a fiscal policy that will promote full employment without inflation for the next twelve months. Be sure to specify what changes (if any) will occur in
   a. Planned investment
   b. Planned saving
   c. Taxes
   d. Government spending
   e. The federal deficit
   f. The rate of interest
4. Using the data from question 3, suppose that you are the monetary authority and possess the following additional knowledge about the economy:

Money stock (M2)	= $600
Bank reserves	= $60
Required reserves	= $60
Elasticity of demand curve for investment goods with respect to the rate of interest	− 1.0
Current rate of interest	= 9%

   Design a monetary policy for the next twelve months to promote full employment without inflation. Be sure to specify what changes (if any) will occur in
   a. Open market operations
   b. Bank reserves
   c. The money supply
   d. All other variables (a through f in question 3).
5. Suppose the consumer price index has risen from 185 to 203 since last year and that this 9.7 percent rate of inflation is not spread evenly over all goods and services. The prices of housing and transportation have risen by 25 percent and 40 percent, respectively, while all other prices in the CPI "market basket" have remained unchanged. Prices are expected to behave this year as they did last year. Newspaper articles say that the inflation was caused by the price increases for housing and transportation. How would you recommend that the expected inflation be controlled? Should Congress pass a law setting a maximum price on these two commodities? Might such a law control inflation? Analyze the micro- and macroeconomic impacts of the law.
6. Discretionary monetary policy is often used to control or reduce inflation. Can you think of any economic reason for using discretionary monetary policy to reinflate the economy?

7. Find the latest employment rate figures for the United States and the rate of inflation over the past six months. Using the diagrammatic analysis developed in figures 8.4 through 8.5 describe the macroeconomic situation in the United States today. Which term best describes today's macroeconomy: recession, inflation, stagflation, or full macroequilibrium? Using the best data you can find on recent monetary and fiscal policies (try some back issues of the *New York Times* or the *Wall Street Journal*), determine whether they are appropriate, given your assessment of the policies needed at this time.
8. Indexing wages through cost-of-living adjustments protects wage earners from inflationary shocks to the economy.[2] Is this always optimal for the economy?
9. If government expenditures and taxes are increased by the same amount, will there be any effect on GNP? Explain.
10. A short-run solution to eliminating the government deficit, (G − T), is to raise tax rates and the tax base. What are the long-run implications of this tactic?

Chapter 11

Monetary and Fiscal Policies in Action

Outline

Objectives

After reading this chapter, the student should be able to:

Describe the appropriate monetary and fiscal policy responses in 1930 and compare these with the actual policies used.

Describe the monetary and fiscal policies used in 1931 and their effects on the macroeconomy.

Explain how the monetary policy used in 1932 contributed to the Great Depression.

Explain how fiscal and monetary policies in 1966 led to the onset of an inflationary episode and what policies could have been used to combat the inflation.

Discuss the monetary policies used in the 1970s and early 1980s and explain the resulting stagflation.

▸ Introduction

Ask your grandparents or any other relatives old enough to have lived through the Great Depression of the 1930s how their lives and attitudes were changed by economic conditions then. Each story differs, but every one conveys a chilling picture of how mean and fearful the times were.

One relative tells us how he became a truck mechanic in 1933 with only one year of college behind him. He responded to an ad for the job by standing in line with about 600 other men. When he got to the front of the line, he was asked why he should be hired instead of one of the others. He recalls saying, "Because I have a wife and baby at home, and I'll do anything I have to to take care of them." He got the job, working eighty hours per week for $15.

In this chapter, we will explain the critical role that monetary and fiscal policy played in the depressed conditions of the 1930s, the accelerating inflation of the late 1960s, and the "stagflation" of the 1970s and early 1980s. In the process we will explain why our understanding of macroeconomic theory and policy leads us to believe that there is no reasonable expectation that we will experience a replay of the Great Depresssion in the future.

Our discussion will be "realistic" in that we take into account the fact that the government may not possess all of the information it needs—or the political will—to conduct effective macroeconomic policy. The specific questions we will answer are (1) What fiscal and monetary policies were followed by the government during these episodes? and (2) Did the government do everything possible to stabilize the economy at a position of macroeconomic equilibrium? We will specify the most effective policies that the government could have employed in combating recession and inflation and then compare them with the policies actually adopted.

▸ The Great Depression

During 1929 the United States economy was in a fairly prosperous position and, as table 11.1 shows, produced a real value of GNP equal to $316 billion (as measured in terms of 1972 dollars). Real GNP in 1929 was 6.7 percent higher than in 1928.[1] This is a fairly high rate of economic growth for the United States economy, based on historical experience in this century. Toward the end of 1929, however, world events adversely affected the expectations of United States citizens about the future of the economy.

The United States Economy in 1929 and 1930

The stock market crash in October 1929 was symptomatic of a collapse in confidence. Because stock ownership represents a claim on *future* profits, the present value of the *expected* stream of future profits is crucial in determining current stock prices. (This is also the case in determining the demand for investment goods.) A collapse in confidence about the future will lead investors to revise their estimate of future profits downward, and the net effect will be lower current prices for shares of common stock.

In terms of our macroeconomic model, this change in expectations in 1929 produced a decline in investment demand and, therefore, the demand curve for loanable funds. (You may wish to refer back to figure 10.2.) This meant that the economy was about to enter a period of falling production and declining prices, that is, a recession.

Table 11.1 shows that in 1930 the economy in fact displayed all of the characteristics associated with a recession. Real investment spending fell 33 percent, from $51.2 billion to $34.7 billion. Real GNP dropped 10 percent, to $284.4 billion. The consumer price index fell 2.5 percent from 40.9 to 39.9. Table 11.2 illustrates what was happening in the financial sector of the economy. The yield (nominal interest rate) on corporate bonds fell slightly, from 6.2 percent in 1929 to 5.9 percent in 1930.

Table 11.1 **Real GNP, real investment, real government expenditures (federal, state, and local), and the consumer price index during 1929–1932**

Year	Real GNP[a]	Real investment[a]	Real government expenditures[a]	Consumer Price index[b]
1929	315.7	51.2	41.0	40.9
1930	284.4	34.7	45.3	39.9
1931	262.4	21.3	47.3	36.3
1932	223.5	6.0	45.1	32.6

Source: From *Economic Report of the President, 1983.*
[a]Billions of 1972 dollars.
[b]1972 = 100.

Table 11.2 **Money supply, commercial banks' reserves, and yield on corporate bonds for 1929–1932**

Year	Money supply[a]	Banks' reserves[a]	Yield on corporate bonds[b]
1929	$26.3	$3.25	6.2%
1930	25.3	3.23	5.9
1931—first half	24.2	3.25	6.5
1931—second half	22.8	3.12	9.0
1932	20.5	2.91	9.3

Source: Milton Friedman and Anna Jacobson Schwartz, *A Monetary History of the United States,* 1867–1960. Copyright © 1963 by NBER. Table adapted with permission of Princeton University Press; and Federal Reserve System, *Banking and Monetary Statistics,* 1914–1941 (bond yields).
[a]Billions of current dollars.
[b]Implicit interest rate received by lenders.

Appropriate Fiscal and Monetary Policies in 1930

Assuming that the government wanted to prevent or at least reduce the severity of the recession in 1930, appropriate policy responses would have been for the monetary authority to expand the reserves of the banking system and for the fiscal authority to increase government expenditure or reduce taxes. An expansion in banks' reserves produces a rightward shift in the supply curve for loanable funds, a lower real interest rate, and a narrowing of the gap between planned aggregate expenditure and production in the goods market. An increase in government expenditure is a direct addition to the planned aggregate expenditure for goods and also narrows the excess production in the goods market.

Actual Fiscal and Monetary Policies in 1930

Table 11.1 shows that real government spending rose slightly in 1930 as compared to 1929, but the increase was not large enough to offset the reduction in the investment component of planned aggregate expenditure.

Contrary to popular belief, the fiscal policy associated with the New Deal played only a minor role in the economy during the 1930s. Government spending on average rose only $1 billion per year over the decade. The federal government operated with a budget *surplus* in fiscal year 1930 that was almost as large (in current dollars) as in 1929.[2]

Turning to the monetary policy followed by the Fed in 1930, table 11.2 shows that banks' reserves *declined* slightly in 1930 from 1929. Accompanying this decline was a 4 percent *reduction* in the United States money supply from $26.3 billion in 1929 to $25.3 billion in 1930. While this policy is exactly the *opposite* of the one that our macromodel prescribes, it should be noted in fairness to the Fed that its policy error was not a major one. Rather, it appears as though the Fed maintained a hands-off attitude in 1930 with respect to the aggregate economy. Thus, we conclude that in 1930 fiscal policy was slightly expansionary but not large enough to be of major significance in stopping the recession. At the same time, monetary policy was basically playing a neutral role in influencing the United States economy, a role that amounted to an inappropriate contraction in the money supply.

The United States Economy in 1931 and 1932

Table 11.1 also shows us that during 1931 the United States economy experienced a continued reduction in real GNP, real investment, and the consumer price index. At first glance, these trends suggest that the private economy was incapable of returning to a position of full-employment macroeconomic equilibrium through its own devices. Before accepting this viewpoint, however, let us examine the course of monetary and fiscal policies in 1931.

Monetary and Fiscal Policies in 1931

As table 11.1 shows, fiscal policy was slightly stimulative during 1931, with real government expenditures rising by about 4.5 percent to $47.3 billion. Monetary policy, on the other hand, turned sharply *contractionary* in 1931. Commercial banks' reserves began to fall, especially in the second half of the year. As a result, the United States money supply declined by $3 billion from 1930 to the second half of 1931—this is roughly a 12 percent reduction in the United States money supply over the course of the year. Based on the smaller amount of reserves made available by the Fed, banks curtailed the number of new loan contracts they were willing to purchase. For the loanable funds market as a whole, this produced a *leftward* shift in the supply of loanable funds curve instead of the *rightward* shift called for in figure 10.4.

As a result of this leftward shift in the supply of loanable funds, the interest rate *increased*. Notice in table 11.2 that the yield on corporate bonds rose to 9 percent in the latter half of 1931. This increase in the interest rate probably explains much of the $13.4 billion drop in investment expenditures in 1931. Why? Because a higher interest rate induces investors to *move up* along their planned investment demand curve, thus lowering the quantity of investment goods purchased. One explanation for the behavior of the Fed in this period is that it thought a low interest rate might lead to an inflation. In order to prevent the inflation, the Fed decided to follow a contractionary monetary policy that ultimately contributed to the Great Depression. In addition, a number of banks experienced runs by nervous depositors. Between 1930 and 1933, 8,000 banks failed. No doubt those bank failures contributed to the sharp contraction in the money supply. Inaction by the Fed was sufficient to ensure a decline in the money supply.

The effect of this higher interest rate on the goods market, already in a state of disequilibrium, was disastrous. In 1931, producers' sales started to plummet dramatically as more and more investors reduced their purchases of goods in the face of a higher interest rate. The gap between supply and demand in the goods market widened after the Fed engineered a contraction in the banking system's reserves. Firms acquired still greater incentives to reduce prices and production as unsold inventories piled up.

If, at the end of 1931, the Fed had ceased interfering in the loan contract market, its mistake in 1931 would have been felt principally as a lengthening of the recessionary period. Even though the excess aggregate production of goods was large after the Fed's miscalculation, there is reason to believe that price reductions would have eventually produced a rightward shift in the supply curve of loanable funds. As this happened, the interest rate would have fallen, investment expenditure increased, and producers' sales risen. The aggregate economy would most likely have eventually returned to a position of macroeconomic equilibrium.

Monetary Policy in 1932

The severe depression persisted, however, because the Fed continued to follow a contractionary monetary policy. Table 11.2 shows that both banks' reserves and the money supply fell again in 1932. The reserves of the commercial banking system were 11 percent lower in 1932 than in 1931. (Fiscal policy was also contractionary.) Notice in table 11.1 that real government expenditures fell by more than 11 percent ($2 billion) in 1932. In terms of figure 10.4, the Fed's *contractionary* monetary policy prevented the loanable funds supply curve, SLF, and the aggregate demand curve from shifting to the right when prices fell in the early 1930s. The interest rate therefore stayed high, and firms observed little change in their total sales. The next step is obvious. To cut back on their inventories, firms began to lay off workers on a large scale and to contract sharply the aggregate amount of production.

In 1932, real GNP declined 15 percent to $223.5 billion. The entire economic system was in the grip of a gigantic collapse. The price level had fallen by over 20 percent since 1929, a price decline unequaled at any time since then. Over one-fourth of the labor force was unemployed, a human catastrophe that many economists believe could have been made much less severe if not entirely avoided. If blame must be assigned for the Great Depression, should we place it on a collapse of the private economy or on the discretionary monetary policy used in the 1930s? On the basis of evidence, it appears that the Fed's mistakes contributed substantially to the Great Depression. In fairness, it must be pointed out that economists and policymakers simply did not know as much about macroeconomics and the appropriate monetary and fiscal policies as they do now.

▸ The Great Inflation: 1965–?

The production of goods and services in the United States economy during 1965 was at or very close to the full-employment level. Late 1965 also marked a fundamental change in United States foreign policy—large-scale commitments of American troops and equipment were made to aid the South Vietnamese government in its fight against North Vietnam. For the United Sates economy, the decision to wage war in Southeast Asia was translated into a significant increase in the amount of goods and services purchased by the United States government, and this had a dramatic effect on the economy.

The Economic Setting in Late 1965 and Early 1966

Table 11.3 shows us that total government spending was nearly 10 percent higher in 1966 than in 1965, with most of the increase taking place in national defense. Figure 11.1 depicts the state of the United States economy both before and after the nation's entry into the Vietnam War. In part (a) of the figure, curve DLF represents the demand for loanable funds at the end of 1965—the sum of the government's budget deficit plus planned investment. DLF intersects SLF, the supply of loanable funds, at interest rate r(0). Hence, the loan contract market is in equilibrium. Since the planned saving equals planned investment plus the government deficit at the

Table 11.3 **Total real government expenditures, federal expenditures, and defense expenditures for 1964–1966[a]**

Year	Total government expenditures	Federal government expenditures	Defense expenditures
1964	$202.6	$100.2	$77.8
1965	209.8	100.3	70.3
1966	229.7	112.6	79.1

Source: From *Economic Report of the President, 1968 and 1983* and *Historical Statistics of the United States, Colonial Times to 1970.*
[a]All are in terms of billions of 1972 dollars.

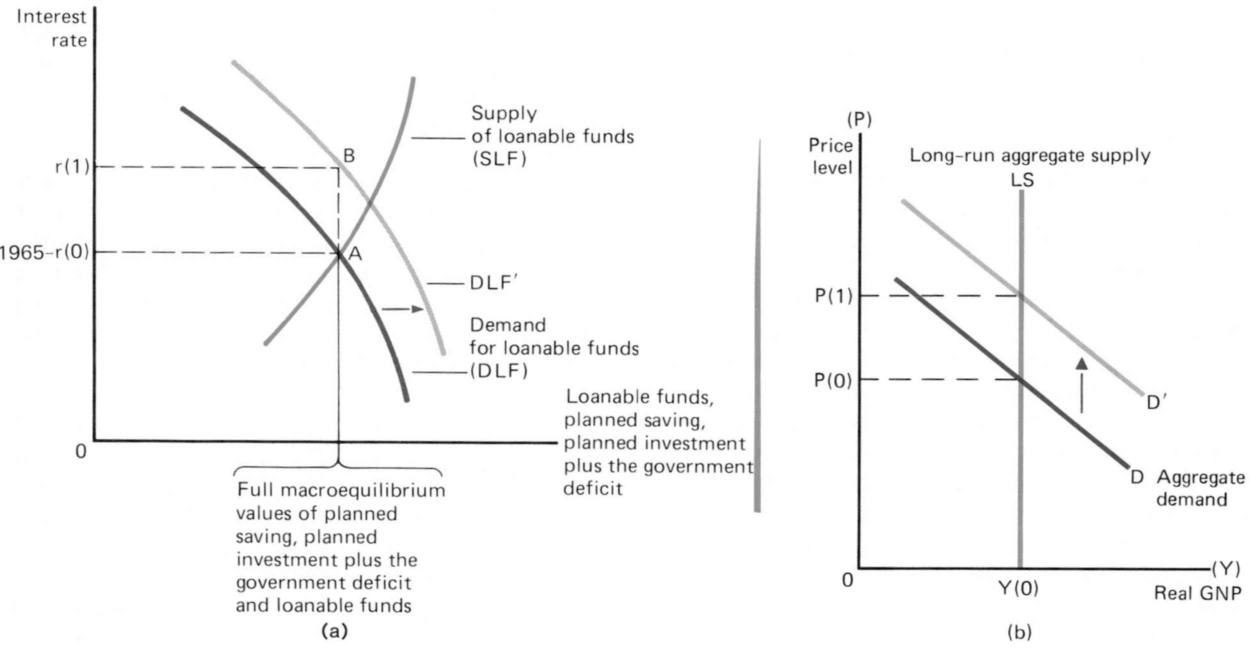

Figure 11.1 The initial impact of the Vietnam War on the United States economy and possible offsetting policy
The arrow in part (a) indicates that government expenditure increased because of the war in Vietnam. This is inflationary unless the government takes action through monetary or fiscal policy to offset the impact of increased expenditure. One possibility would have been to raise taxes, thus offsetting the effect of increased expenditures so as to keep the macroeconomy in full equilibrium at point A in part (a) and at the price level P(0) in part (b). Another possibility would have been to sell government bonds to reduce the reserves of the banking system and thus restrict the money supply. This would have reduced the supply of loanable funds, raised the real interest rate, "choked off" some private investment, and returned the economy to a full macroeconomic equilibrium at point B. Under a restrictive monetary policy a new (reduced) SLF would intersect DLF′ at point B and the price level would remain at P(0).

interest rate r(0), we have depicted a state of full-employment macroeconomic equilibrium as prevailing in the United States economy at the end of 1965. Part (b) of figure 11.1 restates the situation of full macroequilibrium, with full-employment GNP of Y(0) and a price level of P(0).

The War and Increased Government Expenditure

The government increased its expenditure in 1966 to acquire the military equipment and personnel needed for war. For the most part it chose not to increase taxes to finance this expenditure, although as figure 11.1 explains, increased taxes could have prevented inflation. Rather, the government took the alternative route of borrowing the necessary dollars in the loan contract market. It seems likely that this decision was made for political reasons. Higher taxes would have made the costs of the Vietnam War quite evident to the average United States citizen, and the war's unpopularity with the general public might have increased a good deal earlier than it did. As a result of this decision, the government's budget deficit rose. To finance this larger budget deficit, the government had to increase its demand for loanable funds.

When we add the larger government demand for loanable funds to the private investors' demand, we obtain the new, higher aggregate demand for loanable funds, curve DLF′ in part (a) of figure 11.1. Thus, at the beginning of 1966, the budget deficit due to the war in Vietnam led to a rightward shift in the demand curve for loanable funds, and the economy was at the beginning of an inflationary episode.

How Monetary Policy Could Have Prevented Inflation

Today it seems that the Fed's task in 1966 was clear-cut: to choose the monetary policy that would control the inflation stemming from the excess demand created by the increase in government wartime expenditure. Selling government bonds, which would have reduced the reserves of the commercial banking system and thus money supply growth, would have shifted the supply of loanable funds through point B in part (a) of figure 11.1. If the Fed had taken such action, the resulting increase in the interest rate to r(1) would have raised the cost of all investment projects, thereby signaling investors to curtail their expenditures. Overall macroeconomic equilibrium would have been reattained without an inflationary episode had the interest rate increase caused a reduction in investment expenditure to offset the increase in the government's purchases of goods and services.

The function of a higher interest rate is to bring the message of scarcity to the private economy. Basically, participants in the private economy are being "told" by the marketplace that their share of goods must now fall because the government has decided that it wants more.

The point here is to clarify the macroeconomic repercussions of the Vietnam War. If society demands tanks and guns for the purpose of making war, it must be willing to reduce the demand for new homes, new buildings, and other new capital goods if inflation is to be avoided. If taxes had been increased to match the higher level of government expenditure, the inflation we experienced might not have occurred. The war, however, was deficit-financed.

Had the Fed taken action to prevent the onset of an inflationary episode, the new position of macroeconomic equilibrium would have been point B in part (a) of figure 11.1 with price level P(0) as shown in part (b) of figure 11.1. Therefore, aggregate expenditure on goods and services would have reflected more government goods and fewer private investment goods. This is somewhat similar to what would have happened had taxes been raised to pay for the war. (Can you explain how the composition of expenditure on GNP would have been different if taxes had been raised compared to what it would have been had the Fed engaged in contractionary monetary policy?)

Table 11.4 Money supply and commercial banks' reserves, December 1965 to December 1966[a]

Time period	Money supply	Banks' reserves
December 1965	$172	$22.7
January–September 1966	168	22.5
October–December 1966	173	23.4

Source: From *Economic Report of the President, 1968.*

[a]In billions of dollars.

Table 11.6 Housing starts and the consumer price index for 1965–1967

Year	Housing starts	CPI[a]
1965	1.5 million	75.4
1966	1.2 million	77.6
1967	1.3 million	79.8

Source: From *Economic Report of the President, 1968 and 1983.*

[a]1972 = 100.

Table 11.5 Yield on corporate bonds from December 1965 to March 1967

Time period	Yield
December 1965	4.68%
January–March 1966	4.81
April–June 1966	5.00
July–September 1966	5.32
October–December 1966	5.38
January–March 1967	5.08

Source: From *Economic Report of the President, 1968.*

Monetary Policy in 1965 and 1966

Table 11.4 shows that from January to September 1966, the Fed pursued a policy of restricting the reserves of the banking system. Along with the contraction in the banks' reserves, the United States money supply declined over the same period. A direct consequence of the Fed's policy was an increase in the rate of interest. Table 11.5 shows that the yield (the implicit interest rate paid to lenders) on corporate bonds rose from 4.81 percent at the beginning of 1966 to 5.32 percent during July through September of 1966. The higher interest rate caused investors to move up along the demand curve for investment goods. This means that the supply of loanable funds in part (a) of figure 11.1 was beginning to shift to the left and move the economy toward point B. As table 11.6 suggests, the resulting reduction in investment expenditures narrowed the gap between demand and supply in the private goods market so that the consumer price index rose by nearly 3 percent over the course of 1966.

The Reversal of the Fed's Monetary Policy

The investors principally affected by the Fed's contractionary monetary policy were in the housing industry. In table 11.6, we can see that new housing starts fell by approximately *20 percent* between 1965 and 1966. This decline prompted both private citizens and government officials to complain about the high costs that the Fed's contractionary monetary policy imposed on the housing industry. However, as macroeconomic analysis indicates, the decline simply reflected the basic problem of scarcity. The economy was unable to produce more war goods without producing fewer goods of other types, such as housing. When the government demands more war goods, some people must lose out in the competitive struggle for the limited amount of full-employment production. In this instance, the housing industry was the principal loser.

In response to the outcry against its policy and fearing congressional investigation, the Fed decided to reverse its stand and pursue an *expansionary* monetary policy in late 1966. Table 11.4 shows us that increases in the reserves of the banking system and the United States money supply occurred from October to December 1966. Perhaps the Fed hoped, along with everyone else, that the problem of scarcity would suddenly disappear. It did not.

The Effects of the Fed's Expansionary Monetary Policy

As more reserves were created for the banking system, the market supply of loanable funds in figure 11.1, part (a), actually shifted *rightward* from SLF, instead of *leftward,* toward full equilibrium. Notice in table 28.5 that the yield on corporate bonds *declined* from a peak of 5.38 percent in October–December 1966 to 5.08 percent in the January–March period of 1967.

As far as the goods market was concerned, the Fed's expansionary monetary policy led to a larger amount of planned investment and thereby created an even larger excess of aggregate demand in the markets for goods and services. With investors placing more orders for goods and nobody curtailing demand in the private sector, firms found their sales growing by leaps and bounds. (As table 11.6 shows, the number of new housing starts rose in 1967 as compared to 1966.) Inventories fell drastically, and producers began to raise the prices of goods at faster rates. Of course, they attempted to acquire more factors of production, but since the economy was at a position of full employment, the price of resources—such as labor—also began to climb. Under the stimulus of the Fed's expansionary monetary policy, the United States economy in the mid-1960s entered a period during which the prices of its goods and services *continued* to rise at a rapid rate. In the next section we analyze the economy's behavior during the inflationary period of the late 1960s and 1970s.

Stagflation: The United States Economy in the 1970s and early 1980s

Under the impetus of the deficit-financed Vietnam War, the Fed instituted highly expansionary monetary policies. During 1967 and 1968 it permitted the nation's money supply to grow much faster than the economy's capacity to produce goods and services. As we have seen, if the money supply grows faster than is consistent with full macroeconomic equilibrium, an inflationary episode is inevitable. If the Fed continues to increase the ability of the banking system to create new money balances faster than they can be spent on output, when there already is full employment, the price level will continue to rise. A continuing increase in the price level is, of course, a full-blown inflation. The inflation will not stop until the Fed slows down money supply growth to a rate consistent with equilibrium in the goods market.

Money Growth, Inflation, and Unemployment

In the decade prior to 1965, real GNP grew at a rate of about 3.5 percent per year. The annual rate of growth of the money supply as measured by M2 was 4.5 percent, and the average annual rate of increase in the price level—the rate of inflation—was 2.0 percent, relatively low by standards of the 1970s and 1980s. There is no reason to believe that the productive capacity of the United States was growing more rapidly after 1965 than before. Therefore, a significant increase in the growth of the money supply was very likely to result in an increase in the rate of inflation. Between 1965 and 1980, the annual growth rate of M2 was about twice as high—8.9 percent—as it was during the period between 1955 and 1965. The rate of inflation rose dramatically to an average of 6 percent per year over the fifteen years between 1965 and 1980. The average annual growth of M2, annual inflation, and the average annual rate of unemployment from 1965 to 1982 are all shown in figure 11.2.

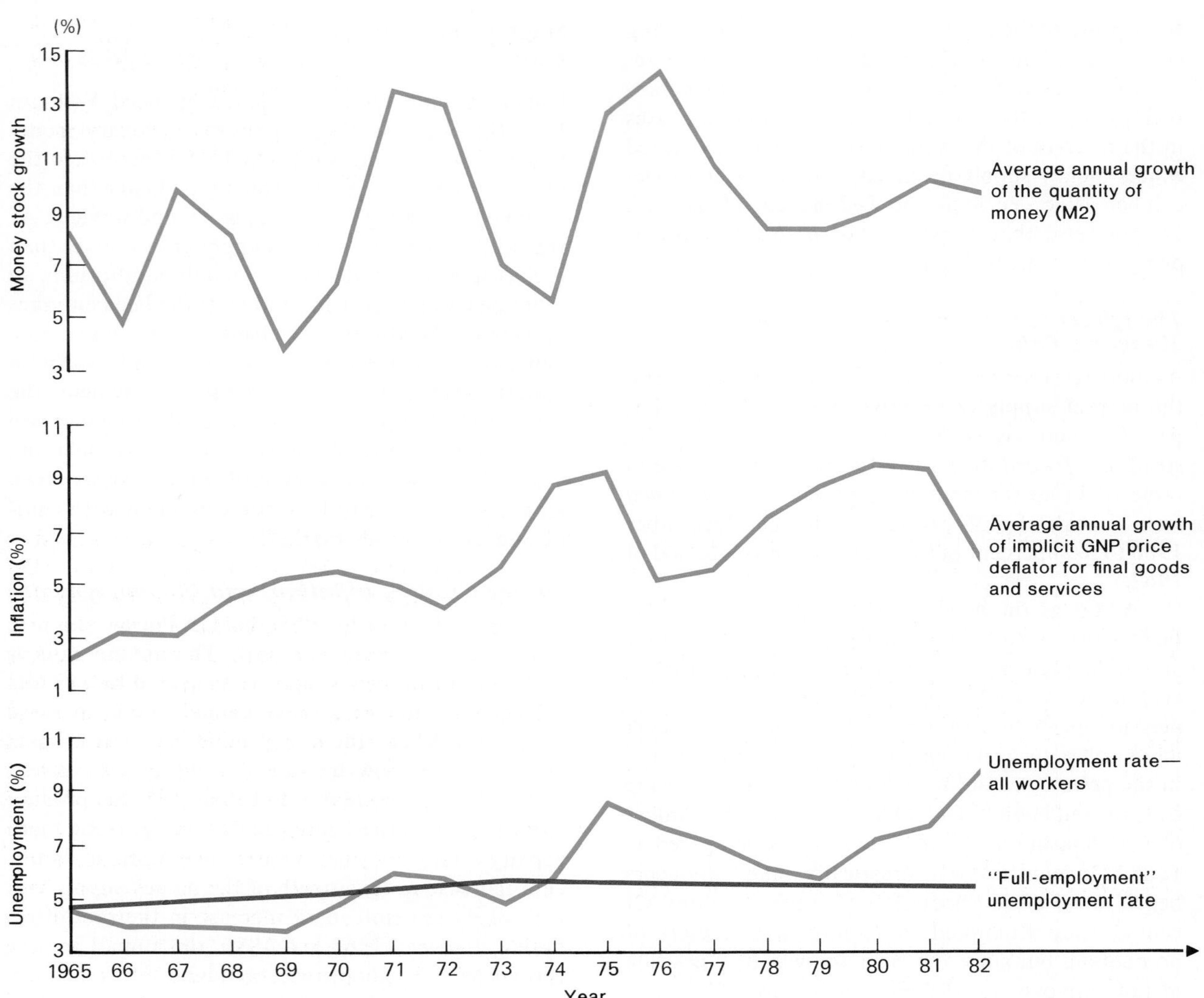

Figure 11.2 Money growth, inflation, and unemployment, 1965–1982
A high rate of monetary growth *temporarily* lowered unemployment while creating inflation. Source: *Economic Report of the President, 1983* and Michael L. Wachter, Personal Communication.

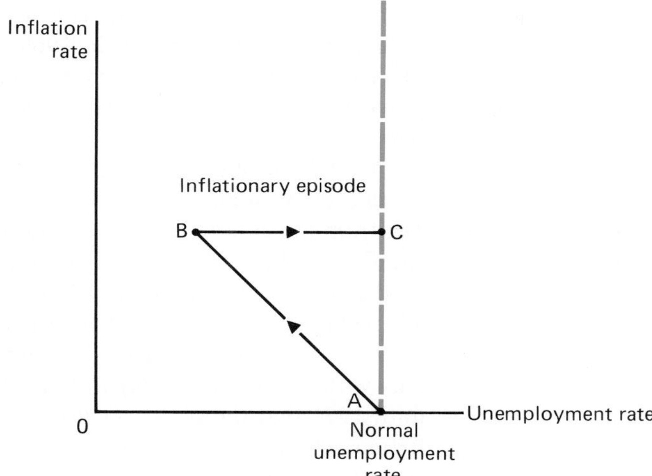

Figure 11.3 The short-run and long-run relationships between the inflation and unemployment rates: A period of inflation
When workers and firms come to expect inflation as the usual state of affairs, the unemployment rate returns to its normal level.

As our model of the macroeconomy predicts, the inflation caused by increased planned aggregate expenditure led to a *short-run* reduction in unemployment. In the late 1960s the unemployment rate was consistently *less* than the normal, or "full-employment" unemployment rate, which is also depicted in figure 11.2. The typical short-run and long-run behavior of the unemployment rate during an inflationary episode is summarized in figure 11.3. During the initial stages of an inflationary episode, unemployment falls to a level below the normal unemployment rate. However, workers eventually realize that an increase in the price level has reduced the real wage rate to a level below what they thought they were earning. As a result, unemployed workers take extra time to find jobs with acceptable wages. The outcome of these two events is that the unemployment rate eventually returns to its normal level as people become accustomed to inflation. In terms of the labor market and aggregate market for goods and services, as their expected real wage declines, workers move back along the aggregate labor supply curve. The economy's short-run aggregate supply curve begins to shift upward. As it crosses the aggregate demand curve at a higher price level, GNP begins to fall, paralleling the decline in the quantity of labor supplied.

This scenario begins with people accustomed to little or no inflation. As a result, they view an inflationary episode as unusual. In a period such as that beginning in 1965, however, business firms, workers, and consumers soon learn that a stable price level can no longer be expected. They then adjust their expectations to try to anticipate inflation in the future. Not to do so would result in economic losses to workers who commit themselves to work for money wages that buy less than expected and in losses to firms who fail to adjust the wages they pay and the prices they charge to the higher price level tomorrow is expected to bring.

In general, consumers, workers, and firms all have a strong incentive to learn from their past mistakes and forecast future events more accurately. They can do this by using available information to develop correct anticipations of the future course of inflation and other economic variables. In chapter 9 we pointed out that the idea that businesses and households do not waste information—that in their self-interest they use available information to correctly forecast the outcomes of economic events and government policy—is called the *theory of rational expectations.*

What does the theory of rational expectations imply concerning an inflationary episode that does not end itself because the Fed permits the money supply to grow at an inflationary rate over a prolonged period? It says that while inflation may *initially* be accompanied by a reduction in unemployment, if the inflation persists, unemployment will start to return to its normal level *without* a decline in inflation. Thus, in figure 11.3, the economy first moves from point A to point B and then to point C during an inflationary episode. The end result is inflation with no permanent reduction in the unemployment rate. Why? The answer was given in our analysis of labor markets in chapter 3. Specifically, the normal unemployment rate is a *real* phenomenon. As such, it can only be affected by policies and events that change the basic structure of labor markets. However, in the long run it will *not* be influenced by a general change in an economy wide *nominal* variable such as the aggregate price level. The upward adjustment of unemployment when inflation becomes the norm is illustrated by unemployment rate data for the United States in figure 11.2.

Periodically, the Fed temporarily decided to reverse its policy of "easy money." This further complicated the behavior of unemployment. The first sharp contraction in monetary growth after 1966 occurred in 1969. In that year the Fed decided to reverse its easy money policy by reducing the annual rate of growth of the money supply to 3.8 percent.

Our macroeconomic model predicts that such a rapid switch in monetary policy will lead to a recession. Why? Although a 3.8 percent annual growth rate of the money supply would have been the norm in the early 1960s, by 1969 the public had become accustomed to inflation and adjusted its behavior accordingly. Thus, slowing down the rate of the growth of money from 8 or 9 percent to only 3.8 percent had a macroeconomic impact similar to *reducing* the quantity of money (a negative growth rate) in the earlier period.

In terms of our macromodel, a contractionary monetary policy reduces the availability of loanable funds and shifts the supply curve of loanable funds (SLF) leftward. This reduction in the supply of loanable funds raises the interest rate and leads to reduced aggregate demand for goods and services and to increased unemployment. As a result of the Fed's reduction of money growth in 1969, the unemployment rate began to rise. Such an increase in unemployment is shown in figure 11.4 as a movement from point C toward point D.

In 1970 the unemployment rate averaged 1.5 percentage points higher than in 1969—4.9 percent. Notice from the data in figure 11.2, however, that while the Fed's policy slowed inflation, it did not immediately halt it. In fact, for all of 1970 inflation averaged a little higher than in 1969. Because inflation had become a way of life, the Fed's 1969 actions took effect only with a considerable *lag in time*. Thus, it was not until 1971 that the twelve-month average rate of inflation actually declined. (If we were to examine the *monthly* rate of inflation during 1970, however, we would notice that the growth of prices began to slow down before the end of the year.)

In 1971, the unemployment rate continued to rise. This rise in unemployment is consistent with our generalizations concerning the short-run and long-run relationships between inflation and unemployment. In the short run, it takes time for firms, workers, and consumers to "unlearn" their inflationary anticipations. As *actual* inflation declines, the *expected* rate of inflation does not fall immediately. Consequently, unemployment rises above its full-employment, or normal, level. If the Fed were to *persist* in restraining inflation, then the public would eventually revise its expections about the future, and the unemployment rate would eventually return to normal (from point D to point E in figure 11.4).

Two other influences on unemployment in the 1970s contributed to the simultaneous appearance of inflation and higher unemployment, which is labeled *stagflation*. One of them was not generally recognized at the time. As figure 11.2 shows, the normal or full-employment rate of unemployment had risen by about 0.7 percentage points since 1965. This was due primarily to the rapidly increasing fraction of young workers in the labor force. Thus, while the 5.9 percent average annual unemployment rate in 1971 was sharply higher than the previous year's rate, it was not much higher than the level to which the normal unemployment rate had grown.

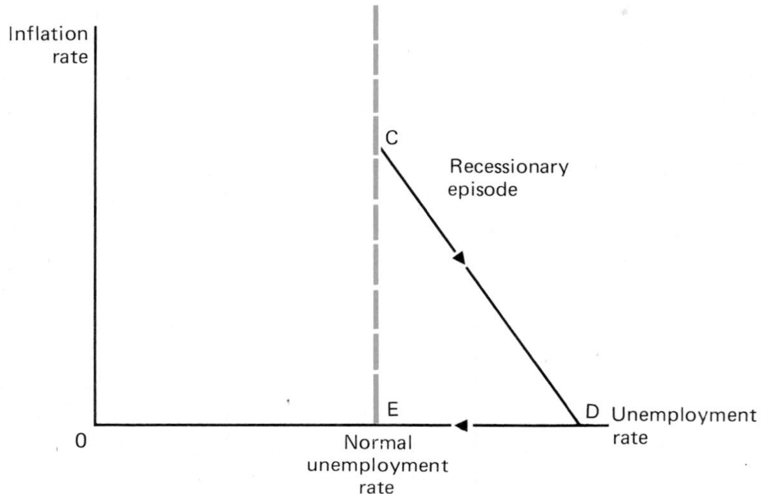

Figure 11.4 The short-run and long-run relationships between the inflation and unemployment rates: A recession following an inflationary episode
When workers and firms come to realize that inflation has ended and expect a stable price level, the unemployment rate returns to its normal level.

In the minds of many people, the appearance of stagflation seemed to contradict the basic laws of economics. This misunderstanding about the events unfolding in the economy during a period of simultaneously *decelerating* inflation and rising normal unemployment led to the establishment of a price control program in the summer of 1971. During that year, the rate of inflation declined to 4.1 percent. This slowing trend has sometimes been viewed as "proof" of the success of price controls in reducing the rate of inflation. The data indicate, however, that a substantial reduction in the inflation rate had occurred *prior* to the introduction of price controls in the summer of 1971. Price controls *appeared* to work because the economy was *already* approaching a position of macroeconomic equilibrium, with inflation proceeding at a more moderate rate. As figure 11.2 shows us, the average growth rate of the money supply from 1969 to 1971 was only about 5 percent, which was lower than any year since 1966. Notice also that the unemployment rate hit a peak of 5.9 percent in 1971 and then in 1972 declined to 5.6 percent, equal to its full-employment level.

In 1971, the Fed again sharply reversed its monetary policy, apparently "protected" from the evidence of its inflationary actions by the camouflage of price controls. As figure 11.2 shows, the money supply grew at the extremely high annual rate of 13.5 percent in 1971 and 13.0 percent in 1972, more than double the average growth rate of the previous two years. On the basis of high money supply growth rates, sharply increasing inflation in 1973, 1974, and 1975 should not have been surprising. The Fed's policy was predictably inflationary. Why did the Fed accelerate money growth in 1971 and 1972? Some observers have argued that Fed policy had become politicized. Arthur Burns, then chairman of the Fed, was a close friend of President Nixon. Expansionary monetary policy in 1971 and 1972 would assure that the president would be running for reelection without having to worry about a recession.

The Fed sharply reduced the growth rate of the money supply in 1973 and 1974, producing a recessionary trend similar to that which developed in 1969 after a contraction in the money supply growth rate. In 1975, the United States unemployment rate exceeded 8 percent. Inflation, however, persisted at a high rate well into the recession for reasons we have already discussed. It appeared to many that stagflation had become characteristic of the United States economy.

To be fair, we must mention the second factor other than monetary policy that may have contributed to stagflation in the United States in the mid-1970s and later. In 1973 and 1974, the Organization of Petroleum Exporting Countries (OPEC) sharply increased its power over world oil markets, and the price of imported oil in the United States began to rise sharply. The effect of OPEC on the United States economy is illustrated in figure 11.5.

Because of OPEC's actions, the United States had to make costly adjustments to use less oil and products made with oil. These adjustments required resources that had previously been used to produce other goods and services. This had an affect on full-employment GNP similar to what would have happened if we had suddenly lost some of our own capacity to produce petroleum. That is, the long-run aggregate supply curve shifted to the left. As figure 11.5 shows, the result of a leftward shift in the long-run aggregate supply curve is to lower GNP and raise the price level. In the aggregate labor market, unemployment increases, just as if the economy has entered a recession.

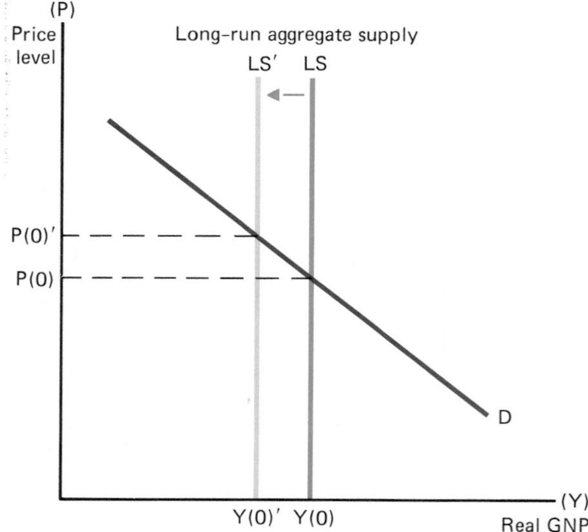

Figure 11.5 The effect of OPEC on aggregate supply and stagflation in the United States
OPEC's success in raising world oil prices had an effect on the United States similar to a leftward shift in the long-run aggregate supply curve. This contributed to stagflation by reducing GNP and raising unemployment and the price level.

Economists disagree on the extent to which the increase in world oil prices contributed to stagflation in the United States. One fact that leads many economists to believe that its overall impact on inflation and unemployment was minor is the experience of other nations that import a much larger share of their petroleum than the United States does. In most Western European nations and in Japan, for example, stagflation was not the severe problem that the United States experienced. However, it is probably fair to conclude that events in the world oil market contributed to, if they did not dominate, the rising prices and high unemployment experienced during the middle to late 1970s in the United States.

As figure 11.2 illustrates, the monetary authority did not mend its ways after the recession of 1975. The cycle of high and accelerating monetary growth followed by "jamming on the brakes" continued. During the latter part of the Carter administration and the early years of the Reagan administration, the Fed sharply curtailed monetary growth compared to its peak in 1976. The first result was an increase in the unemployment rate. In 1982, unemployment reached 10.8 percent, a level that was the highest of any period since the Great Depression. The second, later, result was a decline in the rate of inflation. By late 1982, inflation had been reduced dramatically.

Unfortunately, during 1982 and more so in 1983, the Fed claimed that its ability to determine the "correct" rate of monetary growth was harmed by the decontrol of the banking system (described in chapter 6). Whether banking deregulation actually did this by altering the quantity of money the public desired to hold remains a hotly debated issue. What is certain, however, is that the rate of growth of M1 and M2 sharply *increased* during 1983. Many economists

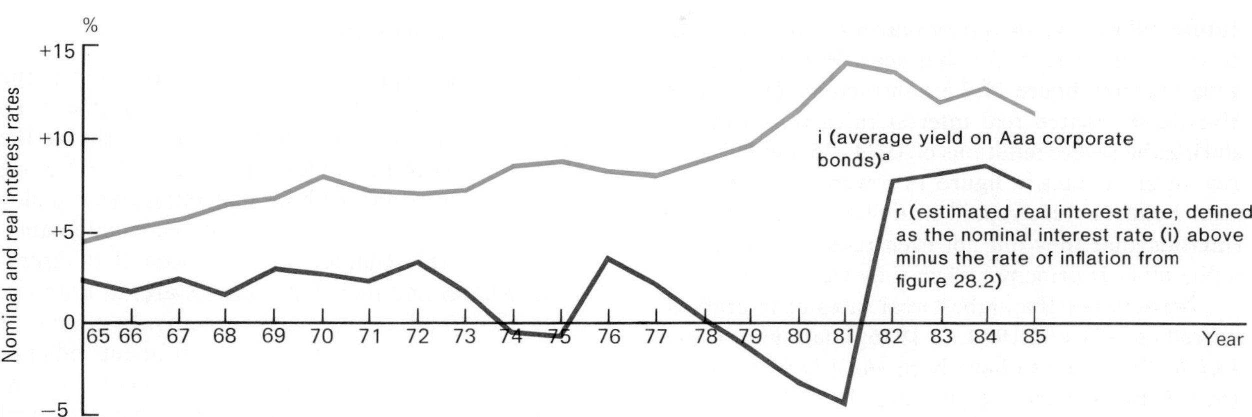

Figure 11.6 The real and nominal rates of interest in the United States, 1965–1985
From *Economic Report of the President,* 1983, 1986, B-59, p. 320 and B-68, p. 332.

and policymakers were very worried that this increase in the growth of the money supply would lead to a resurgence of inflation in 1984 and beyond if it were not curtailed.

It is interesting that inflation did *not* regain its force in 1984 and 1985, as many economists had predicted. The reasons are as yet unclear. One explanation is that the drastic weakening of OPEC and the resulting decline in world oil prices had the reverse effect of the increase of the 1970s. As we noted earlier, the inflation of the 1970s cannot be blamed entirely on OPEC, and not all oil-importing nations experienced the same degree of inflation that the United States did. Perhaps the United States inflation resulted in part from validation of cost-push inflation due to oil price increases, while other nations, such as Japan and Germany, refused to validate such cost-push inflation. It is not unlikely that oil price declines did help slow down inflation in the United States. That is, a rightward shift of the aggregate supply curve may have permitted a monetary growth rate in the United States that would have been more inflationary under "normal" circumstances.

Money Growth, Inflation, and the Interest Rate

As we emphasized in chapter 7, the interest rate that represents the cost of loanable funds to borrowers and the return to lenders is the *real* rate of interest. The real rate of interest is defined as the *nominal,* or market, rate of interest minus the expected rate of inflation. Remember, lenders and borrowers determine the value of loan contracts they wish to offer and purchase, respectively, on the basis of their *expected* rate of inflation. Thus, during a period in which inflation turns out to be greater than expected, lenders turn out to be losers. Once inflation is correctly anticipated, however, loan contracts will be negotiated to reflect fully the inflationary conditions that have prevailed in the recent past and that are expected to continue in the future.

In figure 11.6, the average interest rate on high-grade (low risk of default) corporate bonds in each year from 1965 through 1985 is labeled i. The period is characterized by a gradually rising trend through 1982. We can calculate an *estimate* of the real interest rate by assuming that the public's forecast of future inflation in any given year was equal to the actual rate of inflation for that year. When the rate of inflation from figure 11.2 is subtracted from i, we derive the estimated real interest rates (r). Note that during the severe inflations of 1974–75 and 1979–81, real interest rates in figure 11.6 were actually negative. Lenders were repaid in dollars so devalued by inflation that they did not even receive the full real value of their principal when they were paid back.

Notice that the highest real rates of interest occurred in 1976 and 1984. In 1976 inflationary *expectations* are likely to have been *sharply* increased by the inflation experienced in 1975. In 1984 the public was still forming expectations based on the inflationary experience of the late 1970s and early 1980s. Moreover, lenders who had recently been badly hurt by their underestimate of future inflation were less likely to lend at accustomed interest rates. In 1984, the real interest rate averaged 12.7 percent, one of the highest ever experienced in the economic history of the United States.

Phenomenally high real interest rates helped contribute to the unusually severe recession starting in 1982. This illustrates the heavy cost of the uncertainty created by the "jump on the gas, jam on the brakes" macroeconomic policies (especially monetary policy) in the United States during the period beginning in 1965. It is also important to point out that in addition to the effects of inflationary anticipations, high real interest rates may have also stemmed from the federal deficit. As discussed in chapter 10, our macroeconomic model indicates that an increase in the deficit, other factors unchanging, will probably raise the rate of interest.

▸ Summary and Conclusions

Will you ever experience as severe a recession as the Great Depression? Will you or your children ever go through an inflationary period as severe as that of the United States in the middle and late 1970s? No one can say for sure, although we understand what policy tools can prevent such unfortunate economic catastrophes. In this chapter we have seen that discretionary fiscal and monetary policies are, in practice, quite able to affect the macroeconomy. In pursuit of macroeconomic stabilization, government officials often make mistakes. These errors, especially in monetary policy, are made by people who are constrained both by political realities and by incomplete information about the complicated events that occur in an economy as large as that of the United States. *Theoretically,* monetary and fiscal policies can exert a *stabilizing* influence on the economy. Given our present state of knowledge about the macroeconomy, however, an important question that will continue to be debated is: Should society allow monetary and fiscal authorities to use these powers at their discretion as they see fit? The following main points were emphasized in this chapter.

Expansionary or restrictive monetary and fiscal policies can in practice have powerful effects on macroeconomic activity.

Incorrect discretionary monetary policy contributed to the Great Depression of the 1930s.

Discretionary fiscal policy had little effect on the Great Depression.

Monetary policy has been largely responsible for the great inflation that began in 1965.

The real interest rate has been quite high in recent years as lenders' expectations of inflation have fallen less rapidly than the actual rate of inflation.

▸ Questions for Discussion and Review

1. Are the following statements true, false, or uncertain? Defend your answers.
   a. The Great Depression was exacerbated by monetary policy.
   b. The Great Depression was exacerbated by fiscal policy.
   c. The great inflation was exacerbated by monetary policy.
   d. The great inflation was exacerbated by fiscal policy.
2. List four years during which the United States economy experienced high cyclical unemployment and four years during which the United States economy experienced rapid inflation. In which years, if any, did the economy experience both high unemployment and rapid inflation? Explain the macroeconomic causes of rapid inflation and high unemployment in these years. What type of monetary and fiscal policies could have reduced inflation and unemployment then?
3. Read chapter 1 of *The Economic Report of the President, 1983*. On the basis of this discussion, write a one-page essay on whether or not the recession of 1981–82 was "necessary." Be sure to include in your essay some mention of what caused the recession.
4. Society dislikes both inflation and unemployment. Concerning the long-term relationship between inflation and unemployment, what is society's optimal (preferred) combination of inflation and unemployment in the long term? Explain and support your answer graphically.
5. Write a three-page paper discussing whether or not the great inflation has ended.
6. During 1983 the interest rate on *three-month* Treasury securities averaged about 8 to 9 percent (on an annual basis). During the same period the inflation rate averaged 3 to 4 percent (on an annual basis). Were real interest rates low or high on the basis of historical experience? Explain. If high, why do you think they were?

Chapter 12

Summing Up

Macroeconomic Controversies

Outline

Objectives

After reading this chapter, the student should be able to:

Discuss how monetarists and Keynesians disagree on monetary and fiscal policies and their effectiveness in stabilizing the macroeconomy.

Explain the recession of the early 1980s and the continued high interest rates from both the monetarists' and the Keynesians' point of view.

Describe the supply-siders' view of the macroeconomy.

Discuss the history of the government deficit and reasons for its recent surge.

Compare the recent United States debt experience with that of other industrialized nations.

Discuss the economic significance of the budget deficit (including long-term crowding out).

Introduction

When President Kennedy submitted his budget proposal to Congress for 1962, he and his political advisers were concerned about how the public would react to a federal budget in excess of $100 billion. The federal deficit that year was $4.2 billion. By 1974 federal expenditure had more than tripled to $356.6 billion, and the deficit of $69.36 billion was the largest this country had ever experienced. President Carter made a point of running against big government in 1976 and promised to balance the budget in 1980. The 1980 levels of federal government expenditures and deficit were $602.1 billion and $61.2 billion, respectively. Ronald Reagan promised to rein in big government and eliminate the deficit by 1984. Expenditures increased 46 percent to $879.9 billion in 1984, and the deficit nearly tripled to $176.4 billion. In the 1984 presidential campaign, Walter Mondale accused President Reagan of mortgaging the future of the nation by running high deficits.

We will return to a discussion of presidential campaigns and economic issues in the latter part of this chapter. However, this brief sketch of the politics of big federal budgets and deficits suggests several questions we will want to address. Are federal deficits bad for the economy, and if so, how do they hurt overall economic performance in the United States or other countries? If the federal deficit were to suddenly double relative to GNP, would we be twice as badly off? Why has it become so common for presidential contenders to promise to balance the federal budget and then fail to do so when they are elected? Is it really possible to mortgage the country's future?

Areas of Agreement and Disagreement among Economists

The United States economy has experienced wide fluctuations in unemployment and inflation. Matching the wide swings in economic performance, there is also wide disagreement among economists, politicians, and informed members of the public regarding the best course for macroeconomic policy to follow.[1] Before discussing and evaluating these controversies, however, we should emphasize that among the overwhelming majority of professional academic economists, there is a broad area of agreement on economic policy that we do not usually read about in the newspapers or see and hear on the television and radio.

In the *U.S. News & World Report* article in reference 1, you will find disagreement about such issues as the proper timing of monetary or fiscal policies and the degree to which our knowledge of the economic system, recognition and legislative lags, and political considerations permit effective "fine-tuning" of macroeconomic variables. These are factual issues about which opinions can change as knowledge and experience increase. Despite these differences in opinion—which are very strongly and emotionally held in many cases—there is also much common ground. For example, there is virtually unanimous agreement that the inflation we experienced after 1965 would not, and could not, have occurred without excessive money supply growth. Furthermore, there is no doubt expressed that over the long run, increases in our standard of living can result only from expansion of available resources or increases in productivity. What sparks disagreement are questions of *how* monetary control is to be implemented and *which* actions are most likely to promote productivity growth.

Monetarists and Keynesians are economists who hold different sets of views on monetary and fiscal policies.

Controversies over Short-run Macroeconomic Policy: Is Fine-tuning Practical?

Among professional economists, probably the most significant debate is over the possibility of fine-tuning macroeconomic policy in the short run by "twirling the knobs" of monetary and fiscal policy to assure a stable price level, full employment, and real output growth consistent with the economy's productive capacity. To a large extent these controversies have involved a division between the so-called **monetarists and Keynesians,** who are economists with different views about appropriate short-run macropolicy. The latter group takes its name from the famous economist John Maynard Keynes, whose publications in the 1930s revolutionized our understanding of macroeconomic relationships. (It is not at all clear that Keynes, were he still alive, would be a "Keynesian." However, we will use the terms *Keynesian* and *monetarist* because they represent useful distinctions today.)[2]

Monetarism and Keynesianism

There is no way to describe all of the differences between monetarism and Keynesianism in a brief space. Moreover, it would probably be impossible to differentiate the two groups in such a way that some members of each would not strongly disagree with our description of their beliefs. Therefore, our description of the monetarist versus Keynesian debate can only capture its major features.

The most distinctive principle of monetarism is probably that the money stock (M) and changes in the money supply (ΔM) are thought to be the most important variables influencing short-run fluctuations in the price level, output, and employment. The economist whose research and policy recommendations are most closely tied to the precepts of monetarism is Milton Friedman, who received the Nobel Prize in economic science in 1976.

Keynesians do not deny the importance of money's influence on macroeconomic performance. However, they differ—often markedly—from monetarists in their view of the way in which money affects the economy and, hence, on appropriate short-run policy. Keynesians represent a considerably broader spectrum of beliefs and policy recommendations than monetarists. Therefore, it is more difficult to name a typical Keynesian than a typical monetarist. Two prominent Keynesians, both of whom have also won Nobel Prizes, are Paul Samuelson (in 1970) and James Tobin (in 1981). Keynesians, as reflected in these two economists' policy recommendations, emphasize that the rate of interest is at least as important a guide to macroeconomic policy as the money stock or its rate of growth.

▸ Different Views of How the Economy Works

Keynesian and Monetarist Views about How Monetary Policy Affects the Economy

If one reviews textbook presentations of the Keynesian model, it is clear that monetary policy is viewed as primarily affecting the credit market. Expansion or contraction of the money supply shifts the supply of loanable funds to the right, lowers the real interest rate, and stimulates investment as investors move down the demand for loanable funds schedule in response to lower interest rates. If one believes that the real impact of monetary policy on the economy is through its impact on the real interest rate, then it is tempting to choose the interest rate as an appropriate target of monetary policy. Using the interest rate as a target can form the basis for one's judgment that monetary policy is "right" or "wrong." Generally, Keynesians judge monetary policy as too tight if interest rates seem high relative to where they would be at full macroeconomic equilibrium. For example, much of their pessimism about the economic recovery of 1983 and 1984 centered around the Keynesian notion that interest rates were too high and that tight monetary policy would choke off the recovery.

Monetarists disagree with Keynesians on both practical and theoretical grounds. As a practical matter, monetarists believe that we lack the detailed information that is needed to say, in the short run, whether a given interest rate is "too high," indicating excessive monetary restraint, or "too low," indicating an overly expansionary monetary policy. On theoretical grounds, they have an alternative explanation of the high interest rates that prevailed in 1983 and 1984 that is based on their view of the roles of money and inflationary expectations in the macroeconomy.

Basically, monetarists believe that monetary policy is neutral in the long run with respect to real economic changes. That is, they emphasize that full-employment GNP is determined by "real" events as opposed to monetary events. However, monetarists believe that monetary policy is unambiguously the basis for explaining the price level and inflation.

There is another, subtle distinction between monetarists and Keynesians that we have ignored until now in developing the macroeconomic model used in this text. While monetarists accept the impact of monetary policy in the credit market, they tend to believe that changes in the quantity of money also have a *direct* impact on consumption and investment spending. This direct impact does not depend upon, say, an expansionary monetary policy pushing down the interest rate. Rather, it acts *directly* to expand investment and consumption expenditures because with more money to spend, people tend to expand their purchases of all kinds of goods and services. An illustration of the possible direct impact of monetary policy is that an increase in the quantity of money may lead directly to expanded demand for both consumption and investment goods. This increase in expenditure may not, in other words, depend on a decline in the interest rate leading to greater incentives to purchase investment goods. If monetary policy affects expenditures directly, as well as through the interest rate, then the Keynesian view that the interest rate can tell us about the state of monetary policy may be incorrect.

Monetarists conclude that monetary expansion will promote recovery from a recession or, if the economy is at full employment, result in inflation. Monetary contraction (or too slow a rate of monetary growth) will depress aggregate demand and cause or worsen a recession if the economy is at or below full macroeconomic equilibrium. However, the current rate of interest is unlikely to convey much information about the impact of current monetary policy on GNP, employment, or the price level.

Monetarist and Keynesian Explanations for the Recession of the Early 1980s and Continued High Interest Rates through 1985

Monetarists explain the recession of 1981–82 as the result of too abrupt a reduction of the rate of monetary growth. They believe the expansion of the money supply during 1983–84 was in the right direction but too erratic. That is, the average rate of growth was acceptable over the period, but at times it was much too high and at other times, too low. Monetarists explain the relatively high real interest rates of 1983–85 as resulting from the continued persistence in the public's expectations that inflation would accelerate in the near future. From the monetarist standpoint, the federal deficit represented a problem only because the public anticipated that sooner or later the Fed would increase the money supply—monetizing the debt—in a vain effort to reduce interest rates. Then the monetarists held that although interest rates would not fall, the rate of inflation would increase.

To monetarists, then, the continuation of high real interest rates in 1984 and 1985 can be explained by the public's expectations that the rate of inflation would soon increase from 4 percent to about 7 percent. This was the average annual rate of inflation experienced from 1967 to 1981.

Keynesians view the recession of 1981–82 as primarily caused by the rapid run-up in oil prices in late 1979 and early 1980 in conjunction with the continued decline in the United States steel and automobile industries. Monetary policy contributed to the

*A **target of monetary policy** is the variable(s), such as the rate of monetary growth or the rate of interest, that monetary policy attempts to influence for the purpose of smoothing out business cycles.*

severity of the recession in their view by shifting the supply of loanable funds to the left, raising interest rates, and choking off investment demand for loanable funds.

A simple Keynesian explanation for continued high interest rates during the expansion of 1983–85 is that monetary policy was too tight. The rightward shift in the supply of loanable funds associated with expansion of the money supply was not rapid enough to offset the upward drift in interest rates associated with large federal deficits and the consequent rightward shift in the demand for loanable funds. From the Keynesian standpoint, the deficit represented a problem only because, in the presence of a relatively tight monetary policy, it kept interest rates high and discouraged private investment demand. A decline in private investment would tend to reduce the long-term growth potential of the economy. We will return to this point later in this chapter.

Keynesian and Monetarist Differences of Opinion about the Need to Try to Control the Macroeconomy and the Ability to Do So

Notice that both Keynesians and monetarists are very concerned with monetary policy. They differ intensely, however, over the appropriate **target of monetary policy,** which is the principal variable guiding the Fed's monetary policy decisions. The sources of this difference include scientific judgments about whether we possess the knowledge and ability to know what the appropriate interest rate target to shoot at is at any moment and whether it would be technically and politically possible to hit such a target if we knew what it was. The disagreements between monetarists and Keynesians probably also involve a difference in their tastes for government intervention in the economy. Generally, monetarists prefer to avoid government intervention and believe that we lack the knowledge to fine-tune such variables as interest rates in any event. Keynesians are less worried about the political and moral implications of government involvement in the economy and argue that we can control variables such as interest rates in order to improve macroeconomic performance.

This difference in approach is also related to fundamental difference in views these two groups have about how the economy works. The Keynesian presumption is that business cycles are basically due to "real" (nonmonetary) disturbances and are inherent in market economies. They are the result of imperfections in the linkages among the aggregate goods, credit, and labor markets in market economies as well as sluggish adjustments to change within these markets. The Keynesian remedy is the judicious application of fiscal policy to bolster aggregate demand when it is too low to sustain full employment and to restrain aggregate demand when it is too great to maintain full employment without accelerating inflation. Without such intervention, Keynesians believe, market economies will break down periodically. Fiscal policy is viewed as the instrument of choice to keep the economy on a smooth growth path. The traditional Keynesian perspective is that monetary policy affects the real economy only indirectly through credit markets and is therefore less predictable and effective than fiscal policy in controlling aggregate supply and demand.

The monetarist perspective is that discretionary monetary and fiscal policies both tend to accentuate rather than dampen business cycles. The presumption is that aggregate demand and supply shifts tend to be self-correcting and short-lived. Many monetarists bolster their pessimistic view of discretionary countercyclical policies by arguing that much of their impact on aggregate production and employment occurs only when the public is fooled into taking actions that it would not take if it had complete knowledge about the policies' timing and effects. They go on to argue that the public quickly learns what the effects of policies will be and adjusts accordingly. For example, an increase in the quantity of money during a period of nearly full employment may be targeted on the interest rate. However, if the public believes that inflation will result, interest rates will remain high. As noted in chapter 9, this idea—that the public cannot be repeatedly fooled by macroeconomic events—is called the theory of rational expectations. According to this theory, making the money supply grow faster would not reduce the rate of interest; rather, it would be more likely to raise it.

Monetarists believe that efforts to eliminate aggregate economic fluctuations with discretionary monetary and/or fiscal policies almost invariably make matters worse because of the timing problems (lags) we discussed in chapter 10. Since the obstacles to discretionary fiscal policy actions are greater than the obstacles to discretionary monetary policy, monetarists prefer discretionary monetary policy, if they must choose one or the other. However, the preferred position for monetarists would be to have a fixed money growth rate, beyond the discretion of the monetary authority, and no discretionary fiscal policy.

The distinction between Keynesians and monetarists regarding the proper size and role of government in the economy is directly related to their differences in perspectives about the primary causes of aggregate economic fluctuations. Keynesians view the aggregate economy as inherently prone to severe and perhaps prolonged fluctuations that necessitate discretionary intervention by the federal government. Monetarists view the aggregate economy as subject to moderate and short-term fluctuations and as inherently stable. Essentially, monetarists place their faith in the public's ability to anticipate the future course of prices quickly enough so that adjustment to full macroequilibrium will not be unacceptably slow. Attempts to smooth aggregate economic activity are viewed as irrelevant at best and often counterproductive. The extreme monetarist view is that discretionary monetary and fiscal policies only magnify business cycles.

Differences in Keynesian and Monetarist Policy Recommendations

We have developed our descriptions of the differences between Keynesian and monetarist views with frequent references to their diagnoses and prescriptions for macroeconomic problems in the United States during the early 1980s. It will help to crystallize the distinctions between Keynesians and monetarists if we summarize the distinct differences in their policy recommendations for stabilizing the macroeconomy.

Monetary Policy and Interest Rates In late 1981, Keynesians agreed that the Fed and other government agencies should, above all, take steps to reduce the interest rate. It would be appropriate, they argued, to increase the quantity of money to whatever level would reduce the interest rate and speed recovery from recession. Monetarists argued, however, that as soon as the public perceived that the quantity of money was rising to higher and higher levels, fears of future inflation would keep interest rates high.

Fiscal Policy As we have seen, monetarists place even less faith in discretionary fiscal policy than in discretionary monetary policy. Keynesians, on the other hand, view discretionary fiscal policy as an essential tool in stabilizing the business cycle. One of their frequent proposals aimed at lowering high interest rates in the early 1980s was to reduce the federal deficit by raising taxes. Notice that Keynesians have something of a difficulty here. Macroeconomic theory suggests that an increase in taxes has a negative multiplier effect on planned expenditure and aggregate demand. Thus, Keynesians' recommendation to raise taxes in order to lower interest rates and boost investment and GNP growth contains an element of self-contradiction. They evidently felt, however, that reducing the deficit by any means would be effective, on balance, in lowering interest rates, increasing investment, and raising GNP growth.

Monetarists viewed the Keynesians' arguments in favor of greater taxes as a subterfuge really aimed at maintaining or increasing the role of government in the economy. They argued that if the deficit was responsible for high interest rates (which they doubted), then the best way to reduce the deficit was to lower government expenditure, not to increase taxes. As you may have guessed, Keynesians argued that monetarists were disguising their distaste for "big government" in the cloak of their theory of the impact of the deficit.

Supply-side economics emphasizes the impact of monetary and fiscal policies on investment and real GNP in the long run.

The Laffer curve is a theory about the relationship between tax rates and tax revenues. It states that tax revenues fall when tax rates increase to the levels that now exist in the United States and many other nations.

"Rules" versus Discretionary Policy As we have seen, an appropriate monetary policy during the 1980s, in the monetarists' view, would have been to instigate a steady and gradual reduction of the rate of monetary growth. This reduction would continue until the money supply was growing at a rate about equal to the rate of growth of the economy's productive capacity, say, about 3 percent per year. Once a 3 percent monetary growth rate is achieved, monetarists would prefer to have it remain at that rate regardless of what may happen to interest rates.

In short, monetarists advocate a "rules" approach to monetary policy. Namely, they believe that the best we can hope for in the way of countercyclical monetary policy is to mandate through legislation that the Fed's monetary target should follow a prescribed rule. The rule would require a constant rate of monetary growth approximately equal to the long-run trend in our capacity to produce goods and services.

As a first approximation, monetarists would use the quantity theory of money and the quantity equation as a guide to selecting the appropriate rate of monetary growth. If velocity (V) is approximately constant, then the quantity theory tells us that the money supply ought to grow at the same rate as the economy's capacity to produce real GNP if there is to be no inflation. Monetarists admit that their proposed monetary policy would not eliminate business cycles. They argue, however, that macroeconomic stability would be greater than has been achieved under discretionary monetary policy.

Keynesians reject the monetarists' "rules" approach. They believe that with improvements in statistical models of the macroeconomy the monetary (and fiscal) authorities will be better able to exercise their "authority" over taxation, government expenditure, and interest rates to improve on past performance. The battle over "rules versus discretion" in macroeconomic policy debates will doubtless continue into the foreseeable future.

Long-run Considerations and the "Supply Side"

In recent years, there have been many discussions of another point of view on macropolicy called **supply-side economics.** Unfortunately, the issues involved with the supply side versus monetarism versus Keynesianism have been almost hopelessly confused in popular discussions of economic issues. It is probably fair to say that the overwhelming majority of professional academic economists are "supply siders" when it comes to appropriate economic policies for the long run. Problems arise, however, when long-run policies aimed at long-term economic growth are confused with strategies for smoothing out business cycles.

Supply-side Economics

The principal targets of supply-side economics are taxation and, depending on which supply sider is speaking, government spending. Supply-side economics emphasizes the effects of high tax rates on incentives to work, to save, and to invest. Lower tax rates, it is argued, will result in greater investment, more rapid capital accumulation, a greater supply of work effort, and hence a faster rate of real economic growth. Few economists disagree with this basic supply-side notion. However, there is profound disagreement on the quantitative impact of a tax reduction on economic growth.

The Laffer Curve

The best-known and most extreme form of supply-side economic policy is associated with the so-called **Laffer curve,** which is a theoretical relationship between tax rates and tax revenues. This concept is named after economist Arthur Laffer, who argues that tax rates in the United States have become so high that further increases in tax rates will reduce the amount of tax revenue. In his view, not only do higher tax rates discourage economic growth, but they also result in enlargement of the "underground economy," consisting of barter transactions and illicit businesses, which escape taxation. It follows, if one accepts extreme supply-side arguments, that a reduction in tax rates will not reduce government's actual tax collections. Real output and income will grow so much faster that tax collections will not fall. Consequently, a reduction in tax rates need not result in a greater government deficit.

Other economists who are sympathetic with supply-side arguments in favor of reduced tax rates favor them not because they accept the idea that lower tax rates will lead to no reduction in tax collections but because they believe that lower tax rates will lead to reduced government expenditure. Thinking in terms of the economy's production possibilities, these economists view much government spending as a "drag" on the economy whether it is financed through taxation or borrowing. They do not view supply-side reductions in government spending or tax rates as means of stimulating recovery from recessions or as tools for preventing inflation. Rather, they are policies to be pursued to achieve long-run goals at the same time that the monetary and fiscal authorities seek to achieve short-run macroeconomic stability.

Most economists are supply siders in the limited sense that they recognize the disincentive effects of taxation on investment and work decisions. This does not mean that there is general agreement that current rates of taxation and levels of government expenditure are too high. Some economists think they are probably about right, although there may be dissatisfaction with the allocation of government spending or the structure of some tax rates. As a rule of thumb, it is probably fair to categorize most monetarists as supply siders who favor reduced taxation because they hope it will accompany reduced government spending. Most Keynesians, on the other hand, are much less likely to advocate substantial reduction in taxation or government spending from their current levels.

Supply-side, Keynesian, and Monetarist Views of Government Spending Cuts during a Recession

The extreme supply siders, who are mainly responsible for recent popularization of the supply-side concept, do not adhere consistently to either Keynesian or monetarist positions on short-run macroeconomic policy. Short-run and long-run policy goals are not carefully distinguished in their arguments and hence cannot be separated for purposes of describing how extreme supply siders view the best way to mitigate the effects of business fluctuations on unemployment and inflation.

An example of this confusion can be seen in supply siders' advocacy of a reduced government deficit (as well as less restrictive monetary policy) in the 1981–82 recession in order to reduce unemployment. They argued that the relatively large deficit created high interest rates. Therefore, they advocated reduced government spending to lower interest rates and promote increased aggregate expenditure via an increase in investment. Our basic macroeconomic model indicates that lowering government spending would probably have reduced interest rates, but it would also have lowered GNP and employment in the short run. Neither Keynesians nor monetarists argue that an increase in government spending during a recession retards recovery toward full employment, although they disagree on whether a discretionary increase in government spending is the best policy.

▸ The Government Deficit: Does It Matter?

Concern over the size of the deficit in federal spending in the United States first appeared in the 1980 presidential campaign. Throughout the 1950s and well into the 1960s the annual deficit averaged around 1 percent of GNP. By the late 1970s federal deficits were averaging close to 2 percent of GNP in the United States. The prospect that federal deficits would continue to grow relative to GNP was viewed with some alarm.

Table 12.1 **The national debt and the deficit**

Fiscal year	(1)		(2)	
	(a)	(b)	(a)	(b)
	Annual budget deficit relative to GNP ([−] indicates budget deficit and [+] indicates budget surplus)		**Publicly held national debt**	
	($ billions)	*Relative to GNP (%)*	*($ billions)*	*Relative to GNP (%)*
1789	+0.000150	+0.09	0.00	0.00
1800	+0.000063	+0.01	.083	19.31
1860	−0.0071	−0.18	.064	1.63
1865	−0.963	−10.70	2.22	24.71
1900	+0.046	+0.25	1.023	5.47
1919	−13.36	−15.87	24.28	28.84
1933	−2.60	−4.66	55.80	39.70
1940	−3.10	−3.09	40.31	40.31
1945	−47.47	−22.40	213.39	100.45
1950	−3.11	−1.09	200.69	70.06
1955	−3.04	−0.80	203.01	53.34
1960	+0.269	+0.05	210.65	42.31
1965	−1.60	−0.24	222.51	33.74
1970	−2.85	−0.29	227.17	23.45
1971	−23.00	−2.23	238.81	23.15
1972	−23.37	−2.07	252.34	22.36
1973	−14.84	−1.19	267.86	21.39
1974	−4.69	−0.34	265.41	19.24
1975	−45.15	−3.05	311.91	21.08
1976	−66.41	−4.05	385.59	23.51
1977	−44.95	−2.41	446.84	23.97
1978	−48.81	−2.34	495.47	23.78
1979	−27.69	−1.18	529.00	22.48
1980	−59.56	−2.32	594.26	23.15
1981	−57.93	−2.03	669.97	23.44
1982	−110.61	−3.56	794.90	25.63
1983	−207.70	−6.20	929.40	27.30
1984	−185.3	−4.9	1,141.80	30.30
1985	−212.3	−5.3	1,312.60	32.90

Source: From James R. Barth and Stephen O. Morrell, "A Primer on Budget Deficits," *Economic Review of the Federal Reserve Bank of Atlanta*, 67 (August 1982), pp. 6–17 and Appendix; *Economic Report of the President*, 1986, Tables B-1 and B-73.
Phillip Cagan, "The Real Federal Debt and Financial Markets," *The AEI Economist* (November 1981), pp. 1–8.

Deficits and Presidential Politics

Apart from wartime emergencies, deficits have always been unpopular with voters. Jimmy Carter ran for president in 1976 promising to balance the federal budget by 1980. By early 1980 it was clear that the federal budget deficit would be close to $60 billion, or 2.3 percent of GNP, as indicated in table 12.1. Ronald Reagan attacked the Democratic administration's inability to control the deficit and promised that if elected he would balance the federal budget by 1984.

As indicated in table 12.1, the deficit decreased slightly in dollar terms as well as relative to GNP in 1981. However, it increased dramatically in dollar amount and relative to GNP in both 1982 and 1983. While the deficit had declined to 5.3 percent of GNP by 1985, it had by no means vanished. The Council of Economic Advisers has projected that the deficit will not decline to as little as 2.3 percent of GNP again until 1989.[3]

During the presidential campaign of 1984, Walter Mondale promised to increase taxes in his acceptance speech at the Democratic convention. At the time, some political analysts suggested that Mondale may have taken a bold and positive position by speaking candidly about the debt issue. Throughout the fall campaign the challenger charged the Reagan administration with "mortgaging" America's future to support current spending.

Whatever other findings may emerge from analyses of the 1984 campaign, most observers agree that former Vice President Mondale's promise to raise taxes was a negative factor in his campaign. The American people elected the Reagan-Bush ticket. Evidently they were signaling that the deficit should be reduced through spending cuts and not through tax increases.

In 1985, Senators William P. Gramm and Warren Rudman of New Hampshire introduced a bill, known as the Gramm-Rudman Deficit-Reduction Act, that calls for Congress to achieve a balanced budget by 1990. Interestingly, Senator Gramm is a former professor of economics at Texas A & M University. The Gramm-Rudman bill sets specific declining deficit targets that reach zero in 1991. It requires the president to submit annual budgets containing deficits no greater than the specific target amount in each year. It also requires Congress to enact particular deficit-reduction measures in an attempt to reach these targets. If Congress fails to act in this manner, most federal programs would automatically be cut across the board by the Gramm-Rudman bill.

This bill won wide support from those favoring smaller government and caught many members of Congress, as well as the president, somewhat off guard when it passed in December 1985. In the political atmosphere of the time, it seemed clear that the public would not support significant tax increases, so the Gramm-Rudman proposal was viewed as an attempt to force Congress to reduce expenditures. Along these lines, President Reagan agreed to submit a budget for fiscal year 1987 that would meet the legislation's required deficit target of $144 billion, even before the proposal was passed by Congress. Finally, while the Gramm-Rudman bill was the product of two Republican senators, President Reagan still had some objections to it. Specifically, he opposed the automatic cuts in certain segments of the budget, primarily defense. Despite his objections, the president signed the bill in December 1985. In July 1986, the Supreme Court ruled that the provision for *automatic* budget cuts, without congressional action in each case, is unconstitutional.

The Sources of United States Deficits in the 1980s

In order to understand the deficit and its economic pluses and minuses, we will first examine federal expenditures and receipts to see why the deficit has grown so much relative to GNP. We will also compare the United States experience with that of other industrialized countries over the same period. Federal government receipts and expenditures are listed in table 12.2 and illustrated in figure 12.1. Notice that in 1960, there was a federal budget surplus of one-tenth of 1 percent of GNP. This surplus was the result of tax revenues that amounted to 18.6 percent of GNP, while expenditures were only 18.5 percent. By 1985, the budget surplus had changed into a deficit of 5.3 percent of GNP. Table 12.2 and figure 12.1 show clearly that the deficit arose not because of plunging revenues but because of a surge in government expenditures. The principal source of this increase is the "other" category of government expenditure, which consists largely of government transfer and subsidy programs (not defense expenditures as is so often asserted).

Table 12.2 Budget outlays and receipts as a percentage of GNP, 1960–85

	1960	1970	1980	1982	1983	1984	1985
Total outlays	18.5	20.2	22.4	23.8	24.7	22.6	23.7
National defense	9.7	8.4	5.2	5.5	6.5	6.0	6.3
Net interest	1.4	1.5	2.0	2.8	2.8	2.9	3.2
Other	7.5	10.3	15.1	15.0	15.4	15.3	14.5
Total receipts	18.6	19.9	20.1	20.2	18.6	17.7	18.4

Source: From *Economic Report of the President,* 1986, Table B-1, p. 252, Table B-74, p. 341.

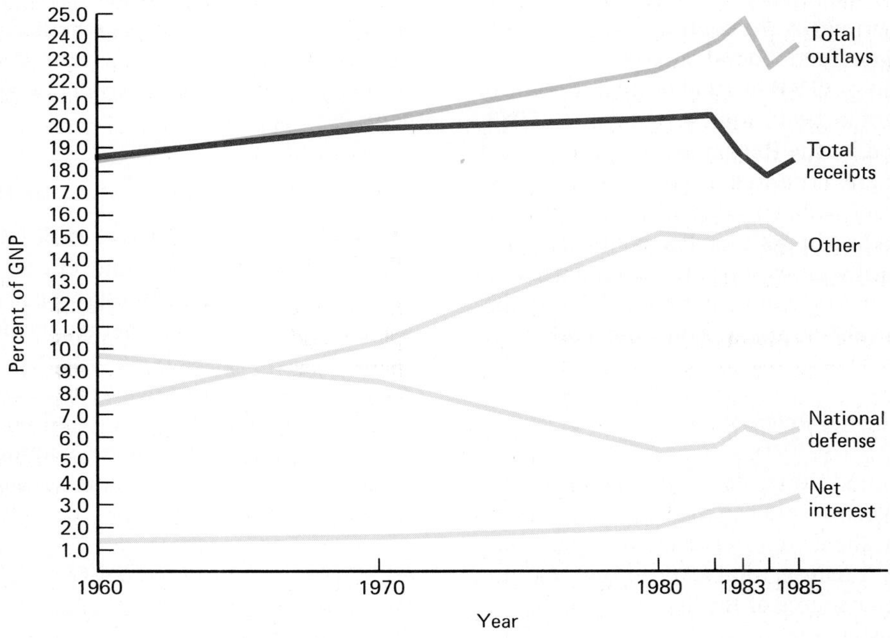

Figure 12.1 Sources of the federal deficit
The federal deficit is the difference between total government outlays and government tax receipts. The deficit has grown primarily because of an increase in outlays, while receipts have remained more or less constant as a share of GNP. The main source of increased outlays has been the category labeled "other," which includes transfer expenditures, subsidies, and related programs.
From *Economic Report of the President,* 1984, Table 1-1, p. 29.

*The **high employment deficit** is the excess of government spending over tax revenues when full employment prevails.*

President Reagan argued in 1980 and 1981 that his proposed tax cuts were intended to arrest the growth of the federal government—not dismantle it. The data in table 12.2 and figure 12.1 bear him out. They indicate that the deficit would be eliminated by a reduction in government expenditure as a share of GNP to the level that prevailed in 1960 or even in 1970. Furthermore, budget projections from the Reagan administration show anticipated tax revenue growing to about 19.8 percent of GNP—about the same as in 1970 but considerably less than the 1985 share of total federal expenditure.[4]

The source of the rapidly rising deficit during the early 1980s was primarily the continued rapid growth in federal spending. Total federal outlays rose steadily from 18.5 percent of GNP in 1960 to 20.2 percent in 1970, 22.4 percent in 1980, and 24.7 percent in 1983. Tax cuts proposed by the Reagan administration and approved by Congress resulted in a decline in receipts to 18.4 percent of GNP in 1985, which was not matched by a decline in outlays. The political debate for the next several years will revolve around whether or not federal spending can be cut enough to significantly reduce the deficit and without resorting to tax increases.

The Recent Debt Experience of Industrialized Nations

How does the United States deficit problem compare with deficit problems of other industrialized nations? As we have seen, the deficit in the United States has grown primarily because total expenditure has increased. The major source of this increase has been a doubling of transfer and subsidy programs and interest payments on the debt. United States experience in terms of changes in general government expenditure and the sources of change has been quite similar to the experiences of other major nations, including Canada, Japan, France, Italy, Germany, and the United Kingdom.[5] Indeed, even in 1984, the share of government expenditure in national income was greater in all of these nations except Japan than in the United States.

The rapid growth in transfer and subsidy programs in the United States in the last twenty years is similar to the pattern observed in other advanced economies. It has occurred both in rapidly expanding economies such as those of Germany and Japan and in slowly growing economies such as those of Italy and the United Kingdom. Similarly, these other nations have, on average, experienced budget deficits that have typically exceeded the deficit of the United States as a share of GNP.[6] Evidently, the existence of a large deficit relative to a country's national income does not tell us much about how healthy an economy is or how good its growth prospects are likely to be. This brings us to the economic issue of whether or not the large deficits of the 1980s are a serious obstacle for an economy to function properly and to grow at a healthy pace.

The Economic Significance of the Debt

In order to establish a framework for understanding the possible macroeconomic effects of the government deficit, we must first establish a standard against which we can measure whether the deficit is large or small. We have already done that to some extent by expressing a country's deficit as a ratio relative to its GNP. However, an important additional step involves recognizing that the economy's automatic fiscal stabilizers assure that the budget surplus will shrink or the deficit will grow during recessions.

Deficits and Business Cycles

When we are interested in the long-term effects of the deficit, we should consider what its size would be if the economy were at full employment; this is what economists call the **high employment deficit.** For example, we saw in table 12.1 that in 1983, the federal deficit was $207 billion. The President's Council of Economic Advisers has estimated that $95 billion of this deficit, or 48.7 percent, would have disappeared if the economy had experienced full employment in 1983. If the economy had been at full employment in 1982, it is estimated that the deficit would have been less than half as large.[7]

Monetization of the debt occurs when the Fed buys government bonds, particularly when the bonds are purchased directly from the Treasury.

A structural deficit is a deficit that persists when the economy is at full employment.

What has created growing concern over the deficit in recent years is that it has not disappeared, or turned into a surplus, during periods of full employment. As we have just seen, although the deficit would have been much smaller in recent years under full-employment conditions, it would still have been significant. Table 12.1 shows that until the 1970s, budget deficits were typically associated with wars and recessions. By far the largest deficits, relative to GNP, have been associated with wartime expenditures. Table 12.1 shows that the accumulated government debt held by the public rose from less than 2 percent of GNP in 1860 to almost 25 percent of GNP after the Civil War. By 1900, however, there had been enough years of budgetary surplus to reduce the publicly held debt to only 5.5 percent of GNP. World War I also was financed largely through deficit spending. The tandem effects of the Great Depression and World War II pushed the amount of publicly held government debt to over 100 percent of GNP.

Since creation of the Federal Reserve System, the public is not the only holder of the federal government's debt. When the government deficit is accompanied by an expansionary monetary policy (the Fed buying government bonds), we say that the Fed **monetizes the debt.** Monetization of the federal deficit has the same impact on the economy as printing dollar bills to finance an excess of government expenditure over tax collections. In 1982, the Fed held a little over 11 percent of the total outstanding federal debt.[8]

Structural Deficits

During the 1950s, the federal budget showed a surplus during three years, during the 1960s there were two years with surpluses, and since 1969 there has been a budget deficit every year. The federal government has become increasingly sensitive to the size and frequency of its deficits. In the thirty years from 1953 through 1982 there was a growing tendency to underestimate the size of the deficit when budgets were formulated.[9] The persistence of budget deficits even during periods of full employment has led to concern about the so-called **structural deficit,** the concept that even at full employment, government expenditure exceeds tax revenue.

Table 12.3 Estimates of the structural deficit as a percentage of GNP, 1980–89

1980	2.1
1981	1.3
1982	1.6
1983	3.2
1984	3.9
1985	4.2
1987	4.1
1989	3.7

The estimates and projections of the structural deficit suggest that even at full employment, the federal deficit will continue to be large relative to GNP, compared to historical standards.

Source: From *Economic Report of the President,* 1986, Table B–1, pp. 252–253.

The question we are concerned with is this: Has the deficit become so large that it harms the economy by raising real interest rates, thus slowing down investment and reducing the growth of productivity and real output? Even if we accept the idea that the federal government was operating with a structural deficit (that is, there would have been a deficit even at full-employment GNP) in the early 1980s, the deficit was not large by historical standards, at least not through 1982. Although 1982 was a recession year, the deficit as a fraction of GNP was lower than during the recession year of 1976. Table 12.1 shows that the deficit for 1983 was, however, rather large compared to previous deficits during times of peace.

Table 12.3 shows estimates of the structural deficit as a percentage of GNP, as estimated and projected by the President's Council of Economic Advisers, for the years 1980 through 1989. The table indicates a structural deficit in 1984 of 3.9 percent and in 1985 of 4.2 percent of GNP. This ratio is expected to remain quite high by historical standards for at least the rest of the 1980s. By contrast, table 12.1 shows that the *total value* of the publicly held national debt relative to GNP was far lower in 1982 than it was in 1960. What is the likely impact of the structural deficit on long-term economic prospects for the United States economy?

"Crowding Out": The Short-run and Long-run Effects of the Deficit

As noted in chapter 10, the process by which the federal deficit may harm prospects of long-run economic growth is referred to as *crowding out,* which means that the deficit, by increasing the total demand for loanable funds, raises interest rates and thus the cost of private investment projects. The quantity of investment goods demanded is then reduced. How likely is crowding out to deter private investment?

Once again, we refer to our macromodel. It tells us that in a recession an increase in the government deficit will reduce the quantity of private investment goods demanded relative to the amount of investment that would occur if the deficit were lower and expansionary monetary policy were used to stimulate economic recovery. However, an increase in the deficit will not lower investment relative to the amount that would occur during a recession if neither expansionary monetary nor expansionary fiscal policy were undertaken.

Under full-employment conditions, however, an increase in the deficit resulting from an increase in government spending will tend to crowd out private investment, at least in the short run, by causing an increase in the rate of interest. An increase in the deficit resulting from a reduction in taxes is more difficult to analyze. To the extent a reduction in tax revenue causes the deficit to increase, *cet. par.,* the rate of interest will rise and investment will be crowded out. However, a reduction in tax rates (particularly if slanted toward encouraging investment by raising depreciation allowances and so on) is likely to shift the investment demand schedule to the right. If reduced tax rates also lead to increased saving and the supply of loanable funds, a deficit caused by a reduction in taxes will result in less crowding out of investment than one caused by an increase in government spending. Thus, it could be that consumption is crowded out, rather than investment, if the deficit is increased by tax cuts that stimulate investment sufficiently.

If one accepts the crowding-out view, one has a pretty good grasp of the underlying economic assumptions in Walter Mondale's argument in the 1984 presidential campaign that the Reagan administration was mortgaging our future with large deficits in 1984 and beyond to stimulate the economy in the short run. The argument would be that deficit spending in 1984 and beyond would keep interest rates high, crowd out private investment expenditure, and reduce the economy's long-term growth prospects. Therefore, Mondale called for higher taxes and reduced government expenditure, at least for defense, in order to reduce the deficit and presumably the crowding-out effect. To the extent that voters rejected Mondale's proposals, they seem to have done so on the basis of favoring expenditure cuts, not tax increases—not because they were unconcerned about possible long-term crowding-out effects.

In contrast, President Reagan's position seemed to consist of three parts. First, he insisted that much of the deficit problem was cyclical and not structural. While that appears to be true for 1982 and 1983, the Council of Economic Advisers data in table 12.3 suggests that just the opposite is the case beyond 1984.

Second, the president insisted that the supply-side effects of the tax cuts of 1981–84 would raise the average full-employment rate of real economic growth in the United States well above the 3 to 3.5 percent rate of the last one hundred years or so. As we discussed earlier, the tax cuts of the early 1980s appear to have succeeded in putting a temporary lid on the federal tax bite out of GNP at a value near that of the early 1960s. While that may stand as a rather remarkable political accomplishment, it is difficult to see exactly how that change could induce supply-side effects large enough to raise the real full-employment growth rate by one full percentage point—almost a third of its historical average.

*The **Ricardian equivalence hypothesis** states that the method of financing government expenditure has no impact on private consumption or investment expenditures.*

Third, the president promised not to raise taxes and to cut federal expenditures enough to halve the projected deficit by 1988. Using the Council of Economic Advisers figures, that would reduce the projected deficit to about only 1.8 percent of GNP. The president's position did not deny the possibility of long-run crowding-out effects. Instead, Reagan forecast sufficient economic growth and expenditure cuts to render the crowding-out effect relatively inconsequential by 1988.

The impact of the government deficit on private investment expenditure is essentially a long-run problem. Moreover, the response of investment to the deficit depends on whether the deficit results from a reduction in taxes or an increase in government expenditure. Unfortunately, the question of whether or not government borrowing crowds out private borrowing cannot be answered completely by reference to our macromodel because the model cannot handle problems of what we shall now call the *very long run.*

In the very long run, the degree of crowding out depends on whether the public views the holding of government bonds as wealth. Why shouldn't government bonds held by the public be viewed as wealth? The answer lies in the theory of rational expectations. Suppose everyone in the economy were to purchase one dollar's worth of government bonds to finance the federal deficit. They would do so in return for the interest payments they expect to receive in the future. However, over the very long run, the public will learn that in order for the government to finance the interest payments, one of the following three events must occur: (1) taxes must be increased; (2) new bonds must be sold to the public (a further increase in government debt); or (3) the government can print the money, increasing the rate of monetary growth. Events 1 and 2 essentially take back the interest the public receives from its government debt holdings. Event 3 takes it back less directly, by using the "tax" of inflation.

The monetarist explanation for continued high interest rates throughout the mid-1980s turns on this third possibility. The argument is that nominal long-term interest rates remained above 10 percent despite inflation rates of 4 percent or less because the public was convinced that the debt would be monetized and that the rate of inflation would return to the 7 to 8 percent range experienced during the 1970s. Of course, if deficits were persistently monetized, the public would soon build inflationary expectations into all its economic behavior, and the government could not succeed in gaining additional resources through deception over the very long run. Persistent attempts to do so have led to hyperinflation in many nations.[10]

If event 1 or 2 occurs the public will eventually transfer back to the government the interest income received from the original debt purchases. By contrast, if each member of the public had purchased one dollar's worth of private debt from business firms, the interest would be paid with the revenues received for selling the additional production made possible by the investment goods financed through the debt issue. The private debt would be viewed as wealth "backed" by an addition to the economy's stock of physical capital.

If the public views a structural deficit as leading to an increase in future taxes, then in the very long run the effect on private investment will be equivalent to that of an equal increase in spending and taxes, with no change in the deficit. This view, that the method of *financing* government expenditure, either by borrowing or by taxation, has no effect on real economic variables, is called the **Ricardian equivalence hypothesis.**[11] It depends on the idea that deficit financing is a means of allowing the public to benefit from government expenditure in the present, while shifting the burden of taxes (payment of interest on the debt) to future generations. However, the Ricardian equivalence hypothesis maintains that the current generation cares about future generations. That is, the typical individual has a *bequest motive*. Thus, the public recognizes that today's deficit will raise future taxes, and it will increase its saving accordingly. This way future generations will be as well off as if current government expenditure were entirely financed through taxation. The increase in saving will shift the supply of loanable funds to the right, offsetting the impact of the government's demand for loanable funds.[12]

If the Ricardian equivalence hypothesis holds or if the public fully anticipates monetization of the debt, then the method of financing government expenditure does not affect the share of GNP that goes to private investment or consumption. It cannot be emphasized too strongly, however, that the level of government *expenditure* does affect private expenditure decisions. This is because, in the long run, whatever resources are used by the government are not available for use in the private sector. In other words, the real course of the economy is independent of the government's monetary and fiscal policies provided the public recognizes the effects of the deficit and the quantity of money on future taxes and the price level. Only "surprises" in the form of unexpected changes in monetary or fiscal policy will affect the allocation of the public's expenditures on consumption and investment goods.

There is considerable disagreement among economists on the existence and significance of long-term crowding-out effects of the public debt. This is because empirical evidence is scarce and subject to widely different interpretations. The political consensus appears to be that it is better to rein in government deficit spending than to wait around to discover what if any adverse effects the deficit may have if we do nothing.

▸ Summary and Conclusions

Now that you have surveyed the major macroeconomic controversies and know who the players are, can you identify them in the political debates leading up to the next congressional and presidential elections? Which side do you favor? In this chapter we discussed the basic differences between Keynesians' and monetarists' viewpoints about how the aggregate economy works. We also analyzed the controversy over the long-run effects of the national debt on the economy. The major points emphasized were these:

Keynesians tend to believe that monetary policy affects aggregate demand indirectly through its impact on the real interest rate and that the impact of fiscal policy on the economy is more significant and direct.

By contrast, monetarists believe that short-run economic impacts of monetary policy are more predictable than are the consequences of fiscal policy actions.

Monetarists also believe that monetary policy affects aggregate spending directly through its impact on consumption and investment expenditure as well as indirectly through its impact on the interest rate.

Monetarists tend to prefer monetary growth rules to either monetary or fiscal discretionary policies.

Keynesians generally believe that the economy can and should be induced to grow more smoothly through the use of discretionary policies.

Monetarists argue that the history of the use of discretionary policies is full of examples of mistakes that have increased the length and severity of recessions and inflations.

United States deficits during the early 1980s were made larger by the adverse cyclical effects of the recession in 1981–82.

United States experiences with respect to deficits, the size of interest payments on the debt, the growth of transfer and subsidy programs, and the size of general government expenditure relative to GNP have been similar to the experiences of other industrialized nations.

An international comparison of public debt shows no correlation with the rate of economic growth or the level of economic well-being.

The growth of the public debt in the United States has been dominated by the growth of expanding federal expenditure after 1965.

Monetarists and economists who accept the rational expectations view tend to view the size of the government debt as relatively unimportant to the long-run growth prospects for the United States economy.

The public debate over the size of the deficit is largely a debate over the appropriate size of government expenditure relative to GNP.

▸ Key Terms

high employment deficit *262*

Laffer curve *257*

monetarists and Keynesians *253*

monetization of the debt *263*

Ricardian equivalence hypothesis *265*

structural deficit *263*

supply-side economics *257*

target of monetary policy *255*

▸ Questions for Discussion and Review

1. Why would a Keynesian prefer the use of fiscal policy to the use of monetary policy to try to regulate the macroeconomy?
2. Why would a monetarist prefer the use of rules rather than discretion in the use of monetary and fiscal policy?
3. Why are we less concerned about the cyclical component of the deficit than we are about the structural component?
4. Explain the economic assumptions underlying the positions on the deficit taken by former Vice President Mondale and President Reagan in the 1984 presidential campaign.
5. How would monetarists and Keynesians explain the high interest rates of the mid-1980s?
6. Would you expect the income tax cuts of 1981–84 to generate substantial supply-side effects? Why?
7. What is the relationship between structural deficits and the possibility of long-run crowding out?
8. Explain the significance of the cyclical component of the deficit to the deficit/GNP ratio in the United States in 1982 and 1983.
9. Are there circumstances under which the public would view government bonds as wealth?
10. Will large deficits lead to long-run crowding out as long as the public views government bonds as a debt to be paid off?
11. Show by means of a graph how a change in the real value of money balances held by the public might *directly* influence consumption and aggregate demand.

Policy Issue: You Decide

Flat Tax

▸ The Action-Initiating Event

The president has decided that he wants to push for a single tax rate on personal income and to eliminate all corporate income taxes despite the problems that such legislation has faced in the past. The staff at the Council of Economic Advisers estimates that a flat tax of 25 percent on personal income will generate enough revenue to balance the current budget if all deductions are eliminated. The president wants to make a major televised address on this issue just before Congress recesses in order to get the public behind his proposal. He wants to be prepared to consider minor changes in his proposal and demonstrate publicly his command of facts regarding the implications with respect to his proposal and possible modifications.

▸ The Issue

Clearly, a single tax rate would substantially reduce marginal tax rates for middle- and upper-income families and individuals. The president is willing to consider a minimum income level below which there would be no tax in order to defuse the fairness issue. By themselves, the elimination of the corporate income tax and the lower income tax rate for many individuals should help to stimulate the economy. The elimination of all personal income tax deductions and business deductions will undoubtedly generate winners and losers with varying amounts of political clout. The president's chief of staff asked me to solicit your opinion on this entire matter. The concern within the inner circle is that the president could be committing political suicide on this issue.

▸ Economic Policy Issues

With respect to both personal and business activities, the president's initial proposal raises several concerns on which I would like to have your opinion. First, with respect to the treatment of personal income, how would the elimination of all deductions affect the housing industry, interest rates, charitable contributions, and any other areas that you might be concerned about? How would the elimination of corporation depreciation allowances and investment tax credits along with the corporate income tax itself affect the structure of industry in the long run? Who would be the big winners in the short run?

▸ Recommendations

If the political judgment is made that some personal deductions cannot be eliminated, we will need answers to the following questions from you: Would you recommend covering any increased deficit associated with retaining particular personal tax deductions by raising the personal tax rate, imposing a minimum corporate tax, or simply allowing the projected deficit to increase? Would a federal consumption tax or national sales tax be worth considering to reduce the deficit? Who would be the winners and losers from these various options? What would be the impact on the economy of the president's proposal as well as the other options? The White House wants the president to understand the implications of various alternatives before he goes public. While the mood in the country continues to favor tax reform, we do not want the president's position to seem unfair or impractical.

Part IV

The International Economy

Chapter 13

Trade among Nations

Outline

Objectives

After reading this chapter, the student should be able to:

Discuss the relative importance of international trade to the United States economy and the world economy.
Derive a nation's import and export curves for a commodity given the nation's supply and demand curves for that commodity.
Show how the world equilibrium price of a commodity is obtained.
Show the international effects of a shift in a nation's demand or supply of a commodity.
Discuss the winners and losers within the importing and exporting countries and the distribution of the gains from international trade.

Real aspects of international trade *are concerned with the flows of commodities among nations.*

Monetary aspects of international trade *deal with currency flows, which are the financial counterpart of international commodity flows.*

Introduction

In a Detroit bar during the early 1980s, a young man of Chinese descent was drinking a beer. Two autoworkers started a fight with him, and when he left the bar, they chased him, attacked him, and killed him. Why? The autoworkers mistook their victim for Japanese, and they equated automobiles imported from Japan with lost jobs and reduced wages in the United States automobile industry. Not long afterward, a South Dakota banker drove to a local farm to discuss a loan that was in default. If the loan was not repaid soon, the bank would have to foreclose on the farm. A member of the farmer's family, hiding inside a barn, shot the banker dead as he started to get out of his car. This killing, too, was related to United States trade with other countries. During the early 1980s, farm exports declined because the dollar rose in price relative to foreign currencies, and this made American farm exports more expensive than those from other nations such as Canada, Argentina, and Australia. The resulting decline in the revenues of American farmers forced many of them into bankruptcy.

These two true stories illustrate the immense importance of international economic relationships in the lives of many individuals. They also reflect stupidly misplaced aggression based on ignorance about international and other economic issues. All of us depend on trade with other nations in many ways that may not be quite as obvious in our everyday lives. The American car you drive may have bumpers plated with chrome from South Africa; the gasoline it burns and the oil that lubricates its engine is almost as likely to be imported as domestically produced; the pencil you use to take class notes is likely to contain tin, graphite, and rubber from three different nations.

Trade between nations occurs for exactly the same reason that individuals and firms within a nation specialize and deal with one another. Comparative advantage, specialization, and trade are crucial to maximizing the benefit we obtain from our scarce resources. In this and the next three chapters we explore how international trade affects the welfare and growth of advanced industrial nations as well as developing countries and examine some causes and effects of barriers to free trade. We will learn why the United States has experienced persistent international trade deficits (importing more than it exports) in recent years and what this means for the typical American citizen and worker. We will also examine the forces that determine the price of one country's currency in terms of another and the means by which inflations and recessions may be transmitted internationally through the international trade connection.

The study of international trade is usually divided into two parts. Issues involving the trade of commodities are designated the ***real aspects of international trade****, whereas matters relating to currency or exchange considerations are called the* ***monetary aspects of international trade****. In this chapter and chapter 14 most of our discussion deals with the real aspects of international trade. The monetary and macroeconomic aspects of international trade and how international currency flows relate to trade are treated* *in chapter 15. In this chapter, we show how supply and demand forces determine exchange rates, how exchange rates in turn affect the international flow of goods and services, and how international trade relates to aggregate employment and production. In chapter 16, we apply the lessons of the earlier chapters to help understand some current problems in today's international economy. We will see what problems led to the international debt crisis of the early 1980s and the way in which some nations have sought to use international trade as an engine of industrialization for their economies.*

▸ Import and Export Patterns in the United States Economy and the World Economy

Foreign trade's importance to the United States economy has grown in recent years. Figure 13.1 shows that using either the value of imports or exports as a measure, the share of foreign trade in GNP has doubled since 1950. Nevertheless, as measured by share of total production, other countries are more dependent on the foreign sector than is the United States. In few other countries do economic relations with foreign nations constitute a smaller proportion of gross

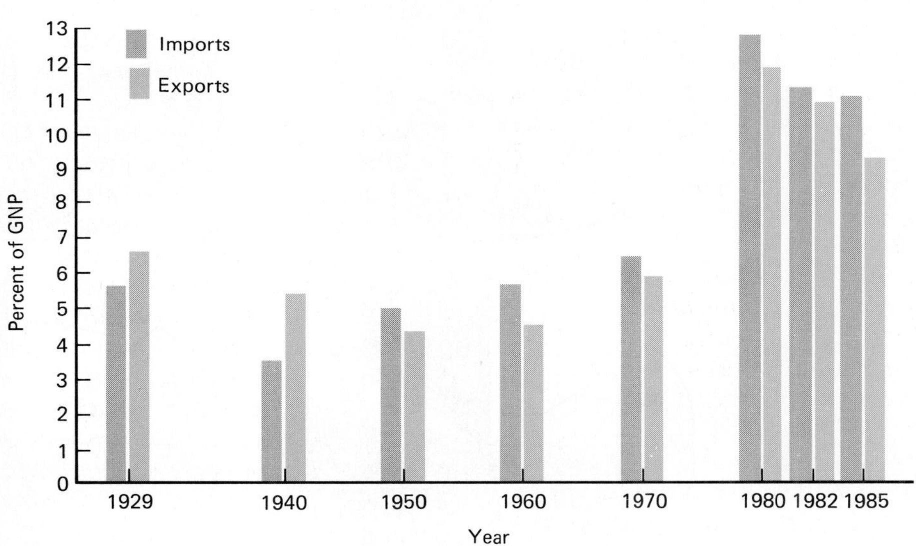

Figure 13.1 Imports and exports of goods and services as a share of GNP in the United States, 1929–1985
Both imports and exports have more than doubled as a percentage of GNP since 1950.
From *Economic Report of the President,* 1986, Table B-1, pp. 252–253.

Figure 13.2 Share of exports from the United States and other nations in total world exports (percent of dollar volume)
From *Economic Report of the President,* 1983, Table B-106, p. 282 and 1986, Table B-106, p. 374.

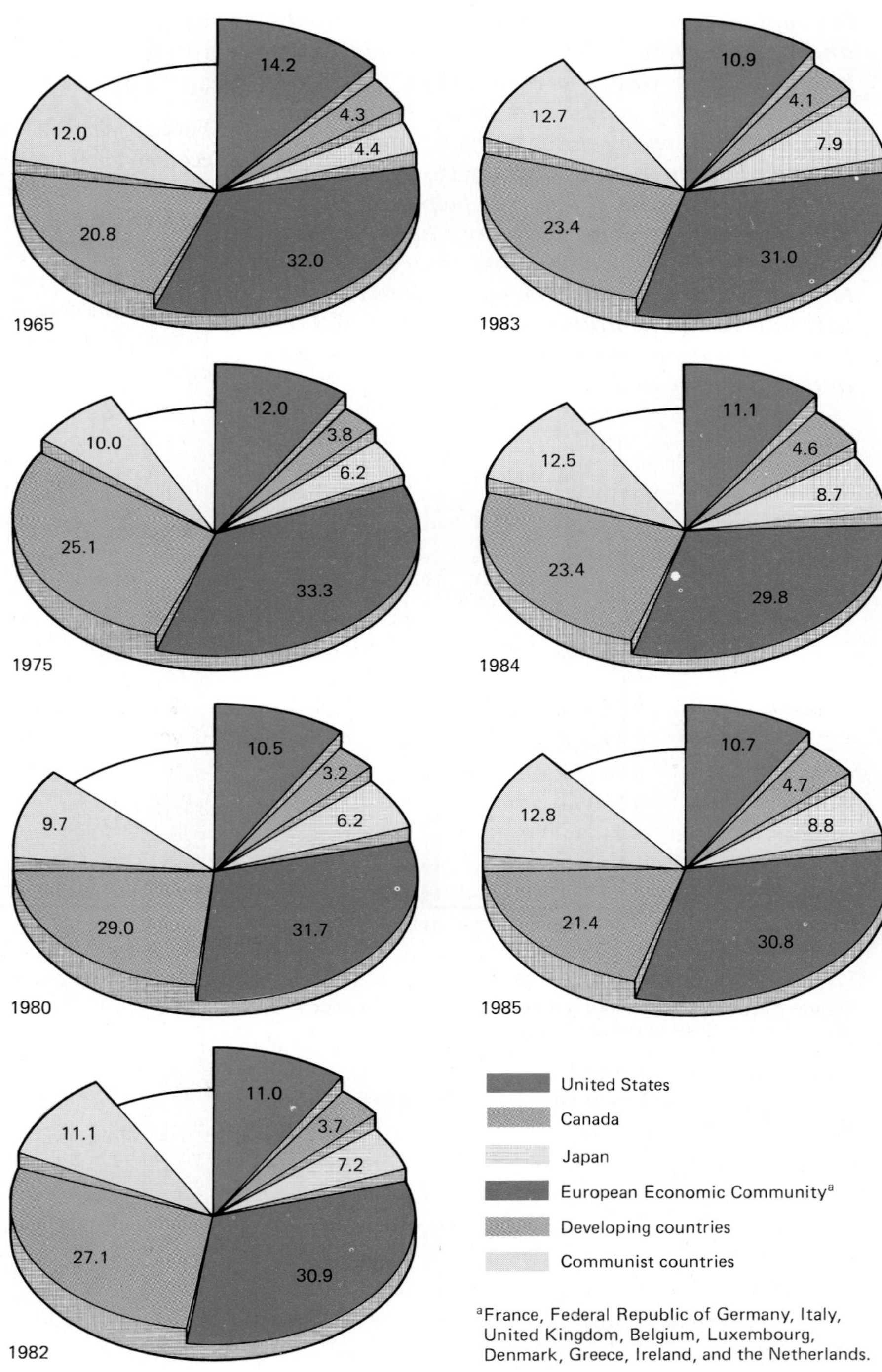

Table 13.1 Net United States imports of minerals and metals as a percentage of consumption, 1983

Mineral		Major foreign sources
Mica	100	India, Brazil, Madagascar
Manganese	99	South Africa, Gabon, Brazil, France
Bauxite	96	Jamaica, Australia, Guinea
Platinum	84	South Africa, Soviet Union, United Kingdom
Chromium	77	South Africa, Philippines, Soviet Union
Zinc	66	Canada, Spain, Mexico, Honduras
Petroleum	28	Saudi Arabia, Nigeria, Venezuela

Source: From *Statistical Abstract of the United States,* 1985, Table 1248, p. 703, Dept. of Commerce-Bureau of the Census.

product. All of the major industrialized market economies listed in figure 13.2 have export shares larger than the United States, and in most of them exports amount to 25 percent or more of their total output. In several of the world's less industrialized nations, exports account for over a third of gross product.[1] Obviously, export earnings are crucial to these nations' ability to import essential consumption goods and investment goods needed for economic growth.

In an important sense, the data in figure 13.1 grossly understate the relationship of the United States to the international economy. In terms of absolute size, the United States economy is so large relative to the rest of the world that even a small share of its GNP constitutes a large fraction of total commerce among nations. Figure 13.2 shows that United States exports constitute over 10 percent of total exports from all nations. Moreover, a number of raw materials essential to our economy are either unavailable within our borders or are much more costly to produce here than elsewhere. Some of these are listed in table 13.1. Even though we import far fewer than half of the petroleum products we use, events since 1973 clearly demonstrate how important trade can be even for a commodity for which we are largely self-sufficient. Table 13.1 shows that the United States is currently almost totally dependent on imports for some important raw materials. What does Gabon have that United States citizens apparently cannot live without? Answer: a large share of the manganese for making high-quality steel. Do you use mica? Many of your electrical appliances probably do. Much of it comes from the remote island of Madagascar. The bauxite used to make your aluminum pots may have originated in the country of Guinea.

Despite the dominant role of the United States in world trade, the international marketplace has become more competitive in recent years. While the United States has been exporting an increasing share of its gross product and importing a larger fraction of the automobiles, steel, and petroleum used by American firms and consumers, other nations have expanded their role in the world economy even faster. For example, between 1965 and 1982, the United States share in total world exports declined by 3 percentage points (about 20 percent), while the share of Japan grew almost three percentage points (about a 60 percent increase in its export share). The share of the world's developing nations in total world exports grew by about six percentage points (about a 30 percent increase).

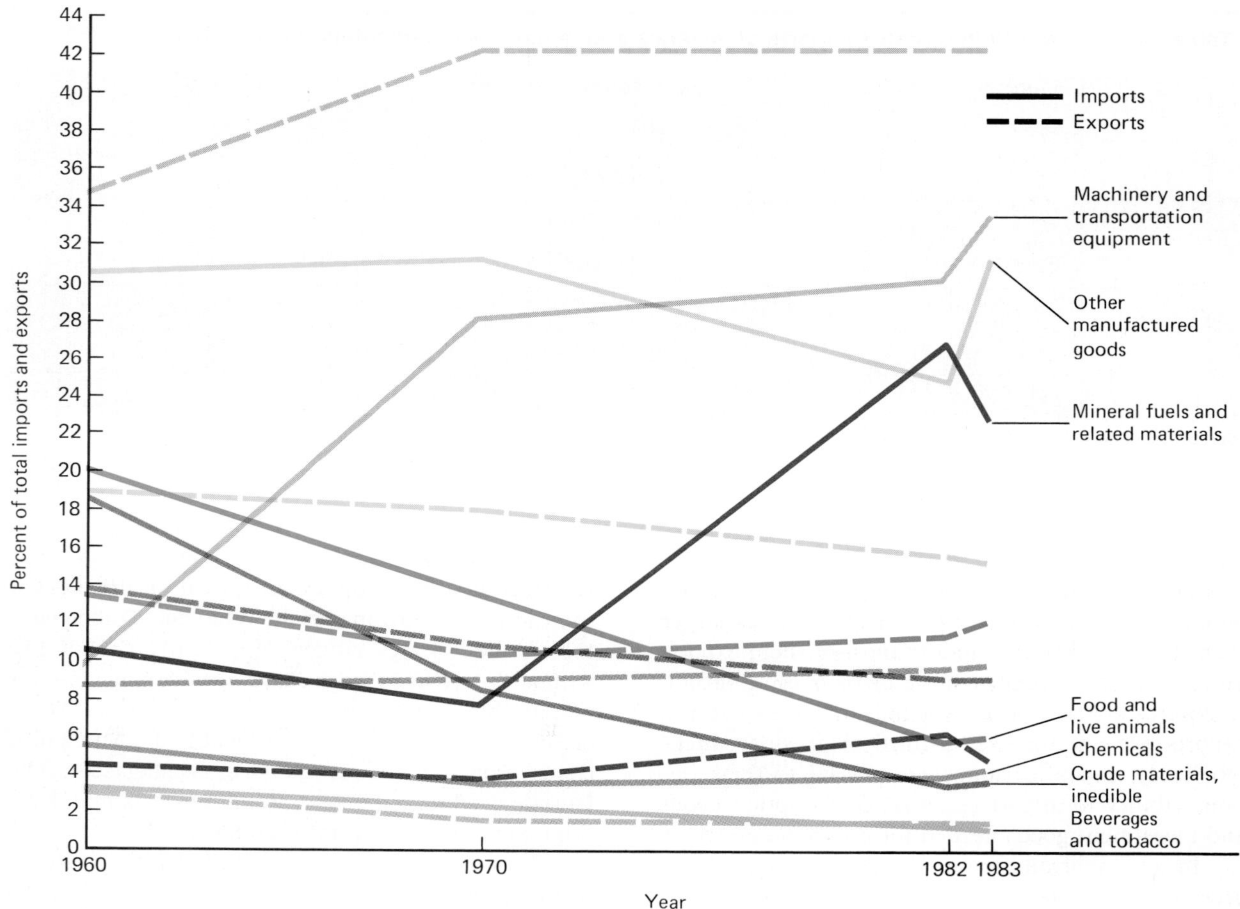

Figure 13.3 Percentage distribution of United States imports and exports by broad commodity groups, 1960–1983
From *Statistical Abstract of the United States,* 1984, Table 1474, p. 838 and 1985, Table 1447, p. 820.

Figure 13.3 shows the pattern of United States foreign trade according to broad categories of final product use. The data there indicate that in terms of dollar value, the United States is a net exporter of food, crude materials, chemicals, and machinery and transportation equipment. It is a net importer of mineral fuels (oil) and other manufactured goods. Figure 13.3 shows how United States imports and exports have changed over the years. The main shift in export patterns has been growth in the share of machinery and transportation equipment. Imports of this broad commodity group have also grown relative to total imports. As you might expect, the most striking change in United States foreign trade has been a

Table 13.2 **United States exports and imports, by country or region, 1984 (percent of total)**

Country or region	Exports	Imports
Canada	24.1	20.7
Japan	10.6	18.0
Western Europe	25.9	21.6
OPEC	6.3	8.0
Eastern Europe	1.9	0.7
Australia, New Zealand, and South Africa	3.6	1.7
Other (includes Latin America)	27.4	29.3

Source: From *Economic Report of the President,* 1983, Table B-103, p. 279.

roughly fourfold increase in the share of mineral fuels and related materials in total imports, from 7.7 percent in 1970 to 22.5 percent in 1983.

Table 13.2 indicates major trading partners of the United States. Measured in terms of either imports or exports, Canada is our single most important international trade partner. Mexico (not included in the table) accounted for 6.8 percent of United States exports and 5.2 percent of imports in 1980.[2] Western Europe accounts for over a quarter of United States exports and a little more than a fifth of imports, while trade with Eastern Europe constitutes a very small share of both United States exports and imports.

Imports, Exports, and the Gains from Trade

Before beginning our analysis of supply and demand in international commerce, it would be helpful for you to review the discussion of comparative advantage in chapter 1. The principle of the gains that arise when two individuals specialize and trade with each other according to their relative opportunity costs is universal. It applies equally to trade among nations when they specialize according to comparative advantage.

The Supply and Demand for Imports and Exports

We will analyze the real aspects of international trade as if the world consisted of only two nations—the United States and Japan. While this is somewhat artificial, you should think of Japan as standing for "the rest of the world" relative to the United States. In other words, Japan stands for all of the other steel-manufacturing countries that export their product to the United States. In our illustration, Japan exports steel to the United States and receives dollars in return. Therefore, to keep everything straight, we will convert all Japanese prices into their dollar equivalents. As we develop the analysis of international trade in steel between Japan and the United States, you should bear in mind that trade essentially involves exchanging one set of *commodities* for another set of *commodities.* So even though we do not treat it explicitly, there is another *flow of currency from Japan* in exchange for *goods and services from the United States.*

*The **world price** is the price of purchasing a given commodity or service on the world market.*

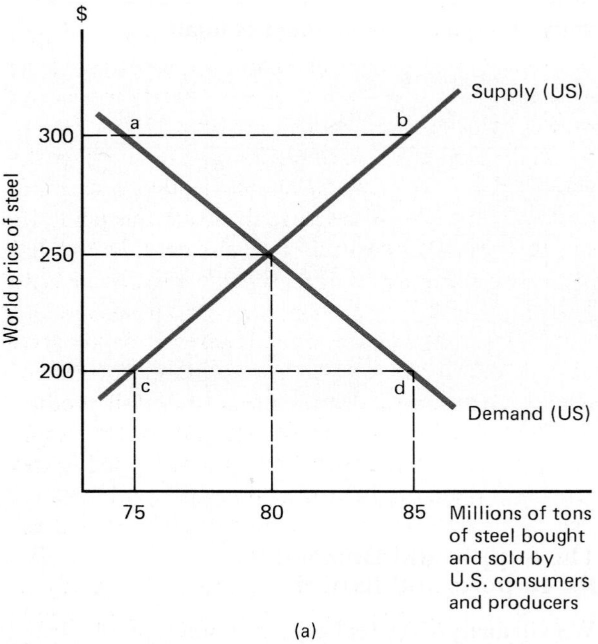

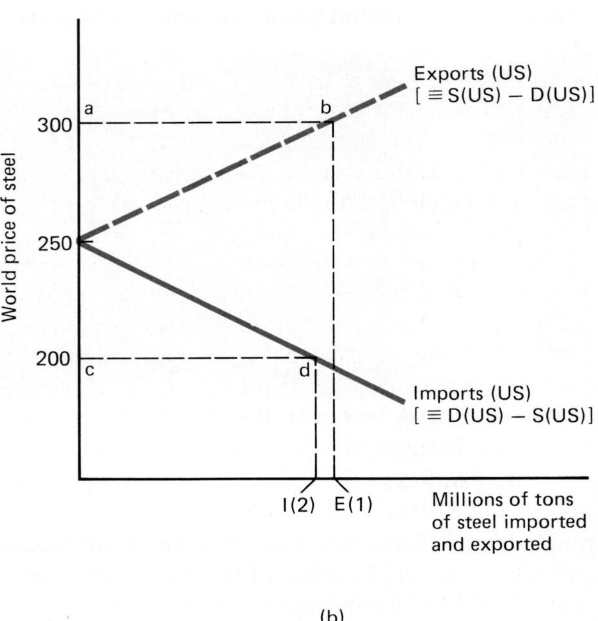

Figure 13.4 Steel supply and demand in the United States and its import and export curves
The world price is the price that prevails in each country when there are no restrictions on trade among nations. At a world price of $200, for example, United States producers wish to supply only 75 million tons of steel, while United States steel users demand 85 million tons. Therefore, imports from Japan will equal I(2) = 85 − 75 = 10 million tons at a world price of $200. At a world price of $300, there will be an excess supply of steel in the United States, which will be exported to Japan. The quantity of steel exported at a world price of $300 is E(1) tons.

The Effect of the World Price on Domestic Production and Consumption

In figure 13.4, part (a), we show the *long-run* supply and demand for steel in the United States. The vertical axis measures the **world price** of steel, which is the amount that it costs to purchase a ton of steel in the worldwide market for it. Suppose the world price of a ton of steel, measured in United States dollars, equals $250. At $250, the United States demand curve intersects the United States supply curve. This means that steel producers in the United States can sell their entire output of steel to United States citizens. At a price of $250, United States steel buyers are willing to purchase the total amount of steel that United States producers wish to sell. Of course, this is the same price that would prevail in the United States if the possibility of international trade in steel did not exist. If there were no international trade, a United States price above $250 would create an excess supply of steel, leading eventually to a reduction in price to $250. At prices below $250, an excess demand would exist and prices would rise to $250. However, with international trade, the price of steel in the United States need not converge to $250 as long as Japanese and American citizens are willing to conduct trade in steel with each another.

To see how trade works, refer to part (b) of figure 13.4. On the horizontal axis we measure the quantity of steel the United States would export or import at various world prices. Since the United States demand

and supply curves intersect at $250 per ton, the quantity of steel exported or imported by the United States at that price is zero. When the world price of steel is $250, no United States producer desires to trade with Japan because the producer can sell all its output to other United States citizens. No citizen needs to import from Japan because domestic production equals the quantity demanded.

Suppose now that the price of steel rose above $250 to, say, $300. We can immediately see in part (a) of figure 13.4 that the amount of steel produced by United States firms would exceed the quantity of steel demanded by United States buyers. Without the possibility of international trade, the excess supply in the United States (equal to the horizontal distance ab would lead to downward pressure on the price of steel in the United States. However, if $300 is the world price of steel and if steel can move freely across the borders of both countries, United States producers have the option of selling not only to United States citizens but also to Japanese buyers. International trade expands the market area in which producers can find potential customers for their output.

Assuming that the cost of transporting goods between the United States and Japan is not prohibitive, United States producers would attempt to export the amount of output that could not be sold to United States buyers at the price $300. By transferring the difference between the quantity supplied and the quantity demanded within the United States from part (a) to part (b) of figure 13.4, we obtain one point, b, on the United States export supply curve. In other words, the amount of steel that United States producers would like to export at price $300 is equal to the difference between United States production and United States demand at that price. If the world price of steel happened to rise above $300, we would observe a further increase in United States production and a reduction in the amount of steel demanded by United States buyers. As a result, the domestic excess supply within the United States would become even larger at prices above $300. In terms of figure 13.4, part (b), this simply means that United States firms would attempt to export a greater amount of steel. We conclude that the United States export supply curve begins at a price of $250 on the vertical axis, with the quantity of United States exports increasing as the world price of steel rises above $250.

A similar analysis demonstrates that whenever the world price lies *below* $250, the United States becomes an *importer* of steel. To illustrate this point, let us suppose that the world price of steel falls to $200 in part (a) of figure 13.4. At this price, United States buyers are willing to purchase the amount of steel indicated by point d on the United States demand curve. On the other hand, the decline in the world price of steel induces United States firms to curtail production to the quantity c on the United States supply curve. Without trade with Japan, some United States demanders find themselves unable to buy all the steel they desire at $200 because there exists a state of excess domestic demand equal to the horizontal distance between points d and c in figure 13.4, part (a). If trade is permitted, however, United States buyers can satisfy their excess demand by purchasing steel from Japanese producers. This excess demand becomes the United States demand for imported steel in part (b) of figure 13.4. At price $200, the demand for imports is derived by transferring the distance between points d and c in part (a) of figure 13.4 to part (b). If the world price of steel falls below $200, the United States demand for steel becomes larger. We conclude that the United States import demand curve in part (b) of figure 13.4 starts at a price of $250 and is negatively sloped with respect to the prices lying below $250 per ton of steel.

Before proceeding, let us summarize what we have just discussed concerning the forces that determine whether the United States imports or exports a particular product. There is some domestic price, $250 in figure 13.4, at which domestic supply and demand in the United States are equal. At that price, the United States will neither export nor import (steel in our example). At prices higher than $250, there is an excess supply of domestically produced steel. This excess supply is what the United States steel industry desires to export to the rest of the world. Combinations of excess supply and prices of $250 and above

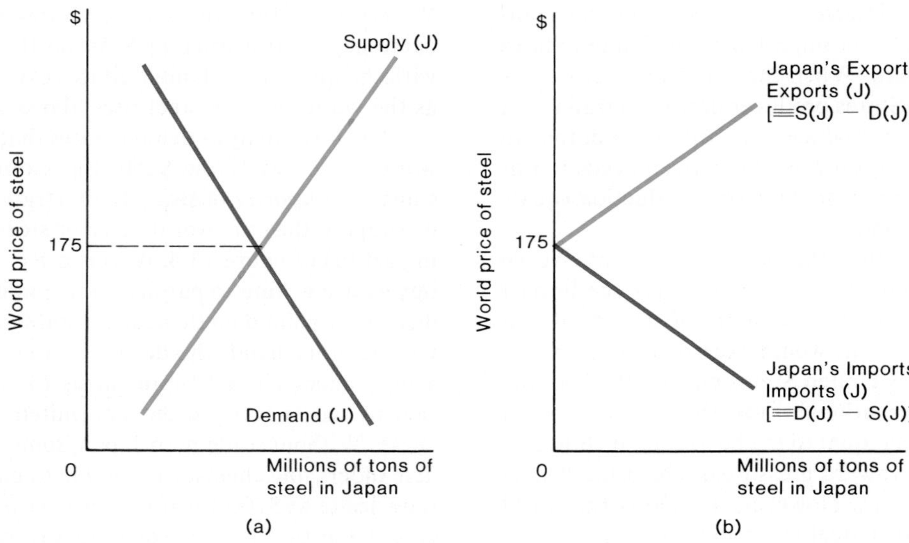

Figure 13.5 Japan's steel supply and demand and its import and export curves
If the world price rises above $175, Japan will export steel to the United States. If the world price falls below $175, Japan will import steel.

plot out the upward-sloping straight line in part (b) of figure 13.4, which is the United States steel-export supply schedule. Similarly, at prices below $250, there is an excess demand for steel by United States consumers. At any given price below $250, this excess demand is the steel that the United States consumers seek to import from the rest of the world. The combinations of excess demand and prices below $250 plot out the downward-sloping straight line in part (b) of figure 13.4, which is the United States steel-import demand curve. Figure 13.4, part (b), is useful because it describes how the United States changes from an importer to an exporter as the price of steel rises. The key question at this point is which of the possible prices in figure 13.4 holds when we consider the fact that there is a world market for steel. It is the *world* market price that determines whether the United States is in reality an importer or exporter.

The Equilibrium World Price and the Flow of Trade

To see whether the United States actually imports or exports steel, we need more information. We must gain knowledge of steel supply and demand in Japan because supply and demand in *both* countries interact to determine their status as importers or exporters.

Figure 13.5 indicates that at a world price of $175, the quantity of steel supplied by Japanese firms equals the quantity demanded by Japanese buyers. Thus, at a world price of $175, Japan would neither import nor export steel. The steel export supply and import demand curves for Japan are derived in the same manner as the corresponding United States curves. Whenever the world price of steel is above $175 the Japanese supply of steel exceeds the quantity demanded by Japanese buyers. Japanese firms will take the quantity of domestically produced steel that remains unsold (to Japanese buyers) and attempt to export this

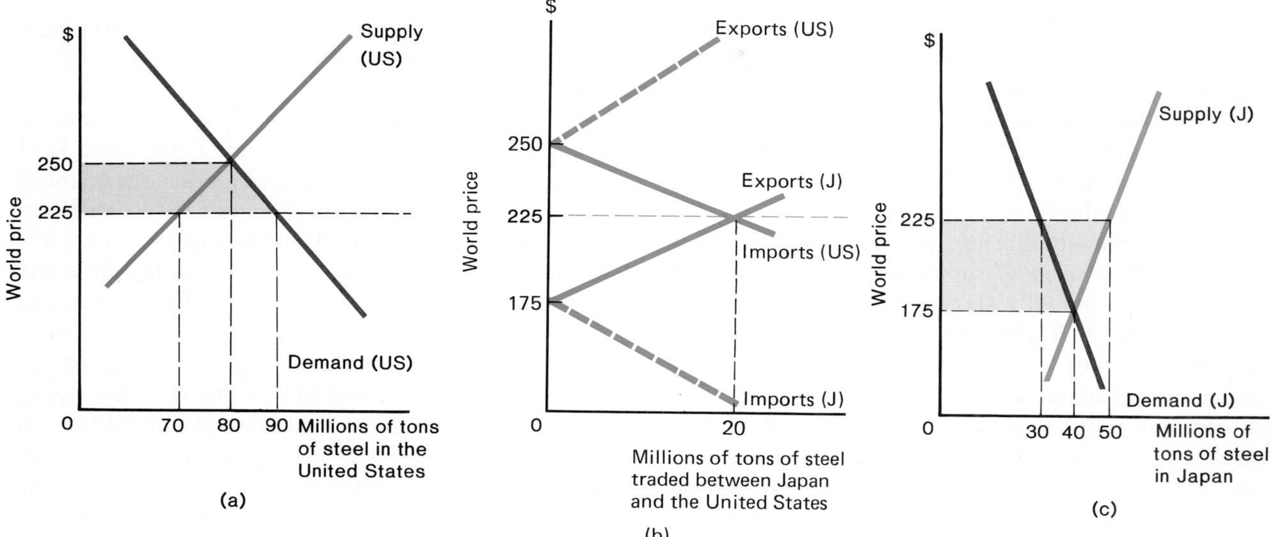

Figure 13.6 International equilibrium in the steel market
The equilibrium world price of $225 is determined by the intersection of the Japanese export supply curve with the United States import demand curve. At this price, the United States imports twenty million tons of steel from Japan. The shaded area in part (a) represents gains from trade to U.S. steel users, the shaded area in part (c) represents gains from trade to Japanese steel producers.

amount to the United States. As the world price of steel rises even farther above $175, the quantity of steel that Japan wishes to export becomes larger and larger. The reverse occurs whenever the world price of steel falls below $175. The quantity of steel that Japan wishes to import increases as the world price of steel falls even farther below $175. The export supply and import demand curves for Japan, therefore, extend from the price $175. The export supply curve for Japan is positively sloped, and the import demand curve is negatively sloped.

To determine the world equilibrium price of steel and to learn which country exports and which country imports steel, we must combine the information in figures 13.4 and 13.5. Figure 13.6, part (a), depicts the United States supply and demand curves, while part (c) depicts supply and demand in the Japanese steel market. Part (b) of the figure contains the import demand and export supply curves for *both* Japan and the United States. Two key prices on the vertical axes in part (b) are $175, the price equating Japanese supply and demand, and $250, the United States equilibrium price without trade. Given the way in which we have drawn the supply and demand curves for the two countries, the equilibrium price of $175 in Japan lies below the equilibrium price of $250 in the United States.

The world equilibrium price of steel is determined by *international* supply and demand. Figure 13.6 does not actually show total world supply and demand directly. Rather, it focuses on *excess* demand and supply. Thus, part (b) graphs the export supply and import demand curves for the two countries. The world equilibrium steel price is determined where one country's export supply curve intersects the other's import demand curve. In part (b) this intersection occurs at a price of $225 per ton of steel, where the Japanese export supply curve crosses the United States import demand curve. Given the positions of the supply and demand curves in the two countries, Japan will export steel and the United States will import steel. The equilibrium quantity of steel traded is 20 million tons. Japanese producers regard 20 million tons as the amount of steel exported to the United States, while Americans consider the same quantity, 20 million tons, as the amount of steel imported.

The 20 million tons of steel traded can also be interpreted in terms of parts (a) and (c) of figure 13.6. Consider first the Japanese steel market. When the world price of steel is $225 per ton, total production within Japan is indicated by the point on the Japanese supply curve corresponding to a price of $225. This quantity is shown on the horizontal axis in part (c) as 50 million tons of steel. The Japanese demand for steel when the world price is $225 is 30 million tons in part (c). At $225 per ton, the production of steel within Japan exceeds Japanese purchases. The domestic output produced but not sold to Japanese buyers is exported to the United States steel market. Similarly, in part (a) of figure 13.6 at the steel price $225 per ton, the quantity supplied by United States manufacturers equals 70 million tons while total purchases of steel is the amount 90 million tons. American buyers demand a quantity of steel that is greater than that produced by United States firms. This difference is, of course, the amount of Japanese exports or, equivalently, United States imports.

To emphasize how international trade equilibrium is reached, consider any price lying above $225 in part (b) of figure 13.6. At such a price, the quantity of steel that Japan wishes to export exceeds desired American imports. Some Japanese manufacturers will be unable to sell all they would like to Japanese *and* American buyers. The higher price has encouraged Japanese producers to expand their output of steel, but unfortunately for them, it has also reduced the quantity of steel demanded in America. This higher price cannot prevail for any length of time because in the face of unsold production Japanese manufacturers will begin to offer lower prices to buyers. The downward pressure on prices is removed only when a steel price of $225 per ton has been reached. A similar analysis applies to any price below $225. In this case, upward pressure on the price of steel is exerted by unhappy buyers who are unable to obtain all of the steel they demand at prices below $225. At $225, the price at which the export supply and import demand curves intersect, there is world equilibrium. At that price *alone* all producers and buyers will be satisfied with the quantity of steel being bought and sold in the world market.

It is very important that you recognize the basic reason for Japan's willingness to export steel to the United States. Ultimately, Japan must be able to import goods it values in return. To see how this reverse flow from the United States to Japan works and to make sure that you thoroughly understand the diagrams illustrating the flow of steel exported from Japan and imported by the United States, take a piece of paper and construct a set of diagrams like figure 13.6 showing exports from the United States to Japan. Suppose, for example, that because of Japan's limited boundaries, it does not have much land to grow rice. The United States, on the other hand, has a great deal of farmland, and United States citizens are not devoted rice eaters. Therefore, the domestic market clearing price in the United States for the rice market, $3 per ton, is *lower* than that in Japan, $5 per ton.

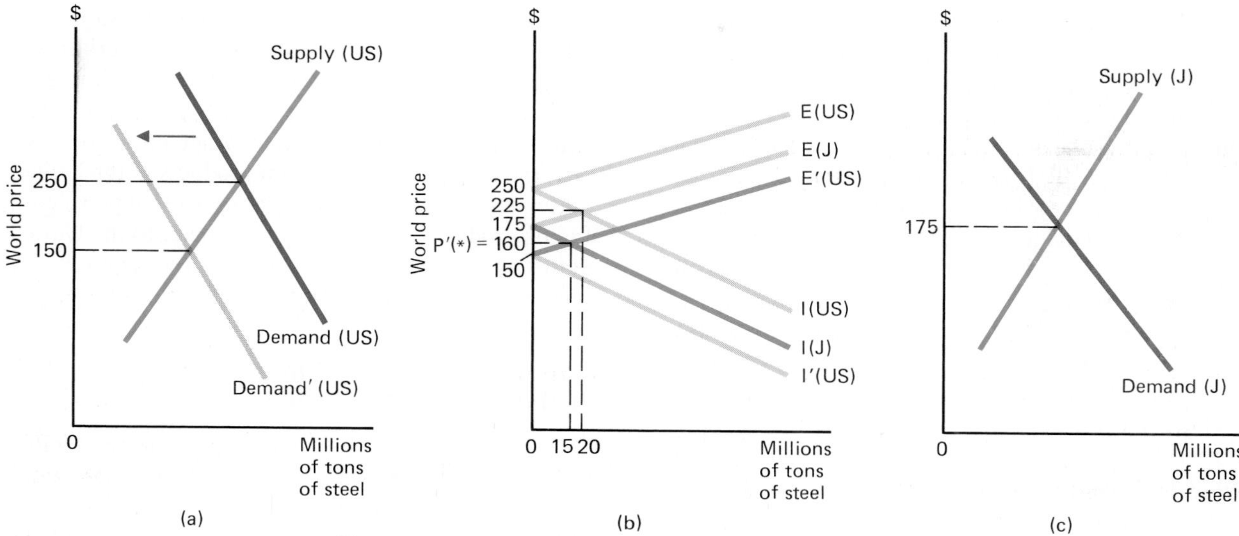

Figure 13.7 A change in import and export patterns caused by a change in steel demand in the United States
Part (a): United States supply and demand. As a result of a change in the U.S. demand for steel, the domestic market-clearing price in the United States has fallen from $250 to $150. Because demand and supply have not changed in Japan, United States producers can sell some of the steel that United States consumers used to buy to Japanese importers.

Part (b): as a result of the decline in steel demand in the United States, the United States has become an exporter of steel and Japan an importer.

Part (c): even though there has been no change in Japanese demand or supply of steel, a decline in the world price of steel means that Japanese consumers can now obtain steel at a lower price than before. The decline in the world price of steel has caused Japanese steel producers to reduce the quantity of steel produced.

With this starting point, construct the United States export supply curve for rice and the Japanese import demand curve. Show the equilibrium world price of rice and the quantity exported from the United States to Japan. Under what circumstances might the United States become an importer of rice?

Supply, Demand, and International Trade Patterns

In the preceding example, Japan exports steel to the United States because the domestic market clearing price in Japan, $175 per ton, is lower than the domestic market clearing price in the United States, $250 per ton. Japan exports steel *in part* because it is a low-cost producer. Yet this is not the whole story. We know prices are also partly determined by demand conditions in the two countries. It is very important to understand that the relationship between prices in the countries without trade, which determines whether Japan exports or imports steel, depends on *both supply and demand conditions*. To see why demand is also a basic determinant of imports and exports, consider the following example.

Suppose that Americans (but not Japanese) suddenly become allergic to products made with steel. As a result, production in the United States uses more aluminum and less steel whenever metal is required. This new situation makes the United States demand curve for steel shift to the left as illustrated in part (a) of figure 13.7. As this happens, the domestic market clearing price that equates the quantity of steel supplied and demanded in the United States falls to $150, which is below $250, the price that existed prior to the allergic reaction to steel. As shown in part (a) of figure 13.7, the United States demand curve shifts so far to the left that the new price in the United States is now also lower than the domestic market clearing price in Japan, $175. Therefore, even though United States *supply* and both Japanese demand and supply are unchanged, the new United States export supply curve, E′(US), now intersects the Japanese import demand curve, I(J), in part (b) of figure 13.7. The United States import demand curve, I′(US), does *not* intersect the Japanese export supply curve, E(J). In other words, Japan becomes the importer of steel and the United States the exporter.

The Japanese might attribute their new status of importer to the "low costs" of American steel. However, we have not hypothesized any change in the technological capabilities of United States manufacturers; the shift in the United States demand curve *alone* is responsible for the reversal of export-import roles. Because the United States demand curve has shifted leftward in our example, the more costly producers of steel in the United States have been forced out of the industry. With only the relatively more efficient United States producers left, the relative international cost positions have shifted between Japan and the United States. The end result is that the United States becomes the relatively low-cost producer of steel.

To make sure that you understand how a shift in demand or supply can change the roles played by two nations in international trade, take a piece of paper and draw three diagrams corresponding to figure 13.7. Now illustrate how the discovery of new, high-grade iron ore deposits in the United States would cause the United States supply curve of steel to shift to the right. Once again, the domestic market clearing price of steel in the United States will fall. Make sure that you shift the United States steel supply curve far enough to the right so that the United States domestic price before trade is below the Japanese pretrade domestic price. This way the United States export supply curve crosses the Japanese import curve in the middle diagram. Show what happens to the world price of steel and the direction of import and export flows. What happens to the price of steel paid by Japanese steel users? What economic effect does the change in United States steel supply have on Japanese steel producers?

An *actual* example of how demand and supply together determine world trade patterns occurs in the petroleum industry. The United States has immense reserves of crude oil, and its annual production is less than that of only three or four other nations. However, the demand for petroleum products in the United States is so great that it is a net *importer* of petroleum and its products. One principal exporter to the United States is Nigeria, whose annual production is far smaller but whose demand for petroleum is lower yet.

Winners and Losers: The Distribution of the Gains from Trade

We will now analyze how *both* Japan and the United States benefit from trade in steel and how these gains are divided between producers and consumers within the two countries. The *within*-country division of the gains from trade explains why governments are continuously tempted to restrict trade patterns that potentially benefit *everyone.*

Winners and Losers in the Importing Country

Imagine what the steel market would be like in the United States if there were no international trade with Japan. In this case the United States market equilibrium position would depend solely on the positions of the United States demand and supply curves. In figure 13.6, part (a), the no-trade steel market equilibrium for the United States occurs at a price of $250 per ton and a quantity of 80 million tons. When international trade in steel is established with Japan, the price of steel drops to $225 per ton. This decline immediately confers a substantial benefit on American consumers. As the price of steel falls, American consumption rises from 80 million tons to 90 million tons. The reduction in steel prices permits American consumers to purchase more goods and services, especially products made with steel. Relatively poor citizens may now be able to buy such items as new stoves, cars, and refrigerators because lower steel prices will make their limited budgets stretch farther.

The gainers from trade, then, are United States consumers who can buy a larger quantity of goods and services. However, some people will be worse off as a result of the competition from Japanese manufacturers. The principal losers are American steel producers. Examining part (a) of figure 13.6, we observe that trade will ultimately curtail United States steel production from 80 million tons to 70 million tons. Trade with Japan will *eliminate* from the steel market those producers whose costs exceed $225 per ton. They will no longer be able to make and sell steel profitably because Japanese producers can do so at a lower cost. These producers, along with the workers they employ, are well aware of such effects and may attempt to prevent them by encouraging trade restrictions. In this way, they resist the competitive pressure on them to exit from the steel market to other industries making products that can be sold to United States buyers or exported.

In our example, the Japanese can produce steel at lower costs than *some* United States manufacturers. This cost advantage does *not* mean there will be *nothing* for *anyone* in the United States to produce. The United States *must* have something to sell to the Japanese or others in return for the dollars paid to import Japanese steel. In a world where people have varied talents, some can do certain tasks at lower opportunity costs than others. Thus, high-cost United States producers of steel will *always* be able to switch and compete effectively in other industries where the United States is *relatively* more efficient. The transition may be an unpleasant experience, but new jobs and industries *are* available to those forced to leave the steel industry.

It is important to remember that transferring resources to nonsteel-producing industries may be a painful process for the workers and the owners of other inputs used in steel manufacturing. During the transition period, they may experience unemployment and depressed incomes. In the long run, however, steel producers will be able to cover all their opportunity costs by shifting their efforts to other industries.

A second group that loses when steel trade with Japan is opened up are the low-cost United States manufacturers of steel. These producers are located in that segment of the United States supply curve lying to the left of 70 million tons in part (a) of figure 13.6. Costs for these producers remain unchanged, but under the pressure of Japanese competition, the price they can charge—and hence the revenue they receive—declines.

Can we determine whether the net benefits associated with international trade are positive or negative? When most economists figure out the tally sheet for all society, the answer comes down unequivocally on the side of net positive benefits. The value of the gains received by buyers of steel outweighs the value of the losses experienced by the producers of steel. In other words, the gainers could *conceivably* compensate the losers and still have some positive gains left over. Instead of providing a complicated graphical proof of this assertion, let us use a simple numerical example. Suppose that in the pretrade situation a United States buyer purchased a ton of steel for $250. In manufacturing this ton of steel, the producer incurred $240 worth of cost, so that the producer received an economic profit of $10 per ton.

When the Japanese begin exporting steel to the United States the price of steel falls to, say, $225 per ton. The United States buyer, who was willing to pay $250 but who now need pay only $225, receives a benefit of $25 per ton. The United States producer must pay $240 for inputs that yield steel now selling for only $225. This results in a loss for the producer equal to $15 per ton of steel instead of the $10 profit the producer was accustomed to receiving. The producer can avoid the $15 loss by not purchasing the resources required to manufacture the ton of steel. These resources will no longer be used to produce steel in the United States and are now available to produce output in *another* industry. We would expect the $240 worth of inputs to yield output in another industry that can be sold for $240.

How do we know that $240 worth of resources will produce output in another industry that can be sold for $240? Assuming that the rest of the United States economy is in competitive equilibrium, we know (from chapter 3) that the cost of an additional extra unit of an input is equal to the value of its marginal product. Remember that when a price-taking firm maximizes its profit, its marginal cost equals the price of the good or service produced. Equivalently, the amount paid for a small additional amount of an input equals the value to the firm of the output it produces with that input. Thus, the $240 worth of resources that had been used to manufacture a ton of steel can be used elsewhere in the economy to produce output valued at $240.

In transferring out of the steel industry, the producer in our example will, of course, lose $10 in profit (or economic rent). That is, in the steel industry, the producer had been able to sell output for $250 that cost only $240 to produce before Japan began exporting steel to the United States. This may be because the producer had a "talent" for steel production. This talent is presumably not transferable to another industry. Yet, if you carefully examine the numbers involved, you will see that the steel buyers could give the producer, say, $20 as a more-than-sufficient compensation to cover the producer's loss in rent. The $20 comes from the benefit the buyer receives because it is now necessary to pay only $225 per ton of steel. The buyer would still be better off by $5 per ton of steel purchased. Trade creates net benefits in the sense that *all* United States citizens engaged in the buying and selling of steel *could* be better off by permitting Japanese firms to enter the United States market and compete with American manufacturers. It is important to note that in fact winners do not tend to compensate losers. The autoworkers in our introductory example were not compensated for their losses, and in their blind rage they killed an innocent young man.

There are additional gains in the United States. The United States demand curve in figure 13.6 shows how much Americans are willing to pay to purchase steel in excess of 80 million tons per year. Since $225 is less than this amount for all but the last ton purchased, American steel buyers are better off than they were. They have the opportunity to increase their steel purchases at a price lower than they were *willing* to pay for more steel.

It cannot be emphasized too strongly that the general principle of the gains from trade does not depend in any way on the particular numbers we have chosen. If consumption of steel in the United States remained at 80 million tons following the introduction of trade from Japan, each consumer would benefit from a reduction in the price of steel. At a *minimum,* each consumer could be "taxed" an amount equivalent to his or her saving in expenditure on steel and steel products, and the proceeds could be given to steel producers who suffered lower revenues. However, steel users *voluntarily* increase their purchases of steel to 90 million tons at the new, lower price. They would not do this if it did not make them better off because they could, if they chose, continue to purchase the original quantity, 80 million tons. Steel consumption increases because the value of additional steel to steel users exceeds its cost. This additional benefit of steel consumption is represented by the shaded area under the United States steel demand curve to the right of 80 million tons in part (a) of figure 13.6. An additional net benefit to the United States comes from the fact that steel producers will not continue to produce 80 million tons of steel. The resources that had been used to manufacture 80 million less 70 million tons of steel, or 10 million tons of steel, will be transferred to other industries. The additional production in these industries represents a net gain to the United States economy because the steel that had been manufactured with these resources has been replaced by imports from Japan. This net gain is represented by the shaded area under the United States steel supply curve to the left of 80 million tons in part (a) of figure 13.6.

Before discussing the winners and losers in the exporting country, let us summarize what we have just found. In the importing country, the winners are primarily the consumers of steel and steel products who now either buy steel when before they did not or now buy steel for a lower price than before. The losers in the importing country include not only the high-cost firms who no longer produce steel but also the low-cost producers who now receive lower economic rents. Of course, it is really the workers and stockholders in these latter steel firms who are worse off because of their reduced profits and job opportunities. It is important for us to remember that the identity of the losers is a key political issue. Even though there is enough economic gain for the winners in the importing country to compensate the losers and have something left over, the politics of the situation are almost never going to make this happen. The losers from trade faced with little or no hope of compensation may simply try to block trade, thus making the country as a whole worse off.

This analysis of the gains and losses from trade is perhaps one of the most widely accepted principles of economics among economists. Nevertheless, it is surprising—indeed shocking—that occasionally an economist is found who claims that unrestricted international trade actually harms losers in an importing country more than it benefits winners. As far as we are aware, such arguments are based on a basic misunderstanding of the reasons countries trade with each other. In one fairly recent example, a well-known economist at a major university claimed that the analysis of international trade we have presented is in error because "There is little comparative advantage in today's manufacturing industries, since they produce the same goods in the same ways in all parts of the world."[3] In other words, this economist claims that the gains from trade depend on trading partners using different technologies. In fact, the entire analysis we have presented is based on the assumption that Japan and the United States (or any two trading partners) have access to exactly the same technology for producing traded goods. The advantage of trade comes from the fact that different countries have different resources and types of labor, as well as different demand curves for the traded goods. This is the reason that they can and do gain, on balance, from unrestricted trade.

Winners and Losers in the Exporting Country

A comparison of pretrade and posttrade positions in Japan reveals that the pattern of Japanese gains and losses is precisely the opposite of that in the United States steel market. Prior to trade, the Japanese equilibrium price equaled $175 in figure 13.6, part (c), while the quantity of steel bought and sold in Japan had been 40 million tons. With trade, the price of steel in Japan rises to the world equilibrium price of $225 per ton. This price increase leads to a reduction of Japanese consumption to 30 million tons and an expansion in steel production to 50 million tons. The losers, then, are the Japanese buyers of steel and steel products who now pay higher prices. Japanese steel manufacturers receive benefits in the form of increased profit (or economic rent). Summing up the gains and losses within Japan will again produce a total positive net benefit for that country. The value of the Japanese steel buyers' losses is smaller than the value of the gains reaped by Japanese steel producers. Conceptually, we could redistribute the gains among all Japanese citizens so that each and every one is made to feel better off as a result of international trade.

How do we know that the value of Japanese steel buyers' losses is smaller than the value of the gains of Japanese steel producers? The analysis is similar to that of the distribution of gains and losses in the United States. To make the discussion simple, we will measure Japanese prices in terms of dollars. Suppose in the pretrade position a Japanese buyer purchased a ton of steel for $175 and in making this steel, the Japanese producer incurred $175 worth of opportunity cost so that economic rent was zero. When trade is opened with the United States, the price of steel rises to $225 per ton. The Japanese buyer now has to pay $225 for the same ton of steel that previously cost only $175.

Obviously, if $50 x 40 million tons of steel (the amount that would be produced in Japan without trade), or $2 billion, were taken from steel producers and distributed to Japanese steel consumers, consumers would be no worse off than before. Japanese steel producers, however, would still have an incentive to increase their production of steel to 50 million tons because the price of steel has risen to $225 per ton. The opportunity cost to the Japanese economy of this increased steel production is represented by the Japanese steel supply curve. Therefore, the shaded area in part (c) of figure 13.6 to the right of 40 million tons represents a gain to Japanese steel producers that does not correspond to a loss for Japanese steel users. They earn increased profit (or economic rent) by producing additional steel for the export market. The reason that Japanese producers can obtain the resources required to produce more steel without causing a loss to others is that producers must pay for the additional resources used. They are willing to pay because they can now sell the additional steel for more than the resources to produce it cost them.

There are additional net gains to the Japanese economy. Even if Japanese steel users were paid $50 for each ton of steel they used to purchase, they would no longer desire to purchase 40 million tons of steel. The Japanese demand curve indicates that at the new price of steel, $225, Japanese steel users prefer to substitute other goods for steel and therefore reduce the quantity of steel purchased to 30 million tons. Since they would have enough money to continue to purchase the amount of steel they used to but would choose to adjust their expenditures, they would be better off as a result of this adjustment. The shaded area above the Japanese steel demand curve to the left of 40 million tons represents an additional net gain from trade to the Japanese economy. It indicates that Japanese citizens can find goods other than steel to satisfy their needs when the price of steel increases. The source of this gain—as well as the gain described in the preceding paragraph—comes from the increase in the price Japanese producers receive for their steel. The higher price reflects the real value of the dollars earned by Japanese exporters when they sell steel to United States purchasers.

We have shown that no one *need* be worse off as a result of international trade. *From the viewpoint of both Japan and the United States, then, unimpeded trade in steel creates net benefits for the two countries.* Although there are likely to be winners and losers in both countries, the gains of the winners (consumers in the United States and producers in Japan) exceed the losses of the losers (producers in the United States and consumers in Japan).

To understand opposition to free trade it is important to realize that the losers from free trade within a country, particularly firms and workers producing goods that can be imported cheaply, are rarely compensated for their losses by the winners. Consequently, protectionist interests are not impressed by the efficiency arguments for free trade.

Summary and Conclusions

Failure to understand the crucial importance of foreign trade to our economic well-being and the cruel hardships that changes in international trading patterns can inflict on citizens of both importing and exporting nations can lead only to tragic consequences for nations and the individuals who live in them. In this chapter we have explored the conditions determining patterns of world trade. The following major points were emphasized.

The United States is a major international trading partner, even though imports and exports make up only a relatively small share of its GNP compared to other nations.

The relative shares of broad commodity groups in United States imports and exports have changed in recent years, reflecting the changing pattern of comparative advantage.

Unrestricted trade benefits all trading nations.

The *distribution* of the gains from trade may result in some groups within each nation being worse off than they would be without trade, even though everyone can *potentially* be made better off through unrestricted international trade. Generally, losers know that they will not be compensated and therefore oppose free trade.

Because international trade involves an exchange of imports for exports and exports for imports, each trading partner has *both* winners and losers.

The major winners in importing countries are consumers, and the major losers are producers and their employees. The major winners in exporting countries are producers and their employees, and the major losers are consumers of the exported products.

Key Terms

monetary aspects of international trade *274*

real aspects of international trade *274*

world price *280*

Questions for Discussion and Review

In questions 1 through 4, judge whether the statements are true, false, or uncertain. Be sure to justify your answer graphically.

1. Even though every nation benefits from trade, some groups within each nation may lose.
2. A country always exports the good that its economy produces the most of.
3. The first country to be the low-cost producer of a good will always be the exporter of that good.
4. A wage increase among Japanese automobile producers will raise only the Japanese domestic price of cars and not the world price.
5. Figure 13.8 depicts international trade in wheat between Egypt and the United States. Which country will export wheat and which will import wheat? Why?
6. In the mid-1970s, a suggested cure for rising food prices in the United States was to restrict exports of United States agricultural output (wheat, corn, etc.). What effect would such a policy have had on domestic food prices, on world food prices, and on United States economic well-being? Illustrate your answer with a diagram.

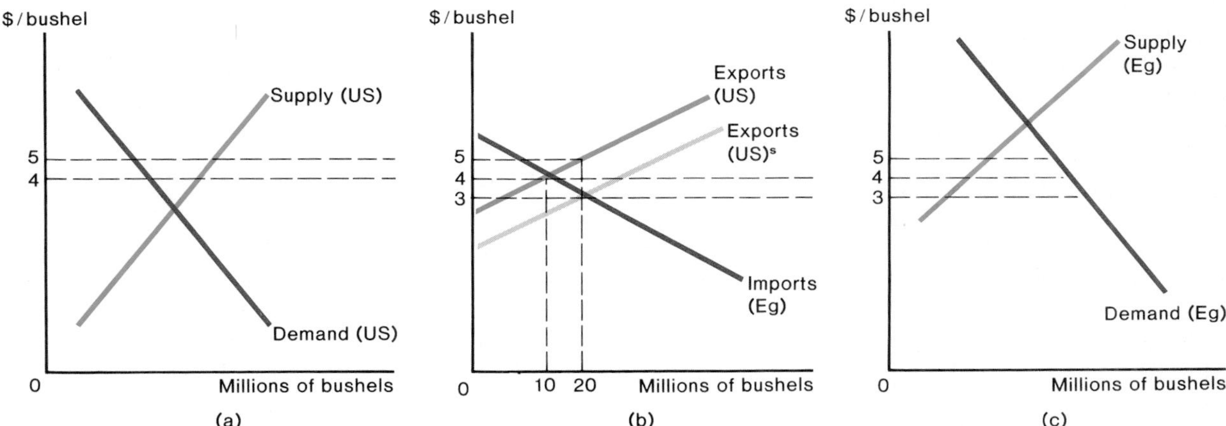

Figure 13.8 Effects of a United States subsidy on wheat exports to Egypt
If the United States subsidizes exports of wheat to Egypt, this is equivalent to lowering the United States export supply curve to (US)ˢ. The equilibrium price of wheat exports to Egypt falls, and exports of wheat to Egypt increase from ten million tons to twenty million tons.

7. True or false: Two countries that produce an identical commodity with identical technologies and labor costs will have no reason to trade. Defend your answer.
8. Draw the export and import functions for a commodity in two different countries. Show the effects of each of the following changes separately.
   a. An increase in demand for the exported good in the exporting country.
   b. A decrease in demand for the imported good in the importing country.
   c. A simultaneous decrease in demand in both countries for the good traded.
9. Suppose Japan exports steel to the United States at the world price of $\overset{*}{P}$. Suppose the Japanese domestic demand for steel increases to where the domestic equilibrium price is equal to $\overset{*}{P}$. Will steel exports cease? Explain.
10. Suppose a strike settlement in the United States steel industry raises domestic steel prices above Japanese domestic steel prices. Identify the posttrade winners and losers.

Chapter 14

The Regulation of International Trade

Outline

Objectives

After reading this chapter, the student should be able to:

Explain why countries frequently restrict international trade flows.

Evaluate the national security and infant industry arguments for import restrictions.

Show the effects of a tariff on the price (in the importing and exporting countries) of a commodity and the quantity traded.

Discuss the losers and winners in each country from the imposition of a tariff.

Explain how the textile and steel industries used specific duties to protect low-quality goods.

Discuss the losers and winners in each country from a nontariff trade barrier such as a quota.

Discuss the effects of a voluntary quota on Japanese automobile exports to the United States.

Describe the provisions of the General Agreement on Tariffs and Trade (GATT) and the Trade Expansion Act of 1962.

Show the gains and losses associated with the formation of a customs union.

Introduction

Textiles have been an important industry in the state of North Carolina and other states in the South. In 1985, a chain of grocery stores used bags carrying the following message: "If you and every other American shopper would redirect only $20 of your clothing purchases to American-made products rather than imports, you would immediately help create 100,000 American textile and apparel jobs. Think of what that would do for our textile-producing friends."

The grocery bag message recognizes the link between purchases of a product and job opportunities. It plays on our love of country and feelings of guilt at perhaps creating a job for a Korean instead of an American through our textile purchases. Such a campaign may fail to maintain job opportunities, however, if Americans basically prefer the quality and styling of foreign-made products. In 1985, a survey by the University of Detroit in cooperation with the Detroit News *found that people who live in Detroit, the heart of the American auto industry, felt that Japanese cars were better than American cars. In particular, 45 percent versus 15 percent of those polled felt Japanese cars were of higher quality than American cars. Lee Iacocca, the head of Chrysler Corporation, has often said that the government should do more to protect the American auto industry from "unfair" foreign competition. Recently, however, Chrysler bought a company airplane. The plane it chose was manufactured by a Canadian firm. When asked why a company that is such a proponent of "Buy American" would purchase a foreign-made airplane, the Chrysler Corporation's representative replied, "It was the best airplane available for what we wanted." In chapter 13, we saw that individual countries and the world as a whole benefit from free trade. Free trade permits each country to specialize in the production of goods and services that it can produce relatively most efficiently. These gains from trade increase the total amount of goods and services that the world has to distribute among countries and that countries have to distribute among their citizens. We also saw in chapter 13 that not all groups automatically benefit from international trade. Some groups, primarily workers and stockholders of firms in import-competing industries, would prefer to restrict trade in one form or another. We should not forget, however, that firms and workers in the export sector and consumers in general benefit from free trade. Thus, the regulation of international trade will also create winners and losers. An additional subtlety is that the government can profit in terms of political and financial power by paying attention to who the winners and losers from trade policy are and regulating trade to its (the government's) own best advantage.*

A primary focus of this chapter will be on some of the more popular forms of trade restraints. We will also explain why trade restrictions are so pervasive when free trade is such a good economic idea. Third, we will explain how different forms of trade restriction work. Fourth, we will investigate why some forms of trade restriction are proliferating at the same time international negotiations are succeeding in reducing other forms of trade barriers. Finally, we will try to see why developing countries feel that international agreements to reduce trade restrictions have failed to address their particular concerns adequately.

▸ Why Interfere with a Good Thing?

One of the earliest motives for restricting international trade was to raise money for the government. When nation-states were first established, sovereigns had to secure their nations' borders from possible attack. Once armies have secured borders and therefore gained control of crossing points, much of the administrative structure necessary to collect taxes on anything going in or out is in place. Historically, border taxes—particularly taxes on imports—played a primary role in providing central governments with revenues with which to conduct their business. In case after case, one finds central governments moving toward freer trade only after alternative sources of revenue to import taxes have been found.

Internal Taxes as Substitutes for Tariffs: British and United States Experiences

Britain is often cited in textbooks as the historical leader in promoting freer trade in the nineteenth century. The dismantling of trade restrictions in Britain began in earnest in the mid-1820s. By the late 1830s the average tax rate on imports in Britain declined to 31 percent. However, the most dramatic steps in trade liberalization in Britain occurred along with the adoption of the income tax by the Peel government in 1841. When the income tax was renewed and made permanent in 1845, import taxes were eliminated on 450 items.

Throughout the post-World War II period, the United States has assumed a leadership role in the movement to deregulate international trade. Yet efforts to reduce or eliminate import taxes in the United States were largely frustrated after the Civil War until the income tax amendment was submitted to the states in 1909 and adopted in 1913.

Not surprisingly, today many developing countries that lack a well-developed system of internal taxes rely upon import and export taxes to provide revenue for their central governments. As governments develop alternative means of raising revenues, trade barriers generally decline.

Income Distribution Considerations

Following tax revenue, the most important reason for restrictions to international trade involves income distribution considerations. This is particularly true for restrictions on imports. While the aggregate gain from trade may be substantial, any individual buyer enjoys only a relatively small part of the total gain in his or her country. The total gain is widely diffused through the entire economy. Losers, however, are concentrated in one or several industries in importing nations. For example, in 1977 the value of all textiles (a United States industry that experiences severe foreign competition) shipped by United States manufacturers plus net imports (imports less exports) amounted to $173 for every member of the United States population.[1] The losers from import competition, on the other hand, lose big and are usually concentrated within particular regions, such as New England and the South in the case of textiles. In 1977, there were 876,000 textile workers in the United States, each earning an average of $9,000 per year.[2] Thus, in a very real sense, each worker's interest in the textile industry and in protecting it from foreign competition is about fifty times greater than that of a typical consumer. This is not to mention the *owners* of textile firms.

Textile workers and the firms that employ them fully recognize that the hypothetical compensation we discussed in the steel industry example of chapter 13 is unlikely to be translated into voluntary dollars and cents payments by those who gain from unrestricted trade. The losers see themselves as victims of unfair competition from exporting nations. Their strategy is quite simple: The losers must convince the government to limit the ability of foreigners to compete in domestic markets. Of course, this objective is seldom stated openly. Emotional appeals may be more effective—producers arguing about the unfair advantages of foreign manufacturers who exploit their workers by paying them sweat-shop wages. In conjunction with their employers, American workers will also complain that foreigners are stealing American jobs.[3] Textile production may even be labeled as vital to our national security and part of our cultural heritage. (We cannot have the United States Army depend on foreigners for boots and uniforms. Textile weaving dates back to the early colonial settlers of the Atlantic seaboard.) Congress, as a result, will be under great pressure to appease the parties who claim injury from foreign import competition.

The study of the politics and economics of international trade restrictions can be traced back to the eighteenth-century economist Adam Smith and his contemporaries. But the efforts to quantify the extent to which trade is regulated and to explain how political and economic forces combine to succeed in restricting trade have been the focus of an expanding body of research in the last fifteen years. Throughout our discussion in this chapter, we will refer to that literature for insights into the nature and scope of trade regulations today.

Strategic Goods and Infant Industries: Bases for Import Barriers?

Arguments other than those based on revenue needs of the central government or income distribution considerations can be used to support government restrictions on international trade. (1) It is dangerous to rely on foreign countries to supply goods that are indispensable for national defense; and (2) our country's relative price disadvantage in producing a good may change to an advantage once domestic firms gain sufficient experience to become internationally competitive.

There is doubtless merit in avoiding the risk of being deprived of some strategic resource such as steel or petroleum should international trade be restricted or cut off entirely by war. Even if the supplier of such a resource is not a military antagonist, air and sea transportation could become extremely difficult. There are sound reasons why a government, as part of overall defense strategy, should make sure that it is able to supply military needs in time of war. It does not follow, however, that restrictions on international trade in time of peace constitute the best policy. There are alternatives. One is simply to stockpile the materials that may be needed for military purposes. The United States government does, in fact, maintain strategic stockpiles of various metals and minerals, even of morphine, for military and civilian emergency use. There is also a strategic oil reserve of underground caverns designed to be filled with crude oil to be used in the event of a national emergency.

It may be argued that, in addition to material stockpiles, it is also necessary to preserve production capability of items such as steel and other key manufactured goods. This may require barriers to foreign competition in order to keep strategically needed firms from going out of business. Carried to its extreme, however, the strategic industry argument can be used to justify protecting almost every industry. After all, soldiers need all of the consumer items that civilians do, in addition to military goods. Thus, why not protect the industries that produce shoes, soap, movies to relieve boredom, rice for a varied diet, and sugar for desserts to maintain morale? As with any other defense strategy, protecting domestic industries has costs that must be weighed against the strategy's prospective benefits. Most economists are generally skeptical of arguments in favor of restricting trade for strategic purposes. Generally, there are less costly means of insuring military preparedness than protecting high-cost industries from international competition.

*The **infant industry argument** for trade restriction states that if an industry is protected in its early years of development, when it is unable to compete on the world market, it will be saved in the long term because the production experience it gains will ultimately make it competitive.*

Strategic Supplies of Steel

The United States steel industry has used national security as an argument to bolster its frequent demand for restrictions on imported steel. From the mid-1970s until today, United States producers of steel have faced stiff competition in the form of imports from Japan and Europe, particularly West Germany, and more recently from South Korea and Brazil. Capacity utilization has remained at or below 60 percent in the United States steel industry throughout this period and fell to a low of 38 percent during the 1982–83 recession. The national security argument has been a significant part of the steel industry's successful battle for systematic restrictions on steel imports into the United States. Yet actual military needs for steel require no more than 10 percent of the economy's existing capacity. Contrary to industry claims, when stiff import competition started the process of shaking out inefficient firms that use outdated production technologies, our ability to satisfy strategic demand for steel was never threatened.

Infant Industries and Technology Transfers

A second reason sometimes stated by engineers and economists to support foreign trade restrictions is based on technical considerations. It is generally recognized that firms learn to be more efficient as they gain experience with new products or production techniques. The **infant industry argument** for trade restrictions states that the reduction in costs that occurs with accumulated production of a good can ultimately reverse a nation's relative price disadvantage in world trade. It does not follow, however, that trade restriction is the best means of securing these cost reductions. By definition, if a nation has a comparative disadvantage in international trade because its firms lack experience in production, there are firms in other nations that do have this expertise. Unless there are legal restrictions on exporting their technology or knowledge, it should be possible to purchase it or to pay foreign firms for their assistance in developing domestic capabilities. If this is possible, then the cost of purchasing foreign technology outright must be weighed against the costs of restricting trade. While the cost of outright purchase is confined to the industries directly involved, the cost of trade restrictions can be much broader. This is especially true if economic warfare results in barriers that affect trade in a wide variety of unrelated goods and services.

Historically, some international restrictions on the transfer of technology might have justified the infant industry argument as a valid reason for international trade restrictions. For example, during the late eighteenth and early nineteenth centuries, England attempted to prohibit the international transfer of information on modern textile production technology. Originally, China was the only country in which knowledge of silk production from silkworms was known, and China guarded its knowledge zealously. (It is said that among Marco Polo's acquisitions on his legendary journey to China were knowledge of silk technology and of the noodle. Both industries, of course, have greatly benefited the Italian economy.) Today, the United States and other nations protect many trade secrets through patents and other means. Moreover, restrictions are imposed on transfer of strategically valuable technology to potentially unfriendly nations. Nevertheless, international transfer of technology and expertise does occur, and it is generally an efficient substitute for trade barriers. One example is the attempt by General Motors to gain knowledge of Japanese methods for producing relatively inexpensive small cars by forming a joint venture with Toyota in the United States.[4]

Just as with the strategic goods and industries argument, the infant industry argument can easily be used as an excuse to support government protection for high-cost industries. This protection cannot typically be justified on efficiency grounds, however. Again, most economists tend to believe that unless exceptional circumstances can be documented, the domestic firms directly involved can arrange to acquire improved technology by purchasing it from foreign firms or negotiating joint ventures whereby both

Import substitution is the use of trade restrictions to promote domestic production of manufactured goods that are currently imported.

sides benefit. If such arrangements are expected to prove unprofitable, this is evidence that protection from foreign competition would also provide benefits that are smaller than the costs to society at large.

Import Substitution

One of the broadest applications of the idea that trade restrictions can be useful in promoting new industries has been the adoption by developing countries in the post-World War II period of a strategy for industrialization referred to as **import substitution.** Import substitution is based on the idea that by restricting imports of manufactured goods a government can provide an incentive for domestic industrial firms to produce substitutes for imports. The desire to promote more rapid industrialization in developing countries was based on two general beliefs. First, throughout much of the 1950s and 1960s, policymakers in developing countries believed that long-term changes in international prices favored manufactured goods rather than the kinds of agricultural and natural resource based products exported by developing countries. This perception led to the belief that developing countries could not benefit much from expanding their role in international commerce.

The second major reason used to support the import substitution policies in developing countries has been the belief that agricultural and natural resource based product prices and output are subject to wide variations in international demand—more so than are the prices and output of manufactured goods. To the extent that production could be diversified by promoting domestic manufacturing industries capable of competing in world markets, policymakers believed that export earnings could be stabilized. This would presumably provide stable foreign currency earnings needed to continue imports of critical products needed for further industrialization.

The behavior of the relative prices of imports and exports for developing nations is analyzed in chapter 16. Briefly, the data reveal that both developing nations and major industrial nations that do not export oil suffered during the period from 1975 through the early 1980s as a result of the rising world prices for petroleum. However, even if one believes that developing nations have a sensible desire to try to speed up the industrialization process, the case for trade restrictions is by no means obvious. If government intervention should be required because of incomplete or underdeveloped internal capital markets, then investment tax credits, direct subsidies, accelerated depreciation laws, and so on would all seem to be more direct and efficient ways of promoting domestic industrialization than the use of import taxes or other import restrictions. Unfortunately, many developing countries currently find themselves in much the same circumstances as Britain in the early nineteenth century and the United States in the early twentieth century; they lack well-developed internal tax and income redistribution mechanisms. Therefore, as crude as import taxes or other trade restrictions may be for the purpose of promoting particular domestic industries, they may in fact represent the best that domestic policymakers can do at the moment.

Barriers to International Trade

We have looked at the many reasons why nations have traditionally imposed restrictions on international trade, even though free trade potentially provides benefits for everyone. In the remainder of this chapter we will analyze the most common forms taken by trade barriers and examine who wins and loses when they are imposed. We will also look at efforts toward international economic cooperation to promote free trade and evaluate what they have accomplished.

*A **tariff** is a tax on imported goods that is collected by the government of an importing country.*

Figure 14.1 Tariffs as a percentage of the value of imports: United States, 1821–1983
Tariffs as a percentage of the value of imports are much less important today than they were prior to World War II. Throughout the nineteenth century tariff revenues constituted a major source of income for the United States government.
From *Historical Statistics of the United States Colonial Times to 1970* Series U211 and U212, and *Statistical Abstract of the United States:* 1982/83, Table 1482, p. 833, and 1985, Table 1450, p. 823.

Tariffs

Probably the most common response by the United States Congress to the demand for international trade protection has been to legislate a **tariff** on imported goods, which is a tax that must be paid to the government of the importing country. Its effect is to raise the cost of selling imported goods in the nation with the tariff. This shields domestic industry from foreign competition.

United States Tariff History

As you can see in figure 14.1, tariffs in the United States currently average about 5 percent of the value of imported goods on which tariffs have been imposed. (Imports on which there are no tariffs currently constitute about half of the value of all United States imports.) While these tariffs raise the prices of goods to United States consumers, they are currently lower than at other times in our history. The peak of protectionism occurred before the Civil War, when tariffs were imposed on most imports and amounted to about 60 percent of their value. (Tariff revenues, as we have discussed, were also the major source of federal government revenue at that time.) Since the Civil War, our willingness to tax imports has fallen gradually and very irregularly. As figure 14.1 illustrates, tariff rates also reached peaks around 1870 and again during the Great Depression.

To some extent, the high post-Civil War tariffs were part of the spoils of war for the winning North. The North, with emerging industries, had been losing the battle for protection in Congress before the war. With the conclusion of the Civil War and the exclusion of southern states from congressional votes, the

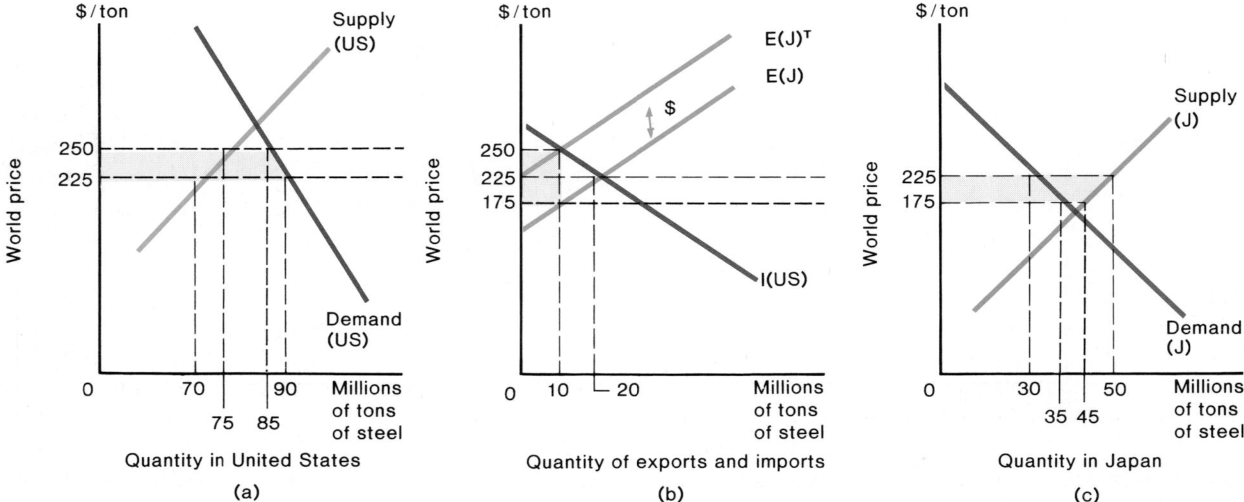

Figure 14.2 Effects of a United States tariff on steel imports
When the United States imposes a tariff on steel imported from Japan, the supply of Japanese exports is shifted upward to $E(J)^T$. As a result, the price of steel to United States buyers rises to $250 while the price received by Japanese producers falls to $175 per ton. Both Japanese producers and United States consumers lose some of their gains from trade as shown by the shaded areas in parts (a) and (c). The United States does gain tariff revenues (customs duties), however, as shown by the shaded area in part (b).

northern states obtained the tariff protection they wanted. The Smoot-Hawley tariff of 1930 raised the average tariff to 59 percent. This tariff was a hysterical attempt to shield the United States from a worldwide depression. Instead, the domestic and international economies were adversely affected by the increase in protection for United States import-competing industries.

A Tariff on Steel Imports from Japan

Figure 14.2 illustrates the effects of a tariff on the price, quantity demanded, and production of steel.[5] If there were no tariff, international trade between Japan and the United States would occur at the equilibrium price of $225 per ton. (You may wish to review the discussion of the gains from trade on pages 286–90 before going on.) Suppose that the United States government levies a tariff of, say, $75 per ton of steel, which must be paid by Japanese exporters for every ton they sell to the United States. As a result, the Japanese export supply curve in part (b) of figure 14.2 will shift to the line $E(J)^T$. At any given quantity of steel exports, the difference between the line $E(J)^T$ and the initial export supply curve E(J) equals the fixed dollar amount of the United States tariff. This shift occurs because the price of steel must reflect its production costs plus the tariff if exporters are to avoid losses. Given the upward shift of Japan's export supply curve, the price of $225 per ton no longer equates United States imports and Japanese exports. The tariff has increased the selling costs of Japanese firms whenever they ship goods to United States buyers. As a result, the volume of steel that Japanese producers wish to export to the United States at each price will decline. This is illustrated by the shift from E(J) to $E(J)^T$.

The tariff raises the price of Japanese steel in the United States. As a result, United States consumers will switch expenditures from high-priced Japanese steel to domestic steel. The switch in consumer demand to United States products will induce United States firms to expand production in response to higher prices. The excess demand pressure within the United States market increases the United States price of steel until it finally reaches $250 per ton. At this price, $E(J)^T$ crosses I(US), and the sum of United States production plus Japanese exports again equals the total quantity of steel demanded by United States buyers.

Equivalently, United States steel importers must pay enough for the steel they purchase from Japan to cover Japanese producers' opportunity costs plus the tariff now imposed by the United States government. Thus, it makes no difference to our analysis whether we show Japan's export supply curve shifting upward by $75 per ton or the United States import demand curve shifting downward by the same amount. To make sure you understand that it makes no difference whether United States importers or Japanese exporters actually write the check paying the United States government's tariff bill, redraw part (b) of figure 14.2, shifting I(US) down by $75 instead of shifting E(J) up. Show that exactly the same effects on the price in the United States and the level of production in the United States occur.

The price effects of the United States tariff on imported steel are precisely the opposite in the Japanese steel market. Notice in part (b) of figure 14.2 that the volume of Japanese exports has declined from 20 million tons to 10 million tons. (Remember that the price Japanese producers now actually receive for their steel is $175 per ton, which is less than the domestic United States price of $250 per ton by the amount of the tariff that has to be paid.) Since Japanese exports equal the difference between Japan's supply and demand curves for steel, the tariff induced decline in United States exports will make this difference smaller. The gap between supply and demand in Japan will close only if the Japanese price of steel falls. In other words, at the initial world price of $225 per ton, the tariff creates a state of excess supply in the Japanese market that can only be eliminated by a reduction in the Japanese price of steel. In part (c) of figure 14.2, the price of steel prevailing in Japan after the introduction of the United States tariff is $175.

The tariff, then, raises United States prices and lowers Japanese steel prices. In Japan, the lower price induces a reduction in the quantity of steel produced by Japanese firms and an increase in the quantity purchased by Japanese buyers. As part (c) of figure 14.2 shows, Japanese production now equals 45 million tons, while consumption is 35 million tons. In the United States, on the other hand, the higher price stimulates United States production of steel and reduces the quantity purchased by United States steel users. In part (a) of figure 14.2, the new quantity of steel supplied by United States firms equals 75 million tons, while purchases fall to 85 million tons.

Aggregate Economic Losses

We will now evaluate the tariff in terms of benefits and losses for United States citizens. For the same reasons that introducing free trade leads to an aggregate gain for society, reducing the amount of trade by means of a tariff results in an aggregate economic loss. Needless to say, the principal victims of the tariff are United States buyers, who now pay a higher price and

*A **specific duty** is a tariff equal to a specified amount per unit of an imported item.*

*An **ad valorem tariff** is defined in percentage terms rather than a specific amount.*

purchase a smaller quantity of steel. Because of the tariff, fewer goods requiring steel will be bought by United States citizens over a given period of time. The winners are United States steel producers, who had been threatened with elimination from the steel market by Japanese competitors or who would have remained in the market, receiving lower economic rents than they do with a tariff. Another group of winners are those who benefit from the tariff revenues (customs duties) collected by the United States government.

We can see the extent to which the tariff on steel imports into the United States would reduce economic efficiency in the United States by again referring to part (a) of figure 14.2. The total shaded area represents the total losses to United States steel users from tariffs on steel imports from Japan. The shaded area bounded by the price axis and the United States supply curve is redistributed from consumers to producers in the form of increased sales revenues above and beyond the costs of expanding United States production from 70 million tons to 75 million tons. The part of the shaded area below the United States supply curve between an output of 70 million tons and 75 million tons is the increased expenditure by steel users needed to cover increased United States production costs. That part of the shaded area is called the *deadweight loss* associated with having the additional 5 million tons of steel produced in the United States when Japanese steel producers could have supplied that same steel at a price of $225 per ton rather than $250 per ton. It represents a net loss to society, resulting from reduced economic efficiency. A deadweight loss simply means that the decreased economic well-being of steel users is not offset by increased income for steel producers. This deadweight loss arises even though producers receive additional revenue from steel users. The additional revenue is just sufficient, however, to cover their costs, which are higher than the costs of Japanese steel producers.

The shaded area between 75 million tons and 85 million tons is equal to the consumer loss that is transferred from steel users to the government in the form of tariff revenue. Finally, the loss equal to the shaded area under the United States demand curve bounded by 85 million tons and 90 million tons is also called *deadweight loss*. That area represents lost economic well-being resulting from the artificial rise in the price of steel, which reduces total domestic consumption of steel from 90 million tons to 85 million. By artificially raising the price of steel in the United States from $225 per ton to $250 per ton the tariff induces consumers to reduce their consumption of steel. Remember that the area under the demand curve and above the price paid for steel represents the value steel users receive over the price they pay. Therefore, reducing consumption of steel artificially by imposing a tariff eliminates a portion of the value that steel users had received from their purchases.

To summarize, the tariff reduces total economic well-being by diverting steel production from efficient Japanese producers to more expensive domestic producers in the United States and by inducing United States purchasers to reduce their consumption of steel. The benefits they receive from the goods they substitute for the steel they no longer purchase are not perfect substitutes for the steel. Thus, consumers cannot completely offset the increased cost of steel by switching to other goods.

Specific Duties versus ad Valorem Tariffs

In discussing the effects of tariffs, we have taken the simplest possible example, in which the government imposes a specific dollar tax, called a **specific duty,** on a particular good, such as steel. Most countries today impose tariffs in percentage terms (for example a 5 percent tariff or a 10 percent tariff) rather than in specific duty form. A tariff defined as a percentage import tax is called an **ad valorem tariff,** which means that the tariff depends on the value of the imported item.

Nontariff trade barriers (NTBs) are nonprice trade restrictions.

A quota is an NTB that limits the quantity of an imported good that may be sold in a country.

Prior to the twentieth century, almost all tariffs were in the form of specific duties. Unlike ad valorem tariffs, which tend to raise the relative price of all grades of a particular product to the same extent, specific duties represent a higher *percentage* tax on relatively cheap varieties of a product than on the more expensive ones. A specific duty of $75 per ton on imported steel would represent a 50 percent tariff on low-quality steel costing only $150 per ton but only a 25 percent tax on high-quality steel that costs $300 per ton. Therefore, a specific duty is more protective of domestic production of low-quality brands than high-quality brands of products. By contrast, an ad valorem tariff is neutral in its protective effect on the various grades of a product.

We will now discuss two historical examples of the use of specific duties in the United States that did promote the production of low-quality goods rather than high-quality goods within given product lines.

Protection of United States Textile Manufacturing In the period preceding the Civil War, the United States was struggling to become competitive with Britain in textile production. The British had an overwhelming comparative advantage in the production of fine fabrics of all kinds and a modest advantage in the production of coarse fabrics of various types. The tariff of 1828 included a specific duty on cotton textiles. All imported cloth that cost $0.35 per yard or more was taxed at the ad valorem rate of 25 percent. However, all imported cloth costing less than $0.35 would be treated as if it cost $0.35 and taxed $0.0875 per yard. Thus, the United States tariff schedule indicated a tariff rate of about 25 percent on imported cotton textiles. However, the actual price of plain cotton sheeting imports in 1830 was close to $0.11 per yard. Therefore, the actual average percentage tariff in 1830 was close to 80 percent (0.0875/0.11), with the rate higher for low-quality than high-quality imports.[6] The United States produced mostly low-quality cotton sheeting at a price of $0.13 per yard. Obviously, then, the specific duty of $0.0875 per yard favored United States production of low-quality cotton textiles while not prohibiting imports of high-quality fabrics from Britain.

Protection of the United States Steel Industry In the last part of the nineteenth century—particularly prior to 1896—the United States developed a strong domestic pig iron industry. At the same time it remained highly dependent on Scotland and England to provide imports of high-quality alloy steels. Throughout the period 1870–99 the specific duty averaged $6.43 per ton. Empirical evidence suggests that the specific duty directly induced a shift of imports away from the low-price steels, which competed directly with emerging United States production. Imports shifted toward high-quality iron and steel products needed but not yet produced in the United States.[7]

In each of the cases described here, there was a definite preference on the part of domestic producers to have protection skewed toward low-quality goods that they produced without needlessly raising the price of high-quality imports substantially. Specific duties work quite well in such cases.

Quotas and Other Nontariff Trade Barriers (NTBs)

Nontariff trade barriers (NTBs) are simply nonprice forms of international trade restrictions. Probably the most common form of NTB is the **quota,** which assigns a definite limit to the amount of goods that can be imported into a country. In our example of the steel market, the United States government can establish a quota on steel by arbitrarily declaring the maximum quantity of steel that it will permit Japan to ship to the United States market.[8] The basic effects of a quota are parallel to those of a tariff, and similar winners and losers emerge from quota intervention as from tariff legislation. When a quota is applied to imports from a specific country like Japan, the main issue is the selection of the lucky exporters from among the entire set of Japanese firms and whether the United States government will collect any revenue from the quota arrangement. One can envision many possibilities, ranging from a lottery system to a collection of license fees by the United States government.

Revenue Needs and the Shift to NTBs

Unless the government can conduct a competitive auction for licenses to purchase quota-restricted imports, government revenues will be less with a quota or other NTB than with an equally restrictive tariff. Therefore, until a government finds suitable alternatives to tariffs to meet its revenue needs, policymakers will have a natural preference for tariffs over quotas. The general shift in protectionism away from tariffs in the last fifty years may partially reflect the decline in government preferences for tariffs relative to other forms of trade restrictions. For many developing countries, tariff revenue is critical as a source of government funding. Ad valorem tariffs have the advantage that during periods of general inflation and resulting increased government expenses, tariff revenues increase automatically.

NTBs and the Tariff Revenue Equivalent

NTBs result in price increases that must be paid by buyers who can no longer obtain imports, just as tariffs do. However, the shaded area in part (a) of figure 14.2 that represents tariff revenue is no longer received by the government of the importing country because there is no tariff. Different NTBs will result in different distributions of the increased amount paid for imported items that might have ended up as tariff revenue. The government of the importing nation can direct the price increase benefits to either domestic or to foreign producers or their government. This added element of flexibility associated with NTBs may make it possible for domestic industry pressure groups to lobby successfully for nontariff barriers to trade when it might prove impossible to gain tariff protection.

The most common NTB is a quota. However, there are other devices. One is a "domestic content" requirement that a certain proportion of the value of imported items be made with parts manufactured in the importing nation. Another is "minimum quality" requirements for imported items, such as a minimum size for tomatoes imported from Mexico. If Mexican farmers' comparative advantage is in producing small tomatoes, a minimum-size requirement makes it more difficult for them to export tomatoes to the United States and thus protects United States tomato growers.

"Voluntary" Quotas

International trade currently operates under a set of rules governing what are "fair" and "unfair" trade practices. We will have more to say about the generally accepted rules governing appropriate and inappropriate barriers to trade later in this chapter. When it cannot be established that an exporting country has engaged in an unfair international trade practice, it violates international rules to increase a tariff or to impose a quota to protect domestic producers. However, another tactic that produces the same effect as a quota is to negotiate a "voluntary" export restraint with the exporting country. Clearly, any act, "voluntary" or not, that reduces imports below the level that would prevail in unimpeded international trade has many of the effects discussed for mandatory quotas.

Imports and the United States Auto Industry "Voluntary" quotas on Japanese auto exports to the United States have been used to protect United States automobile manufacturers in recent years. Japanese automobile producers have developed a significant cost advantage over United States producers of small cars. One analysis comparing the Toyota Corolla and the Chevrolet Chevette in 1983 found that the Japanese could deliver a car to the United States at a cost of $1,718 less than the cost of a comparable vehicle produced within the United States. None of this cost differential was attributable to a Japanese government subsidy. Over half was due to better Japanese management systems and less than a third to lower Japanese labor compensation.[9] Quotas of any kind, of course, limit the degree to which this Japanese cost advantage is passed on to United States consumers. In 1983, the Japanese government announced the intention to end its voluntary quotas on auto exports to the United States.[10]

In fact, however, the Japanese extended their voluntary restriction on total exports of automobiles to the United States market into 1986. When President Reagan indicated in March 1985 that the United States would not ask Japan to continue to limit its automobile exports to the United States, the Japanese themselves indicated that they would continue to limit exports anyway. Why do you suppose the Japanese would voluntarily restrict their own sales of automobiles in the United States?

Imports were a fairly small share of the total automobile market in the United States until the late 1960s.[11] Rising imports were probably stimulated by rapidly rising United States automobile prices and increasing skepticism about the United States automobile industry's ability to meet federally mandated emission control standards and still produce high-quality automobiles. Between 1973 and 1974–75, a recession sharply reduced automobile purchases. Total new registrations fell by almost 30 percent, and most of this represented reduced purchases of domestically produced cars. Import sales were buoyed during the recession by rapidly rising gasoline prices as consumers switched to fuel-efficient foreign cars. By 1978, both total and domestic automobile sales were close to their 1973 levels. The rapid rise in the price of oil following the Iranian revolution in 1979 depressed total car sales and promoted an even larger shift of consumer demand toward fuel-efficient imports. The one-third drop in domestically produced new car sales between 1978 and 1981 led to considerable pressure on the United States government to limit foreign automobile imports into the United States.

By 1981, Japanese imports were judged by consumers to be much better than cars made in the United States.[12] Chrysler's financial woes in the early 1980s were surely related to the low-quality ratings given to Chrysler cars by consumers. At the same time, the hourly wage in automobile production in the United States remained more than 50 percent above the hourly wage rate in United States manufacturing in general and, as recently as 1983, 140 percent higher than the hourly wage rate in automobile production in Japan.[13]

In response to the disaster rapidly approaching for the United States automobile industry, Congress threatened to impose severe barriers on Japanese car exports to the United States. To avoid what might have been a worse outcome for them, the Japanese "volunteered" to restrict their exports to an agreed quota.

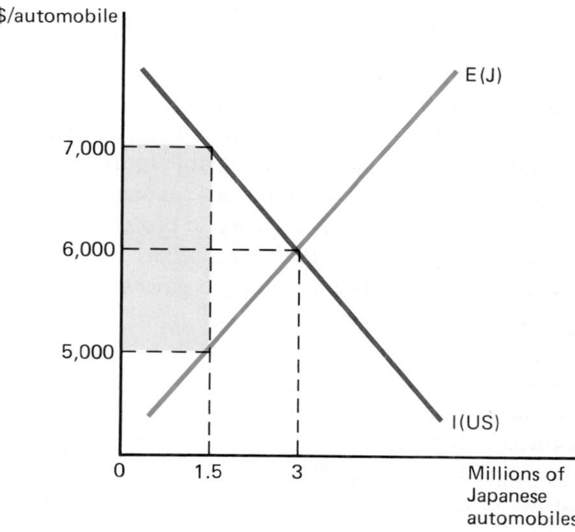

Figure 14.3 A "voluntary" quota on Japanese automobile exports to the United States
I(US) is the United States import demand for Japanese automobiles, and E(J) is the Japanese export supply. Without voluntary quotas, the United States price of Japanese automobiles would be $6,000, and 3 million cars would be sold to the United States. The voluntary quota system reduces Japanese cars exported to the United States to 1.5 million. The actual marginal cost of supplying cars to the United States falls to $5,000. Japanese automobile producers benefit to an extent indicated by the shaded area, which is equal to $3 billion.

Quota Rents to Japanese Exporters Figure 14.3 illustrates the United States import demand for Japanese automobiles and the Japanese export supply curve. The curves I(US) and E(J) represent the United States import demand for Japanese automobiles and the export supply curve for automobiles from Japan. Unrestricted trade would result in imports equal to 3 million automobiles at a price of $6,000 each. With imports from Japan artificially restricted by an export quota of 1.5 million automobiles, the United States price of Japanese automobiles will rise to $7,000. The shaded area in figure 14.3 would have amounted to tariff revenues if a tariff had been used to restrict imports to 1.5 million automobiles. This area now represents additional profits of $3 billion to Japanese producers who are lucky enough to gain government permission to export automobiles to the United States.

*The **General Agreement on Tariffs and Trade (GATT)** is an agreement that was reached by most nations after World War II to reduce trade barriers, such as tariffs and quotas, and to discourage "unfair" competition on the world market through the use of export subsidies.*

Recall that even when President Reagan indicated in March 1985 that the United States would not ask Japan to continue to voluntarily restrict exports, the Japanese indicated they would do so anyway. Clearly, existing major producers in Japan who have obtained export licenses and are able to export autos to the United States will lobby the Japanese government to keep the quotas in order to protect their monopoly rents and protect themselves from other Japanese manufacturers trying to gain access to the United States market.

Estimates of Gains and Losses Our discussion of quotas and tariffs has indicated that producers in the United States gain and consumers lose when imports are restricted. Through early 1985, the accumulated cost of restricting Japanese automobile imports to the United States economy was $3.6 billion. This resulted from a loss of $4 billion to consumers and a gain of only $0.4 billion to domestic producers. The cost of each dollar of automobile workers' earnings protected in the United States was estimated to be $23.90 to consumers and $21.41 to the economy at large. The accumulated deadweight loss of quotas on Japanese auto imports was estimated to be approximately $3 billion. This is an indication that the deadweight loss to the United States of restrictions on imports of Japanese cars was quite high.[14]

The General Agreement on Tariffs and Trade (GATT), "Fair" Competition, and Trade Restrictions

Following World War II, the vast majority of nations signed the **General Agreement on Tariffs and Trade (GATT),** which is intended to promote trade among the nations of the world by lowering tariffs, quotas, and other barriers. As a result of several conferences, the nations participating in GATT have greatly reduced trade barriers since the late 1940s. This is reflected in the decline in average tariff rates shown in figure 14.1.

The Rules of the Game and "Unfair" Trade Practices

The GATT also defines a number of "unfair" trade practices. If a nation engages in certain proscribed behavior, such as subsidizing its exports so that they compete "unfairly" with those of other nations, the countries whose exports are affected can retaliate with countervailing measures. Export subsidies can occur through various channels besides direct payments to companies that export goods or services. A government may provide low-interest loans, remit taxes, or take any action that lowers the cost of exported goods relative to those sold domestically. If a country thinks it is harmed by such subsidies, it can impose import duties (tariffs) to offset the subsidies of a nation that violates GATT, or it can impose quotas on imports from that nation.

It is an open question whether a nation is well advised to retaliate against "unfair" trade practices that lower the costs of its imports. If Great Britain uses its taxpayers' money to subsidize exports to the United States, it is essentially taxing its citizens to raise the standard of living of American citizens. Producers in Great Britain do benefit, of course, but not as much as British consumers lose. To see this, review figure 14.2 and the discussion of the winners and losers when a tariff is imposed. If Japan were to subsidize steel exports to the United States by, say, $75 per ton, this would lower the E(J) curve in part (b) of figure 14.2 by $75. You may wish to redraw figure 14.2 to show the impact of an export subsidy by Japan. You will see that the effects are opposite those of the $75 tariff. The subsidy-distorted export supply curve will be shifted downward to the right of E(J). Steel trade will increase, the price of steel in Japan will rise, and Japanese consumers will be worse off. Moreover, the difference between the marginal cost of steel and the new, lower export price is paid by Japan's taxpayers. This amounts to a gift from Japan to the United States. In the United States, the price of steel will fall, consumers will be better off, and producers will suffer, along with their employees.

Following the analysis in our discussion of the distribution of the gains from trade in chapter 13, it is fairly easy to show that the subsidy will benefit American consumers more than it harms American producers and workers. However, the same pressures that might lead the United States government to restrict any trade with Japan will also tempt it to retaliate against Japan's export subsidy. It is a question of the distribution of the gains within the United States. Furthermore, retaliation against real or alleged unfair trade practices may spill over into other markets, resulting in a general increase in trade barriers. Probably the most forceful argument against one country's subsidizing its exports to another, then, is that such practices increase the political pressure by producer groups for general protection from imports. To the extent that the rules of the game seem unfair to some, it is more difficult for governments to resist the ever present pressure to erect international trade barriers.

As you might expect, domestic firms frequently charge that foreign governments unfairly subsidize exports to obtain protection from import competition. Sometimes these charges are well founded, but it is often very difficult to document the exact amount of such subsidies. Domestic firms and their employees naturally tend to see the main problem they face as unfair foreign export tactics rather than their own high costs, less advanced technology, or poorer management techniques.

Two industries in which import competition has been particularly severe in the United States are steel and automobiles. We have already discussed the use of "voluntary" quotas to protect the United States automobile industry.

When the United States had rich iron ore deposits, it had a comparative advantage in the production of many forms of steel. Over the years, the richest United States iron ore deposits were exhausted. As a result, this advantage began to shift to other countries that do not necessarily have access to rich iron ore but that do have lower cost labor. In addition, some of these steel exporters have subsidized steel exports. This underlies why steel producers in the United States petitioned the United States Department of Commerce and International Trade Commission to impose countervailing tariffs on steel imports from countries violating GATT.[15]

The principal reason for growing steel imports into the United States, however, is not export subsidies but rather lower manufacturing costs in exporting nations. For example, in 1981 almost one-third of United States steel imports came from Japan, which was not found to subsidize its exports.[16] Moreover, the most rapid growth in world steel production capacity is occurring in several "advanced developing countries" (ADCs). Among ADCs, only Brazil was found to subsidize its steel exports. In the United States, average total hourly compensation (wages plus fringe benefits) of steelworkers in 1981 was $19.42 compared to $12.18 in petroleum refining, $11.89 in coal mining, and $11.01 in motor vehicles.[17] Even in Canada, where wage rates are frequently as high as those of the United States, steelworkers' hourly compensation was only $12.63 in 1981. (Canada supplied about 15 percent of United States steel imports in 1981.) In Japan, the average steelworker received $10.15 per hour.[18] In ADCs, compensation was still lower. It is evident that significant wage adjustments must occur if the United States steel industry is to retain a significant share of the domestic market for steel. The collective bargaining agreement signed in 1983 between the United Steelworkers' Union and the major United States steel producers reflected an attempt to bring labor costs more in line with those of steelworkers in other countries.[19]

The Trade Expansion Act of 1962

Despite all of the pressures for protection from industries harmed by import competition, Congress also responds to the desires of consumer groups and export industries, which benefit from free trade. To reduce political pressure for tariffs and quotas, Congress

*The **Trade Expansion Act of 1962** authorized government financial assistance to workers who were designated as displaced and firms that went out of business because of foreign competition.*

*A **customs union** is a group of nations that impose a common set of trade barriers against the rest of the world but none among themselves.*

*A **common market** is a customs union that also allows the free movement of labor and capital among its member countries.*

passed the **Trade Expansion Act of 1962,** which provided trade adjustment assistance (TAA) in the form of financial aid to workers and firms judged to have been displaced by international competition. Other countries have passed similar legislation. Under TAA, financial aid was paid for retraining and relocation into industries less threatened by imports. By 1981, the costs of adjustment assistance in the United States had become much larger than anticipated, and most forms were eliminated. One reason the costs became so large is that firms and workers increasingly sought compensation for harm from all forms of competition—international and domestic. Moreover, a majority of workers who received TAA either returned to jobs in their original industries or retired when their TAA benefits ran out. It is often difficult to discover why a company is failing when others in the same industry survive. It seemed to many observers that it was no fairer to protect workers and firms from the effects of foreign than of domestic competition. This weakened support for adjustment assistance in principle.

Customs Unions

The GATT agreement and the successive rounds of tariff reductions to liberalize international trade are examples of attempts to coordinate trade policies to the mutual benefit of participating nations.

Another example of an attempt to coordinate trade policies with a view toward mutual benefit is the establishment of a **customs union,** which is a group of nations that remove international trade restrictions among themselves while maintaining common external barriers with nonmember nations. Such arrangements are permitted under GATT even though they clearly discriminate against trade with some nations and in favor of trade with other nations. The simple argument for the GATT exception is that any move toward free trade, even among a few nations, is a step in the "right" direction.

Clearly, the best-known example of a customs union is the *European Economic Community (EEC),* which was established in 1957–58 by the Treaty of Rome. France, West Germany, Italy, Belgium, the Netherlands, and Luxembourg agreed to eliminate trade barriers among themselves and to develop common external trade barriers over time between 1958 and mid-1968. Only a few years earlier, Belgium, the Netherlands, and Luxembourg integrated their economies in the form of Benelux. The Stockholm convention of 1960 created the European Free Trade Association, EFTA, as a rival trade agreement. The seven original members Austria, Denmark, Norway, Portugal, Sweden, Switzerland, and the United Kingdom agreed to remove trade barriers among themselves in stages over the period from 1960 to 1965. Finland and Iceland joined EFTA in 1961 and 1970, respectively.

Denmark, Ireland, and the United Kingdom joined the EEC in 1972–73, Greece in 1981, and Spain and Portugal in 1985. In the interim, trade barriers were removed among the nine (prior to the addition of Greece) and with the remaining EFTA countries during the mid-1970s. Trade preference agreements have also been reached with most nonmember Mediterranean countries similar to those reached earlier with developing countries (most of which were former colonies of EEC countries). The earliest agreements included those with Greece in 1961, Turkey in 1964, and Spain and Malta in 1970. In fact, Turkey is likely to become the next full member of the EEC.

Before turning to an assessment of the gains and losses associated with forming a customs union, we should note that beginning in late 1968, the members of the EEC agreed to form the Common Market. A **common market** differs from a customs union by permitting labor and capital to move freely among member nations. That process of further integration was fairly complete by the late 1970s. The next step is to form an **economic union,** which is an integrated community in which monetary and fiscal policy are fully coordinated. The European community has been wrestling with this next step for more than ten years.

Figure 14.4 illustrates the potential short-term gains and losses associated with the formation of a customs union. The demand and supply curves are domestic demand and supply for computer terminals. With no trade, the domestic price would be $400 per

*An **economic union** is a common market in which the member countries coordinate their monetary and fiscal policies.*

*The **trade creation effects of a customs union** are the increased gains from trade resulting from expanded imports and exports within the union.*

*The **trade diversion effects of a customs union** are the reduced gains from trade resulting from diminished imports from countries outside the union.*

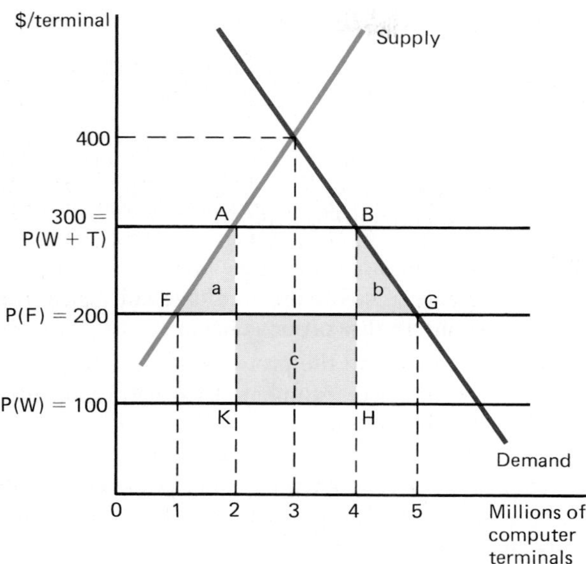

Figure 14.4 The effect of a customs union on the gains from trade
This diagram shows the domestic demand and supply for computer terminals. P(W) = $100 is the world supply curve for computer terminals, and P(F) = $200 is the foreign trade partner's supply curve. The curve P(W + T) = $300 is the world supply curve facing domestic consumers when a tariff, T = $200, is imposed. Before the customs union is formed, imports are from the world market at price P(W) = $100. At the domestic price of P(W + T) = $300, imports equal two million, and tariff revenue equals the area ABHK, or $400 million. A customs union expands trade by lowering the domestic price to $200. Imports expand to 5 million. The expansion of trade leads to trade creation gains equal to the shaded areas a and b, or $150 million. Tariff revenue is zero, and area c represents the trade diversion losses associated with the increased cost of the original two million imports from a less-efficient trade partner. The diversion losses in this case equal $200 million.

terminal and the domestic output would be 3 million units. If we assume that the country depicted in figure 14.4 would benefit from trade with another country in a customs union or with the world as a whole, we would expect trade to lower the price of traded goods and lead to gains from trade as discussed in chapter 13.

The horizontal line P(W) = $100 represents the world supply curve of traded goods facing this country, and P(F) = $200 is the supply curve of a potential trading partner within a customs union. (We assume these supply curves are completely elastic because the country depicted in figure 14.4 is small relative to the world market for traded goods. Hence, it is a price taker in international trade.) Initially, the home country imposes a specific duty of T = $200 per unit of imports on all its trading partners. Imports will come exclusively from the world market—that is, there is no trade with the potential trading partner. The domestic price of imports is therefore equal to P(W + T) = $300, and imports equal 2 million terminals. Domestic production equals 2 million terminals, and tariff revenue equals the area ABHK, or $400 million.

If a customs union is formed with a potential trading partner, the domestic price of imports from that partner will fall to P(F) = $200, while the domestic price of the same product from the rest of the world will still be P(W + T) = $300. Imports will shift entirely from the world market to the new trading partner. Since the domestic price falls, domestic production, which is relatively inefficient, falls to 1 million terminals. The decline in price benefits consumers who can now buy more imported goods at lower prices. Imports expand from 2 million terminals to 5 million terminals. Areas a and b represent the net improvement in economic well-being arising from the gains from increased trade and are called the **trade creation effects of a customs union.** In the case illustrated, areas a and b are equal in total value to $150 million.

Once the customs union is formed, all of the imports are purchased from the trading partner within the customs union rather than from the more efficient world market. Therefore, tariff revenue falls to zero. Some of the income that had gone to the government before the customs union was formed has been redistributed to consumers through cheaper import prices. However, the shaded area c, representing income that had been collected as tariff revenue, now goes to the trading partner to pay for imports. The cost of the initial level of imports of 2 million terminals has increased by an amount equal to area c, or $200 million because trade has been diverted from the lowest-cost world producers to a less efficient customs union partner. That loss of gains from trade is referred to as a **trade diversion effect of a customs union.**

If you study figure 14.4 carefully, you will see that the more inelastic the domestic demand and supply curves are, the smaller the trade creation effects of a customs union will be. The less efficient are trading partners within the union relative to the world market—that is, the higher is P(F) relative to P(W)—the greater will be the trade-diverting effects of a customs union. Demand and supply curves for agricultural products tend to be fairly inelastic, and European agricultural production is not very efficient relative to the rest of the world. Therefore, it is not surprising that one of the most divisive issues within the EEC has been the structure of its common agricultural plan, which includes import restrictions on agricultural exports from nonpartner countries. This protection against non-EEC agricultural products is the source of some estrangement between the EEC and the United States because the United States is a lower-cost producer of agricultural products than the EEC countries. Note in the simple case of the computer terminals that the trade diversion costs actually exceed the trade creation effects by $50 million.

It is hoped that in the long run the benefits associated with access to a larger and freer market will offset any short-term negative effects of a customs union. However, clear-cut evidence on whether the gains from trade creation exceed the costs of trade diversion does not yet exist in the case of the EEC.

▸ Summary and Conclusions

What do you now think of the message on the grocery bag that illustrated our introductory discussion? In this chapter we explored the reasons why most nations have erected some barriers to free international trade and the means chosen to do it. The following major points were emphasized.

Tariffs have been important revenue sources for governments of countries that have not developed effective internal taxation schemes.

National security and the protection of infant industries are two arguments used by proponents of import restrictions.

Tariffs and quotas reduce international economic efficiency and create winners and losers that were among the groups of losers and winners from unrestricted trade.

Specific duties protect relatively cheap varieties of products, whereas ad valorem tariffs are financially neutral in this regard.

Legal and voluntary quotas are the primary forms of nontariff barriers to international trade. Quotas typically create economic rents for the holder of the import license.

The General Agreement on Tariffs and Trade (GATT) has led to reduced trade barriers and defines a number of "unfair" trade practices.

Customs unions exhibit both trade creation and trade diversion effects by encouraging trade between member nations and discouraging trade with countries outside the customs union.

Key Terms

- ad valorem tariff *302*
- common market *308*
- customs union *308*
- economic union *309*
- General Agreement on Tariffs and Trade (GATT) *306*
- import substitution *298*
- infant industry argument *297*
- nontariff trade barriers (NTBs) *303*
- quota *302*
- specific duty *302*
- tariff *299*
- trade creation effects of a customs union *309*
- trade diversion effects of a customs union *309*
- Trade Expansion Act of 1962 *308*

Questions for Discussion and Review

1. Why might a developing country use a tariff rather than subsidized loans or tax credits to promote industrialization?
2. Why do developing countries want to develop export markets for manufactured goods?
3. Illustrate and explain the net production and consumption losses from a tariff.
4. Illustrate and explain the distribution of quota rents to exporters when voluntary export restrictions are imposed on a product.
5. Illustrate and explain government revenue gains from the competitive auction of import licenses for a quota-restricted commodity.
6. Explain why a specific duty tends to limit imports of low-quality goods more than high-quality goods.
7. Explain why governments in developed countries might have a relative preference for NTBs to restrict trade while governments in developing countries might have a relative preference for tariffs to restrict trade.
8. What is the infant industry argument for import restrictions?
9. What factors help to explain the rapid rise of the import share in United States automobile sales between 1965 and 1985?
10. Illustrate and explain the welfare effects of trade creation.

Chapter 15

Monetary and Macroeconomic Aspects of International Trade

Outline

Objectives

After reading this chapter, the student should be able to:

Explain how systems of fixed and flexible exchange rates operate in terms of the supply and demand for foreign currency.

Discuss the balance of trade and its significance compared to the balance of payments.

Analyze the effects of foreign exchange intervention.

Show how a macroeconomic disturbance in one nation can be transferred to another nation.

Explain the trade deficit of the United States during the 1970s and early 1980s and why it was not eliminated by changes in exchange rates.

Discuss the past and present roles of the International Monetary Fund and the World Bank.

Discuss the role of Eurodollars and Eurocurrency banks in the international economy.

Introduction

In early 1980 two young business people founded promising international firms. One was Rick, a whiz-kid computer technician in Dallas, Texas. The other was Helga, a bright computer scientist in West Germany. Each began producing and selling what are called dumb computer terminals (used with minicomputers for word processing and scientific computing) for sale in Germany. Both Rick and Helga are capable business people who produced quality products. Nevertheless, by February 1985 their businesses had failed. The common link between them was the rapid rise in the value of the United States dollar relative to the West German deutsche mark (DM). This was the primary cause of their financial ruin. The change was something that neither of them had anticipated or understood. Between the beginning of 1980 and February 1985 the deutsche mark price of United States dollars rose 55 percent, from DM 2.1 to DM 3.25. Let us briefly consider what happened to each business.

Rick began selling his terminals in West Germany for $200 each and found that he could hardly produce enough of them to meet his customers' needs. By early 1985, Rick had managed to keep producing his terminals for $200 each but could find no one to buy them.

Helga borrowed $2 million from a large New York bank to finance her business. She sold her terminals in West Germany for DM 210 each and paid about DM 50 on each terminal she sold to meet her loan payments. By early 1985, it was clear that to maintain the 1980 level of sales she would have to recover DM 77.4 for loan payments. Since none of her other costs of production had changed, she could not cover all of her costs unless she charged DM 237.4 for each of her computers. Unfortunately, at that price she could not find many buyers and had to discontinue production.

In this chapter we will explain how changes in the price of one currency in terms of another can occur and how such changes interact with the flow of goods and services among nations. This will explain how the changes in the deutsche mark price of the United States dollar between 1980 and 1985 caused Rick's and Helga's businesses to fail. We will then extend our analysis of international economic relationships to show how the macroeconomic performances of the world's economies are related by trade. We will use the macroeconomic model developed in chapters 2 through 12 to explain how the United States and other economies have performed in the recent past and how their macroeconomies have been affected by international trade and finance.

*A **foreign exchange rate** is the amount of one country's currency (money) that it takes to buy one unit of another country's currency.*

Paying for Foreign Trade: Currency's Role

In chapters 13 and 14 we analyzed international trade in terms of the exchange of exports for imports. An example would be the United States exporting wheat to Japan in exchange for Japanese automobiles. Although treating trade between two nations as though it involved *bartering* one set of goods for another emphasizes many important aspects of international markets, it is incomplete. After all, a Kansas wheat farmer may prefer American cars to Japanese imports. More important, if the farmer did accept a Japanese car as payment, how would he find an American car dealer who would accept the Japanese car in exchange? What if the farmer did not want an automobile at all but preferred to use the income received from selling wheat to Japan to buy clothes or pay college tuition for the children? These problems do not usually arise as a result of international transactions for the same reason that they do not plague trade among domestic firms and consumers: *Money is used as a medium of exchange in international transactions just as within every market economy.* The farmer does not receive automobiles for the wheat sold to Japan; the farmer receives dollars that the Japanese importers purchased with yen. Similarly, the Japanese auto exporters receive yen that American importers purchased with dollars.

Trade among nations requires the use of *money* for the same reasons that trade among individuals in the same country does. Money greatly facilitates *specialization* in international trade just as it does at home. If means did not exist to exchange one nation's currency for another's, the production possibilities of the world's economy would be much smaller. Money is also used for international transactions that do not directly involve the exchange of one nation's goods for another's. It is used, for example, when a United States citizen wishes to purchase financial assets in another country, such as foreign government bonds or common stock of a firm in Japan, Great Britain, or Italy. Money is used when the United States government grants foreign aid to another nation to assist in its economic development. Money is used when a United States bank lends funds to, say, the Mexican or Brazilian government, and it is required when these debts are repaid. The complication that arises in international trade is that each country uses its own currency so that foreign sales and purchases will inevitably involve exchanges of the currencies of the countries involved. This fact quickly gives rise to questions like how many Japanese yen can I buy with one United States dollar.

Because of the multiple uses for international currencies, the price of one nation's money in terms of another's, which is called the **foreign exchange rate,** can have an important influence on the quantity and type of goods traded among nations. For example, in 1984 and early 1985 the price of many European currencies—the British pound, the West German deutsche mark, the French franc, and others—fell abruptly in relation to the United States dollar. United States citizens found that they could purchase cashmere sweaters in Britain, luxury automobiles in Germany, and fancy dinners in Paris at bargain rates. Foreign travel accelerated as many Americans decided to take vacations abroad rather than at home. European firms catering to travelers were delighted; many United States firms lost sales and suffered lower profits.

Governments recognize the effect of foreign exchange rates on the volume and direction of trade. They frequently buy and sell their own currencies and those of other nations to influence exchange rates and thus control international trade. We will explore the impact of such actions in this chapter and chapter 16.

There are almost as many different currencies as there are nations—dollars for the United States, yen for Japan, pesos for Mexico, cruzeiros for Brazil, zlotis for Poland, and so on. To find out how the existence of different currencies affects the international economy, we must explore how foreign exchange rates are determined. We must also examine how countries settle their financial accounts with one another through the international balance of payments.

*The **foreign exchange market** is where currencies are bought and sold; it is where foreign exchange rates are determined.*

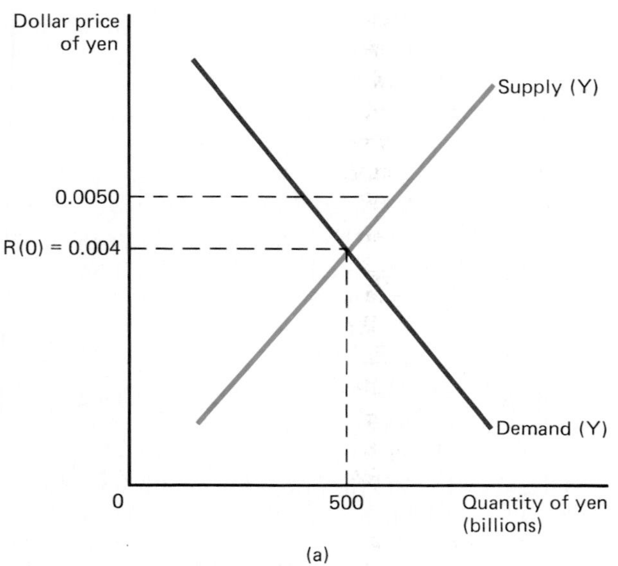

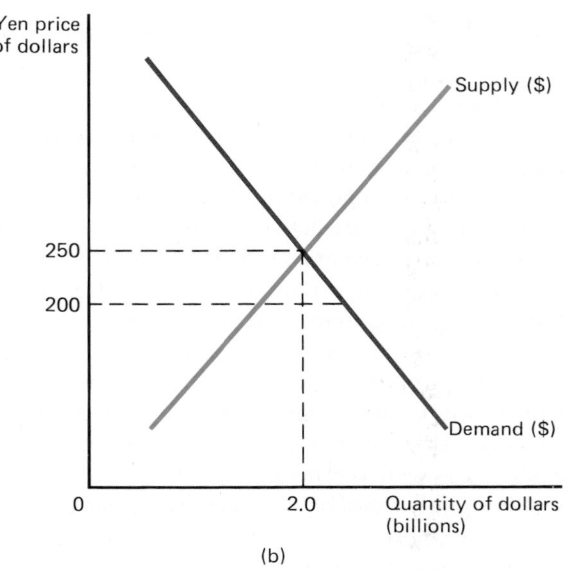

Figure 15.1 The supply and demand for foreign exchange
The exchange rate equates the quantity of yen demanded by United States citizens with the quantity of yen supplied by Japanese citizens. At the same time the quantity of dollars supplied by the United States is equated with the quantity demanded in Japan. If the price of yen in terms of dollars is above equilibrium, say, $0.005, then there will be an excess supply of yen. If the exchange rate falls below R(0), there will be an excess demand for yen. If the equilibrium price of yen in terms of dollars is $0.004, then the equilibrium price of dollars in terms of yen is 1/$0.004 = 250 yen. The equilibrium quantities of yen and dollars are 500 billion yen and $2 billion, respectively.

The Supply and Demand for Foreign Currency

Suppose a United States exporter sells computer equipment to, say, a Japanese importer. The United States exporter, being a United States citizen and employing United States factors of production, will demand payment not in yen but in dollars. How, then, does the Japanese importer *convert* yen into dollars? The importer goes to a financial dealer in the **foreign exchange market,** where yen can be sold in return for dollars. The price determined in this foreign exchange market is the foreign exchange rate measuring the dollar price of yen and the yen price of dollars. For example, suppose the Japanese importer wants to purchase 5,000 yen worth of dollars and the exchange rate of dollars for yen is $0.004. (That is, the price of one yen is 4/1000 United States dollars.) Given this exchange rate, our importer could exchange 5,000 yen for $20.

The key question, of course, is what determines the exchange rate? Before answering this question, let us construct the demand and supply for foreign exchange (yen and dollars, for example). Figure 15.1 illustrates the foreign exchange market in which dollars and yen are traded. Because two currencies are involved, two sets of supply and demand curves are required. Part (a) of figure 15.1 illustrates the supply and demand for yen in terms of dollars, and part (b) depicts the supply and demand for dollars in terms of yen. On the horizontal axes we measure the quantities of yen and dollars, respectively; the vertical axes measure the dollar price of yen and the yen price of dollars. The supplies of yen and dollars to the foreign exchange market are drawn with a positive slope.

The main reason the supply curves are positively sloped is that as their respective exchange rates rise, Japanese citizens are able to acquire more dollars for each of their yen and Americans can purchase more yen with each dollar. That is, American products (expressed in dollar prices) become cheaper to Japanese citizens as the dollar price of yen increases, and Japanese goods (expressed in yen prices) become cheaper to United States citizens as the yen price of the dollar increases. For example, suppose an American-made microcomputer has a $100 price tag and the exchange rate is $0.004 per yen. This means that the computer costs 100/.004 = 25,000 yen. If the dollar price of the yen rises to $0.008 per yen, you can see that the Japanese price of the computer has fallen to 12,500 yen. Given an increase in the exchange rate of dollars for yen, Japanese citizens would have an incentive to buy larger quantities of American items. As Japanese importers expressed this desire in various United States markets, United States exports of many different items would rise. Japanese importers would need dollars, and they in turn would obtain them by supplying yen to the foreign exchange market. In other words, the supply of yen in figure 15.1, part (a), represents the demand for United States dollars by Japanese citizens depicted in part (b). Everything we have said about the supply of yen and the demand for dollars applies, of course, to the supply of dollars in part (a) of figure 15.1 and the demand for yen in part (b).

Suppose Japanese consumers demand ten American microcomputers with price tags of $100 each when the exchange rate is $0.004 per yen. Thus, Japan imports 250,000 yen worth ($1,000) of computers from the United States. If the value of the yen rises to $0.008 per yen, from the Japanese perspective this is equivalent to a decline in the unit price of microcomputers from 25,000 yen to 12,500 yen. The quantity of yen supplied will increase if Japanese consumers decide to spend *more* than 250,000 yen on United States computers now that their price (in terms of yen) has fallen. For example, if the Japanese now want to purchase twelve microcomputers, they will cost only 150,000 yen, and the quantity of yen supplied to the foreign exchange market *may fall, not rise.* But if the Japanese decide to buy 25 microcomputers at the lower yen price of 12,500 yen, the quantity of yen supplied to the foreign exchange market will rise to 312,500 yen.

Under what conditions would an increase in the dollar price of yen lead to an increase in the quantity of yen supplied? Suppose that in response to the *50 percent reduction* in the yen price of United States computers, Japanese importers wish to *more than double* their purchases of United States microcomputers. As indicated above, if Japan now imports, say, twenty-five microcomputers, it will take 312,500 yen to purchase them. This would imply that the Japanese demand for United States microcomputers is elastic—that is, greater than one. The more elastic is a country's demand for imports, the more elastic is its supply of currency to the foreign exchange market, *ceteris paribus.* If the elasticity of demand for imports is less than one, as in our first example—when a 50 percent price decline increased the quantity of microcomputers demanded from ten to twelve, or 20 percent—the supply of yen will actually decline.

What we have just seen is that Japan's supply curve of yen will be upward sloping if its *elasticity of demand* for United States goods *is greater than one* in absolute value. Is this likely? As long as we think of the supply of yen with respect to the dollar-yen exchange rate, *holding constant* the exchange rate of yen for other currencies, the answer is yes. The reason is that as the *yen* price of United States goods falls, *ceteris paribus,* United States imports become cheaper relative to those that might be bought in Japan or purchased from countries other than the United States. Because United States computers, wine, and wheat are close substitutes for similar goods produced elsewhere, Japan's elasticity of demand for them is likely to be quite high. The same logic applies to the United States supply of dollars to the yen-dollar foreign exchange market.

The demand curve for yen in part (a) of figure 15.1 is drawn with a negative slope. This demand curve ultimately represents the desires of American citizens for Japanese items ranging from steel to digital watches to the common stock of Japanese companies. As the dollar price of yen falls, the dollar cost of Japanese exports (whose prices are expressed in yen) falls. For example, suppose a Japanese television costs 120,000 yen and the dollar price of yen is $0.004 per yen. Translated into dollars, the television's price

Fixed exchange rates *are exchange rates that governments arbitrarily set between their countries' currencies.*

Devaluation *occurs when a country makes its currency cheaper in terms of other countries' currencies under a system of fixed exchange rates.*

Revaluation *occurs when a country increases the value of its currency in terms of other countries' currencies under a system of fixed exchange rates. (Revaluation is the opposite of devaluation.)*

is 120,000 × .004 = $480. If the dollar price of yen fell to $0.002 per yen, the television's dollar price would decline to $240. A reduction in the dollar price of yen gives Americans a greater incentive to purchase Japanese imports. Since Americans need yen to pay Japanese exporters, the demand for foreign exchange (yen) reflects the desire of American citizens to purchase Japanese products. The demand curve for yen will be downward sloping as long as the United States demand for Japanese imports is downward sloping. The same analysis applies, of course, to the Japanese demand for dollars in part (b) of figure 15.1.

It is important to emphasize the symmetry involved in transactions in the foreign exchange market. In figure 15.1, the American demand for yen is also the American supply of dollars to the Japanese. Japan's supply of yen to the United States is also Japan's demand for dollars. Similarly, a *change* in the demand for yen is also a change in the supply of dollars, and a change in the demand for dollars is also a change in the supply of yen. Finally, also remember that an exchange rate can be expressed in either of two ways. In our example, it can be dollars per yen or yen per dollar.

Fixed Exchange Rates

Given the supply and demand for foreign exchange, what determines the exchange rate? After World War II and prior to 1971, there was a system of **fixed exchange rates** whereby governments maintained exchange rates at predetermined levels. The fixed exchange rate system caused problems for the international economy whenever the fixed exchange rate differed from the one equating demand and supply in the foreign exchange market. To see how these problems developed, suppose the United States and Japan agreed at some point in the past to fix the exchange rate of yen for dollars at 200 yen per dollar (equivalent to $0.005 per yen). Presumably, this exchange rate at one time represented the intersection of the supply and demand curves—that is, the equilibrium exchange rate. Suppose that today, as figure 15.1 indicates, conditions in the United States and Japan have changed so that the agreed-upon dollar price of yen is too high and the agreed-upon yen price of dollars is too low.

With the quantity of yen supplied exceeding the quantity demanded, Japanese importers who want dollars cannot obtain all they would like from people who want to sell dollars. They must therefore go to the Japanese central bank, the Bank of Japan, and hand over yen. In exchange, they receive dollars. As long as the Bank of Japan has a sufficient quantity of dollars in reserve, it can maintain the exchange rate at $0.005. The United States might also be willing to cooperate in maintaining the artificially low value of the dollar by printing dollars and supplying them to Japanese importers on demand.

It is also possible that under a fixed exchange rate system economic forces would be set in motion to correct the excess supply of yen at $0.005. For example, as the Bank of Japan accepted larger quantities of yen from its citizens, the amount of yen in circulation would be reduced. This would reduce the Japanese money supply and lead to a recession. The end result would be lower prices for Japanese goods and services. Japanese products would then become more attractive to American buyers. The demand for yen would shift rightward, thus narrowing the excess supply gap in the foreign exchange market. Alternately, if the United States government supported the $0.005 price of yen by printing dollars, inflation might result in the United States, leading to a reduction in the demand for United States exports and an increase in demand for Japanese imports within the United States.

Recessions and inflations are a high price to pay for equilibrium under a fixed exchange rate system. What happens if the United States is unwilling to risk inflation to support the price of the yen? Then Japan is left with the task of financing the demand from its dollar reserves. What may well happen before a

*In a **flexible exchange rate system** the forces of supply and demand in foreign exchange markets determine exchange rates for currencies.*

***Depreciation** refers to a decline in a currency's exchange rate under a flexible exchange rate system.*

***Appreciation** refers to an increase in an exchange rate under a flexible exchange rate system.*

recession in Japan restores equality between demand and supply in the foreign exchange market is that the Bank of Japan exhausts its supply of dollars. When that happens, Japan will be forced to lower its exchange rate, a process known as **devaluation.** To restore equilibrium, it must lower the dollar value of the yen to $0.004, where the demand and supply for yen exchange are equal. In the opposite case, in which Japan increased the dollar value of the yen officially, we refer to the change as **revaluation.**

Historically, countries have used tariffs, quotas, subsidies, and other trade restrictions to try to maintain fixed exchange rates. Such policies can induce severe distortions in resource allocation throughout an economy.

Flexible Exchange Rates

Foreign exchange crises during which substantial devaluations occur with little warning can be avoided with a **flexible exchange rate system,** a system in which exchange rates are allowed to fluctuate freely in response to changes in demand and supply in the foreign exchange market. In this case the exchange rate of yen for dollars would have moved of its own accord from $0.005, which equated demand and supply at some point in the past, to $0.0042, the current equilibrium exchange rate. Under a flexible exchange rate system, a decline in the equilibrium price of a currency is called **depreciation,** and an increase in the equilibrium price is called **appreciation.** The presumption in favor of flexible exchange rates is based on the idea that allowing currency prices to vary moderately from day to day as international demand and supply conditions change is less disruptive than sudden and often large changes that occur under a fixed exchange rate system. There is now some concern that the post-1971 flexible exchange rate system has been characterized by large swings in currency prices. In this chapter and the next we will investigate why exchange rates have fluctuated so much in recent years.

The need for government intervention—and the occasions for media descriptions of international monetary crises—prior to 1971 would have been less under flexible exchange rates. In a flexible system, buyers and sellers can *always* buy and sell all the foreign exchange they want at the current equilibrium exchange rate.

Since 1971, the governments of most non-Communist countries have allowed their exchange rates to increase and decrease with the forces of supply and demand with only modest amounts of intervention. (While the central banks of some countries have occasionally voluntarily intervened to dampen swings in their exchange rates, such intervention is not required by international banking rules.) So far, the system of flexible exchange rates has worked well. International monetary crises like those that occurred under the fixed exchange rate standard have been avoided. As you will see in the next section, the supply and demand for foreign currencies depends not only on the flow of exports and imports but also on the desire of one country's citizens to invest in another country. Basically, however, exchange rates are determined by the costs of trading partners' goods and services and the trading patterns that result. Thus, we would expect a shift in United States consumers' demand in favor of British rock records to lead to an appreciation of the pound and a depreciation of the dollar, *ceteris paribus,* while an increase in the popularity of American-made movies in Britain would lead to an appreciation of the dollar and a simultaneous depreciation of the pound.

The demand for another country's currency is also affected by *speculation* that its value (exchange rate) will change in the future. Most economists agree that speculation does not alter the main effects of the forces we have outlined so far. Although we will not look at the complicating effects of speculation on foreign exchange markets, a brief word is in order. In our example, if United States citizens expect the price of

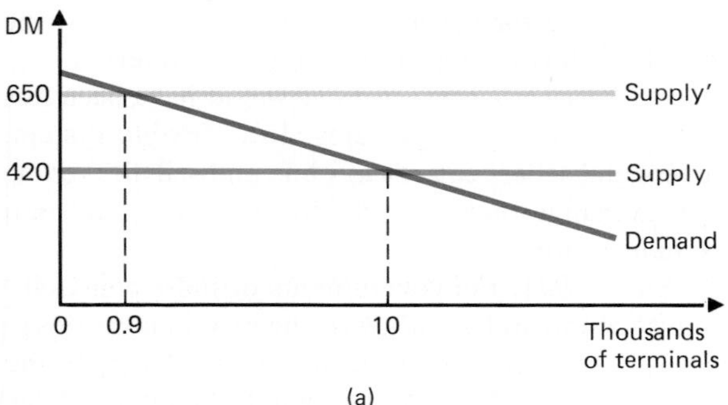

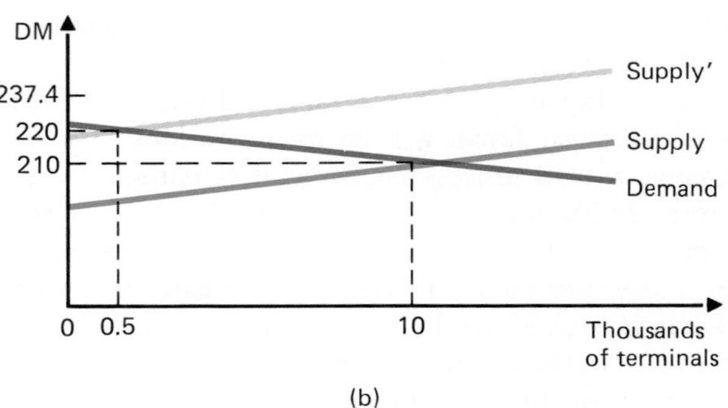

Figure 15.2 The effect of a change in foreign exchange rates on exports and imports of computer terminals
Part (a): initially, Rick sold 10,000 terminals for 420 deutsche marks (DM) each. The rise in the deutsche mark price of the United States dollar from DM 2.10 to DM 3.25 between 1980 and 1985 shifted the supply curve to Supply′. Even though demand was unchanged, the price of terminals rose to DM 650 and sales fell to 900 units.

Part (b): initially, Helga sold 10,000 terminals for DM 210 each. The rise in the deutsche mark value of the United States dollar had the effect of shifting Helga's supply curve to Supply′ as the deutsche mark cost of her loan payments rose from DM 500,000 to DM 773,809. Despite the fact that Demand did not change, sales dropped to 500 units as the price rose to DM 220 and Helga defaulted on the loan by mid-year.

yen in terms of dollars to rise over time, it may be profitable for them to buy yen now. Suppose they expect the price of yen to rise from $0.004 to $0.005. An American can withdraw, say, $10,000 dollars from a United States bank account and purchase 2.5 million yen. Then, if the yen actually appreciates as expected, these yen can be used to purchase $12,500—a profit of $2,500. Notice that speculation that the yen will appreciate shifts the demand for yen to the right in part (a) of figure 15.1, causing the *expected* exchange rate increase to occur in the present. Since the speculation is carried out in terms of United States dollars, the supply of dollars shifts to the right, causing a simultaneous depreciation of the United States dollar in part (b) of figure 15.1.

Returning to our introductory example, part (a) of figure 15.2 illustrates what happened to Rick's computer business. The diagram shows Rick's supply curve for terminals and the demand for his terminals in West Germany in 1980. Equilibrium price is DM 420 or $200, and equilibrium sales are 10,000 terminals. By 1985, the demand for Rick's terminals was unchanged, but because the deutsche mark price of the United States dollar had risen from 2.10 to 3.25 the West German price of $200 per terminal had risen to DM 650. The effect was the same as if Rick's costs of production had risen 55 percent or as if his supply curve had shifted up to Supply′. As illustrated, sales fell to less than 1,000 terminals. In effect, the rise in the deutsche mark price of the dollar raised the delivered price of Rick's terminals to the West German market by 55 percent, and he was no longer competitive. By late 1985, Rick had stopped production and was looking for a new job.

Part (b) of figure 15.2 shows the initial demand and supply curves for Helga's terminals in West Germany. Initial sales were equal to 10,000 and the price for her somewhat less fancy terminals was DM 210. The fifty deutsche marks she had to pay for each sale to cover her loan payments amounted to total payments of DM 500,000, or $238,095. With the rise in the deutsche mark value of the dollar from 2.1 to 3.25, that same loan payment of $238,095 each year increased from DM 500,000 to DM 773,809. As a result, Helga could not continue to sell 10,000 terminals for DM 210 each. Instead, to earn the same profit in 1985 that she earned in 1980, she would have to have charged DM 237.4, with sales unchanged. As illustrated in figure 15.2, part (b), the higher cost of the United States loan in terms of deutsche marks had the effect of shifting up the supply curve to Supply′. As shown, the result was a dramatic loss of sales. Helga declared bankruptcy in mid-1985.

*The **balance of payments** is the accounting for the flow of goods and services and the means of paying for them among international trading partners.*

Table 15.1 United States balance of payments (millions of dollars)

Current account (international flows of goods, services, and gifts)	**1970**			**1980**			**1983**		
	Credits less debits[a]	**Credits**	**Debits**	**Credits less debits**[a]	**Credits**	**Debits**	**Credits less debits**[a]	**Credits**	**Debits**
Merchandise (except military) "balance of trade"	+2,603	42,469	39,866	−25,342	223,966	249,308	−61,055	200,257	261,312
Military goods and services	−3,354	1,501	4,855	−2,515	8,231	10,746	515	12,737	12,222
Services (investment income, foreign travel)	+6,375	21,704	15,329	+38,636	112,470	73,834	27,628	119,208	91,580
Gifts (foreign aid, private gifts; includes government pensions to persons living abroad)	−3,294			−7,056			−8,651		
Current account balance	+2,330			+3,723			−41,563		
Capital account (international currency flows, borrowing and lending, changes in foreign assets in the U.S. and U.S. assets abroad, and special drawing rights[b]**) (will be negative when current account is positive)**	−2,111	7,226	9,337	−33,363	51,415	84,776	32,232	81,722	49,490
Statistical discrepancy	−219			29,640			9,331		
Balance of payments[c]	−0−			−0−			−0−		

Source: From *Statistical Abstract of the United States,* 1985, Table 1425, pp. 800–801.

[a]Positive balance indicates credits exceed debits. In the current account, a credit refers to goods and services exported to other countries. A debit in the current account refers to goods and services imported from other countries. When credits exceed debits, the United States exports more than it imports. In the capital account, a credit refers to dollars or other currencies sent from the United States to other countries or an increase in the amount owed to other countries by the United States. A debit refers to dollars or other currencies received by the United States from other countries or an increase in the amount owed to the United States by other countries. When credits exceed debits, the United States has sent more dollars or other currencies abroad than it has received, or it has increased the amount it owes to (has borrowed from) other countries. This shows how the United States has paid for its net imports or was paid for its net exports.

[b]See the appendix to this chapter.

[c]Statistical discrepancy is a balancing item that assures that the balance of payments will equal zero.

The Balance of Payments and the Balance of Trade

To see how the international flows of goods and services and currencies mesh, it is necessary to understand the international **balance of payments,** which is a set of accounts that keeps track of the flows of currencies in international transactions. A country's balance of payments records all of the economic transactions between residents of that country and the residents of foreign countries during a given period. To understand the information contained in balance of payments accounts, we will analyze data for the United States' balance of international payments in three different years. These data appear in table 15.1.

The flow of international payments is recorded, accounting-style, in credit and debit columns. In the balance of payments accounting system, a *debit* is a

The ***balance of trade*** *is equal to a country's merchandise exports minus its merchandise imports.*

transaction that is recorded in a right-hand column, and *credit* is a transaction recorded in a left-hand column. In the international payment accounts, a credit entry records an export of some valuable item from the United States. A debit entry records a flow in the opposite direction, an import. For example, if a business firm in Italy purchases a computer from IBM for $1 million, this will appear as a $1 million credit entry in the row labeled "merchandise" in table 15.1. Another entry records the payment for the computer. For example, the payment might consist of IBM's increasing its holding of lira worth $1 million. In this case, the second entry will be a debit to United States holdings of Italian currency. Another possibility, however, is that IBM executives and other United States citizens purchase $1 million worth of Ferraris during the same year and pay for them with lira purchased on the foreign exchange market. The exchange of dollars and lira in these transactions would cancel each other. Therefore, at the end of the year all that would appear in the balance of payments accounts would be a credit for $1 million worth of computers exported from the United States to Italy, and a debit for $1 million worth of automobiles imported by the United States from Italy.

All international transactions must be accounted for as either purchases or gifts, and all purchases must be paid for either in cash or by issuing a promise to pay (an IOU). Thus, *the flow of payments among nations must always balance.* It is *impossible* for a country to be out of balance in its foreign transactions because of this accounting definition. That is why the bottom line of table 15.1 contains *only* zeros. Unfortunately for an accountant's peace of mind, the documents from which the international payments statistics are gathered are imperfect and incomplete. Many transactions are represented by inaccurate or missing sales slips, so to speak. Therefore, it is necessary that the next-to-bottom line in the balance of payments accounts be something called "statistical discrepancy." Statistical discrepancy is the same type of entry that many of us use in our checkbooks each month to reconcile our balance with that shown on our bank statements. If we (and our banks) never made addition or subtraction errors and always remembered to record each check, charge, and deposit, then the statistical discrepancy in our checkbooks would be zero.

Let us examine the balance of payments accounts of the United States for 1970, 1980, and 1983, starting in 1970 at the top of table 15.1. During 1970, the United States exported merchandise valued at $42,469 million ($42.5 billion). This flow of value from the United States is recorded as a *credit* in the merchandise row. During 1970, merchandise valued at $39,866 million ($39.9 billion) also flowed *into* the United States. This is recorded as a *debit* in the merchandise row of the balance of payments accounts. The difference between merchandise exports and imports is called the **balance of trade** and is sometimes given quite a bit of attention in the media.

The United States balance of trade in 1970 was $2,603 million, meaning that the United States exported about $2.6 billion more merchandise than it imported. The United States balance of trade was also positive in 1975. But it was negative in 1980, when the United States imported $25,342 million ($25.3 billion) more merchandise than it exported. If we were to accept the news media evaluations, we would usually conclude that a positive balance of trade is "good" and a negative balance is "bad." However, such an interpretation generally has no basis in economic analysis. In a fundamental sense, if other countries were willing to accumulate claims on the United States indefinitely, by holding its dollars or IOU's (both claims on the production of the United States), would it not be better always to have a *negative* trade balance? A country's citizens can consume *more* goods to the extent that their country imports *more,* not *less,* than it exports. The same logic applies to our relationship with nations that have a heavy debt to us. How can we ever expect this debt to be repaid if we are unwilling to import more goods and services from our debtors than we export to them? Such a negative balance of trade for the United States provides developing countries that have large loans from United States banks with the dollars to pay off their financial obligations to the United States.[1]

The ***balance of payments on current account*** *is equal to the exports of merchandise, military items, and services plus gifts to the United States less imports of merchandise, military items and services, and gifts to other countries.*

The ***capital account*** *is the section of the balance of payments accounts that indicates how the current account balance has been financed; it indicates international currency flows plus borrowing and lending.*

Another reason why the news media emphasis on the balance of trade is generally misplaced is that *merchandise* is not the only flow generating payments or IOUs among nations. Services are imported and exported, also. Service exports include services bought by foreigners when they visit the United States on business or vacation and payments to United States shipowners for carrying freight to other countries. Service exports also include interest and dividend payments on United States investments abroad. For example, Americans buy securities in foreign countries or accept foreign IOUs in exchange for United States exports. Their investments generate returns that flow back to the United States over time in the form of interest and dividends. These flows back to the United States have the same effect on the United States balance of payments as exports of goods, which also generate payment flows from foreign countries. In 1970 and 1980, the United States was a net *exporter* of services, which generated a net flow of claims on foreign countries ranging from $6.4 billion in 1970 to $38.6 billion in 1980. In 1983, the United States imported $41.6 billion more in total goods and services than it exported.

During the decade from 1970 to 1980, the United States spent more on military purchases in foreign countries than the value of military goods it exported to them. This was largely the result of the goods and services purchased to maintain American military personnel stationed around the world. By 1983, however, the balance of military goods and services had reversed itself. Between 1970 and 1983, private gifts and foreign aid generated a net flow of claims from the United States. To the extent the United States government or its individual citizens send benefits abroad, foreigners do not have to pay for the merchandise, services, or military goods the United States exports to them.

When all of the *net* flows (shown in the "credits less debits" column) are added up, we obtain the **balance of payments on the current account.** (Exports of merchandise, military items, and services less imports are what comprised *net exports* in our discussion of GNP in chapters 2 and 3.) Notice that the United States current account balance was positive in both 1970 and 1980, despite a substantial negative balance of trade in 1980.

The **capital account** shows how the current account balance is financed. Consider the +$3,723 million ($3.72 billion) current account balance in 1980. This means that despite the fact the United States imported $25,342 million ($25.3 billion) more merchandise than it exported, money claims *by* the United States on foreigners exceeded their claims on the United States by $3.7 billion. How were these claims settled? Since the current account balance indicates a net flow of value *from* the United States (positive net exports of goods and services), the capital account must represent a flow of payments or IOUs equal in value *to* the United States. The capital account summarizes these settlements. It includes increases in United States investments in foreign countries whereby United States investors, on net, accept stock in foreign companies as payments for United States exports to them. It also includes increases in foreign IOUs held by the United States government, exporters, and banks. Finally, it reflects increases in United States holdings of foreign currency relative to foreign holdings of United States currency. If there were no statistical discrepancy, the entry in the *capital account* would be equal, and opposite in sign, to the *current account balance*.

One way to settle a positive balance of payments on the current account is for foreigners to draw down their dollar balances and pay United States banks and exporters. However, foreigners may not keep dollar balances, or if they do, they may not want to use them up. Then what foreigners can do is simply to purchase dollars on the foreign exchange market. Thus, if foreigners owe the United States more than the United States owes them, this will tend to push up the price of dollars in terms of foreign currencies. However, to the extent foreigners offer Americans investment opportunities or IOUs with attractive rates of return or interest rates, United States citizens might prefer to accept these claims on future payments from foreigners instead of currency. Thus, relatively high real interest rates or returns on investments in foreign

Foreign exchange intervention *means that the government of a country (through its central bank) buys or sells foreign exchange for the purpose of affecting the exchange rates for its currency in a particular way.*

countries will tend to cause the dollar to increase in value less rapidly or to decrease in value more rapidly relative to other currencies than it otherwise would, given the balance of payments on current account. The reverse situation partly explains the strength of the United States dollar relative to other major currencies between 1980 and 1985. Relatively high real interest rates in the United States caused the dollar to increase in value more rapidly relative to other currencies than it otherwise would have, given the balance of payments on current account.

Before proceeding, make sure you are clear on the difference between the balance of payments and the balance of trade. Moreover, be sure that you can give some examples of a credit as opposed to a debit item in each. Suppose the United States were to get foreign aid. Where would it appear in the balance of payments? How do purchases of United States corporate bonds by foreigners (loans to United States businesses) appear? You will find the answers to questions such as these in table 15.1. If you can answer them, you are ready to proceed to the issues in the rest of this chapter.

Equilibrium and Disequilibrium

In concluding our discussion of the balance of payments, we cannot emphasize too strongly that there is *no economic meaning to the concept of balance of payments disequilibrium* under a system of flexible exchange rates. Every transaction reflected in the balance of payments accounts represents a choice among alternatives, given the price of imported and exported goods and services, exchange rates, and interest rates in the countries of the world. If residents of the United States need to pay West Germans for *any* reason, to finance imports, to purchase West German IOUs, or to invest directly in West German business firms, they can *always* purchase West German deutsche marks in the foreign exchange market. Any tendency to develop an excess demand for deutsche marks will be quickly eliminated by an increase in the value of deutsche marks relative to United States dollars. The United States dollar price of deutsche marks will rise. This will make it more expensive for Americans to import goods and services or to invest in West Germany. Thus, United States citizens will not be as eager to purchase deutsche marks. As a result, the potential balance of payments deficit in the United States that would have resulted from, say, an increased demand in the United States for West German automobiles—the potential excess demand for deutsche marks and excess supply of United States dollars—is offset by the appreciation of West Germany currency (and depreciation of United States dollars). This adjustment of exchange rates automatically eliminates the deficit. Figure 15.3 illustrates the shift in the United States demand for West German goods from Demand(1) to Demand(2) and the subsequent appreciation of West German deutsche marks, which eliminates the excess demand for West German currency in the United States.

Persistent, long-term disequilibrium in the balance of payments has economic meaning only if one country's government desires to maintain a particular value of its currency in terms of other currencies at some fixed value regardless of the forces of supply and demand. For example, suppose that the Canadian government wishes to promote exports to the United States to maintain the political support of workers in its export industries. To do this, the government may choose to try to keep the Canadian dollar cheap relative to the United States dollar by intervening in the foreign exchange market. In this case, **foreign exchange intervention** requires that the Canadian government *buy* United States dollars with Canadian dollars.

One way to obtain these Canadian dollars is for the Canadian government to tax its citizens. This amounts to a gift from Canadian taxpayers to the United States. The reason is that it allows United States citizens to purchase Canadian goods with Canadian dollars that would otherwise have been available for Canadian citizens to purchase Canadian

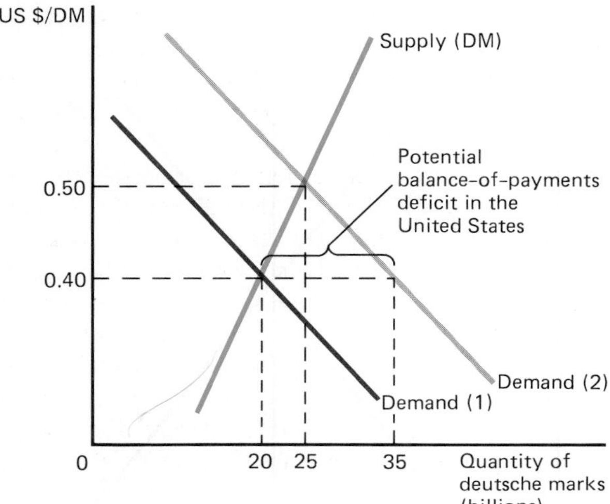

Figure 15.3 The effect of a shift in demand for West German goods on the price of West German deutsche marks in the United States
A shift in demand for West German goods in the United States will shift the United States demand for deutsche marks to Demand(2). At the initial price of deutsche marks in America, \$0.40, an excess demand for deutsche marks equal to DM 15 billion would emerge. This excess demand represents America's balance-of-payments deficit and West Germany's balance-of-payments surplus. The appreciation of the deutsche mark represented by the price rise from \$0.40 to \$0.50 eliminates the United States potential balance-of-payments deficit and West Germany's potential surplus.

goods. The flow of Canadian dollars to the United States is something like an international payments disequilibrium. It occurs only because the Canadian government is unhappy with the exchange rate that would be determined by the forces of supply and demand without intervention. The international payments account will still balance, however. When Canada buys United States dollars, this will appear as a *credit* in the United States balance of payments capital account with Canada, because the United States is exporting dollars to Canada. If Canada is successful in its strategy, the offsetting entry will be an equivalent *debit* reflecting United States imports of goods or services from Canada.

To see how arbitrary it is to think of this scenario as representing balance of payments disequilibrium, suppose that the Canadian government decided to be more forthright and explicitly stated it was granting foreign aid to the United States. (We ignore the absurdity of trying to defend such an action to Canadian voters.) Then, the "gifts" row in the credit less debits column for the United States in table 15.1 would show a positive entry with respect to Canada, and United States citizens would need fewer Canadian dollars to pay for Canadian imports. The Canadian government would use taxes collected from Canadian citizens to pay Canadian producers for exports to the United States. The effect on the United States-Canadian exchange rate would be the same as an equivalent intervention in the foreign exchange market, but we would be less likely to define this set of transactions as reflecting a balance of payments disequilibrium.

Some news media interpretations and political discussions of balance of payments disequilibrium either reflect ignorance or are disguises for promoting the special interests of groups that see themselves as being harmed by some aspect of international trade. More likely than not, such groups will consist of firms (and their employees) who see themselves as being harmed by import competition. They will shout with horror at a negative balance of trade or balance of payments on current account, perhaps defining a negative balance as "disequilibrium." Since "disequilibrium" sounds like a rather uncomfortable situation that might cause harm unless "equilibrium" is restored, use of the term may bolster calls for import protection. Why a positive balance is not also a "disequilibrium" is not usually spelled out. The use of rhetoric to make one's position look more reasonable is not new. In our discussions of trade regulations, you could easily imagine United States autoworkers and steelworkers calling for fair, rather than free, trade. During the 1950s and 1960s these same groups were quite happy with our strong export sales and never suggested that perhaps we were being unfair to Europe or Japan.

The International Transmission Mechanism

The macromodel developed in chapters 2 through 12 tells us how macroeconomic disturbances are transferred from one country to another. The key relationship is that one country's imports are exports from the point of view of other nations. Figure 15.4 shows, for example, how a recession that begins in the United States is transmitted to Canada. Exports to the United States constitute a significant component of Canada's GNP—about 20 percent in 1984.[2]

A nation's exports make up part of *exogenous expenditure* on GNP. Therefore, a change in exports exerts an impact on equilibrium GNP through the *exogenous expenditure multiplier.* The effect of a change in exports can be illustrated by using the aggregate demand and supply curves. When the United States enters a recession, production and income fall. Consequently, consumption and imports decline. Because exports from Canada make up a large share of United States imports, Canada experiences a reduction in its exports and, hence, aggregate demand. The leftward shift in Canada's aggregate demand indicates that Canada is entering a recession. The recession in the United States has been transmitted to Canada through their international economic relationship.

The aggregate demand and supply curves also illustrate that an inflationary episode in the United States will lead to a rightward shift in Canada's aggregate demand curve. If Canada happens to be in a recessionary phase of the business cycle, then the international transmission mechanism will lead to a faster recovery for Canada. However, if Canada's macroeconomy is at full employment, then an inflationary episode in the United States will be transmitted to Canada, leading its economy into an inflationary period, too.

In general, economic disturbances in the United States are transmitted to any nation whose exports to the United States make up a significant fraction of that nation's GNP. By contrast, it is much less likely that a macroeconomic disturbance in any *individual* foreign nation will have a dramatic impact on the United States economy. The reason is that most other nations' GNPs are much smaller than the GNP of the United States. Consequently, a given change in their imports constitutes a fairly small fraction of United States GNP. Consider the United States-Canada relationship for example. Canada's GNP is only about one-tenth the size of that of the United States.[3] Therefore, so long as Canada's imports from the United States roughly equal its exports to the United States, United States exports to Canada amount to only about 0.1×0.2, or 2 percent of United States GNP. The point is not that Canadian economic changes have no impact on the United States economy but rather that on balance the net transmission of economic disturbances across international borders is generally from the United States to Canada and its other trading partners.

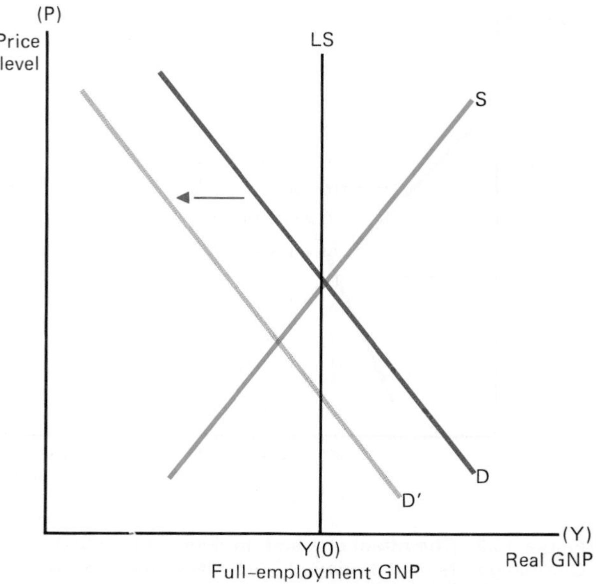

Figure 15.4 The international transmission of a recession from the United States to Canada
This diagram depicts the macroeconomic situation in Canada when the United States experiences a recession. When the United States enters a recession, production and income fall. Consequently, consumption and imports decline. Because exports from Canada to the United States make up a large share of Canadian GNP, Canada experiences a reduction in aggregate demand. The leftward shift in Canada's aggregate demand indicates that Canada is entering a recession. The recession in the United States has been transmitted to Canada through their international economic relationship.

Macroeconomic Influences on the United States Balance of Trade and International Financial Flows

We have seen how international financial flows, exchange rates, and features of the *monetary* aspects of international trade interact with the *real* flows of goods and services to determine the balance of trade and balance of payments. In this section we will relate this knowledge to our discussion in this chapter of international macroeconomic relationships. Throughout much of the post-World War II period the United States had a positive merchandise, or commodity, balance of trade. By 1973, however, merchandise exports barely exceeded imports. Thereafter, the United States commodity balance of trade turned negative, and in 1985 the trade deficit exceeded $120 billion. In chapter 16 we shall see that one reason for this trade deficit was our growing dependence on imported oil. Related to increasing oil prices was a shift in demand for small foreign-made cars—especially from Japan. Indeed, our balance of trade deficit with Japan was particularly worrisome to many United States citizens and policymakers. In 1983, for example, United States merchandise exports to Japan were only half as large as its imports.[4] By 1985, the United States trade deficit with Japan exceeded $40 billion.

Inflation and the Trade Balance

In addition to the shift in demand for Japanese cars, another important reason for the Japanese trade imbalance with the United States was the lower rate of inflation in Japan. Throughout the 1970s and the first half of the 1980s, Japan had a much lower inflation rate than the United States. (The reasons for this are discussed in chapter 16.) We would expect that a tendency to import more from Japan than the United States exports to Japan would lead to an increase in the demand for yen to pay for these imports. Moreover, inflation in the United States would lead Japanese producers to export less to the United States as the purchasing power of the dollars they receive fell; Japanese importers would find it less attractive to purchase American-made goods as their price rose. These two effects of United States inflation would *reduce* the supply of yen to the foreign exchange market.

We have seen that the combined impact of the increased demand for yen and reduced supply would be expected to lead to *appreciation of the yen in terms of the dollar* (that is, an increase in the dollar price of yen). If no other changes occurred in the Japanese-United States trading relationship, the equilibrium price of yen in terms of the dollar would rise sufficiently to restore equilibrium in the balance of trade between the two countries.

The reason the United States experienced a *continuing* negative balance of trade with Japan and other industrial countries is that the price of foreign exchange did *not* rise sufficiently to increase the cost of imports to United States citizens and reduce the cost of United States exports to foreigners. Between 1978 and 1980 the dollar *appreciated* in value by over 20 percent, after adjusting for the degree of inflation in the United States and in countries with which it traded.[5] Between 1980 and early 1985 the dollar appreciated another 30 percent. In the next section we will explore why changes in the foreign exchange markets did not eliminate the United States trade imbalance.

Macroeconomic Policy, Interest Rates, and International Financial Flows

In chapters 11 and 12 we saw how monetary restraint to control inflation led to higher real interest rates in the United States during the early 1980s. We also discussed how federal deficits relative to GNP increased during the same period. Between 1977 and 1979 United States deficits relative to GNP averaged 2.0 percent. Between 1980 and 1984 the deficit-GNP ratio averaged 4.1 percent. That increase in the United States deficit required immense increases in United States Treasury bond sales. This was a new situation for the United States economy, except in time of war. The combined shocks of unanticipated monetary restraint and the accelerated pace of federal borrowing increased both short-term and long-term real interest

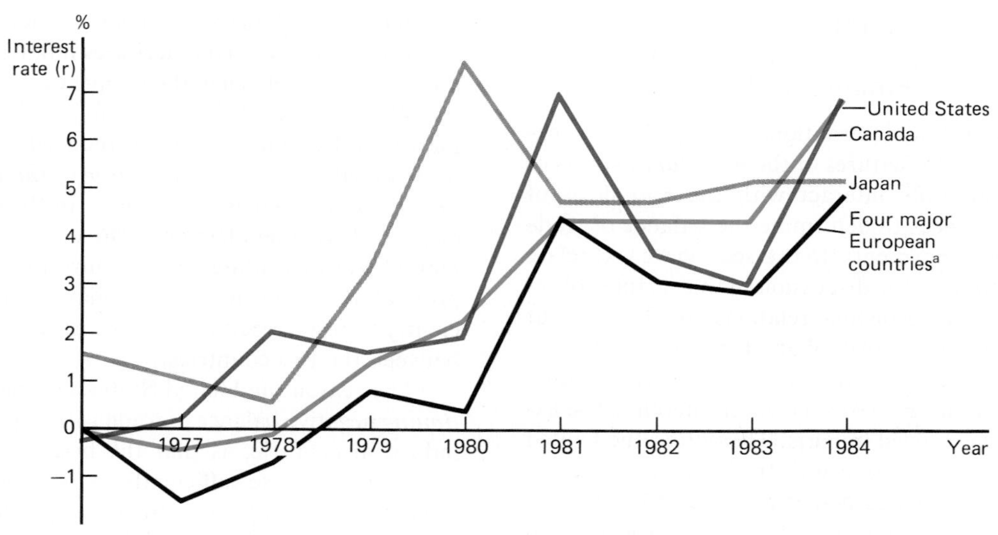

Figure 15.5 Average annual short-term interest rates in the United States and other major industrial countries, 1976–1984
This figure shows the average interest rates for short-term loans corrected for the rate of inflation in the United States and other major industrial nations.
From International Monetary Fund, *World Economic Outlook,* 1984, Table 2.6, p. 120, and 1985, Table 2.7, p. 121.

rates. Figures 15.5 and 15.6 show how real interest rates on short-term and long-term bonds changed over the period 1976–84 in the United States and several of the countries with which it traded.

Remember that *real* interest rates are nominal interest rates adjusted for the rate of inflation. Thus, it is possible for real interest rates to be negative—less than zero—when unanticipated inflation leads to lenders' being repaid in amounts insufficient to maintain their purchasing power. Over the period 1976–79, the average real short-term interest rate in the United States was −0.6 percent and −0.4 percent in the four major European countries shown in figure 15.5. Japanese credit markets are relatively closed to the West, and short-term interest rates there did not closely parallel those in the United States and Western Europe. Later on, over the five-year period 1980–84, average real short-term interest rates in the United States had risen to 4.4 percent, compared to 3.1 percent in the four major European countries.

In the United States, long-term real interest rates increased from an average of 1.4 percent over the 1976–79 period to 5.0 percent in 1980–84. In the four major European nations, long-term real interest rates averaged 0.5 percent and 3.5 percent, respectively. Figures 15.5 and 15.6 show that monetary restraint and deficit financing in the United States helped raise the differential real interest rates on both short-term and long-term bonds between the United States and European countries. This made the United States an

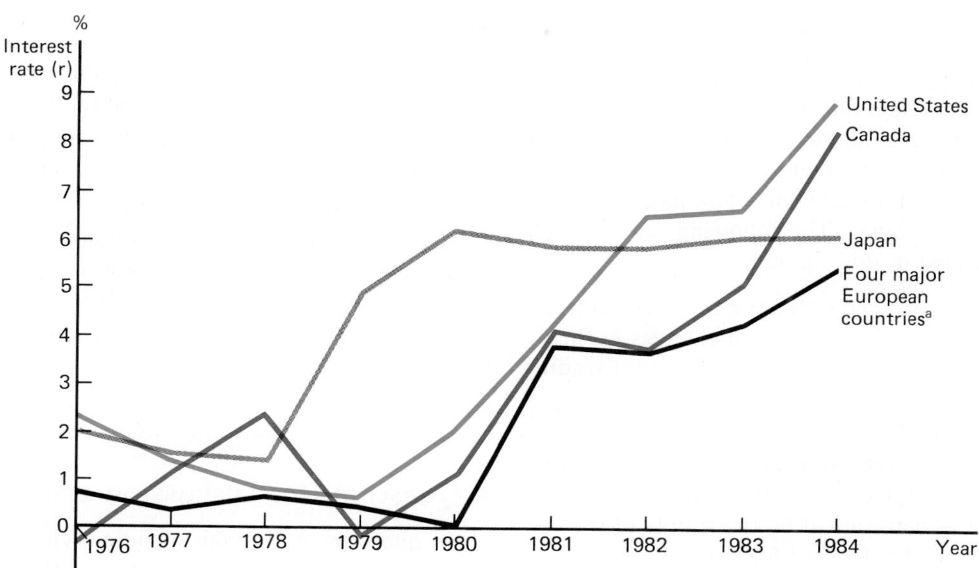

Figure 15.6 Average annual long-term interest rates in the United States and other major industrial countries, 1976–1984
This figure shows the average interest rates for long-term loans corrected for the rate of inflation in the United States and other major industrial nations.
From International Monetary Fund, *World Economic Outlook*, 1984, Table 2.2, p. 121, and 1985, Table 2.7, p. 121.

attractive place for foreign lenders, not only European but also OPEC nations and other major trading partners of the United States, to send their loanable funds. Still another factor influencing foreigners' desire to hold United States financial assets was a high level of political uncertainty in many nations. Particularly after the fall of the Shah of Iran, with the growing political anarchy in Lebanon and the state of unrest among other nations in the eastern Mediterranean, North Africa, and Persian Gulf regions, the United States became a "safe haven" for foreign investments. Economic and political crises in the early 1980s in countries like Chile, Argentina, Brazil, Mexico, Nicaragua, and El Salvador have added to the "safe haven" demand for United States-financed assets and to Miami's development into an international financial center.

To the extent that foreigners were willing to lend the United States money, or simply accumulate dollars as the dollar tended to appreciate in terms of foreign currency, they did not spend their dollars on United States exports. This is what balanced the excess demand for foreign commodities by the United States and allowed the United States to run a prolonged balance of trade deficit.

▸ Summary and Conclusions

Foreign exchange rates and our international economic relations affect all of us daily in our personal and professional lives and will continue to do so in the foreseeable future. That is why it is important to learn about the markets that determine how nations pay for trade with one another. The following major points were emphasized in this chapter.

Under a system of fixed exchange rates, equilibrium in foreign trade occurs through changes in the levels of national income and/or prices of trading partners rather than in their currencies' exchange rate.

In a system of flexible exchange rates, the price of one country's currency in terms of other currencies is determined by the supply of the currency and the demand for it.

In a system of flexible exchange rates, there is no economic meaning to the concept of balance of payments disequilibrium.

When a nation keeps the price of its currency artificially low in terms of the currency of another nation, the result is the same as if it granted foreign aid to that nation.

The shock of monetary restraint and high government deficits in the early 1980s raised interest rates and allowed the United States to maintain a balance of trade deficit that was not offset by depreciation of the dollar.

▸ Key Terms

appreciation *319*
balance of payments *321*
balance of payments on current account *323*
balance of trade *322*
capital account *323*
depreciation *319*
devaluation *318*
fixed exchange rates *318*
flexible exchange rate system *319*
foreign exchange intervention *324*
foreign exchange market *316*
foreign exchange rate *315*
revaluation *318*

▸ Questions for Discussion and Review

In questions 1 through 4, judge whether the statements are true, false, or uncertain. Be sure to justify your answer.

1. Under flexible exchange rates a domestic currency's appreciation will make imports more expensive.
2. A negative balance of trade denotes disequilibrium in the international currency market.
3. An increase in the United States money supply at the full-employment level of GNP will cause the exchange rate to fall.

4. Under fixed exchange rates an excess supply of dollars in France can be eliminated by devaluing the franc.
5. A reduction in domestic income taxes at full employment could decrease the demand for imports through an appreciation in the exchange rate.
6. Under flexible exchange rates an increase in demand for Japanese goods in the United States will raise the price of United States exports to Japan.
7. Why would an exporting nation ever accept increased holdings of another country's currency or its IOUs instead of imports in return for its exports? When an exporter does not demand imports of goods or services as payment, what is the effect on the price of the exporter's currency in terms of the importing country's currency?
8. Use a diagram such as figure 15.1 to show the effects of the following events on the value of the United States dollar in terms of the currencies of other nations.
   a. Inflation in the United States and in other countries.
   b. An increase in interest rates in the United States and in other countries.
   c. A recession in the United States.
   d. Vastly improved investment opportunities abroad.
9. Between 1970 and 1982, the world's major oil-exporting nations experienced the following *cumulative* (total) current account balances with respect to their international payments (in billions of United States dollars).[6]

Saudi Arabia	$165.3	Gabon	1.2 (1970–81)
Kuwait	85.2	Nigeria	−3.3
United Arab Emirates	48.8	Algeria	−16.5
		Venezuela	6.8
Qatar	16.9	Indonesia	2.7 (1970–81)
Omon	4.9	Ecuador	−3.8 (1970–81)
Iran	31.2	Mexico	45.4
Iraq	22.9		
Libya	21.2		

   Use the format of table 15.1 to show how these countries might have balanced their payments with the rest of the world. Which countries were exporting more goods and services than they were importing? What would be the major difference between the balancing entries of the countries with positive current balances and those with negative balances?
10. Suppose you are a foreign exchange trader for a major United States bank. Assume the theory of rational expectations holds. There is a fully anticipated increase in the United States money supply with the money supply of Japan remaining constant. Would you make more profit by buying or selling yen now?

Appendix to Chapter 15

International Financial Cooperation

We have already mentioned that prior to 1971 governments established fixed exchange rates among their currencies. This type of government intervention was called the *gold or gold exchange standard* prior to World War II. According to this standard, each country would define its money in terms of gold. For example, if one ounce of gold cost $30 in the United States and £10 in Great Britain, then the exchange rate was $3 per British pound. Private citizens could, if they wished, *require* payment in gold rather than the currency of a particular country. This system was officially replaced by the dollar exchange standard following the *Bretton Woods Agreement* of 1944. In the Bretton Woods system, each country's money was still defined in terms of gold, but private citizens could no longer require payment in gold. If they did not want a particular country's money, the only other form of payment permitted was in dollars. In effect, the United States dollar price of gold was held constant at $35 per ounce of gold. Other countries then set a fixed price for their currencies in terms of the United States dollar.

▸ The International Monetary Fund and the World Bank

To help implement the change from the gold standard to the dollar exchange standard, the Bretton Woods Agreement provided for the creation of the *International Monetary Fund (IMF),* which began operating in 1946. One of the principal architects of the new system was John Maynard Keynes, senior representative of Great Britain to the Bretton Woods Conference.

The IMF was intended to serve as a kind of international bank. Member countries deposit currency with the IMF and were able to draw on these accounts either in their own currencies or in other currencies in order to finance imports on a temporary basis while maintaining a fixed United States dollar price for their currencies. As already noted, the United States dollar was used to define a fixed price of $35 per ounce of gold. That fixed price was maintained until 1968, when the "official" price of gold among central banks remained $35 per ounce but the private market price of gold was allowed to fluctuate. The United States abandoned the fixed price of gold in August 1971. The collapse of the Bretton Woods Agreement was the direct result of rapid inflation in the United States associated with financing the Vietnam War. The money supply in the United States grew too fast to maintain either a fixed world gold price or fixed prices of other currencies in terms of United States dollars. In particular, there was considerable pressure in currency markets to allow the dollar price of West German deutsche marks and Japanese yen to rise substantially.

Between 1946 and 1971 countries borrowed from the IMF with the objective of maintaining fixed exchange rates for their currencies relative to the dollar. Until 1971 international trade was financed predominantly in United States dollars, and even during the 1970s, after the fixed currency price system ended, three-fourths of all international transactions were made in dollars. However, the relatively rapid rate of inflation in the United States that occurred after the mid-1960s created difficulties with this system. Attempts to reestablish the fixed exchange rate system have not been seriously considered since 1974. Even today, there are occasional discussions among international bankers to try to return to a relatively fixed exchange rate system, but there is no agreement on how that could be done without recreating the problems of the Bretton Woods system. The first serious effort to coordinate monetary policy among industrial nations to influence the value of the United States dollar abroad was initiated by the United States Secretary of the Treasury in late 1985 and early 1986.

Special drawing rights (SDRs) are a kind of international money created by the International Monetary Fund.

The Eurodollar market is a financial market in which Eurodollars are borrowed and lent.

Eurodollars are dollar deposits in European banks.

In order to reduce reliance on the United States dollar as the principal monetary unit of international trade transactions in the late 1960s, the IMF developed a kind of international paper money called **special drawing rights (SDRs)** in 1970. The value of SDRs was originally defined as a weighted average of sixteen currencies but that was streamlined to five currencies in 1981 (the United States dollar, West German deutsche mark, French franc, Japanese yen, and British pound).

The creation of SDRs extended the international central bank nature of the IMF. Member votes to expand allocations of SDRs are qualitatively similar to money creation by, say, the Fed in the United States. Suppose, for example, members of the IMF vote to expand the quantity of SDRs by one billion units. These SDRs then become available for any participating nation to borrow in order to finance imports from other participating nations. Thus, the demand for an exporting country's goods will increase as a result of importing nations' borrowing SDRs from the IMF.

The *World Bank* was created in conjunction with the IMF and serves to provide countries that have international financial problems with low-interest loans to assist in improving their domestic and international competitiveness over time. The World Bank was intended to help countries finance long-term internal changes that would eliminate their recurring short-term international financial problems.

Eurodollars and Eurocurrency Banking

The final international link among countries that we want to introduce here is the **Eurodollar market,** which is not a particular geographic place but rather the sum of transactions outside the United States dealing in United States dollar-denominated assets. Elements of the Eurodollar market can be found in such major financial centers as London, Paris, Zurich, and the Cayman Islands. About 70 to 75 percent of the transactions in banks dealing with currencies of other nations in Europe involve United States dollars.

Eurodollars are dollar deposits in European banks. They are the creation of Eurocurrency banks. *Eurocurrency banks* are banks that simultaneously deal in the currencies of many nations and are exempt from many national banking regulations. Eurocurrency banks exist primarily for the convenience of large international business transactions and usually maintain multimillion dollar minimum amounts for deposits and loans. The Eurodollar market began to develop when these banks needed to find a means for providing United States dollars to finance East-West trade during the 1950s. At that time, the "cold war" between East and West prevented direct trade between the United States and eastern-bloc countries.

The Eurodollar market grew quickly for several reasons. First, by maintaining high minimum balance requirements on deposits and dealing exclusively with large loans, the interest rate spread between deposit and loan rates at Eurocurrency banks could be kept low, which permitted the banks to offer high deposit rates and low loan rates compared to other banks. Since Eurocurrency banks are not subject to many national regulations on banks, they tend to hold lower reserve balances and to pay higher deposit interest than other banks. Another reason for the rapid expansion of the Eurodollar market was that between 1965 and 1974, there was a shortage of dollars to finance international transactions. This shortage resulted from efforts by the United States and a number of other countries to limit international capital flows and to maintain the fixed price currency system that eventually collapsed in 1971. As the central banks limited the availability of United States dollars for international transactions, traders and currency dealers relied more and more on Eurodollar banks to obtain the United States dollars they wanted despite central bank controls.

Key Terms

Eurodollar market *333*
Eurodollars *333*
special drawing rights (SDRs) *333*

Chapter 16

Current Issues in International Trade

Outline

Objectives

After reading this chapter, the student should be able to:

Discuss the role of monetary policy and central government deficits in explaining international differences in macroeconomic performance in the United States compared to other major industrial nations.

Explain how the world oil market in the middle and late 1970s contributed to recessionary episodes and stagflation among major oil-importing nations.

Explain why developing nations often face a highly variable commodity terms of trade and the impact of this on their economies.

Explain why excessive external debt in many developing nations is often accompanied by high domestic inflation rates.

Discuss the recent Mexican experience with overvaluation of the peso.

Discuss the external debt crisis that developed in the late 1970s and early 1980s.

Introduction

In chapters 11 and 12 we discussed actual experience with the use of monetary and fiscal policies in the United States. The problems of defining and assessing policy actions in an international setting are at least as complex. We will begin this chapter with a comparison of economic conditions in the United States and other major industrial nations in recent years. Apart from providing a better perspective on United States policy, that comparison will demonstrate how the effectiveness of domestic monetary and fiscal policy can be influenced by international trade. Economic conditions in the advanced industrial nations as a group strongly influence the macroeconomic options available to the less developed countries. Moreover, in many of the world's developing nations, policy difficulties are often made worse by problems of implementation. For example, while visiting Cairo, Egypt, one of the authors of this book was told about what is mockingly referred to as the "season of fires." It is contended that in the month prior to the deadline for filing income tax statements many businesses are burned to the ground along with all of their financial records. The government official telling us the story said that the practice at times has been so popular that during that month an uninformed observer would think that the night sky was quite beautiful with all the red glow throughout the city. Obviously, forecasting national government revenues can be quite difficult under such circumstances.

In Bolivia the rate of inflation in mid-1985 was estimated to be at least 1,000 percent per year. By that time national elections had become a regular occurrence as each successive regime willingly offered the opposition the opportunity to try to make sense out of a national economic nightmare. No one seemed to know what money growth rates should be over time or to worry much about attaining them.

Chile seemed to be on the road to economic growth and stability in the late 1970s. But by the early 1980s, the unemployment rate was soaring, the economy was in a tailspin, and foreign debt was rapidly expanding. The government of President Pinochet tried to maintain a fixed exchange rate relative to the United States dollar despite the fact that the world price of copper, Chile's major export, had collapsed with no hope for a quick rebound. In retrospect, it was clear that the Pinochet government had erred badly in maintaining the fixed rate vis-à-vis the dollar. But no one could offer any simple remedy to the economic crisis accompanying the rapid fall in copper prices. What could Chile have done to soften the adverse impact of the declining world price of copper, and how much good would it have done?

This chapter explores some of the major international economic problems of the 1970s and 1980s and devotes considerable attention to those facing the world's developing economies. The problems of the world's developing nations are not that much different from those of the United States. However, they are of a much greater order of magnitude relative to these nations' limited productive capacities. We will pay particular attention to the experience of those countries that compete with many others in world export markets. Such countries are essentially price takers—

competitive suppliers of their exports and competitive buyers of imports on the world market. (By contrast, a major exporter of petroleum, such as Saudi Arabia, can and does have a major impact on the world price of oil through its decisions to export more or less oil.)

Small, developing nations often see themselves as subject to domination by wealthier, industrial nations in ways that limit their growth. In this chapter we shall briefly look at evidence bearing on this claim. We will see how some developing nations have borrowed from the industrialized countries to finance imports of desired capital and consumer goods and explore factors underlying the international debt problems that have resulted. We will also see how a strategy of trying to manipulate the value of a country's currency in foreign exchange markets by its own government ties in with alternative approaches to industrialization.

It should be clear by now that the economic prospects of the United States are tied through international trade and finance to the ability of developing nations to deal effectively with their own economic problems. Nowhere is this clearer than in the ramifications of the sharp increase in world oil prices that occurred during the middle and late 1970s. Because the United States is such a dominant force in world trade, due to the sheer size of its economy, we begin this chapter by analyzing recent United States economic performance relative to that of other major industrial nations. We then study the impact of the oil "crisis" before going on to look in more detail at the problems of smaller, less industrialized countries.

▸ Recent United States Economic Performance Relative to that of Other Major Industrial Countries

In chapters 11 and 12 we reviewed some major macroeconomic events in the United States. We will now relate these periods of inflation and recession to the experience of other nations. This comparison will help us to see the strengths and weaknesses of the United States economy in broader perspective. It will also show how changes in aggregate economic conditions in the United States have often caused similar changes in other advanced economies.

Growth, Inflation, and Employment

Figures 16.1 and 16.2 contain data on annual changes in real GNP and the aggregate price level for the United States, Canada, Japan, and four major European countries (France, the Federal Republic of Germany, Italy, and the United Kingdom) between 1967 and 1985. During the nine-year period 1967–76, the United States experienced a rate of economic growth of 2.8 percent annually. Although this was well below the 3.5 percent growth rate the United States enjoyed during the preceding nine years, 1958–67, it was not much below the hundred-year average of 3 percent. During the 1967–76 time span, the United States experienced economic growth that was slower than that of Canada, Japan, or the four major European countries represented in figure 16.1. During the 1967–76 period, the United States initially improved its rate of GNP growth relative to the other countries shown. Between 1978 and 1982, however, the rate of economic growth in the United States fell sharply, and this pattern was matched elsewhere, except in Japan, where economic growth declined but

Figure 16.1 Economic growth in several major industrial economies, 1967–1984
This figure illustrates the annual percentage rates of real GNP growth for the United States and a number of other advanced economies.
From International Monetary Fund, *World Economic Outlook*, 1985, Table 2, p. 206.

not as severely. During the expansion of 1983 through 1985 United States economic growth was as vigorous as that of most of the other major industrial countries. The Japanese economy exhibited a relatively high but declining rate of economic growth throughout the entire period covered in figure 16.1. Japan appears to be moving toward matching, rather than exceeding, the economic growth rates of Canada, the United States, and Western Europe.

Japan is the only major industrial country that sustained substantial economic growth in the 1980–82 time period. No doubt the oil price shock of 1979 contributed to the economic downturn that followed in most of the developed and developing countries by doubling the price of crude oil. But Japan's experience indicates that such an explanation is too simple. Japan imports about 95 percent of the oil that it uses, and most of that oil comes from the Persian Gulf—the heart of OPEC.

Figure 16.2 Inflation rates in several major industrial economies, 1967–1986
This figure illustrates the annual percentage rates of inflation as measured by the GNP deflator for the United States and a number of other advanced economies.
From International Monetary Fund, *World Economic Outlook*, 1985, Table 8, p. 213.

Inflation Rates in Industrial Countries

Figure 16.2 indicates the annual percentage change in a broad measure of domestic prices—the GNP deflator. Inflation increased substantially in the United States after 1967 as a consequence of the monetary and fiscal policies associated with the Vietnam War, as we saw in chapter 11. However, inflation in the United States remained below that in most other industrial countries. During the period of rapidly accelerating inflation (1978–81), the GNP deflator in the United States rose less rapidly than in Canada, or most of Western Europe. (Inflation in the Federal Republic of Germany was less than in the United States.) In 1983 and 1984, only Japan and the Federal Republic of Germany achieved inflation rates lower than that in the United States.

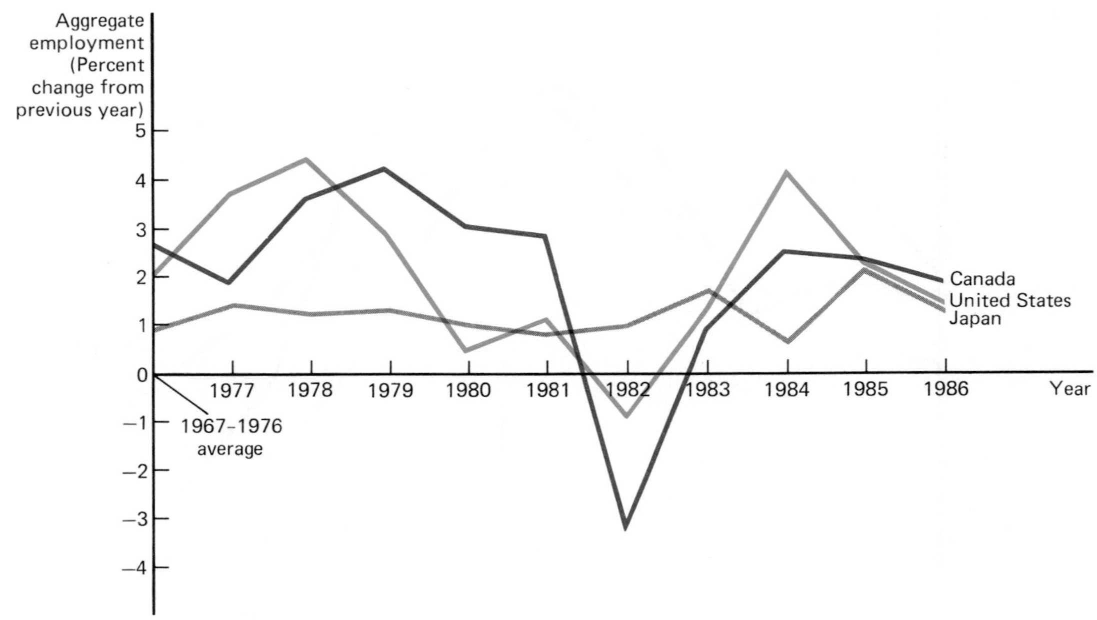

Figure 16.3 Percentage change in aggregate employment in the United States, Canada, and Japan, 1967–1986
From International Monetary Fund, *World Economic Outlook,* Table 6, p. 173, and 1985, Table 4, p. 209.

Employment and Unemployment in Advanced Economies

Figures 16.3 and 16.4 summarize changes in total employment and the unemployment rate for the United States, Canada, Japan, and the Federal Republic of Germany (unemployment only), whose unemployment has been typical of other Western European nations. We saw in chapter 11 how United States unemployment increased during the 1970s and early 1980s. From an average annual unemployment rate of 5.4 percent for 1967–76, the United States unemployment rate rose to 7.5 percent on average during the 1977–85 period, reaching a peak of 9.7 percent in 1982. Unemployment increased less dramatically in Western Europe until the 1980s. One reason was that these countries employed "guest workers" from the Mediterranean region, who were allowed to work when unemployment was low but who were shipped back to their home countries when employment opportunities diminished during the 1970s. However, by the 1980s, a continued decline in new employment opportunities began to raise unemployment rates in Western Europe to levels as high or higher than those in the United States. In Japan, stable economic conditions, along with a tradition of long-term job attachment, helped maintain exceptionally low unemployment rates despite slow employment growth.

Figure 16.4 Average unemployment rates in the United States and other major industrial countries, 1967–1986
From International Monetary Fund, *World Economic Outlook,* 1985, Table 4, p. 209.

Employment growth in Japan during the 1967–84 period was little more than half that in the United States. In fact, although figure 16.3 does not show it, employment growth in the United States exceeded the average for all of Western Europe and Canada during these years. One of the best-kept secrets about United States economic performance between 1967 and 1985 is the dramatic expansion in employment that took place in comparison to most of the other industrialized countries.

Monetary and Fiscal Policies in Industrial Countries

One issue concerning policymakers around the world has been the apparent common pattern of business cycles in the industrialized countries. Politicians in Europe and Canada were quick to argue that the stagflation they experienced during 1979–82 resulted from monetary and fiscal mismanagement in the

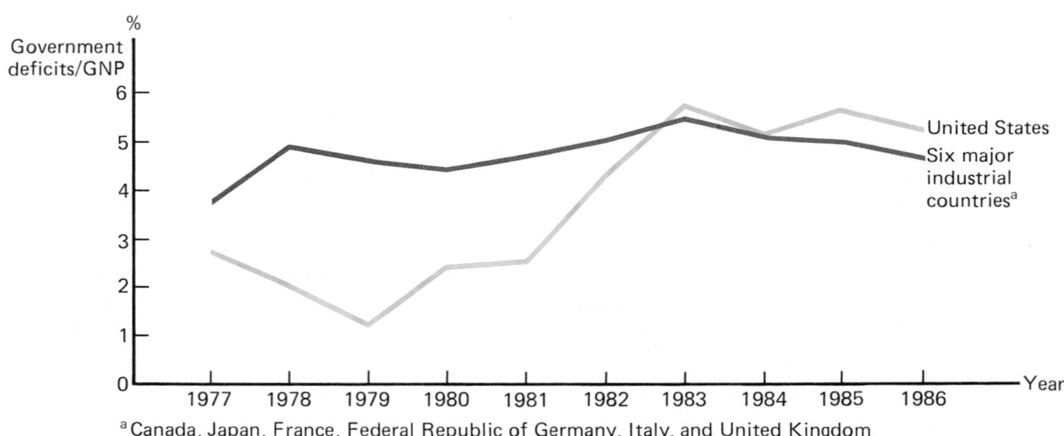

Figure 16.5 Government deficits as a percentage of GNP in the United States and other major industrial countries, 1967–1986
From International Monetary Fund, *World Economic Outlook*, 1984, Table 8, p. 174, and 1985, Table 15, p. 220.

United States. (However, we have seen that an increase in the world price of oil in 1979 and 1980 may have played a part in affecting the fortunes of all oil-importing nations, including Japan and the countries of Western Europe.) It is clear that as a result of its sheer size alone, conditions in the United States would tend to affect its industrial trading partners. Yet both Japan and Germany managed to avoid the pattern of inflation observed in the United States during the late 1970s and early 1980s. Moreover, Japan sustained positive and significant economic growth throughout the period 1977–84. Clearly, the economic ups and downs of the world's economy cannot be explained simply as the result of United States fiscal and monetary policies. Nor can they be explained solely in terms of a common response to OPEC's success in raising world oil prices. In this chapter, we will explore in some detail how macroeconomic policies in the United States have influenced economic conditions around the world.

Central Government Deficits Relative to GNP

One of the issues that has most concerned major trading partners of the United States has been the immense quantity of borrowing on the part of the United States Treasury to finance government expenditure. What evidence is there that deficit spending in the United States or elsewhere has harmed or helped the economies of major industrial countries?

Figure 16.5 shows the size of central (federal) government deficits relative to GNP in the United States and six other major industrial countries. Our first observation is that the much publicized United States deficit to GNP ratio was actually *below* that of other major industrial countries throughout much of the period following 1976. If we were to look at the deficits of the six individual countries other than the United States represented in figure 16.5, we would see that there is no relationship between the size of the deficit relative to GNP and the degree of inflation or economic growth in each country.

Researchers at the International Monetary Fund have calculated the deficits for these countries relative to their full-employment GNP levels, and the results still indicate little relationship between deficits and various measures of aggregate economic performance.[1] The size of the deficit in the United States does not appear to be associated with changes in other countries' GNP, rate of inflation, employment, or unemployment. Moreover, these measures of economic "health" in each country appear unrelated to their own deficits. Within individual countries, the tax structure, marginal tax rates, patterns of government spending, and other details of fiscal policy may help explain the varying macroeconomic patterns exhibited in figures 16.1 through 16.5. The sheer size of the deficits relative to GNP, however, does not stand out as an important variable, at least for the range of values observed in recent years across industrial countries.

Monetary Policy in Major Industrial Countries

In earlier chapters, we have repeatedly stressed the long-run link between monetary growth and nominal GNP. The rationale underlying this relationship is our macromodel. In particular, the *quantity theory of money* implies a close relationship between the quantity of money (M) and nominal GNP (PY), given velocity (V). The quantity theory tells us that relatively rapid monetary growth will be associated with a relatively rapid rate of increase in either real GNP (Y) or the price level (P), or both, depending upon whether the economy is at full employment or in a recessionary phase of the business cycle. Either way, *nominal* GNP is expected to be closely associated with monetary growth. However, our macromodel also tells us that macroeconomic disturbances are transmitted from one nation to another via imports, exports, and currency flows. What evidence can we find to shed light on the relative importance of these two major determinants of macroeconomic fluctuations in major industrial countries?

Figure 16.6 illustrates the relationship between the annual percentage growth rates of the money stock and nominal GNP in the United States, Canada, Japan, and four major Western European countries. Perhaps the most obvious relationship is that on average, over the entire 1977–84 time span, monetary growth rates and nominal GNP growth rates are closely matched. The graphs of monetary growth and nominal GNP growth are very close together for all of the countries shown. In the United States and Canada, the monetary growth lines tend to lie a little above the nominal GNP growth lines, while in Japan and Western Europe, the lines cross each other, indicating that average monetary and nominal GNP growth are approximately equal over the period.

The second obvious feature of figure 16.6 is that the major trends and turning points of monetary and nominal GNP growth in the United States are reflected closely in these series for Canada. They are reflected somewhat less clearly in the Western European nations and still less in Japan. Evidently, the international linkage of macroeconomic performance discussed in chapter 15 is an important force determining the economic experiences of our international trading partners. The closer the partnership, the more closely linked are other nations' macroeconomies with that of the United States. Nevertheless, as the experience of Japan and Western Europe indicates, other nations can and do exert considerable independent control over their aggregate economies.

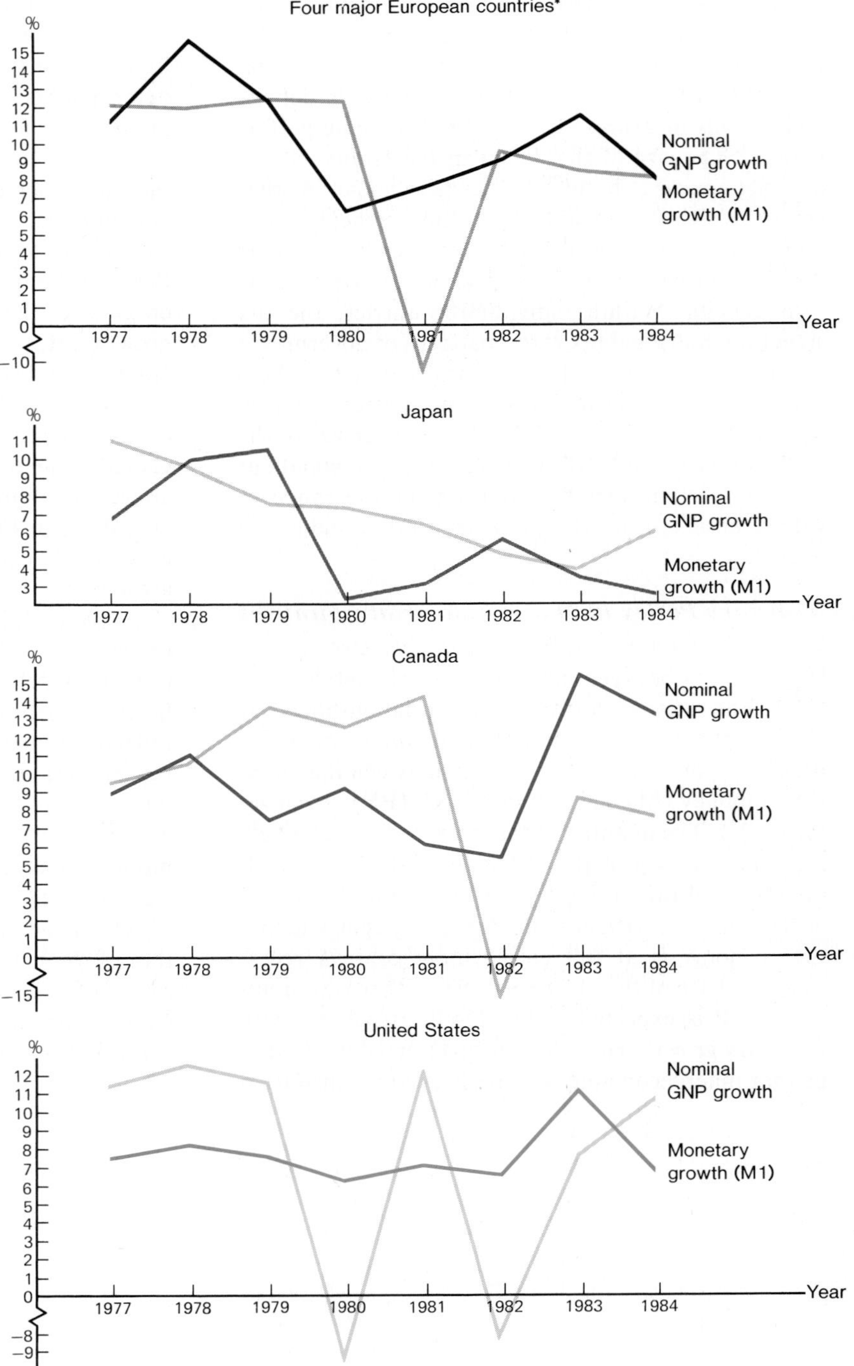

Figure 16.6 Percentage rates of monetary and GNP growth in the United States and other major countries, 1977–1984
This figure illustrates the rate of M1 growth in major industrial nations and compares it to the rate of growth of nominal GNP. This comparison is based on the quantity theory of money, which relates the stock of money (M) to nominal GNP (PY). In these charts, the rate of GNP growth in one year is compared to the rate of monetary growth in the preceding year.
From International Monetary Fund, *World Economic Outlook,* 1985, Tables 2, 8, pp. 206, 213.

▸ The Impact of Changes in the World Oil Market

The United States experienced two major recessions after 1970. The first recession occurred in 1974–75 following the consolidation of the OPEC cartel in the autumn of 1973. Between the autumn of 1973 and mid-1974, Saudi Arabian crude oil rose in price from \$2 to \$3 per barrel up to \$12. During the 1970s, the oil-exporting countries were successful in limiting the world supply of oil by restricting their own production. In 1979, their total production was no greater than it had been in 1973.[2] Because of this restriction in supply, given the growth of world demand for oil, the price of oil rose to over \$30 per barrel (\$20 in terms of 1974 prices) by the early 1980s.

Figure 16.7 depicts the major shifts in demand and supply that accounted for major disruptions in the world oil market in the 1970s and early 1980s. D(1) and S(1) represent the demand and supply of oil in 1973. Equilibrium occurs at point E(1) with a price of \$3 per barrel. The consolidation of the OPEC cartel is illustrated by the shift in supply from S(1) to S(2), leading to the equilibrium indicated by point E(2). Because world demand was relatively inelastic, the rapid increase in price to \$12 per barrel was accompanied by only a small production cutback.

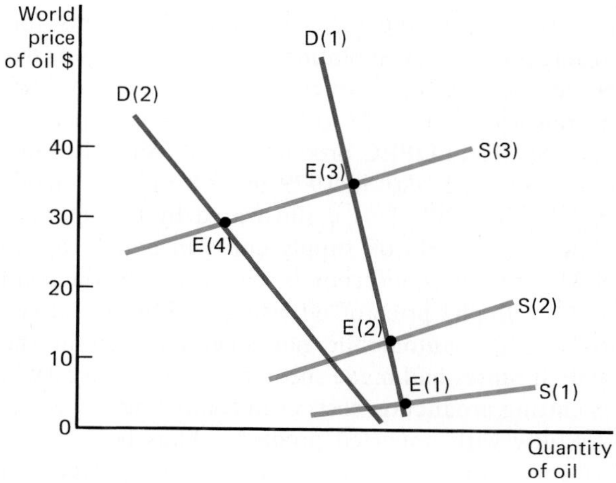

Figure 16.7 Shifts in world demand and supply for oil D(1) and S(1) are the world demand and supply for oil in 1973. Equilibrium is at point E(1) with a price of \$3 per barrel. S(2) represents the world oil supply in 1974 after OPEC established production quotas. Equilibrium shifts to point E(2) with an equilibrium price of \$12 per barrel. S(3) represents the world oil supply in late 1979 after the Shah of Iran was deposed and Iranian oil production fell from 6.5 to 0.5 million barrels per day. Equilibrium shifts to E(3) with an equilibrium price of \$34 per barrel. The world economic recession of 1981–82 plus conservation efforts shifted demand from D(1) to D(2). Equilibrium price fell to \$29 per barrel.

A recession occurred in the United States during 1974 and 1975. As we discussed in chapter 11, this recession was probably linked to the quadrupling of world oil prices. United States auto sales slumped in part because American firms lost sales to manufacturers of fuel-efficient foreign cars. The most dramatic impact was on the steel industry and on manufacturing in general. Relative to other industrialized nations, the United States had previously been able to count on cheap energy to produce goods and services. Differences in the impact of the oil price hike among industrial nations arose because (1) other countries already imposed heavy taxes on oil, most of which was imported, and were accustomed to high energy prices; (2) the United States had traditionally imported relatively little oil, even though it had been quite cheap; and (3) in the 1970s, the United States began to rely more on oil imports because its own oil fields were becoming less productive. Thus, the impact of OPEC on manufacturers in the United States was *relatively* more severe than on manufacturers in other major industrial nations, who had already learned to adapt to high fuel costs.

The United States experienced another major recession in 1980–82. As figure 16.1 shows, real GNP growth was near zero during this period. Unemployment rose from 5.7 percent of the labor force in 1979 to 7.2 percent in 1980, reaching 9.7 percent in 1982.

*The **commodity terms of trade** measures the quantity of imports that a country can obtain for a given quantity of the goods it exports. It is the ratio of the price of exports divided by the price of imports.*

Contributing to the recession were the events following the Iranian revolution. After the Shah was deposed, Iranian oil production fell from 5.4 million barrels per day in 1978 to 1.7 million barrels per day by 1980. Total OPEC production fell from 31.5 million barrels per day in 1979 to 27.8 million barrels per day in 1980. This is illustrated by the leftward shift in the world oil supply curve in figure 16.7 to S(3). The new equilibrium is represented by the point E(3), with the price of oil rising to $34 per barrel. Neither the automobile nor steel industry in the United States had made substantial gains since 1974 in cutting production costs or in competing more successfully with imported products. Thus both industries were once again severely affected by events in the world oil market.

By 1984, the sharp increase in oil prices had finally led to significant conservation efforts, and the 1980–82 recession reduced oil demand worldwide. Conservation and production innovations meant that world oil demand had become more elastic, and the recession also pushed demand leftward, to D(2) in figure 16.7.

The world price of oil began to fall as OPEC found it increasingly difficult to restrict its production enough to maintain its market power. Even though OPEC oil output fell from 31.5 million barrels per day in 1979 to 19.5 million barrels per day by 1984, the world price of oil fell by $5 per barrel. One of the probable consequences of this drop in the cost of fuel was that real GNP growth in the industrialized nations rose to an average of 3.6 percent in 1984. Thus, we have seen how demand and supply shifts in a single important market were linked to aggregate economic activity in the United States and, partially through the United States, to the economies of other countries.

In the remainder of this chapter, we will focus on problems that are especially important to small countries, particularly those that are in the process of developing a modern, industrialized sector.

▸ Export Problems of Small, Developing Economies

Export Prices

For years, policymakers in countries whose principal exports are crops and raw materials (primary products), manufactured foods, and light manufactured consumer products have complained that as price takers in world markets, they are subject to wide fluctuations as well as long-term trends in market prices that they cannot control. Compounding their sense of being victimized is the perception that other participants in world markets, such as the industrialized countries of the United States, Western Europe, and Japan, exercise substantial market power in markets for their manufactured goods. Indeed, one defense offered by the OPEC nations for the dramatic increase in crude oil prices in 1973–74 was that such increases were necessary to maintain their purchasing power over western manufactured goods, whose prices had been rising rapidly.

In short, many small nations, which often must rely on only one or two primary products to earn foreign currency, perceive that the rules of the international trade game favor the major industrial nations. In fact, prices of primary products have traditionally fluctuated severely over short periods, as the complaints of farmers in the United States attest. Thus, small, developing nations' export earnings, which are critical for food and capital imports, are often quite unpredictable from year to year. There is a separate issue from that of how predictable export earnings are from one year to the next—one that is of paramount concern to policymakers in developing countries. This issue is how the purchasing power of exports, which is called the **commodity terms of trade,** is likely to change in the long run. For example, if a small country exports sugar and the world price of sugar declines steadily over time, imports that are critical to that country's economic development will be increasingly difficult to finance.

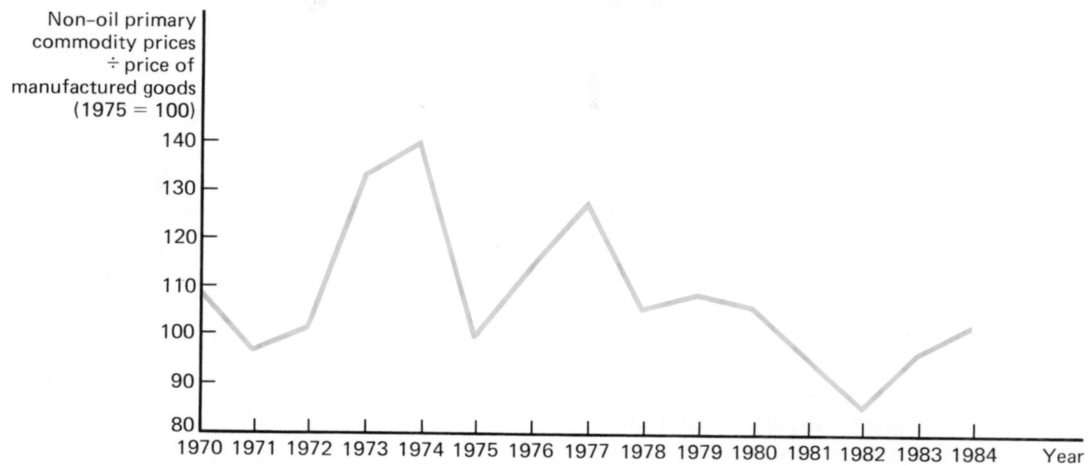

Figure 16.8 Index of the commodity terms of trade for nations that do not export oil, 1970–1984
This figure illustrates the commodity terms of trade for exporters of primary products other than oil. The commodity terms of trade measures the purchasing power of these exports in terms of the manufactures exported by the industrial countries. The commodity terms of trade is expressed in index-number form, with the index taking on the value of 100 in 1975. From International Monetary Funds, *World Economic Outlook,* 1985, Table 3-1, p. 131.

Countries care how their commodity terms of trade change over time because a deterioration in the commodity terms of trade means they have to devote more of their resources to purchase a given quantity of imported goods and services. When this occurs, their economic well-being is reduced or, at best, grows less rapidly than it would have if the purchasing power of their exports had remained higher.

Trends and Variations in Prices of Primary Products Other than Oil

Figure 16.8 indicates what happened to the commodity terms of trade for exporters of primary products other than oil from 1970 to 1984. From 1970 to 1974, the trend in the price of primary products such as food, beverages, agricultural raw materials, and metals tended to favor their exporters when measured against the prices of imported manufactured goods. We mentioned that the OPEC nations defended their price increases in part as an effort to maintain the purchasing power of their oil exports relative to goods manufactured in the West. Ironically, the increases in oil prices in 1974 and again in 1979 caused an acceleration in the rate of price increases for manufactured goods. The linkage between oil prices and manufactured goods prices is easier to understand once we realize that increased oil and energy prices in general will directly increase the costs of producing manufactured goods. This is why the index in figure 16.8 peaks in 1974 and trends downward to a low of only 60 percent of its 1974 peak by 1982. Since OPEC's control over world oil prices has weakened, the commodity terms of trade for these nonoil primary product exporters has begun to increase again.

Industrialized countries, too, suffered from the increase in the OPEC-dominated world price of oil. Between 1967 and 1976, the terms of trade for the world's industrialized nations declined by approximately 1 percent per year. From 1977 through 1983, this downward trend accelerated to 1.4 percent annually. For the entire period 1967 through 1983, the industrialized countries of the world experienced an 18.8 percent decline in their commodity terms of trade.[3] One of the principal effects of OPEC's actions, then, was to seriously lower the purchasing power of the developing nations that do not produce oil in terms of their imports of manufactured goods and also to lower the terms of trade of the industrialized countries somewhat.

Policymakers in developing nations were correct if they viewed the decade after 1974 as unfavorable for their terms of trade. However, they seem to have shared this fate with many highly industrialized countries. Figure 16.8 also shows the year-to-year variability of the commodity terms of trade for exporters of primary products. For example, the highest value reached, in 1974, is about 30 percent higher than the mean value, 40 percent higher than the index value reached only two years earlier, and 40 percent higher than the level to which it fell over the following twelve months. One can imagine the difficulty that buyers and sellers of these commodities have in planning purchases and sales over time. Moreover, governments in many developing countries find that the year-to-year variability in the prices they face for their exports makes it difficult to plan for the use of export revenues to help finance food and capital imports or to pay off government loans from abroad. Many governments have been led to seek industrial diversification by developing domestic manufacturing industries as a means of avoiding the uncertainties they face in the markets for their exports.

One cause of variability of the commodity terms of trade is the business cycle. In the short term, each country's supply curve of, say, a crop or some mineral is relatively inelastic, as indicated in figure 16.9. This means that when there is a recession or an inflationary episode, the shifts in demand for these products tend to cause relatively large changes in their prices. Additional factors affecting primary product prices include weather, national disasters, discoveries of new sources of supplies of minerals, and the development of substitutes for them.

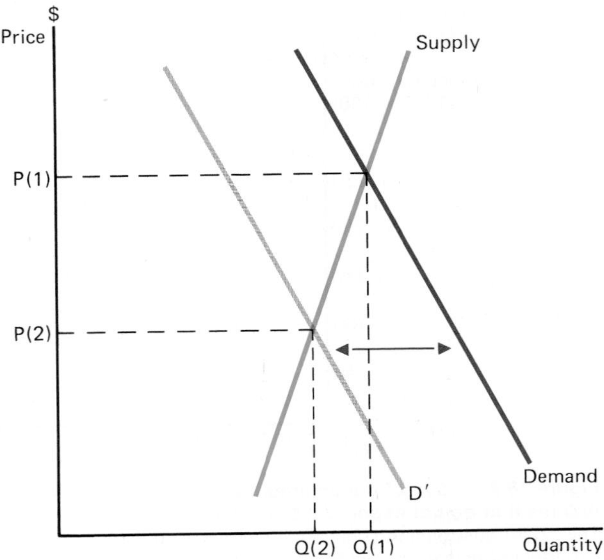

Figure 16.9 The supply and demand for primary products over the business cycle
The supply curves for primary products tend to be relatively inelastic. Therefore, during business cycles leftward and rightward shifts in the demand for these goods lead to relatively large changes in their prices.

Trade Imbalance in Developing Economies

Trade problems in developing countries are frequently linked to their governments' attempts to alter the outcomes of domestic markets. Some frequent forms of government intervention in the markets of developing countries include subsidization of cheap food imports, low-income housing, and investment in industrialization. All too often these commitments are not matched by the financial resources necessary to import the required goods and services. Four sources are available to governments wishing to engage in massive social projects: (1) taxing the general public, (2) borrowing from domestic lenders, (3) borrowing from foreign lenders in order to pay for imports that exceed the value of exports, and (4) printing the money to purchase the goods and services desired.

*The **debt-service ratio** is a country's payments of principal and interest on its external debt divided by the value of its exports.*

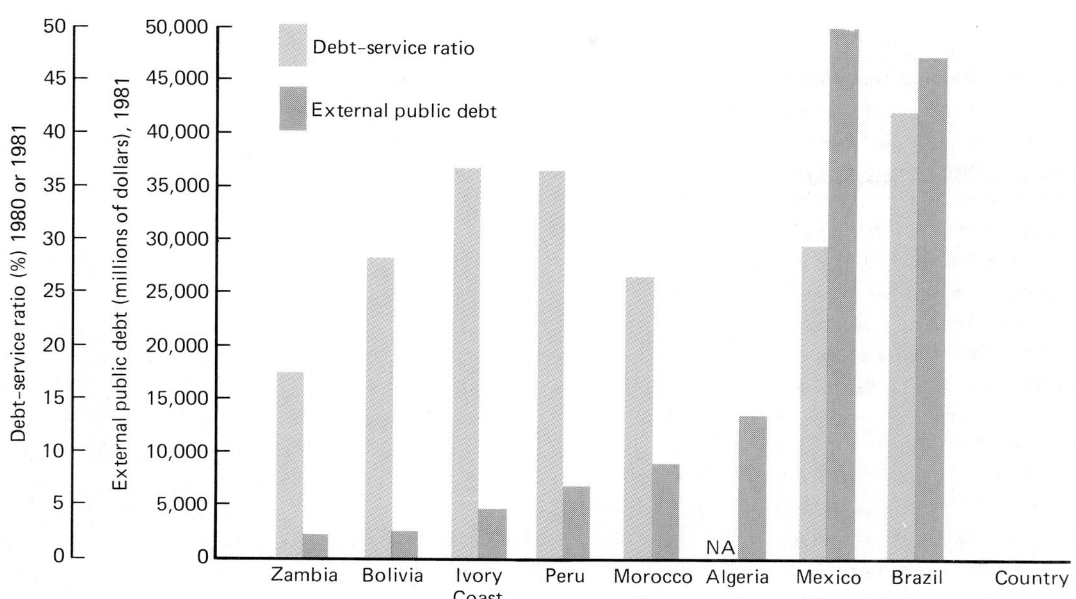

Figure 16.10 External public debt and debt-service ratios for some developing countries
From *Statistical Abstract of the United States*, 1985, Table 1510, p. 864.

Since developing countries are usually not wealthy, foreign borrowing and inflationary monetary growth have been extremely tempting choices.

By contrast, governments of some developing countries have successfully managed to export more than they import, which has led to economic growth stimulated by expanding export industries. In this case, government intervention has been required to maintain a persistent balance of trade surplus.

To summarize, balance of trade deficits and surpluses have been common in many smaller nations. They have resulted from government efforts to attain a wide range of social goals. In the remainder of this chapter, we will explore the successes and limitations experienced by nations that have used international trade surpluses and deficits as means of attaining their economic and political goals. We will also examine policies that some nations have adopted when they have failed to accomplish their goals despite the maintenance of persistent trade imbalances.

The Expansion of External Debt in the 1970s and 1980s

Figure 16.10 contains information on the external debt of several developing nations in the 1970s and 1980s. The first column of figure 16.10 reports the **debt-service ratio,** which measures annual payments on foreign debt relative to export earnings. The debt-service ratio is important because it measures a country's ability to repay its debts to foreign lenders while maintaining a level of imports sufficient to meet its internal economic and political demands. Contrast, for example, the debt-service situations of Zambia and Brazil in 1982. In the former case, \$0.17 of every dollar in export sales (foreign exchange earnings) must be spent to pay off debt. In Brazil, \$0.42 of every dollar of foreign exchange earned from exports is earmarked for debt repayment. To the extent that countries continually rely upon foreign loans to finance domestic public projects, they often experience rapidly rising debt-service ratios. This not only reduces

Figure 16.11 **Average annual money supply growth and inflation rates in developed and developing countries, 1983–1984**
From *Statistical Abstract of the United States*, 1984, Table 1535, p. 886, and 1985, Table 1508, p. 863.

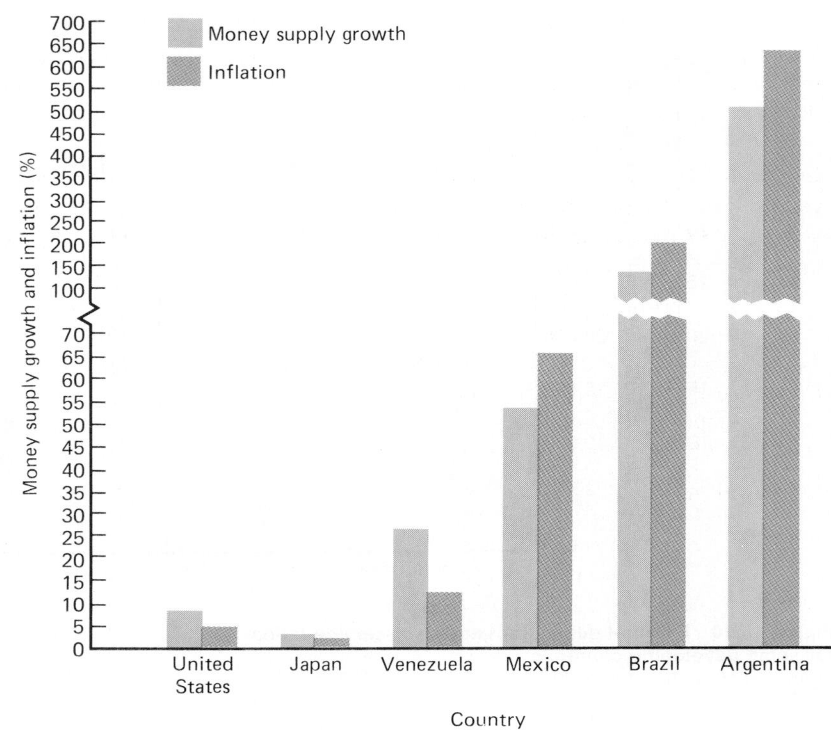

the share of export earnings available to buy imports, but it also makes foreign lenders reluctant to extend further loans.

Figure 16.10 lists countries that have acquired particularly high debt-service ratios in recent years. Brazil and Mexico have been frequently noted trouble spots because the sheer size of their foreign debt is a threat to the solvency of many of the banks that lent money to them. Between 1973 and 1982 the foreign debt of these nations increased from about $20 billion to $566 billion, and in 1982 their combined debt service amounted to over a third of their export earnings.

Developing countries with rising debt-service ratios and a declining willingness of foreign banks and others to provide additional loans to them face a difficult dilemma. Their problem is that they must choose between reducing imports and finding other means of financing the projects that the imports support. Internal political pressures almost always point in the direction of continued imports rather than austerity.

Monetary Expansion

The simplest means of financing desired social projects when external borrowing becomes difficult is to speed up the pace at which money is printed. Figure 16.11 indicates rates of monetary growth for some developed and developing countries. Monetary growth between 1983 and 1984 is used to illustrate the immense differences among these nations in the impact of their monetary policies in recent years. Money supply growth averaged only 6.9 percent annually in the United States and 2.9 percent in Japan. By contrast, money supply growth was 506 percent in Argentina, 138 percent in Brazil, 53 percent in Mexico, and 27 percent in Venezuela.

Excessive monetary expansion leads to inflation in developing nations as well as in industrialized countries. Therefore, we should not be surprised to learn that Argentina, Brazil, Mexico, and Venezuela all experienced inflation rates that exceeded those in the United States and Japan. Whereas inflation in the United States and Japan was 4.3 percent and 2.3 percent per year, respectively, in the other four nations prices rose at a rate of 627 percent for Argentina, 197 percent for Brazil, 66 percent for Mexico, and 13 percent for Venezuela. The simple quantity theory, discussed in chapter 9, tells us that the inevitable result of unrestrained monetary growth is inflation. Therefore, you should not be surprised at the rates of inflation that resulted in the countries shown in figure 16.11.

The Mexican Experience: Domestic Inflation, Balance of Trade Deficit, and Overvaluation of the Peso

We have seen that in the late 1970s and early 1980s Mexico experienced more rapid inflation than the United States and that this was associated with a rate of monetary growth in Mexico several times greater than the rate maintained in the United States. In chapter 15 we saw how inflation in the United States—a major trading partner of Mexico—could be transmitted to other nations. Can we be sure that Mexico's inflation wasn't merely the tail being wagged by the United States dog?

The answer to this question lies in what happens in the foreign exchange market when inflation in the United States increases. As the prices of goods in the United States rise relative to those in Mexico, imports from Mexico increase as does the demand for pesos by United States importers. The increase in Mexican exports to the United States will shift aggregate demand for Mexican goods to the right and may lead to an increase in the Mexican price level. However, the increased demand for pesos will be accompanied by a reduced supply as Mexicans find imports from the United States becoming more expensive. The resulting *appreciation* of the peso will make United States goods cheaper to Mexicans and Mexican goods more expensive to United States citizens.

Thus, under a system of flexible foreign exchange rates, there need not be a prolonged increase in exports from Mexico to the United States or a prolonged decline in imports by Mexico from the United States in response to United States inflation. In short, flexible foreign exchange rates will severely limit the impact of United States inflation on the Mexican economy. We must therefore conclude that the rapid monetary growth and high inflation experienced by Mexico resulted from actions taken by the Mexican government and did not result from transmission of United States inflation abroad. We will now see how Mexican inflation fit in with the political strategies of the Mexican government and how it affected the price of the peso in terms of the dollar.

Mexican Inflation and the Dollar Value of the Peso

Figure 16.12 illustrates the impact of rapid monetary growth and inflation in Mexico on the demand and supply of pesos in terms of United States dollars. The demand and supply curves D and S represent the conditions in the market for Mexican pesos before the Mexican government adopted a policy of rapid monetary growth. The equilibrium dollar price of pesos

An overvalued currency is one whose price relative to some other currency is kept artificially above the price that would clear the foreign exchange market without government intervention.

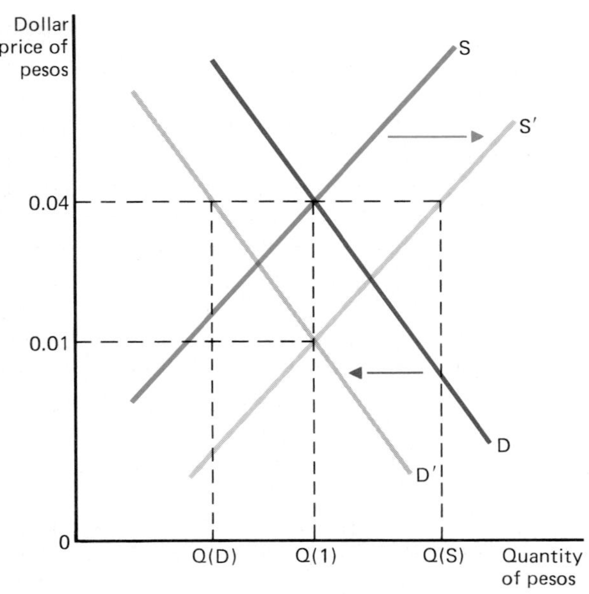

Figure 16.12 Maintaining an overvalued Mexican peso The curves D and S are the initial demand and supply curves for Mexican pesos in terms of United States dollars. Inflation in Mexico that is greater than in the United States results in a rightward shift in the supply of pesos and a leftward shift in demand. With flexible exchange rates, the equilibrium price of the peso in terms of dollars will fall from \$0.04 to \$0.01—a depreciation of the peso. However, if the Mexican government desires to maintain the peso at an overvalued price, \$0.04, there will be an excess supply of pesos equal to Q(S) − Q(D). The Mexican government must therefore be prepared to purchase these pesos. If the government has sufficient dollar reserves, it can achieve its goal, or as long as the Mexican government can borrow dollars, it may also be able to maintain an overvalued peso.

was about \$0.04 (23.3 pesos per dollar) in the mid-1970s. In figure 16.12, the quantity of pesos exchanged for dollars was Q(1). When Mexico began to experience rapid inflation relative to that in the United States, the demand curve for pesos shifted leftward and the supply curve of pesos shifted to the right. If there had been no other changes in factors influencing foreign trade between the United States and Mexico, the market for pesos would have reached a new equilibrium with a depreciated peso selling for about \$0.01.[4]

Overvaluation of the Mexican Peso

If the Mexican government wants to prevent the peso from depreciating in order to maintain low-priced imports for its citizens, it must deal with the laws of supply and demand. If the desired price of the peso is \$0.04, given demand and supply curves D′ and S′ and an equilibrium price of \$0.01, the government must be prepared to deal with an excess supply equal to Q(S) − Q(D) pesos. This excess supply of pesos represented the financial side of a balance of trade deficit with the United States. At the artificially high price of the peso (low price of the dollar), the quantity of imports demanded from the United States remained high and the quantity of exports demanded from Mexico remained low. One means that the Mexican government used to deal with this problem was to borrow dollars from the United States to pay for the excess of Mexican imports over its exports.

Mexico succeeded in maintaining a very high value for the peso compared to the dollar only by means of Mexican government loans from large United States banks. The dollar loans that the government obtained were sufficient to buy up the excess supply of pesos illustrated in figure 16.12. The peso is **overvalued** in this position in the sense that the high price of the peso—\$0.04—is maintained by government borrowing from abroad. It is an artificially high price for the peso compared to the free market price of \$0.01 that would exist without government action as illustrated in figure 16.12.

Winners and Losers from Overvaluation Why did the Mexican government insist on maintaining an artificially high price for the peso rather than let it depreciate? Why did the government allow its foreign debt and the debt-service ratio to rise to levels that wiped out its ability to borrow additional foreign currency? To answer these questions, we need to look more closely at who wins and who loses when a currency is overvalued. One group who may win consists of those who successfully speculate against an overvalued currency. In the case of the peso, it became obvious in the early 1980s that its price in terms of dollars was being kept artificially high and that the Mexican government could not continue to support the peso much longer. If a speculator can purchase dollars with pesos before depreciation of the peso and then, after depreciation, use the dollars to purchase a much larger quantity of pesos than were originally used to buy the dollars, he or she can gain a great deal of wealth.

In every case in which a currency is overvalued, there is an effort by individuals to sell their domestic currency holdings at the overvalued price. The more obvious the overvaluation, the greater the pressure for people to get their money out of the country. Therefore, it is not surprising that in late 1981, just before the Mexican government allowed the dollar price of the peso to fall dramatically, it nationalized the banks and froze private accounts to stem the rapid flow of currency out of the country. One can only guess at the profits captured by corrupt government officials and black market money traders after this strong signal by the Mexican authorities that depreciation relative to the dollar was imminent. The point is that government officials and political insiders may have much to gain personally by interfering with free exchange rates.

The second major group that benefited from an overvalued peso consisted of anyone who desired imported goods. If the peso had been allowed to depreciate to its equilibrium value, it is clear that the price of imported goods would have increased. For example, suppose a United States product costs $1. With the peso valued at $0.04, the product would cost twenty-five pesos. When, in 1982, the peso was devalued to $0.01, the same United States product quadrupled in price to one hundred pesos. Mexican imports included food and other basic items that were used to support the poor in both urban and rural areas. It is not difficult to imagine that the Mexican government found the prospect of rapidly rising imported food prices to be politically unacceptable in 1981, on the eve of the national elections.

Depreciation of the peso would have stimulated exports by making them cheaper in terms of the dollar. Thus, exporters should have welcomed depreciation. However, one of Mexico's major exports is oil, and the OPEC price of oil is set in terms of dollars, not the currency of the exporting country. Throughout the late 1970s and early 1980s, Mexico and other oil-exporting countries were under great pressure not to lower their United States dollar price of oil. In addition, the United States and other industrialized countries were increasingly inclined to limit imports by imposing quotas. A sharp depreciation of the peso might have increased such restrictions and thus offset any gains to Mexican exporters.

To the extent that currency depreciation would have expanded export sales, the domestic prices of exported goods would have increased, too. In Mexico, a large fraction of domestically produced goods is exported, and therefore Mexican consumers would have faced increasing inflation for both imports and domestically produced goods. If the Mexican government had not initially tried to maintain an overvalued peso, it would have depreciated gradually, and the additional impact of depreciation on domestic inflation would not have been as noticeable. However, given the significant overvaluation that had occurred by the early 1980s, any attempt to restore equilibrium in the foreign exchange market was bound to have a large inflationary impact on the Mexican economy.

The Value of Existing and Potential Loans Another effect of peso depreciation was on the value of Mexico's foreign debt. Most of Mexico's external debt is owed to United States lenders and is denominated in dollars, not pesos. So if Mexico has an external debt of $50 billion and the peso depreciates from $0.04 to $0.01, the value of the debt in terms of domestic currency would automatically increase from 1.25 trillion pesos to 5 trillion pesos. For both political and payment purposes, the Mexican government would prefer to keep the value of its external debt denominated in pesos as small as possible. That can be done—but only for a while—by keeping the peso overvalued.

Not only does depreciation of the peso increase the peso value of Mexico's foreign debt, it also makes it more difficult to attract foreign investment into Mexico. Suppose, for example, that a United States company desires to invest $1 billion in a factory to be built in Mexico City. With the peso valued at $0.04, the peso cost of the factory would be 25 billion pesos. Suppose that the United States investor expects to be able to sell the factory for 50 billion pesos one year later. This would amount to a profit of 25 billion pesos, or $1 billion—an attractive return on the initial investment. Now suppose instead that during the year, the value of the peso falls from $0.04 to $0.01. Then, the same sale of the factory for 50 billion pesos would only yield $500 million, or 50 percent of the original investment. Clearly, that would be a very unattractive investment.

The government has every reason to fear that a depreciation of the domestic currency will discourage foreign private investment. Therefore, there is a temptation to delay depreciation as long as possible. Unfortunately, potential foreign investors are well able to read the foreign exchange statistics and will soon anticipate an inevitable official depreciation. Therefore, maintaining an overvalued currency relative to the United States dollar is unlikely to encourage continued foreign investment when the state of disequilibrium becomes apparent to all who care to look.

Overvaluation and Speculation Against the Domestic Currency Earlier we mentioned that one set of gainers from overvaluation consists of "insiders" who manage to purchase dollars at just the right time to reap substantial gains in terms of the domestic currency upon depreciation. As a general rule, when a currency becomes obviously overvalued and market conditions do not change in favor of supporting that value, a depreciation will have to take place sooner or later. This result of the laws of supply and demand encourages speculation against the overvalued currency. For example, if I withdraw 1 million pesos from my bank account in Mexico and transfer them into dollar deposits in the United States, I will receive $40,000 when the peso is worth $0.04. Once the peso has declined in value to $0.01, I can transfer my $40,000 back into 4 million pesos. The potential profit of 3 million pesos is a very attractive return to speculating against the peso. Of course, it increases the excess supply of pesos and adds further pressure toward eventual depreciation.

A government trying to support an overvalued currency will, at least officially, tend to look with extreme disfavor on speculators, who are viewed as troublemakers and profiteers. Because these "undesirables" benefit when depreciation actually occurs, governments tend to find this consequence of ultimate, forced depreciation of the domestic currency particularly galling.

To summarize, currency overvaluation and external borrowing are opposite sides of the same coin when a government is trying to support consumption or investment expenditures beyond the capacity of its economy to produce. Borrowing from abroad acts as a buffer between the demand for foreign currency and currency depreciation. By building up an external debt, the government merely postpones the date at which imported goods must be paid for. If the government ultimately defaults or if the debt is renegotiated with lower interest or stretched out repayments, the result is equivalent to foreign aid granted by the lenders, which are usually privately owned banks. Eventually, countries reach the limit of their capacity to borrow because foreign lenders do not wish to grant aid; they desire to earn a profit in their banking activities. Thus, countries like Mexico with relatively high rates of inflation compared to their major trading partners invariably experience currency depreciation.

We indicated earlier that Argentina and Brazil experienced much more rapid inflation than the United States during the late 1970s and early 1980s. Therefore, it is not surprising that the Argentine peso fell from $5 in 1980 to $0.21 in 1982 and the value of the cruzeiro fell from $0.015 in 1980 to $0.004 in 1982.

Terminology: Devaluation or Depreciation? Unfortunately, much of the press coverage of currency crises in Mexico, Argentina, and elsewhere has contributed to sloppy use of terminology. We indicated earlier that a devaluation (revaluation) consists of a decrease (increase) in the value of one currency relative to all other traded currencies under a fixed exchange rate system such as that prevailing from 1945 to 1971. During that period, all currencies had a fixed price relative to (were "pegged to") the dollar, and the dollar had a fixed price in terms of gold. Since 1971, many countries, like Mexico, continue to peg the value of their currency to the United States dollar. But not all currencies remain pegged to the dollar, and the United States dollar is no longer fixed in terms of the price of gold. When Mexico or another country depreciates relative to the United States dollar, the press often calls it a devaluation. This is not strictly correct, since all currencies are no longer pegged to the United States dollar. However, since nearly 75 percent of all international trade is defined in United States dollar terms, a depreciation of a currency relative to the United States dollar is in effect very much like a devaluation.

The External Debt of Developing Nations

In our discussion of persistent balance of trade deficits that characterize many developing nations, we saw that many governments have tried to postpone the inevitable need to pay for their imports by accumulating more and more foreign debt. Any discussion of worldwide international trade problems requires some assessment of the significance of the external debt of the world's developing nations. Between 1977 and 1984, the ratio of external debt to GNP in the world's developing countries that are not major oil exporters rose by 50 percent.[5] The rapid increase in external debt for many developing countries that do not export oil arose in response to the oil price shocks of 1974 and 1979. Moreover, the interest rates on most of these loans were not fixed. As global inflation accelerated, countries that were paying only 6 percent interest in 1976 were paying as much as 15 percent in 1982.

By 1983, developing and Eastern European countries had $700 billion in debt to the West and more than forty countries could not meet their schedules for debt repayments. The problems of debt repayment for developing countries became a matter of serious concern for the United States and other industrialized nations. Between the beginning and the end of the 1970s, private banks came to be the principal lenders to developing countries. Although by 1983 most developing countries' debt was still owed to other governments, the nine largest United States banks had loans outstanding to Argentina, Brazil, and Mexico alone that totaled more than the combined net worth of the banks! To the extent that such loans might go into default, there was concern that it would lead to a global financial panic. To avoid financial crises the banks began to revise and lengthen the schedule for loan payments from developing countries. The issue remained open, however, as to whether substantial numbers of bank failures could be avoided.

In order to help avoid what many feared would be an international financial catastrophe, the International Monetary Fund (IMF) took an active role in assisting debtor nations. By 1983, the IMF had conditional loans with forty-seven countries. The word *conditional* means that countries receiving these loans had to agree to take steps to reduce domestic government expenditures, deficits, imports, and inflation. Countries were also encouraged to reduce trade restrictions and to move toward free market exchange rates. The loans were financed by increased contributions to the IMF from major industrial nations. These nations—mainly the United States—have contributed their taxpayers' money to subsidize developing country loans. Thus, the developing countries benefit at the expense of taxpayers elsewhere. Perhaps the biggest gainers, however, have been private banks and their stockholders who have been able to rely on international lending agency assistance to make their bad debts good. Again, the primary losers are taxpayers in the countries that support the IMF, who must ultimately pick up the tab for misjudgments of major private banks that overextended their international loans.

What Caused the World Debt Crisis?

Before moving on to other issues, we want to briefly review some of the conditions that contributed to the world debt problem. The debt crisis was not simply the outcome of bad bank practices and irresponsible government borrowing. World economic conditions made several dramatic and unanticipated changes in direction between 1973 and 1983, with OPEC and the United States playing central roles.

World inflation was moderate in 1973, and world trade was expanding at a healthy pace, continuing a twenty-five-year trend. Shortly after OPEC consolidated its position in the world petroleum market in late 1973 and early 1974, the price of crude oil increased fourfold. The United States economy slipped into what at that time was the worst recession in the postwar period, with unemployment rising rapidly from 5.5 percent to over 9 percent. The higher price of oil and the United States economic slowdown both had strong influences on economic conditions in developing countries. First, the oil price increase caused import prices of crude oil to developing countries that do not produce oil to skyrocket. Without either the hard currency (currencies traded in major foreign exchange markets) earnings needed to finance the higher priced imports or popular support for rapid domestic gasoline price increases, governments looked to foreign banks for loans. At the same time, OPEC revenues soared and vast amounts of "petrodollars" flowed into banks of the United States and other industrial countries. With vast amounts of cash on hand, banks lent heavily to developing countries. Other developing countries, like Mexico and Venezuela, found that the price their oil sold for rose rapidly, too. They used their oil export earnings to press on with ambitious public works and industrialization schemes.

The United States economic slowdown in 1974 contributed to a slowdown in other developed countries, too. As a result, the developing nations that do not produce oil found their export earnings stagnating or declining, while oil prices continued to rise. The demand for international loans by developing countries accelerated in line with the flow of petrodollars to banks, which were happy to have customers willing to borrow at higher and higher interest rates.

Throughout the late 1970s, oil prices continued to rise, the Fed and other central banks allowed domestic money supplies to grow rapidly to avoid another recession, and both inflation and interest rates consequently continued to rise. Debtor nations expanded their debts at higher and higher rates, and it seemed that the spiral of rising prices and nominal interest rates would never end. Oil-producing developing nations such as Mexico and Nigeria continued to enjoy high oil export earnings and to plow the money into public programs with no end in sight.

The Iranian revolution in 1979 led to a rapid decline in Iran's oil exports and additional dramatic increases in oil prices. The pace of public spending in oil-producing countries accelerated, along with the international borrowing by developing countries that produce no oil.

Tight monetary policy in the United States to reduce inflation led to a decline in inflation and, in 1981–82, to the worst recession in the United States since World War II. Export earnings for all developing countries took an unexpected downturn, but interest rates remained high because lenders and borrowers remained skeptical that inflation had been arrested in the United States and other industrial countries. Quite suddenly, it became apparent that countries producing oil, such as Mexico, had overcommitted themselves to public works programs and many countries (including those who produce oil and those who do not) had borrowed too much relative to their now less certain ability to sell exports. Large banks that had committed huge sums of money to these countries quickly became less certain that the loans could ever be repaid. All of these elements of the debt crisis story were in place by 1982.

Beginning in 1983 and continuing into 1985, rapid economic growth in the United States played a key role in stimulating world growth and renewed growth of export earnings for the developing countries. During that period, the financial risks to the large banks were reduced by renegotiating loans with developing countries to spread them out over more realistic time periods. Furthermore, moderating inflation in the United States helped to bring nominal interest rates down substantially. By mid-1985 it was clear that very little new money was flowing to developing countries and that many of those countries continued to have serious debt problems. The major banks had weathered the storm, but the verdict was still out for many developing countries.

In July 1985, the newly elected government of Peru announced that it would not repudiate its debts but that it would not pay them as scheduled. This announcement was expected to be repeated by governments of other debtor nations. While such actions may seem to resolve the immediate problem, they also create concern. How will developing countries so desperate for financial resources convince banks to lend them money in the future? How will such countries convince private investors to lend them funds if they cannot be trusted to repay their loans as promised?

▸ Summary and Conclusions

The example that introduced this chapter described some severe economic anomalies in developing economies. We have shown in this chapter how the economic systems of the world's industrialized nations are linked to one another and to those of the developing countries. We have also shown that the economic problems in developing nations are often more severe than in the more advanced industrialized nations and described how they interact with the developing nations' dependence on foreign trade. The following major points were emphasized.

The slowdown in GNP growth in the United States that began in the 1970s was more severe than the slowdown in other advanced economies.

Inflation accelerated in the United States during the 1970s but not by more than in other major industrial countries.

By the mid-1980s, unemployment rates in Japan, Canada, and Western Europe were not, on average, lower than those in the United States.

Record deficits relative to GNP in the United States in the early 1980s were similar to the relative deficits in other major industrial countries and appear unrelated to international differences in the growth of GNP or inflation.

International trade linkages apparently have led to a similar pattern of monetary and nominal GNP growth in the major industrial nations.

The oil price shocks of the middle and late 1970s contributed to a common pattern of recessions and stagflation among major oil-importing nations, primarily through their impact on the United States.

The oil price increase in 1974 and 1979 led to declines in the commodity terms of trade for developing countries that do not export oil and for major industrial nations.

Many developing nations have financed imports by increasing their external debt beyond the level at which they can comfortably repay principal and interest with their export earnings.

Excessive monetary growth and inflation have often accompanied growth of the external debt of developing nations. Mexico is an example of a country that has encouraged domestic inflation and a large external debt and has accompanied these policies with actions to maintain an overvalued currency.

▸ Key Terms

commodity terms of trade *346*

debt-service ratio *349*

overvalued currency *352*

▸ Questions for Discussion and Review

1. What evidence can you point to in this chapter to suggest that a comparison of unemployment rates across industrialized countries in the 1970s understates how well the United States economy performed relative to other advanced industrial countries.
2. Did inflation in the 1970s cause high rates of inflation in other industrialized nations? Support your answer with evidence presented in this chapter.
3. Explain why the oil price shocks of 1974 and 1979 did not have as negative aggregate economic effects on the Japanese economy as they did on the United States economy.
4. Illustrate and explain who wins and who loses if the British pound depreciates relative to the United States dollar.
5. Illustrate and explain conditions under which inflation in the United States can cause inflation in France.
6. Explain why some Mexican citizens tried to transfer their deposits from Mexican banks to United States banks just prior to the collapse in the value of the peso in 1982.
7. What impact would a currency appreciation have on the willingness of foreigners to invest in a country and on the burden of foreign debt?
8. Why do you suppose United States commercial banks became so heavily involved in loans to financially risky countries like Argentina, Brazil, and Mexico?
9. Why does there seem to be a greater bias toward rapid growth in the money supply and domestic inflation in developing countries than in developed countries?
10. Who wins and who loses when a currency is overvalued?

Policy Issue: You Decide

Will Encouraging Workers to Cut Their Wages Save Many Jobs Lost to Foreign Exports?

In early 1983, the United Steelworkers Union signed an agreement to reduce wages in an attempt to restore some employment opportunities for steelworkers. At the same time, approximately 40 percent of workers in the union were on layoff. Here is the issue. When one of your authors was on the staff of the President's Council of Economic Advisers, he was asked to estimate how many job opportunities would be created by the wage cut the steelworkers accepted. How would you do it? After you think about this and sketch your answer, proceed to the following paragraph to find out how your author came up with an estimate.

At the time of the assignment, the following facts were known: (1) the steelworkers took approximately a 5 percent wage cut, (2) labor costs are about 35 percent of total production costs in the steel industry in the United States, and (3) a 1 percent increase in the price of steel is typically associated with about a 1.5 percent reduction in the quantity of steel demanded. Assuming that in the short run a wage reduction does not affect the technology used to make steel, a 5 percent cut in wages will lead to a 1.75 percent (0.35 × 5 percent) cut in the cost of steel production for domestic steel firms. In light of what we have said about the demand for steel, this should generate about a 2.6 percent increase in the quantity of steel demanded. A simple assumption is that the steel industry will use 2.6 percent more of all of its inputs, including labor. Thus, a 5 percent wage cut will probably lead to at least a 2 to 3 percent increase in job opportunities in the steel industry. With 159,000 members of the steelworkers union employed and working at the time of the wage cut, a 2 to 3 percent increase amounted to about 4,000 additional jobs.

There is more to the story, though. In response to a wage cut, manufacturers are likely to use a greater proportion of labor in each ton of steel compared to the amount of machinery and other capital used. Your author estimated that this change in the steel industry's input mix would double the estimate of additional jobs created—to about 8,000.

Unfortunately, 8,000 jobs amounted to only about 8 percent of the 106,000 steelworkers who were out of work in 1983. The moral of the story seems to be that the wage cuts for steelworkers were not likely to go very far in offsetting the previous employment loss due to reduced domestic sales. One reason for this disappointing conclusion is that steel, as currently produced in the United States, uses relatively little labor per ton of steel produced. Thus, a 5 percent wage cut leads to a fairly small cut in production costs because only 35 percent of total costs are labor costs. Another reason is that hourly pay in the steel industry in 1982 was approximately $26. This was at least twice as high as steelworkers in other steel-exporting countries were earning. A much larger wage cut than 5 percent would have been necessary to return a substantial number of the 106,000 laid-off steelworkers to their old jobs.

Part V

Economic Growth and Comparative Systems

Chapter 17

Economic Growth and Change

Outline

Objectives

After reading this chapter, the student should be able to:

Define productivity and describe how it affects economic growth.
Demonstrate economic growth as a shift in the production possibilities frontier.
List possible reasons for the recent slowdown in productivity growth in the United States.
Compare economic growth rates in the United States and other industrial nations.
Discuss major economic changes that have affected economic growth in the United States in recent decades.
Discuss how Japanese industrial policy works and to what degree it has been successful.

***Economic growth** is an increase in the economy's capacity to produce real GNP and can be represented by an outward shift in the production possibilities frontier.*

Introduction

The first thing we learned in this book was that scarcity is the *basic economic problem. Mick Jagger of the Rolling Stones almost got it right when he said you can't always get what you want. Had Mick finished his studies at the London School of Economics, he would probably have refined his statement to you can't always get enough of all the things you want. This is especially true for society as a whole. Scarcity constantly affects our everyday lives because it forces us to choose among alternatives as individuals and as a society. In terms of these choices, every economic system decides what things get produced.*

During the middle 1960s, the United States was engaged in two activities that would leave permanent marks on our country. One was the war in Vietnam, and the other was the establishment of the social programs that comprised what was to become known as the Great Society. During this period, Lyndon Johnson promised us that we could have both *guns and butter. By this he meant that the United States could both wage the Vietnam War and generously spend for social welfare programs. To the casual observer it seemed as though President Johnson was right. After all we* were *doing both at the time. The subtlety here, however, is that although we were waging a war against poverty and a war in Vietnam at the same time, this does not mean that President Johnson found a way to avoid the concept of opportunity costs. While we were fighting the war in Vietnam, we used resources that could have been used on programs in the domestic economy (or vice versa). Even President Johnson could not truly avoid the problem of scarcity.*

A Review of Scarcity and the Production Possibilities Frontier (PPF)

The issue of scarcity and how it forces us to make choices is nicely represented by the concept of a production possibilities frontier (PPF). The production possibilities frontier in figure 17.1 is a general representation of how society must choose among goods (such as automobiles, clothing, and housing) and services (such as education, entertainment, and dry cleaning) at any point in time.

It is important to remember a number of the properties of the production possibilities frontier. First, the graphical representation of PPF is basically limited to two (or at most three) dimensions. This means that even though society produces a myriad of items, we can only represent two general categories of production in our diagram. This does not mean, however, that we are ignorant of the great diversity of production within society. Second, the production possibilities frontier reminds us that when an economy is operating efficiently, it is at a point on its PPF, such as A or B in figure 17.1. Points *inside* the PPF are economically inefficient; society is wasting resources in the sense that it is foregoing both goods and services. In particular, at point C society can have more goods and more services. Finally, combinations of goods and services outside the PPF are currently unattainable. Does this mean that society can *never* get the combination described by point D in figure 17.1?

The answer to this question is that at any moment in time, the economy's PPF defines the limits on what can be produced and consumed. How is it, then, that the typical individual consumed about three times more goods and services in 1984 than fifty years earlier?[1] The answer is that the PPF is not necessarily fixed in one position. Rather, it can shift outward over time; this is known as **economic growth.**

Labor productivity measures the quantity of goods or services produced by a typical worker during a particular period of time.

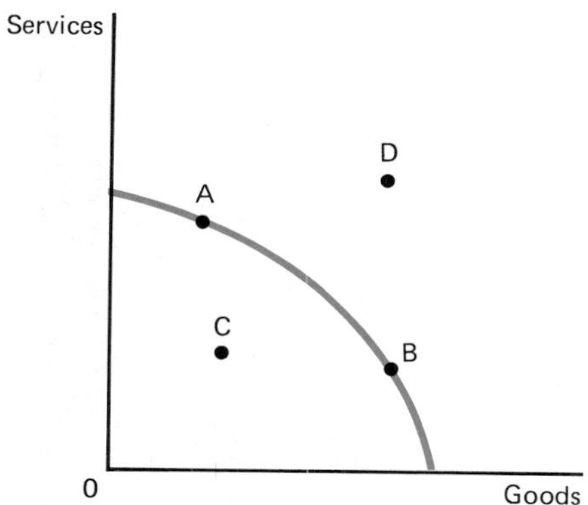

Figure 17.1 Society's production possibilities frontier (PPF) for goods and services
Society's production possibilities frontier for goods and services indicates the options society has for answering the What question of economics. Points inside the PPF indicate wasted resources or economic inefficiency. Points outside the PPF are unattainable in light of current resources and technology.

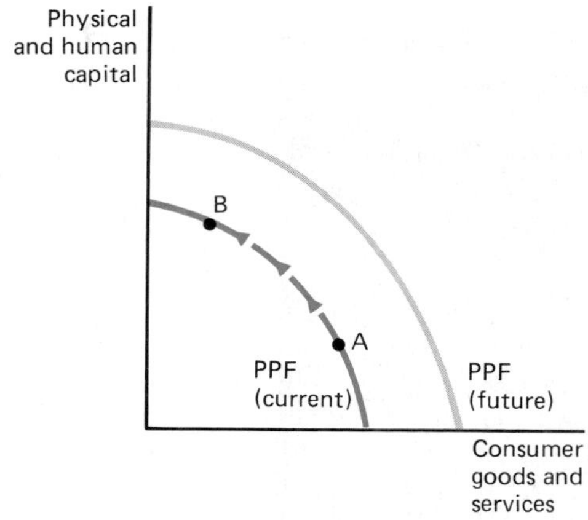

Figure 17.2 Greater investment in physical and human capital leads to expansion of the production possibilities frontier in the future, or economic growth
If society invests more in physical and human capital, there is a movement from a point such as A to a point such as B that occurs along the current PPF. This increased stock of capital allows society to produce more consumer goods and services (and capital) in the future. The increased potential to consume goods and services is known as economic growth.

Figure 17.2 illustrates the key issues involved in economic growth. At any point in time, say, now, society chooses how many consumer goods and services it wants as opposed to using its resources to produce physical and human capital. By definition, producing capital uses up resources that could be available for consumer goods and services but expands production possibilities in the future. Thus, if society chooses to forego some consumer goods and services today and increases its production of physical or human capital, this would be illustrated by a movement from point A to point B in figure 17.2. Ultimately, the physical and human capital that is accumulated expands production possibilities in the future, including the ability to produce physical and human capital itself. Improved and increased amounts of machinery and a more educated population are the key elements in explaining why society can have more in the future. We might also add that economic growth can occur if new, more effective production techniques (such as the assembly line) are developed or if an inefficient economy, such as one at point C in figure 17.1, becomes more efficient, moving toward its PPF.

Factors that Shift the PPF

Suppose there is an outward shift of the PPF, with no additional work effort or employment required. A typical individual can consume more goods and services because of this economic growth. What are some additional details involved in how an increase in physical and human capital ultimately leads to the outward shift in the PPF described in figure 17.2? In the situation we have been describing, economic growth means that more is produced with each hour of work, and this is called an increase in **labor productivity.** Economists are in general agreement that increases in the productivity of labor have been the principal cause of increases in consumption per capita in the United States and most other nations. Thus, the answer to our question requires that we identify a few more details of how investment in human and physical capital causes labor productivity to grow over time. In the process, we will discover additional factors that are related to labor productivity growth.

Figure 17.3 Output per hour of all persons in the business economy, 1909–1985
From Bureau of Labor Statistics, U.S. Department of Labor, June 1983, Bulletin 2172, *Productivity and the Economy: A Chartbook* and *Economic Report of the President*, 1985, 1986.

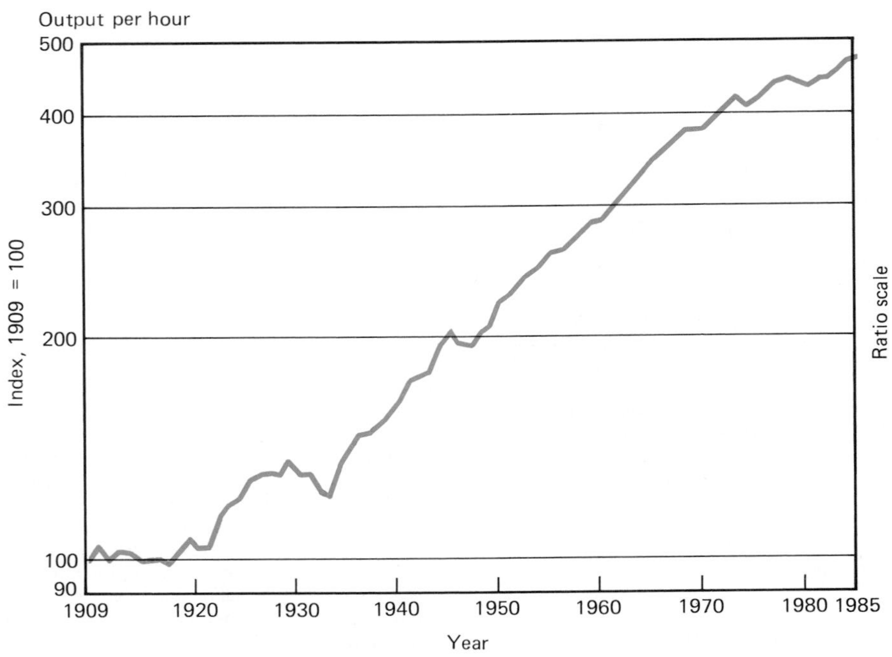

Labor Productivity in the United States

Figure 17.3 illustrates how productivity has grown in the United States since 1909. The measure of productivity used is output per hour of all workers in the business (nongovernment) sector of the economy. One important fact about productivity is immediately evident. Productivity has grown substantially over time. The average American worker was over 4.7 times as productive in the middle 1980s as in 1909.

Table 17.1 tells us that labor productivity has grown about 2.4 percent per year in the United States since 1947. The table also shows that the rate of productivity growth has fluctuated considerably. For example, during 1947 to 1965, labor productivity grew relatively rapidly. In more recent years, productivity growth slowed dramatically. For example, annual productivity growth between 1973 and 1982 was less than 1 percent, and between 1984 and 1985 it was only 0.3 percent. Only during the recovery from severe recession, 1982–84, did productivity growth rise above 1 percent per year. This slowdown is sometimes misinterpreted in the mass media as a decline in the *level* of productivity of United States workers. This is clearly incorrect, as indicated by the fact that the line in figure 17.3 has not sloped downward in recent years. Put differently, the data of table 17.1 and figure 17.3 show us that the production possibilities frontier of the United States has continued to shift outward in recent years, although at a relatively slow rate.

Forces Behind Recent Productivity Growth in the United States and Other Industrial Nations

Figure 17.4 compares labor productivity in the United States to that of some other industrial nations. Notice that only the Federal Republic of Germany, France, and Canada approached the United States in terms of labor productivity in 1981. Despite what you may have thought, labor productivity in Japan was only about two-thirds of that in the United States. This is

Table 17.1 Productivity growth in the United States, 1947–85

Period	Output per hour of all persons in the business economy (average annual percentage change)
1947–85	2.4
1947–65	3.4
1965–73	2.4
1973–82	0.9
1982–84	2.1
1984–85	0.3

Rates of growth in the productivity of the business economy have slowed significantly since 1965. Explanations for the slowdown have included the effects of change in the composition of the labor force as the proportion of younger and less experienced workers has increased; a slower rise in the capital-labor ratio, resulting from lessened investment in equipment and structures at the same time that employment and hours rose strongly; a leveling off in research and development expenditures; diversion of investment funds to pollution abatement; the maturation of some industries with little new technology; and changes in attitudes toward work. No simple explanation for the decline exists; nor is there general agreement on the quantitative impact of the various factors.

Source: From Bureau of Labor Statistics, U.S. Department of Labor, June 1983, Bulletin 2172, *Productivity and the Economy: A Chartbook* and *Economic Report of the President,* 1985, 1986.

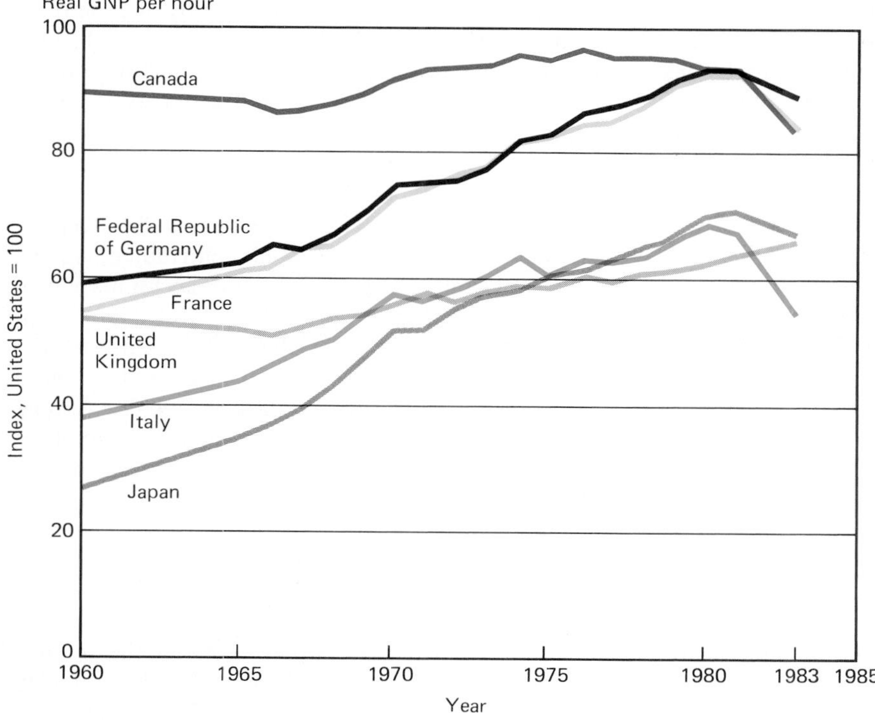

Figure 17.4 Relative levels of real gross domestic product per employed person, selected countries and years, 1960–1983 From Bureau of Labor Statistics, U.S. Department of Labor, June 1983, Bulletin 2172, *Productivity and the Economy: A Chartbook and Economic Report of the President,* 1985; and *Statistical Abstract of the United States,* 1986.

Table 17.2 United States productivity growth compared to that of other major industrial countries, 1950–81

Country	Real gross domestic product per employed person (average annual percentage change)		
	1950–81	1965–73	1973–81
United States	1.6	1.6	0.2
Canada	1.9	2.4	0.1
France	4.1	4.6	2.4
Federal Republic of Germany	4.5	4.3	2.5
Japan	6.3	8.2	2.9
United Kingdom	2.2	3.2	1.3

Between 1950 and 1981, real gross domestic product (GDP) per employed person increased at substantially different rates among the six major industrial countries compared here. It grew about 1.5 percent per year in the United States and 2 percent per year in Canada and the United Kingdom compared to 6 percent per year in Japan and 4 and 4.5 percent per year in France and the Federal Republic of Germany.

Each country experienced a slower rate of growth in real GDP per employed person in the period 1973 to 1981 than in previous periods. The slowdown was greatest in the United States and Canada and least in France and the Federal Republic of Germany.

Source: From Bureau of Labor Statistics, U.S. Department of Labor, June 1983, Bulletin 2172, *Productivity and the Economy: A Chartbook* and *Economic Report of the President*, 1985.

not to say that we should ignore the fact that the *rate of growth* in our ability to consume goods and services has slowed recently. Economists have studied the reasons for this slowdown and have reached agreement on some, but not all, of the factors responsible. One of the interesting facts they have discovered is that the decline in productivity growth in the the late 1970s and the beginning of the 1980s was not confined to the United States economy. Others shared this experience. This is documented by the data in table 17.2. In every country in this table, labor productivity grew on an average much more slowly between 1973 and 1981 than during 1965–73.

Probably the most important factor behind this slowdown was a decline in the rate at which business firms purchased or invested in new buildings and equipment for their employees. Workers produce goods and services with the aid of machinery, tools, buildings, trucks, computers, and myriad other forms of investment (capital) goods. The larger the amount of annual investment per worker, the higher is the rate of productivity growth.

One of the principal concerns of economic policy in recent years has been to encourage more investment spending, which is expected to foster more rapid productivity growth. This concern is especially acute because of recent slowdowns in the rate of capital accumulation in the United States and other industrial nations. For example, data indicate that the rate of net (after depreciation) nonresidential fixed investment as a fraction of GNP declined by over one-fourth between the late 1960s and the late 1970s. In particular, the rate was 4 percent of GNP during 1966–70 and just under 3 percent during 1976–80. This reduction in the rate of investment contributed, in part, to a noticeable deceleration in the accumulation of capital per worker in the United States. Net capital stock per worker grew at about 4 percent per year during 1966–70 but only about 0.4 percent (one-tenth as much) during the latter half of the 1970s.[2] Among the possible explanations for this reduced rate of investment are government regulation, increasing energy costs, high real interest rates, and a possible change in the time horizons of businesses toward a more short-term versus long-term profit orientation.[3]

The importance of the rate of investment to productivity growth is evident when we look at table 17.3, where we see that those nations investing the greatest percentages of their gross domestic products tended to have the highest rates of growth of output per hour of work.

Table 17.3 Comparison of capital formation in six countries, 1971–80 (percent)

Country	Gross investment as a percentage of gross domestic product	Growth rate of output per hour in manufacturing
France	24.2	4.8%
Federal Republic of Germany	23.7	4.9
Italy	22.4	4.9
Japan	34.0	7.4
United Kingdom	19.2	2.9
United States	19.1	2.5

Source: From *Economic Report of the President,* 1983, p. 81.

Another important influence on productivity growth—one that rivals investment in new plant and equipment—has been changes in the *quality* of labor. The American labor force is better educated today than at any time in the past. Increased schooling was an important contributor to productivity growth during the first half of this century in the United States. However, now that the vast majority of United States workers are high school graduates, the contribution of increased education to productivity growth is not as dramatic as it used to be. Moreover, some people argue that the quality of education in the United States has actually fallen in recent years. This issue will probably continue to be hotly debated.

Schooling is only one determinant of labor quality, however. Other determinants are experience and training. Two changes in the composition of the United States labor force affected the average level of worker experience and training during the 1960s and 1970s. One of these was the decline in the average age of the labor force. As people born in the late 1940s through the early 1960s (the "baby boom" generation) entered the labor force, the proportion of workers with no prior labor market experience increased. Not only were those new jobholders less productive than their older counterparts already in the labor force, but providing them with training also used up some effort of other workers that could have otherwise been devoted to current production of more goods and services. Of course, training young workers contributes to productivity growth in the future. Another change in the labor force was a sharp increase in the fraction of married women working. Newly hired women typically had less prior job experience than previously hired men. More than half of all married women now work in the labor force, and it seems unlikely that this fraction will continue to grow in the future as rapidly as it did in the past. Thus, this cause of decline in productivity growth should be much less important in the near future than it was in the last three decades.

In preceding paragraphs we have discussed the forces impinging upon productivity growth about which there is general agreement. However, they are not the only factors that have been suggested for the slowdown in output per worker that characterized the United States during the late 1970s and early 1980s except for the 1982–84 recovery period. The others are more speculative, and we will mention them with little discussion. One is the difficulty in measuring productivity itself. Some evidence suggests that workers are now using less of their time on the job actually working than they did twenty years ago and that if this were taken into account, much of the reported slowdown in productivity growth would disappear.[4] Other factors that have been cited include the slight slowdown in expenditures for research and technology development, the rising divorce rate (which presumably makes people less happy and therefore less productive), increases in drug abuse among workers, greater white-collar crime (which reduces industrial output), and a general malaise.[5] Some have even gone so far as to blame the slowdown in productivity growth on the sexual revolution.[6]

Economic change, or structural shifts, refers to changes in the pattern of economic activity, such as the level and distribution of output or employment, in any economy over time.

It is important to recognize that even if greater government regulation in the form of safety requirements and antipollution devices is responsible for the slowdown of measured productivity growth, this is not necessarily bad. It simply means that society has made a choice to trade greater productivity growth for increased job safety and a cleaner environment. Remember that economic decisions such as these must always be phrased in terms of their trade-offs or the opportunity costs involved. Specifically, what are the costs of the productivity slowdown, and what are the benefits that go with it?

It is also important to realize that while the slowdown in labor productivity growth is disturbing to many people, it is impossible to conclude on the basis of economic analysis that this slowdown is "bad." After all, this is what conservationists and proponents of slow growth want when they argue that "small is beautiful." Preserving our nation's natural and scenic resources will certainly slow the rate of industrial development and growth of labor productivity. Some people view this as a desirable outcome and others do not. Economists find it extremely difficult to say whether more or less productivity growth is a good thing. The reason is rooted in problems of market deficiencies in the form of externalities and the public-good nature of some forms of conservation. These difficulties make measuring the growth of economic well-being much more difficult than measuring productivity growth as it is usually defined.

Productivity growth started to rebound in the United States after 1982. In particular, output per hour of all persons in the business sector grew at an annual rate of 4 percent during the first quarter of 1983 and at an annual rate of almost 5 percent during the second three months of 1984.[7] Although it seemed reasonable, there is reason to believe that higher productivity growth would continue into the future,[8] these hopes have evidently not materialized because productivity growth slowed down to 0.3 percent per year after 1984.

Adjusting to Economic Change

Economic growth is only one of many aspects of a dynamic economy. In recent years policymakers have also been greatly concerned with the issue of **economic change,** or **structural shifts,** which means an alteration of the distribution of economic activity within the economy. During periods of economic change, some industries grow and others shrink; similarly, new jobs are created in some areas and disappear in others. The policy issue involves who will reap the benefits and who will pay the costs of economic change.

Has the United States Been Deindustrializing?

Some observers of the United States economy feel that it has been "deindustrializing" in recent years. What do they mean by this? Is so-called deindustrialization a cause for alarm? It is not easy to give a precise definition of deindustrialization. However, it generally refers to a situation in which manufacturing's share of the economy has been eroding because markets have allocated capital and other resources away from heavy manufacturing industries (automobiles, steel, and anything with a smokestack) and toward service industries (such as fast-food restaurants and boutiques). Thus, deindustrialization could also be called "servicization." The concern over possible deindustrialization is that it may lead to the elimination of high-paying blue-collar jobs, which will be replaced by lower-paying service-sector jobs.

The facts suggest that if the United States *has* been deindustrializing, it has not been doing so very rapidly. During the period 1950–80, for example, production, capital stock, and employment all grew in manufacturing. This is shown in table 17.4. While the rate of growth was somewhat slower in the 1970s than during the 1960s, the growth was still there.

The ***industrial policy debate*** *concerns the proper role of government in fostering economic change and helping the losers from economic change.*

Table 17.4 Size and share of the United States manufacturing sector, selected years 1950–84

Year	Manufacturing			Share of total		
	Output (billions of 1972 dollars)	Employment (millions)	Capital stock (billions of 1972 dollars)	Output	Employment	Capital stock
				Percent		
1950	131.1	15.2	106.4	24.5	33.7	28.4
1960	171.8	16.8	140.4	23.3	31.0	25.8
1970	261.2	19.4	202.2	24.1	27.3	23.5
1980	351.0	20.3	287.0	23.8	22.4	23.4
1984	471.0	19.4	306.0	21.8	20.6	22.1

Source: From *Economic Report of the President, 1986,* pp. 264, 298, and *Statistical Abstract of the United States, 1986,* p. 527.

The data in table 17.4 also indicate the share of total output, capital stock, and employment in the manufacturing sector of the United States economy. Notice that total output and capital as shares of the United States total remained roughly the same between 1960 and 1980. While manufacturing output as a share of total GNP declined somewhat between 1980 and 1984, only manufacturing's share of total employment has not fallen to any great extent in the period of time covered by this table. Thus, the data in table 17.4 suggest that manufacturing productivity increased rather than that the manufacturing sector experienced a decline. The pattern of relative slowdown in the growth of manufacturing production and employment also occurred in other industrialized countries, including France, Germany, Japan, and the United Kingdom.[9]

There have been some important shifts *within* the manufacturing sector of the United States economy since 1960. In particular, there has been a trend toward more high-tech manufacturing. High-tech industries have relatively large components of research and development expenditures as proportions of their total production costs. The importance of research and development expenditures in these industries can be measured by examining *value added,* which is industry revenue minus the cost of inputs purchased from other industries. Between 1960 and 1980, value added increased by 40 percent and employment increased by more than 20 percent in high-tech manufacturing.[10] The United States is switching from being the world's producer of steel and automobiles to being the world's engineering consultant and banker. Whether this is good or bad, there are winners and losers from this change. An important issue is how the costs and benefits are shared within the United States economy. Do the beneficiaries of economic change—the stockholders and employees of growing industries—owe anything to the losers in declining industries? What, if anything, do the members of society who are not affected directly owe the losers? These important economic policy issues form the core of what has been called the **industrial policy debate.**

A Critical Look at Industrial Policy

Suggestions for a formal industrial policy (that is, one explicitly recognized through the establishment of a bureau, commission, or cabinet post) in the United States and existing industrial policy in Japan and Western Europe have several common elements. First, there is a central planning body to make the government's industrial policy decisions. This agency is typically advised by a group of representatives from business, labor, and the government itself and seeks to gather information on the problems and growing pains of particular industries. It then tries to form a consensus for action. In keeping with the stated goal of industrial policy, there is also some form of development bank, which invests money in industries that are selected as targets for relatively high growth. The justification for such a bank is that the targeted industries supposedly receive inadequate capital from private financial markets. We will examine this argument in more depth shortly. Finally, industrial policy typically contains some form of government aid for declining industries coupled with import protection while they adjust to changing economic conditions. With these ideas in mind let us examine Japanese industrial policy. Our goal is to discover whether industrial policy appears to be a cost effective way to smooth an economy's adjustment to economic change.

Japanese Industrial Policy

At the center of Japanese industrial policy is the Ministry of International Trade and Industry (MITI). One function of the MITI is to identify those industries likely to have relatively high growth in the future. The MITI seeks information from leaders in the major industrial centers around the world, as well as Japanese bankers, industrialists, traders, and academics.[11] Once the MITI feels it has determined those industries offering the most promise for future growth, plans are made to foster that growth. The plans are formulated in councils including representatives of banks, the news media, academic institutions, trade unions, and the firms involved. One of the key purposes of these councils is to create a consensus among the "key players" so that MITI's plans will not be opposed once they are begun.[12]

On the basis of the information it has gathered and the consensus it has built concerning the likely emerging industries, the MITI utilizes a number of tools to try to stimulate economic growth in the targeted industries. First, it provides subsidies for research to develop new technology. It has done this, for example, in the computer, semiconductor, and commercial aircraft industries. The MITI has also encouraged joint research among firms where competition might otherwise have prevented them from cooperating. Another way the MITI has encouraged certain emerging industries economically is by providing low-interest loans from the government-owned Japan Development Bank (JDB).[13]

Finally, the MITI has tried to provide emerging industries protection from competition or excess capacity caused by recessions and possible overly rapid expansion. During periods of excess capacity, the MITI has organized "recession cartels." These cartels are designed to restrict output and thus prevent prices and profits from falling as far as they would during a competitive industry's typical adjustment to a recession. The MITI has also organized production quotas when foreign governments put pressure on the Japanese government to restrain Japanese exports.[14]

We have seen what Japanese industrial policy has done for new industries. What are the key components of Japanese industrial policy for declining industries? In this case, the basic goal has been to facilitate the flow of resources out of such industries. The MITI has tied its help to declining industries to an agreement on an explicit plan by the industry for reducing production. After an agreement has been reached, the MITI has approved subsidized loans and recession cartels to restrict production and keep profits and prices from falling as much as they might normally. Aid to declining industries has also included formal protection from foreign trade, although such protection has not always been used. However, informal trade barriers must still be present to protect the domestic Japanese cartels from foreign competition.[15]

Recently, there has been some in-depth examination of how important Japanese industrial policy has been to the country's relatively rapid economic growth. In an extremely insightful and clearly written discussion, Charles Schultze, head of President Carter's Council of Economic Advisers, took a close look at Japan's success.[16] Schultze argued that reasons other than the MITI have contributed most to Japan's rapid economic growth. Among other things, Japan saved 30 to 35 percent of its GNP versus 17 to 20 percent for the United States during the past two decades or more. Japan also had less capital stock to begin with. This is likely to have contributed to a relatively large proportionate payoff to investment. Schultze also cited the unique set of employer-employee relations in Japan that makes labor-management strife relatively infrequent.

However, risk taking by entrepreneurs, rather than by the JDB, has probably played the most important role in Japan's economic development. Schultze noted that about three-fourths of the Japan Development Bank's funds went to merchant shipping, electric utilities, and regional and urban development. These are hardly high-growth industries. Moreover, JDB loans to the electrical machinery sector, which includes computers and semiconductors, were only 0.6 to 0.8 percent of total bank lending to those industries during the 1960s and 1970s.[17] Since the 1970s, public investment in Japan, as in the United States, has emphasized energy and pollution control. Very little money has been devoted to developing new technology. He concluded that public funds have been divided up according to political criteria rather than directed to industries targeted for economic growth. This is no different from the ordinary practice in the United States, which does not have a formal industrial policy.

Finally, Schultze pointed out that the MITI has tried (and fortunately for Japan has failed) to implement some incredibly bad decisions. These include an attempt to keep Honda out of automobile production and Sony out of the development of transistors. Schultze argued that the government cannot regularly predict the winners involved in economic change. Who would have predicted Japan's dominance in motorcycles, Sweden's in ball bearings, or that of the United States in pharmaceuticals and design? In any case, the private market has an incentive to move resources in the economically "right" direction. In particular, rates of return to investment in capital and wages will be high in growth sectors; this will draw resources away from the rest of the economy. As declining sectors shrink, the removal of resources will tend to make the remaining firms profitable and the remaining capital and labor more productive and remunerative.

Even though most economists would agree that Japanese industrial policy has influenced Japan's industrial structure, it is clearly debatable whether it has enhanced or slowed down economic growth.[18] While the MITI has chosen to support some industries that have turned out to be winners, it has also backed losers. The MITI has tried to help industries that would have become successful without any help at all. The most objective thing to say about the Japanese industrial policy is that its net contribution to rapid Japanese economic growth is unclear.[19]

Summary and Conclusions

We will never be able to get *all* that we want, but the way an economic system promotes economic growth is crucial in helping us to obtain *more* of what we would like than we would get in a stationary economy. In this chapter we have examined economic growth and change. The following major points were emphasized.

Economic growth refers to an increase in the economy's ability to produce and is represented graphically by an outward shift of the production possibilities frontier.

A common measure of economic growth is the proportionate change over time in labor productivity (output per employee hour).

Economic growth stems from an increase in the resources available to society or from an increased capacity to produce output from those resources due, say, to technological innovation.

Although the level of labor productivity in the United States has remained the highest of all countries in recent years, productivity growth has slowed relative to earlier periods and relative to some other industrialized countries.

Factors underlying the slowdown in productivity growth in the United States include comparatively low capital formation and a change in the compositon of the labor force toward greater numbers of less-experienced workers.

Economic change produces winners and losers. A crucial policy issue is how the losers will be helped to ease their situations and who will pay for that help. A second policy issue is whether the government should take an active role in selecting winners and attempting to accelerate economic change.

Industrial policy in Japan is a conscious effort by the government to help the winners and losers involved in economic change. On the basis of available evidence, it is difficult to conclude that Japanese industrial policy has fostered economic growth, although it has undoubtedly influenced the pattern of economic activity in Japan.

Key Terms

economic change or structural shifts *370*

economic growth *364*

industrial policy debate *371*

labor productivity *365*

Questions for Discussion and Review

Are the statements in questions 1 through 5 true, false, or uncertain? Defend your answers.

1. A decline in the average education level of the population causes the production possibilities curve to shift inward.
2. Low real interest rates today could encourage economic growth in the future.
3. Society can provide unlimited medical care to all who want it.
4. A decline in the growth rate of labor productivity indicates that output per worker hour in all sectors of the economy has fallen.
5. An important reason for owning your own home is to increase the level of domestic investment and thus ensure future economic growth.
6. Illustrate the following situations with respect to the production possibilities frontier.
   a. The Great Depression
   b. The Vietnam War era
   c. Devoting all resources to medical care
   d. The innovation of a 32-bit microchip
7. Would expectations of future inflation have any effect on an entrepreneur's risk taking?
8. Compare the recession cartels concept with the infant industry argument regarding international trade.
9. Who would benefit if research and development costs were disallowed as ordinary business expenses on corporate income taxes?
10. Is there any possibility that a country can consume more of a commodity than its production possibilities frontier shows it can produce? Explain.

Chapter 18

Alternative Economic Systems

Outline

Objectives

After reading this chapter, the student should be able to:

Describe the primary differences between capitalist and socialist economies.
Describe how output decisions are made in a centrally planned economy such as the Soviet Union.
Illustrate graphically how shortages and surpluses are eliminated in a centrally planned, socialist economy.
Compare economic performance in capitalist and socialist economies.
Discuss the economic approach to government activity in a mixed economy.
Explain why government intervention in a mixed economy frequently sacrifices economic efficiency to alter the distribution of economic gains and losses.
Cite examples of government economic activity in a mixed economy that are substitutes for production by privately held firms.

An ***economic system*** *is the set of institutions, such as free markets or planning agencies, rules, and laws that determines the answers to the basic economic questions in a country.*

▸ Introduction

When you think about it, it is really quite difficult to imagine everyday life in another country's economy. It takes some facts and figures to get any kind of feel for life there. Here are some numbers for China that you may find surprising. The China Daily *reports that there are only about sixteen washing machines per 100 families in Beijin. There are only two refrigerators for every 100 families.*

In China, a bicycle is a very prized possession. It is like a car in the United States in terms of how it is used for an individual's transportation needs. However, bicycles have been quite difficult to obtain in China and thus have been rationed. Those who are lucky enough to get a ration coupon are allowed one month to find a shop that has a bicycle in stock. Those who pass this hurdle must then raise $82.50, the equivalent of about two months' wages in China.

The purpose of this chapter is to paint a picture of the various economic systems in effect around the world and to compare and contrast their goals and performance. In earlier chapters we discussed the relative economic performance of different industrialized economies and of developing economies. We also touched on the causes and consequences of varying degrees of government involvement in those market-oriented economies. In contrast with earlier chapters, this chapter focuses on market versus centrally planned economies. As we shall see, market and planned economies are generally quite different in terms of their expressed goals, the mechanisms for achieving those goals, and the incentive schemes they use.

An ***economic system*** *is a set of mechanisms and institutions that determines the methods by which a country's production, consumption, and income distribution decisions are made and implemented. In this chapter we will focus on the two most important types of economic systems: capitalist systems such as those found in the United States, Japan, and many nations of Western Europe and planned, socialist systems such as those of the Soviet Union, China, and many of their allies.*

A ***capitalist economic system*** *is one in which private property and free markets are the principal institutions determining the answers to the basic economic questions.*

▸ Basic Issues to Be Addressed by Every Economic System

In chapter 1 we discussed three basic economic questions that every economic system must address. We can sharpen our focus on the essential characteristics of capitalist and socialist systems by discussing how they generally address these basic issues. The three basic questions are (1) What gets produced? (2) How are goods and services produced? and (3) For whom are goods and services produced? To these three questions, we will now add a fourth: (4) What are the incentives within a system that make it work? Question 3 will help us understand the essential differences between capitalist and socialist systems and see the crucial importance of the fourth question when we also consider the question of who owns or controls property.

Throughout this book we have discussed the characteristics of individual product markets and the aggregate markets of industrialized and developing countries. The term **capitalist economic system** is applied to all countries in which the market is the primary instrument with which the four basic economic questions are answered. Almost all capitalist economies are mixed economies in the sense that some industries may be nationalized, as is the case with basic industries like steel and coal in some European nations, or heavily dependent on government contracts as opposed to private expenditures, as is the case with the defense industry in the United States. What binds capitalist economies like the United States, the United Kingdom, and Japan together is not that markets alone determine *what* is to be produced but that markets play the dominant role in answering this question.

Similarly, *how* goods are produced is not determined solely by market forces even in the United States. Regulations exist with respect to health and safety conditions in the workplace. Environmental regulations affect both the location of various kinds of production facilities and production techniques. Zoning laws are the most obvious example of the former kind of restriction, while limitations on strip-mining of coal and the use of high-sulfur coal (through emission controls) in electricity generation are examples of the latter type of limitation. Nevertheless, among the varied mechanisms that do determine how goods and services are produced, markets are of primary importance in capitalist economic systems.

The question of who owns property is critical in determining how wealth is distributed and, therefore, *for whom* goods and services are provided. Capitalist economic systems have the common characteristic that property is primarily privately owned. Thus, private demands for goods and services are the major ingredients on the demand side of each market. Private demands tend to determine what is produced and for whom. All capitalist countries have some nationalized industries that amount to state property, not private property (such as the United States Postal Service, federal land holdings, and some public transportation systems in the United States). Moreover, virtually all capitalistic economic systems use their taxing powers to redistribute income and wealth. Nevertheless, most property is privately owned in capitalist societies.

Table 18.1 Attributes and examples of capitalist and planned, socialist economies

Questions	Answers	
	Capitalism	**Socialism**
What gets produced?	Market determined (decentralized)	Centrally planned
How are goods produced?	Primarily market determined	Primarily planned
Who owns property?	Primarily private property	Primarily state property
What motivates productive effort?	Primarily material gain	Both private and collective material gains
	Examples	
	United States	Bulgaria
	Canada	China
	Federal Republic of Germany	Czechoslovakia
	Greece	Democratic Republic of Germany
	Japan	Hungary
	Spain	Poland
	Turkey	Romania
	United Kingdom	Soviet Union

The final basic question is this: *What is the incentive mechanism in the society that motivates the production of goods and services?* Clearly, if individual and household incomes depend largely on how we supply productive factors, such as our labor, to the production process and if individuals and households own these resources, private material gain will be the dominant incentive mechanism of our economic system. Even in capitalist economies, tax collections amount to between one-fourth and one-half of national income.[1] An important use of tax revenues is to provide income maintenance and welfare services to various groups in society. Private charitable contributions are also substantial in capitalist countries. For example, in 1984, total contributions by private philanthropy funds amounted to $74.3 billion, which was more than total outlays under all major federal and state income maintenance programs.[2] While it is clear that collective social welfare is of considerable concern and therefore does motivate economic activity in capitalist societies, the primary motivation is private material gain.

Table 18.1 contains a summary of the attributes of capitalist and planned, socialist economic systems and gives examples of specific countries that can be classified as mainly either capitalist or socialist.

The Relative Importance of Market Forces and State Planning in Capitalist and Planned, Socialist Economies

None of the countries listed in table 18.1 is either a "pure" capitalist or socialist system. In the world's socialist economies the answer to the question of what gets produced is determined primarily by central plans rather than market signals. However, free markets exist in certain areas. For example, in the Soviet Union, private plots within agricultural cooperatives yield an important part of total farm output. Planned, socialist economies often use the term *second market* to describe the mix of goods and services that is market determined. These markets are not limited to agriculture, even in the Soviet Union. In recent years, Eastern European countries including Hungary and Czechoslovakia have preferred to be thought of as modified centrally planned economies in which market forces are important in determining what gets produced. Although it would be theoretically possible for a country's government to own all property but to allow market forces to guide what is produced and how, the primary mechanism for deciding what gets produced in socialist countries is primarily central planning and not the forces of market demand and supply.

In capitalist countries the primary source of information on the appropriate methods for producing goods and services is the market-determined profits and losses of enterprises. In planned economies market signals are largely bypassed or at least heavily filtered out. Thus, historical experience and the technical know-how of central planners will be the primary determinants of how to produce goods and services. In the controlled sectors of planned economies the forces of demand and supply will not signal how goods can be produced most efficiently. Planners may use information gleaned from unregulated markets to guide decisions in methods of production in centrally planned sectors. Observations on how capitalist countries produce goods whose production is controlled in centrally planned economies may encourage planners to adopt techniques of production that are not dramatically different from those signaled by unconstrained market forces. Thus, we tend to observe the same basic production methods used to produce steel, automobiles, and other items in the Soviet Union as in capitalist countries, even if many inefficiencies plague socialist firms.[3]

In contrast to capitalist economic systems, in which property is primarily owned by private individuals, in planned, socialist economies property is primarily owned by the "state." As indicated earlier, small plots of land and the output produced on them by workers in agricultural cooperatives in the Soviet Union are privately owned. Recognizing the power of private incentives in promoting effort, China has recently permitted small businesses to be run as private enterprises.[4] A number of East European countries have permitted limited private ownership of land, farm animals, and so forth, in recent years.[5] Evidently, the Soviet Union will not risk the efficiency of its arms production program to satisfy socialist incentive norms. One analyst believes that incentives for productive efficiency in arms production are more effectively harnessed in the Soviet system than in the United States because the Soviets in this case have used the capitalist incentive system more effectively than has the United States government.[6]

On a more cynical note, one might ask how the "state" can be defined as anything other than a particular set of private individuals with the political power to obtain the property rights to the means of production. Presumably, the "state" is different from private property owners in that its expressed goal—in socialist economies—is to create a more even distribution of wealth among workers and households. Theoretical models of socialism certainly spell out equality as a major justification for doing away with private property. If income or wealth inequality is comparable in capitalist and planned, socialist economies, it can be argued that this principal justification for socialism is a facade for a more basic motivation. One of the major issues on which we will focus in this chapter is the extent to which capitalism and planned socialism *as actually practiced* in specific countries lead to consistent differences in the quality of life and distribution of wealth.

Differences in Performance Criteria for Capitalist and Planned Economies

To the extent that there are real differences between capitalist and planned, socialist economies with respect to their methods of operation and their institutions, there are likely to be differences in their overall economic goals. Therefore, simple comparisons of economic data across capitalist and planned, socialist economies may tell us little about how effective countries are in achieving their aims. A rather extreme example may help to illustrate our point. Suppose you were to visit a very strict religious monastery in a remote country to study its economic and social organization. You might find that the members of the monastery eke out a perilous standard of living by using archaic production methods. If you suggested that the monastery should resort to private ownership of the means of production and a capitalist incentive system in order to increase its output per person and its level of material well-being, you would probably be misunderstanding the principal reason for the monastery's existence—the renunciation of material welfare in order to promote spiritual welfare.

Table 18.2 Gross national product in constant (1981) dollars and rates of growth, 1975–82

	GNP (billions of dollars) 1975	1980	1982	Per capita GNP (dollars) 1975	1980	1982	Per capita growth rate 1975–82 (percent)
Capitalist economies							
United States	2,416.1	2,883.0	2,897.2	11,290	12,661	12,482	10.6
Canada	230.5	264.6	261.0	10,153	11,026	10,610	4.5
Federal Republic of Germany	576.1	686.7	679.6	9,321	11,148	11,032	18.36
Greece	30.9	38.3	37.9	3,438	3,992	3,870	12.57
Japan	857.7	1,094.7	1,157.3	7,685	9,372	9,774	27.18
Spain	166.4	183.1	186.0	4,700	4,894	4,894	4.13
Turkey	49.8	56.6	61.6	1,229	1,230	1,279	4.07
United Kingdom	467.3	508.9	501.4	8,344	9,087	8,954	7.31
Socialist economies							
Bulgaria	31.8	33.4	35.3	3,659	3,747	3,969	8.47
China	420.8	603.5	658.4	446	595	630	41.26
Czechoslovakia	125.6	139.5	138.7	8,485	9,115	9,007	6.15
Democratic Republic of Germany	143.1	160.7	165.6	8,469	9,622	9,914	17.06
Hungary	57.8	63.8	65.2	5,500	5,962	6,092	10.76
Poland	187.2	193.8	176.2	5,504	5,444	4,868	−11.56
Romania	78.8	95.6	98.9	3,717	4,308	4,394	18.21
Soviet Union	1,382.0	1,556.6	1,617.7	5,430	5,863	5,991	10.33

Source: From *Statistical Abstract of the United States, 1985,* Table 1481, p. 846.

Although the different values and aims of socialist and capitalist societies make comparisons of how effectively they achieve the goals of high average material well-being and equality somewhat difficult, such comparisons are still meaningful. Both economic growth and equity are stated goals of most societies today. To the extent that one form of economic and social organization achieves more in one direction and no less in the other, it probably is possible to draw positive conclusions about the effectiveness of one system over the other.

A common goal in both capitalist and socialist economies is to have a high and stable real rate of economic growth. Most planned, socialist economies are not highly industrialized. Because of the strong drive to develop heavy industry, they have frequently emphasized high rates of growth, even if this has meant severely limiting the production of consumer goods. Table 18.2 indicates real aggregate output, output per capita, and growth in output per capita for the same countries listed in table 18.1. Except for the Democratic Republic of Germany and Czechoslovakia, the levels of per capita output in the socialist economies are quite low by western industrial standards. For most of the socialist economies, including the Soviet Union, this measure of the standard of living suggests that they are at a level comparable to that of countries like Greece, Spain, and Turkey rather than the United States, the Federal Republic of Germany, and Canada. Despite the high priority claimed for growth in these semideveloped economies, only China, the poorest of the lot, has achieved a degree of expansion that is remarkable by the standards of capitalist countries.

One rationale given for planning is to avoid the "chaos" of capitalist societies as reflected in their recurring business cycles. Therefore, the socialist economies also tend to emphasize stable economic growth as part of a central plan. With respect to inflation and employment, socialist economies tend to use more price controls to keep "necessities" affordable and to

*The **materials balance approach** is a planning device in which a set of accounts is formulated by a central planning agency and used to coordinate the quantities of inputs and outputs needed to achieve production goals for an economy.*

guarantee jobs for workers to a greater extent than is the case in capitalist economies. Both price controls and job guarantees create economic waste and resource misallocations, but they are viewed as effective means of protecting the standard of living of working people and avoiding unemployment. After all, socialist planning is advertised as a means of avoiding the deterioration of living standards and growing unemployment of the working classes that Karl Marx viewed as an inevitable by-product of capitalist economic development.

If we take the popular socialist statement "to each according to his needs" as a goal of socialist economies, then there should be a commitment to a substantially more equal distribution of income across households in socialist economies, in which property is mainly owned by the state, than in capitalist economies, which are characterized by private property arrangements. The argument for nationalizing property in the socialist economies has been to avoid the rich-poor contrast with which the socialist governments characterize capitalist societies.

▸ Characteristics of a Planned, Socialist Economy

We can learn a great deal about differences between socialist and capitalist economies by discussing specific examples. Our examples will be the two archetypes of their respective economic systems, the Soviet Union and the United States. We have already devoted most of this book to examining the United States economy. Now we will look at how the economic system of the Soviet Union works. This will represent our benchmark of the level of economic performance in socialist economies. The Soviet Union is the oldest continuously planned socialist economic system in the world. It has served as a model for Eastern Europe, China, and other socialist states. In a way, different planned, socialist economies can be usefully described as variants of the Soviet centrally planned economy. The relative importance of the Soviet Union in world affairs and the relative ignorance among westerners of how its economic system works makes it an important case to analyze.

How Annual Output Plans Are Developed in the Soviet Union

In terms of general command structure, the Communist Party of the Soviet Union (CPSU) is the principle organ of control and supervision in the Soviet Union. The CPSU decides what the overall objectives of the economy ought to be in terms of a plan and prepares directives that eventually filter down through the economy to local plant managers. The state planning agency is called Gosplan. It has the tasks of providing the CPSU with information that can be used to determine future plans. It also must establish the instructions that tell each industry and firm what should be done to put the plan into effect. The major organizing unit for each industry is called the ministry of that industry. In the early stages of planning, the ministry transmits the tentative output targets and other instructions to individual enterprises for comments and informational input. Then the proposed targets, along with proposed modifications, work their way back up through the system to Gosplan.

To complete the plan, a **materials balance approach** is used, which means that physical units of inputs and outputs are added up to ensure that quantities demanded and supplied are all equal to each other. In principle, the questions of what to produce and how to produce it are answered simultaneously during this last round of planning. Finally, Gosplan directives are sent out in the *techprominplan* (technical industrial financial plan). These disaggregated unit enterprise targets are legally binding. Only a few thousand basic commodities are centrally planned this way. Most products are subject to planning at the regional or local level, and many are not subject to planning at all. Plans are revised annually.

Incentives

Individual enterprises are run by managers who are on fixed base salaries. In addition to their base salaries, managers receive bonuses for achieving or exceeding planned output targets. These bonuses can be as much as 35 percent of base salaries. There are two interesting negative side effects of the bonus system. First, in the early stages of formulating the plan, managers have an incentive to convince Gosplan to set low targets. Often, fraudulent information is provided in efforts to deceive Gosplan into setting lower targets than originally proposed. The more successful the deception, the more certain and substantial will be the bonus a manager receives. Second, if targets are expressed in terms of quantities only, without specification of quality standards, there is an obvious incentive to produce large quantities of shoddy output in order to exceed target and qualify for bonuses.

Market-Clearing Mechanisms

As we have seen, the complexity of planning production of all commodities and coordinating inputs is too great a task for Gosplan. Much coordination is left to regional and local subunits of the CPSU and planning agency. The materials balance approach is simply insufficient to assure a balance of supply and demand in all markets. Consequently, other mechanisms must be used to help eliminate shortages and surpluses of various goods and services.

Product Markets Under Price Controls

Each planned enterprise in the Soviet Union has a budget. Budgets go through the state bank, which is called Gosbank. Included in the budgets are investment funds, subsidies, profits, and all sales and purchases. Prices are usually set by administrative authority to equal estimated average cost plus a small profit. Prices at the wholesale level were set in 1955 and remained fixed until 1966. The last general reform of wholesale prices occurred in 1966–1967. At the retail level, prices are adjusted to equate demand and supply by using a system of taxes and subsidies. Figures 18.1 and 18.2 illustrate how taxes and subsidies are used to clear markets in the Soviet Union.

In figure 18.1, the demand and supply curves, D and S, would determine an equilibrium market-clearing price of P(0) and a quantity of Q(0) in a market economy. Suppose, however, that historical precedent has determined that the controlled price is P(C). At this price, there is an excess demand for the

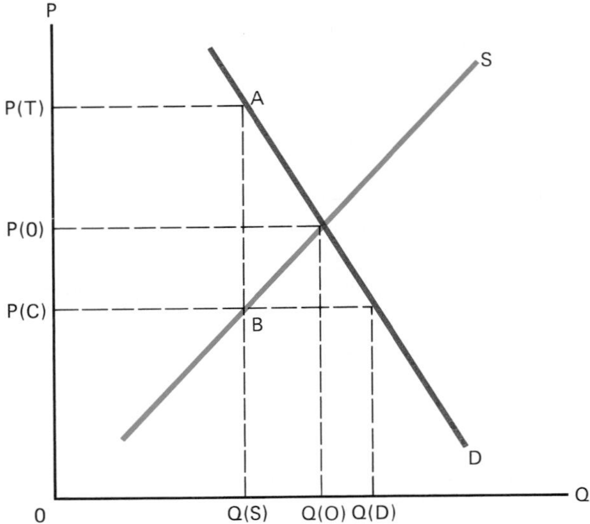

Figure 18.1 Setting prices in the Soviet Union
D and S are the demand and supply curves for some commodity. Since prices are centrally planned and seldom revised, the price is not likely to be the market-clearing (equilibrium) price P(0), associated with the equilibrium output Q(0). If the controlled price is set at P(C), output Q(S) will be less than the quantity demanded Q(D). A "turnover" tax is added to P(C) to reach price P(T) and clear the market. Turnover tax revenue equals the area of the rectangle P(C)P(T)AB.

product equal to Q(D) − Q(S). In order to eliminate this shortage, a "turnover" tax is imposed, equal to P(T) − P(0). This tax, when added to the controlled price, results in a market price of P(T). Notice that the new price, including the tax, clears the market in the sense that the quantity Q(S) also becomes the quantity demanded. The government then collects turnover tax revenue represented by the rectangle P(T) A B P(C). If the turnover tax is paid out to the enterprise producing this good, it may increase its output. However, if the government retains the tax revenue, consumers end up paying a higher price for less output than they would in a market economy. Given the inertia inherent in bureaucratic systems and the absence of a profit incentive to meet consumer (as opposed to Gosplan) demands, controlled prices and targeted output levels are not likely to respond quickly or fully to market signals.

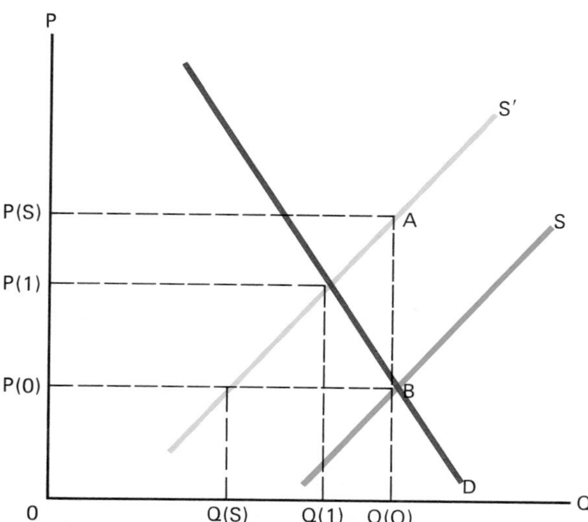

Figure 18.2 Price adjustments in the Soviet Union
D and S are initial demand and supply conditions for some commodity, and P(0) and Q(0) are equilibrium price and quantity. An adverse supply shift to S′ will shift equilibrium price and quantity to P(1) and Q(1) in a market economy. In the Soviet Union an excess demand of Q(0) − Q(S) results at the old price. A production subsidy of P(S) − P(0) causes the quantity supplied to equal the quantity demanded.

Figure 18.2 illustrates what happens when there is a change in the initial demand and supply conditions. Suppose the production of some good is reduced because a supplier fails to provide a necessary input or because of a weather-related shortfall of some raw material. The supply curve shifts from S to S′, reflecting the changed condition. At the controlled price of P(0), a shortage of Q(0) − Q(S) will result where none had existed before. The free market response would be an increase in the equilibrium price from P(0) to P(1). However, in a controlled economy, a consumer price of P(0) might be maintained and the market cleared by providing producers with a payment, or subsidy, equal to P(1) − P(0). The monetary cost of this program to the government is represented by the area of the rectangle P(S) A B P(0). In this response to an excess demand, the government has encouraged more output than a free market would.

Setting controlled prices and then adjusting them with taxes and subsidies to eliminate shortages (or gluts) may appear to lead to relatively smoothly working "markets" under the best of circumstances. However, this practice is almost certain to result in overproduction of some goods and underproduction of others when judged against the criterion of economic efficiency. Even though consumers can purchase all they want in figures 18.1 and 18.2 at the posttax and postsubsidy prices, they would prefer to have more of the good in figure 18.1 and less of the good in figure 18.2 than Gosplan has chosen to provide. Moreover, as we previously noted, product quality often suffers as a result of the planning emphasis on meeting quotas, which are set in quantity terms.

Factor Price Determination and the Allocation of Factor Inputs

Factor prices in the Soviet Union are not designed to signal firms to economize on relatively scarce inputs or to direct labor, machinery, and raw materials toward their most productive uses. Land and buildings are primarily owned by the state. Land is allocated to enterprises and farms administratively, and no rent is charged. Private saving decisions have virtually nothing to do with the allocation of aggregate production between consumption and investment. The Soviet Union has a strong desire for economic growth as reflected in a ratio of investment to GNP of between 35 and 40 percent. Note that even though this is more than double the ratio in the United States, the GNP growth rate in the Soviet Union has tended to be less, not more, than in its major capitalist competitor.

We indicated earlier that in the Soviet Union the choice of production technique is generally made by a planning agency. The expressed goal of planning is to minimize cost, that is, to satisfy the plan efficiently. However, without market-determined wage rates, capital costs, interest rates, and so on to guide them, planners are often wide of the mark when it comes to cost minimization. Furthermore, planners often have political goals that may lead to decisions that are non-cost minimizing. For example, heavy industries such

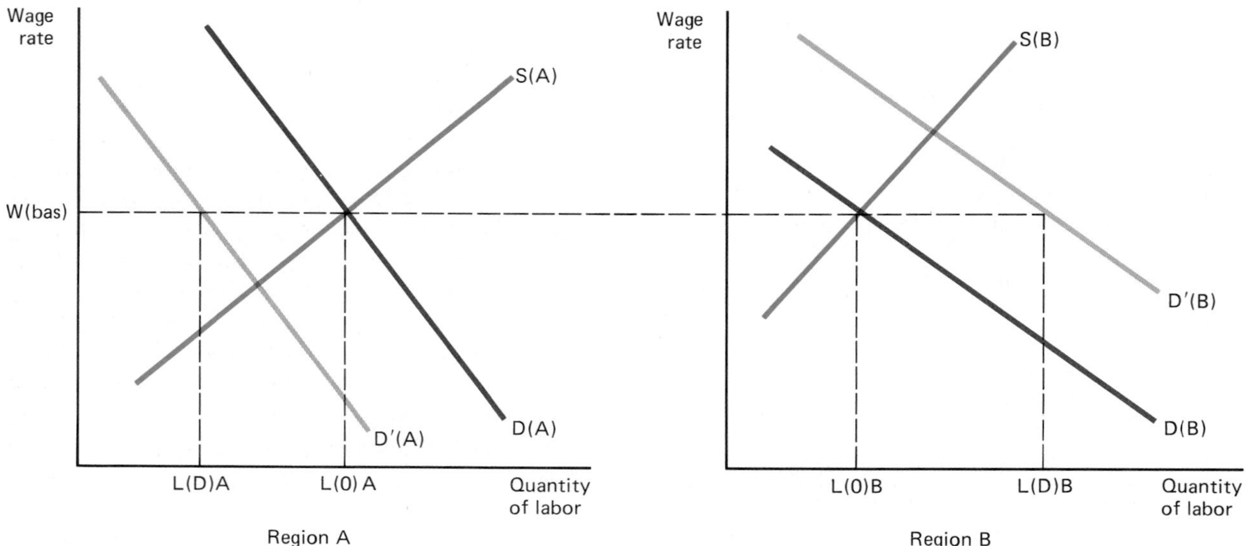

Figure 18.3 Shortages and underemployment of labor in the Soviet Union
D(A), D(B), S(A), and S(B) are the initial labor demand and supply curves in regions A and B, respectively. The equilibrium wage rate in each region is initially W(bas), the basic wage rate. Equilibrium employment is initially L(0)A and L(0)B, respectively. A leftward shift in the demand for labor in region A creates underemployment equal to L(0)A − L(D)A, while an increase in demand in region B creates a shortage equal to L(D)B − L(0)B.

as steel production and armament manufacturing may be promoted to lend an appearance of military strength to the nation. Some national regions may be favored with new facilities in order to please local political leaders even though other locations would be less costly. Finally, the immense discretion and power in the hands of strategically located planning officials opens the door to personal gain through bribery and corruption.

Once we recognize the maze of administrative levels, directives, plans, and individuals that directs the allocation of resources, it becomes easy to understand the immense possibilities for distortions and misallocations, to understand why all recent Soviet administrations have been plagued by widespread corruption.

Workers in the Soviet Union have some discretion in their choice of job and where they work. Nevertheless, basic wage rates and differentials associated with different skills are set administratively rather than in the marketplace. The government manipulates wage differentials to adjust labor supplies.

Figure 18.3 illustrates how the manipulation of wage rates can generate shortages of labor in some areas simultaneously with a glut, or unemployment, of labor in other regions. The curves D(A), D(B), S(A), and S(B) represent labor demand and supply in regions A and B, respectively. The planning authority has set a basic wage rate for both regions, W(bas), that initially equates the quantity of labor demanded and supplied. Suppose now that the demand for output from region A declines while that in region B increases. Labor demand in region A falls to D′(A), while that in region B rises to D′(B). In a free labor market we would expect the wage rate in region A to fall and the wage rate in region B to rise, leading to a shift of labor to region B from region A. This migration of labor would cause the labor supply curve in region A to shift leftward and the labor supply curve in region B to shift rightward. This shift of the labor force would continue until wage rates in the two regions were once again equal.

With administratively set wage rates, a labor shortage equal to L(D)B − L(0)B will appear in region B. In the Soviet system, any evidence of unemployment is looked upon with great disfavor. Therefore, enterprise managers in region A would be risking their reputations if they laid off the workers no longer desired. Thus, the excess supply of labor in region A—L(0)A − L(D)A—takes the form of disguised unemployment. *Disguised unemployment* amounts to making work for employees who are no longer required in order to avoid direct evidence of more workers than jobs. This problem of simultaneous disguised unemployment and labor shortages across occupations and geographic regions is common in the Soviet Union. When shortages become particularly acute, planners will adjust wage rates and working conditions to attract workers. However, as in administration of the turnover tax and subsidy schemes described above, the adjustments are too few and too slow to avoid substantial misallocation of labor.

The Soviet system of administered prices and wages creates unfilled demands for goods and workers in many areas. This creates numerous opportunities for workers to increase their incomes substantially if they can help fill these demands either legally or illegally.[7] One interesting result has occurred in agriculture. In addition to guaranteed wages earned on state-owned or collectively owned farms, families are allowed to own small (half acre) plots and to sell their produce on the open market. Since the end of World War II the private agricultural sector has provided a very large share of the fresh meat, fruit, and vegetables in Soviet markets and is estimated to have provided about 40 percent of all farm income. The second way in which workers can enhance their incomes is to provide services to the underground economy of illegal activities. This does not necessarily involve dealing in illicit commodities, but perhaps providing services such as auto repair, plumbing, and so on, outside the system. The amount of production carried on in this fashion can only be guessed at.

▸ Economic Performance of Capitalist and Socialist Economic Systems

The bottom line in evaluating comparative economic systems is how well they perform in meeting general social goals. We will now briefly examine the success that a sample of socialist economies and capitalist economies have had in providing their citizens with some broad measures of economic well-being. In evaluating these performance measures we should also bear in mind that in addition to material measures, many individuals would also include political and economic freedom as desired characteristics of economic and social organization. While measures of freedom cannot be made as precisely as measures of production and consumption, it is generally agreed that citizens in planned, socialist economies have less than do those of most capitalist economies. If the two economic systems turned out to perform equally well on purely economic criteria, then, a case could be made that greater freedom of choice and action makes capitalism the preferred system. This is a consideration that each reader should bear in mind when comparing capitalist and socialist economic performance.

Another point that should be considered when comparing the relative performance of capitalist and socialist economies is that the *level* of economic development (as measured by per capita income) is also an important determinant of various performance measures. For example, the proportion of total production devoted to health and welfare services, or to education, depends on per capita wealth as well as on the political-economic system of a country. The process of economic development itself has historically been associated with increased equality of the relative income distribution and increased quality of social services. We can suggest two explanations for this observation. One explanation, as Adam Smith observed, is that rapid economic growth often provides benefits for even the poorest elements of society. The second explanation is that advanced capitalist societies have had at least one or two centuries to observe the social and political stresses that emerge in market economies. They have had the time and experience to develop systems that reduce poverty, social alienation,

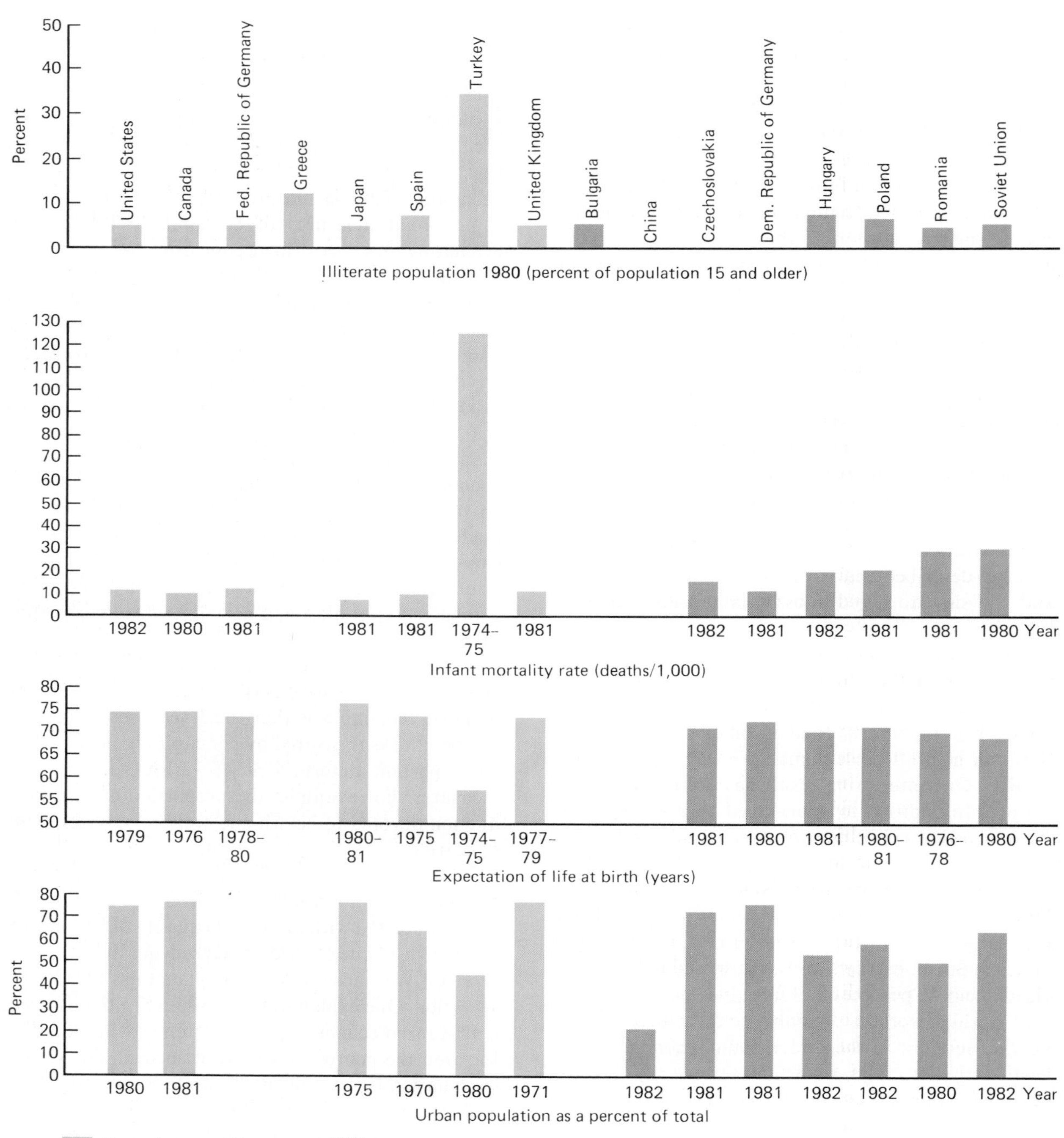

Figure 18.4 Population characteristics in capitalist and planned, socialist economies

From *Statistical Abstract of the United States,* Table 1505, p. 861, Table 1506, p. 862, and Table 1508, pp. 863–64.

and political unrest. To avoid confusing the effects of a country's economic system with its level of economic development, remember that countries such as Greece and Spain are at about the same level of economic development as most planned, socialist economies. In our evaluation of relative performance, we will examine several different characteristics of countries that are related to the quality of everyday life.

General Measures of Health and Literacy

Figure 18.4 contains data on several measures of the welfare of the population of capitalist and socialist countries. First, we see that the proportion of the population that is urban in the socialist countries (with the exception of Czechoslovakia and the Democratic Republic of Germany) is similar to that of Spain. The least developed capitalist and socialist economies in our sample, Turkey and China, respectively, are predominantly agrarian societies.

Estimates of life expectancy at birth in the socialist economies are generally less than in the advanced capitalist economies and even less than in Spain. Surprisingly, life expectancy at birth in the Soviet Union (69 years) is less than in all of the other Eastern European countries for which we have data. The relatively low life expectancy at birth in the socialist countries is partly attributable to their high infant mortality rates. The infant mortality rate reflects live births that result in death by age one per 1,000 live births. The worst figure (125) is for Turkey, the poorest country for which we have data. The infant mortality rate among socialist economies for which we have data is highest in the Soviet Union (28–30), and it is three times the infant mortality rate in Spain. Mothers' health, the quality of prenatal care, and the availability and quality of infant medical care all affect the infant mortality rates. These figures raise some doubts about the quality of health care provided under planned socialism.

On the other hand, if literacy is important to the quality of life, the planned economies fare well relative to Greece and Spain. In fact, for several planned economies, including the Soviet Union, the illiteracy rates compare favorably with those of the most advanced capitalist economies.

Health and Health Services

Figure 18.5 provides information on the commitment of material resources and personnel to health care services in capitalist and socialist economies. As one might expect, the least developed capitalist and socialist economies, Turkey and China, have the highest ratios of population per hospital bed and per physician. In terms of the availability of hospital beds, physicians, and dentists, the socialist economies fare well in comparison with the most advanced capitalist economies. It is of course important to bear in mind that the data in figure 18.5 reflect the quantity of health care facilities and personnel available but do not inform us about the quality of those facilities or the skills of the health care personnel.

Communication and Education Services

Figure 18.6 contains data on various communication and education services. The first four sections report on the relative availability of telephones, newspapers, televisions, and radios in our sample countries. The relative availability of televisions and radios in the socialist countries is comparable to availability in Spain and Greece. Daily newspapers are as readily available in socialist economies as in the more advanced capitalist economies and more available than in Spain. In contrast, telephones are much more readily available in Greece and Spain than in any of the socialist economies. Since telephones permit private individuals to send and receive information from one another, the relative scarcity of telephones in socialist states may have more to do with the security of the government than with the ability of planned economies to provide telephone services. Try to imagine how different United States society would be if eight out of every nine telephones were removed to replicate the relative scarcity of telephones in the Soviet Union. The failure of the trade union movement in Poland to prevent martial law through more effective coordination of strikes and work slowdowns in 1980 may be easier to understand when one realizes that there is one telephone for every ten people in Poland compared to almost eight telephones for every ten people in the United States.

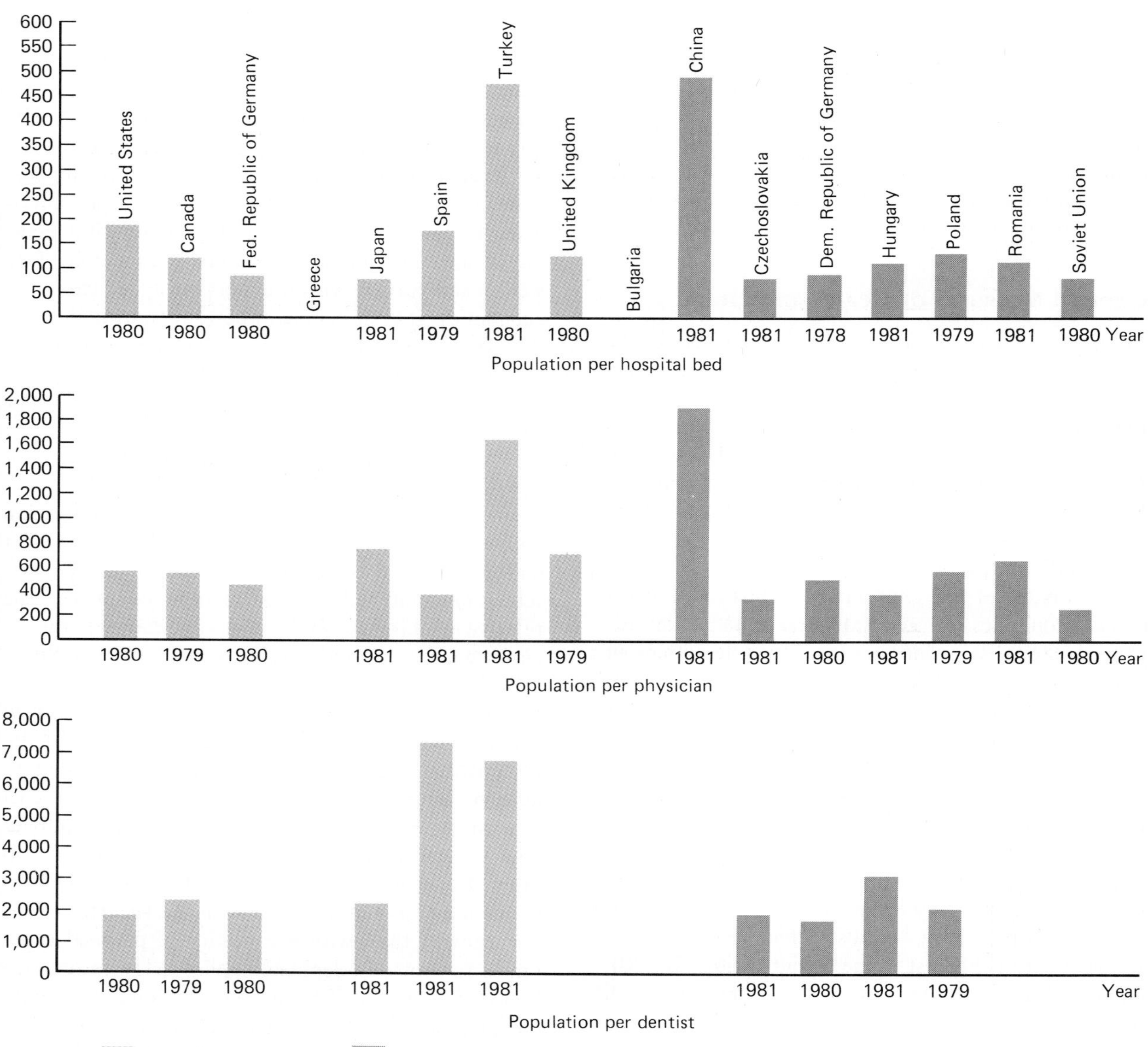

Figure 18.5 Provision of health services in capitalist and planned, socialist economies
From *Statistical Abstract of the United States,* Table 1506, p. 862, Table 1508, pp. 863–64, and Table 1531, pp. 881–82.

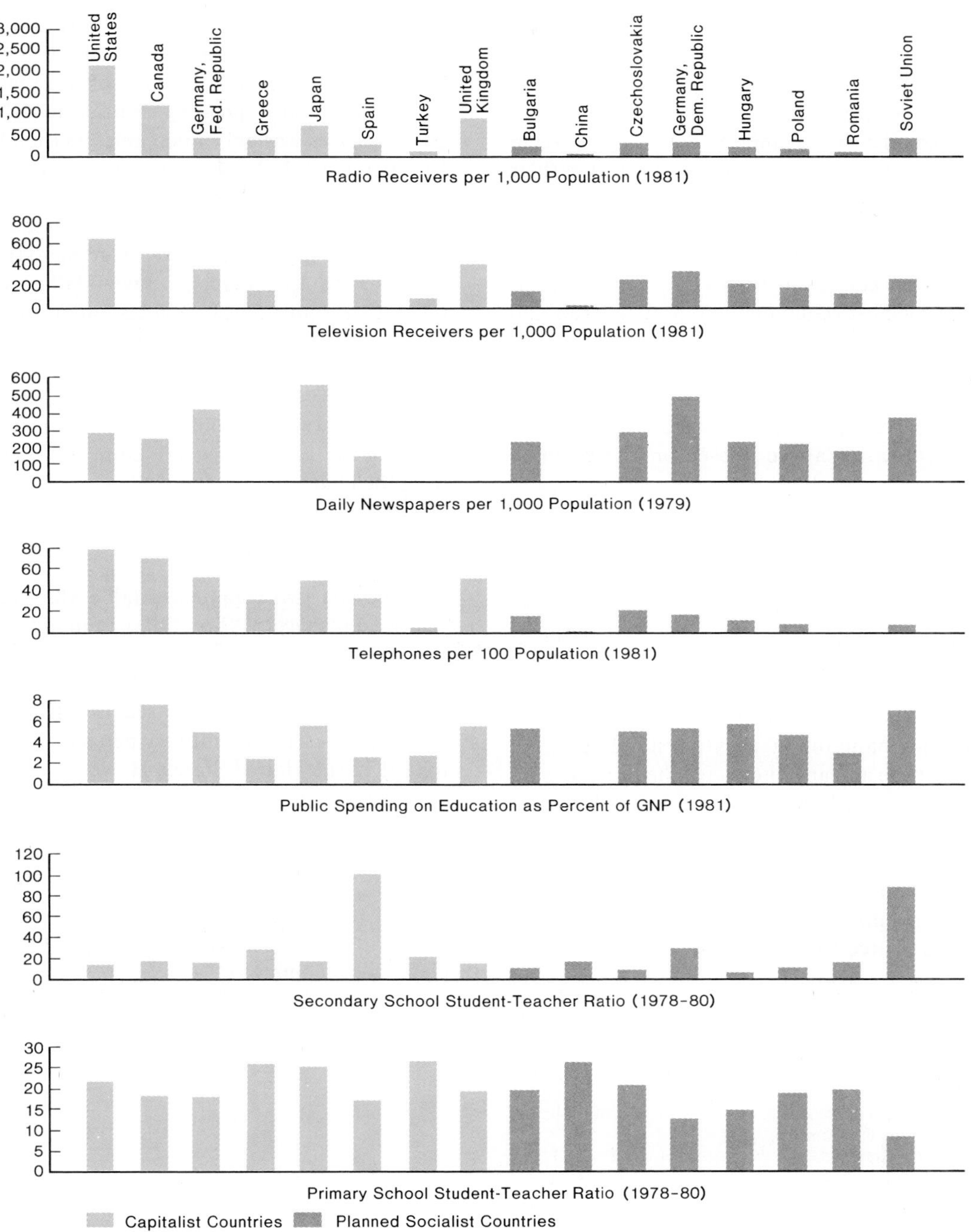

Figure 18.6 Education and communication services in capitalist and socialist economies

From *Statistical Abstract of the United States,* Table 1508, pp. 863–64, Table 1531, pp. 881–82, 1985, Table 1480, p. 845, and Table 1487, p. 849.

Figure 18.6 also illustrates public expenditures on education relative to GNP and student-teacher ratios. Student-teacher ratios for primary and secondary schools are similar across capitalist and planned economies. Spain and the Soviet Union seem to have extremely high student-teacher ratios in their secondary schools. Spain and Greece have lower shares of GNP going to public education than any of the socialist economies for which we have data. Public expenditures on education relative to aggregate income in the socialist economies compare favorably to the corresponding shares observed in the most advanced capitalist economies. Adding in private school expenditures relative to GNP would no doubt raise the aggregate educational expenditure-GNP ratios in capitalist economies above those for the socialist countries.

Military Spending and Military Presence

Americans have traditionally been concerned about the role of the military in society. There are frequent expressions of concern about the potential diversion of economic resources to wasteful military projects that benefit only the "military-industrial complex." Opposition to maintaining a large standing army during peacetime and arguments for the draft in wartime have often rested on the belief that a substantial professional military force is always a threat to democracy.

The first four columns of table 18.3 contain data on military spending in several economies. Not surprisingly, the United States and the Soviet Union are the capitalist and socialist economies that spend the highest share of GNP on the military. It is surprising, however, that even at the height of the Vietnam War in 1971, military spending relative to GNP in the United States was only 7 percent, less than half of the 14.9 percent GNP share going to the military in the Soviet Union. By 1982, United States military expenditure relative to GNP was 6.4 percent, whereas the Soviet Union's share of GNP going to the military increased to 15.0 percent. Soviet military expenditures were equivalent to $242.4 billion in 1982 compared to $185.2 billion in the United States. It is interesting to note that in his biography, deposed Soviet Premier Nikita Khrushchev echoed President Eisenhower's warning about the danger to society of a growing military-industrial complex.[8] Even apart from the United States and the Soviet Union, the share of GNP going to the military tends to be higher in planned, socialist economies than in capitalist economies.

The last two columns of table 18.3 indicate the relative presence of the military among the population. In 1975, the number of armed forces personnel was lower in the United States than in the Soviet Union, 0.99 percent compared to 1.61 percent. By 1982, the presence of military personnel had declined to 0.91 in the United States. However, it had risen to 1.63 percent in the Soviet Union.

Other socialist economies also tend to have more military personnel relative to their populations than do other capitalist countries. Whatever the explanation for that difference may be, to many people it reflects a relatively unattractive characteristic of the planned economies.

Table 18.3 Military spending and armed forces personnel in capitalist and socialist economies

	Military expenditures in constant 1981 dollars (millions)						
			Percent of GNP		Armed Forces (thousands)	Armed forces per 1,000 population	
Capitalist countries	1975	1982	1975	1982	(1982)	1975	1982
United States	141,213	185,205	5.8	6.4	2,108	9.9	9.1
Canada	4,392	5,790	1.9	2.2	82	3.4	3.3
Federal Republic of Germany	20,924	22,970	3.6	3.4	480	8.0	7.9
United Kingdom	23,068	25,815	4.9	5.1	322	6.2	5.8
Planned socialist countries							
China	48,909	46,691	11.6	7.1	4,490	4.6	4.3
Democratic Republic of Germany	8,060	9,655	5.6	5.8	233	13.0	14.0
Soviet Union	206,351	242,419	14.9	15.0	4,400	16.1	16.3

Source: From *Statistical Abstracts of the United States, 1985,* table 1513, p. 866.

Summary and Conclusions

Having completed an extensive introduction to how capitalist economies allocate resources and a comparison with socialist allocation mechanisms, you should now be able to form your own opinion about which system forms the best basis for society to deal with the ever present problem of scarcity. This chapter has focused on the ways in which planned, socialist economies find answers to the basic economic questions that must be answered by all economic systems. The following major points were emphasized.

The questions of what to produce, how to produce it, and for whom to produce it are determined primarily by market forces in capitalist economies and by central planning in socialist economies.

Except for the Democratic Republic of Germany and Czechoslovakia, the levels of per capita output in socialist countries are quite low by western industrial standards. By this measure, the standard of living in the Soviet Union and most socialist countries is at a level comparable to that of countries like Greece, Spain, and Turkey.

Real economic growth during the 1970s was no greater among the socialist economies than among capitalist economies.

While basic commodities are produced subject to central plans in the Soviet Union, most products are subject to planning at the regional or local level. Plans are revised annually.

Prices at the wholesale level in the Soviet Union were last set in 1966/1967. Government taxes are used to eliminate excess demands, and government subsidies are used to eliminate excess supplies of goods subject to controlled prices.

Wage rates and wage differentials associated with different skills are set administratively rather than by market forces in the Soviet Union. Consequently, there tend to be persistent labor shortages in some regions and occupations, while at the same time there are labor surpluses in other regions and occupations.

Estimates of life expectancy at birth in the socialist economies are generally less than in the advanced capitalist economies.

The infant mortality rate in the Soviet Union is three times as high as it is in Spain. Life expectancy at birth is sixty-nine years in the Soviet Union, which is less than in the socialist countries of Eastern Europe in general.

The relative availability of hospital resources, doctors, and dentists in the socialist countries compares favorably with the availability of such resources in the advanced capitalist economies.

Public expenditures on education relative to aggregate income in the socialist economies compares favorably to the corresponding shares observed in advanced capitalist economies.

Television sets and radios are about as available in the socialist countries as they are in Greece and Spain. Telephones are much less available in socialist economies than in Spain and Greece.

Military spending relative to GNP is twice as high in the Soviet Union as it is in the United States. In 1982, military expenditures equaled $242.4 billion in the Soviet Union and $185.2 billion in the United States.

Military personnel are almost twice as large a share of the population in the Soviet Union as in the United States.

▸ Key Terms

capitalist economic system *377*

economic system *376*

materials balance approach *381*

▸ Questions for Discussion and Review

1. What are the four basic issues confronting any economic system, and how are they generally dealt with in capitalist and socialist economies?
2. Give specific examples of production techniques in capitalist countries that are not primarily market determined and explain them.
3. Give specific examples in which the answer to the question "what gets produced" is not primarily market determined in capitalist economies and explain your examples.
4. Explain how final annual production targets are established by the state planning agency in the Soviet Union.
5. Explain the positive and negative effects of bonus incentives for enterprise managers in the Soviet Union.
6. Illustrate and explain how a poor wheat harvest would be reflected in the Soviet Union if the price of wheat is fixed at P(W).
7. Illustrate and explain how a shortage of skilled labor could develop in the Soviet Union.
8. What, if any, incentive problems could arise if the United States tried to use taxes to reduce income inequality to equal that in the Soviet Union?
9. What political, social, and economic forces do you suppose could explain why income is as evenly distributed across households in a capitalist country like the United Kingdom as in the Soviet Union?
10. Explain how the size of the military-industrial complex could slow real economic growth in socialist economies and why they commit relatively more resources including personnel to the military than is generally true in capitalist economies.

11. Are the following statements true, false, or uncertain? Be sure to justify your answers.
    a. Government's primary economic role is to enforce property rights in a market economy.
    b. Government facilitates voluntary exchange in a market economy by protecting workers and consumers from exploitation.
    c. Individual self-interest is likely to lead to more ignorance in political decisions than in market decisions.
    d. The profit motive leads bureaucrats to supply public needs at the lowest possible cost to society.
    e. The principal difference between the behavior of politicians and that of business leaders is that business firms are operated solely to achieve the self-interest of their owners, while politicians cannot win elections if they do not strive for maximum social welfare.
12. A number of states and localities have passed legislation in the past few years limiting the power of their legislators to raise taxes without explicit voter approval. However, these restrictions do not govern which tax-expenditure issues will be placed on the ballot and which will be financed from general funds. Given this legislator discretion, which of the following activities are most likely to be submitted to the electorate for approval or rejection and which reserved for control of the legislative bodies? Defend your answers in terms of the analysis of government behavior developed in this chapter.
    a. Financing an ambulance and emergency squad.
    b. Subsidizing local bus transportation.
    c. Funding day-care centers for the children of working mothers.
    d. Supporting a local junior college.
    e. Urban redevelopment.

*The **economic approach to government activity** uses the tools of modern economic analysis to study government behavior.*

Appendix to Chapter 18

The Government's Role in Mixed, Capitalist Economies

Capitalist economies are mixed economies in that government plays a role in many branches of economic activity. In this section we will analyze government's goals, its means of achieving its ends, and the important behavioral characteristics of governments in mixed, capitalist economies. The **economic approach to government activity** is a theory of government activity in the same spirit that theory guides the economist's analysis of the behavior of households and business firms. Capitalist economies, as opposed to socialist economies, generally have representative governments, such as in the United States. In representative governments individual citizens affect government policies indirectly through their elected representatives. It is this process of indirect representation via the voting process that leads to different governmental behavior in capitalist systems than in most socialist systems, where the democratic process is much less well-developed, if it exists at all.

Bear in mind that a politician cannot work toward any desired goals without being elected. In other words, political survival is necessary, just as economic survival is necessary for a firm. Recall that in a competitive environment, surviving firms are forced to maximize profits. Similarly, the need to win elections serves as an effective constraint on politicians' desires to work toward "good government" when achieving that goal conflicts with the expressed goals of certain groups of voters in a democracy.

▸ Voting Behavior in a Democracy

We will now develop a simple analysis of voting behavior in a representative democracy. Then we will explore the actions of politicians, the voters' elected representatives. Finally, we will use the concepts of the "demand" and "supply" of government activities to derive some implications for government behavior in a mixed economy.

Self-Interest, Rational Ignorance, and Voting Behavior

The problems of financing public goods also affect citizens' voting behavior. By voting behavior, we mean the activities leading up to the act of voting, whether or not a citizen actually votes in an election, and the choice expressed if a vote

Logrolling is the mutual exchange of political support among special-interest groups.

is cast. To what extent does it make sense for an individual voter to gather information about the choices offered in an election or even to vote? When the voting population is large, say, 1,000 voters or more, the probability is extremely low that any single vote will determine which candidate or which proposition wins. However, the cost to an individual of acquiring information and casting a vote can be significant. Moreover, an individual citizen will benefit or be harmed by an election's results independently of whether or not he or she participates in the election.

These considerations imply that in public choices involving issues not likely to affect individuals, either significantly or directly, voters are likely to be free riders. They have a tendency to spend very little time becoming informed about, or even voting in, those elections where their own special interests are not involved. Suppose for the purpose of discussion that you would prefer an election outcome that transfers income to people below the median level of income in society. How much time and money would you be willing to spend to discover the probable effect of law X or candidate Y on this aspect of the income distribution? Probably not very much if you do not expect your vote to matter.

By contrast, if you are a member of the United Auto Workers Union, you are much more likely to learn about each candidate's position on tariffs on imported automobiles and other import restrictions. While you may fully understand that an increase in the tariff on Japanese autos will harm your fellow citizens, your relatively large gain compared to their relatively small individual losses is likely to influence you to vote against free trade in automobiles. The payoff to acquiring information and voting is relatively greater where private choices are involved. Thus, it is much more likely for ignorance to be rational in a public choice situation than when deciding whether to buy a particular item and how much of it to buy. An implication of this "principle of rational ignorance" is that public choice outcomes are likely to reflect individual preferences much less accurately than private choices.

▸ Social Choices in a Democracy: Outcomes of the Political Process

The behavior of voters and politicians can be thought of as roughly equivalent to the demand for and supply of public choices that determine government behavior in a democracy. Let us now examine how the interactions between voters and politicians affect government's role in a mixed economy.

Special Interests and Logrolling

Those of you who are budding politicians may have already developed some strategies to win elections when you run for office. One strategy is probably that you will align your platform to appeal to the strongly held feelings of certain important special-interest groups. One of the implications of our analysis of voters' and politicians' behavior is that voters with special interests will have a much stronger impact on legislation than one would expect on the basis of their proportion of the electorate. Anyone who doubts this need only reflect on agricultural policy in the United States and other industrial democracies of the world. Farmers account for only about 3 percent of the United States labor force and less than 10 percent of the Japanese and Western European labor forces. Yet their influence on public policy is immense in those nations.[1]

A second strategy to win elections is **logrolling,** whereby a politician convinces various special-interest groups to support him or her and vice versa. In this way certain minority held, but strongly felt, views may prevail in public choices. For example, votes from the arid South for flood control in the North may be exchanged for New England's support for massive irrigation projects in the South. Legislators who are not willing to make deals are not likely to get very far in promoting constituents' interests.

Frequently, logrolling has a negative connotation in the mass media and other public forums. On the one hand, it can serve as a means whereby citizens engage in mutually beneficial exchange of their votes in a manner similar to voluntary exchange in goods markets. On the other hand, it can also lead to expenditures on projects that cost more than the value to their beneficiaries. This is economically inefficient. For example, if southwesterners and New Englanders logroll at the expense of residents of the Midwest, then midwesterners may pay for part of projects in other regions that do not benefit them and that New Englanders and southwesterners would be unwilling to pay for in full. Why would midwesterners pay? They may be in a minority, or more importantly, their lack of a special interest in the projects that benefit other regions may lead to their ignorance of the relatively small amounts they pay per individual.

Shortsightedness and Obfuscation

Surviving politicians may emphasize the present relative to the future and obfuscate (confuse) rather than clarify issues. Forming an opinion about the future requires close attention and a willingness by voters to spend time weighing the facts and hypotheses involved in forecasting. The principle of rational voter ignorance works against politicians' supplying citizens with information they do not want to use, and this is likely to lead to rational shortsightedness on the part of voters. That is, voters are not likely to take the time or devote much effort to evaluating the effects of policies that they do not expect to have a major impact on their well-being.

It is difficult to test the hypothesis that people are often shortsighted when it comes to political issues. Concrete data on this topic are not available. Still, informal observations lend support. One example is in the area of national defense. Military preparedness involves substantial current cost in return for uncertain future benefits. Moreover, the information required to make informed decisions is extensive and costly to acquire and evaluate. Who knows whether we will really need a larger air force or more nuclear missiles in Europe to protect us and our allies from the Soviet Union? The costs are borne now and are readily perceived. The benefits—costly and difficult to evaluate—are at best uncertain. Thus, there would appear to be a tendency in societies with representative, democratic governments to allocate fewer resources to defense than do countries with totalitarian governments. As table 18.3 indicates, reality apparently bears out this tendency. In evaluating this comparison, it is important to keep in mind that the cost of a given amount of military protection is likely to be inflated by government decisions, and this will also influence the amount of protection chosen in a democratic process. We will deal with the costs of government activities shortly.

Another example of shortsightedness is "government by crisis." Immediate solutions to severe problems are more appealing than preventing problems over the long term. For example, the long-term impacts of price controls on quantities supplied are frequently less persuasive than their immediate and short-lived effects on the amount that must be paid for a good. Excessively accelerating the money supply is known to be ultimately inflationary, but it may yield short-term political gains by temporarily increasing the pace of economic activity. Another example of the tendency to put off dealing with problems until they reach the critical stage is Social Security funding. Only when there is imminent danger of exhausting funds for current payments has Congress been willing to address the problems of financing Social Security and determining benefits. Even then, there is a strong bias toward quick and temporary fixes rather than long-term solutions.

Because of rational ignorance, present benefits or costs are more readily apparent to an average citizen than benefits or costs that will occur in the future. Thus, present benefits or costs are more likely to influence public choices in a democracy. At the same time, politicians who want to pool the support of special-interest groups through logrolling will do well to exploit the principle of rational ignorance. It will in general be harmful to a politician's political survival to clarify and emphasize project costs to the general public. Special-interest groups will be willing to learn about the benefits and costs of projects that concern them directly. However, as far as members of the general public are concerned, the politician will be inclined to act as if what they don't know won't hurt them. It may even pay to cloud the issues with extraneous facts and misleading arguments. For example, the average voter is unlikely to take the time to learn why it is *fallacious* to argue that lowering dairy industry price supports will lead to milk shortages and higher prices. Thus, this is a popular argument used by supporters of minimum prices for fresh milk.

Another example of obfuscation is government's eagerness to use conscription in obtaining military personnel, especially in time of war. Many people sincerely believe that a military draft is necessary to preserve civilian control over the military in a democracy and to share defense burdens fairly. However, when military forces are staffed through conscription rather than by paying wages high enough to attract voluntary armed forces, much of the cost is borne by draftees in foregone earnings and other lost opportunities in the private sector of the economy. If the costs were more obvious to nondrafted citizens through increases in their taxes or reductions in nonmilitary government expenditures, it would be more difficult to maintain armed forces of a given size, and popular support for military activities in wartime would probably be reduced. Thus, whatever the moral arguments in favor of a draft may be, they are reinforced by conscription's appeal as a cost-hiding way to finance military expenditures.

The Budgetary Process: Separation of Taxes from Expenditures

Logrolling and obfuscation of costs are more difficult in situations where taxpayers are presented with a tax bill for each individual government project. If each dam, income-maintenance program, and change in agricultural price supports were accompanied by the need to vote on the taxes to finance them, politicians would probably find it more difficult to commit government to expenditures from which many voters receive little or no benefit. State constitutions and local charters often specify that certain types of expenditures, such as public schools, libraries, and public transportation, must be linked to specific property tax levies or sales taxes or to other earmarked tax receipts. However, financing from a general fund appears to be politicians' method of choice when possible because it makes it easier to benefit special-interest groups at the expense of all taxpayers.

Bureaucratic Behavior and the Cost in Output of Government Services

How does government provide the services politicians or voters decide upon in a democracy? In the private sector the firm provides goods and services. Government also purchases the output of private firms, however. These government purchases are usually inputs into the process by which governments produce the services they ultimately furnish to their constituents. Within governments, *agencies* or *bureaus* correspond to private-sector firms in their role of producing government services from purchased inputs. Knowing how bureaus function in comparison to private-sector firms is crucial to understanding government's economic role in the mixed economy.

The key to understanding the difference between bureaucratic and firm behavior is profit and how it is affected by revenue and cost. Competitive firms must minimize costs if they are to survive. While monopoly power reduces survival pressures as a motive to lower costs, monopolists still benefit directly if they act to reduce their costs. This is not so with bureaucrats. A government official's salary is not in general linked, even indirectly, to success in reducing costs or increasing the value of government services to citizens. Because a bureau's services are not sold in the marketplace, its revenues are derived from legislative appropriations. A bureaucrat who reduces his or her agency's costs may actually receive a smaller appropriation next year rather than earn a promotion or salary increase.

If, through diligence, an agency's costs are reduced, the official in charge may receive a letter of commendation or possibly a promotion. However, the opposite may occur insofar as salary and prestige depend upon the number of employees supervised or the size of the agency's budget. Thus, the direct gain from cost saving is likely to be far less than to a private firm. Moreover, reducing costs may involve laying off workers who are friends or political supporters. Cost savings that arise from cutting down office space, reducing the quality of the office environment, or moving to a cheaper location are likely to reduce bureaucrats' satisfaction on the job. And they are unlikely to receive monetary compensation for such sacrifices. We conclude, then, that bureaucratic costs per unit of service provided are likely to be higher than the costs of a private firm.

How is the output of a government bureau likely to differ from that of a private firm? First, consider the demand for a government agency's services. Most government activities involve goods or services that are not 100 percent "public." There is a private component, for example, to police protection insofar as individual citizens may ask a patrol car to drive through their neighborhood to quiet a rowdy party. Therefore, individual users' demands can affect government agencies' output directly in many cases. Generally, these services are not priced on a fee-per-use basis. This means that a user will typically face a zero marginal money cost and will demand a greater quantity of the service than if he or she were directly confronted with the true marginal cost of providing it. If an agency meets all demands, rather than engaging in formal or informal rationing, the tendency to charge users less than marginal cost will cause bureaucratic output to be larger than that of a private firm.

Bureaucrats' goals and constraints affect their willingness to meet individual citizens' demands for government services. We assume that government employees, like politicians, act in their own self-interest. Of course, they may wish to satisfy altruistic motives, and they may place a high value on the services their particular agencies provide to the public. Nevertheless, their behavior will be affected by the constraints they face in government employment, just as employees of private firms must function within the constraints imposed by the marketplace.

How, then, will bureaucrats respond to the demand for their output? There is no certain answer to this question. Remember that the management of a government agency is unlikely to do anything to reduce an agency's budget. We have shown that the quantity of government services demanded is likely to be larger than the quantity of comparable services demanded from the private sector because government is likely to charge less than the marginal cost of providing those services. A bureau will meet demand if its budget is large enough, but there is little incentive to avoid a shortage if to do so would require reducing its costs per unit of service. A shortage, after all, will create political pressure to increase the agency's budget. Thus, it is uncertain whether a government agency will supply more or less output than would a private firm providing the same good or service.

Labor Costs in Government

Our analysis of government costs is difficult to test against the facts because there are few data comparing government and private costs of producing similar products or providing similar services. (We do report some interesting empirical cost comparisons in the next subsection, however.) Bear in mind that government costs are likely to be higher than private costs *even if government pays the same price for its inputs as private employers do.* As we pointed out, a government official who lays off workers in order to reduce costs may well reduce political support in a democracy. The same line of reasoning suggests that government employers will not seek to hire workers of given skills at the lowest possible wage rates.

The principle of rational ignorance implies that if governments pay their employees more than market wage rates, a typical voter will not know. However, government employees have an intense interest in making sure their employee organizations and unions exert political pressure for high wages. In addition, it may hurt a politician's popularity with many voters to acquire a reputation of being hard on labor. There is evidence that government employees do earn more than workers in the private sector who are similar in such wage-related characteristics as experience, schooling, and health. This differential is most apparent at the federal government level, where workers have earned about 20 to 30 percent more than their private-sector counterparts in recent years.[2]

Some Illustrations of Public Choice

It is difficult to be precise in assessing the degree to which the democratic political process influences economic decisions made in the public sector. The reason is that for many important government functions, similar choices are not made in the private sector of a mixed economy. National defense is typically a government activity, for example. In those nations where mercenary armies are used, data on costs and effectiveness are virtually nonexistent. As we have already seen in chapter 18, another interesting comparison is with the government provision of military activities and national defense in planned, socialist economies, where government operates under a different set of constraints than in democracies.

Despite difficulties of little or no data, it is possible to gain some factual insights into the costs and quality of government services in a mixed economy, and we will now summarize information available on some areas of economic behavior at the local and national levels of government in the United States.

Government and Private Costs Compared

Government does not often compete directly with private industry in the United States, but there are some cases in which comparisons between government and private industry costs and quality can be made. Even without precise data, casual impressions of the success of United Parcel Service, Federal Express, Purolator, and other private package delivery services suggest that they outperform the United States Postal Service in certain instances. Some detailed analyses provide evidence that government's cost, and perhaps quality of service, disadvantages are by no means confined to package delivery. One study compared the efficiency of private and public provision of services in five industries.[3] One of these comparisons is for another country—between a government and a privately owned airline in Australia. The other comparisons involve the provision of fire protection, electricity, hospital services, and garbage collection in the United States. Each study was designed to compare the government and private costs of providing services of approximately equal quality. In every case, the government spent at least as much—and usually significantly more—to furnish a given quantity of service as did suppliers from the private sector.

The fire protection study is particularly interesting because it involved a government service that is traditionally organized and provided by the public sector. Scottsdale, Arizona, elected to hire a private firm to provide fire protection.[4] Payments to the private firm were financed from tax revenues, so this is an excellent illustration of the distinction between government's financing and government's providing a public service. Using detailed data on the production of fire protection, the study predicted that if Scottsdale had used a traditional government-operated fire department, its annual costs would have been 88 percent higher than what it actually paid the private firm.

▸ Key Terms

economic approach to government activity *393*

logrolling *394*

Policy Issue: You Decide

An Industrialization Plan

▸ The Action-Initiating Event

The opposition have been claiming that the country will never approach real economic growth rates like those experienced during the mid-1960s in the United States without systematic planning at the federal level. This is not a new presidential campaign issue. In fact, the opposition have been playing the same tune since the last presidential election campaign. However, our pollsters reported at last weekend's high-level campaign strategy meeting that the public is starting to take the opposition seriously. Apparently, voters have lost patience with the rate of economic growth in the country under the free market policies popularized by the government forces in the early 1980s. The leadership is afraid that the campaign could be hurt if we appear to have no position on the issue of federally directed growth programs. Obviously, the government cannot embrace the opposition proposals. The issue is whether we should offer a less government-directed program of our own or oppose any such program. We need some hard-headed analysis of the pros and cons of getting involved in the business of industrial planning at the national level.

▸ The Issue

There are three sets of issues to be addressed. First, there is the simple question of whether the slow rate of economic expansion in the United States in the last few years has in any way been attributable to a lack of economic planning that could have been undertaken at the national level. If recent economic performance in the United States could not have been improved upon by national planning, what could have been done that was not done? Other countries such as France, West Germany, the Soviet Union, and all of the Eastern bloc countries use some degree of central planning. How well have those countries performed in terms of economic growth compared to the United States in recent years? We all know that Japan has continued to experience rapid economic growth and that the Ministry for International Trade and Industry (MITI), is somehow involved in planning or making loans or conducting other activities related to economic development. The opposition are running all over the country claiming that MITI did this and MITI did that. How does MITI operate, and what if any evidence is there that MITI was at all responsible for Japan's rapid economic expansion in recent years?

A second set of issues that our political people will focus on involves the consequences for a democracy of moving toward central planning. Any philosophical thoughts you may have would be appreciated. However, we really would prefer that you concentrate on the economic issues.

The final set of issues we must consider is also economic rather than political. Suppose we opted not to endorse some form of national industrial planning. What economic reasons can we give for rejecting it? We know that the people at the top of the government's ticket lean in that direction philosophically. If we suppose for the sake of argument that voters are getting more sophisticated in their thinking on economic issues, we cannot simply wave the flag and say that planning is un-American. We will have to explain the kinds of economic nightmares that could emerge from federal industrial planning.

▸ Economic Policy Issues

To treat all of the foregoing systematically, you must pull together answers to the following set of economic questions: What have been some of the major reasons for slower than promised economic growth in the United States in recent years? Have countries that rely somewhat on central planning of industrial activities done as well or better than the United States in terms of economic growth in recent years? What is the planning role of MITI in Japan, and is it all that the opposition makes it out it to be? Can you give us some examples of how economic planning works in other countries? To the extent that we come down on the side of opposing federal industrial planning, can you provide some specific examples of how such planning creates more problems than it solves?

▸ Recommendations

We all know that the final decision on which direction the campaign takes will be made at the next level up in the election committee. However, there may be some second thoughts as election day gets closer—especially if it looks like a close race. For the moment, I want your best judgments regarding the specific questions that have been raised in this memorandum. However, I would appreciate your taking a litle extra time to pull together your own thoughts after responding to the questions posed above to provide me with your opinion on whether there is any role for federal industrial planning in our economy. If you think there could be such a role, what form would it have to take? I need that deeper insight from you in case we are ever faced with one of those eleventh hour strategy sessions and someone asks, "Now, what the hell do we do?"

Appendix A

Graphs

The economic models throughout this text are illustrated in diagrams called *graphs*. Graphing skills are essential for the analysis of economic problems, and this appendix is intended to outline the techniques and mechanics of graphing so that you may better understand and interpret these graphs. The following sections will familiarize you with the tools you will need. The best approach is to work through all of the examples in this appendix until you are satisfied that you can use the material confidently. A major mistake some beginning students of economics make is to try to memorize the graphs and then reproduce them for exams. You will find that this approach has a low probability of success. You should view the material presented here as essential not only for this course but any future courses in economics or other subjects in which graphs are important.

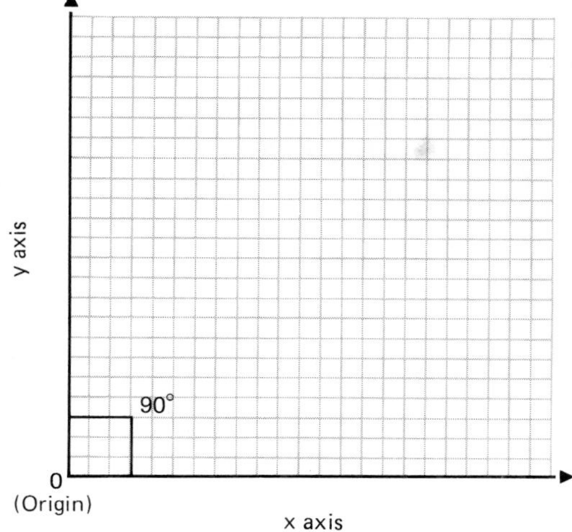

Figure 1

▸ What Is a Graph?

By illustrating economic relationships instead of merely talking about them, we can be much more precise, thus reinforcing your understanding of the subject matter. We depict many economic relationships by borrowing graphing techniques from mathematics. The basic idea of graphing is to illustrate the relationship between two measurable quantities that vary. These quantities are called *variables*. The basic layout of a graph is depicted in figure 1. Since we are going to examine the relationship between two variables, the graph is called a two-dimensional graph. We measure the two variables by means of two perpendicular lines called *axes*. Each axis represents the values of one of our two variables. The point of intersection for the axes is called the *origin* of the graph and is usually zero on both axes.

The next step is to assign values to our variables and then represent the values on the graph. This process is called *plotting* and begins with some representative values of the variables arranged in a table called a *schedule*. The schedule of values in table 1 will be used to plot the relationship between the two variables. The variables in this table represent the expected score on an economics midterm exam and the hours spent watching television the night before the exam. The two variables form associations called *ordered pairs,* which can be plotted on the graph. The first element of the ordered pair is associated with the horizontal or *x axis* on the graph. The second element of the ordered pair is associated with the vertical or *y axis* on the graph. In figure 2, the hours spent watching television the night before the exam are plotted on the x axis, and the expected scores on the exam are plotted on the y axis. After we plot the points from the schedule, we then connect the points to form a line. Notice that this straight line exhibits a downhill tilt from left to right. We call such a straight-line graph a *linear* graph that illustrates an *inverse* or *negative relationship* between the two variables. In other words, when one of the variables increases the other variable decreases. In this example, we say that your exam score is inversely or negatively related to the number of hours you spend watching television.

Some schedules of variables exhibit a *direct* or *positive relationship.* This means that as one variable becomes larger, the other variable also increases. Such a schedule is shown in table 2. We illustrate this data in figure 3 by plotting the number of hours spent studying for an economics exam on the x axis and the expected exam scores on the y axis. The

Table 1

Exam scores	Hours spent watching television
100	0
90	2
80	4
70	6

Table 2

Expected exam scores	Hours spent studying
60	1
70	2
80	3
90	4

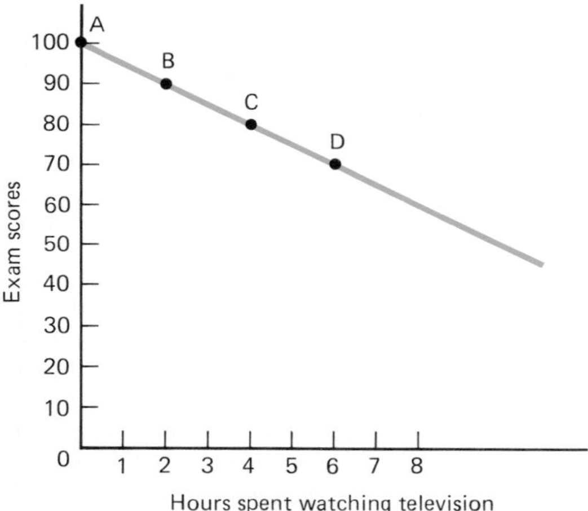

Figure 2

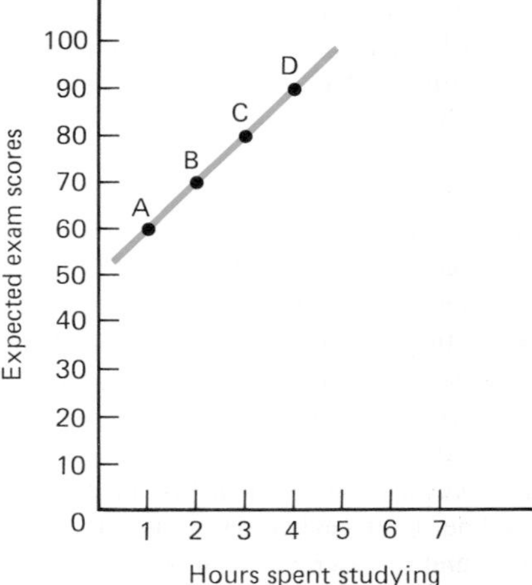

Figure 3

interpretation of this graph is that the more hours you spend studying for the exam, the higher you can expect your exam score to be. Notice that this linear graph tilts uphill from left to right. This indicates a positive or direct relationship between two variables. You should be able to see by now that one of the key advantages of using and understanding graphs is to be able to tell at a glance whether two variables are positively or negatively related without examining every line of a schedule.

A third type of relationship is frequently encountered in economics. Certain variables exhibit no relationship between each other. This situation is graphed in figure 4. The number of hours in a week (168) is constant and therefore is not influenced by the value of the other variable on the graph, the scores on the exam. We represent the fixed number of hours in a week by drawing a horizontal line parallel to the x axis at 168 on the y axis. This illustration indicates that no matter what the score on the economics exam, the number of hours in a week is still 168.

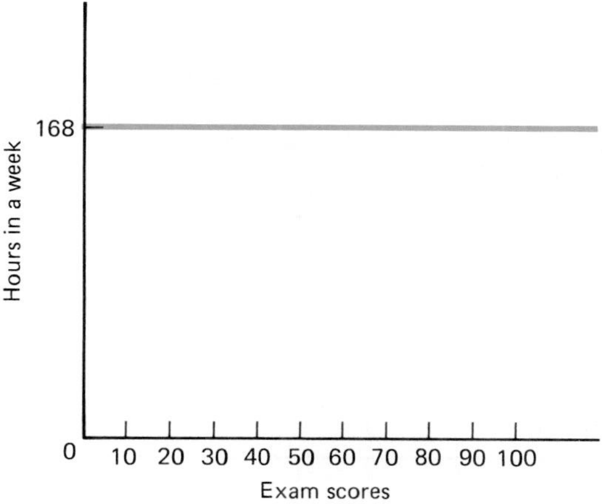

Figure 4

Not all relationships between variables in economics are linear. Variables sometimes exhibit a *nonlinear* or *curvilinear relationship* with each other. In general, a nonlinear relationship between two variables indicates that the relationship changes as the variables change value. (In the previous examples, the variables exhibited the same relationship regardless of their size.) We illustrate a curvilinear relationship between two variables in figure 5. The y axis shows the number of pages typed per hour, and the x axis shows the number of hours spent typing. The hill-shaped curve that shows the relationship between the two variables indicates that as the typist begins to type, typing speed accelerates as the typist becomes familiar with the typewriter and the material being typed. The maximum number of pages typed per hour occurs at six hours. After that, the number of pages typed per hour begins to fall, probably because the typist is tired and makes more mistakes. The curvilinear graph in figure 5 exhibits both uphill and downhill tilt.

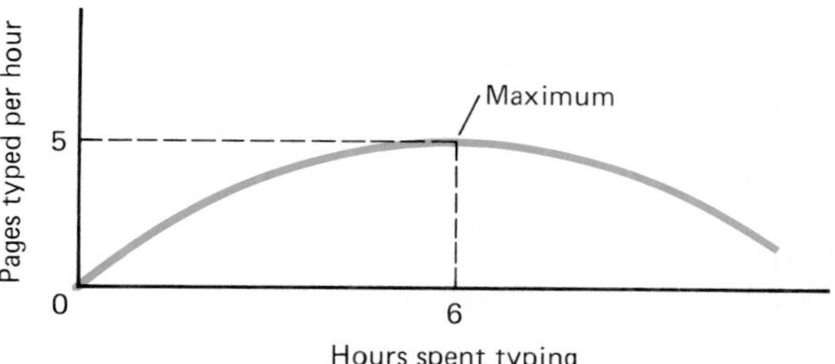

Figure 5

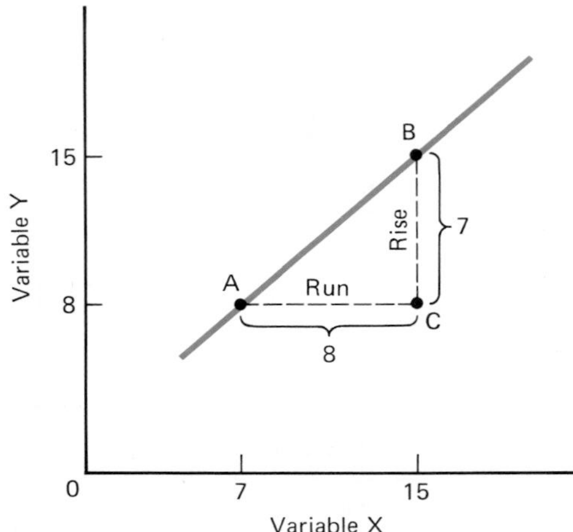

Figure 6

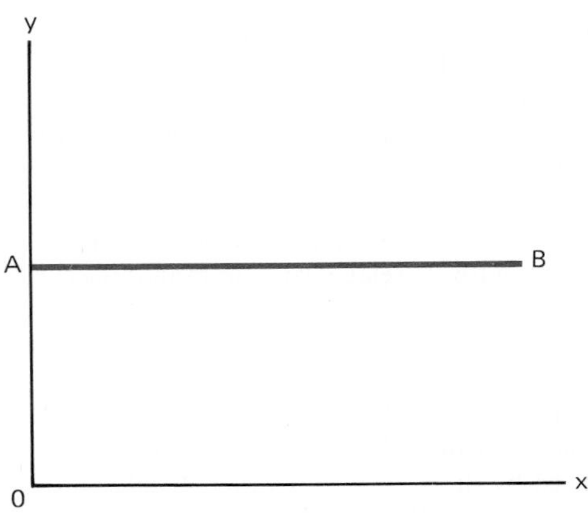

Figure 7

▸ Slope

Until now, we have referred to the tilt of the line as being either uphill or downhill. The tilt of the line can be measured more precisely with a concept known as *slope*. The slope of a straight line measures the relative change in the two variables that are graphed. Specifically, the formula for slope is the ratio of the difference between two values of the y-axis variable to the difference between the corresponding values of the x-axis variable. In the language we previously used, the slope measures the degree of the tilt of the line. In figure 6, a positive linear relationship is illustrated between two variables called X and Y. Notice the triangle ABC. The height of this triangle, CB, measures the amount of *rise* in the line between points A and B. The base of the triangle, AC, measures the horizontal distance between A and B. This distance is referred to as the *run* between two points. Therefore, a good way to remember the formula for the slope of a line is "rise over run," or in our figure, the distance BC divided by the distance AC. Having an intuitive feel for what slope is, we can measure precisely the slope of a line with the following formula:

$$\text{Slope} = \frac{Y_2 - Y_1}{X_2 - X_1},$$

where Y_2 and X_2 represent the ordered pair associated with point B, and Y_1 and X_1 represent the ordered pair associated with point A. In the text, we usually use the symbol Δ to indicate a change in a variable, such as the change in Y between Y_1 and Y_2 or in X between X_1 and X_2. Using this symbol, the formula for slope becomes

$$\text{slope} = \frac{\Delta Y}{\Delta X},$$

where ΔY represents $Y_2 - Y_1$ and ΔX represents $X_2 - X_1$. Substituting for the variables in the slope formula, the slope of this line is $+7/8$. The slope of a straight line is always the same everywhere on the line so it does not matter which pair of points we choose to calculate the slope. If the sign of the slope is positive, the line exhibits a positive or direct relationship. If the sign of the slope is negative, the line exhibits an inverse or negative relationship. Go back to figure 2 and prove to yourself that the slope of the line shown there is negative. (Hint: What value of $X_2 - X_1$ is required to increase your score by ten points?)

Figures 7 and 8 illustrate two special cases of slope. In figure 7, the horizontal line drawn parallel to the x axis has a slope equal to zero. This line has zero slope because there is no rise to the line regardless of the length of the run. Figure 8 depicts a line drawn parallel to the y axis. This line has infinite slope because the rise is infinite and the run is zero.

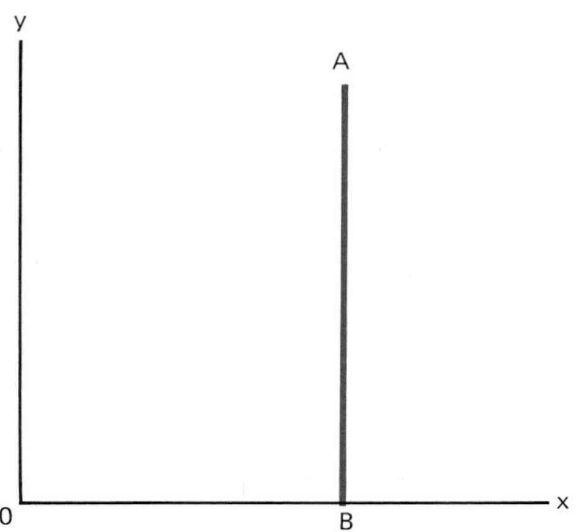

Figure 8

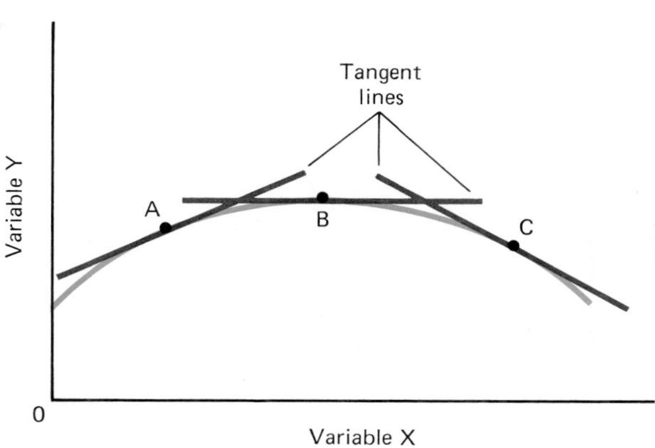

Figure 9

These special cases are used frequently in economics, and it is therefore necessary to recognize and understand them.

How do you measure the slope of a curvilinear relationship? We can see by inspection that the slope of a curve such as that in figure 5 is not always the same. It continually changes at each point along the curve. The answer to the question is surprisingly simple because we can apply the previous method for measuring the slope of a straight line. Figure 9 depicts a curvilinear relationship between the variables X and Y. Since the curve does not have a constant slope, we have to measure the slope at particular points along the curve. The procedure is to draw straight lines that touch the curve only at the points at which we want to measure the curve's slope. Such lines are called *tangent lines* and are illustrated in figure 9. The next step is to calculate the slopes of the tangent lines using the previous formula. In figure 9, the curve has a positive slope at point A. At point B, the maximum, the curve has zero slope, and at point C, the curve has a negative slope.

An important but often ignored problem with slope measurements is that they are sensitive to the units of measurement used for plotting the variables on the graph. This problem often leads to misinterpretations of the graph. For example, suppose that you want to measure the altitude of an airplane at various points in time after the airplane leaves the ground. You can measure the altitude in feet or miles. But when you plot your results with altitude on the y axis and time on the x axis, the slope of the graph measured in miles will be much smaller than the slope of the graph measured in feet. With slope interpreted as the rate of change of altitude with respect to time, the graph measured in miles will give the impression of a slowly climbing airplane. The graph measured in feet will give the impression of a rapidly climbing airplane. Since data in economics are often measured in different units, economists frequently avoid this problem with slope by emphasizing *percentage changes* for the variables. In this example, when the altitude of the airplane increases from 500 feet to 1,000 feet, there is a percentage change of 100 percent. If you measured the same altitude change in miles, you would still have a 100 percent change in altitude. This approach to plotting data avoids the pitfalls in the interpretation of the slope.

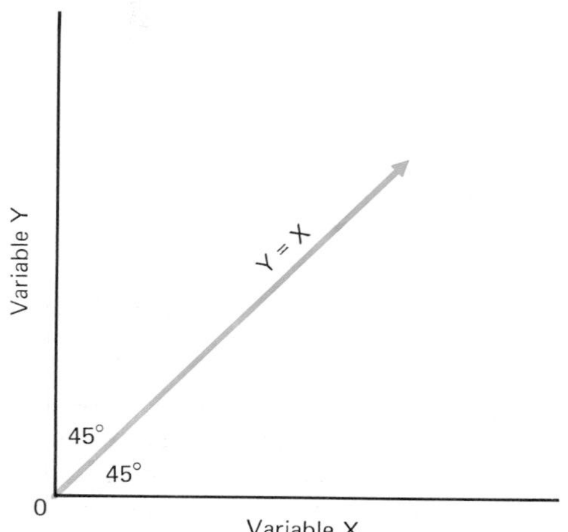

Figure 10

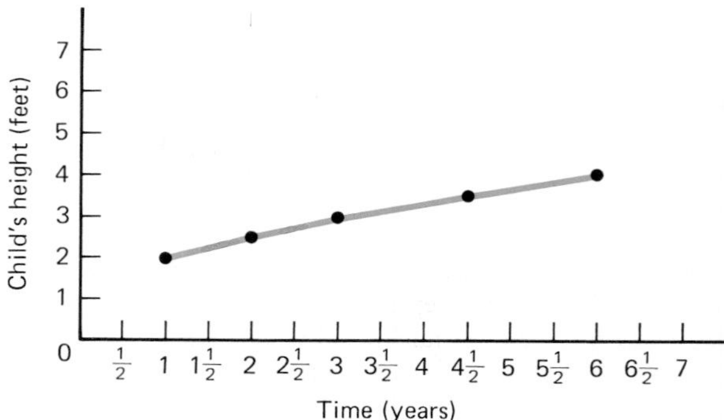

Figure 11

Special Graphs

Certain graphs in this text are designed for special situations in which measuring the sign or magnitude of the slope is not the focus of the analysis. This section explains these graphs and their purpose.

A linear graph starting at the origin is called a *ray*. A particular ray that makes a 45-degree angle with the x and y axes has the slope of +1. It has the special feature that for every point on the ray, the variables X and Y are equal as in figure 10. In other words, this ray is a plotting of the points Y = X. The ordered pairs on this ray would be (1,1), (2,2), (10,10), and so on. This line is used as a reference line in economics to illuminate other economic relationships.

A *time-series graph* is useful in illustrating certain economic variables. Such graphs are characterized by the variable time's being plotted on the horizontal axis. The basic idea is to show how some variable changes over time. In figure 11, a child's height is plotted against time. We can see that as the child ages, his or her height increases. Not all economic variables change smoothly over time and are illustrated by time-series graphs that resemble the teeth of a handsaw.

Another graph that is frequently used to illustrate changes in a variable over time is the *bar chart*. The focus here is not on the rate of change on the variable as much as on comparing the levels of the variable over time or among different groups of people. Figure 12 shows hypothetical data on average income among different age-groups in the form of a bar graph. Notice that the bar graph emphasizes the difference in the levels of income among the age-groups.

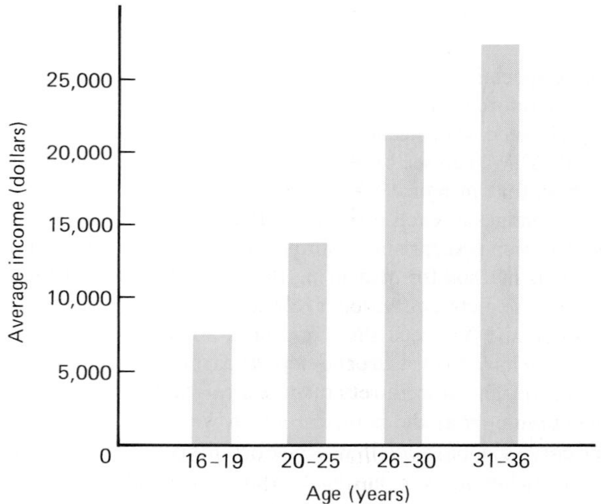

Figure 12

Conclusion

The purpose of this appendix is to illustrate and explain various graphing techniques and the uses of special graphs in economics. Remember these two key points: (1) This material should be well understood now so that graphs will become a useful tool for economic analysis and not an obstacle. (2) It is not sound strategy to memorize various graphs in the text and try to reproduce them for an exam. Instead, try to understand how the graphs are drawn so that you can use them yourself to illustrate various topics in economics.

Appendix B

How to Solve the Policy Issues

You will find a policy issue at the end of each major section of this book. These issues represent puzzles to help you apply basic economics to important social decisions. The purpose of these puzzles is to give you a chance to use the information you have learned to analyze important economic issues. Most puzzles assume that you are a staff economist for a government agency and require you to provide input into a decision that will be made by your boss, who holds a major political office. We want to get you off to a good start by listing the steps you should follow for solving the policy issues, which all have some common major features. We will use the puzzle following section 1 to illustrate a basic approach to the policy issues that follow later sections.

▸ Steps for Solving the Policy Issues

1. *Identify the problem*
   Identify the main issue or problem to be addressed. List any subproblems that may exist. Be able to distinguish between the main problem and the subproblems.
2. *Sort out the issues*
   What groups are involved? What are their objectives/priorities? What concerns do they have regarding the main problem? What discrepancies and overlaps exist between the objectives of the various groups?
3. *List and evaluate alternative solutions*
   Develop various solutions to the main problem identified in step 1. Analyze how the solutions affect the groups identified in step 2. Who are the winners and losers? Do the "wins" offset the "losses"? Are the priorities of some groups more significant than those of others? If you cannot develop a priority list of the objectives of the various groups, is a compromise possible? What are the benefits and drawbacks of a compromise?
4. *Recommend a solution to the problem*
   Given your analysis in step 3, select and defend a solution to the problem.

Now, together, let's work through the policy issue that follows Part I, "Who Should Pay for Clean Air?"

▸ Identifying the Problem

The first thing you may have noticed is that the policy issue asks you to address several related questions at the same time. The puzzle embraces a number of economic policy issues that vary in difficulty and clarity. Each member of the city council will have his or her own idea regarding which issues are more important than others. One member may decide whether or not to support the ordinance primarily on the basis of its potential effects on business owners. Another may feel that the impact on workers deserves more consideration, while still another member of the council may view the interests of taxpayers as a group as most important. You will also need to consider whether the council has asked you all of the important questions. If not, what other questions do you think the council should consider in deciding how to vote?

As an economic analyst you will often have to make your own decisions about the relative importance of the questions asked of you and whether or not to try to convince your employer to consider other questions that you think are important but have not been asked explicitly. Moreover, since those who ask you the questions will not usually have your expertise, you will have to figure out how to provide an answer that will clearly sort out the issues but without too much technical jargon.

Any social policy issue will involve both objective, or positive, questions about how a particular policy will work and value, or normative, questions about what should be done. Since your value judgments may be different from those of some council members, you will want to provide the council with as clear an indication as possible of the positive and normative elements of your analysis.

▸ Getting Started

Recall that in chapter 1 we introduced the idea of developing a model in order to focus on the key elements of an economic issue. What economic models and concepts have you learned about in chapter 1 that you can use to discuss the pros and cons of providing the city with clean air? What kinds of data will you need to give council members quantitative measures of the opportunity costs of different amounts of improved air quality? What sources of statistical information do you know of that will enable you to obtain these data? (Hint: Look in the source notes to various tables and figures in the text and in the reference section for each chapter at the end of the text for some suggestions.)

With respect to affected parties, can you think of conditions that would increase the likelihood that clean air legislation would actually cause some manufacturing enterprises to leave the city? Under what circumstances would you expect the ordinance to lower wages and/or create serious unemployment problems? Are there conditions under which the tax burden would be so severe that taxpayers would rebel and vote council members out of office? Are there circumstances under which you would recommend that compliance with the new clean air standards be required immediately? Would you ever recommend that firms be allowed several years to comply with the new standards?

In summary, you will be most successful in providing council members with the information they need if you can help them identify the important issues. Each question you have been asked can be broken down into several related questions that help to clarify the pros and cons of the proposed ordinance. Furthermore, your judgments about what will happen if the law is passed will be clearer if you can provide facts instead of mere guesses about the consequences of the clean air legislation.

Now go ahead and draft your memo for the city council. Later, after you have studied additional chapters and added to the simple tools of analysis now at your command, take another look at the clean air issue. We guarantee that your added study of economics will have changed some of your judgments about the likely impact of the ordinance. You will have a clearer idea of what the relevant issues are and how to present them to the council members for consideration.

References

Chapter 1

1. "Economics of Life and Death Arises in Debate over Kidney Therapy," *New York Times*, 25 May 1982.
2. This discussion is based on Charles Lave, "The Cost of Going 55," *Newsweek*, 23 Oct. 1978.

Chapter 2

1. *Economic Report of the President* (Washington, D.C.: U.S. Government Printing Office). Copies may be obtained from the Superintendent of Documents, U.S. Government Printing Office, Washington, D.C. 20402.
2. See, for example, *Economic Report of the President, 1983* (Washington, D.C.: U.S. Government Printing Office), Tables B–76, B–77, and B–78.
3. See Organization for Economic Cooperation and Development (OECD), *The Hidden Economy in the Context of National Accounts* (Paris: OECD, 1981); John W. Kendrick, "Expanding Imputed Values in the National Income and Product Accounts," *Review of Income and Wealth*, Dec. 1979, pp. 349–63; Edward F. Denison, "Is U.S. Growth Underrated Because of the Underground Economy? Employment Ratios Suggest Not." *Review of Income and Wealth*, 1982.
4. *Economic Report of the President, 1983*, Table B–34, p. 202.
5. *Economic Report of the President, 1983*, p. 30.
6. See, for instance, Belton M. Fleisher, *The Economics of Delinquency* (Chicago: Quadrangle Books, 1966).

Chapter 3

1. For more discussion, see the *Economic Report of the President, 1983* (Washington, D.C.: U.S. Government Printing Office), pp. 46–49.
2. If your local library has a collection of videotapes of television documentaries, view the NBC White Paper, "America Works When America Works," originally broadcast 25 June 1981. This program deals with structural unemployment, and it contains interviews with steelworkers who refused to move from their hometown of Youngstown, Ohio, despite tremendously reduced job opportunities in the steel industry. The interviews are a chilling reminder of the substantial emotional upheaval that can accompany the thought of leaving home for a job in another part of the country.
3. See the *Economic Report of the President, 1983*, p. 44.
4. Ibid., pp. 46–47.
5. See "Labor Seeks Less," *Business Week*, 21 Dec. 1981, pp. 82–88.
6. See *Economic Report of the President, 1983*, p. 29.

Chapter 4

1. "Socking It Away, Drop in Inflation Spurs Many to Cut Spending and Increase Saving," *Wall Street Journal*, 9 Dec. 1982, p. 1.
2. *The Economic Report of the President, 1983* (Washington, D.C.: U.S. Government Printing Office), Table B-24.
3. "Taking a Chance, Accent Is on Growth as Tax Law Changes Many Investors' Ways," *Wall Street Journal*, 13 Jan. 1982.

Chapter 5

1. Milton and Rose Friedman, *Free to Choose* (New York: Harcourt Brace Jovanovich, 1980), p. 252.
2. See J. Huston McCulloch, *Money and Inflation*, 2d ed. (New York: Academic Press, 1982). For those who would like to study money and inflation in greater depth, McCulloch's book is an excellent and highly readable source.
3. See *Federal Reserve Bulletin*, Feb. 1983, p. A18.
4. For a fascinating, easy-to-read history of money in the United States, see Arthur Nussbaum, *A History of the Dollar* (New York: Columbia University Press, 1957).
5. For more precise definitions of M1, M2, and M3, see a recent issue of the *Federal Reserve Bulletin*, which is published by the Board of Governors of the Federal Reserve System and is available in most libraries.

Chapter 6

1. *American Banker*, 6 Jan. 1986, p. 10.
2. See two opposing articles by Jeffrey E. Garten and William M. Isaac under the title "Dealing with a Changed Banking System," *Wall Street Journal*, 29 May 1984; Michael J. Boskin, "Going Overboard on Bank Bailouts," *Wall Street Journal*, 23 Aug. 1984; and George J. Benston, "Why the Government Can't Run a Bank," *New York Times*, 29 July 1984.

3. See "Extra Duty: Fed's Chief Took on Big Role in Attacking World's Financial Ills," *Wall Street Journal*, 14 Mar. 1983; "FDIC Surprise," *Wall Street Journal*, 15 Apr. 1983; "U.S. Will Invest $4.5 Billion in Rescue of Chicago Bank, Vowing More if Needed," *New York Times*, 27 July 1984; and George A. Benston, "Why the Government Can't Run a Bank," *New York Times*, 29 July 1984.

Chapter 7

1. For example, between 1940 and 1959, the federal government had budget surpluses during eight years. See *Economic Report of the President, 1983* (Washington, D.C.: U.S. Government Printing Office, 1983), table B-75.
2. *Statistical Abstract of the United States 1986*, table 781.

Chapter 8

1. Victor Zarnowitz, "Recent Work on Business Cycles in Historical Perspective: A Review of Theories and Evidence," *Journal of Economic Literature*, June 1985, pp. 523–580, tables 2 and 3.

Chapter 9

1. All data are taken from *Historical Statistics of the United States, Colonial Times to 1970*.
2. Ibid., Series F125.
3. The Phillips curve is so-named because of research reported by an Australian economist, A. S. H. Phillips, "The Relationship Between Unemployment and the Rate of Change of Money Wage Rates in the United Kingdom, 1861–1967," *Economica*, Nov. 1958. However, it would have been fairer to name it the Fisher curve, after the famous American economist Irving Fisher, who pointed out the relationship between unemployment and inflation over thirty years earlier in an article entitled "A Statistical Relation Between Unemployment and Price Changes," *International Labour Review*, June 1926; reprinted in *Journal of Political Economy*, Mar./Apr. 1973.

Chapter 10

1. "State Highway Work on Hold," *Columbus Dispatch*, 29 Apr. 1983. Further examples of the implementation lag of government expenditures are contained in the *Economic Report of the President, 1983*, pp. 39–41.
2. Stephen A. Holland, "The Impact of Inflation Uncertainty on the Labor Market," *Federal Reserve Bank of St. Louis Review*, Aug./Sept. 1984, pp. 26–27.

Chapter 11

1. *Historical Statistics of the United States, Colonial Times to 1970*, p. 226.
2. James R. Barth and Stephen O. Morrell, "A Primer on Budget Deficits," Federal Reserve Bank of Atlanta *Review*, Aug. 1982, pp. 6–17.

Chapter 12

1. For an informative overview of the areas of agreement and disagreement among economists, see "How to Get the Country Moving Again: Advice from Six Nobel Prize Economists," *U.S. News & World Report*, 31 Jan. 1983, pp. 66–71.
2. For an interesting discussion of Keynes' impact on economics, see Paul A. Samuelson, "The House That Keynes Built," *New York Times*, 29 May 1983. See also the four articles by Nobel Laureates Sir John Hicks, Paul Samuelson, Friedrich Hayek, and Milton Friedman entitled "The Keynes Centenary," *The Economist*, 4, 11, 18, and 25 June 1983.
3. *Economic Report of the President, 1984*, table 1.1, p. 29.
4. Ibid.
5. For detailed statistics on the government budgets of other nations, see International Monetary Fund, *World Economic Outlook* (Washington, D.C.: International Monetary Fund, 1984), table 1.1, p. 100.
6. Ibid.
7. *Economic Report of the President, 1984*, table 1.2, p. 36.
8. *Economic Report of the President, 1983*. See also Alan S. Blinder, "Monetization of Deficits," Working Paper No. 1052 (Cambridge, Mass.: National Bureau of Economic Research, Inc., 1983).
9. "Budget Estimates and Realities," *New York Times*, 9 Feb. 1982.
10. See "When Inflation Rate Is 116,200%, Prices Change by the Hour," *Wall Street Journal*, 7 Feb. 1985.
11. The Ricardian equivalence hypothesis, or theorem, is named after the famous nineteenth-century economist David Ricardo. See Robert J. Barro, *Macroeconomics* (New York: John Wiley & Sons, 1984), chap. 15.
12. See Robert J. Barro, "A Deficit Nearly on Target," *Wall Street Journal*, 19 Jan. 1985.

Chapter 13

1. *Statistical Abstract of the United States 1981*, table 1551.
2. *Statistical Abstract of the United States 1981*, table 1514, p. 846.
3. John M. Culbertson, " 'Free Trade' Is Impoverishing the West," *New York Times*, 28 July 1985. For a view that is much more widely accepted among economists, see Herbert Stein, "Best-Selling Fiction: 3 Million Jobs," *Wall Street Journal*, 29 July 1985.

Chapter 14

1. *Statistical Abstract of the United States 1981*.
2. Ibid.
3. See, for instance, "Coast Jobs Disappear through 'Gateway to Pacific,' " *New York Times*, 26 Nov. 1982.
4. See "GM Needs Toyota Efficiency," *New York Times*, 16 Feb. 1983.
5. This example is especially relevant because the United States imposed a new set of tariffs on so-called *specialty* steel, which is a low-

volume, high-value product considered vital for national defense, telecommunications, aerospace, and oil refining. In 1982, specialty steel accounted for about 2 percent of tonnage but about 10 percent of the value of total steel production in the United States. See "U.S. Places Tough Curbs on Imports of Specialty Steel," *Washington Post,* 6 July 1983, p. A1.

6. Bennett D. Baack and Edward J. Ray, "Tariff Policy and Income Distribution: The Case of the United States 1830–1860," *Explorations in Economic History,* Winter 1974, pp. 103–121.
7. Bennett D. Baack and Edward J. Ray, "Tariff Policy and Comparative Advantage in the Iron and Steel Industry: 1870–1929," *Explorations in Economic History,* Fall 1973, pp. 3–24.
8. Recent United States trade restrictions on specialty steel also include quotas; see "The Fight Over Steel Quotas," *New York Times,* 22 Aug. 1984.
9. For data on United States automobile imports, see *The Brookings Review,* Summer 1984, table 1, p. 9.
10. Ibid., table 4, p. 11.
11. Ibid., table 5, p. 11.
12. David G. Tarr and Morris E. Morkre, "Aggregate Costs to the United States of Tariffs and Quotas on Imports," Bureau of Economics Staff Report to the Federal Trade Commission, Dec. 1984, table 4, p. 4.
13. Ibid.
14. Ibid.
15. See John M. Starrels, "Steel's Stiff Competition," *Wall Street Journal,* 9 July 1982.
16. Ibid.
17. United States Department of Labor, reported in "Steel's Elusive Search for a New Deal," *New York Times,* 18 Nov. 1982.
18. Ibid.
19. For details, see "Steel Union Leaders Ratify Concessions," *New York Times,* 1 Mar. 1983.

Chapter 15

1. See David Glasner, "The Much-Maligned U.S. Trade Gap," *New York Times,* 21 Oct. 1984.
2. *Statistical Abstract of the United States 1986,* tables 1433 and 1472.
3. *Statistical Abstract of the United States 1982/83,* tables 693 and 1524.
4. *Economic Report of the President, 1984,* table B101, p. 335.
5. International Monetary Fund, "Exchange Rate Volatility and World Trade," *Occasional Paper No. 28.* (Washington, D. C.: International Monetary Fund, 1984), p. 43.
6. "Oil Cut to Hurt Poorer Nations," *New York Times,* 7 Mar. 1983.

Chapter 16

1. International Monetary Fund, *World Economic Outlook, 1984* (Washington, D.C.: International Monetary Fund), table 3.2, p. 130.
2. Ibid, table 8, p. 174.
3. Ibid., table 10, p. 176.
4. For values of foreign exchange rates, see *Statistical Abstract of the United States 1984,* table 1538, p. 887.
5. International Monetary Fund, *World Economic Outlook, 1984,* table 36, p. 206.

Chapter 17

1. *Economic Report of the President, 1985,* table B-24.
2. *Economic Report of the President, 1983,* chapter 4.
3. See Ibid.; Ralph E. Winter, "Multiple Choice, Many Culprits Named in National Slowdown of Productivity Gains," *Wall Street Journal,* 21 Oct. 1981, p. 1; and Ralph E. Winter, "Paper Weight, Many Businesses Blame Governmental Policies for Productivity Lag," *Wall Street Journal,* 28 Oct. 1981, p. 1.
4. Ralph E. Winter, "Gauging Growth, Productivity Debate Is Clouded by Problem of Measuring Its Lag," *Wall Street Journal,* 14 Oct. 1981, p. 1.
5. Ralph E. Winter, "Multiple Choice."
6. Barbara Toohey, "Sexual Revolution Wrecks U.S. Productivity," *Wall Street Journal,* 8 May 1981, p. 26. Ms. Toohey is a librarian who formulates economic theories for pleasure in her spare time.
7. *Economic Indicators, December 1984* (Washington, D.C.: United States Government Printing Office), p. 16.
8. John Kendrick, "Productivity Gains Will Continue," *Wall Street Journal,* 29 Aug. 1984, p. 22.
9. *Economic Report of the President, 1984,* p. 90.
10. Ibid., p. 89.
11. Geoffrey Carliner, "Japanese Industrial Policy and U.S. Trade Policy," memorandum to the Council of Economic Advisers, Executive Office of the President, Washington, D.C., 25 July 1983.
12. Ibid.
13. Ibid.
14. Ibid.
15. Ibid.
16. Charles L. Schultze, "Industrial Policy: A Dissent," *The Brookings Review,* Fall 1983, pp. 3–12.
17. *Economic Report of the President, 1984,* p. 97.
18. For such a debate, see "Do We Need Industrial Policy? The True Cost of Economic Change," *Harper's,* Feb. 1985, pp. 35–48. See also, Kim Kiwhan "A Case Study in the Perils of Industrial Policy," *Wall Street Journal,* 22 June 1983; and "Helping Business, Japanese Style." *New York Times,* 17 Nov. 1981.
19. For discussion of an attempt to introduce industrial policy into the United States, see Tamar Lewin, "Putting Industrial Policy to a Vote," *New York Times,* 10 June 1984; and Howard Kurtz, "A 'New Idea' Fizzles on Launch, Skeptical Rhode Islanders Wouldn't Go for 'Industrial Policy,' " *Washington Post,* 15 July 1984, p. B5.

Chapter 18

1. *Statistical Abstract of the United States 1982/83,* table 1530, p. 870.
2. *Statistical Abstract of the United States 1986,* table 655, p. 385.
3. See, for example, "Russian Economy Gives Andropov Huge Problems," *New York Times,* 12 June 1983.
4. See Martin Feldstein, "An Economist Looks at China's New Economy," *Wall Street Journal,* 8 July 1982; and D. Gale Johnson, *Progress of Economic Reform in the People's Republic of China* (Washington, D.C., American Enterprise Institute, 1982).
5. "Hungary Builds Lively Economy on West's Ideas," *New York Times,* 3 Dec. 1981.
6. Bruno Koeppl, "Tricks of the Arms Trade," *Newsweek,* 21 Apr. 1980, p. 21.
7. See, for instance, Gregory Grossman, "Notes on the Illegal Private Economy and Corruption," in Joint Economic Committee, *Soviet Economy in a Time of Change,* vol. 1 (Washington, D.C.: U.S. Government Printing Office, 1979).
8. N. Khrushchev, *Khrushchev Remembers,* ed. and trans. Strobe Talbott (Boston: Little, Brown, 1970), pp. 519–520.

Appendix to Chapter 18

1. See, for example, "Trade War Feared Over Food Export Issue," *New York Times,* 22 Feb. 1983.
2. See "VA May Face Crisis as Veterans Turn 65 and Seek Free Care," *New York Times,* 26 Feb. 1983.
3. Sharon P. Smith, "Pay Differentials between Federal Government and Private Sector Workers," *Industrial and Labor Relations Review,* (Jan. 1976), pp. 179–199.
4. Robert M. Spann, "Public Versus Private Provision of Government Services," in *Budgets and Bureaucrats,* ed. Thomas E. Borcherding (Durham, N.C.: Duke University Press, 1977), pp. 71–89.

Glossary

▶ **accelerated inflation** An accelerated inflation is one in which the percentage rate of increase of prices increases from year to year.

ad valorem tariff An ad valorem tariff is defined in percentage terms rather than a specific amount.

aggregate demand and supply curves The aggregate demand and supply curves describe the relationship between the price level and the quantities of GNP demanded and supplied, respectively.

aggregate demand for labor [D(L)] The aggregate demand curve for labor [D(L)] illustrates the total number of workers that society's firms wish to hire at various real wage rates.

aggregate demand for loanable funds (DLF) The aggregate demand for loanable funds (DLF) is a schedule illustrating the total amount of loanable funds borrowers seek to borrow at various real interest rates.

aggregate economics Aggregate economics is a synonym for macroeconomics that reminds us that in order to be manageable, macroeconomic analysis must summarize the workings of an entire economy as the behavior of a few aggregate measures of economic performance including the inflation and unemployment rates.

aggregate supply curve of labor [S(L)] The aggregate supply of labor [S(L)] illustrates the total number of people in society who want employment at the various real wage rates that might exist.

aggregate supply of loanable funds (SLF) The aggregate supply of loanable funds (SLF) is a schedule illustrating the total amount of loanable funds lenders offer at various real interest rates.

appreciation Appreciation refers to an increase in an exchange rate under a flexible exchange rate system.

automatic fiscal stabilizers Automatic fiscal stabilizers are fiscal policies that do not require new legislation or executive decisions to become effective because they are built into existing laws.

▶ **balance of payments** The balance of payments is the accounting for the flow of goods and services and the means of paying for them among international trading partners.

balance of payments on current account The balance of payments on current account is equal to the exports of merchandise, military items, and services plus gifts to the United States less imports of merchandise, military items and services, and gifts to other countries.

balance of trade The balance of trade is equal to a country's merchandise exports minus its merchandise imports.

bank A bank is a financial institution that accepts deposits and makes loans.

bank run A bank run occurs when a large proportion of a bank's depositors want to withdraw their funds all at once.

barter economy A barter economy is one in which money plays an unimportant role and in which goods and services are traded directly.

base year The base year is the date at which a cost of living index is set equal to 100 for the purpose of comparison with other years.

basic accounting identity The basic accounting identity describes the structure of all balance sheets; it says that net worth is defined as the difference between assets and liabilities.

business cycle The business cycle is the pattern of recession followed by recovery that characterizes the United States and other market economies.

▶ **capital account** The capital account is the section of the balance of payments accounts that indicates how the current account balance has been financed; it indicates international currency flows plus borrowing and lending.

capitalist economic system A capitalist economic system is one in which private property and free markets are the principal institutions determining the answers to the basic economic questions.

cash drain Cash drain is the flow of money into the public's holding of currency when there is an increase in the total money stock.

central bank The central bank is a nation's monetary authority and is responsible for determining the quantity of money under a paper monetary standard.

ceteris paribus *Ceteris paribus* means that all but one factor influencing some form of economic behavior (such as demand) are assumed not to change.

change in supply A change in supply or a change (shift) in the supply curve is a movement of the supply curve to the right (an increase in supply) or left (a decrease or reduction in supply). A change in the quantity supplied at every price results when the supply curve shifts to the right or left. Such a shift occurs when there is a change in a factor that affects the supply of a good or service other than the good's or the service's own price.

circular flow of GNP The circular flow of GNP refers to the flow of money back and forth between the buyers and sellers of society's output and means that GNP can be calculated in either of two ways—as the flow of payments for the products of society or as the payments for the inputs used to make society's output.

commodity standard of money Under a commodity standard of money, the quantity of money is determined by the amount of a specific commodity, such as gold.

commodity terms of trade The commodity terms of trade measures the quantity of imports that a country can obtain for a given quantity of the goods it exports. It is the ratio of the price of exports divided by the price of imports.

common market A common market is a customs union that also allows the free movement of labor and capital among its member countries.

comparative advantage Comparative advantage is determined by which producer has the lowest opportunity cost of producing a good or service. Since opportunity cost is measured in terms of the quantity of one good or service that must be sacrificed to produce one more unit of another good or service, *everyone* has a *comparative* advantage in producing *something.*

competitive firms Competitive firms are price takers in the market for the good or service they produce and in the markets for the inputs that they use.

consumer price index (CPI) The consumer price index (CPI) for the United States is a number that represents the cost of purchasing a representative group of goods and services relative to some time in the past.

consumption Consumption refers to households' expenditures on goods and services to be used primarily during the year in question.

consumption function The consumption function is a schedule, or equation, indicating society's total intended consumption expenditures at various levels of aggregate real income.

controlled economies Controlled economies are characterized by controlled markets, in which prices, and sometimes quantities bought and sold, are mandated by law or government decree. Some transactions may occur in uncontrolled markets.

corporate profits Corporate profits represent the income people receive from dividends paid to them on the stocks they own and earnings retained by the corporation for reinvestment.

cost-push inflation Cost-push inflation is caused by increases in costs that shift the aggregate supply curve to the left.

countercyclical fiscal policy Countercyclical fiscal policy is fiscal policy designed explicitly to moderate fluctuations in GNP and employment.

credit markets Credit markets are markets in which loans of various time lengths are arranged between borrowers and lenders.

crowding out Crowding out means that an increase in the government deficit raises the interest rate, leading to a reduction in planned private investment expenditure.

current prices Current prices are the prices of goods and services actually in effect during the year in question.

customs union A customs union is a group of nations that impose a common set of trade barriers against the rest of the world but none among themselves.

cyclical unemployment Cyclical unemployment results when workers are laid off because the aggregate demand for output declines and firms cut back on production.

▶ **debt-service ratio** The debt-service ratio is a country's payments of principal and interest on its external debt divided by the value of its exports.

demand Demand is the relationship between the desire to buy various quantities of a good or service and its price.

demand curve A demand curve for a good or service is a geometric representation of demand.

demand deposits Demand deposits include any bank account from which the owner may demand immediate payment to the owner or to a third party by means of a check, telephone call, or telegram.

demand for labor The demand for labor is the relationship that defines the quantity of labor a firm would like to hire at various real wage rates.

demand-induced inflation Demand-induced inflation is caused by forces that shift the aggregate demand curve to the right.

depository institution A depository institution accepts deposits from the general public and from other banks.

Depository Institutions Deregulation and Monetary Control Act of 1980 The Depository Institutions Deregulation and Monetary Control Act of 1980 extends control of the Fed to all depository institutions and provides for greater competition among banks and for eventual decontrol of most interest rates they charge and pay.

depreciation Depreciation refers to a decline in a currency's exchange rate under a flexible exchange rate system.

depression A depression is a very severe recession, a period of time when a very severe decline in real GNP is occurring.

devaluation Devaluation occurs when a country makes its currency cheaper in terms of other countries' currencies under a system of fixed exchange rates.

direct credit controls Direct credit controls allow the Fed to tell banks how much they can lend and to whom.

discount rate The discount rate is the interest rate banks must pay when they borrow from the Fed. The term discount refers to the payment of the interest charge in advance so the actual loan is the net of the total interest payment.

disposable income (YD) Disposable income (YD) is the total income consumers have to spend after their taxes (T) are paid, so that $YD \equiv Y - T$.

dissaving Dissaving occurs when people consume more than their disposable income.

durable consumer goods Durable consumer goods are pieces of equipment that provide services to households over a number of years.

▶ **economic approach to government activity** The economic approach to government activity uses the tools of modern economic analysis to study government behavior.

economic change, structural shifts Economic change, or structural shifts, refers to changes in the pattern of economic activity, such as the level and distribution of output or employment, in any economy over time.

economic growth Economic growth is an increase in the economy's capacity to produce real GNP and can be represented by an outward shift in the production possibilities frontier.

economic profit Economic profit is the excess of a firm's revenue over *all* its costs of production.

economic rent Economic rent arises from the difference between the price of a good or service and its opportunity cost.

economic system An economic system is the set of institutions, such as free markets or planning agencies, rules, and laws that determines the answers to the basic economic questions in a country.

economic union An economic union is a common market in which the member countries coordinate their monetary and fiscal policies.

efficient economy An efficient economy derives as much benefit as possible from its available resources; in this sense it wastes no resources.

endogenous consumption Endogenous consumption is that part of planned consumption that depends on GNP.

equilibrium interest rate The equilibrium interest rate is the real interest rate that equates the aggregate supply and demand for loanable funds; at the equilibrium interest rate borrowers want to borrow exactly the amount of funds that lenders want to lend.

equilibrium in the aggregate labor market Equilibrium in the aggregate labor market occurs when an employment–real wage combination is found that leaves no buyer or seller of labor unsatisfied.

equilibrium price The equilibrium price is the price at which the quantity of a good or service demanded equals the quantity supplied.

equilibrium quantity The equilibrium quantity is the quantity that results from the equilibrium price. It is both a quantity demanded and supplied.

equilibrium real GNP Equilibrium real GNP occurs when the aggregate real quantity of goods and services produced exactly equals planned aggregate expenditure.

eurodollar market The eurodollar market is a financial market in which eurodollars are borrowed and lent.

eurodollars Eurodollars are dollar deposits in European banks.

excess demand An excess demand, or shortage, is the amount by which the quantity demanded exceeds the quantity supplied.

excess reserves Excess reserves are banks' deposits at the Fed and other reserves in excess of their required amount.

excess supply, or glut An excess supply, or glut, is the excess of the quantity supplied over the quantity demanded.

exogenous consumption Exogenous consumption is that part of planned consumption that depends on factors other than GNP.

expected real wage (W/P^e) The expected real wage (W/P^e) is the nominal (paycheck) wage in terms of its purchasing power expected in the near future.

▶ **Federal Deposit Insurance Corporation (FDIC)** The Federal Deposit Insurance Corporation (FDIC) insures "small" bank deposits (those not exceeding $100,000) against losses if a bank fails.

Federal Open Market Committee (FOMC) The Federal Open Market Committee (FOMC) is the part of the Fed that controls bank reserves.

Federal Reserve notes Federal Reserve notes are our paper currency.

Federal Reserve System (Fed) The Federal Reserve Bank, or Fed for short, is the central bank of the United States.

fiat money Fiat money is money because the government has declared it to be so.

financial instrument A financial instrument is an asset for one party and a liability for another party.

financial sector The financial sector consists of the economy's money and credit markets.

firm A firm is the basic economic unit that makes production decisions in a market economy, just as the household is the basic unit that makes consumption decisions.

firm's labor demand curve [d(l)] A firm's labor demand curve [d(l)] is a graph illustrating the firm's desired labor force at various possible real wage rates.

fiscal policy Fiscal policy is the adjustment of taxes or government spending.

fixed exchange rates Fixed exchange rates are exchange rates that governments set between their countries' currencies.

flexible exchange rate system In a flexible exchange rate system the forces of supply and demand in foreign exchange markets determine exchange rates for currencies.

foreign exchange intervention Foreign exchange intervention means that the government of a country (through its central bank) buys or sells foreign exchange for the purpose of affecting the exchange rates for its currency in a particular way.

foreign exchange market The foreign exchange market is where currencies are bought and sold; it is where foreign exchange rates are determined.

foreign exchange rate A foreign exchange rate is the amount of one country's currency (money) that it takes to buy one unit of another country's currency.

45° line The 45° line exactly divides the right angle created by the two axes of the consumption function graph. Along this line, whatever expenditure components are measured along the vertical axis exactly equal GNP, which is measured along the horizontal axis.

fractional reserve system In a fractional reserve system, required reserves are less than the banks' deposit liabilities.

free market economies Free market economies are those that operate with the least amount of government control over the prices and quantities of goods and services bought and sold; few such economies operate with absolutely no government influence, however.

frictional unemployment Frictional unemployment occurs because it takes time for newly unemployed workers to find jobs even though there are enough jobs to go around.

full employment Full employment occurs when there is no cyclical unemployment.

full-employment GNP Full-employment GNP requires that there is equilibrium in the aggregate market for goods and services and full employment in the aggregate labor market at the same time.

full macroeconomic equilibrium Full macroeconomic equilibrium occurs when equilibrium exists in the labor, goods, and credit markets simultaneously.

▶ **General Agreement on Tariffs and Trade (GATT)** The General Agreement on Tariffs and Trade (GATT) is an agreement that was reached by most nations after World War II to reduce trade barriers, such as tariffs and quotas, and to discourage "unfair" competition on the world market through the use of export subsidies.

GNP deflator The GNP deflator is a special index number that expresses the average price of current GNP in terms of prices that prevailed in a base year.

government spending Government spending is the total dollar value of the purchases of goods and services by all government units—federal, state, and local.

gross national product (GNP) Gross national product (GNP) measures the total value of all final goods and services the economy produces during a year.

▶ **high employment deficit** The high employment deficit is the excess of government spending over tax revenues when full employment prevails.

hyperinflation Hyperinflation is an *extremely* rapid and continuous increase in the price level.

▶ **import substitution** Import substitution is the use of trade restrictions to promote domestic production of manufactured goods that are currently imported.

income effect The income effect refers to the tendency of people to demand more of most goods and services when their purchasing power rises and to demand less when their purchasing power falls.

indexing Indexing is a means of adjusting nominal payments by referring to a price index so that their real value is unaffected by the rate of inflation.

indirect business taxes Indirect business taxes are those taxes paid by firms on the basis of the value of production taking place.

industrial policy debate The industrial policy debate concerns the proper role of government in fostering economic change and helping the losers from economic change.

infant industry argument The infant industry argument for trade restriction states that if an industry is protected in its early years of development, when it is unable to compete on the world market, it will be saved in the long term because the production experience it gains will ultimately make it competitive.

instruments of monetary policy The Fed's instruments of monetary policy are the different types of actions it can take to control the money supply.

interest rate The interest rate is the percentage of a dollar that a borrower must pay a lender per year for each $1 borrowed.

intermediate goods Intermediate goods are goods purchased by a firm to use in further production.

investment Investment occurs when businesses add to their collection of physical capital (plant and equipment) and inventories. It also includes the purchases of new dwellings, even if by individuals or families.

▶ **labor force** The labor force is the sum of employed plus unemployed people in the population.

labor productivity Labor productivity measures the quantity of goods or services produced by a typical worker during a particular period of time.

Laffer curve The Laffer curve is a theoretical relationship between tax rates and tax revenues. It illustrates tax revenues falling when tax rates increase to the levels that now exist in the United States and many other nations.

lag A lag is the time that elapses between the occurrence of an event and a reaction to the event.

law of demand The law of demand states that there is a negative relationship between desired purchases and the price of a good or service, *cet. par.*

law of supply The law of supply states that the quantity of a good or service firms desire to sell is greater the higher the price of the good or service, *cet. par.*

loanable funds Loanable funds consist of money borrowed and lent in the credit market.

loan contract A loan contract is an agreement created when one party borrows from another. It is a financial instrument specifying a repayment schedule along with interest owed to the lender.

loan contract, financial, or credit market The loan contract, financial, or credit market is where borrowers and lenders of money arrange the terms of loans.

logrolling Logrolling is the mutual exchange of political support among special-interest groups.

long-run aggregate supply curve The long-run aggregate supply curve is a vertical line relating the price level to the full macroeconomic equilibrium value of real GNP.

▶ **M1** M1 includes all deposits (except those of the United States Treasury) in the banking system's consolidated balance sheet on which checks can be written plus currency and traveler's checks in the hands of the nonbank public.

M2 M2 includes M1 plus "small" certificates of deposit, savings accounts, money market mutual fund accounts, and certain other bank obligations that banks' depositors treat as readily available to carry out transactions.

M3 M3 includes M2 plus "large" CD's and other deposits that are relatively liquid but are inconvenient to use in day-to-day transactions.

macroeconomics Macroeconomics analyzes the behavior of an entire economy.

marginal product of labor (mpl) The marginal product of labor (mpl) measures the additional output a firm produces when it hires an additional unit of labor, all other inputs such as machinery held constant. (The marginal product of capital is defined as the additional output obtained from using one more unit of capital with a given amount of labor.)

marginal propensity to consume (MPC) The marginal propensity to consume (MPC) is the additional aggregate consumption spending that occurs out of each additional dollar of disposable income; MPC is a fraction (b) between 0 and 1.

marginal propensity to save (MPS) The marginal propensity to save (MPS) is the extra aggregate saving that occurs out of each additional dollar of disposable income; $MPS \equiv 1 - MPC = 1 - b$ and is therefore a fraction between 0 and 1.

market A market may be an actual location, but in economics it is best thought of as an idealized concept that describes how buyers and sellers of a particular good or service come together.

market economy A market economy is one in which most goods and services are bought and sold in markets rather than each good and service being produced by each person or family that uses it.

materials balance approach The materials balance approach is a planning device in which a set of accounts is formulated by a central planning agency and used to coordinate the quantities of inputs and outputs needed to achieve production goals for an economy.

medium of exchange A medium of exchange is something that is widely accepted by people in return for the sale of commodities or services or as payment for a loan.

mixed economies Mixed economies contain many government-owned industries that are typically privately owned in free market systems.

model An economic model is an abstract, simplified representation of how decision makers interact, how their decisions are affected by the economic environment, and the behavior that results from these decisions.

monetarists and Keynesians Monetarists and Keynesians are economists who hold different sets of views on monetary and fiscal policies.

monetary aspects of international trade Monetary aspects of international trade deal with currency flows, which are the financial counterpart of international commodity flows.

monetary authority A nation's monetary authority is usually its central bank, which is responsible for determining the quantity of money under a paper monetary standard.

monetary base The monetary base is the raw material from which banks create deposit liabilities and is equal to the sum of banks' reserves, currency in their vaults, and currency in the hands of the public.

monetary policy The Fed's monetary policy determines how much money circulates in the United States economy.

monetary standard A monetary standard defines the basis of an economy's money.

monetization of the debt Monetization of the debt occurs when the Fed buys government bonds, particularly when the bonds are purchased directly from the Treasury.

money Money consists mainly of checking account balances owned by business firms and individuals (not those owned by banks and the government) plus paper money and coins (currency) outside banks' vaults.

money multiplier The money multiplier is the ratio of the change in the quantity of money that results from a change in banks' reserves.

moral suasion Moral suasion is one of the Fed's methods of encouraging banks to lend more or less than they would like or to favor certain classes of customers.

multiple deposit expansion Multiple deposit expansion means that when the banking system's reserves increase, the quantity of checking account liabilities can be increased by a larger amount.

multiplier, exogenous expenditure multiplier The multiplier (also called the exogenous expenditure multiplier) is the ratio $1/(1 - b)$, where b is the marginal propensity to consume, which shows how changes in exogenous expenditure (planned investment, government spending, or exogenous consumption) are related to changes in equilibrium GNP.

▶ **net exports** Net exports represent the dollar value of a country's exports minus the dollar value of its imports.

nominal, or paycheck, wage (W) The nominal, or paycheck, wage (W) is the pay a worker receives measured in dollars per hour.

nominal GNP Nominal GNP is the observed value of GNP during a given time period, say, a year, with goods and services evaluated at current prices.

nominal interest rate A nominal interest rate is sometimes referred to as the market rate of interest; it is the interest rate borrowers and banks agree to and is unadjusted for the rate of inflation.

nondurable consumer goods Nondurable consumer goods are goods used up by households in the year they are purchased.

nonlabor income Nonlabor income is income someone receives that is independent of the amount worked.

nonmarket activities Nonmarket activities are the production of goods and services at home that are not sold for a price on a market.

nontariff trade barriers (NTBs) Nontariff trade barriers (NTBs) are nonprice trade restrictions.

normal employment (L^n) Normal employment (L^n) is the amount of employment denoted by the aggregate labor supply curve at a given real wage.

normal unemployment rate (u^n) The normal unemployment rate (u^n) is the unemployment rate when the labor market is in equilibrium; it is the percentage of the labor force that is frictionally or structurally unemployed.

normative view A normative view concerns the ethics of an issue or what is "right" or "just" versus "wrong" or "unjust."

▶ **open market operations** Open market operations are the purchases and sales of government bonds by the Fed on the open market (the market for government bonds).

opportunity cost Opportunity cost is the amount of one good or service that must be given in order to produce a unit of another good or service.

overvalued An overvalued currency is one whose price relative to some other currency is kept artificially above the price that would clear the foreign exchange market without government intervention.

▶ **paper standard of money** Under a paper standard, the quantity of money is determined by a monetary authority and is unrelated to any commodity.

Phillips curve The Phillips curve is a statistical relationship between the unemployment rate and the rate of inflation that is observed in the short run during inflationary episodes and recessions.

planned aggregate expenditure ($\overset{*}{E}$) Planned aggregate expenditure ($\overset{*}{E}$) is the sum of aggregate planned consumption by households ($\overset{*}{C}$), investment planned by firms ($\overset{*}{I}$), and government spending (G)—as well as net exports (X).

positive economics Positive economics is the study of how economic variables are related to one another.

price index A price index is a number that indicates the ratio of the cost of purchasing or producing a given bundle of goods and services relative to some base year, multiplied by 100.

price taker A price taker is a buyer or seller that has no direct control over the market price of a good or service. All competitive firms are price takers.

prime interest rate The prime interest rate is the standard or base rate of interest that banks charge borrowers for one-year loans.

production function A production function quantifies the relationship between a firm's output and its inputs.

production possibilities frontier (PPF) A production possibilities frontier (PPF) illustrates the alternative output levels for an economy that gets the most it can from its given set of resources and available technology. It shows the maximum production possible for each good or service, given the output of all other goods and services.

proprietors' income Proprietors' income is the income earned by the self-employed from their business activities.

quantity equation The quantity equation expresses the quantity of money as proportional to nominal GNP.

quota A quota is a nontariff trade barrier (NTB) that limits the quantity of an imported good that may be sold in a country.

rate of inflation The rate of inflation is the percentage change in the general price level and is typically measured by the percentage change in the CPI between two years.

real aspects of international trade Real aspects of international trade are concerned with the flows of commodities among nations.

real GNP Real GNP is the value of the economy's total production adjusted to ignore changes in the prices of goods and services over time.

real interest rate The real interest rate is the nominal (market) interest rate minus the expected rate of inflation.

real wage (W/P) The real wage (W/P) is equal to the nominal (or paycheck) wage (W) divided by the aggregate price level (P); the real wage expresses a worker's pay in terms of its ability to purchase goods and services.

recession A recession is a period of time when real GNP declines for two or more consecutive quarters.

recognition lag A recognition lag is the time that elapses between the occurrence of an event and the observation that the event has occurred.

rental income Rental income is the income produced by renting out machinery or buildings for use in production or consumption.

required reserve ratio The required reserve ratio is the amount of reserves that banks must keep with the Fed or on hand, expressed as a fraction of the banks' deposit liabilities.

reserves Reserves consist of assets banks retain to pay their depositors when they wish to withdraw from their accounts. In today's banking system, reserves include a bank's cash on hand and demand deposits it holds in other banks. The most important component of commercial banks' reserves are deposits they hold with the central bank—the Fed in the United States.

revaluation Revaluation occurs when a country increases the value of its currency in terms of other countries' currencies under a system of fixed exchange rates. (Revaluation is the opposite of devaluation.)

Ricardian equivalence hypothesis The Ricardian equivalence hypothesis states that the method of financing government expenditure has no impact on private consumption or investment expenditures.

saving Saving is the difference between total income and the amount spent on the consumption of goods and services or paid to the government in taxes.

saving function The saving function is a schedule, or equation, indicating how much society plans to save at various possible levels of aggregate real income.

scarcity Scarcity means that human wants or desires far exceed the capacity of the world's limited resources to satisfy those wants or desires.

short-run aggregate supply curve The short-run aggregate supply curve shows what happens to the price level and real GNP during inflationary episodes and recessions.

short-run macroeconomic equilibrium Short-run macroeconomic equilibrium occurs when equilibrium occurs in the aggregate market for goods and services but not all aggregate markets.

special drawing rights (SDRs) Special drawing rights (SDRs) are a kind of international money created by the International Monetary Fund.

specialization Specialization occurs when people produce a good or service to trade or sell to others, not because they may wish to use the good or service they are producing.

specific duty A specific duty is a tariff equal to a specified amount per unit of an imported item.

stagflation Stagflation is the coexistence of inflation and above-normal unemployment.

store of value A store of value is any means of keeping wealth over time.

structural deficit A structural deficit is a deficit that persists when the economy is at full employment.

structural unemployment Structural unemployment arises from the job losses people suffer when firms move out of a region, the skill requirements of the work force change, or when there is a minimum wage rate.

structure of interest rates The structure of interest rates refers to the variation in interest rates across loans by the type of borrower and the term of the loan (loan period).

substitution effect The substitution effect refers to the tendency for desired purchases of a good or service to rise when its price falls and to fall when its price rises relative to the price of others goods and services, *cet. par.*

supply Supply is the quantity offered for sale at each possible price.

supply of labor The supply of labor is the relationship that defines the amount of labor offered to firms by individuals.

supply-side economics Supply-side economics emphasizes the impact of monetary and fiscal policies on investment and real GNP in the long run.

▶ **target of monetary policy** A target of monetary policy is the variable(s), such as the rate of monetary growth or the rate of interest, that monetary policy attempts to influence for the purpose of smoothing out business cycles.

tariff A tariff is a tax on imported goods that is collected by the government of an importing country.

theory of rational expectations The theory of rational expectations says that firms and households correctly incorporate available information in making decisions about their work effort, level of production, willingness to borrow and lend, and so forth; they are not fooled over and over by the effects of persistent or repeated economic events and government policy actions.

the **three fundamental economic questions** Every economic system must answer the three fundamental economic questions: What? How? For whom?

trade creation effects The trade creation effects of a customs union are the increased gains from trade resulting from expanded imports and exports within the union.

trade diversion effects The trade diversion effects of a customs union are the reduced gains from trade resulting from diminished imports from countries outside the union.

Trade Expansion Act of 1962 The Trade Expansion Act of 1962 authorized government financial assistance to workers who were designated as displaced and firms that went out of business because of foreign competition.

transfer payments Transfer payments are the opposite of taxes: payments from government to individuals or firms to raise their incomes.

▶ **unemployed** The unemployed are people who did not work during the week before the CPS, but were available for work that week *and* (1) made specific efforts to find a job within the four weeks prior to the survey, (2) were waiting to be called back to jobs from which they had been laid off, or (3) were waiting to report to a new job within the next month.

unemployment rate The unemployment rate is the percentage of the labor force classified as unemployed.

unit of account A unit of account is the way in which an economy's prices are expressed (such as in dollars or yen).

▶ **value of the marginal product of labor (vmpl)** The value of the marginal product of labor (vmpl) is the increase in a competitive firm's sales revenue resulting from the sale of the extra output produced when an additional worker is hired.

velocity of money (V) Velocity (V) tells us the constant of proportionality in the quantity equation: $1/V$ is the constant of proportionality between nominal GNP and the quantity of money required to sustain it.

world price The world price is the price of purchasing a given commodity or service on the world market.

Index